Highlights from reviews of *She's A Rebel*:

"[*She's A Rebel*] is as thoroughly entertaining as it is researched . . . It's exhaustive and exhilarating." —*Billboard*

"A smart and lively celebration of its subject . . . Gaar brings female savvy to her study, and that in itself is a milestone in rock history."—*Entertainment Weekly*

"[An] encyclopedic range . . . Gaar includes all the major developments, from girl groups to Motown to punk." —*New York Times Book Review*

"An exhaustive inventory of Women in Rock—one that includes not just key performers, but producers, DJs, and record company executives." —*Village Voice*

"*She's A Rebel* shakes us out of the pervasive attitude that women's place in rock & roll is to provide anonymous backup scenery. At last we have a lively history of our rock heroines whose raw talent and bravado liberate the rock & roll rebel in every woman." —Naomi Wolf, author of *The Beauty Myth*

"Gillian Gaar proves that American rock & roll is not a boys' club. Even though we hear them on our radio every day, the voices of women in rock have been largely ignored by our pop-culture's chroniclers. At last, they have a historian of their own." —Susan Faludi, author of *Backlash*

"*She's A Rebel* is a long overdue work and a must-read for rock historians who, prior to this, have been presented with only half the story. Gaar does a superb job in charting the strides that women have made in the rock world while also making it clear that sexism in the music industry is alive and well." —*Goldmine*

"A first-rate rock n' roll history with enough lively detail and thoughtful analysis to put to shame the marginalization of women rockers decried by Gaar . . . Essential reading for rock fans—particularly those with large record collections and open minds." —*Kirkus Reviews*

"Gaar's careful research and lively writing make this book required reading for anyone interested in rock 'n' roll in all its dimensions." —*The Bloomsbury Review*

"*She's A Rebel* goes some way beyond the standard 'Girls are as good as men and here's why' approach . . . The main thrust is simply to document their lives, times and most important of all, their music."—*Alternative Press*

"*She's A Rebel* is not a book that merely fits women outsiders inside the male-defined rock and roll tradition; it is a book that subverts the assumptions of value that have long determined the story of that tradition. Gaar combines her astute reassessment of rock and roll trends with details on a myriad of women rockers . . . What emerges is a rich and lively tapestry documenting the full range of women's involvement in rock and roll." —*Choice* (ALA)

"There is something inherently thrilling about this collection of women's lives that I can't express. It is perhaps just holding all these stories in one hand, the weight of it, the voluminous amounts of research . . . Gaar has done a fantastic job." —*Seattle Gay News*

"Gillian Gaar is a demon researcher whose book graphically documents the stupid, nasty sexism that so many women have encountered in the pop music business. At the same time, she splendidly captures all the flash, trash and energy that make rock & roll so alluring in the first place." —Lindsy Van Gelder, *Ms.* magazine

"At last—a long overdue antidote to the male-dominated view of rock history, by an author who combines scholarship, insight and readability in equal doses."—Peter Doggett, *Record Collector*

SHE'S A REBEL

THE HISTORY OF WOMEN IN ROCK & ROLL

EXPANDED SECOND EDITION

GILLIAN G. GAAR

PREFACE BY YOKO ONO

SEAL PRESS

SHE'S A REBEL
THE HISTORY OF WOMEN IN ROCK & ROLL
Expanded Second Edition

Seal Press
An Imprint of Avalon Publishing Group Inc.
161 William St., 16th Floor
New York, NY 10038

First printing, October 1992
First printing, second edition, December 2002
Interior design by Paul Paddock

Acknowledgment is hereby made for permission to quote song material and prose from the following publishers and copyright holders, to whom all rights are reserved: *Folksinger* by Phranc. Copyright (c) 1989 Folkswim Records. All rights reserved. Used by permission. *Penis Envy* by Andrew Ratshin & Arni Adler. Copyright (c) 1984 Liv Tunes. All rights reserved. Used by permission. *I Am Women* by Helen Reddy and Ray Burton. Copyright (c) 1971 Buggerlugs Music. All rights reserved. Used by permission. *Stepping Out of Line* by L. Woods, P. Ford, J. Munro, P. Hammond. Copyright (c) 1982 Ideal Home Noise Productions. All rights reserved. Used by permission. *The Real Roxanne* by Shaun Fequiere, Frederick Reeves, Jeffrey Campbell, High Clark, Maurice Bailey, Lucien George, Brian George, Curtis Bedeau, Gerald Charles, Paul George. Copyright (c) 1985 Adra Music, K. E. D. Music & Mokojumbi Music. All rights reserved. Used by permission. Cowboy Mouth by Sam Shepard and Patti Smith. Copyright (c) 1976 Bantam Books, Inc. All rights reserved. Used by permission. *Gloria* (Van Morrison. Copyright (c) 1965 Hyde Park Music Co. Ltd., Bernice Music Inc., January Music Inc.) prelude by Patti Smith. Copyright (c) 1975 Arista Records. All rights reserved. Used by permission.

Library of Congress Cataloging-in-Publication Data is available.

ISBN: 1-58005-078-6

Printed in the United States of America
Distributed by Publishers Group West

Acknowledgments

This book was put together with the generous help and support of a number of individuals and organizations. I am especially grateful to all the women who agreed to be interviewed, including: Arni Adler, Annette Aguilar, Laurie Anderson, Michele Anthony, Roma Baran, Ivy Bauer, Pamela Brandt, Ruth Brown, Bonnie Buckingham, Charlotte Caffey, Kristi Callan, Exene Cervenka, Linda Clark, Gail Colson, Danielle Dax, Judy Dlugacz, Carol Dodds, Lisa Fancher, Celia Farber, Rachel Felder, Ferron, Karen Finley, Lita Ford, Deborah Harry, Nona Hendryx, Una Johnston, Leslie Ann Jones, Peggy Jones, Holly Knight, Lene Lovich, Carol MacDonald, Lisa Macek, Rachel Matthews, June Millington, Holly Near, Roberta Peterson, Phranc, Helen Reddy, Poison Ivy Rorschach, Donna Russo, Boden Sandstrom, Lori Seid, Lisa Shively, Michelle Shocked, Jane Siberry, Susan Silver, Penelope Spheeris, Alison Steele, Teresa Trull, Maureen "Moe" Tucker, Vicki Wickham, and Nancy Wilson. Thanks also to those who were interviewed but whose stories were not ultimately used. Special mention should be made of Lori Twersky, who was not only interviewed for *She's A Rebel*, but who also referred me to other potential interviewees, provided me with a near-complete set of *Bitch* magazines, and who telephoned frequently to convey a piece of news or gossip. Regrettably, Lori Twersky died in November 1991 in the midst of compiling her own book on women performers; I am thankful for the time we did get to spend together. Other people who provided me with referrals or source material include: Sam Andrew, Beth Berkley, Leon Berman, Pete Blecha, Kelly Curtis, Brian Hendel (*Yoko Only*), Faith Henschel, Bob Jeniker, Jim Keaton (The Helen Reddy Fan Club), Ken Keiran, Kathy Kelly, Chris Knab, Terry Morgan, Lisa Orth, Jesse Reyes, Kerri Uretz, Dennis White, and David A. Young. I am also grateful to the record companies, public relations firms, and organizations who also provided me with material: Atlantic, Capitol, Chameleon, Chrysalis, Fantasy Inc., Enigma, MCA, Mute, the New Music Seminar, Next Plateau, Shorefire Media, and Tommy Boy, with the following individuals being especially helpful: Bill Bentley, Marge Falcon, and Howie Klein (Warner

Bros.), Bev Chin (A&M), Steve Levesque (Solters, Roskin, Friedman, Inc.), Brett Milano (formerly with Rhino), Bob 'Beak' Myers (formerly with Island), Howard Paar (Mercury), Carrie Anne Svingen (Rykodisc), and Tim Thompson (Sony Music). Very special thanks are in order to my transcriptionists: Susannah Iltis, Mary Nugent, and especially the tireless Cydney Gillis; those who took on the task of securing photo and lyric permissions: Gillian Anderson, Ingrid Emerick, Megan Knight, and Jennifer Rose; all the photographers and other individuals who provided us with photos; and my ever-scrupulous copy editor Cathy Johnson. Thanks also to those who provided a home away from home during my travels while researching this book: the Brooklyn Boys (Kimble Mead, Alan Neil, and Dan Romer), Eileen Money, and Shirley Solomon. Additional thanks are due to: William B. Abbott IV, Ed Beeson and Cynthia Payne at the Backstage, Dr. Helen Caldicott, Cloud 9 Prods., Susan Despenich (R.I.P., Dec. 2001), Group Health Cooperative, The Literary Center, V. Mary, S. J. McCarthy, Mary McFaul, Michael Phillips, Larry Reid and the Center on Contemporary Art, the entire staff at *The Rocket* magazine (especially Grant Alden, Art Chantry, Charles R. Cross), Shoreline Community College, The Swedish Housewife, Steve Wells, and Re-bar. My deepest thanks and appreciation to Yoko Ono for writing the preface. Finally, thanks to all the women at Seal Press who have helped make this book a reality, and especially my editor, Faith Conlon, who offered me the opportunity to write my first book in addition to providing me—on a sometimes daily basis—with advice, materials, encouragement, support, and, of course, home cooked meals. They were all much appreciated.

Acknowledgments 2002

Thanks to everyone who was interviewed: Kirsty MacColl, Lucinda Williams (1990); Lori Barbero, Kat Bjelland, Jean Smith (1993); Suzi Gardner, Donita Sparks (1997); Tristin Laughter (2000); Carrie Brownstein, Julie Butterfield, Carla DeSantis, Laura Love, Molly Neuman, Cheryl Pawelski, Candice Pederson, Corin Tucker, Janet Weiss, Meryl Wheeler, Kaia Wilson, and Allison Wolfe (2002). Thanks also to: Faith Conlon for agreeing to do a second edition; Anne Mathews for editorial direction, photo research, and general support; Christina Henry de Tessan for editorial assistance; Annie Decker for copyediting; Jennie Goode for proofreading; Elizabeth de Noma for transcription and editorial support; Neal Tamburro for transcription; Cinnamon Stephens for legal work; Diana Adams for the author photograph; Matt Kumma for additional support; all the photographers who contributed to this edition; Yoko Ono for her updated preface and L7's "Fast and Frightening" (*Smell the Magic*, Sub Pop, 1991). And mom.

To my mother
who told me
"We had rocking before Elvis!"

CONTENTS

Preface

The time was 1946; place, Tokyo. I was confronting my father who, as usual, sat in a deep comfortable leather chair with his pipe and suede jacket. I had just told him that I wanted to be a composer. I would not have dreamt of making such a bold statement unless it just jumped out of my mouth, which it had. Initially, my father had called me to his study only to tell me that I should give up on being a pianist. "You're not good enough. Just give up practicing. It's a waste of time." It was said in a kind and gentle tone. My becoming a pianist, however, had been my father's wish, not mine. I felt relieved that I did not have to practice anymore. "Actually, I want to be a composer, father," I said. There was a silence. I sensed I had inadvertently dropped a bomb, and felt butterflies in my stomach. "Well," my father said after a considerable silence, "there are not many women composers in the world, Yoko. At least I haven't heard of one yet. Maybe there's a reason for that. Maybe it's a question of women's aptitude. I know you are a talented and intelligent child. But I wonder . . . I don't want to see you struggle in vain." How could he have known that it may not have been a question of gender aptitude? In those days, the fact that a father would discuss a daughter's career was already considered quite unusual. Daughters were brought up to go to finishing schools and hoped to get married before people started to raise their eyebrows. I am still thankful that my father cared at all about my career. Eventually, he made me take voice lessons to sing German lieders, saying that that would be a vocation which would satisfy both my love for poetry and music. "Women may not be good creators of music, but they're good at interpreting music," was what he said. I rebelled, gave up my voice lessons, and went to a Japanese university to study philosophy while being a closet songwriter.

She's A Rebel by Gillian Gaar is a powerful document of Herstory in rock and roll, a book equal in its importance to *The First Sex* by Elizabeth Gould Davis. How many of us know the names of the pioneer women songwriters/singers/musicians of the '50s? How many of us are aware of the fact that women have been successfully breaking ground in the business side of the music industry since the '60s? How many of us remember the role women producers/singers/songwriters played in the upsurge of the feminist movement in the early '70s? And how many of us have cared to learn the continuing plight of women artists in the "material world" of the '80s even after gaining fame and money? Gillian covers the four decades of women in rock from the '50s, when rock and roll was still considered off-shoot music by the public, to when it finally received respectability at the end of the '80s and the early '90s. Through her thorough and precise writing, with many direct quotes from women rockers, we discover the important role women played in the development of rock music. We are reminded of individual women artists who kept making music despite overwhelming odds till finally the music industry had to realize that women were there to stay. Their struggle was not in vain. It opened doors for the next generation of women rockers, turned the heads of parents who would have otherwise discouraged their daughters from getting into the field, lent power to the music industry, and gave good music to the world.

Once I started reading this book, I could not put it down, even though it was a somewhat painful process for me as it reminded me of my own unresolved hurt. It also uplifted my spirit to realize that I was not alone. We all went through pain, we all went through the struggle, and, together, we have indeed come a long way. I am thankful to Gillian for giving me this insight.

—Yoko Ono
New York City
March 1992

In the beginning there was music. Two sounds playing with each other and generating energy have created the Universe. In the new millennium, we see that women rockers have come a long way. We are now seeing the world dancing to our songs and our music. One day, we will come together and the world will be as one, and a better place for all. Till then, sisters, let's keep rocking!

—Yoko Ono
New York City
May 2002

Note to the New Edition

When I first began to work on *She's A Rebel* in 1989, the music press was in the throes of the latest women-in-rock "trend," when acoustic-oriented acts like Suzanne Vega, Tracy Chapman, and the Indigo Girls were enjoying unexpected chart success. By the time of Rebel 's publication in 1992, the new women-in-rock trend had become riot grrrls and other "angry" acts such as Hole and Babes in Toyland.

Since then, so many women have become involved in every level of the music industry that it would seem impossible to cram them all under the heading of "women-in-rock." But that hasn't stopped the media from trying. During the '90s, riot grrrls became the so-called "quiet grrrls" of Lilith Fair, *Spin* and *Rolling Stone* each put out women-in-rock issues, and when and *Music Connection* noted that "Female Artists Dominate The Top 10 in '96" in a December cover story, the magazine still lumped all related stories in the issue under the heading "Women In Music." When would women be able to stand on their own, and not perennially seen as part of a trend?

At times, it has seemed as if women in the music industry would forever be perceived as women first and performers (or managers or publicists or record label owners) second. But change has happened. Sleater-Kinney's Carrie Brownstein is frequently referred to as a "best guitarist" in alternative rock rather than "best female guitarist." Anyone who doubts the commercial appeal of female artists needs only to be reminded of the massive success of Mariah Carey, TLC, and the Spice Girls. Even women-in-rock articles have become increasingly self-aware, as in a 1997 *Newsweek* story, headlined "The Girl Problem," which praised Shania Twain and Celine Dion for being able to "soar above" women-in-rock categorization in the hopes of giving "rise to a whole new genre: Just Plain People in Rock."

But perhaps the most notable change is more women are determining the course of their careers outside conventional boundaries. Virtually every performer in the first edition of *Rebel* strove to secure a major label contract. But in the '90s, an increasing number of artists—Bikini Kill, Ani DiFranco, and Sleater-Kinney among them-turned down offers from the majors in favor of maintaining full control over their careers, achieving their own idea of success on their own terms. And those who see gaps in what the industry has to offer women are now more likely to fill those holes themselves, which has led to the creation of such endeavors as Lilith Fair, Mr. Lady Records, *ROCKRGRL* magazine, and Ladyfest.

In light of all these events, it became obvious that *Rebel* would need to be updated.

The book's three new chapters chart the progress women have made during the '90s and continue to make in the new century. To preserve the integrity of the original edition, the 1992 epilogue has been retitled "Note to the Nineties" and provides a transitional link to the new material. Like the first edition, the new chapters cover the period selectively, but hopefully touch on most of rock's major developments over the past ten years. There has also been selective updating in the book's original chapters.

It's been exciting—then and now—to watch women in all facets of the industry come into their own. Their success, particularly in overcoming obstacles, is what makes *Rebel* as much a celebration of women's achievements in the music industry as it is a history of those achievements. And as long as rock music remains an art form with a potent ability to inspire, those achievements will continue to be made.

Gillian G. Gaar
Seattle
August 2002

Introduction
to the Original Edition

I n 1988, both the music press and the mainstream press were busy writing about a new "trend" they had recently discovered: women-in-rock. This "trend" had come into being due to the success of Suzanne Vega's 1987 single "Luka," which reached the Top 10, followed by the emergence of such performers as Tracy Chapman, Sinéad O'Connor, Natalie Merchant of 10,000 Maniacs, Michelle Shocked, Melissa Etheridge, and the Indigo Girls, among others, on the music scene.

The underlying premise of the articles on this "trend" was that an unprecedented number of female performers were now carving out a substantial place for themselves in the rock world—for the first time. In fact, many of the performers were not new-comers to the music scene; Vega, 10,000 Maniacs, Shocked, and the Indigo Girls had all released at least one album before their "discovery" by the media. More importantly, there had been similar women-in-rock trends noted in the media in previous years, when women of varying musical styles were lumped together primarily because they were women. In the mid-'80s, "videogenic" performers like Annie Lennox of Eurythmics, Cyndi Lauper, Madonna, and Tina Turner were the women-in-rock of the MTV era. In the late '70s and early '80s, Debbie Harry of Blondie, the Go-Go's, Chrissie Hynde of the Pretenders, and Pat Benatar were all considered the women-in-rock of the new wave. In the late '60s and early '70s, the singer-songwriter movement was spearheaded by Carole King, Laura Nyro, Joni Mitchell, Carly Simon, and Janis Ian, paralleled by the feminist-oriented women's music movement of the same period. And in the early '60s, before the British Invasion conquered the U.S. airwaves, vocal groups like the Shirelles, the Chiffons, the Crystals, the Ronettes, and the Shangri-Las popularized the "girl group" sound.

Far from being a unique trend, women-in-rock have instead been a perpetual trend. With the arrival of the feminist movement of the early '70s, women who were asked about their role as women-in-rock invariably answered that the idea of a woman assuming a "non-traditional" performing role (such as playing an electric guitar) was only deemed unusual because there weren't many women in such positions, and that as more women became rock musicians the idea of women-in-rock would lose its validity. But, as the recent trend of 1988 demonstrates, this has not yet occurred. Women in rock are still by and large defined in that order—as women first, and rock performers second.

One of the more obvious reasons for the recurrence of the women-in-rock trend is that women as a gender are not integrated into society but are still seen as an "other" that deviates from a male norm. This is communicated in even the most innocuous settings, as in a headline about the 1988 Democratic Presidential Convention that read, "Democrats Pick Woman to Deliver Keynote Address" as opposed to, for example, "Democrats Pick Ann Richards to Deliver Keynote Address." Parallel examples can be easily found in the rock world when an artist is identified as the "best female guitarist" as opposed to, simply, "best guitarist."

The attitudes underlying such distinctions provide a partial explanation as to why women's roles in the music industry have frequently been overlooked and downplayed in many rock histories. If women performers (or songwriters, DJs, managers, etc.) are only seen as exceptional because they are women, this justifies the relegation of women-in-rock to an obligatory chapter, where their contributions are acknowledged but are also portrayed as being a step removed from the history as a whole. The implication is that these women-in-rock were able to make a impression in spite of the fact that they were female. This in turn perpetuates stereotypical views regarding women's capabilities to be anything other than entertainers of the most passive kind: a malleable "body with a voice." Such an inherently sexist perspective denies women the chance to avail themselves of career opportunities in other areas of the industry as well.

Another factor contributing to female invisibility in the rock industry is how a performer's works are valued. The history of rock is in some ways a history of commercial, rather than artistic, success, with records that sell in large quantities often seen as "better" than those that do not. This type of reasoning effectively eliminates the stories of any number of female performers who may not have achieved success on a large—or even a moderate—scale. As a result, if you go to a standard rock history, you will usually find that very few female performers are listed, giving the erroneous impression that women played an insubstantial role in the creation and development of rock & roll.

The irony is that women performers have often been caught in a double bind. Female artists were (and are) frequently not seen as having the commercial potential of a male artist, and so were not given the chance to demonstrate that they could indeed sell records on their own merits. In the late '50s, for example, the all-female vocal group the Chantels were nearly denied a record contract solely because they were female. Fortunately for the group, they did manage to secure a contract and ultimately landed four singles in the Top 40 charts over the course of their career. When given the opportunity, women performers have proved again and again that they can sell records, but doubts about the ability of women artists to make records that people will actually want to buy remain—even today, managers relate that they still have trouble finding a record deal with companies who continue to claim, "But we already have a girl singer."

The focus on commercial success, along with the secondary status women have in society, has meant that lesser-known female performers—unlike their male counterparts—are more likely to be absent from rock histories. This is particularly true of rock's early years, and extends well into subsequent decades; not until the arrival of punk in the late '70s would "cult" or underground female performers begin to be covered in a comparable fashion to male artists at a similar level. The recovery of this "lost" history is a major aspect of *She's A Rebel*, intending to show that the sheer number of women who have been involved in the rock industry is actually much greater than can be deduced from most sources. It is an attempt to flesh out one-line references into something more substantial. And though *She's A Rebel* can only offer a selective look at the large number of women who have been involved in rock, the book would not be as comprehensive as it is without the assistance of many people—frequently the artists themselves—who provided clippings and oral interviews about groups whose stories merited more than the few obligatory sentences they had received in other histories. This excavation also brought to mind the possible number of female performers who undoubtedly existed but never rated a one- or two-line mention in any rock history. Are their stories lost forever?

She's A Rebel also covers—again selectively—the careers of female performers who are well known, examining the experiences these artists have faced as women and placing them in the larger context of how those experiences have had an effect on their work as rock performers. Too often, one well-known female performer has been seen as representing all women performers. In interviews, the artists themselves sometimes comment on their being the only female rock performer in a certain position, when, in fact, there have been others; there is little sense of an ongoing tradition of women in the music industry. And the so-called "breakthrough" artists, who have confidently stated that their position as women-in-rock only seems unusual because of the lack of well-known women involved in the rock industry, might be dismayed to know that the same type of comments have been made by female performers a decade earlier—and may well be made a decade hence.

Yet there has been a substantial increase in the visibility of women in the rock world, even if women-in-rock are still presented as something of a novelty. Ask someone to name a woman-in-rock from the '50s and you're likely to be met with a blank stare, while the same question about performers in the '80s would probably elicit a variety of responses. There are also more women working within the industry itself. Even in rock's early years, women were record label owners, managers, and songwriters, though again, their histories have often been obscured. Though the executive suites in the music industry as a whole remain male-dominated, women continue to move beyond the "publicity ghetto" (one of the few areas of the music industry that has traditionally been female-dominated) into other areas of the business. In these "behind the scenes" positions, women can have an even more influential role in bringing about changes for women in all areas of the music industry.

When one considers the gains women have made on an industry-wide basis in the music business since the '50s, it becomes readily apparent how misleading a tag like "women-in-rock" is. Ultimately, it promotes a perceived musical similarity between performers based on the fact that they are women—a similarity that is, in reality, non-existent. The flaw in this perception becomes clear when you take it to its logical conclusion, which would mean devising a category for "men-in-rock"—writing articles on the new crop of "all-male bands," and, perhaps, identifying the Beatles as "separatists" because they made "all-male records."

Though sometimes unacknowledged, women have made a broad contribution to both the rock industry and to rock history. *She's A Rebel* presents an exploration of the many roles women have played in the development of the rock industry, both onstage and off. Women-in-rock do have a similarity between them, but it is not simply because they are women. It is in the experience they have faced as women working in a male-dominated industry. *She's A Rebel* chronicles their side of the story.

Gillian G. Gaar
Seattle
June 1992

SHE'S A
REBEL

1

Roots

"At what point did rhythm & blues start becoming rock & roll?"
"When the white kids started to dance to it."
—Ruth Brown to Rolling Stone, April 19, 1990

On July 25, 1984, Willie Mae Thornton died in Los Angeles of heart and liver complications, probably brought on by years of alcohol abuse which had reduced the one-time 350-pound "Big Mama" Thornton to a mere ninety-five pounds. She was fifty-seven years old. It was an inglorious end for an influential rock & roll pioneer: Thornton had sung and played harmonica and drums for a variety of rhythm & blues bands from the 1940s on, appeared on stages from New York City's famed Apollo Theatre to the Newport Jazz Festival, performed with blues legends such as Muddy Waters, B. B. King, and Eddie "Cleanhead" Vinson, wrote "Ball and Chain," revived in the '60s by Janis Joplin, and recorded one of the seminal records in rock & roll history—"Hound Dog."

"Hound Dog" was Big Mama's only substantial hit. Written especially for her by the songwriting/producing team of Jerry Leiber and Mike Stoller, it reached number 1 in 1953 on the rhythm & blues (R&B) charts, compiled by music industry trade magazines like *Billboard*, which rated the weekly popularity of current records. Though the R&B charts ostensibly reflected the musical tastes of the black audience, R&B was also attracting a growing white audience that was beginning to tune into the "underground" sounds on R&B radio stations, and "Hound Dog" no doubt gained exposure among white R&B aficionados during its seven-week stay at the top of the R&B charts. But Thornton's success with "Hound Dog" was due to be eclipsed by Elvis Presley's cover of the song in 1956, which went on to top not only the R&B charts, but the Top 40 charts as well.

It was a familiar pattern, one which frustrated the rise of many black performers: as the white musicians performing R&B moved it further from its black roots, eventually transforming it into rock & roll, the originators of the sound were left with little to show for their hard work. Big Mama was one of those lost in the shuffle. When interest in her had cooled, she was dropped by her record company in 1957. And though she continued to tour and record throughout the rest of her life, she never regained the momentum generated by "Hound Dog." Nor would her biggest hit provide her with financial compensation—Thornton later claimed that though "Hound Dog" had sold more than two million copies, she received only one royalty check for five hundred dollars.

Born in Montgomery, Alabama, in 1926, Willie Mae Thornton was one of seven children. In her early teens she moved to Atlanta, where she appeared as a dancer in a variety show and in the early '40s became a member of Sammy Green's Hot Harlem Review. An admirer of blues singers Bessie Smith and Memphis Minnie, Thornton's own musical education came through observation. "My singing comes with experience," she once explained. "I never had no one teach me nothing. I taught myself to sing and to blow the harmonica and even to play drums, by watching other people."

Thornton toured with the Hot Harlem Review until 1948, after which she settled in Houston, Texas. It was in Texas that she launched her recording career, with her first single, "All Right Baby"/"Bad Luck Got My Man," released in 1951 on E&W Records and credited to the Harlem Stars. She was then signed to Peacock Records, and began releasing records under her own name, including "Partnership Blues" in 1951, and "No Jody for Me" and "Mischievous Boogie" in 1952. She also traveled to Los Angeles, where she became a featured artist with the Johnny Otis Show, an R&B combo formed by Otis, a former jazz drummer who had made the move into R&B in the late '40s. While touring with Otis, Thornton made her debut at the Apollo, where she delivered such a powerful rendition of the Dominos' hit "Have Mercy Baby," she graduated from opening act to headliner in one night.

Otis produced Thornton's third session for Peacock on August 13, 1952, in L.A. He had also invited Jerry Leiber and Mike Stoller, two aspiring songwriters, to drop by the session to see if they could provide any material for Thornton, and after meeting her they wrote "Hound Dog." "It was as much her appearance as her blues style that influenced the writing of 'Hound Dog,' " Stoller later recalled in Rolling Stone. "We wanted her to growl it. Which she rejected at first. Her thing was 'Don't you tell me how to sing no song!'" Thornton had her own memories of the session: "They were just a couple of kids then," she told columnist and jazz writer Ralph Gleason. "And they had this song written on a paper bag. So I started to sing the words and join in some of my own. All that talkin' and hollerin'—that's my own."

As originally recorded by Thornton, "Hound Dog" moves with a lazy blues drawl that has Big Mama bawling at her errant suitor that his days are numbered; she sees through his smooth-talking jive and even his wagging tail can't entice her anymore. Released in late 1952, it hit the top of the R&B charts by early 1953 and spawned a number of "answer" songs from men seeking to get in the last word, such as disc jockey Rufus Thomas's "Beat Cat" and John Brim's "Rattlesnake." In the wake of her success, Thornton appeared on a package tour that included Bobby "Blue" Bland, Junior Parker, and up-and-coming R&B star Johnny Ace (Thornton was allegedly in the same back-stage dressing room as Ace when he accidentally killed himself during a game of

Big Mama Thornton, 1965
Photo by Chris Strachwitz, courtesy of Arhoolie Productions, Inc.

Russian roulette). But none of her subsequent eight singles for Peacock matched her success with "Hound Dog," and when her contract with the label expired in 1957, it was not renewed.

Thornton then moved to California, playing clubs in San Francisco and L.A. and recording for a succession of labels. While signed to Baytone Records in the early '60s she recorded her own "Ball and Chain," and though the label chose not to release the song (Thornton later recorded it for different labels), they did hold on to the copyright—which meant that Thornton missed out on the publishing royalties when Janis Joplin recorded the song later in the decade.

As interest in the blues was rekindled during the '60s, Thornton began appearing at blues and jazz festivals around the world and she continued releasing records: *Big Mama in Europe*, which featured backing from guitarist Buddy Guy, *Big Mama Thornton with the Chicago Blues Band*, with backing from Muddy Waters, James Cotton, and Otis Spann, and *Stronger Than Dirt*, which featured contemporary material like Wilson Pickett's "Funky Broadway" and Bob Dylan's "I Shall Be Released." The '70s saw the release of *She's Back* and, in 1975, Thornton's final albums, *Sassy Mama!* and *Jail*, a live album recorded in two prisons. In 1980, Thornton shared the bill at the Newport Jazz Festival in a "Blues Is a Woman" showcase with Sippie Wallace, Koko Taylor, and other female singers. One of her final performances was a free R&B concert at L.A.'s Variety Arts Theatre in March 1984, with Lowell Fulson and Joe Liggins and His Honeydrippers, among others, also on the bill, which was filmed for British television. But Thornton's heavy drinking had made her live appearances infrequent by this time, and she died four months later at the Los Angeles boarding house where she was living.

In contrast to Thornton's version, Presley's lively rendition of "Hound Dog" was considerably speeded up and far closer to bright-eyed pop than the earthy blues of Big Mama—or even the raw rockabilly swing of Presley's earlier Sun Records hits. Presley had been touted as the ultimate crossover artist, who "sounded" black but was in fact white, so he could perform R&B material with some measure of credibility and gain exposure through media still closed off to most black performers, such as television and Top 40 radio. Having white artists cover material originally performed by black musicians may have diluted the power of R&B, but such covers made the music "safe" for consumption by a white audience. Presley's move from Sun to RCA Records (who signed Presley at the end of 1955) illustrated both the transformation of R&B into "rock & roll"—a hybrid that could be seen as either jumped-up country or watered-down rhythm & blues, depending where you stood on the musical spectrum—and the gradual absorption of the new music from its roots in the realm of independent, or "indie," record labels into the major label mainstream.

Major label record companies (which in the '50s included such labels as Columbia, RCA, Decca, Capitol, MGM, and Mercury) ran their own disc-pressing plants and distribution networks and had the potential to maximize their profits because they were able to get their records into the largest number of shops. But their size could also put them at a disadvantage, for they needed to sell more records in order to break even. As a result, major labels were usually more interested in promoting the type of middle-of-the-road music that sold to the majority of America's record buyers, artists with broad popular appeal like Rosemary Clooney, Bing Crosby, Doris Day, and Frank Sinatra. Indies, who might operate out of a one-room office and distribute their records from the trunk of the owner's car, were nonetheless small enough to take chances on records that didn't have to sell in large numbers. Being unable to compete in markets dominated by major labels, indies had to find their own markets, and as a result they were able to pick up on developing trends overlooked by the majors and break new and innovative artists.

One of the markets indies had initially specialized in was the blues. The first blues hit, recorded in 1920 and released on the Okeh label, was "Crazy Blues," performed by Mamie Smith, who was also the first African-American to make a record. "Crazy Blues" surprised the record industry by eventually selling over seven thousand copies a week, and Ralph Peer, the record's producer, dubbed this newly discovered market "race" music (he later dubbed the early country market "hillbilly" music, after recording Jimmie Rodgers and the Carter Family in 1927). The post–World War I years were boom years for the record industry (record sales totaled over 106 million in 1921 alone), but the arrival of radio curtailed its growth, and by the time the Depression arrived in the 1930s, many of the independent labels had been bought up by the majors (Okeh's catalog was acquired by Columbia) or had simply gone bankrupt. World War II brought with it a shortage of shellac, leading the majors to retreat into producing middle-of-the-road pop records instead of expending energy on "specialized" markets, as the blues and country genres were considered.

But the war years had also led to the evolution of a new audience for another type of "race" music that came to be called rhythm & blues. World War II had brought an influx of African Americans into America's major cities in search of work, and black radio stations and record labels sprang up to take advantage of this burgeoning market. Rhythm & blues was then "discovered" by a white audience who tuned into R&B stations out of curiosity and ended up going out to their local record shops in search of the music they'd heard. By 1949 "race" music had officially become "rhythm & blues" in the venerated pages of *Billboard*; the same year the magazine also dropped the term "hillbilly" in favor of "country and western." The Top 40 charts were still dominated by the mainstream pop of artists like Frank Sinatra and Doris Day, but as the interest in R&B continued to grow, songs that would previously have only hit on the R&B—black—charts would begin to have an impact on the Top 40—white—charts as well.

It was this phenomenon—a white audience buying black music—that led to the creation of radio shows like Alan Freed's *The Moondog Show.* Freed, a DJ at radio station WJW in Cleveland, had persuaded the station management to add an R&B program in the early '50s after a local record shop owner tipped him off to the growing white audience that was taking an interest in R&B music. Freed later moved to New York, where he hosted his radio show on station WINS—and also took credit for originating the term "rock & roll" to distinguish the music from black-identified rhythm & blues, though the phrase was a familiar one in any number of R&B songs (such as Roy Brown's "Good Rockin' Tonight," Wild Bill Moore's "Rock and Roll," and Trixie Smith's "My Daddy Rocks Me (With One Steady Roll)," among others). The term was also a euphemism for sex, making the idea that rock & roll was "cleaner" than R&B somewhat ironic.

Rock & roll finally broke solidly into the pop charts in 1955 when Bill Haley & His Comets' "Rock Around the Clock," on Decca Records, went to number 1 more than a year after it had originally been released, having gained a welcome degree of exposure when it was played over the opening credits of the film *The Blackboard Jungle.* As a result, the major labels began waking up to the commercial potential of rock & roll, but for the moment, indie labels were still able to rule the scene: Chess, with Chuck Berry, the Moonglows, and later Etta James; Specialty, with Little Richard and Fats Domino; Sun, with Presley, Jerry Lee Lewis, and Carl Perkins; and Atlantic, home to LaVern Baker and one of the first R&B stars of the '50s, Ruth Brown.

Atlantic Records was founded in 1947 by Ahmet Ertegun, a longtime music fan who arrived in America in his early teens, the son of the Turkish Ambassador to the United States. When Ertegun decided to start his own label, he brought in Herb Abramson, formerly an Artists and Repertoire (A&R) staffer at National Records, as his partner; Abramson's wife, Miriam, was also hired to look after Atlantic's business affairs, and she eventually became responsible for working with the pressing plants to ensure that Atlantic's product was delivered on time. Ertegun's brother Nesuhi became a partner in the mid-'50s and also worked as a producer for the label. Working out of Ertegun's Manhattan apartment, the Atlantic staff soon found that R&B was more profitable than jazz, and the company had their first hit in 1949 with Stick McGhee's "Drinkin' Wine Spo-Dee-O-Dee," which reached number 3 on the R&B charts in April.

Ruth Brown's performing career was also launched in 1949 on Atlantic with the May release of "So Long"/"It's Raining," which eventually reached number 6 on the R&B

charts. It was the first in a series of records that would prove to be such hot contenders that Atlantic was referred to as "The House That Ruth Built." Born Ruth Weston in Portsmouth, Virginia, in 1928, Brown began singing in the local church where her father was the choir director. "You had to sing in church," she remembers. "That was required learning. If you could carry a tune, it would start in the church and then, naturally, in the school groups. I never thought, though, that music would be my livelihood. For years I never thought I was ever going to get out of that little town. So for those reasons I used to dump music class—I never learned to read it. My music teacher used to say, 'You'll regret that someday.'"

Skipping music class didn't keep Brown from singing. "I was always singing," she says. "That's all I've ever done. It's my gift. I sang when my daddy didn't know I was singing, for the USO shows, sneaking out and singing at the army bases. I was a little rebel. I wasn't a little angel, by no means, singing the so-called devil's music. Then I fell in love, got married, and ran away. Isn't that always the way?" After escaping Portsmouth, Brown continued singing, and while performing in Detroit was hired by Lucky Millinder, whose band had backed a number of blues artists, including Wynonie Harris.

But her stint with Millinder was short-lived, for he fired her after a few weeks on the road ("He changed his mind. They said I couldn't sing") and left Brown stranded in Washington, D.C. She found work when a friend introduced her to Blanche Calloway, the sister of bandleader Cab Calloway, who hired Brown to sing at her club, the Crystal Caverns, and later became her manager. One night Duke Ellington and DJ Willis Conover, from radio's *Voice of America* program, caught Brown's set, and Conover was impressed enough to phone his friend Ahmet Ertegun. Ertegun dispatched Herb Abramson to D.C. to meet with Brown, and she was on her way to New York to sign the contract and make an appearance at the Apollo when a car accident waylaid her for a year. But Ertegun was prepared to wait; he visited Brown in the hospital to get her signature on a contract, and on her twenty-first birthday he brought her some birthday presents: a pitch-pipe, a book on sight-reading, and a writing tablet.

After her success with "So Long," Brown had her first number 1 hit on the R&B charts with "Teardrops From My Eyes," released in 1950. The hits firmly established Brown as an R&B singer, a direction Atlantic hadn't originally considered for her. "Basically they weren't really sure what position I was going to be in," she says. "When I first started to sing for Atlantic, I wasn't doing rhythm & blues, I was doing standards. I was singing Bing Crosby songs. I could sing anything, and that was what the problem was. And rhythm & blues kind of just popped up there. 'Teardrops' was probably the one that turned it around. So if this is what they wanted to hear, good, I could do it. And

Ruth Brown, 1950s
Courtesy of Ruth Brown

if they had turned around and said, 'Well, I want you to do gospel,' I could do that too." But the commercial success of Brown's R&B songs led to a string of further hits, including "5-10-15 Hours," "(Mama) He Treats Your Daughter Mean," and "Mend Your Ways." "Miss Rhythm," as she was dubbed by singer Frankie Laine, finally crossed over into the pop charts in 1957 with Leiber and Stoller's "Lucky Lips," which reached number 25.

Brown's success on the label was followed by that of LaVern Baker—"The Countess"—who signed with Atlantic in 1953. Born Delores LaVern Baker in Chicago in 1929, Baker, like Brown, got her start in music by singing in church. By the time she was in her teens, Baker was performing in local clubs, including Chicago's Club DeLisa, where she was billed as "Little Miss Sharecropper," a name she also recorded under for RCA and National Records. At a later engagement at Detroit's Flame Show Bar, Baker met her manager, Al Green, who got Baker a recording contract with Columbia Records, for whom she recorded as "Bea Baker" in 1951. Baker also recorded on the Okeh label with Maurice King, and for King Records with Todd Rhodes, later touring Europe with Rhodes.

Baker made her Atlantic debut in 1953 with "Soul On Fire"/"How Can You Leave a Man Like This," and by 1955 she became one of the first Atlantic artists to cross over to the pop charts with "Tweedle Dee," which reached number 14 (number 4 on the R&B charts). Baker subsequently released a number of records with similarly playful titles and lyrics: "Bop Ting-a-Ling," "Fee Fi Fo Fum," the jaunty "Jim Dandy," which reached number 17 on the pop charts and topped the R&B charts in 1957, "Jim Dandy Got Married," and "Humpty Dumpty Heart." Baker had no problem working with such light material, which she described as "cute." "Every novelty song I recorded was a hit, like 'Jim Dandy,'" she told *Goldmine*. "Maybe my voice was good for novelty songs."

Baker's most successful pop hit came in 1958 with the bluesy waltz-tempo ballad "I Cried a Tear," which went to number 6, and she had further Top 40 hits with such songs as "I Can't Love You Enough," "I Waited Too Long," and "See See Rider." But her material ultimately proved to be more successful on the R&B charts and by 1962 she'd landed eleven songs in the R&B Top 10. In 1965, Baker left Atlantic for Brunswick (a subsidiary of Decca) and continued her live performance work. In the late '60s, she began performing at military bases overseas, and later became the entertainment director at the Subic Military Base in the Philippines before returning to the U.S. in the late '80s. She continued performing until her death on March 10, 1997.

Etta James was another performer with roots in the R&B scene who eventually found success on the pop charts. Born Jamesetta Hawkins in 1938 in Los Angeles, James sang in the church choir as a child. She later moved to San Francisco with her mother and in her teens formed a vocal trio with sisters Abbye and Jean Mitchell. The trio auditioned for Johnny Otis when his band was appearing at San Francisco's Fillmore, and Otis brought them to L.A., where he had the girls record a song they had written, "Roll With Me Henry." The song was an answer record to the decidedly raunchier "Work With Me Annie" (a number 1 R&B hit in 1954 for Hank Ballard and the Midnighters, another act Otis had worked with) and was later given the less suggestive title "The Wallflower." Released on Modern Records in 1955, "Wallflower" went to number 2 on the R&B charts. James, who had changed her name on the record's release, spent the next few years touring with Otis and enjoying further success with such R&B hits as "Good Rockin' Daddy" (a number 12 R&B hit) and "Most of All." By 1960 James had moved to Chess Records, where she recorded for their subsidiary labels Argo and Cadet and landed in the pop charts with such Top 40 hits as "All I Could Do Was Cry" (her first Top 40 appearance), "Pushover," and "Tell Mama."

But the growing commercial success rock & roll and R&B were experiencing was matched by a growing number of attacks on the music from political and religious leaders and conservative powers in the music industry itself. That rock & roll had its roots in the black community was reason enough to condemn it; the presence of "suggestive" lyrics, the emotional frenzy the music generated in live performance, and the fact that blacks and whites were able to freely mix at such performances added considerable fuel to the fire. Songs, rock & roll shows, and films featuring rock music were regularly banned: when Clare Boothe Luce, then-ambassador to Italy, denounced *The Blackboard Jungle*, the U.S. entry to the Venice Film Festival, as "degenerate" due to its depiction of juvenile delinquency in public schools, the film had to be replaced by the more genteel *Interrupted Melody*; back in the U.S., performances by black artists in rock films were routinely cut from prints distributed in the South. Frank Sinatra took the time to denounce rock & roll as "the most brutal, ugly, desperate, vicious form of expression it has been my misfortune to hear"; Alan Freed lost his TV show on WNEW due to complaints received when Frankie Lymon, of Frankie Lymon and the Teenagers, was shown dancing with a white girl; and even the mild-mannered Nat "King" Cole was attacked during a 1956 concert in Birmingham, Alabama, by a group called the White Citizens Council, whose aim was to eradicate all "bop and Negro music."

The artists who took their music out on the road were able to see the crossover impact of rock & roll in action as they confronted the attempts of a racist society to restrict such musical integration. "Now, ninety percent of my audience is white," says Ruth Brown, "but in the '50s it was just the other way around. And we performed mostly through the Deep South, where segregation was at its worst, so we were not allowed to live in the better hotels and eat in the restaurants and that kind of thing. It was a music that came out of some kind of difficulty." For some of the performers, touring gave them their first exposure to such rigid segregation. In her first trip to Nashville, LaVern Baker was surprised to discover that she was only allowed to ride in cabs bearing a sign that said "colored" ("All the cabs in Chicago were yellow and that's all I knew," she told *Goldmine*). Etta James, on her first tour of Texas with Johnny Otis, incurred the wrath of a local who was angered by her curt refusal to use the insect-infested "colored" bathroom at his establishment. "That guy came around the corner with a shotgun," she told *Pulse*. "'I'm gonna blow all of your brains out if you don't make her apologize' . . . [Otis] said, 'Etta, you've never experienced this, but this man is not playing. If you don't apologize, he will kill all of us.' So I apologized, and from that day on I knew what kind of pressure we were under in the South."

But segregation—both in and outside of the theaters—wasn't enough to keep away a curious white audience. "There were always white spectators," says Brown. "But they were either upstairs or separated on the main floor because of the rules of the South." Meanwhile, a different kind of segregation began taking place on the radio once rock & roll's commercial viability had been established and white artists began covering material initially popularized by black performers. Cover versions offered record companies—particularly the majors—a way to circumvent the potential controversy of rock & roll while still exploiting its commercial potential by "cleaning up" questionable lyrics in the original version, as Georgia Gibbs did in "Dance With Me, Henry," a cover of Etta James's "Wallflower." And despite the frequent lack of fire in cover versions (a lack amply demonstrated in Pat Boone's covers of Little Richard's "Tutti Frutti" and Fats Domino's "Ain't That a Shame"), being on a major label often gave covers the edge over original versions as far as distribution was concerned. Hence Gibbs could rack up sales of over a million with "Henry" while James's "Wallflower" only managed sales of four hundred thousand.

Georgia Gibbs, a performer who represented the acceptable face of female pop of the 1950s, made her first appearance in the Top 40 charts with another R&B cover, LaVern Baker's "Tweedle Dee," which reached number 2 (in contrast to Baker's version, which reached 14); she also later covered Baker's "Tra La La," which she took to number 24 while Baker's version, released as the flip side of "Jim Dandy," stalled at 94. Baker's response was to contact Michigan State Representative Charles Diggs, Jr., in an attempt to revise the Copyright Act of 1909 to prohibit a song's arrangement from being copied verbatim (an attempt which proved to be unsuccessful). Baker didn't necessarily mind having her songs covered, but she did object to having a song's arrangement—which she would have paid for out of her royalties—copied note-for-note without receiving any financial compensation.

Nor did those recording R&B originals necessarily see their music as inherently "purer": Ahmet Ertegun stated that his own R&B artists recorded "watered-down versions of real blues. The real blues were too hard for [white kids] to swallow." Etta James, in a 1973 interview in *Rolling Stone*, was somewhat more cynical in analyzing Leonard Chess's ability to assess a potential hit for his Chess Records label: "He'd sit there . . . and he wouldn't pat his foot until I'd see him sneaking a look at *my* foot," she said. "And sometimes, just for evilness, I wouldn't pat my foot. And if he couldn't see it patting, he'd say 'Etta, I don't think that tune's any good.' And then I'd wait till some old jive tune that wasn't anything came on, and I'd pat my foot . . . and he'd say 'That's it! That's going to be a hit record! Believe what Leonard tells you.' He knew nothing about it."

Nonetheless, the prevalence and acceptance of

Etta James
1984 at the Vine Street Bar and Grill, Hollywood,
Photo by Sherry Rayn Barnett

covers by Top 40 radio meant that black artists like Ruth Brown, whose songs were also covered by artists like Gibbs and Patti Page, faced the frustration of being shut out of the pop charts. It was an experience Brown found "devastating." "Rhythm & blues was getting ready to be called rock & roll," she remembers. "It had become interesting enough; white kids were starting to pay attention to it. And then on the scene came Alan Freed. On the scene came Elvis Presley. On the scene came Jerry Lee Lewis. But we already had Jackie Wilson. We already had Bo Diddley. We already had B. B. King. We had it all in place. But it was not feasible for us as black artists to be the innovators or to be the performing acts that did this in person. So once you got rock & roll creeping in, the cover records got to be tremendous, and we didn't get the media exposure. I never got to do *The Ed Sullivan Show*. And I had never, until September 1990, been on *The Tonight Show*, ever. I mean, never!"

But while racial barriers were being challenged with varying degrees of success, gender barriers in rock & roll rarely came in for the same kind of reassessment, and most women in the early days of rock made their mark as singers. But there were other women who did challenge the assumptions about what a woman's role in rock was "supposed" to be. Peggy Jones not only wrote and produced her own material, she also earned the nickname "Lady Bo" through her association with Bo Diddley, having played with the pioneering guitarist both on tour and on his records of the late '50s—early '60s. Jones's role in Diddley's band has been obscured over the years for a number of reasons. Recording credits were never as inclusive in rock's early years as they are today, and the mistakes frequently remain uncorrected when the records are reissued. The situation for Lady Bo was further complicated when she took a "leave of absence" from playing with Diddley and was replaced by his half-sister, dubbed "The Duchess," and articles have been confusing the two ever since.

Born in New York City, Jones grew up in a household where her artistic development was encouraged. Beginning as a dancer at age three, Jones appeared at Carnegie Hall at nine. At twelve she took up the ukulele—a popular first instrument for many female performers—later learning the guitar. "I thought it was kind of stupid to go into entertainment with the ukulele!" she says. "That's why I switched over to something I thought someone could accept . . . but little did I know that a female playing any instrument was like a new thing. I was breaking a lot of barriers."

Jones soon began writing songs and later had her own singing group. "I came out of the era where all the doo-wop groups were singing on the corner," she says. "It's like when you get out of school, guys and girls would bunch together, and sometimes they would trade off homework or what have you; then, for leisure time, it's vocalizing. This was during the times groups like the Bobbettes were out, the Chantels were out. And we were just a girl group; we'd get together after school. We'd do a lot of programs at different high schools, junior high schools. Would you believe at that age I was doing stuff like Ruth Brown? Oh, she is fantastic still! I was doing a little bit of Etta James, some cover stuff like the Chantels to keep in touch with the recording people, and I did a lot of writing, so we did a lot of original stuff. It was a real combination there."

A scholarship enabled Jones to move on to New York's High School of the Performing Arts, where she studied drama and modeling in addition to working with her girl group. In 1957, Jones recorded her first single, "Baby"/"So Why" with the Bopchords, and further records and session work followed. "I was doing a lot of session work, believe it or not," she says. "I was the third guitar player on a lot of sessions; you had your two main guys and sometimes there was room for a third. And being the type of person I was, I wanted to get into as many things as I could, even if it became standing outside a studio door, with someone saying, 'Do you play guitar? What do you do? Okay, come on in,' you know, get invited in."

Her own singles included "Honey Bunny Baby"/"Why Do I Love You," recorded with Gregory Carroll of the Orioles and released under the name Greg and Peg in 1958, and "Everybody's Talking"/"I'm Gonna Love My Way," recorded with Bobby Bakersfield, later Jones's first husband, and released credited to Bob and Peggy in 1959. "That was one of my first singles that I produced and wrote both tunes," she says. "Anything that I couldn't write down I got someone to help me out. I did the arrangements and I said, 'I would like to have some strings in this section . . . how do we write for violins?' It was really a challenge for me. I was like, what, seventeen."

Jones and Bakersfield next brought in drummer Brian Keeny (who later played with the Chambers Brothers) to form a trio, the Jewels, which soon began playing area clubs. "We were a mixed group," says Jones, "being not only female and male, but colored and white, so we were mixed all the way round. And we were told that a mixed group would not make it, people would not accept that, because you're still coming in from that era where they did not know where to put R&B people, let alone a mixed group. And being a guitarist, that didn't set too good with a lot of people, because it was also that time where, well, why aren't you singing with a girl group or doing girlie things? A lot of people felt that a guitar is a male instrument, you know what I mean?

"I just hung in there because this is what I wanted to do, and I had a real strong constitution as to the way I thought I should go about it," she continues. "A lot of times, even now, when you see a new thing, the first thing you do is criticize. So you go, okay, there's some that criticize and some that will check into what you're doing, and then the people that are criticizing, eventually they're going to stop criticizing and say, 'Well, let me check this out.'"

1957 was also the year that Jones met Bo Diddley during one of his appearances at the Apollo. Diddley's distinctive, choppy guitar playing had made him a major R&B performer, with such hits as "Bo Diddley" and "I'm a Man." Jones, on her way to a session, had come by the theater to check out the day's showtimes and her guitar case caught Diddley's eye. "I ran into him in the street, outside the theater," she says. "I was always a subject of someone coming up to talk to me; you're automatically different anyway when you're walking down the street with a guitar. I guess that's one way instead of saying, 'Hey baby, what's happening?' And we got to talking about the guitar, which was my favorite subject anyway, so he invited me in to the show and told me, 'Why don't you come backstage and bring your guitar and we'll see what you're doing.'"

As a result, Jones found a mentor in one of the leading instrumentalists of the day: Diddley began playing with her backstage, showed her the basics of the "Diddley rhythm," and eventually invited her to sit in with the band. "To me, it was like training," she says, "because the hardest thing in the world for me at that time was the rhythm, that Bo Diddley rhythm. That alone would make your toes curl up. You'd roll over in your grave. I tell you, my hands were so sore. I thought I was going to have a permanent lock on holding my pick trying to play this rhythm." And though Jones was still working with the Jewels, the chance of working with Diddley was an opportunity she couldn't pass up. "He asked me to be in the band for the simple reason, he said then, that I was beginning to sound so much like him he wanted to see how I turned out," she says. "He was trying to keep an eye on me because the first thing that was odd was I was a female, and number two, I sounded like him. So with him being the macho Bo Diddley, I think he wanted to keep a tab on me. Even though a lot of people thought I wasn't playing, you know, that I had a tape recorder or something and was not really playing!"

Jones's work as a guitarist and vocalist appeared on many of Diddley's best known songs, including "Mona," "Who Do You Love," and "Hey Bo Diddley," among others. Her stint with Diddley not only gave her her first experience in touring, but also her first encounters with the kind of segregation other black performers had experienced on the road. "We were touring in this hearse," she says. "Now you could not draw more attention: a band in a hearse. But that was touring on the road with Bo Diddley. And if you pulled over and you couldn't get served in a restaurant, Bo had a way he could cook in the car." While touring in Ohio, Jones inadvertently used the "wrong" bathroom at a club, though with far fewer ramifications than Etta James had experienced. "I went to go to the ladies' room," she says, "and I went down off the stage and walked across the dance floor. I didn't know that I wasn't supposed to walk across the dance floor. See, the people of color would have to go this way to the bathroom, everything

Lady Bo with Bo Diddley
1973 in Denver, Colorado, Lady Bo Archives, courtesy of Lady Bo

was divided up. All this was new to me, man. I think Bo got a little paranoid because when I came back he said, 'Did you know you weren't supposed to do that?' I said, 'Do what?' Well, how the hell did I know? This is my first time in town. It was a trip. He said, 'Don't do that no more. We might get in trouble.' Just funny stuff like that."

In the early '60s, Jones took a break from Diddley's band to concentrate on working with the Jewels, who released the single "I'm Forever Blowing Bubbles"/"We've Got Togetherness," also written and produced by Jones, in 1961. The band's label, MGM, had originally wanted to sign only Jones, but eventually signed the whole group when Jones refused to sign as a solo act. But Jones's career stalled because of marital problems with Bakersfield, who had become increasingly abusive. "I had a lot of opportunities," says Jones, "but at the time I was just not available, because you're fighting for your life here. I would say it was almost as bizarre as the Tina Turner and Ike issue, except I didn't wait sixteen years to leave!" The Jewels disbanded as a result, and Jones joined the King's Paupers in an effort to start with a clean slate, but Bakersfield continued to harass her and her family. After enduring innumerable threats on her life, Jones finally got Bakersfield to leave her alone by purchasing a gun and convincing Bakersfield she'd use it—on him. Jones later married another bass player, Wally Malone, and moved to California's Bay Area at the end of the '60s. Today Jones and Malone continue to perform in their band, the Family Jewel; the group also backs Bo Diddley when he appears in the area and in 1987 accompanied Diddley on a European tour.

On the other side of the country there was another woman juggling the duties of producer, studio musician, and recording artist: Bonnie Buckingham, who, recording under the name "Bonnie Guitar," faced the same sort of resistance Peggy Jones had encountered over her choice of instrument. "You were almost not really acceptable if you were an instrumentalist at that time," she says. "It just wasn't believed that females could do that. Keyboard was acceptable, but guitar didn't seem to be. I think I was accepted because I never thought of it any other way; I don't think I went in with any attitude that 'Oh, oh, I'm a girl, they're not going to like my playing.' So probably that might have been my savior, because I just went in as a musician and expected to be accepted as a musician."

Born in 1924 in Auburn, Washington, Buckingham came from a musical family. "All my family played some kind of instrument," she says, "and we had every kind of music in our home." After getting her start on clarinet, Buckingham moved to the guitar, which she played in school groups and later in area clubs, working on maintaining the diversity she'd grown up with. "I played in Western bands, I played in pop bands, I played in everything," she says. She was equally receptive to the sounds of rock & roll when it arrived on the music scene in the '50s. "Of course it was an exciting thing to have that kind of music coming in," she says. "And as a guitar player, I wanted to learn to play those kinds of things." She also identified with the country roots of rock. "In those days, they were taking country licks and putting them to rock beats, just using a different feel with them," she says. "And that was what was a part of '50s rock and R&B—it all had a kind of between blues-country flavor. We don't have that today. A country hit never crosses over today into your hard rock field. But then, a song could be real hardcore country and become a hit in the Top 40."

Buckingham and one of her early bands had released a record locally, but when that didn't take off she busied herself with other work, hosting a daily TV show and performing in local clubs at night, playing a solo set in the early evening followed by a full-band set at night. Then, in 1955, Buckingham recorded a demonstration tape (demo) for a songwriter she knew. The tape was sent off and caught the attention of Fabor Robison in Malibu, California, who ran his own studio and record label, but it was Buckingham, not the songs, he was interested in. "He called and asked me if I'd come down and talk with him," says Buckingham. "So I went down, and he hired me as a staff guitarist. I was surprised, delighted, and elated out of my mind. I was in California before you could say the name!"

Buckingham's time at Fabor Records Studios gave her an excellent opportunity to learn every aspect of recording. "From morning to night we were in the studio," she says. "I was learning the studio 'cause that's what I wanted to learn. I was learning the mixing board and how to mike rooms and how to mike voices. And we were all writing together; we were writers and singers and that's all we did. It was the perfect thing for me." Buckingham also did session work, playing on records by Dorsey Burnette and on Ned Miller's hit "From a Jack to a King," in addition to releasing her own records as "Bonnie Guitar," a name she adopted in 1956. "Every time I had a record, *Billboard* would say, 'If this girl gets the right song she'll have a hit.' And I had wonderful reviews, but the first two or three were not hits. And then 'Dark Moon' came along." A country-flavored ballad written by Miller, "Dark Moon," released in 1957, was also covered by Gale Storm and released on the same label as Buckingham's version, Dot. "I was so naive," says Buckingham. "I was just basking in the glory of being a studio musician and having a record being played on the air. It never occurred to me that someone was not doing me a favor by covering it." She changed her mind when she saw a number of juke-boxes purporting to carry her record that actually had Storm's version of "Dark Moon," and Storm eventually edged out Guitar on the charts, with her version peaking at number 4, while Guitar's peaked at number 6. But Guitar's Top 10 success nonetheless won her a spot on *The Ed Sullivan Show* as well as tour dates with Gene Vincent and the Everly Brothers.

Guitar had further success with the song "Mr. Fire Eyes," which she co-wrote, and tied with Johnny Mathis and Polly Bergen for "Most Promising New Vocalist" of the year, when her career ground to a sudden halt. "I was getting offers for some pretty big things," she says, "and my producer wanted to become my manager, and wanted to have all the rights to direct my financial gain in the directions he chose. He had artists that had left him when they got successful [including Jim Reeves, the Browns, and the DeCastro Sisters], and he didn't want that to happen with me." When Guitar was reluctant to agree to the offer, Robison presented her with an ultimatum: accept or leave the company. Guitar chose the latter, and since her contract forbade her from working in the area, she decided to move back to Seattle.

But Guitar's next project returned her to the charts, albeit as producer, with "Come Softly to Me" by the Fleetwoods, a vocal trio from Olympia, Washington. The group, Barbara Ellis, Gretchen Christopher, and Gary Troxel, had attended high school together; Ellis and Christopher originally sang as a duo, later bringing in Troxel on trumpet, which he soon dropped in favor of becoming a third vocalist. After making a tape of "Come Softly to Me," which Ellis and Christopher had written, the group brought it to Bob Reisdorff, a record promoter, who in turn brought it to Guitar. "I knew it was a hit," she remembers. "When I heard that tape I said, 'This is absolutely a hit and we can cut a hit on it even in Seattle!'" Guitar and Reisdorff were so excited by the song they decided to set up their own label, Dolphin—later Dolton—Records. Guitar produced the song and played guitar on the track, which was then leased to Liberty Records, who released the single in 1959.

There had been pressure from Liberty to change the record's soft and intimate sound to a "hot" sound, but Guitar resisted. "The sound that I put on the record, with the gut-string guitar, was not used by anybody until I used it with the Fleetwoods," she says. "And that became one of the new sounds, and people started using it. At that time, if you could find a new sound that was a good sound and well recorded, well produced and well presented, you had a chance of getting a hit. And I mean a pretty big chance. Even somebody who never had recorded before. All of a sudden something would come from nowhere, that was recorded in a basement—and I mean that literally!—and have a hit record. That was happening all the time, that was not an unusual thing." "Softly," which went to number 1, was the beginning of a string of hits for the Fleetwoods, including a second number 1, "Mr. Blue," also released in 1959, and "Tragedy," which reached number 10 in 1961. But the group's run of success was put on hold when Troxel was drafted into the army in 1960, and though he rejoined the group later, the momentum was broken. Guitar eventually returned to Dot, where she worked as the head of A&R for their country department; today, she continues to perform and record as Bonnie Guitar.

If women being instrumentalists was something that didn't "set too good" with people, it also appeared that being a vocalist could have its limitations as well. In comparison to the white male rockers making dents in the Top 40 charts, the white female performers having Top 40 hits were in no sense as wild and abandoned as Jerry Lee Lewis, Eddie Cochran, or Elvis Presley. Of course, the male rockers did not necessarily escape public censure; when Presley appeared on *The Ed Sullivan Show*, it was under the condition that he be shot from the waist up in order to spare the television audience the sight of his "suggestive" pelvic gyrations. Accordingly, it was unlikely that a female rock & roller was going to find ready acceptance from a mainstream America that found it difficult to tolerate the sight of Presley's pelvis in motion. Nonetheless, there were some women who did dare to rock more than Georgia Gibbs or Patti Page ever did, though they found little success in the pop charts. These performers included Janis Martin, Wanda Jackson, Cordell Jackson, Rose Maddox, Jean Chapel, and a host of other regionally popular performers.

Rockabilly emphasized the country roots of rock & roll, so it was not surprising that many female rockabilly performers got their start in the country field. Chapel, who appeared on the country variety show *The Grand Old Opry* as Mattie O'Neill, became

Jean Chapel when she recorded such material as "Oo-Ba La Baby" at the Sun Records Studios in Memphis, where Jerry Lee Lewis, Carl Perkins, and Elvis Presley, among others, had recorded. Janis Martin was even billed as "The Female Elvis" when she was signed to his label, RCA, later recording the song "My Boy Elvis" as a tribute. Born in Sutherlin, Virginia, in 1940, Martin had started playing the guitar at age four, and by age eight she had entered her first talent show. At eleven she became a member of the WDVA Barndance in Danville, and eventually worked her way up to the Old Dominion Barndance based in Richmond, at that time the third largest show of its kind in the country. In 1956, a demo Martin recorded was taken to RCA, who signed Martin and released the song, "Willyou, Willyum," as her first single, with one of her own compositions, "Drugstore Rock and Roll," as the flip side.

"Drugstore" was the livelier of the two, but the bright bop of "Willyou, Willyum" led to sales of over 750,000 copies, and Martin was voted "Most Promising Female Artist of 1956" by *Billboard*. The "Female Elvis" subsequently began touring the U.S. with performers like Carl Perkins and Johnny Cash, later touring as a member of Jim Reeves's show, including a 1957 tour of army bases in Europe. Back in the States, Martin formed a band called the Marteens and continued touring, but following the birth of her son in 1958, she gradually limited her live performances to appearances in local venues in order to spend more time with her family (the sleeve notes on a 1979 compilation of Martin's songs observed, "She is presently booking on weekends only until her son graduates in June"). She continues to perform with her husband Janis Martin and The Variations.

In contrast to Martin, Wanda Jackson had more of an authentic rock growl in her rockabilly material, though she had also started out recording country music. Born in 1937 in Oklahoma, Jackson was given a guitar while her family was living in California in the '40s, and her father taught her to play. After returning to Oklahoma, Jackson won a spot hosting a show on Oklahoma City's radio station KLPR while in high school. The show brought her to the attention of singer Hank Thompson, who invited her to join his Brazos Valley Boys as a vocalist on weekends. She signed with Decca in 1954 and had her first hit with "You Can't Have My Love," a duet with the Brazos Valley Boys' bandleader Billy Gray, which reached number 8 on the country charts. In 1956, at age eighteen, she signed with Capitol Records, and met Elvis Presley while on tour in the South. Presley suggested Jackson try singing in a rockabilly style, and after considering his advice, Jackson recorded "I Gotta Know," released in 1956. The song humorously alternated between a drawling country beat and a hiccuping rockabilly swing and proved to be a success, reaching number 15 on the country charts.

After the release of "I Gotta Know," Jackson's next singles usually combined a country song on one side with a rocker on the other. Jackson's rock material is largely compelling because of her voice, which bristles with an appealingly raw feistiness. Jackson added to the sizzle by telling her producer, Ken Nelson, that she wanted her records to sound like those of Gene Vincent (who had a Top 10 hit with the rock & roll classic "Be-Bop-A-Lula"). Jackson was able to take inspiration from Presley and Vincent yet make the sound her own, taking a stance that savored her proud, defiant attitude: "Hot Dog! That Made Him Mad" is a primer on how to keep one's man in line, and "Fujiyama Mama" had Jackson drawing favorable comparisons between herself and atomic weaponry. Jackson also wrote or co-wrote some of her own material, which laughingly dismissed any notion of submissiveness; her "Mean Mean Man" is awarded the title because he won't give Jackson a goodnight kiss, and "Cool Love" has her despairing about her would-be lover's tendency to treat her like "a square" instead of being eager to "live it up" with her. This was a recurring theme in a number of rockabilly songs recorded by women, who did not hesitate to make their demands known, whether they were seeking a date, as in Donna Dameron's "Bopper 486609" (an answer record to the Big Bopper's "Chantilly Lace") or looking for physical gratification, as in Janis Martin's "Just Squeeze Me."

Jackson's Presley connection continued when she covered "Let's Have a Party," featured in Presley's film *Loving You*, and recorded "Honey Bop," written by the same team that had written "Heartbreak Hotel." "Party" provided Jackson with her first Top 40 hit in 1960, two years after it had originally been recorded. By that time, interest in rockabilly had declined, but Jackson continued to record rock & roll material, including covers of Little Richard's "Long Tall Sally," the Coasters' "Yakety Yak," and Jerry Lee Lewis's "Whole Lot of Shakin' Going On." She had two further Top 40 hits in 1961 with the country-flavored ballads "Right or Wrong" and "In the Middle of a Heartache" before moving back solidly into country, and eventually gospel, performing a mix of songs from each genre in her present day appearances. "My lifestyle is a Christian lifestyle, but I have no problems doin' those early rock things," she explained in the liner notes of a 1990 Rhino Records compilation of her rock and country material.

Cordell Jackson was one of the few female rockabilly artists who not only wrote her own material and played guitar, but ran her own record label, Moon Records. Born Cordell Miller in Pontotoc, Mississippi in 1923, Jackson gained her first performing experience with her father's band, the Pontotoc Ridge Runners. She moved to Memphis after graduating from high school in 1943, where she joined the Fisher Air Craft Band. By the early '50s, Jackson was writing her own songs and recording demos at Sam Phillips's Memphis Recording Service. She launched Moon Records in 1956 with her own single, "Rock and Roll Christmas"/"Beboppers Christmas," which she also produced. Jackson went on to produce records by other local performers and kept Moon an ongoing concern while holding down a series of day jobs, in addition to releasing her own records, including "Football Widow," and, in 1983, the four song EP (extended play record) *Knockin' 60*. She also became the producer of a contemporary Christian radio show, *Let's Keep the Family Together America*. "I have always stayed out of the mainstream because I love freedom," she told the *Memphis Star*, but she nonetheless took the opportunity to introduce herself to the mainstream on a large scale when she appeared in a 1991 commercial for Budweiser beer, besting Stray Cat Brian Setzer in a battle of dueling guitars. She continues to peform today.

Brenda Lee, though not strictly a rockabilly artist, was another white performer who crossed over from the country charts to the

Cordell Jackson, "Rockens First Lady of the '50s"
Courtesy of Cordell Jackson

pop charts and back again. Her young age made her something of a novelty: when she began recording for Decca at age eleven, "Little Miss Dynamite" was billed as being nine years old. Born Brenda Mae Tarpley in Atlanta in 1944, Lee began her career at six, appearing on radio, and soon moving on to television work. She signed with Decca in Nashville in 1956, working with Owen Bradley, who had also worked with Patsy Cline, as her producer. After successes with such songs as "One Step at a Time," which went to number 15 on the country charts, and equally successful appearances in Europe, Lee had her first Top 40 hit in 1960 with "Sweet Nothin's," which reached number 4. Her next release, "I'm Sorry," became her first number 1, and went on to sell over ten million copies, though there had been some initial hesitation that the ballad

Cordell Jackson, 1990
Photo by Pat Blashill

was too "adult" for a fifteen-year-old to sing. She rounded out the year with four more Top 40 hits, including a second number 1 with "I Want to Be Wanted," and a Top 20 hit with "Rockin' Around the Christmas Tree," originally recorded in 1958 and a seasonal radio staple ever since. But her subsequent hits never quite matched the sharp bounce of "Sweet Nothin's," and she eventually returned to the country field.

Ironically, if there was a lack of commercially successful female rock & roll performers, female songwriters had a hand in a number of notable rock & roll songs. Dorothy La Bostrie provided Little Richard with the lyrics for "Tutti Frutti," his first pop chart hit. Richard, in his initial recording session for Specialty Records, had spent the morning unable to deliver the goods, but later cut loose with a raucous, lewd number during a break at a local restaurant. Hoping to sustain the energy, producer Robert "Bumps" Blackwell pulled in La Bostrie (Richard had recorded her "I'm Just a Lonely Guy" earlier in the day) and asked her to "clean up" Richard's raunchy lyrics; the result was "Tutti Frutti." Mae Boren Axton, a schoolteacher, was the co-author of Elvis Presley's first RCA hit, "Heartbreak Hotel," having been inspired by a news story about a young man's suicide and the note he left behind. The married songwriting team of Felice and Boudleaux Bryant provided the Everly Brothers with a number of their early hits, such as "Bye Bye Love," "Wake Up Little Susie," and "All I Have to Do Is Dream." Sharon Sheely wrote Rick Nelson's number 1 hit "Poor Little Fool"; she was later involved in a key incident in rock & roll history, being a passenger in the same car wreck that killed Eddie Cochran in April 1960 while on a tour of England, a wreck both Sheely and Gene Vincent, another passenger in the car, survived.

In addition to radio and live performance, the media of film and television had begun to explore ways of presenting rock & roll to the public. Following Bill Haley's success with "Rock Around the Clock," a film of the same name was released in 1956, kicking off the era of "jukebox musicals," a seemingly endless series of look-alike films with sound-alike titles: *Don't Knock the Rock*; *Shake, Rattle and Rock*; *Rock, Rock, Rock*; *Mister Rock and Roll*, ad infinitum. Elvis Presley's popularity also ensured a profitable series of starring roles for the singer. Most of the plots dealt with teen concerns—getting a date for the prom, or convincing narrow-minded adults that a Saturday night rock & roll dance wouldn't transform their children into juvenile delinquents.

Women were usually relegated to the role of "the girlfriend" in such films, and rarely appeared in the lineup of singing stars. One exception was LaVern Baker, whose association with Alan Freed (she regularly headlined the rock & roll concerts he promoted in New York) led to appearances in two of his films, *Rock, Rock, Rock* and *Mister Rock and Roll*. Zola Taylor, one fifth of the vocal group the Platters, was about the only other female performer that turned up regularly in rock films, including *Rock Around the Clock*, *Rock All Night*, and one of the most notable films of the period, *The Girl Can't Help It*. Released in 1956, *The Girl Can't Help It* was a lively satire on rock & roll, with Jayne Mansfield as "Jeri Jordan," a would-be singing star pushed into the music business by her gangster boyfriend (Edmund O'Brien). The music industry as a whole is shown as being inextricably linked to organized crime: when a rival mobster keeps Mansfield's records off his company's jukeboxes, O'Brien and his assistant "shake down" hapless cafe owners into carrying O'Brien's jukeboxes. But it was all played for laughs (the rival mobster even signs O'Brien to a long-term recording contract), and in addition to the Platters (who performed "You'll Never Know"), there were appearances from Julie London, performing "Cry Me a River," and Abbey Lincoln, among others.

Television was quick to pick up on the visual appeal of rock & roll, and top acts of the day appeared on such variety programs as *The Ed Sullivan Show*, *The Steve Allen Show*, and *The Milton Berle Show*. Soon there were also shows specifically designed to cater to the newly discovered market of the "teenager" which featured pop and rock music exclusively, such as *American Bandstand*. Initially a local program on ABC-affiliate WFIL in Philadelphia, *Bandstand*, as it was originally called, made its debut in 1952, with host

Bob Horn introducing film clips of singing stars like Patti Page and Bing Crosby. In 1956, Horn was fired after a scandal erupted when he was arrested for drunken driving, accused of income tax evasion, and charged with statutory rape (the latter charge was dropped). Al Jarvis, an R&B DJ and the network's first choice as a replacement host, turned down the job due to ABC's hesitation to feature black artists on the show, so Dick Clark, who had worked at WFIL since 1951, was hired. The show went national in 1957, airing every afternoon Monday through Friday, with Clark eventually assuming the mantle of the World's Oldest Teenager and hosting the show until 1989.

The presence of the show in Philadelphia encouraged the development of the so-called "teen idol" market in the city, catering to a young female audience, wherein polite, pleasant-faced boys, such as Bobby Rydell, Fabian, and Frankie Avalon, could get a record deal, cut a song, and get national exposure via *Bandstand*. A similar situation developed on the West Coast, where television gave a boost to the singing careers of Edd "Kookie" Byrnes from *77 Sunset Strip* and Rick Nelson from *The Adventures of Ozzie and Harriet*, along with a number of other young television and film performers.

There were also female "teen idols," such as *The Mickey Mouse Club*'s Annette Funicello, Connie Stevens from *Hawaiian Eye* (who sang with Edd Byrnes on "Kookie Kookie (Lend Me Your Comb)"), and Shelley Fabares from *The Donna Reed Show*, who used their television exposure as the foundation for a potential singing career, though, like their male counterparts, their music was limited to pleasant, insubstantial pop. Connie Francis, a *Bandstand* regular, had more of an impact chartwise, notching up thirty-five Top 40 hits between 1958 and 1964, including sixteen in the Top 10. Born in 1948 in Newark, New Jersey, Concetta Rosa Maria Franconero was probably the most popular female performer of the late '50s and early '60s who wasn't a holdover from the pre–rock & roll Doris Day–Rosemary Clooney era, though her music was clearly more pop than rock. Francis began her career at age ten on the TV talent show *Startime* and signed to MGM Records in 1955. The hits started to arrive with "Who's Sorry Now," which reached number 4 in 1959, followed by, among others, "My Happiness," "Lipstick On Your Collar," and "Everybody's Somebody's Fool." By the '60s, Francis had moved into films, beginning with *Where the Boys Are* (for which she also sang the title tune), and ultimately left the pop arena behind to become more of an all-round entertainer as evidenced by the titles of her later releases: *Folk Song Favorites, Connie and Clyde: Hit Songs of the Thirties, German Favorites, Modern Italian Hits, At the Copa,* and, cashing in on the latest dance craze, *Do the Twist*.

After the initial period of using film and television to promote new rock & roll artists, the two mediums began drawing upon their own ranks to "create" rock & roll stars, as in the case of the teen idols. The end result diluted the music just as much as cover versions had, but this was of little concern to the record companies that continued to make money. For if the music was bland in comparison to the first wave of R&B and rock & roll (and performed by artists who, not coincidentally, were all white), its very blandness also made it safe and non-controversial. The fading of many of the original rock & roll pioneers from the music scene in the late '50s also coincided with the payola investigations of 1960, which gave the music industry further incentive to avoid controversy.

"Payola" referred to the bribing of DJs with cash or gifts to ensure airplay of a particular record, for maximum radio exposure was a vital ingredient in attaining maximum sales. Payola had long been an accepted practice in the music industry, but to conservative powers relentlessly seeking out new ways to attack rock & roll, payola provided a logical avenue to explore; why else would otherwise respectable radio stations flood the airwaves with such degenerate music unless they were being paid? The 1960 hearings were prompted by the revelation in 1959 that TV game shows were being rigged, and the investigations soon spread to the record industry. As a result, a congressional subcommittee, chaired by Owen Harris, held its first payola hearings in February 1960— also an election year—which continued through May. The subcommittee concluded that $263,000 in payoff money had been given to DJs in forty-two cities, and cited 255 with accepting such money.

This number constituted a mere fraction of the ten thousand DJs then working in the U.S., but an atmosphere of paranoia set in nonetheless, heightened by the actions of the Federal Communications Commission (FCC). The FCC had gone to work before the congressional hearings, filing payola complaints against record manufacturers and distributors, and asking radio station management to collect their own data on payola activities at their stations. And though payola did not become illegal until after the 1960 hearings, when Congress passed a statute making it a misdemeanor, nervous radio station owners fired DJs who admitted accepting payola in order to avoid scandal. Dissent was not tolerated: when Jack LeGraff, station manager at WJBK in Detroit, defended payola as being "part of American business," his comments cost him his job.

Others were prosecuted under their state's commercial bribery laws, a scenario that brought Alan Freed's career to an end when he, along with seven other DJs, was charged with accepting payola by a New York grand jury. Freed's unwillingness to cooperate (he refused to testify at the grand jury hearings) probably did not endear him to the authorities, in contrast to Dick Clark, who was also investigated due to his involvement in thirty-three music-related businesses in addition to his work on *Bandstand*. When Clark was told to either give up his interests in outside businesses or quit the show, he readily complied, electing to stay with *Bandstand*, and came through the investigations relatively unscathed, even being proclaimed "a fine young man" by the investigating subcommittee.

During this same period, a new musical movement was growing in which female performers would play a key role: the era of the "girl groups." The girl group sound had been developing throughout the rock era, and had its roots in the vocal harmonizing of doo-wop groups. The softer sounds of doo-wop had coexisted with the wildness of rock & roll from the beginning, in songs like "Earth Angel" by the Penguins, "Sh-Boom" by the Chords, and "In the Still of the Night" by the Five Satins, and similarly styled groups were now rising to prominence in the wake of the original rock & roll boom. Doo-wop's greatest attraction for aspiring performers was that it required little in the way of financial setup—all that was needed was your voice. In major urban cities, particularly in black, Latino, and Italian communities, groups of friends assembled to practice in schoolyards, in apartment building stairwells, or on street corners.

The white female vocal groups of the '50s tended to be more oriented toward pop than the bluesier strains of doo-wop. The "barbershop" vocal stylings of the Chordettes, an all-female quartet from Sheboygan, Wisconsin, gave them a series of hits, including "Mr. Sandman" and "Lollipop." There were also innumerable "Sister" combos that appeared in the Top 40, such as the Fontane Sisters, the Shepherd Sisters, the Lennon Sisters, the DeJohn Sisters, the DeCastro Sisters, and the McGuire Sisters. The growing interest in R&B and doo-wop over the decade inspired some of the groups to sing cover versions of songs first performed by black groups: the McGuire Sisters had a number 1 hit with "Sincerely," originally recorded by the Moonglows, and also recorded "Goodnight, Sweetheart, Goodnight," originally recorded by the Spaniels, and the Chordettes covered the Coasters' "Charlie Brown" in addition to recording such obviously rock-influenced material as "A Girl's Work Is Never Done," a supposed lament about the drudgery of housework that was nonetheless performed with inordinate cheerfulness.

Some of the doo-wop groups featured a female singer in their ranks, such as Lillian Leach of the Mellows and Trudy Williams of the Six Teens, and there were also black all-female groups, including the Bobbettes and the Chantels. The Bobbettes were essentially a one-hit group, having their greatest success with the song "Mr. Lee" in 1957. They were also one of the youngest girl groups, with the five members all between the ages of eleven and fifteen when they were signed to Atlantic Records in 1957. The group, originally eight members who attended the same school, had formed in 1955 and was initially called the Harlem Queens. Two years later, the group had trimmed down to five, Jannie and Emma Pought, Helen Gathers, Laura Webb, and Reather Dixon, and was gaining experience performing at school functions and local amateur shows, including Amateur Night at the Apollo. In 1957, the group found a manager, James Dailey, who brought the group to Atlantic.

The group was also notable in that they wrote much of their own material. "Mr. Lee," which they recorded at their first session for Atlantic along with three of their other compositions, was originally a derisive song about one of their teachers, but Atlantic insisted that the words be changed before it could be recorded. "Instead of 'He's the ugliest teacher I ever did see,' we changed it to 'the handsomest teacher I ever did see,'" Reather Dixon later recalled. The song, released in May 1957 under their new name, the Bobbettes, was enormously successful, topping the R&B charts and reaching number 6 on the pop charts, and the group spent much of the next two years on the road capitalizing on this success. Being the sole girl group on the touring bus, they were befriended by other female singers such as Ruth Brown and LaVern Baker, who helped the teenagers adjust to life on the road.

Surprisingly, the Bobbettes failed to have another hit, something they attributed to Atlantic's preference for more "gimmick songs" in the style of "Mr. Lee." In an attempt to dispense with "Mr. Lee" once and for all (in addition to ending the spate of answer records about him), the group released a "sequel" to the story with "I Shot Mr. Lee," which reached number 52 on the pop charts in 1960. Using the same bouncy melody line as their earlier hit, the song told how the unfortunate Mr. Lee met his untimely end because of his unfaithfulness, though the mood is clearly a celebratory one, as the group relates how they "shot him in the head boom-boom" with barely restrained glee. The Bobbettes originally recorded the song in 1959 for Atlantic, who chose not to release it. But when the number was re-recorded and released the following year on Triple-X Records, Atlantic, who had tried to acquire the master of the Triple-X version, then released their own version and managed to secure half of the publishing rights as well.

The Chantels, who released their first single three months after the Bobbettes released "Mr Lee," were one of the first all-female vocal groups to maintain their success beyond a single hit. They also had a clear rock sensibility, as opposed to the altogether more wholesome qualities of previous female vocal groups like the Chordettes and the various "Sister" combos. When the group began touring after the success of their second single, "Maybe," in 1958, they would also find themselves the only girl group on the bill, but by the time of their last Top 40 hit in 1961, the music scene would have progressed to the point where "girl groups" were no longer seen as a novelty, due in large part to the gains made by groups like the Bobbettes and the Chantels.

The Chantels were five schoolgirls who attended St. Anthony of Padua school in the Bronx, with Arlene Smith as lead singer, along with Sonia Goring, Rene Minus, Lois Harris, and Jackie Landry. The girls had been singing together since second grade in their Catholic school choir, and when they began singing as a group, they took the name "Chantel" from a rival school, St. Francis de Chantelle. Inspired by the youthful vocals of Frankie Lymon on the Teenagers' hit "Why Do Fools Fall in Love," the girls got backstage at a Teenagers' show and met up with the group's manager, Richard Barrett. A performer, songwriter, and producer in addition to being a manager, Barrett brought the group to George Goldner, who owned a number of New York indie labels, Gee, Gone, Rama, and End among them. Goldner was not initially interested in the group, as he didn't believe that girl groups were "saleable," but when Barrett threatened to withhold his songs from Goldner's empire, he relented and the group began recording for Goldner's End label.

The Chantels' first single, "He's Gone"/"The Plea," with both songs written by the fifteen-year-old Arlene and arranged by Barrett, was released in August 1957. The group's impressive harmonies provided a solid background for Smith's strong, soulful lead vocal, but the single only managed to reach number 71. But their next single, Barrett's "Maybe," featuring another powerful lead vocal from Smith, went all the way to number 15, winning the group an appearance on *American Bandstand* and a spot on one of Alan Freed's tours, where they were looked after by a solicitous LaVern Baker. They had two subsequent hits in 1958 with "Every Night (I Pray)," which reached the Top 40, and "I Love You So," which peaked at number 42.

But there were also growing tensions within the group, primarily because the Chantels were not making any money in spite of their chart successes, for the profits were swallowed up by expenses ranging from recording costs to "promotion." The lack of monetary compensation was an unfortunate fact of life for many recording artists, particularly black performers, for haphazard accounting procedures, along with frequent disregard for an artist's welfare, kept artists from earning money no matter how substantial a hit was. "In those days we paid for everything," explains Ruth Brown. "The recording studio, the scores being written, all the records given out for promotions, the musicians. So you thought you were doing all right with advances and whatnot, but all that money came back off the top before you saw a dime, and you always ended up in debt. We were just out there taking you at your word if you said, 'Okay, you're going to make $700.' I look for $700, no questions asked. I don't know what happened to that other $7,000 over there, but the $700 was what I was promised."

Smith ended up leaving the Chantels in 1959 due to frustration over the group's finances, and Lois Harris also left at the same time. Barrett then brought in Annette Smith (no relation), a singer in another group he managed, the Veneers, as the Chantels' new lead singer. Her voice was no match for Arlene's, but the group had two further Top 40 entries in 1961 with "Look in My Eyes" and "Well, I Told You," an answer record to Ray Charles's "Hit the Road, Jack." The group continued to record for a variety of labels throughout the '60s. Arlene Smith also recorded as a solo artist in the early '60s; she eventually became a teacher, and continues to perform live with her new group. Though Landry died in 1997, the Chantels continue to peform as well.

As the '60s began, women had managed to work their way into every area of the newly created rock & roll industry, as performers, songwriters, instrumentalists, producers, and record label owners. But progress had been slow, and the gains women had made had not necessarily cleared the path for the women who followed. The joint obstacles of sexism and racism combined to downplay, overlook, or erase women's contributions to the development of rock & roll. Nonetheless, female rock & roll pioneers had laid a substantial foundation upon which to build, enabling other women to ben-

efit from their hard-won experience: the endurance of Big Mama Thornton, whose drive would keep her performing virtually all her life, with or without the appearance of royalty checks; the patience of Lady Bo, who proved night after night that it was she, not a tape recorder, who was playing her guitar on stage; and the popularity of the Chantels, who showed once and for all that a group of girl singers could indeed be considered "saleable." Each step that these and other women had taken cracked open the door that much further, allowing an increasing number of women to emerge in the coming years.

Big Mama Thornton
July 1981 at the Hollywood Bowl, Photo by Sherry Rayn Barnett

2

Girl Groups

"Nobody in the business really took female performers too seriously back then. The system just wasn't
open to women. If a man's career wasn't successful anymore, he could move into A&R or production, or
into the company hierarchy—but we couldn't do that."
—Lesley Gore, in *Girl Groups: The Story of a Sound*

I n early 1961, the Shirelles became the first all-female group to top the singles
charts with "Will You Love Me Tomorrow." In the next two years they would have
ten more hits in the Top 40, including five in the Top 10. But more important than
their string of hits was their role in popularizing the "girl group" sound, the first major
rock style associated explicitly with women. Its roots lay in the '50s, in the music of
groups like the Bobbettes and the Chantels, but where those groups had been rarities in
the male-dominated landscape of vocal groups, by the early '60s there was a veritable
explosion of all-female groups on the music scene.

The girl groups provided a voice for a generation of adolescents, female and male,
in literally thousands of songs that addressed the issues of romance, heartbreak, and
the endless search for true love. The appealing honesty and sincerity of the genre was
underscored by the fact that the girls in the groups were primarily in their teens themselves, and many of the best songwriters of the era were also in their early twenties.
Though the groups occasionally wrote their own material, it was their image that made
the greatest impact with audiences, especially the female audiences that comprised most
of the record-buying public at the time. Suddenly, aspiring female performers didn't
have to look to the likes of a Frankie Lymon to provide inspiration, as the Chantels
had—they could now find ready role models in girls their own age.

The importance of the girl group image and its effect on the female rock audience has traditionally been overlooked by rock historians, who tend to regard girl groups as interchangeable, easily manipulated puppets, while the ones with the "real" talent were the managers, songwriters, publishers, and producers who worked behind the groups. And because the life expectancy of the groups was usually brief, and because their successors appeared in a seemingly never-ending stream, the role of the "girls" in the girl group equation has been diminished. An equally persistent stereotype has been the assumption that any group of girls with the ability to carry a tune could have a hit—as long as they remained malleable to the whims of the male Svengalis who really called the shots.

Unfortunately for the groups, their dependence on the manager/songwriter/producer teams around them did put them at a disadvantage as far as maintaining their careers after the initial flush of success. Once a winning formula for a group had been identified, it was repeated in subsequent singles until the group stopped having hits. The group was then left to return to obscurity, while the production teams moved on to the next formula and the next group. It was a scenario that would be repeated innumerable times during the girl group era. Because of their age and lack of experience, the groups were unsure how to go about voicing their own concerns, leaving them at a further disadvantage. In later interviews with these performers, a recurring complaint is the complete lack of involvement, let alone control, they were allowed in decisions affecting their careers. With the focus on getting hits the primary goal, it was all too easy to overlook the feelings of, again, the most expendable element in the unit: the performers.

Ultimately, trying to single out who played the most "important" role in the creation of a girl group hit record is an exercise in futility. A poor vocal has the capability of ruining the best written, best produced song; among the girl groups, the whole was certainly greater than the sum of its parts. There was also the fact that the "man behind the scenes," whether producer, songwriter, or manager, was sometimes a woman—so much for the "male Svengali" theories. To the public, it was the overall sound—the vocal harmonizing of doo-wop with a bright, uptempo backbeat—that was important, not the offstage machinations. And unlike the male "teen idols," with their placid musings on eternal devotion, the material performed by the girl groups often went beyond one-dimensional Moon-and-June sentimentality in its examination of adolescent emotions, creating engaging, well-crafted, and impassioned songs that changed the simple scenario of boy-meets-girl into something far more complex.

After the success of previous hits like the Bobbettes' "Mr. Lee" and the Chantels' "Maybe," the Shirelles' "Will You Love Me Tomorrow" heralded the true start of the girl group era. It was the first major hit for the group (and the first major success for the songwriters, Carole King and Gerry Goffin), who had been performing together since the late '50s. Shirley Owens, Beverly Lee, Doris Coley, and Addie "Micki" Harris, who attended the same high school in Passaic, New Jersey, had been inspired by groups like the Chantels to form their own group, originally called the Poquellos. After making their debut at a school show, a classmate introduced the group to her mother, Florence Greenberg, who ran her own record label, Tiara. Greenberg signed the group, now called the Shirelles, and released their first single, "I Met Him on a Sunday," in the spring of 1958. A group composition, "Sunday" was the story of a weeklong romance, set against a backdrop of the Shirelles' vocal harmonies with handclaps and finger-snapping providing a smooth, steady beat. After being leased to Decca Records, the single eventually reached number 49 on the charts.

Further singles followed, but none were able to match the mild success of "Sunday." In 1959, Greenberg started a new label, Scepter, and brought in a new producer to work with the Shirelles, Luther Dixon, a former member of the Four Buddies and a songwriter for such artists as Pat Boone, Perry Como, and Nat "King" Cole. Dixon's first collaboration with the Shirelles was producing and arranging "Tonight's the Night," a song written by Shirley Owens. Released in 1960, "Tonight" offered a personal perspective of teenage romance, with Owens (who sang the lead vocal) preparing for her big date in a mood of nervous anticipation, vacillating between the doubts and excitement of beginning "a great romance." The single cracked the Top 40, reaching number 39, and set the stage perfectly for "Will You Love Me Tomorrow," a song Dixon brought to the group.

Dixon had heard "Tomorrow" while visiting the offices of Aldon Music, the publishing company where Carole King and Gerry Goffin worked. King and Goffin had originally offered "Tomorrow" to Johnny Mathis, but when it was turned down, Dixon was able to persuade the songwriting team to give it to the Shirelles, in addition to having them shorten the song, which was originally over four minutes long. The Shirelles had their own reservations about recording "Tomorrow," feeling the song sounded "too white." But "Tomorrow" was a logical follow-up to "Tonight's the Night," taking the teenage drama to the next level. If Owens had pondered, somewhat obliquely, the dangers of going "too far" with her boyfriend in "Tonight's the Night," she had now clearly decided to give in to his demands, but wondered about the consequences of her actions by asking, "Will you still love me tomorrow?" The directness of the question was a startling one from a teenage girl, and unusual in a genre that generally assumed a lifetime of happiness would follow once you'd attained the boy of your dreams. In "Tomorrow" Owens had attained the boy, but her feelings about the permanence of love appeared to be more uncertain than ever.

Released in late 1960, "Tomorrow" (which also featured Carole King on kettle drums) hit the top of the charts in early 1961, and the hits continued for the next two years. "Soldier Boy," released in 1962, became the Shirelles' second number 1 hit, and they had further Top 10 successes with "Baby It's You," "Mama Said," and "Dedicated to the One I Love," a song which only reached number 83 on its original release in 1959, but which climbed up to number 3 after the success of "Tomorrow." But the Shirelles' dependence on Dixon as their producer, arranger, and song provider meant that the foundation of their success was shaky, as they discovered when Dixon quit working with the group at the end of 1962. The group managed another Top 10 hit with "Foolish Little Girl," but by the end of 1963 they'd made their last appearance in the Top 40.

Nor was there any financial compensation to enjoy now that their run on the charts was over, for on turning twenty-one the group members found that the money they had earned, supposedly held in trust for them by Greenberg, had been spent in the usual

The Shirelles, circa 1962 (left to right: Beverly Lee, Doris Coley, Shirley Alston, Micki Harris)
Courtesy of David A. Young collection

manner—for recording costs, promotion, touring, and so on. The fact that they were also legally forced to remain with Scepter did nothing for the Shirelles' quickly disintegrating morale, though they continued recording for the label until 1968. Afterwards, Shirley Owens—now Shirley Alston—formed her own group called Shirley and the Shirelles, and later recorded two solo albums as "Lady Rose"; the other group members formed their own "Shirelles" combinations and found work on the "oldies" circuit.

In contrast to the performers, the women songwriters of the early '60s were in a better position to both exert control over their careers and make the kind of money the girl groups themselves rarely saw. Three of the main female/male songwriting teams of the time were also husband and wife: Carole King and Gerry Goffin, Ellie Greenwich and Jeff Barry, and Cynthia Weil and Barry Mann. King and Goffin and Weil and Mann worked for Aldon Music, which was formed by Al Nevins and Don Kirshner in 1958. The company had their first hit that same year with Connie Francis's "Stupid Cupid," which was also the first hit for the songwriters, Neil Sedaka and Howard Greenfield. Sedaka, a solo performer as well as a songwriter, had grown up in the same Brooklyn neighborhood as Carole King and had a number 9 hit in 1959 with a song written for her, "Oh Carol" (King later answered Sedaka with "Oh Neil").

Born Carole Klein in 1942, King began playing the piano at age four and was writing songs and performing in vocal groups by her teens, recording some unsuccessful singles for ABC-Paramount and singing on demo records with another neighborhood friend, Paul Simon. While attending Queens College she met aspiring songwriter Gerry Goffin, whom she married when she was eighteen. The two quit college to see if they could make their mark in music, and were hired by Aldon in 1959. King also continued her recording career and had a Top 40 hit in 1962 with "It Might as Well Rain Until September," originally written for Bobby Vee. But she quickly abandoned performing for the work she really preferred: writing, arranging, and producing.

As songwriters, it was relatively easy for women to get involved in the different aspects of record production, especially in the whirl of activity surrounding the Brill Building. Located at 1619 Broadway in Manhattan, the building was seen as the home of the hits, though in fact all manner of music industry offices were located in surrounding buildings as well (Aldon, for example, was located across the street at 1650 Broadway). Still, the Brill Building became synonymous with hit records, and the area was full of hopeful singers, songwriters, and producers, all looking for that one deal that would lead to a hit. Songwriter Ellie Greenwich's reflections on the girl group era in Charlotte Greig's *Will You Still Love Me Tomorrow?* demonstrate the energized atmosphere of the times: "There were many small labels in the Brill Building . . . If you played a song and they liked it, they'd say, 'Let's think. Do we know anyone who can do this? Do you?' So then you could go out and look for an artist, and a record label would give you a shot to produce a single. If it did well, great, you started getting a name for yourself. If it didn't, so what, no big deal."

After their success with the Shirelles, Goffin and King went on to work with a wide range of female vocalists in the early '60s, maintaining a longer presence in the Top 40 charts than the performers they wrote for were able to match. Little Eva was one such performer, who became virtually an overnight star when she recorded the team's "The Loco-Motion," but who disappeared from the charts completely in less than a year. Born Eva Narcissus Boyd in Belhaven, North Carolina, in 1943, Boyd had moved to New York in 1960, where she met Earl-Jean McCrea, a singer with the Cookies. Boyd then decided to try singing herself and auditioned for Goffin and King, not only winning a place as an alternate Cookie, but also netting a job as the songwriters' live-in babysitter. At the time, Goffin and King were working on a follow-up for Dee Dee Sharp, who'd had a number 2 hit with "Mashed Potato Time" in March 1962. Inspired by Boyd's dancing while listening to the radio, the team wrote "The Loco-Motion" and also had Boyd sing on the demo of the song.

There are differing accounts as to whether "Loco-Motion" was ever actually offered to Sharp at all, but the end result was the same: Sharp did not record it, and it was Boyd's demo that was released as the first single on the new Dimension record label, credited to "Little Eva." Released in June 1962, the song's pulsing, driving rhythms took "Loco-Motion" to number 1 by August, and "Little Eva" was a star at age nineteen; in the wake of her success, even Boyd's sister, Idalia, was brought in to release her own single, "Hula Hoppin'"/"Some Kind of Wonderful" in early 1963. By that time, Boyd's own career was in descent. Her second single, "Keep Your Hands Off My Baby," was released in November 1962 and reached a respectable number 12, but her next single, another "dance" song called "Let's Turkey Trot," was her last Top 40 entry. Boyd retird from the music business in the Æ70s, but returned in 1989 with the album *Back on Track*, and performed on the oldies circut.

The Cookies, who had provided backup vocals on "Loco-Motion," also had their own string of Top 40 hits by Goffin and King. The group, Ethel "Earl-Jean" McCrea, Dorothy Jones, and Margaret Ross, had started in Brooklyn, and after winning an Apollo Theatre Amateur Night contest, had become backup vocalists; in addition to Boyd's records, they also sang on records for Tony Orlando, Ben E. King, Neil Sedaka, Carole King, and on Eydie Gorme's hit "Blame It on the Bossa Nova" (written by Barry Mann and Cynthia Weil). Their first Top 40 entry as the Cookies came in 1962 with "Chains," followed by "Don't Say Nothin' Bad (About My Baby)" in 1963 (both written by Goffin and King) and their final Top 40 hit, "Girls Grow Up Faster Than

Boys," came in 1964. McCrea also pursued a solo career as "Earl-Jean," and had a minor hit with Goffin and King's "I'm Into Something Good," which reached number 38 in 1964, three months before Herman's Hermits would take their version of the song into the Top 20. In the late '60s, the Cookies broke up; some of the members later reformed the group in the late '90s.

The Chiffons were another group that found success with Goffin and King songs. Hailing from the Bronx, Judy Craig, Barbara Lee, Patricia Bennett, and Sylvia Peterson attended high school together and, in the expected fashion, had put together a group. Their first record, released on the Big Deal label in 1960, was a cover of the Shirelles' "Tonight's the Night," after which the group recorded for a number of other small labels. The Chiffons were then signed to Laurie Records on the strength of a demo tape they recorded for their friend Ronnie Mack, an aspiring songwriter who also became the Chiffons' manager.

"He's So Fine," one of the songs on the demo the Chiffons recorded for Mack, became their first single for Laurie, released in early 1963. The song's opening "doo-lang doo-lang" phrase proved to be an irresistibly catchy hook, and "He's So Fine" spent five weeks at number 1. The follow-up, "One Fine Day," was written by Goffin and King and had originally been intended for Little Eva but was given instead to the Chiffons to tie in with the "fine" theme of their first hit. Little Eva had already recorded her version of the song, but her vocals were erased from the master recording (which also featured a vibrant piano part from Carole King) and new vocals by the Chiffons were dubbed in. "One Fine Day," released within a few months of "He's So Fine,"

The Chiffons, circa 1963 (left to right: Barbara Lee, Judy Craig, Patricia Bennet, Sylvia Peterson). Courtesy of David A. Young collection became a number 5 hit for the Chiffons—while Little Eva was stuck with releasing a "Loco-Motion" tie-in called "Old Smokey Locomotion," which didn't even crack the Top 40. The Chiffons had a final "fine" hit at the end of the year with "A Love So Fine," which reached number 40. The group also recorded under the name the Four Pennies and attempted to move beyond the girl group genre, recording the psychedelic-flavored "Nobody Knows What's Going On (In My Mind But Me)" in 1965 (the Shirelles had tried a similar ploy with "One of the Flower People"). When this proved to be unsuccessful, the group reverted to their earlier style and had a final Top 40 hit in 1966 with "Sweet Talkin' Guy." Bennett and Craig continue to perform as the Chiffons on the oldies circuit.

Ellie Greenwich's work as a songwriter soon rivaled Carole King's in the girl group sweepstakes. Born in Brooklyn in 1940, Greenwich moved to Levittown, Long Island, in 1951, picking up the accordion as her first instrument before moving to piano. Like King, she recorded a number of singles beginning in the late '50s, under a variety of names (Ellie Gaye, Ellie Gree, Kellie Douglas) with little success. After graduating from college in 1961, she taught high school for three and a half weeks, but quit to pursue a career in music, which ensured her arrival at the Brill Building soon after. Initially mistaken for Carole King when she visited the offices of Jerry Leiber and Mike Stoller, who were now running their own publishing company, Trio Music, Greenwich was hired as a staff writer at one hundred dollars a week.

The Exciters were one of the first groups Greenwich worked with. The group, based in Jamaica, Queens, was originally an all-female quartet (Brenda Reid, Lillian Walker, Carol Johnson, and Sylvia Wilbur) called the Masterettes who sang with a male vocal group called the Masters. After recording the single "Follow the Leader"/"Never Never" for a local label, the group auditioned for Leiber and Stoller, who suggested a name change and gave them a record by Gil Hamilton, "Tell Her," to learn. Herb Rooney, a singer with the Masters, helped the group arrange the song (he added the "doop-dee-doop" background phrase), and ended up becoming a member of the newly named Exciters.

Released in 1962 (by which time Wilbur had quit the group), "Tell Him" raced up the charts to number 4, powered by Reid's energetic lead vocal, Leiber and Stoller's bright production, and, of course, the "doop-dee-doops." Unfortunately, "Tell Him" proved to be the high point in the Exciters' career, for none of their subsequent singles reached the Top 40. Their second single, "He's Got the Power," written by Greenwich and Tony Powers and released in 1963, featured another gutsy vocal from Reid, but failed to crack the Top 40. The Exciters' original version of "Do-Wah-Diddy," written by Greenwich and her new collaborator (and husband) Jeff Barry, and also released in 1963, again fared poorly, peaking at number 78; the following year the song would become a number I hit for the British group Manfred Mann as "Do-Wah-Diddy-Diddy." The group broke up in 1974, but a revamped line up was formed in the late '80s.

In 1963, Greenwich began working with record producer Phil Spector, who used her material for the roster of girl groups he was producing; Greenwich and Tony Powers wrote for Darlene Love ("(Today I Met) The Boy I'm Gonna Marry"), and Greenwich and Jeff Barry wrote for such groups as the Crystals ("Da Doo Ron Ron" and "Then He Kissed Me") and the Ronettes ("Be My Baby"). Greenwich also inadvertently found herself back in the performing arena briefly in 1962 via a song written with Barry, "What a Guy." The two recorded the song as a demo for the Sensations, overdubbing all the voices themselves, but when their publishers decided to release the demo itself as the single, it was credited to a nonexistent "group" called the Raindrops. When "What a Guy" reached number 41, and a second record by the two, the lively "The Kind of Boy You Can't Forget," was a Top 40 hit the following year, a real group was needed for live work, and Greenwich, her sister, and Bobby Bosco (who replaced Barry) were assembled to lip-synch songs for the Raindrops' "live" performances.

Greenwich and Barry also became the primary songwriting team for Red Bird, a label Leiber and Stoller started in 1964. Leiber and Stoller had also brought in George Goldner, who'd previously released the Chantels' records, to help with promotion, promising him a partnership in the company if the first record was a hit. While listening to an assortment of demos at home, Goldner's wife suggested choosing a Greenwich/Barry/Spector song, "Chapel of Love," an ode to everlasting marital bliss previously recorded, though not released, by the Ronettes and the Crystals. A New Orleans trio called the Dixie Cups ultimately released the song, giving Red Bird their first number I record. In addition to the Dixie Cups, Barry and Greenwich provided songs for a number of Red Bird acts, including the Jelly Beans, the Butterflies, and, most notably, the Shangri-Las.

The records of the Shangri-Las plumbed the depths of teenage angst with a high sense of melodrama that had been completely absent from other girl group records. The group, twins Mary Ann and Margie Ganser, and sisters Betty and Mary Weiss, grew up in Queens, and began singing together in high school, performing at local sock hops and talent shows. They eventually found a manager/producer/songwriter in George "Shadow" Morton, and recorded two singles for Smash and Spokane Records before Morton, who had met Greenwich in high school, brought a demo of the Shangri-Las singing his own "Remember (Walkin' in the Sand)" to Red Bird. Initially over seven minutes long (complete with a spoken intro from Morton), Greenwich and Barry tightened up the song and created a lament to lost love that was an epic on a grand scale, from the opening piano chords relentlessly banged out on the keyboard to the fade-out that mixed seagull cries with the Shangri-Las' own finger-snapping chorus.

"Remember," released in 1964, reached number 5 in the charts, but the Shangri-Las' next record created even more of a sensation. "Leader of the Pack," a Morton-Barry-Greenwich collaboration, was another melodramatic epic, a Romeo and Juliet teenage tragedy with all the contemporary trappings—a leather jacketed rebel without a cause, a good girl whose love will save him, and (via the appropriate sound effects), a motorcycle. Released in the fall of 1964, the record's focus on death (after the singer's parents forbid her to date the rebellious "Leader," he dies in a motorcycle accident) kicked off considerable controversy, resulting in the song's being banned in Britain. But in the U.S. (where the record was "unofficially" banned at some stations), it went to number 1, and paved the way for a further two years of hits from the group.

Barry and Greenwich wrote much of the Shangri-Las' subsequent material, including "Out in the Streets," "He Cried," "The Train from Kansas City," and "Give Us Your Blessings," another "death disc" where both the young lovers die in a car accident. "Blessings," which only reached the Top 30, was a genteel rewrite of "Leader" minus the allure of a "bad" boy; "I Can Never Go Home Anymore," written by Morton and released in 1965, was a far more effective tale of untimely death, and the Shangri-Las' final Top 10 hit. In this story, it is the singer's mother who dies as the result of the loneliness brought on by the selfishness of the daughter, who has left home to be with her boyfriend. As the

The Shangri-Las, circa 1966 (left to right: Mary Ann Ganser, Mary Weiss, Marge Ganser). Courtesy of David A. Young collection

thoughtless daughter, Mary Weiss sang the lead with a tortured intensity, her heart-rending cries of "Mama!" ringing out like a primal scream.

The Shangri-Las' image was as striking as their music. Unlike most of the girl groups, who wore matching frilly dresses and heels, the Shangri-Las projected a more streetwise look in their hipster trousers, ruffled shirts, and go-go boots. The girl groups were usually promoted more as "groups" than as individuals, and the substitution of one girl for another in the studio and on the road was rarely noticed, much less commented on; and though the Shangri-Las were no exception in this regard (the group's four members rarely appeared together), their "tough" look gave them a greater individuality than most other girl groups of the time.

But the circumstances of the group's demise were painfully familiar. Despite their hits and frequent tours, the Shangri-Las saw little of the generated profits, which were eaten up in the black hole of management and studio costs. The group had a Top 40 hit in 1966 with "Long Live Our Love," an uncharacteristically chipper song of support for a boy no longer a rebel but a patriot serving his country overseas, but two subsequent singles, "Dressed in Black" and the haunting "Past, Present, and Future" (based on Beethoven's "Moonlight Sonata") failed to chart. The Shangri-Las moved on to Mercury Records, but never regained their previous momentum, and after a brief turn on the oldies circuit in the '70s, monumentally dropped out of sight. Mary Ann Ganser died of encephalitis in 1971, and the remaining Shangri-Las reunited in 1980, but the group broke up for good when Marge Ganser died of breast cancer in 1996.

In spite of the contributions to the girl group genre made by Florence Greenberg, Carole King, and Ellie Greenwich—or, for that matter, Don Kirshner and Shadow Morton—when rock historians write about the "male Svengalis" who called the shots behind the girl group scene, they are usually referring to one man in particular: Phil Spector. The creator of the glorious "wall of sound" is revered in countless rock histories which gloss over the price Spector exacted in creating that sound. Born in New York City, Phil Spector moved to Los Angeles with his family when his father died, and while in high school wrote a song taken from a line on his father's tombstone, "To Know Him Is to Love Him." The song was his first number 1 hit as a songwriter, producer, and performer, having been recorded by his own group, the Teddy Bears (which included Spector, Marshall Leib, and lead singer Annette Kleinbard) in 1958. When the group found themselves short-changed as far as their royalties were concerned, they wasted no time in confronting the matter head-on, declaring the contract with their record company (Dore) void because they weren't twenty-one when they signed. But a move to Imperial Records resulted in no further hits, and additional tensions within the group led to their breakup.

Spector had by this time made the acquaintance of Lester Sill, a music industry figure and, later, Spector's partner in his record company Philles Records. Sill set him up with Leiber and Stoller, then working for Atlantic Records in New York, where Spector moved in 1960. He quickly gained experience working with such performers as Arlene Smith (who was trying for a solo career after leaving the Chantels), Ruth Brown, LaVern Baker, and the Paris Sisters, producing the latter group's Top 5 hit "I Love How You Love Me." In 1961, Spector started Philles Records, and latched on to the growing girl group boom by signing the Crystals. The Crystals, who consisted of Barbara Alston, Dolores "La La" Brooks, Dee Dee Kennibrew, Mary Thomas, and Patricia Wright, were from Brooklyn and had been brought together by their manager (and Alston's uncle) Benny Wells. After meeting them, Spector produced the group's (and Philles') first record, "Oh Yeah Maybe Baby"—though it was the B-side, the doo-wop flavored "There's No Other (Like My Baby)," that became the hit, reaching number 20 in early 1962.

Though a dispute over money made the Crystals hesitant about working with Spector again, the group relented and recorded Barry Mann and Cynthia Weil's "Uptown" (originally intended for Tony Orlando) for Philles, and the song hit the Top 20 in the spring of 1962. But the group's suspicions about Spector's treatment of them were hardly assuaged when he then had them record Goffin and King's stark "He Hit Me (And It Felt Like a Kiss)." Goffin later claimed that he and King were "inspired" by Little Eva's explanation that the black eye her boyfriend had given her was proof that "he really loves me," though he did admit the song's blatant masochism was "a little radical for those times." Lester Sill was more critical in his assessment, calling the tune a "terrible fucking song." Nor were the Crystals happy with the number. "We didn't like that one," Alston told writer Alan Betrock. "We absolutely hated it. Still do."

But the feelings of the Crystals were hardly uppermost in Spector's mind. Hearing a demo of a new Gene Pitney song, "He's a Rebel," while visiting the offices of Liberty Records (who were planning to have Vikki Carr record it), Spector managed to acquire a copy of the demo from Pitney and flew to Los Angeles, where he decided to record the song as the next Crystals record—without the Crystals, since they were proving so troublesome. A group of L.A. backup singers, the Blossoms, were pulled in to provide the vocals (with Darlene Love on lead), though the song was released as a "Crystals" record, which Spector was able to do since his contract with the group gave him ownership of their name. "He's a Rebel," like "Leader of the Pack," explored the redemptive power of a "good" girl's love for a "bad" boy, but where "Leader" was darkly melodramatic, "Rebel" was bright and optimistic. Released in the fall of 1962, "Rebel" went straight to number 1, neatly beating out Carr's version.

The real Crystals were on tour in Ohio when they learned, to their surprise, that they had recorded the number 1 song in the country—and now had to learn it so they could include it in their live act. The Blossoms also recorded the next "Crystals" hit, Mann and Welli's "He's Sure the Boy I Love," which went to number 11; meanwhile, the real Crystals found themselves recording "(Let's Dance) The Screw," another ploy of Spector's to fulfill a royalty obligation. Their next two hits, Greenwich and Barry's infectiously happy "Da Doo Ron Ron" and "Then He Kissed Me," were the first Crystals records to reach the Top 10 that featured their own voices and not those of the Blossoms, but they were also the last records by the group to make the

The Crystals, circa 1962
Courtesy of David A. Young collection

Top 40. By the end of 1963, Spector was involved with a new group, the Ronettes, and the Crystals were no longer of any interest to him. In an effort to try and salvage something from their career, the Crystals actually sued Spector for unpaid royalties, a move rarely undertaken by any girl group. The Crystals lost their suit, but they did manage to secure the rights to their name again, enabling them to continue performing.

If his eye (or ear) for detail, as well as his relentless drive for perfection had resulted in a string of hits readily identifiable as "Phil Spector records," Spector's obsessiveness was also about to manifest itself in a particularly unpleasant fashion in the case of the Ronettes. The Ronettes were two sisters, Veronica (Ronnie) and Estelle Bennett, and their cousin Nedra Talley, who grew up in New York's Spanish Harlem. Ronnie was already a budding performer when she found further inspiration from Frankie Lymon; as she quite candidly says in her autobiography *Be My Baby*, "If he hadn't made a record called 'Why Do Fools Fall in Love,' I wouldn't be sitting here writing this today." It wasn't long before Ronnie and a variety of other relatives became a group, making their debut at Amateur Night at the Apollo. After that performance, the group slimmed down to Ronnie, Estelle, and Nedra, and billed themselves as Ronnie and the Relatives. The group then began building their career by taking singing lessons and next found a manager who got them live work at neighborhood bar mitzvahs.

Their manager also got them a deal with Colpix Records, who released the Relatives' first single, "I Want a Boyfriend"/"Sweet Sixteen," in August 1961. The group continued recording for Colpix until 1963—with little to show for it except a name change to the Ronettes, which they'd adopted in 1962—in addition to working as backup singers on records for Del Shannon and *Gidget* star James Darren. But as a live act, the Ronettes were moving up with greater results, graduating from the bar mitzvah circuit to neighborhood sock hops and, shortly after the release of their first single, to the Peppermint Lounge, one of New York's hot spots. The three had dressed up for a night on the town in form-fitting gowns and beehive hairdos ("stacked up to the ceiling," in Ronnie's words) and while waiting in line to get into the Lounge were mistaken for the girl group hired to dance at the club and told to come in. Their dancing skills won them a regular gig at ten dollars each per night, as well as the chance to occasionally sing with the house band, Joey Dee and the Starlighters (who had a number 1 hit with "Peppermint Twist" in 1962). Their stint at the Peppermint brought them to the attention of WINS DJ Murray "The K" Kaufman, who hosted his own rock shows at Brooklyn's Fox Theater and booked the Ronettes as his "dancing girls." Their Peppermint connection also got them hired as extras in the Starlighters' film *Hey, Let's Twist.*

Though some accounts relate that the Ronettes connected with Phil Spector via a misdialed phone call, Ronnie's book maintains the call was no "accident"; Estelle had simply worked up the courage to dial Spector at his office, and her courage was rewarded with a chance to audition. Spector was immediately taken with Ronnie and tried to sign her as a solo act, but when the Bennetts' mother refused to let him break up the group, Spector signed all three Ronettes. Nonetheless, he set about dividing the group internally anyway, singling out Ronnie for preferential treatment from the start. When the group recorded their first material for Spector in Los Angeles, Ronnie was allowed to fly out, while Estelle and Nedra had to drive cross-country in the company of Bobby Sheen (from Bob B. Soxx and the Blue Jeans, another Spector group). Ronnie and Phil also began what would end up being a very tumultuous affair.

After recording a number of tracks during 1963 that were initially unreleased (including versions of "The Twist," "Mashed Potato Time," and "Hot Pastrami" that later turned up as "Crystals" songs when they appeared on the album *The Crystals Sing Their Greatest Hits*), the Ronettes made their official Philles debut with a bang: "Be My Baby," co-written by Spector, Greenwich, and Barry. It was a tune that couldn't miss, an evocative ode to love dripping with Spector's extravagant production and Ronnie's sultry voice coming out on top. Released in September 1963, the song quickly reached number 2 in the charts. But what should have been a spectacular beginning for the group turned out in retrospect to be the high point, for by the end of 1964 the Ronettes had their last Top 40 hit, and two years later they disbanded.

Spector's increasing possessiveness of Ronnie helped to accelerate the group's decline. When the group toured England with the Rolling Stones in early 1964, Spector sent the Stones a telegram forbidding them to speak with "his" Ronettes. When the group

The Ronettes, circa 1964
Courtesy of David A. Young collection

was scheduled to tour with Dick Clark's Caravan of Stars in 1963, and on the Beatles' final U.S. tour in 1966, Spector kept Ronnie in the studio and had her replaced in the Ronettes' road lineup by another cousin of the Bennetts', Elaine. Spector continued recording Ronettes material, but little of it was released. He began not only separating Ronnie from the group on the road and in the studio, but also keeping her away from anyone on hand while she was recording, bringing her into the production booth with him and then refusing to let her leave.

Yet even after learning from Darlene Love that Spector was married, Ronnie was reluctant to end the relationship, since the Ronettes were so dependent on him for providing their material and producing their records. But after having one of his biggest hits with the Righteous Brothers' "You've Lost That Lovin' Feeling" (written by Mann and Weil), the U.S. failure of Ike and Tina Turner's "River Deep, Mountain High" in 1966 (which Spector co-wrote with Greenwich and Barry) was partially responsible for Spector's temporary withdrawal from recording, effectively ending the Ronettes' career. During this sabbatical, Spector divorced his first wife and married Ronnie, who then became a virtual prisoner in their Los Angeles mansion. Though Ronnie maintains

Spector was never physically abusive, his psychological torture proved to be sufficiently demoralizing. Ronnie was allowed to roam the estate—now surrounded by an electrified gate—during the day, but was locked up in the house at night, when the servants' entrance in the kitchen was closed. Her only chance of gaining access to the outside world was if one of the servants unlocked the gates for her—but only with Spector's permission. Spector also provided Ronnie with her own car, complete with inflatable male "decoy," for those times when she was allowed to venture beyond the gates.

Ronnie eventually escaped from Spector, with help from her mother, in 1972, though she'd developed a drinking problem she wouldn't kick for another decade; in *Be My Baby* Ronnie relates that toward the end of her time with Spector she deliberately went on drinking binges in order to get sent to the local rehab center, finding it a pleasant alternative to her life at home. But the years she'd spent with Spector had left their mark. "Darlene and I saw Ronnie after the divorce and we were shocked at how she looked," Blossom Gloria Jones said in a later interview. "She was not the same person . . . Ronnie was like the cheerleader in the old days, happy-go-lucky. Phil took that away from her."

For his part, Spector did resurface to produce the occasional record (most notably for the Beatles and solo LPs for George Harrison and John Lennon), but eventually became as well known for his eccentricities as for his production skills. In the British television documentary *Rockin' and Rollin' with Phil Spector*, Ronnie charitably attributed Spector's behavior to the intense media scrutinization he received as the "Tycoon of Teen," a title Tom Wolfe had bestowed on him in an article which had originally appeared in the *New York Herald Tribune.* "I think Phil was a very normal person at the very beginning of his career," Ronnie said, "but as time went on, they started writing about him being a genius, and then he'd say, 'Yeah, I am a genius.' Then they say he's the mad genius, so he became the mad genius." She quoted a line from the song "When I Saw You" ("I knew I would lose my mind") to further illustrate her point. "It kinda happened to him," she said. "Not meaning losing his mind over me, but just losing his mind!"

Dee Dee Kennibrew of the Crystals, while calling Spector "obnoxious," also shared some of Ronnie's perceptions: "He was a normal enough person," she told *Rolling Stone.* "But after he began to be successful, I think he tried to be more of a star than his groups—you know, 'Without me, there would be nothing.'" But others who worked with Spector have been more critical in their assessment of his behavior. Miriam Abramson, the business manager at Atlantic Records, recalling Spector's time at the label in the book *Music Man*, stated, "I thought he was insane. I think now, in some sense, you would excuse it as . . . 'star quality.' But at the time he did it he was no star— he was a pain in the neck."

Ronnie, like many performers who worked with him, had feared that breaking with

Spector would cause irreparable damage to her career. But as the later career of Annette Kleinbard, the lead singer in Spector's first group, the Teddy Bears, demonstrates, breaking with Spector might have been the one thing that could have saved the Ronettes' career from being relegated to the oldies circuit. After the Teddy Bears' split, Kleinbard changed her name to Carol Connors and became one of the few women to write and record songs in the hot-rod/surf music genre of the '60s (including "Little Red Cobra" and "Go Go G.T.O."), having later successes as co-author of "The Night the Lights Went Out in Georgia," "Gonna Fly Now (Theme from *Rocky*)," and "With You I'm Born Again," as well as serving on the Academy Awards music nomination committee.

Darlene Love was another "Spector Survivor," managing to work for him yet not wind up completely under his thumb (though she did change her last name from Wright to Love at his suggestion). Love, the daughter of a Pentecostal minister, had been asked to join the Blossoms by Fanita James, who heard Love singing in church. The group, which also included Gloria Jones and Bobby Sheen, was initially managed by Johnny Otis; they also recorded for a variety of labels in the late '50s and by the early '60s had become well-respected backup singers. The group enjoyed the stability studio work offered, which could also be more lucrative than live work. By the time the Blossoms recorded "He's a Rebel" for Spector, Love had enough financial savvy to ask to be paid triple scale for her work, though she received no royalties. When Spector next approached her to record "He's Sure the Boy I Love," she pressed for better financial compensation, and recorded the song, thinking it would be released under her own name—only to see it released as another Crystals record. Leery about the same thing happening again, she never recorded a final version of "Da Doo Ron Ron" for Spector, who ended up having an actual Crystal, La La Brooks, provide the lead vocal.

Love eventually got her contract and was able to release other singles under her own name in addition to recording as a member of Bob B. Soxx and the Blue Jeans. But the contract made little difference when it came to being paid; Love later claimed to have received only one royalty statement for three thousand dollars during the years she worked with Spector. "That's when we started not really getting along," she said in *Rockin' and Rollin' with Phil Spector.* "It didn't bother me as much then because I was young, inexperienced, and never thought at the time that I was being used. It wasn't till years later that I started feeling like that. Because the records were still being produced and still being put out . . . and nobody was getting paid." Love and the Blossoms went on to appear as regulars on the TV rock series *Shindig*, and Love continued doing session work, singing for performers as varied as the Mamas and the Papas, the Beach Boys, Luther Vandross, U2, Dionne Warwick, and Whitney Houston. She also branched out into acting in the '80s, most notably as Danny Glover's wife in *Lethal Weapon* and *Lethal Weapon 2*.

Love sang lead vocals on some of the most memorable records in rock history—and yet, ironically, her face would probably be unfamiliar to many of the people who have bought her records over the years. The same was true for a number of acts in the girl group era, regardless of the fact that the groups, unlike Love, toured regularly and were also having substantial hits. The attacks that branded rock as "nigger music" may have faded, but racism was still very much a part of American society, and despite the beginnings of a civil rights movement, the black girl groups were rarely given the exposure their white counterparts received. As Ruth Brown had found in the '50s, radio may have been colorblind, but television was not: none of the black girl groups of the early '60s appeared on *The Ed Sullivan Show* no matter how many hits they had, whereas a minor contender like Britain's Cliff Richard, who had only two U.S. Top 40 hits at the time, appeared three times. This attitude was common throughout the industry. When producer Jack Good first enlisted Love and the Blossoms to appear as regulars on the TV rock show *Shindig*, he faced opposition from the ABC network because the group was black; only after threatening to take the show elsewhere did the network concede. Love wryly remarked that the Blossoms had been a successful studio act "because nobody knew whether we were black or white." The racial mix in the Ronettes' heritage (the Bennetts' mother was black and Cherokee, their father was white) presented further confusion: initially considered to play the Starlighters' girlfriends in *Hey, Let's Twist*, the group was rejected by the casting director, who found them "too light to play black girls and too dark to play white girls." Fan magazines, primarily catering to a female audience, tended to cover male stars over women, and white performers over black ones.

The denial of such mainstream exposure also eroded the groups' slim grasp on their careers; if the audiences had never seen them, it was easy enough for them to be replaced on the road by other performers—and hard to establish their own image if they did manage to break away from management with the right to use the group's name. Both black and white groups were likely to face monetary disputes, but white acts still had greater opportunities as far as film and television work—though sexism in these fields was powerful enough to undercut women of any race. It was an assessment of the entertainment industry that singer Lesley Gore readily agreed with. Gore might have made it to *The Ed Sullivan Show*, and sung "Sunshine, Lollipops and Rainbows" in the film *Ski Party*, but when remembering the era in *Girl Groups: The Story of a Sound* she stated: "Even though I was a big seller, they only cared about males. That was always clear to me. They just thought it was easier to sell males. It really got to me after a while."

Born in 1946 in Tenafly, New Jersey, Gore was readily accepted as the all-American girl-next-door from the moment she burst onto the music scene in 1963 with "It's My Party." After spending her childhood years practicing songs in front of her bedroom mirror ("Behind that closed door, I slicked my hair back in a fairly credible Elvis imitation," she later told *Ms.*), Gore decided to try for a larger audience, and recorded a demo tape after her sixteenth birthday. The tape got her a contract with Mercury Records, and Gore worked with her producer, Quincy Jones, in choosing her debut single, going through a box of 250 demo tapes. "It's My Party" was eventually selected, partially because Gore liked its "rebellious attitude," and she recorded it on March 30, 1963. The single was released within a week, and shortly afterwards shot to number 1. "It's My Party" had Gore lamenting the loss of her steady boyfriend to an unprincipled rival, and its good-girl-done-wrong theme firmly established Gore as a Nice Girl (who was nonetheless able to exact her revenge in the follow-up single, "Judy's Turn to Cry," which went to number 5).

Lesley Gore, circa 1963
Courtesy of David A. Young collection

But though Gore's songs by and large focused on girl group scenarios of love lost and found, she threw a curve ball at her audience with the song "You Don't Own Me," a feisty statement of independence released in 1963, the same year that Betty Friedan's groundbreaking feminist work, *The Feminine Mystique*, was published. In a radical departure from the norm, Gore, in the song, refuses to be seen as the "possession" of a boy, not because she prefers the company of a different boy, but out of a desire for establishing her own autonomy and making her own decisions, whether deciding what to wear or whom to date. This was a defiant attitude at a time when having a boy who hit you instead of kissing you was preferable to having no boy at all, but it was evidently one Gore's audience was more than pleased to hear—the song (written by John Maera and Dave White) went to number 2 and became Gore's second-biggest single.

Gore's subsequent material returned to more conventional ground, and she continued having Top 40 hits through 1967, among them Greenwich and Barry's "Maybe I Know" and "Look of Love." Though her run on the charts gave Gore little in the way of financial reward ("I saw one check and then I didn't see any money until two years ago," she told *Ms.* in 1990), she continued working in the music business, eventually moving into songwriting, co-writing Irene Cara's hit singles for the film *Fame*, and continuing to perform live.

Nona Hendryx is another performer who managed to persevere after the monetarily dry girl group period despite the hardships. "We got ripped off really badly over the years, especially from the Bluebelles era," she says. "We ended up with nothing but our name—I don't know who had the brains enough to ask for that at the time, but somehow we ended up with the name so we could work without any limitations. But we lost a lot of the money that we were entitled to." Born in Trenton, New Jersey, in 1944, Hendryx's career as a performer developed almost by default, for despite growing up in a household where "there was always music around . . . it was very much a part of everyday existence," she had little desire to pursue a musical career herself. That began to change in her teens when her friend Sarah Dash invited Hendryx to sing in a local group, the Del Capris. "So I said sure," Hendryx says. "It sounded like fun to me. It wasn't something that I considered as a living, as a vocation. It was just something that was fun to do; it was not something that I felt I was going to be doing for the rest of my life."

Hendryx and Dash eventually met the manager of a Philadelphia group called the Ordettes, who joined them with Ordettes singers Patti LaBelle and Cindy Birdsong to form the Bluebelles in the early '60s. "He put us together initially because a man in Philadelphia was looking for girls to be a group," Hendryx says. "But I wasn't seeking anyone to make me a star at that time because it just did not enter my mind. I didn't want to be a recording artist, I didn't want to be a songwriter, I didn't want to be any of those things! I was just sort of going along with friends." But the Bluebelles became recording artists nonetheless, making records for Newtown Records. Typically, the group had little input regarding the songs they recorded. "The managers pretty much chose material," Hendryx says. "We did very standard material—'Somewhere Over the Rainbow' or 'You'll Never Walk Alone.' We would rework the standard songs into gospel renditions or more soulful renditions. And then we would do our songs about teenage angst, our hearts being broken—you know the stuff!"

It turned out to be the standards that provided the group (now billed as Patti LaBelle and the Bluebelles) with their other Top 40 hits, including "Down the Aisle (Wedding Song)" in 1963 and "You'll Never Walk Alone" in 1964 (they also recorded the original version of "Groovy Kind of Love," later a number 2 hit for the Mindbenders). And despite their forays into "teenage angst," the group gave little thought to being part of the girl group scene at the time. "I don't really look back on it at all to tell you the truth!" says Hendryx now. "When I do, I see that we were a part of the history, but you never know that you're making history when you're doing it. You just don't. And certainly when you're a teenager you really don't know anything. You're just doing stuff and hoping you get good grades and graduate."

But if the Bluebelles were unaware of making history as a girl group, they soon became well aware of the financial hazards of being a girl group, eventually taking their record company to court for lack of financial compensation. The group had already observed standard music industry swindles: "We would record songs, and listed on there as the writer would be his eight-month-old grandchild!" says Hendryx of their record company's owner. "It was just ridiculous. He owned the recording studio, he owned our contracts, we had his lawyers . . . I mean, talk about conflict of interest! But I didn't know anything about conflict of interest. I was fifteen years old. What do I know about conflict of interest, and making a recording contract deal?"

Problems with their label led to the Bluebelles' departure in 1964, by which time the music scene was beginning to change drastically. In February of that year, the Beatles arrived in America, an event that launched the "British Invasion." The Beatles' U.S. success opened the doors for a wide range of British acts, who were no longer dismissed as second-rate imitations of American performers. British beat groups had found their own voice, creating an innovative sound that was now making a sizeable impression on the American charts. The irony was that many of the British groups had been raised on a diet of American rock & roll and rhythm & blues, and were merely reintroducing U.S. audiences to their own musical heritage. The Beatles themselves started out playing songs by Little Richard, Chuck Berry, Buddy Holly, and Elvis Presley, and were now recording Motown and girl group covers (the Shirelles' "Baby It's You" and "Boys," the Marvelettes' "Please Mr. Postman," and the Cookies' "Chains," among others), and as songwriters, John Lennon and Paul McCartney aspired to be the new Goffin and King.

More importantly, the Beatles are credited with re-establishing the idea of a performer's self-sufficiency; they played their own instruments and wrote much of their own material, as the early rock & rollers had. This made the assembly-line techniques of the Brill Building seem obsolete, and as the Beatles and the ensuing wave of cute boy bands in neat suits began to dominate the charts, the girl group production teams seemed all too willing to concede defeat. As a result, the groups that depended on the production teams for their material naturally began to disappear from the charts.

In the changing climate, even the women who had previously been seen as integral to the hit-making process found their power eroded. Ellie Greenwich ultimately lost her production credit on the "Barry and Greenwich" records due to her husband's argument that it was more important for him to establish his name as sole producer; according to him, she'd be having children one day and would be staying home to take care of them. As a result, when the marriage and songwriting partnership crumbled, Greenwich had a hard time re-establishing her own credentials as a producer. The Goffin and King songwriting team and marriage also split (though King remarried soon after her divorce), and after the girl group era had ended, King curtailed her production work to concentrate on developing her skills as a musician and songwriter.

King's career as a performer was revived with great success in the early '70s after the release of the album *Tapestry*, and her records regularly featured covers of the songs she'd written during her girl group days. Greenwich also recorded albums with covers of her girl group hits (1968's *Ellie Greenwich Composes, Produces and Sings* and 1973's *Let It Be Written, Let It Be Sung*). Her songs also provided the basis for the musical *Leader of the Pack*, which opened on Broadway in 1985. Loosely based on Greenwich's life story, *Leader of the Pack* featured Darlene Love in a starring role and also closed with a solo spot from Greenwich. Three years earlier, in a more tongue-in-cheek homage to the era, the musical *Little Shop of Horrors* opened Off-Broadway, featuring a sassy, black, girl group–styled trio of backup singers—named Ronnette, Chiffon, and Crystal.

But if the death knell had been sounded in the Brill Building by the mid-'60s, the Beatles' example of self-sufficiency gave inspiration to rock's next generation of artists, and young men began grabbing guitars and rushing to their parents' garages to practice—an idea which seemed to bypass young women of the time completely. Women folk singers were able to hold acoustic guitars, since the emphasis in folk music was on the song rather than the singer's instrumental skills, but in general women instrumentalists were still too rare in the music community to provide much of an example to budding female musicians. "I really think that had to do with the roles that were put forward of what girls do and what boys do," says singer Holly Near, who was a high school student at the time when the British Invasion was inspiring the birth of hundreds of groups in America and Britain. "All the kids started putting together bands," she remembers. "Everybody wanted to be in a band, everybody wanted to play guitar. Well, the 'everybody' were boys. And I played the acoustic guitar, probably knew more chords and more about music than any of the guys who were diving in and plugging in their guitars. And it never even occurred to me to plug in. It's not even that I was told not to, it just didn't even cross my mind. 'Louie Louie'—how many chords does it have, right? But it just wasn't something girls did. So I put the guitar away and became a girl singer."

In fact, "girl singers," or solo vocalists, were beginning to replace the girl groups in the charts by the mid-'60s, and again, the lead came from England, though America was not quite as receptive to Britain's female solo artists as it was to the cute boy bands. Singers like Petula Clark and Dusty Springfield enjoyed the greatest success, while the response to others, such as Marianne Faithfull, Lulu, Cilla Black, and Sandie Shaw, varied greatly. And while these singers didn't cover the girl group songs with the regularity that the boy bands did, Lulu, Black, and Springfield still reflected a brassy, soulful delivery that owed an obvious debt to the girl group era and especially the high energy sounds that were now coming out of Detroit (Springfield in particular was an unabashed fan of Motown artists). The new singers also presented a more sophisticated image to their audience—grown-up, yet hip, giving the impression of independence, unlike the "little girl" dependence of the girl groups. Most significant, despite slack periods, each singer was able to maintain a long-term career, instead of sinking into obscurity like the U.S. girl groups, who, if they did survive, found themselves with few options other than toiling on the oldies circuit.

Petula Clark was the oldest of Britain's new "girl singers," in her thirties at the time she broke through in the American market with "Downtown" in 1965, after several years of chart success in Britain and Europe. In contrast, most other female soloists were in their teens or early twenties. Lulu, born Marie McDonald McLaughlin Lawrie, was discovered in Glasgow as the lead singer of the Luvvers (formerly the Gleneagles) at age fifteen, and with the renamed Lulu and the Luvvers began her career in 1964 with a cover of the Isley Brother's "Shout." Lulu was immediately dubbed "the Scottish Brenda Lee" and her first American hit came in 1967 with the theme song of the film *To Sir With Love.* "Swingin' " Cilla Black, who released her first record at age twenty, was the only female artist handled by Brian Epstein, manager of the Beatles. Just as the Beatles had been tidied up by Epstein, forsaking their leather gear for suits and ties, Black's act was toned down, and the former nightclub coat-check girl who sang rock songs with the band on her break was put in a dress to sing Burt Bacharach–Hal David ballads. Black enjoyed far greater success in the U.K., where she had a total of eleven Top 10 hits (including two number 1's), as opposed to the U.S., where her sole Top 40 hit was "You're My World," which went to number 26 in 1964. The same was true of Sandie Shaw (Sandra Goodrich), who launched her singing career at age seventeen and whose trademark was performing in her bare feet. Shaw had three number 1 hits in the U.K. and became the first British artist to win the Eurovision Song Contest (an annual song competition among European countries) with "Puppet on a String," but she couldn't even crack the U.S. Top 40. Lulu and Shaw also had female managers, Marion Massey and Eve Taylor respectively.

Marianne Faithfull was the odd-woman-out in this crowd, at least musically, for her clear voice and folk-tinged material had more in common with the work of folk singers like Joan Baez than with the realm of pop music. Faithfull was, in fact, a reluctant pop star who preferred the music of Baez and Bob Dylan to pop music, and had arrived in the music business almost by accident. Born in 1946 to a university professor and an Austrian baroness, Faithfull had grown up in Reading, England, where she attended a convent school and played folk music in local coffeehouses in her teens. In 1964, her boyfriend John Dunbar (later her first husband) brought her to a party Paul McCartney was giving in London, where she met Andrew Loog Oldham, the manager of the current "bad boys" of rock, the Rolling Stones. Upon learning Faithfull was a singer, Oldham offered her a record contract and co-wrote her first single, the melancholy "As Tears Go By," with the Stones' Mick Jagger and Keith Richards (the song which finally got the Jagger-Richards songwriting partnership off the ground).

At the time, Faithfull was not especially concerned about the record's success. "I didn't think anything would come of it," she said later. "It came out in the summer, I did a few TV shows, and that was all very boring, and I thought 'Oh God, this is a big fuss about nothing.' And I just went back to school in the fall." But when the song went to number 9 in the British charts (number 22 in the U.S.), she left school and began pursuing a singing career in earnest. Though she continued having pop hits, Faithfull was also able to record folk albums (only released in the U.K.): *North Country Maid* featured highly effective renditions of "She Moved Through the Fair," "Scarborough Fair" (recorded two years before Simon and Garfunkel would have a Top 20 hit with the song), and the title track. Another folk album, *Come My Way*, had Faithfull performing traditional songs like "Fare Thee Well" and "Once I Had a Sweetheart," and reading Lewis Carroll's poem "Jabberwocky" from his book *Through the Looking Glass*. Yet despite her success, Faithfull still felt some uncertainty about her career in music. "The only thing that was—that *is*—difficult, is I wonder why I ever did it," she said in 1990. "I wonder if it was a good idea; maybe I should have just not done it and stayed at school. Now I love it and I'm glad it all happened, but I have thought that sometimes. I'm enjoying it . . . but it took a long time to get there."

Dusty Springfield was a more familiar face to American audiences. Born Mary Isabel Catherine Bernadette O'Brien in 1939 in London, Springfield first sang in a group called the Lana Sisters in the late '50s; after their breakup in 1960, she formed the Springfields, a folk trio that also included her brother Tom and their friend Tim Field (later replaced by Mike Hurst). The Springfields had a few British hits—and a Top 20 hit in the U.S. with the song "Silver Threads and Golden Needles"—before disbanding in 1963. Springfield wasted no time in starting a solo career and had an immediate hit with "I Only Want to Be With You," which captured the spirited, danceable fun inherent in her favorite Motown dance hits. Released in December 1963, "I Only Want to Be With You" reached the Top 10 in England and went to number 12 in the U.S., the first in a string of ten Top 40 hits in the '60s.

With her dramatic use of black eyeliner and her elaborate hairdo, Springfield reflected the cool of "Swinging London," as the British capital was now dubbed; by the mid-'60s London was the center of the pop universe, home to everything that was with-it and hip in music and fashion. But while America was won over by such exports as the British Invasion bands, Mary Quant mini-skirts, and Diana Rigg's "Emma Peel" character (the stylish, leather jumpsuit-clad heroine of the British TV spy series *The Avengers*), Britain's musical in-crowd championed black American soul music (as R&B was beginning to be called). Springfield's love of black music led to her hosting the British television special *The Sounds of Motown* when the "Motown Revue" package tour arrived in England in 1965, and in 1968 she traveled to the States to record *Dusty in Memphis*, produced by Jerry Wexler, who had revitalized Aretha Franklin's career by bringing her to Atlantic Records (unsuccessful at the time of its release, *Dusty in Memphis* is now considered a classic album). When Franklin turned down the opportunity to record "Son of a Preacher Man," Springfield (who was occasionally referred to as "the white Aretha Franklin") recorded it for *Dusty in Memphis* and also had a Top 10 hit with the song. Vicki Wickham, producer of the British television rock show *Ready, Steady, Go! (RSG)*, credits Springfield with introducing her—and *RSG*—to a variety of black performers, many of whom ended up receiving greater television exposure in Britain than in the U.S. "We did specials with Otis Redding and James Brown and it was great because nobody in England had ever seen these people," says Wickham. "Only people like Dusty or the Beatles or the Rolling Stones, who were going to America and buying their records. England was still a very virgin country when it came to that music, so we made a big impact."

Ready, Steady, Go! debuted in 1963 to capitalize on the British beat group explosion (which took off in the U.K. a year earlier than in the States), and bubbled with freshness. In some ways a U.K. equivalent to *American Bandstand, RSG* traded in Dick Clark's paternalistic image for youthful hosts whose age matched the show's audience. "There just hadn't been anything like it," says Wickham. "People, the same as myself, were sitting at home and didn't realize that there was fashion out there, that there was art, that the music was very much a part of what was going on, that really the focal point of everything creative or artistic was coming from the music." Wickham had left her previous job as a production assistant at BBC Radio with the hopes of landing a job in television; she was taken on as a secretary by the independent station then planning *RSG* with a promise for advancement within a year. She ended up becoming the show's producer—at age twenty-one. "I was lucky because in every situation I always ended up being the only person there," she says. "I'm naturally pushy, so I always was doing the next thing because there was nobody else to do it, and then it was always much easier to find a new secretary than it was to get somebody who should have been doing my job. So there was never a real promotion; it was just because I was doing it—booking it, writing it, producing it, everything. By the time we'd done the pilot, I was the producer. There wasn't anybody else."

RSG quickly established itself as *the* music show to appear on in Britain, with a healthy roster of current stars and new acts, chosen by Wickham, Michael Lindsay-Hogg, the show's director, and the show's presenters, Michael Aldred and Cathy McGowan. "We were conscious of the charts and what was happening," Wickham says. "You have to be. And you had to be slightly visual, otherwise it just wasn't going to work. We really stayed away from what I would call the more middle-of-the-road people even if they were number 1 in the charts. And, honestly, it was who we liked. Luckily, we liked a lot of different things, and the four of us truly depended on somebody telling us about somebody we'd go see, and if we liked them, they were on. So we were mixing between the Kinks and the Swinging Blue Jeans, then we would have John Lee Hooker."

Patti LaBelle and the Bluebelles were among the black groups that appeared on the show, and after striking up a friendship with Patti, Wickham later became the group's manager. "Not many acts were on two weeks running, but the Bluebelles were because they were just phenomenal," she says. "They sang 'Groovy Kind of Love,' which was brilliant." For their part, the Bluebelles enjoyed the less racially charged atmosphere of Britain as compared to what Nona Hendryx describes as "the usual prejudice" they'd faced in the U.S.—"traveling and not being able to go in certain restaurants, and actually having someone point a gun at us to get out of his restaurant, not being able to stay in certain hotels. Whereas when you'd go to England, yes, there are less black people there, and if prejudice was in somebody's heart, in their mind, I don't know, but there were not black and white water fountains. It just did not exist."

Another American group that made a strong impression on *RSG* was Goldie and the Gingerbreads, one of the few all-female bands of the time who did play instruments. "I think they were the only girl group that played live that we ever had on," Wickham says. "I don't think there was anybody else in those days, so it was perfect for us. They had quite a good following at one point." It was a following the group hadn't been able to find in the U.S., where the Gingerbreads had been working since the early '60s, defying convention by trying to make it as an all-female rock band. But despite their success in England, the group was unable to make a dent in the American market, and today there are few rock histories that make even a passing reference to the band. Yet the Gingerbreads should certainly stand out to historians if for no other reason than the fact that they were one of the few female rock bands playing their own instruments at a time when the very idea was still seen as a contradiction in terms.

Carol MacDonald, the Gingerbreads' guitarist, had been playing guitar for many years before meeting up with the rest of the group, who had been busy perfecting their skills on their instruments too. Born in Wilmington, Delaware, MacDonald started out on ukulele at age nine and graduated to guitar at ten; by high school she was performing in a doo-wop group called the Tranells and with a rock band from Maryland that played the Bainbridge Naval Base on weekends. After graduating in 1960, an illicit trip to a local nightclub led to her first offer to record. "This guy gave me his card and said, 'We want to record you,' so I said okay," she recalls. "I was really torn because I wasn't supposed to be in this place. But then I had to tell my mother and father because the record company was in Philadelphia! So I had to end up telling them the truth because I really wanted to do this."

Armed with her parents' permission, MacDonald traveled to Philadelphia and made her first record, "I'm in Love"/"Sam, Sam, Sam, My Rock and Roll Man," for a local label before starting college. After two years, MacDonald quit college and moved in with an aunt in Trenton, New Jersey. In 1963, having tried to figure out a way to get back into music, an invitation MacDonald accepted for a night out provided the answer. "I met this guy who said to me, 'You want to go to New York? I gotta take you to this club in the Village, you won't believe it,'" she remembers. "I was so naive, I didn't even know what 'the Village' was. This is at twelve o'clock at night, and I said, 'Isn't everything closed?' He said, 'No, they stay open until four in the morning!' So he takes me to this place and it was the hippest jazz club, the Page Three. I go in with him, and we sit down and I looked at the hippest jazz trio I'd ever heard in my life, and I just flipped out. I said, 'Oh my God, this place is fantastic!'"

A few drinks later, MacDonald was ready to ascend the stage herself. "I said to the MC, 'I want to sing,' and he said, 'Oh, do you?' like who-the-hell-are-you type of thing," she says. "And I said, 'Yeah, I'd really like to get up.' I had all the nerve in the world. I had no idea what I was doing, I just said, 'Let me get up and sing.'" Her nerve won her a weekend spot at the club, making ten dollars a night, sharing the billing with Tiny Tim. "He was making eight dollars, so I was really highly paid!" MacDonald says. "And we had to sit there all night long; little did I know I was like a B-girl. They'd tell you who you could go sit with and have a drink with—I thought it was great, I'm getting free drinks! Little did I know I'm selling the drinks for them! I was very, very naive."

A short time later she met Goldie and the Gingerbreads, who paid a special visit to the Page Three to ask her to join them. "The MC said, 'There's this girls' group that just came off the road; they're in the back, and they want to talk to you.' And I thought, 'Girls' band? This is interesting, let me go check this out!'" she says. "So I go in the back, and here is this ragged bunch of women, because they had really, literally, just come off the road. They had heard about me and they asked if I wanted to play guitar in their band, and I said, 'No, no, no, I don't think so; I'm really happy with this job.' They looked ragged and scary to me . . . this turned out to be so funny later on."

If the Gingerbreads had appeared "ragged and scary," MacDonald's introduction to the realities of the music industry were more unpleasant, as she found when she acquired her first manager, Milton Ross. "He was one of the most obnoxious men I'd ever met in my life when I first met him," she remembers. "Really, he was disgusting. Every other word out of his mouth was 'fuck.' I couldn't believe this mouth. This was just the way he was, your typical New York manager—at that time! They're a lot different now. I will say that because I'm one now! He was into showing me the sleazier side of the industry. Now they put record deals together with drugs . . . in those days it was sex, and they'd set the executives up with girls. It was really weird—this was how they used to make record deals, I swear to God. In the '60s you got your money stolen because you were naive. In the '70s it got stolen because you were stoned. But you still got your money stolen! It's the truth! And I just kept singing. My whole thing was, I don't want to know about that, I just wanted to write."

A recording contract with Atlantic didn't make MacDonald much happier, as she bristled against the company's intended manipulation of her. "They wanted me to be Lesley Gore," she says. "My first record, 'Jimmy Boy,' was that type of thing. So they give me this image, and I'm not happy. I'm not playing guitar, number one, and I'm not doing my own music. They changed my name, too—they didn't like MacDonald, so it was Carol Shaw." The fact that her record was starting to sell offered little consolation, but shortly after getting her record deal, she encountered Goldie and the Gingerbreads again—and this time she liked what she saw. "We went up to 45th Street, to the Wagon Wheel," she remembers. "And I see on the thing 'All Female Band, Goldie and the Gingerbreads.' So I walk in and these girls are up on stage, and my socks are knocked off. I just stood there with my mouth hanging open. They go on break, and I run up and say, 'Listen, remember me? You asked me to play—you don't have a guitar, do you still need a guitarist?' They said, 'Yeah, you want to get up and sit in?' So we picked a song, and I fit in like I had been there forever. I was like the missing piece of that puzzle. And then Goldie looked at Margo, and Margo looked at Ginger, and they were looking at me, and I'm smiling. I'd never felt so good on stage. I had to be there, and that was it. I started working with them."

When manager Ross was unable to persuade MacDonald to not join the band, he relented and got the group—Goldie Zelkowitz (later Genya Ravan), Margo Lewis, Ginger Bianco, and, now, MacDonald—a deal with Atlantic (the group had previously recorded for Scepter before MacDonald joined). And though MacDonald admits the group was perceived as a "novelty" by the industry, the members themselves remained nonplussed. "We didn't think anything of it," she says. "We got more jobs because they were exploiting the hell out of us. All Girl Band! They'd do the whole thing, tits and ass. And we didn't care. We were happy because we knew we could play, and we were knocking the socks off of most of the male bands. And the guys couldn't believe it. They'd start off laughing, and then they'd walk out crying." As a joke, the group would also deliberately play up to the expectations club owners had about "girl bands" in order to turn the tables later, as Genya Ravan later recalled on a panel at the New Music Seminar in New York in 1990: "We'd walk into a club with all our instruments and you could see the owner going 'Oh my God, these broads? They know how to play? They really know how to play?' We'd set up and have a sound check and play totally out of tune, and I would sing the wrong lyrics. And the guy'd be chewing on his cigar going 'Oh my God! Oh my God! Oh my God!' And by the time we went on and counted off the song, we were cookin'. You could see the cigar drop and the guy had a heart attack . . . We had fun with this."

As "the darlings of the New York scene" the Gingerbreads met many of the visiting musicians when the British Invasion began, usually while playing society parties and debutante balls. They also met the Rolling Stones when they played at the band's U.S. welcoming party, but were unimpressed. "We all went in their dressing room and we were thinking, 'My God, they're such pigs!'" MacDonald remembers. "They were so dirty. They really were—but that was their image." When the British band the Animals arrived, the band's manager, Michael Jeffery, was impressed by the Gingerbreads and extended an offer to bring them to England, which the group accepted. On their arrival in Britain the

Pop Weekly Pin-up   No.
Goldie and The Gingerbr

Goldie and the Gingerbreads, circa 1965 (left to right: Goldie Zelkowitz, Ginger Bianco, Carol MacDonald, Margo Lewis). Courtesy of David A. Young collection

band was put in the studio to record the song that became the Gingerbreads' first hit, "Can't You Hear My Heartbeat." "I hated the song," says MacDonald. "We're doing stuff like 'Harlem Shuffle,' and then they give us this 'Every time I see you . . . dee de dee de dee.' Eeeow! I said, 'Goldie! What are we doing?' She said, 'We gotta do what they say!' It's like we had to do everything they said or we were not going to be successful. So we record this stupid song, and then they shove us off to the Star Club in [Hamburg] Germany because we don't have our working visas yet."

While playing in Hamburg's notorious red-light Reeperbahn district (where the Beatles also received an education—musical and otherwise), "Can't You Hear My Heartbeat" landed in the British Top 10, and the Ginger-breads were called back to England to appear on the comedy program *Not Only, But Also.* The Ginger-breads were now on a roll and were soon touring England in the company of the Yardbirds, the Hollies, the Kinks, and the Rolling Stones, though the group's negative impression of the Stones was reconfirmed in an unwanted "groping" incident between Mick Jagger and Margo Lewis. "Margo almost punched his head off his neck," remembers MacDonald. "She came around and slapped his head off his shoulders and said, 'Who do you think you are? How dare you!' Because he thought he could do that! He's the star so he could do that. That's the kind of shit we'd have to put up with."

As always, live performance gave the band greater satisfaction. "They put us in what they called the 'hot seat,' which was right before the main act," MacDonald says.

"Because we could hold their attention. By that time, these kids have sat through nine million groups—they want to see the Stones already! The kids would jump out of the balconies and break their teeth, bleeding, they didn't care. They'd dive under the fire curtain after these guys, almost get chopped in half—I never saw anything like it. And now they're screaming and yelling for us too. They would try to jump on our van while we were going out. It was unbelievable. We couldn't even go to the post office without getting bombarded by kids, little girls coming and falling asleep on our doorsteps, finding out where we lived, camping out, wanting to go with us and live with us—oh, forget it! We were very big stars over there."

Unfortunately for the Gingerbreads, Atlantic only released three singles by the group, on their subsidiary label Atco. The group's launching in the States was further botched by Michael Jeffery's eagerness to have the group record "Heartbeat," when his partner, Mickie Most, who managed Herman's Hermits, felt he had first rights to the song. "That little song was on Mickie's desk," MacDonald explains. "So when Michael took the song and gave it to us, Mickie got pissed off with him and said, 'All right, I have Herman's Hermits, I'm gonna record it with Herman, and I'm gonna release it in the States.' And he released it two weeks before ours." The Hermits' version went all the way to number 2. "That blew our hit," says MacDonald. "It really ruined it for us because they were already known. Talk about bad timing! And that was our bad luck. We never got a hit."

Nor did the Gingerbreads end up making any money. After three years of continual touring in Germany and England and three British Top 10 singles, the group learned their finances had been misappropriated by their management. In the wake of this dispiriting blow, the group returned to the U.S., where they remained relatively unknown and soon broke up. (They would play a reunion show in New York in 1997.) It was not the first time an American group found a larger audience overseas than it would at home, nor would it be the last, though later bands would be able to build on their success overseas to win equal recognition at home. In 1980, an all-female band called the Go-Go's, who released their first single in England, would be able to maintain the momentum and eventually become the first all-female band to reach number 1 in the album charts. The Gingerbreads, while receiving little recognition themselves, helped to lay the groundwork that enabled other female performers to break out of the conventional roles women were still expected to play in the music industry.

The girl group era as a whole had brought an unprecedented number of female artists to the charts, and more women were able to develop their roles in offstage positions during the era as well. The years between the first wave of rock & roll in the '50s and the arrival of the British Invasion in the '60s have generally been regarded as a musically barren period, save for the bland offerings of the male teen idols. But songs like "Will You Love Me Tomorrow," "Be My Baby," "I Can Never Go Home Anymore," and "You Don't Own Me" were bold statements of desire, anguish, and independence that could hardly be considered bland or tame. Some performers, like Carole King, Lesley Gore, and Nona Hendryx were able to use the momentum of the period to generate substantial careers for themselves. Others, like Goldie and the Gingerbreads pushed beyond the stereotypes for female performers to forge a path for later groups to follow. And as the decade progressed, women would find the atmosphere of social change providing them with further opportunities they were now in a better position to take full advantage of.

3

Talkin' 'bout a Revolution

"How important were the musicians during the civil rights years? They were crucial.
You couldn't call black people together in any committed way without a ritual
that involved an enormous amount of singing."
—Bernice Johnson Reagon, in *When the Music's Over: The Story of Political Pop*

In the summer of 1964, the Supremes had their first number 1 hit with "Where Did Our Love Go," the first out of a total of twelve number 1 singles they would have by the end of the decade. It was an impressive record that established the Supremes as the top female group of the '60s, and helped make their label, Motown, one of the most successful black-owned businesses in the country. At a time when British Invasion acts were giving the Brill Building production teams stiff competition, Motown was in large part responsible for keeping, as their company slogan put it, "The Sound of Young America" firmly on the charts. The company headquarters in Detroit, Michigan, an unprepossessing building with a sign above the door that read "Hitsville U.S.A.," was now as much of a hit-making center as the Brill Building had been.

And as their slogan implied, Motown's music was designed to cross over to all of America's youth, not just black youth. In contrast to the "dangerous" R&B and early rock & roll of the '50s, Motown had hit upon, as Steve Chapple and Reebee Garofalo noted in *Rock 'n' Roll is Here to Pay*, "a perfect pop formula: music that was clearly black, but not threatening, and very danceable"—and so readily acceptable to white America. The rise of Motown coincided with the rise of the civil rights movement in America (two weeks before "Where Did Our Love Go" made its debut in the Top 40, Congress passed the 1964 Civil Rights Act), and its presence as a highly visible, and successful, black-owned business made a considerable impact. "Blacks and whites were making efforts to change things, and music helped bridge the gaps," wrote Mary Wilson in *Dreamgirl: My Life as a Supreme*, identifying the role Motown and its artists played in confronting and challenging attitudes toward racism. As a member of Motown's most successful group, Wilson would see over and over again how the Supremes' crossover to the pop mainstream did challenge people in that mainstream; in her book she remembered being approached while the group was appearing in Miami by a woman who told her, "I usually don't let my children watch Negroes on television, but the Supremes are different." "Fortunately, we knew where they were coming from," Wilson added, "but these comments said a lot about what the Supremes meant . . . We were living examples of the slogan 'black is beautiful.'"

Berry Gordy, Jr., Motown's founder and owner, also invested more time and money in launching and maintaining the careers of the company's artists than black acts had received before. With few exceptions, black performers before the rock era of the '50s found that their potential audience was limited by the constraints of recording for poorly distributed indie labels and performing on the "chitlin' circuit," the name given to the circuit of clubs and halls located in black neighborhoods. Gordy set out to change that, forming publishing and management companies (Jobete and Talent Management, Inc., respectively) at the same time he started the Motown Record Corporation, enabling him to oversee every aspect of his performers' careers. Gordy extended his control to all areas of his company as well: the songwriters' work was continually evaluated, records were repeatedly remixed until they were deemed acceptable, and the artists themselves, when not working in the recording studio or out on tour, were sent to Motown's "school," the Artist Development Department, which taught performers how to behave both onstage and off. Motown's aspirations were well conveyed by Maxine Powell, who ran a local modeling school that she closed in order to work full-time for the Artist Development Department. In between the pointers of etiquette she passed on to her students, Powell reminded the artists they were being groomed for performances at venues of the utmost respectability—namely Buckingham Palace and the White House.

Gordy, a former boxer, record shop owner, and Ford assembly-line worker, began his career in music as a songwriter, composing melodies while working on the assembly-line. His first songs, co-written with his sister Gwen and her friend Billy Davis (who wrote under the name Tyran Carlo), were recorded by Jackie Wilson, whom Gordy knew when they were boxers in the '40s, and included such R&B hits as "Reet Petite," "Lonely Teardrops," and "I'll Be Satisfied," all released in the late '50s. In 1960, Barrett

Strong took Gordy's song "Money (That's What I Want)," co-written with Janie Brad-ford, to the Top 30 in the pop charts and number 2 in the R&B charts. "Money" had been released on Anna Records, a label started by Gwen and Billy Davis (and named after another Gordy sister) in 1959, and, inspired by his sister's example, Berry launched Motown (a contraction of "Motortown," a nickname for Detroit) with a seven-hundred dollar loan from his family the same year.

Gordy ran the company out of a house found by his second wife, Raynoma Liles, at 2648 West Grand Boulevard, and soon other members of the Gordy family joined Motown (by the mid-'60s, ten members of the Gordy family would be working for the company). Berry's sisters Esther and Louyce became vice presidents, in charge of management and billing, respectively, and Gwen worked as a publicity aide. Berry's wife Raynoma, also known as "Mother Motown," served as executive vice president, and was involved in a variety of activities at the company, from writing lead sheets for the musicians to use during recording sessions to providing background vocals at ses-sions herself (in her book *Berry, Me, and Motown* Raynoma claimed to have co-founded Motown with Berry, but had taken her name off the business registration papers at his request). Berry's occasional songwriting partner Janie Bradford became a receptionist. Also on hand was Martha Reeves, hired as the secretary for William "Mickey" Stevenson, the head of Motown's A&R department. Reeves, a member of the Del-Phis, had auditioned for Motown as a singer, but when she was offered the secretarial job instead, she decided to take it and wait for the opportunity to develop her singing career at a later date.

"Come to Me" by Marv Johnson became the first record released on Motown's Tamla label in January 1959, though not until the release of the Miracles' "Way Over There" in 1960 would the company begin to distribute its own records. The Miracles, who originally included Claudette Rogers (who later married another member of the group, Smokey Robinson) in their lineup, also gave Tamla its first big success in the white market in 1961 with "Shop Around," which went to number 2 in the pop charts, and topped the R&B chart. By the end of the year Tamla would have its first pop number 1 with the Marvelettes, Motown's first girl group, whose "Please Mr. Postman" topped both the pop and R&B charts.

The Marvelettes—Gladys Horton, Katherine Anderson, Georgeanna Dobbins, Juanita Cowart, and Wanda Young—had attended the same high school in the Detroit suburb of Inkster. Originally called the Marvels, the group had entered a talent contest at Inkster High which offered the prize of an audition at Motown. The group won the contest, and their Motown audition (where they performed the Chantels' "Maybe") generated enough interest that they were asked to come back and bring along some original material. The group returned with "Please Mr. Postman," co-written by Dobbins. Gordy signed them, changed their name to the Marvelettes, and released "Postman" as their first single. Released in the fall of 1961, "Postman," with its light pop beat, fit in well with other girl group songs then on the market. Motown's choice of a follow-up single, "Twistin' Postman," released in 1962, used the familiar ploy of exploiting a previously successful theme, with "Twistin' Postman" attempting to cash in on both the latest dance craze while continuing the "Postman" theme of the group's previous hit. "Twistin' Postman" only reached number 34 in the charts, but the Marvelettes were soon back on track with "Playboy," co-written by Horton, which reached the Top 10 in the spring of 1962. Unfortunately, the Marvelettes wouldn't have another Top 10 hit until 1966, by which time the Supremes were established as Motown's top act; and though the group continued having Top 40 hits through 1968, they never regained their previous momentum. The group broke up the following year.

In 1962, Mary Wells emerged as Motown's first solo star. Born in Detroit in 1943, Wells had sung in church as a child and was singing at school functions by her teens, in addition to performing with all-male bands: "[They] didn't want me in there, but I

Mary Wells, circa 1964
Courtesy of David A. Young collection

was persistent," she explained. At eighteen, she auditioned for Berry Gordy, not as a singer, but a songwriter, performing an a capella rendition of her own "Bye Bye Baby," which she'd written for Jackie Wilson. Gordy not only liked the song, he liked Wells, and signed her to Motown. "Bye Bye Baby" was released as Wells's first single in 1961 and reached number 45 on the pop charts, but by the next year Wells and the Motown label would break into the pop Top 10 with "The One Who Really Loves You," followed by "You Beat Me to the Punch" and "Two Lovers," both of which also reached the Top 10.

In contrast to the teenage image of the Marvelettes, Wells was presented as more adult, though in fact she was still in her teens. In songs like "Two Lovers," Wells was clearly beyond adolescent yearnings for a boyfriend, and was now coolly assessing her "two lovers" (actually the two sides of the man's personality) from a perspective of maturity. After "Two Lovers," Wells's subsequent singles placed lower in the charts, but her success was re-established in 1964 with the release of "My Guy." "My Guy," written by Smokey Robinson, was Wells's biggest hit, a number 1 smash (the first number 1 for the Motown label) that remained in the Top 10 for two months. Motown followed up this success by pairing Wells with Marvin Gaye, and the two had Top 20 hits with "Once Upon a Time" and "What's the Matter with You Baby" in May and June of 1964. In the fall of 1964 Wells became the first Motown act to perform overseas, appearing with the Beatles on a tour of England.

But by that time, Wells's chart run and her time at Motown were over, for in addition to being Motown's first solo star, Wells was also to become Motown's first casualty. Urged on by her then-husband, Herman Griffin (also a Motown employee and songwriter), Wells began negotiations with Twentieth Century Fox about signing to their record label, with the additional hope of moving into films. When she turned twenty-one in May of 1964, Wells announced she was leaving Motown, declaring her contract with the company void, as she'd signed when she was a minor. Upon officially breaking with Motown after a legal battle, Wells signed with Fox, but the move proved to be disastrous; only one subsequent single cracked the Top 40 ("Use Your Head," which reached number 34 in 1965) and no film contracts materialized. Wells moved on to the Atlantic subsidiary Atco in 1966, but was unable to revive her career, and she eventually wound up on the oldies circuit. Nonetheless, she tried to maintain a positive attitude in regard to her situation. "I used to be very hurt by this oldie goldie thing," she told Gerri Hirshey in *Nowhere to Run.* "But really, the term is 'oldie but *goodie*,' right? And we all have a ball . . . I say, let me just sit back with the kids and relax, just go off and work." Wells died of throat cancer on July 26, 1992.

Martha Reeves and the Vandellas were the next female act to provide Motown with hits. Reeves and her group, the Del-Phis (Gloria Williams, Rosalind Ashford, and Annette Sterling), had been providing backing vocals on various Motown records, such as Marvin Gaye's hits "Stubborn Kind of Fellow" and "Hitch Hike." The Del-Phis had also managed to get a contract with Check-Mate, a subsidiary of Chess Records, which released a single from the group. The Del-Phis finally got the chance to cut their own record for Motown in 1962 when Mary Wells missed a recording session and the Del-Phis stepped in to record "There He Is (At My Door)," though there were spec- ulations that Wells "missed" the session because she didn't like the song. As the group was still under contract to Chess, the record was credited to "The Vels" and released on Motown's Melody label (not to be confused with the country label Melodyland Motown started in the '70s).

If Wells had deliberately missed the session, her instincts proved to be correct, for "There He Is" made no impression on the charts, and Gloria Williams quit the Del- Phis shortly after its release. The group then recorded another song turned down by Wells, "I'll Have to Let Him Go," and with the group now signed to Motown, Reeves thought up a new name, combining the "Van" from Detroit's Van Dyke Avenue with "Della" from the name of singer Della Reese to create the Vandellas. "I'll Have to Let Him Go," released on the Gordy label, was equally unsuccessful, but the group's third single, "Come and Get These Memories," released in 1963, managed to crack the Top 30, and that summer, the group reached the Top 10 with "Heat Wave." Fortuitously released at the time of an actual heat wave, "Heat Wave" reached number 4 in the pop charts and number 1 in the R&B charts. But its lively, raucous dance rhythms would no doubt have made the song a hit at any time of the year, and the group followed up their success with another Top 10 hit, "Quicksand," which reached number 8 in early 1964.

After two less successful records, "Live Wire" and "In My Lonely Room," the Van- dellas landed in the Top 10 again in the fall of 1964 with "Dancing in the Street." Reeves had sung on the original demo of the song, which was intended for another Motown singer, Kim Weston. But when Weston turned it down, the Vandellas were allowed to record it for official release and took it to number 2, their biggest success with Motown. The song also generated a minor controversy, for some people inter- preted it as a call for the black community to riot, to the amazement of Reeves. "My Lord, it was a *party* song!" she told Gerri Hirshey, and though a few stations banned the song, the vast majority seemed to share Reeves's opinion. But along with their success, the group was also feeling a sense of dissatisfaction, for 1964 was the year the Supremes finally developed into a major act, and the Vandellas' two Top 40 hits didn't hold up as well against the Supremes' four Top 40 hits (which included three number 1's) during the same year.

Reeves in particular felt the energy being put into the Supremes was having a negative effect on the Vandellas' chances for greater success: their song "Jimmy Mack," for example, a Top 10 hit in 1967, had been held back from release for almost two years because it reportedly sounded too much like the records the Supremes were making. And though the Vandellas continued to find chart success with such songs as "Nowhere to Run" in 1965, "I'm Ready for Love" in 1966, and "Honey Chile" in 1967, the hits came too infrequently to help the group grow and develop. A series of personnel changes also began to plague the group, making it difficult to maintain continuity: Annette Sterling left in 1963, replaced by Betty Kelly (who sang in another Motown group, the Velvelettes); Kelly left in 1968, replaced by Reeves's sister Lois; and Rosalind Ashford left in 1970, replaced by Sandra Tilley, another Velvelette.

In spite of these difficulties, Reeves persevered, though her unhappiness over the group's treatment at Motown did not subside; she suspected the songs the Vandellas were given had been rejected by the Supremes, and she was equally suspicious about the company's accounting system. "I think I was the first person at Motown to ask where the money was going," she told Gerri Hirshey. "Did I find out? Honey, I found my way out the door." The group's name change in 1967 to Martha Reeves and the Vandellas (following the pattern set by other Motown groups who were now pulling their lead singers out for special mention—such as Diana Ross and the Supremes) made little difference to the Vandellas' declining fortunes; after "Honey

Martha Reeves and the Vandellas, circa 1966 (clockwise from the top: Annette Beard, Martha Reeves, Rosalind Ashford). Courtesy of David A. Young collection

Chile" the group had no further Top 40 hits. In 1971, the Vandellas disbanded; Reeves has since appeared on the oldies circuit, with innumerable permutations of the "Vandellas" also in circulation.

Reeves and the Vandellas were not the only performers at Motown to feel overshadowed by the success of the Supremes: the Velvelettes, Brenda Holloway, and Kim Weston also felt lost in the shuffle. The Velvelettes—Carolyn and Milly Gill, Bertha and Norma Barbee, and Betty Kelly—were brought to Motown by Gordy's nephew, Robert Bullock, who attended Western Michigan University with two members of the group. Their singles had little impact on the charts. "Needle in a Haystack" charted the highest at number 45; "There He Goes" and "He Was Really Sayin' Something" didn't even make it that far, though the latter did get to number 21 in the R&B charts and went on to be a number 5 hit in the U.K. for Bananarama in the 1980s. "Motown was product oriented and primarily interested in results rather than the vehicle used to accomplish the results," Carolyn Gill told Charlotte Grieg—a lament typical of a record company's attitude toward its girl groups, whether based in New York City or Detroit.

Brenda Holloway seemed at first set to be a successor to Mary Wells. Born in 1946 in Atascadero, California, Holloway moved to Los Angeles in her teens, where she recorded singles for the Catch and Minasa labels, but her dream was to sign with Motown. In 1964, Holloway attended a DJ convention held in L.A., assuming someone from Motown would be there, and Berry Gordy caught her impromptu performance singing along to a record of "My Guy." Gordy signed Holloway, and her first single, "Every Little Bit Hurts" (released on the Tamla label in 1964), went to number 13. Holloway's prospects for the future looked good, but two months later, the Supremes had their first number 1 hit, and Holloway suddenly found her career was no longer that much of a priority. Out of nine subsequent singles, only two reached the Top 40, "When I'm Gone" and "You've Made Me So Very Happy," co-written by Holloway and her sister Patrice, along with Gordy and Frank Wilson, which peaked at number 39 in 1967. The latter song became a number 2 hit for the white, jazz-based group Blood, Sweat, and Tears in 1969; ironically, Holloway had wanted to give her own version a jazzier flavor, but was opposed by Gordy. Other conflicts, including disputes over money, led to Holloway's decision to leave the label when her contract expired in 1967. She released a gospel album in 1980, and returned to live performances in the mid-'90s.

Kim Weston was another singer seen as a possible successor to Mary Wells. Born Agatha Natalie Weston in Detroit, Weston got her start singing in church and later joined the gospel group the Wright Singers. After signing with Motown in 1963, she released her first single, "Love Me All the Way," which reached number 24 in the R&B

charts, where she also had successes with "Take Me in Your Arms" and "Helpless." She recorded duets with Marvin Gaye, and in 1967 reached number 14 in the Top 40 charts with "It Takes Two," but found no success on her own in the pop charts. She also recorded a solo album, but it was not released, and she left Motown in 1967 when her husband, Mickey Stevenson, quit the company.

Tammi Terrell was another Motown singer paired with Marvin Gaye for a series of duets which proved to be far more successful than her solo work for the label. Born Tammy Montgomery in Philadelphia, Terrell had been discovered by Luther Dixon, the Shirelles' producer, and had recorded for Wand Records, James Brown's Try Me label (she also toured with Brown), and Checker Records before signing with Motown in 1965. Her first single with Gaye, "Ain't No Mountain High Enough," was released in 1967 on the Tamla label and went to number 19, followed by six more singles that all made the Top 30, four of them in the Top 10. Most were written and/or produced by the team of Nick Ashford and Valerie Simpson, including "Your Precious Love," "Ain't Nothing Like the Real Thing," and "You're All I Need to Get By." But Terrell's career was cut short when she died of a brain tumor in 1970.

If performers like Martha Reeves, Brenda Holloway, and the Marvelettes were understandably upset by the way their careers had drifted after promising starts, their hurt was intensified by the fact that they could be treated this way at Motown. To those who worked for the company, Motown was more than just another record label. In addition to being one of the country's most successful black-owned businesses, Motown was offering blacks a wealth of opportunities in the music industry. Even when they had grievances, the performers' pride in Motown's accomplishments remained: in a letter Brenda Holloway sent to Berry Gordy expressing dissatisfaction with the way Motown had handled her career, she nonetheless added the postscript, "I will always LOVE Motown and you!" But pride in Motown also led those working for the company to believe they would receive better treatment at Motown than they would at other companies. As Mary Wilson of the Supremes noted in the preface to *Supreme Faith*, "Of course other labels treated their artists badly; we all knew that. We also thought Motown was different." The realization that Motown was not, in the end, that different from other record companies, was often what stung the most.

Supreme Faith was Wilson's second memoir: her first book, *Dreamgirl* (taken from the title of the Broadway musical *Dreamgirls*, loosely based on the Supremes' story), had covered the origins and first decade of the group in detail and was one of the first major books written about the Supremes. From Wilson's perspective, even being a member of one of the most successful groups of the 1960s had its downside, for the inner tensions that eventually ripped the original group apart left the members with destinies that ran the gamut from superstardom to disillusionment to death. But during their heyday in the '60s, the Supremes' achievements were truly remarkable, with a total of twenty-three Top 40 singles and a further eight Top 40 singles in the '70s. As the most commercially successful all-female group in rock at the time, the Supremes smashed through the stereotype of the anonymous "girl group" collective; each member of the Supremes mattered, and, more importantly, everyone knew their names. At their height during the mid-'60s, the Supremes helped to establish a new image for female performers, particularly black women singers.

The Supremes first cracked the Top 40 in 1963, but they'd actually been with Motown since 1961, releasing singles with so little success they were known around the company as the "no-hit" Supremes. The group had formed in the late '50s as the Primettes, and included Florence (Flo) Ballard, Diana (originally Diane) Ross, Betty Travis, and Mary Wilson. Ballard, Ross, and Wilson lived in the same Detroit neighborhood, in the government-subsidized Brewster-Douglass housing projects. Ballard and Wilson had met when they performed in the school talent show (Wilson donning a leather jacket to lip-synch her way through the Frankie Lymon and the Teenagers' hit "I'm Not a Juvenile Delinquent," and Ballard performing a classical number), and when Ballard was contacted by a male vocal group, the Primes (who later became the Temptations), to form a "sister" combo called the Primettes, she brought Wilson into the group. Travis and Ross had been approached by other members of the Primes to round out the group, and the Primettes were soon appearing at local sock hops and a variety of social functions, performing contemporary hits, standards, and ballads.

The Primettes eventually got an audition with Smokey Robinson, a former neighbor of Ross's, who listened politely and then hired the group's guitar player. The group then secured an audition with Berry Gordy himself, who also listened politely and suggested they come back when they'd graduated from high school. Undaunted, the group began hanging out at Motown's offices after school, hoping to be noticed, though Travis soon left to get married and was replaced by Barbara Martin. Before Martin joined, the group cut their first single, "Tears of Sorrow," for another local label, Lu-Pine, which went unreleased at the time. But the group's persistent presence around Motown eventually began to pay off; they were enlisted to provide backup vocals and hand-claps during recording sessions, and they became Motown's first all-female group when they were finally signed by the company in 1961 (eight months before the Marvelettes would release "Postman").

At Gordy's suggestion, the group also changed their name, Ballard picking out "Supremes" from a list of potential names the group had compiled. The group's first single, released on the Tamla label, was "I Want a Guy" and featured Ross on lead, setting a precedent for future releases. Up to that time, lead vocals had been traded off among the group, but Gordy had decided that Ross's voice was the one he wanted promoted. When "Buttered Popcorn," the group's second single, began generating attention locally, Gordy declined to put a big promotional push behind it, because Ballard was the lead singer on the song. When Martin left the group at the end of 1961, the remaining Supremes decided not to replace her but continue as a trio; though neither Ballard nor Wilson was happy about being denied the chance of singing lead vocals on the group's singles, both still hoped the situation might change in the future.

For the next two years, the Supremes, having now moved to the Motown label, continued releasing singles that hovered around the bottom of the Top 100 if they entered at all. In late 1962, they joined the roster of acts that went out on the road as the Motor Town Revue (later shortened to the Motown Revue), giving Ballard and Ross their first taste of life down South. Wilson, who had been born in Mississippi and returned on occasion to visit her family, had experienced the South's racism firsthand, but for others in the Motor Town Revue it was the first time they'd been refused service at restaurants, hotels, and gas stations—or been shot at as their bus drove out of town. The tour ended on a high note with a successful run at the Apollo Theatre, but the Supremes were disappointed with their lack of progress in the charts compared to Motown's other performers; the Marvelettes and Mary Wells each had Top 10 hits during the year, while the highest charting Supremes single had been "Let Me Go the Right Way," which reached number 90.

In October 1963, the Supremes began working with the songwriting/producing team of Brian and Eddie Holland and Lamont Dozier (known as Holland-Dozier-Holland or H-D-H), the team responsible for most of the Vandellas' hits, including "Heat Wave," though their work with the Supremes would be oriented more toward cool, breezy pop. The Supremes' first single with H-D-H, the bouncy "When the Lovelight Starts Shining Through His Eyes," became their first Top 40 success, reaching number 23. But the group would not break out fully until the release of "Where Did Our Love Go." Ironically, the group had been reluctant to record this song—Wilson in particular referred to the early material H-D-H wrote for the Supremes as "teenybop"—wishing they could record a number with the soulful fire of the Vandellas' hits. Wilson had also hoped she would be able to sing the lead this time and found a supporter in Eddie Holland, but he was outvoted by his brother Brian and Lamont Dozier. Released in June 1964, "Where Did Our Love Go" was the first of an unprecedented string of five number 1 singles the group would have: "Baby Love" and "Come See About Me" in 1964 and "Stop! In the Name of Love" and "Back in My Arms Again"

The Supremes (left to right: Flo Ballard, Mary Wilson, Diana Ross). September 1966 at the Flamingo, Las Vegas, Courtesy of the Las Vegas News Bureau

in 1965; the group also had Top 10 successes in the album charts with *Where Did Our Love Go* and *More Hits by the Supremes.*

The Supremes were now Motown's number one priority, and their career advanced rapidly. By the end of 1964, the group made their debut on *The Ed Sullivan Show*, and other prestigious bookings followed: the Supremes shared the bill at the opening of the Houston Astrodome with Judy Garland, performed at the Olympia in Paris and the Flamingo Hotel in Las Vegas, and recorded their Top 20 LP *Live at the Copa* during their debut appearance at New York's Copacabana club. Their numerous television appearances included spots on *The Tonight Show*, *The Sammy Davis Show*, *The Dean Martin Show*, and *Hullabaloo.* They recorded commercials for Coca-Cola and Arrid Deodorant, had their own food product on the market with "The Supremes White Bread," and appeared on the covers of *Time* and *Ebony.* They also kept on turning out the hits, including another run of consecutive number 1's in 1966–1967 with H-D-H's "You Can't Hurry Love," "You Keep Me Hangin' On," "Love Is Here and Now You're Gone," and "The Happening."

But along with their success, the Supremes were also experiencing their share of difficulties. The fact that Ross seemed to be receiving most of the attention became a sore point with the other Supremes, who felt themselves pushed out of the spotlight both on record and in public appearances, for while the Supremes had become Motown's favorites, Ross had become Berry Gordy's special favorite. Ballard, being the group's founder, took it the hardest and became increasingly resentful, expressing her anger by showing up late for rehearsals or press conferences and drinking to the point where she had to be replaced in shows by a member of one of Motown's backup groups, the Andantes. In 1967, she was fired from the group, replaced by Cindy Birdsong (from Patti LaBelle and the Bluebelles), and the group's name was then changed to Diana Ross and the Supremes.

From that moment on, it was only a matter of time before Ross would be launched on a solo career, but for the next two years the group kept working as much as they ever had, though their records were not always as successful as they had been. They reunited with their old "Primes" brother band, the Temptations, for a series of television specials and records, including "I'm Gonna Make You Love Me," which went to number 2, and the soundtrack for their *TCB* (Takin' Care of Business) television special, which went to number 1. They also made a guest appearance on the TV show *Tarzan* (cast as a trio of nuns), performed at a fundraiser for President Lyndon Johnson and later for presidential candidate Hubert Humphrey. And, if they didn't quite make it to Buckingham Palace, they did perform for Britain's Royal Family at London's Palladium Theatre as part of the Royal Command Performance variety show.

But to Mary Wilson's dismay, she found that she and Cindy Birdsong were becoming more and more a part of the background. Ross rarely rehearsed with the group anymore, and often served as the sole representative of the Supremes in interviews; she was also at times the only Supreme who sang on the group's records, including, ironically, "Someday We'll Be Together," Ross's last single with the group. In late 1969, it was officially announced that Ross would leave the group in the new year; she performed with the Supremes for the last time on January 14, 1970, at the Frontier Hotel in Las Vegas. Jean Terrell (no relation to Tammi) was brought in as a replacement for Ross, and the rechristened Supremes continued as a group until the mid-'70s, initially having more success than Ross did in her early solo career, with the hits "Up the Ladder to the Roof" and "Stoned Love," and their Top 30 album *Right On*.

Things did not go nearly as well for Ballard. Her initial settlement with Motown gave her only twenty-five hundred dollars a year for six years, and she was forced to relinquish her right to use the Supremes' name in any way; she was also to receive no further royalties. With the help of a lawyer, she was able to negotiate a much larger settlement, and then signed with ABC Records, who released two singles by her, "It

Doesn't Matter How I Say It" and "Love Ain't Love." The singles failed to take off, and Ballard suffered a further blow when she found her lawyer had misappropriated her funds. The lawyer was eventually disbarred, but Ballard managed to recover only fifty thousand dollars from her settlement. Her financial situation rapidly deteriorated: the management company she started with her husband folded, she lost her house, and she was finally forced to go on welfare to support her three children. When a story about her impoverished condition ran in the *Detroit Free Press* and was later picked up by the *Washington Post*, letters of support and offers of work poured in, but Ballard was too dispirited to accept most of them and in June 1975 made her final appearance at a benefit concert in Detroit, performing "Come See About Me" and Helen Reddy's "I Am Woman." In February 1976, after complaining of chest pains, shortness of breath, and hot flashes, Ballard was found lying on her floor paralyzed from the waist down. She was taken to the hospital, but died the next day of a heart attack, at age thirty-two.

The Supremes themselves broke up the following year, the end of a remarkable sixteen-year run. The group's influence had waned during their later years, in part because of the rise of soul, an altogether more aggressive style of music than the smooth, stylish pop that emanated from Hitsville (though Motown launched a subsidiary label called Soul in 1964). By the late '60s the term "soul" not only referred to the riveting musical blend of blues and gospel, but also a collective black identity, or, as Nelson George put it in *Where Did Our Love Go?*, "a special quality that blacks possessed and whites didn't." By this standard, black artists who found success in the pop mainstream were sometimes seen as "selling out" their inherent "soulfulness"—an accusation the Supremes faced from a British journalist who suggested they should "Get back to church, baby!"

As Mary Wilson noted in *Dreamgirl* with some exasperation ("What was this church business?"), none of the Supremes had ever sung in church—though they had attended services to hear other Detroit gospel singers, such as Aretha Franklin, sing. And when they did make statements of racial pride, they were criticized by the same press so eager for them to return to their "roots." In November 1968, Diana Ross included a brief eulogy to civil rights leader Dr. Martin Luther King, Jr., who had been assassinated the previous April, in the Supremes' performance of "Somewhere" (from *West Side Story*) at their Royal Command Performance appearance in London, an act that sparked an immediate controversy. The sequence was cut when the show was later televised and Ross defended herself at a press conference by stating, "It wasn't meant to shock . . . I didn't say anything bitter, it was more like a prayer." She then acknowledged her support for Stokely Carmichael, former head of the civil rights activist group the Student Nonviolent Coordinating Committee (SNCC), and the sentiments of James Brown's recent Top 10 hit, "Say It Loud—I'm Black and I'm Proud." But if the Supremes were in the curious position of having to defend themselves for not being "black" enough for some of their critics and for being too militant for others, their success undeniably helped to break down color barriers in the pop scene, evidenced by the breakthrough of the first major black solo female artist, Aretha Franklin, who burst onto the pop charts in 1967 with four Top 10 hits.

Aretha Louise Franklin was born in Memphis in 1942, but grew up in Detroit, where she moved with her family as a child. She became involved in music at a young age, as her father, Reverend Clarence LaVaugh Franklin (known as C. L. Franklin), was the pastor of Detroit's New Bethel Baptist Church. Reverend Franklin's electrifying sermons regularly drew packed houses and were eventually broadcast on radio and released on Chess Records.

Aretha began playing piano at age eight, initially taking lessons but stopping when she found them too constricting—she preferred teaching herself. She was soon appearing in church alongside her father, singing her first solo at age twelve, where she was an instant success; she also played piano for the church choir and sang in a gospel quartet with her sister Erma. When her father put together a traveling show, featuring singing acts and a sermon, Aretha joined them on the road during school vacations. At fourteen, she recorded her first album, *Songs of Faith*, for Chess.

Aretha's musical apprenticeship was further enhanced by the house guests her father entertained, many of whom were significant black performers, including Mahalia Jackson, Clara Ward, Art Tatum, Sam Cooke, Dinah Washington, and Reverend Cleveland, who taught Franklin how to play piano by ear. Franklin credited Ward with giving her initial inspiration: "Clara knocked me out!" she told Mark Bego in *Aretha Franklin: The Queen of Soul.* "From then on I knew what I wanted to do—sing! I liked all of Miss Ward's records." Dinah Washington was another favorite, as was Sam Cooke, whose successful shift from gospel to pop was a move that Franklin began considering for herself.

In early 1960, she made her decision and moved to New York City to try and make it as a blues singer. Shortly after her arrival, she recorded a demo of "Today I Sing the Blues," produced by Major "Mule" Holly, a bass player for pianist Teddy Wilson and a friend of her father. The song's author, Curtis Lewis, then brought the demo, along with other songs he'd written, to John Hammond, then working for Columbia Records. Hammond, who had produced Bessie Smith's last recordings and had discovered and produced Billie Holiday, was impressed with Franklin's performance and signed her to Columbia. Her first album, *Aretha*, was released the following year, the first of ten albums she would record for the label. But though a number of the songs she recorded were hits on the R&B charts, only one would land in the pop Top 40, and none of her albums would have any crossover hits.

Columbia initially decided they wanted to present Franklin as a jazz artist, and following the release of *Aretha* she toured on the nightclub circuit and appeared at the Newport Jazz Festival in 1962. But as she began working with different producers, the songs she recorded spanned a wide range of material that included jazz, blues, show tunes, standards, and ballads: "God Bless the Child," "Over the Rainbow," "Ol' Man River," "Why Was I Born," and "Try a Little Tenderness." Her sole Top 40 hit on Columbia came in 1961 with "Rock-A-Bye Your Baby with a Dixie Melody," which reached number 37. She also recorded cover versions of contemporary hits like "My Guy," "Walk on By," "Every Little Bit Hurts," and Betty Everett's "The Shoop Shoop Song (It's in His Kiss)" as well as a tribute album of Dinah Washington songs, *Unforgettable*, released in 1964 after her idol's death the previous year. Her albums also featured some of her own piano work and included backup vocals from the Warwick Singers, run by Dionne Warwick's sister Dee Dee and featuring Cissy Houston (Whitney Houston's mother) and Myrna Smith; later Houston and Smith would form their own group, the Sweet Inspirations, who would provide backup for Aretha's records at Atlantic.

Franklin's first husband, Ted White, was also her manager during her years with Columbia. Franklin met White when he visited her father's house while traveling with Dinah Washington. They married in 1961 and had two children; Franklin also had a son she'd given birth to at age fifteen. Once White became Franklin's manager, he was frequently in conflict with Columbia over the direction her career should take. He also attended her recording sessions, where some of the producers, particularly Clyde Otis, who became Franklin's producer in 1964, found his presence inhibiting to Aretha: "He'd come in, and if she wanted to have a little bit of fun by cutting loose, he'd look at her, and that was it," Otis told Mark Bego. For his part, White found Otis a "dictator" who wanted to push Franklin in the wrong musical direction. The one thing everyone did agree on was that when Franklin's contract with Columbia ran out in 1966 she would not re-sign with the label, and after leaving Columbia she was immediately picked up by Atlantic Records' Jerry Wexler.

Wexler had been following Franklin's career since her Chess Records days and felt what she lacked during her stay with Columbia was a clear focus. He also wanted to push her as a major R&B artist, a direction Aretha was eager to pursue. After signing Franklin, Wexler arranged for her to record at the Fame Studios in Muscle Shoals, Alabama, to add an authentic southern sound to Franklin's music. Unfortunately, the recording session lasted a single night; while recording "I Never Loved a Man (The Way I Love You)," White got in an argument with one of the white trumpet players, and the next morning both White and Franklin returned to Detroit. Franklin ended up recording the rest of her Atlantic debut album in New York, again playing keyboards on a number of cuts, using her sisters Erma and Carolyn as backup vocalists.

When "I Never Loved a Man" (also the title of her first Atlantic album) was released in February 1967, it quickly found success on both the pop and R&B charts, reaching number 9 and number 1, respectively; the LP went to number 2. Her second single, "Respect" (written and recorded by Otis Redding, whose version went to number 35 in 1965), did even better, topping both charts. Aretha and Carolyn had been working on their own arrangement of "Respect" for some time, incorporating the phrase "sock it to me" ("Another in the long list of sexual terms from blues or jazz that have passed into respectable everyday language," *Time* magazine would helpfully note) and spelling out the song's title. The contrast of Franklin's subdued work at Columbia with the passionate new songs she was recording for Atlantic was immediately apparent; her powerful voice, which sang out with a clear purity in her Columbia work was now burning with a fire that the public found irresistible.

"Respect" hit a potent nerve in 1967, the same year Black Power activist H. Rap Brown became the new leader of SNCC. Riots broke out in the black neighborhoods of several cities across America throughout the summer; the Vandellas were performing their "inflammatory" number "Dancing in the Streets" in Detroit on the very night a four-day riot was sparked by the arrest of seventy-four black men charged with drinking alcohol in an unlicensed establishment after-hours. "Newspapers, periodicals and television commentators pondered the question of 'Why?' as Aretha Franklin spelled it all out in one word, *R-E-S-P-E-C-T!*" wrote Phyl Garland in *The Soul Scene*, and *Ebony* writer David Llorens dubbed 1967 "the summer of 'Retha, Rap and Revolt!" But "Respect's" broad appeal was also due to the fact that the song could be read in a number of different ways. "It could be a racial situation, it could be a political situation, it could be just the man-woman situation," Tom Dowd, the recording engineer for the song, told *Rolling Stone*, adding, "Anybody could identify with it. It cut a lot of ground."

After spending most of the decade well out of the public eye as far as commercial success was concerned, Franklin spent the next few years making up for lost time. "Respect" was followed into the Top 10 by "Baby, I Love You," Goffin-King-Wexler's "(You Make Me Feel Like) A Natural Woman" and the LP *Aretha Arrives*. She began 1968 with a smash hit single and album, "Chain of Fools" (which featured Ellie Greenwich on backing vocals) and *Lady Soul*; each went to number 2 in the charts. During the rest of 1968 and 1969 she would have eleven further Top 40 singles, three more Top 20 albums (including the live set *Aretha in Paris* and a greatest hits package), and win the first two in a string of ten consecutive Grammy awards. In addition to their work on her records, Aretha's sisters were also signed to record labels, Carolyn recording for

Aretha Franklin
June 1969 at Caesar's Palace, Las Vegas, Courtesy of the Las Vegas News Bureau

RCA and Erma recording for the Shout and Brunswick labels; Erma would have a Top 10 hit in the R&B charts in 1967 with "Piece of My Heart," later recorded by Janis Joplin.

By the end of the decade Aretha Franklin was clearly one of America's top female singers and an international star. But problems in her personal life continued to intrude on her professional life. In 1968, she was traumatized by a cover story in *Time*, which painted a picture of Franklin as the shining, if "chunky," star suffering from the pain inflicted by her "private demons," quoting her as saying, "I might be just twenty-six, but I'm an old woman in disguise— twenty-six goin' on sixty-five." The article also identified White as one of her primary "burdens," alleging that he had assaulted Franklin in public. White sued the magazine over the statement (the case was later dismissed), but his status as a "burden" was to be short-lived, for the couple divorced in 1969. If groups of the time were often perceived as being easily manipulated—as the girl groups had been—the problem was magnified for a solo performer, particularly those managed by spouses or relatives who were assumed to have more of a "genuine" interest in working for the performer's benefit. Women, traditionally expected to maintain a subservient role even if they were stars, were in an even weaker position to question whether the authority over their careers might be misplaced. In Franklin's case, her divorce from White allowed her to fully establish her own identity and give full rein to her musical talents.

In contrast, Tina Turner was a performer who found herself caught in a deteriorating and abusive relationship with her husband/manager that eventually threatened to destroy the gains she'd made in eighteen years in the entertainment business. Turner's work as part of the Ike and Tina Turner Revue was neither the cool pop of Motown nor the gospel-tinged fire of Aretha Franklin, but earthy, sweaty R&B that was generally thought to have little crossover potential unless covered by a white artist. Tina Turner was born Annie Mae Bullock in 1939 in Nutbush, Tennessee, where she and her family were field workers. Tina's parents separated when she was a child and at age sixteen she and her sister Alline joined their mother in St. Louis, where Alline, three years older than Tina, began frequenting local clubs. She eventually brought Tina to see one of her favorite groups, the Kings of Rhythm, led by Ike Turner. Ike had been a musician since childhood, and formed the Kings of Rhythm in the late '40s. The group had recorded one of the first rock & roll records in 1951, "Rocket '88," (credited to "Jackie Brenston with the Delta Cats") and toured with artists like Howlin' Wolf and B. B. King. They also recorded for a variety of indie labels, and by the late '50s were one of the most popular live acts in St. Louis.

Though Tina's singing experience had been limited to the church choir ("I had gotten into the choir as soon as they found out I could sing," she remembered in her autobiography *I, Tina*), she was confident enough to send word to Ike via another band member that she was interested in singing with them. Ike ignored her requests until one night Tina got hold of a mike and began to sing while the band was on a break. "That blew [Ike] away," Tina said. "He ran down off that stage and picked me right up! He said, 'I didn't know you could really sing. What else do you know?'" Tina joined the band soon after, and made her first appearance on record in 1958 on the song "Box Top," which the group released on another local indie label.

Tina made her debut as a lead singer on record in 1960 when the singer Ike had enlisted to sing his composition "A Fool in Love" failed to show up for the group's session. Tina stepped in as lead vocalist, and her raw, gritty wailing helped push the song, credited to Ike and Tina Turner (as Annie Mae had been renamed by Ike though the two did not marry until 1962), into the Top 30, while peaking at number 2 on the R&B charts. The Kings of Rhythm were now rechristened the Ike and Tina Turner Revue, embellished by a female trio called the Ikettes, and the group continued recording for a variety of labels during the decade. But despite an occasional appearance on the Top 40 charts, the Revue's audience seemed destined to be limited to R&B aficionados. One record which might have reached the rock audience was "River Deep, Mountain High," written by Ellie Greenwich, Jeff Barry, and Phil Spector. Spector had arranged for the Ike and Tina Revue to appear in *The Big TNT Show*, a concert film released in 1966, and he then arranged to produce "River Deep" with Tina on vocals— though released as an Ike and Tina Turner single, Tina was the only member of the group who performed on the record. It was a typically extravagant Spector production in the best wall-of-sound tradition, with Tina's impassioned vocal performance adding a new and exciting element to that sound. But the record failed to take off in the U.S., peaking at number 68, a failure that led to Spector's withdrawal from the music business for three years.

Tina had welcomed the opportunity to work with Spector, and not only because "River Deep" was different from the R&B "shouting and screaming" she was used to doing with the Revue. "This was the first time I'd been given the freedom to go anywhere alone," she explained in *I, Tina*. "I was only allowed to go to the studio or the airport. For the first time, I really felt like a professional." Against her better judgment, Tina had become personally involved with Ike after joining the band, and her fears proved to be correct; for the next decade and a half, Tina endured frequent beatings from Ike, demoralizing her to the point that she attempted suicide when she was twenty-eight. Ike's abusive behavior extended to other members of the Revue as well. There was a frequent turnover among the male musicians, who found it difficult to work with Ike. Conversely, the female members of the group, who often became romantically involved with Ike and experienced the same kind of physical assaults as Tina, were too frightened to leave. Ike's possessiveness also had an impact on the professional lives of the Revue's members. When the Ikettes began

Tina Turner
December 1973 at the Hilton, Las Vegas, Courtesy of the Las Vegas News Bureau`

having Top 40 hits of their own in the '60s (at a time when the Revue had disappeared from the pop charts), Ike would not allow them to tour and promote their records, hiring other sets of "Ikettes" to send out on the road. When the original Ikettes tried to fight back, quitting the Revue in 1965 and setting up their own tour, Ike took out restraining orders to prevent them from performing.

But by the end of the '60s, the fortunes of the Revue began to pick up. In 1967, Tina Turner was featured on the cover of the second issue of *Rolling Stone* magazine, which had just been launched in San Francisco. The group was also invited to be the opening act on the Rolling Stones' British tour in 1966 and their American tour in 1969, due to the success of "River Deep" in England, where it reached the Top 5. In 1970, Ike and Tina Turner had their first Top 40 hit in the U.S. in eight years with "I Want to Take You Higher," and in 1971 their cover of Creedence Clearwater Revival's "Proud Mary" made it to number 4. Their next Top 40 entry came in 1973 with a song Tina had written immortalizing her hometown—"Nutbush City Limits," which reached the Top 30 in the U.S. and was a number 2 hit in Britain. Until their breakup in the mid-'70s, the Revue continued as a popular live act, appearing in Vegas and on television, with extravagant costumes and suggestive interplay between Ike and Tina that was quite different from anything a black (or white) act had presented to a mainstream audience before. But Ike's ill treatment of Tina continued, and it was only when Tina walked out on Ike and the Revue at the beginning of a tour in 1976 that she would be able to find greater success for herself as a solo artist.

In contrast to the fiery emotions generated by soul music, which produced anthems like "Respect" that fairly burst with racial pride, the folk music popularized by other artists during the '60s was decidedly restrained. But lyrically, the disparate genres often had a common denominator in their support of the growing civil rights movement. The alliance of folk music with political issues had been very much a part of the earlier work of performers like Woody Guthrie and the Weavers. Joan Baez and Peter, Paul and Mary were among the first folk singers of the '60s to carry on this tradition, helping to re-establish the link between music and political activism for a new generation, addressing not only civil rights but also protesting the escalating military conflict in Vietnam and other social issues, both in their music and in their appearances at rallies and marches.

Joan Baez, born in 1941 on Staten Island to a Mexican father and a Scottish mother, spent much of her childhood moving around the country due to her father's work as a professor. Previously a physicist doing armaments work, Baez's father had left the field when he began attending Quaker meetings, and by her teens, Baez was moving in a similar direction, having discovered Gandhi's teachings of nonviolence. In 1957, she committed her first act of "civil disobedience" while a high school student in Palo Alto, California, by refusing to leave the building during an air raid drill; her picture ran on the front page of the town paper after the incident, accompanied by an article speculating on the "communist infiltration" in the school system.

This incident took place around the same time that Baez received her first guitar, having already been taught to play the ukulele by a friend of her father. She was also singing in the school choir and listening to her favorite R&B/doo-wop songs on the radio, like the Penguins' "Earth Angel" and Johnny Ace's "Pledging My Love." After learning the guitar, she discovered the music of Harry Belafonte, Pete Seeger (a member of the Weavers), and Odetta. Her family moved to Boston after she graduated from high school and Baez enrolled at Boston University as a drama student. But she soon left college to become more involved in the city's flourishing folk music scene, where her clear, soaring voice gained her an immediate following in local coffeehouses. Baez took her performances seriously and demanded that her audience do the same. "If some innocent student wandered into the coffeehouse thinking it was like all the others, namely a place to relax and read, he was mistaken," she wrote in her book *And a Voice to Sing With.* "I'd stop in the middle of a song and tell him that if he wanted to study he could use the library."

In 1959, Baez was invited to make her first recording, as one of three folk artists on the album *Folksingers 'Round Harvard Square,* released on a local label. The same year, she was also invited by singer Bob Gibson to appear with him at the Newport Folk Festival, where they sang "Virgin Mary Had A-One Son" and "We Are Crossing Jordan River." Her performance was a success and manager Albert Grossman stepped in to try to secure Baez a record contract. Grossman began negotiating with Columbia Records, but Baez was not enthusiastic about working with the label and eventually signed with Vanguard, a smaller label. Vanguard was notable to Baez for being the only record company willing to release records by the Weavers when three of the members were accused of being members of the Communist Party, including Pete Seeger, who also came under fire from the House Un-American Activities Committee during the McCarthy Hearings in the mid-'50s. She also rejected Grossman's offer to be her manager, and instead hired Manny Greenhill, a promoter and manager she knew from Boston.

Joan Baez (which featured guitar contributions from the Weavers' Fred Hellerman) was released in 1960 and quickly became one of the biggest selling albums by a female folk artist, the first of six gold albums she would receive (an award given to albums selling half a million copies or more). Baez was one of the few performers of the time who found greater success on the album charts than on the singles charts—she would not have a Top 40 single hit until 1971 with "The Night They Drove Old Dixie

Down"—but nine of her records hit the Top 40 albums chart, three in the Top 10. She was also one of the first performers to succeed with a decidedly "unglamourous" image in comparison to the make-up, wigs, and gowns adopted by most female singers at the time. With her long straight hair and simple, comfortable style of dress, Baez undermined standard perceptions about female performers by keeping the focus on her music. Baez's appearance also allowed her to be seen as a "serious" musician by the mainstream media—who nonetheless were able to make the "look" of the performers the focus once again. "It is not absolutely essential to have hair hanging to the waist—but it helps," began an article entitled "The Folk-Girls" in *Time* in June 1962. "Other aids: no lipstick, flat shoes, a guitar. So equipped, almost any enterprising girl can begin a career as a folk singer."

Baez later appeared on the cover of *Time* in November 1962, the same year she released her third album, *Joan Baez in Concert.* The following year, she introduced a new singer to her audience, Bob Dylan. Baez had met Dylan in 1961 at the Greenwich Village club Gerde's Folk City, and in 1963 she invited him to join her at the Newport Folk Festival, where he was as much a success as Baez had been at her own debut at the Festival in 1959. The two also became romantically involved and were dubbed "The King and Queen of Folk Protest." Baez also included Dylan songs in her repertoire, and in 1968 released a double album set of his songs, entitled *Any Day Now.*

Though Baez's early material was not explicitly political, she became increasingly politically active as the decade progressed and she worked hard to keep her political convictions an integral part of her career. In 1962, in order to make live appearances in integrated venues while touring the South, she performed only at black colleges. An ardent supporter of Dr. Martin Luther King, Jr., whom Baez had first heard speak while in the eleventh grade, she marched with King at various rallies, and she was one of the performers who appeared on the platform with King at the historic March on Washington in August 1963, singing "We Shall Overcome." She also refused to appear on the television folk program *Hootenanny* because of the ABC network's blacklisting of Pete Seeger, she informed the "Eternal Revenue Service" that she would not pay the percentage of her taxes that were marked for defense spending, and she served two jail sen-

Joan Baez and Mimi Farina
1973 at the War Resisters League Conference, Pacific Grove, California, Photo by Sherry Rayn Barnett

tences for protesting at draft induction centers. As a result of her political beliefs, in 1967 she became the first performer in twenty-eight years to be denied use of the Daughters of the American Revolution's Constitution Hall in Washington, D.C. (singer Marian Anderson had been denied use of the hall in 1939 because she was black). She also began performing more contemporary songs, and such politically oriented material as "What Have They Done to the Rain" and "Joe Hill," culminating in the release of *Where Are You Now, My Son?* in 1973, which documented her 1972 visit to Hanoi, which had coincided with a fierce bombing raid by the U.S.

Peter, Paul and Mary were another folk act who became involved in the political activities of the times. Peter Yarrow, Noel Paul Stookey, and Mary Travers had each been involved in the Greenwich Village folk scene before being brought together by Albert Grossman: Yarrow performed as a solo artist and had appeared at the 1960 Newport Folk Festival, Stookey was a stand-up comic, and Travers had worked with different folk groups and appeared in the unsuccessful Broadway musical *The Next President.* Grossman had the group rehearse for seven months before their 1961 debut at New York's Bitter End club.

Being part of a group where all members sang (Stookey and Yarrow also played guitar), Travers would seemingly not have been the object of special attention because of her gender, though apparently the management had different ideas: "It was Albert's edict that Mary should not speak," Yarrow said in the book *Off the Record.* "His premise was for her to maintain a mystique. Mary was the sex object for the college male." It's doubtful whether Travers's "mystique" was indeed enhanced by Grossman's "edicts," for Peter, Paul and Mary were generally regarded as a group, not individuals, by their audience. Like Baez, Travers also adopted a simple manner of dress in performance, which emphasized the fact that her primary contribution to the trio was a musical one.

The group followed their Bitter End appearance with shows at other folk clubs around the country, and in 1962 Warner Bros. released their first LP, *Peter, Paul and Mary.* The album, called "an instant classic" by *Billboard,* stayed at the top of the charts for seven weeks and remained in the Top 20 for two years. Like the Kingston Trio, an all-male group whose success in the late '50s had rekindled the general public's interest in folk music, Peter, Paul and Mary performed traditional songs and ballads, but they were soon caught up in the politically progressive spirit of the times. After a moderate Top 40 success with "Lemon Tree" in 1962, their stirring, lively version of the Weavers' "If I Had a Hammer" reached the Top 10. "Peter, Paul and Mary were very much the Weavers' children," said Travers in the 1982 documentary film on the Weavers, *Wasn't That a Time.* "We learned from them . . . that the folk tradition was one of social commitment as well as just old fashioned have fun together."

The following year, Peter, Paul and Mary's cover of Dylan's "Blowin' in the Wind" became a number 2 hit (beating Dylan—also managed by Grossman—into the singles charts by two years), as well as an unofficial civil rights anthem, solidly linking the group to progressive causes. Like Baez, the group also appeared at the August 1963 March on Washington and other civil rights rallies and protests against the Vietnam War; they also boycotted the *Hootenanny* program. And whereas political commentary had been an area many popular performers preferred to shy away from, Peter, Paul and Mary showed that it was possible to stand up for your beliefs and still enjoy substantial commercial success. Their first five albums all hit the Top 10 (*In the Wind*, the group's third LP, reached number 1) in addition to receiving gold record awards.

The success and popularity of performers like Joan Baez, Bob Dylan, and Peter, Paul and Mary resulted in a blend of music and politics that had rarely been experienced on so large a scale in American popular culture. The same political leanings that had led to the Weavers' demise in the '50s were an asset to the folk singers of the early '60s, who in turn popularized the songs of their predecessors: in addition to "If I Had a Hammer," Peter, Paul and Mary also performed Woody Guthrie's "This Land Is Your Land." The performers of the '50s and '60s frequently worked together as well. After sharing a bill at Carnegie Hall with Pete Seeger in 1962, Bernice Johnson Reagon (who later formed the black women's vocal groups the Harambe Singers and Sweet Honey in the Rock) enlisted Seeger's wife, Toshi, to handle bookings for a group Reagon had recently joined, the Freedom Singers. Then, at Reagon's request, Pete Seeger began performing at benefits for SNCC, an organization Reagon was involved with. The fact that the outspokenness of these performers on political issues only enhanced their credibility with the record-buying public sent out a powerful message to other entertainers.

Folk made an impact on musical styles as well, especially when it began to "go electric" and eventually emerged as folk rock. 1965, the year Bob Dylan was booed off the stage at the Newport Folk Festival for using electric instruments in his set, was the same year Joan Baez started to "go electric," using an electric guitar for the first time on her album *Farewell, Angelina*. But this bending of musical boundaries also resulted in a gradual erosion of the political commentary of folk lyrics, with the new emphasis on the sound of the music rather than its message. The resulting lack of potentially controversial lyrics made folk rock more palatable to the mainstream, while the adoption of a hip look and sound theoretically allowed the performer to retain the interest of the youth market. It was a look and a sound readily and successfully conveyed by Sonny and Cher, folk rock's grooviest couple despite their decidedly un-hip adherence to convention—they were, after all, happily married at the height of the Swinging '60s, when an alleged "sexual revolution" was supposedly rendering such marital unions passé.

Though a number of folk rock groups had their roots in the East Coast folk community, Sonny and Cher came from the West Coast rock scene in Los Angeles. Cher, born Cherilyn LaPierre in El Centro, California, in 1946, had originally planned to pursue acting, and had taken acting lessons as a child. She met Salvatore Phillip Bono when both were working for Phil Spector. Bono was an aspiring songwriter and performer who had previously worked for Specialty Records and was now handling promotion for Spector. Cher was a backup singer, singing on records by the Crystals and Ronettes ("Be My Baby" was the first record she ever appeared on), in addition to serving as one of Ronnie Spector's "minders," assigned the job of accompanying Ronnie on trips around town when she was not needed at the studio and was out of sight of Phil's watchful eye.

Cher and Sonny married in 1964, and Sonny then arranged for Spector to release a solo Cher single on his Annette record label. The song, capitalizing on the Beatlemania craze of the time, was "Ringo, I Love You" and was credited to Bonnie Jo Mason. After failing to break out, Sonny and Cher began recording for the Vault and Reprise labels under the name Caesar and Cleo. But their singles failed, and in 1965 the two moved on to the Atlantic subsidiary Atco, and Cher signed as a solo artist with Imperial. Their first singles, Sonny and Cher's "Just You" and Cher's "Dream Baby," were both strongly reminiscent of the rich texture of Spector's girl group records, but again the songs made little impression on the charts. That would change dramatically with the release of Cher's "All I Really Want to Do" (a Dylan cover), which went to number 15, and Sonny and Cher's "I Got You Babe," their first and only number 1. This ode of mutual admiration had very nearly been relegated to the B-side of the single, as Atco believed "It's Gonna Rain," a song about the dissolution of a love affair, was the stronger track.

In the wake of their new success, "Just You" now became a Top 20 hit, and a single the two had recorded for Reprise, "Baby Don't Go," was re-released and hit the Top 10; Cher also had solo hits with "Bang Bang (My Baby Shot Me Down)" (which reached number 2) and "You Better Sit Down Kids," among others. Though their preference for hip-hugging trousers, striped shirts, and fur vests gave the two a measure of unconventionality, Sonny and Cher represented a safe aspect of youth culture. When the two did address contemporary issues, they were not controversial issues like the Vietnam War, but less volatile situations, such as divorce in "You Better Sit Down Kids," and Sonny's "Laugh at Me," which dealt with his experience of being thrown out of a restaurant because of his attire. But by the end of 1967, their bright pop paled in comparison to the heavier sounds coming out of the new home of the counterculture, San Francisco, and Sonny and Cher's career went into a slump, reviving in the early '70s with the success of their television series, *The Sonny & Cher Comedy Hour.* The couple eventually divorced in 1974 and Cher went on to have a successful solo career as a singer and actor, winning an Oscar in 1987 for her performance in the film *Moonstruck.*

The Mamas and the Papas were an equally colorful, safe, and commercially successful folk rock outfit, who parlayed their folk roots into a pop context that netted them nine Top 40 hits in two years. The group had formed in New York City, where the four members, Cass Elliot, Michelle and John Phillips, and Denny Doherty had performed with a variety of folk-oriented groups. John Phillips, the group's guitarist, began his musical career in Virginia, eventually moving to New York, performing and recording with a group variously named the Abstracts, the Smoothies, and the Journeymen. While on tour with the Journeymen, John met model Holly Michelle Gilliam, who became his second wife in 1962. When the Journeymen disbanded, John persuaded Michelle to join him in the New Journeymen, a group that also included Denny Doherty. Doherty, born in Halifax, Nova Scotia, had previously recorded with a group called the Halifax Three before joining the Big Three—later the Mugwumps—which also included Cass Elliot.

Born Ellen Naomi Cohen in 1941 in Baltimore, Maryland, Elliot had grown up in the Washington, D.C. area, taking piano lessons as a child and switching to guitar when she developed an interest in the growing folk boom. After briefly attending Washington, D.C.'s American University, she formed the Big Three, whose original members included Tim Rose and Jim Hendricks (Elliot married Hendricks to keep him from being drafted, and they later divorced). By 1964, Doherty had joined the group, which eventually became the Mugwumps (the group also included Zal Yanovsky and John Sebastian, who later formed the Lovin' Spoonful). The Mugwumps signed with Warner Bros., releasing a single in 1964 which was unsuccessful; they also recorded an album which was not released until the group disbanded and the former members found greater success with their subsequent groups. Following Denny's stint with the New Journeymen, he accompanied Michelle and John on a trip to the Virgin Islands, and though Cass was not yet a member of the group, she soon joined them, getting a job as a waitress at the club where the trio performed.

Cass's persistence eventually paid off when John finally agreed to let her into the group, and the resulting combination of voices, matched with John's careful musical arrangements, resulted in a rich harmonic style. When the group returned to the States, they moved to Los Angeles, where one of John's friends from his New York days, singer Barry McGuire (who'd had a hit with the anti-war credo "Eve of Destruction"), introduced them to record producer Lou Adler. The group, now called the Mamas and the Papas, started out as backup vocalists for McGuire's *This Precious Time* LP, and they launched their own career with "Go Where You Wanna Go," released on Adler's Dunhill Records label in 1965. But Adler recalled the single shortly after its release, in favor of releasing another song the group had recorded that he felt had a lot more potential: "California Dreamin'."

Written by John (Michelle was initially also credited as co-author, but the credit was dropped on later compilation albums), "California Dreamin'" was originally intended for Barry McGuire's album, and the Mamas and the Papas had already recorded the backing vocals. But Adler had Doherty record the lead vocal, and "California Dreamin'" was released in the winter of 1966, a time when the song's rhapsodies of the state's warm climate were certain to make an impact. With the West Coast becoming a musical and cultural center for young people, the song was also a clear reflection of the belief that nirvana awaited all true believers who made the journey out west. But unlike Phillips' other West Coast anthem, "San Francisco (Be Sure to Wear Flowers in Your Hair)," written for fellow ex-Journeyman Scott McKenzie, "California Dreamin'" has not dated over time; instead of linking the Golden State to such hippie accoutrements as flowers, bells, and "gentle people," as "San Francisco" does, all "California Dreamin'" promises is better weather (though both reached the same position in the charts, peaking at number 4). The Mamas and the Papas followed up this success with further Top 5 hits, including "Monday, Monday," the Shirelles' "Dedicated to the One I Love" (chosen by the group after rejecting Michelle's suggestion of recording "He's a Rebel"), and "Creeque Alley," a humorous account of the group's origins. They were equally successful on the album charts, with their first four LPs all reaching the Top 5.

The sound of the Mamas and the Papas was obviously dependent on the singing skills of all four members, but John and Cass soon emerged as the dominant figures in the group, due to their strong personalities and creative skills, John being the group's sole instrumentalist and primary songwriter, and Cass having the most powerful voice of the four. Elliot's size also presented the pop world, traditionally concerned with a performer's appearance (particularly a female performer's), with a situation it had never dealt with before, but which now had to be confronted because of the group's success. The liner notes of the group's number 1 debut album, *If You Can Believe Your Eyes and Ears*, dealt with Elliot's weight somewhat obliquely, stating "To end up with, there's Cass. You couldn't really end up with anybody else" when describing the group, and though admitting Elliot was "large," quickly paired that observation with the word "lovely." Elsewhere, the group's manager, Bobby Roberts, stated, "She was overweight, but she carried it off like she was a beauty queen."

Elliot herself was more down-to-earth about the matter. "I've been fat since I was seven," she told *Rolling Stone*. "Being fat sets you apart, but luckily I was bright . . . I got into the habit of being independent, and the habit became a design for living." Her deep-rooted feelings of independence led Elliot to fight against a "Mama" Cass image she had never asked for. "I never created the Big Mama image," she said. "I fought it all my folk-singing life . . . then came the Mamas and the Papas and I was stuck with it." That the "Mama" Cass image was a direct reference to her weight was evident in that Michelle Phillips was not generally referred to as "Mama" Michelle, but was described as the quiet, sexy, "sylph-like" member of the group. And unlike her husband, who had been reluctant to let Cass in the group because of the strength of her personality (in the liner notes of the Mamas and the Papas compilation *Creeque Alley* Michelle states, "John didn't really want her in the group because she was so independent"), Michelle admired Cass's sense of self-worth. "Cass was the first real emancipated woman I ever knew," she said. "She had an enormous effect on me, both personally and musically . . . She gave me the confidence to sing things I didn't think I could."

Elliot was also the member of the group most anxious to start a solo career and in 1968 released her first single, "Dream a Little Dream of Me," recorded by the Mamas and the Papas but credited to "Mama Cass with the Mamas and the Papas." By the end of the year, the group had split, aside from a short-lived reunion in 1971 to record *People Like Us* to fulfill a contractual obligation. Elliot recorded four albums for Dunhill, but left the label in 1970, frustrated by the lightweight material she was recording and after collaborating with Dave Mason on *Dave Mason and Cass Elliot* for Blue Thumb, she signed with RCA in 1971. In addition to recording material ranging from Broadway show tunes, standards, and songs by songwriters like Randy Newman, Bruce Johnston ("Disney Girls"), and her sister Leah Kunkel, Elliot continued to work at leaving her "Mama" Cass image behind, with her final RCA LP, released in 1973, entitled *Don't Call Me Mama Anymore*.

Though most of her recorded material fared poorly on the charts (as a solo artist, she had only three Top 40 hits, including "It's Getting Better" and "Make Your Own Kind of Music"), Elliot proved to be a popular live performer after a shaky start. Preparing for her solo debut in Las Vegas in the fall of 1968, Elliot went on a strenuous diet, losing one hundred ten pounds, which resulted in her becoming seriously ill. On opening night, her throat started hemorrhaging during the first set, with Elliot in a state of near-disorientation. "When I walked out on stage I didn't know what was going on," she later wrote in an article for *Ladies' Home Journal* entitled "How to Lose 110 Pounds in Three Months." "There were 1,200 people out there and I couldn't sing. All I could do was cry."

The show's run was cancelled, but after a period of recovery, Elliot was able to rebuild her career, branching out into television and making her film debut in the 1970 feature *Pufnstuf*. In 1973, she returned to Vegas for a successful engagement, and was eventually performing at nightclubs around the country. In July 1974, she made one of her most prestigious appearances in a two-week engagement at London's Palladium Theatre. But on July 29, two days after the Palladium show had closed, Elliot was found dead in the flat where she was staying at the time. She was thirty-two. Initial reports attributed Elliot's death to her choking on a ham sandwich, but the true cause was later said to be a heart attack, brought on by Elliot's weight, the health problems she incurred in dieting, and her drug use. But in spite of the continual focus on Elliot's weight throughout her professional career, she had nonetheless managed to project a strong, confident sense of self, and was the sole member of the Mamas and the Papas to find success as a solo artist.

The emergence of vocal groups and singers like the Mamas and the Papas, Sonny and Cher, the 5th Dimension, Spanky and Our Gang, and Jackie DeShannon, along with the success of the Motown acts, helped keep women on the music charts after the disappearance of the girl groups and the arrival of the British Invasion bands. But their roles remained overwhelmingly conventional, a situation which was rarely challenged. Women were not encouraged to develop as songwriters, they were almost never instrumentalists, and they remained under constant pressure to appear "feminine" in the public eye. But as the teenage "baby boomers" of the '60s began maturing into adulthood, they began questioning societal attitudes on everything from racism to sex to the ethics of the Vietnam War, and these attitudes were beginning to be reflected in rock music, which was now moving from being "rock" to "progressive rock," an amalgamation of musical styles ranging from blues to folk rock to the endless drone of Indian ragas. In this atmosphere of change, women also theoretically had the freedom to experiment, but since underlying attitudes toward women's roles in society were not undergoing the same degree of change at the time, such experiments inevitably led to contradiction, and women who challenged these attitudes usually paid a price for their audacity in some way.

Janis Joplin, the next major female solo singer to emerge after Aretha Franklin, was never able to find a positive alternative to this contradiction and the end result killed her. Her contemporary, Grace Slick, who came from the same San Francisco music scene, did, and she survived. San Francisco was now becoming a focal point for the burgeoning progressive rock culture, home to the hippie mecca that convened around the intersection of Haight and Ashbury streets, where Joplin's Big Brother and the Holding Company and Slick's Jefferson Airplane shared the scene with the Grateful Dead, Country Joe McDonald and the Fish, the Quicksilver Messenger Service, and others, playing such venues as the Fillmore, Avalon, and Matrix ballrooms or at "cultural events" like the "Trips Festivals" hosted by Ken Kesey (author of *One Flew Over the Cuckoo's Nest*), which brought together the key ingredients of rock music, a light show, and LSD-laced punch to be enjoyed by the faithful. The link the counterculture had now forged between rock music and youth culture was made clear in an ad taken out in the *New York Times* by the new rock music bi-weekly *Rolling Stone* (which published its first issue in San Francisco in November 1967), which stated: "Rock and roll is more than just music, it is the energy of the new culture and youth revolution."

The Jefferson Airplane was the first Bay Area group to give this energy nationwide exposure, being the first band to get a contract with a major label, RCA. The group was started in the mid-'60s by Marty Balin, and consisted of Paul Kantner, Jorma Kaukonen, Jack Casady, and Skip Spence. Balin also added a female vocalist to the band, Signe Toly (later Anderson), feeling that the inclusion of a woman in the lineup would distinguish the group from others in the scene. Originally more of a folk-flavored band, the Airplane's sound began to lean more toward rock, and in 1966 the group met their first manager, Bill Graham, at a benefit he was hosting for the San Francisco Mime Troupe at the Fillmore Auditorium. Graham soon began booking the Fillmore on a regular basis, and he helped the Airplane get their record contract with RCA. Their debut LP, *The Jefferson Airplane Takes Off*, was released in August 1966, and though not making an appearance in the Top 40, sold enough copies to become the group's first gold album.

Following its release, Toly, who had married and had a baby, quit the band, and the group approached Grace Slick, then singing with the band Great Society, to replace her (Skip Spence was also replaced by Spencer Dryden on drums). Born in Evanston, Illinois, in 1939, Slick grew up in Chicago and had worked as a model to help put her first husband Jerry through college. The two had been living in Palo Alto, a nearby suburb of San Francisco, and had been inspired to form Great Society after witnessing an early Jefferson Airplane performance; the group also recorded two albums for Columbia, but these were not released until Slick's later success with the Airplane. When she joined the band, she also brought along two of her songs that had previously been recorded with Great Society, "Somebody to Love" and "White Rabbit," which provided the Jefferson Airplane with their only Top 40 singles hits.

Slick's first album with the group, *Surrealistic Pillow*, was released in February 1967, and included both singles; the singles, and the album, all hit the Top 10. Slick downplayed her songwriting, referring to it as "glots of thought, slams of insanity" (though in a 1989 interview she admitted her inability to find happiness as a housewife was because "I couldn't stay away from the piano"), and her vocal skills, which she described as more "talking" than "singing." She was equally low-key about her role in the group: "I'm nothing except possibly more aggressive than most females my age," she told Aida Pavletich in *Rock-A-Bye Baby* (later published as *Sirens of Song*). Yet her piercing voice

("When she reached for a high note, it was as if she were zeroing in on something in order to throttle it," wrote Charles Perry in *The Rolling Stone Illustrated History of Rock & Roll*) became as much of a Jefferson Airplane trademark as her song "White Rabbit," a perfect depiction of a psychedelic drug experience seen through the surreal haze of Lewis Carroll's *Alice in Wonderland.* Slick's sarcastic, sometimes menacing demeanor also made her one of the strongest female rock personalities of the time.

The Jefferson Airplane continued releasing albums through the end of the decade, but by the early '70s, the group's tastes were beginning to diverge: Slick married Kantner and had a baby, and the two began recording their own solo projects along with Airplane albums. Slick and Kantner eventually reinvented the Airplane as Jefferson Starship—later simply Starship—a band that found greater commercial success than they had in their previous incarnation, though without being granted the cultural importance the Jefferson Airplane received during their peak in the late '60s. By the '90s, Slick had retired fom performing.

Unlike Slick, who had the sanctuary of the band and their "Airplane House" to retreat into, Janis Joplin, singing her gut-wrenching blues alone at the mike, always appeared to be more vulnerable. It was a lack of support that ultimately proved to be fatal for the singer who had dared to sing with an abandon no white female had ever attempted before. Born in 1943 in Port Arthur, Texas, Joplin was marked as "different" (or in her words, "a weirdo among fools") by her peers because of her interest in music, poetry, art, and reading, and her reluctance to engage in the local sport of "nigger-knocking" (knocking over blacks with a wood plank while driving by in a car). As a teenager, she fell in with an all-male gang and did her best to be "one of the boys," a defiant stance in conservative Port Arthur and one not even totally acceptable to the others in the group: "When Janis was outrageous she was totally outrageous," remembered one of the "gang" in Myra Friedman's *Buried Alive.* "It was unheard of for a woman to yell, 'Well, fuck you, baby!' It even embarrassed *us.*"

After graduating from high school in 1960, Joplin attended Lamar College and later the University of Texas in Austin, where she listened to and was deeply influenced by the music of Odetta, Jean Ritchie, Leadbelly, and Bessie Smith (she would later put up half the money to buy Smith a tombstone). She also began singing in local clubs, joining a trio called the Waller Creek Boys, and made her first recording, a commercial for a local bank to the tune of "This Land Is Your Land." But she found no more acceptance in Austin than she had in Port Arthur and she quit the university soon after being voted "Ugliest Man on Campus" by her fellow students.

In early 1963, Joplin hitchhiked to San Francisco with another university student, Chet Helms. Feeling a lot more at home in San Francisco's freewheeling atmosphere,

Joplin continued singing in clubs, appeared at the Monterey Folk Festival, and also visited New York, where she sang in Greenwich Village. The continual hustle to survive, along with her indulgence in alcohol and speed, eventually took its toll, and she retreated to Port Arthur in 1965 in an attempt to clean up, re-enrolling at Lamar. But she soon returned to singing, and to Austin, where her sizzling blues vocals now generated instant attention. On the verge of joining Austin's Thirteenth Floor Elevators, Joplin was suddenly contacted by Helms to become the lead singer for a band he was now managing, Big Brother and the Holding Company. Joplin agreed and returned to San Francisco in June 1966.

Ironically, at a time when the Supremes were dressing up in evening gowns and wigs, and Aretha Franklin had not yet escaped from Columbia Records, the crowds in San Francisco were going crazy over a woman who belted out songs with a soulfulness no one had thought a white singer could pull off. "Janis's voice was right on the money from the first minute she sang with us," wrote Sam Andrew, a guitarist with Big Brother, in an unpublished memoir. By September the group had signed with the Chicago-based label Mainstream Records and recorded their debut album in Chicago and L.A. The group soon regretted their decision in signing with Mainstream, particularly when their self-titled LP was not released for several months. But 1967 began on a strong note, with Big Brother joining the Jefferson Airplane and the Grateful Dead, among others, at "the first Human Be-In," a festival held in San Francisco's Golden Gate Park on January 14, attracting twenty thousand people. In June, the group made an even more memorable appearance at the first Monterey Pop Festival, billed as a celebration of "music, love, and flowers," and organized in part by John Phillips and Lou Adler. In addition to the expected "regulars" (Big Brother, the Airplane, the Dead), the three-day festival also gave major national exposure to performers like the Who, Otis Redding, and Jimi Hendrix.

Big Brother performed twice at the festival, on Friday and Sunday, the latter being a moment when everything crystallized for the band. "That second performance at Monterey was the moment we crossed some line between being a good time local group to being an international phenomenon," said Andrew. "Reporters were demanding interviews and photographers were asking us to sign releases" (their performance was also captured for the documentary film *Monterey Pop*). The band also acquired Albert Grossman as a new manager, and a contract with Columbia, who released the live album *Cheap Thrills* the following year (originally titled *Sex, Dope and Cheap Thrills* but changed at the company's request). The album featured a cover of Erma Franklin's "Piece of My Heart" (Janis referred to Erma's sister Aretha as "the best chick singer since Billie Holiday"), the honky-tonk melancholy of Joplin's own "Turtle Blues," and climaxed with a stunning interpretation of Big Mama Thornton's "Ball and Chain," a song Big Brother had seen Thornton perform in a San Francisco club. Released in the fall of 1968, *Cheap Thrills* went straight to number 1, where it stayed for eight weeks.

By the end of the year, Joplin had split from Big Brother as a star in her own right, but she remained insecure about her success: "What's gonna happen to me when I'm not number 1 anymore?" she once asked Grossman. She tended to disregard aspects of her work, playing down her songwriting by saying that her songs were something she just "made up." Yet she also felt frustrated by what she saw as the tendency by the media and the public to ignore her work in favor of her "image." "Interviewers don't talk about my singing as much as about my lifestyle," she told Mary Campbell of the Associated Press, adding, "Maybe my audiences can enjoy my music more if they think I'm destroying myself." The strain of maintaining her tough-talkin'-hard-drinkin' persona for the benefit of others was not something she enjoyed ("It's not easy living up to Janis Joplin, you know"), but endured for the sake of her career, as Myra Friedman (who worked for Grossman) noted when she suggested Joplin take a break from the rock world: "Janis sobbed, these horrible, wrenching sobs, and said over and over, 'I don't have anything else.'"

Joplin had also begun to use heroin, an addiction that marred the sessions for her second album, *I Got Dem Ol' Kozmic Blues Again Mama* (recorded with the "Kozmic Blues Band") and her appearance at the counterculture's most historic event, the Woodstock Festival, where Joplin came across as a pale copy of the feisty, gyrating firebrand she'd been two years earlier at Monterey. By the end of 1969, the Kozmic Blues Band had split, but the following spring, Joplin formed a new group, the Full Tilt Boogie Band, to support her latest persona, "Pearl." She also managed to kick heroin for a while. On the surface, her career seemed to be progressing well; the *Kozmic Blues* album had reached the Top 5 and she was soon back on the road with the Full Tilt Boogie Band. But crowd attendance was down; her arrest the previous November for using "vulgar and indecent" language at a concert made some promoters reluctant to book her, while others worried about the property damage an overly enthusiastic rock audience would inflict on their venues. Joplin responded to the latter charge with the disarming rejoinder, "My music ain't supposed to make you want to riot! My music's supposed to make you want to fuck!" But it was also apparent that the reaction to her behavior had not changed appreciably since her days in Port Arthur—as the city of Houston demonstrated when they announced the rock acts banned from performing in town, including Joplin on their list "for her attitude in general."

In September 1970, Joplin and Full Tilt Boogie began recording in L.A. The sessions went well, and Joplin was also occupied with arranging the details of her upcoming wedding. But she had also started using heroin again. In the early hours of October 4, 1970, after an evening of drinking and bar hopping with her band members, Joplin returned to her current base at L.A.'s Landmark Hotel and died of a heroin overdose; she was twenty-seven years old. *Pearl* was released posthumously in 1971, and both the album and the accompanying single, "Me and Bobby McGee," went to number 1. In the wake of her death, other Joplin product soon began to seep into the market: *Big Brother and the Holding Company* was reissued by Columbia in 1971, the double-album set *In Concert* came out in 1972, a greatest hits compilation was released in 1973, and a double-album soundtrack of the documentary *Janis* came out in 1974. There were also four biographies issued within the same

Janis Joplin
August 1970 at Forest Hills Tennis Stadium, New York,
Photo by Sherry Rayn Barnett

time, and the 1980 Bette Midler film *The Rose* was said to be loosely based on Joplin's life.

In fact, *The Rose* was based more on the masochistic, hedonistic lifestyle that the media and the public identified with Joplin, rather than any specific incidents directly relating to her life. Following the death of Jimi Hendrix and preceding that of the Doors' Jim Morrison, Joplin's death was perceived as just another rock & roll casualty, but the fast living had different implications for Joplin than it did for the male musicians. In her own way, Joplin was still trying to be "one of the boys," though again, as in high school, the penalties were different for girls: they could only be "good" or "bad," not some combination of both. Joplin had opted for the latter, and glamourized her "bad" image in the creation of Pearl, but in the end the role of "bad" girl turned out to be as limited (if more interesting) as the role of "good" girl. Country Joe McDonald, who had been romantically involved with Joplin for a brief period in San Francisco, understood this contradiction when he told Deborah Landau in *Janis Joplin*: "Sexism killed her. Everybody wanted this sexy chick who sang really sexy and had a lot of energy . . . and people kept saying one of the things about her was that she was just 'one of the guys' . . . that's a real sexist bullshit trip, 'cause that was fuckin' her head around . . . she was one of the women. She was a strong, groovy woman. Smart, you know? But she got fucked around." Joplin's role as a rock & roll martyr does have elements of truth, but her daring in confronting the stereotypes available for female rock singers at the time and trying to find a viable alternative provides a much worthier legacy.

In contrast to the West Coast, the bands on America's East Coast were experimenting with a completely different definition of "rock." The group that best exemplified this experimentation during the late '60s was the Velvet Underground, often reviled during their existence, but now considered one of the most influential bands in all rock music. The group, who took their name from a pornographic novel, formed in New York City in the mid-'60s, founded by guitarist Lou Reed and also including Sterling Morrison on guitar, John Cale on bass and viola, and Maureen Tucker on drums. Tucker was one of the very few female drummers on the rock scene at the time aside from Ginger Bianco, of Goldie and the Gingerbreads, and Lily Lantree, of the British group the Honeycombs, but to her surprise she found her presence in the band generally provoked little reaction. "I'm sure in the audience there were many people going, 'Holy cow, that's a girl!'" she says. "But in an interview it wasn't a big issue, which is very odd when you think about it. Or maybe they were afraid to ask!"

Born in 1944 in Jackson Heights and growing up on Long Island, Tucker's musical experience prior to the Velvet Underground consisted of playing clarinet with the school band and a three-week stint as a drummer with a local group called the Intruders when she was twenty. "It was fun to play," says Tucker, "but at that point the bother of dragging off to some ridiculous bar on Long Island to play cover songs was more trouble than it was worth." Tucker had listened to the music of classic rock & roll artists like Chuck Berry and Bo Diddley as a teenager (she later covered the song "Bo Diddley" as a solo artist) and at eighteen taught herself to play guitar. The arrival of the British Invasion bands inspired Tucker to switch to the drums ("I bought a snare drum and I would spend hours playing Stones records and banging this drum," she says), and shortly after leaving the Intruders she was introduced to the Velvet Underground by her brother, who had gone to college with Lou Reed.

At the time, the Velvets were looking for a replacement for their original drummer, Angus MacLise, who had quit the band before their debut performance in November

1965. "They got a job to play at a high school in New Jersey," explains Tucker. "So Lou came out to our house to see if I could actually play anything. And he said, 'Yeah, cool,' and we practiced the songs a few times and played the show." Following their debut, the band's next gig was a short residency in early 1966 at Greenwich Village's Cafe Bizarre, where they came to the attention of artist Andy Warhol. Warhol hired the band to provide the music for his Exploding Plastic Inevitable "total environment" road-show productions and also paired them with German-born singer Nico, whose pale, European countenance and deadpan vocals gave another enigmatic dimension to the group.

Warhol's Exploding Plastic Inevitable shows, held at the Dom, a former Polish National Hall on St. Mark's Place, were an East Coast counterpart to Ken Kesey's Trips Festivals. "We would play and there would be movies on a screen behind us," remembers Tucker. "An Andy movie, of course. And there would be a light show and sometimes slides instead of a movie, and all this would be going on at the same time. It was very exciting. I really wished I could've slipped out of my body and sat in the audience to see what it was like. Many times I would get chills on stage thinking, 'Holy shit, this must be incredible!'" The free-form nature of Warhol's work further encouraged the band's musical experimentation. "The songs really worked themselves out during live performances," says Tucker. "We did a lot of improvising. We'd do some specific songs, like 'Heroin,' but just as often we'd improvise for half an hour or forty-five minutes or whatever. It must have been as interesting as hell, because Andy's movies were so wacky!"

In 1967, the group released their first album (which they had recorded in eight hours), *The Velvet Underground & Nico*, on Verve. The songs were an extension of the garage rock punk of earlier '60s groups like the Kingsmen, the Standells, and the Sonics, though the Velvets' subject matter was dramatically different— the fuzzy, droning slash of the music provided an unkempt bed for the band's nihilistic tales of seedy urban life,

Maureen "Moe" Tucker of the Velvet Underground 1969 at a recording session for the band's third LP, Los Angeles, Courtesy of the Velvet Underground Appreciation Society

replete with drugs ("Heroin") and sadomasochism ("Venus in Furs"). The music had already provoked confusion and alarm, as evidenced by the review quotes of the group's live shows included on the album's inner sleeve: "A three-ring psychosis that assaults the senses" *(Variety)*, and "An assemblage that actually vibrates with menace, cynicism and perversion. To experience it is to be brutalized, helpless" *(Chicago Daily News)*. But such reactions did not displease the group. "I'm sure it *was* like being brutalized . . . but happily so!" says Tucker. "So much of the music in those days was flower power and love and peace. It bored the shit out of us. Not that we were dark hulking figures who hated everybody, we just weren't interested in it. Now, if Lou had written a song about flower power I'm sure it would have been interesting if we'd played it!"

The band's next album, *White Heat/White Light*, was released in December 1967, by which time Nico and Warhol had gone on to other projects. The band toured sporadically, but by 1969 Cale left the group to pursue a solo career, replaced by Doug Yule. Following the release of *The Velvet Underground*, also released in 1969, Tucker quit the band to give birth to her first child and was replaced by Doug's brother Billy. The band finally split shortly before the release of *Loaded* in 1970. The group then reformed in the early '70s with a lineup that included Tucker, Morrison, Doug Yule, and bassist Walter Powers, but it proved to be short-lived; Morrison was soon replaced by Willie Alexander and the band broke up for good in 1972 following a tour of England. According to Tucker: "It wasn't a lot of fun anymore, and I felt like a phony because it wasn't really the Velvets." By that time, other performers like Detroit's MC5, the Stooges (whose first album was produced by Cale), and Yoko Ono were testing the limits of what rock could endure, laying the groundwork for the punk explosion later in the '70s, an explosion in which women would participate on an equal basis with men. Tucker later released solo albums and the Velvet Underground reunited for a tour in 1993.

As progressive rock became big business, record companies, promoters, and radio stations moved in to take advantage of it. This development gave an unexpected opportunity to a DJ in New York, Alison Steele, who became the first female DJ at a major radio station, WNEW, then one of the leading radio stations in the country. Steele had started in New York's entertainment industry in the 1950s while still in her teens: she was the first woman to lead exercises on TV and later graduated to "Weather Girl." "I did all the things that girls did in the early days of television, thirty years ago," she says. "I backed into radio accidentally because in 1966 the FCC decreed that AM stations split from FM stations instead of simulcasting. WNEW had to hire DJs for the FM station, and the scale set by AFTRA [the American Federation of Television and Radio Artists] for the FM station at that time was $125 a week. Now the guys across the hall [at the AM station] were getting $150,000, $200,000—who were they gonna get for a hundred and a quarter? So somebody came up with the idea of an all-female station. And I was hired."

When WNEW-FM debuted its all-female air staff on July 4, 1966, Steele found she was one of the few jocks who had prior broadcasting experience; aside from one woman who'd worked at a radio station in Bermuda, the other DJs were actresses or models. Unsurprisingly, the "great experiment" failed, and WNEW decided to switch over to a progressive rock format, firing the female air staff in September of 1967. "America, New York, was not ready for lady DJs," explains Steele. "And I still don't know whose idea it was because everybody claimed ownership of the idea until it bombed, and then nobody would admit to it!" But Steele had managed to take advantage of her situation, conducting celebrity interviews she would then work into her show and doing stints as a theater critic. Her hard work paid off, for she was the only DJ who survived the September purge. "Shortly before they decided to go for the change they had done a survey and found that ninety percent of the people they surveyed knew my name and liked me," she says. "So when they found out that many people liked me they said, 'Ok, if you want to stay, you can stay.' And I said, 'Thank you, thank you, thank you.'"

Steele was set to begin her overnight shift, midnight to 6 A.M., on January 1, 1968. "I knew nothing about rock music," she admits. "Not progressive rock. Nobody knew anything about it, least of all the station management. There was no such thing as a playlist." After asking for guidance and being told to "do your thing," Steele decided to turn the late hours of her shift to her advantage. "I wanted to create something at night that was different," she says. "I felt that night was a very special time. When you don't feel well, you feel worse at night. If you're lonely, you're lonelier at night. And I felt if I could make this bond visible between people who are feeling things at night, then I'd have something going. So I came up with the idea of 'The Nightbird.'"

Steele also felt it was important to incorporate an element of fantasy in her "Nightbird" persona. "For the opening for the show I wrote something like, 'The flutter of wings, the sounds of the night, the shadow across the moon, as the Nightbird lifts her wings and soars above the earth into another level of comprehension, where we exist only to feel. Come fly with me, Alison Steele, the Nightbird at WNEW-FM until dawn,'" she says. "That opening poetry became so popular, and what it stemmed from was my philosophy of life. I'm a very positive person and I believe you can do anything you want to do in life—I've proved it—and I used to give that philosophy to my listeners. When I started I knew instinctively I could not pontificate to my audience, because they'd say, 'Who the hell is this?' So I would translate my feelings into the great works: Shakespeare, the Bible, John Donne, Robert Frost, and everybody in between. I

Alison Steele
In the studio with John Lennon, May 1968, Photo by Bill Stone, courtesy of Alison Steele

would pick a forty-second passage of poetry that made my point and then segue into the music, and the music always echoed the feelings of the poetry. And that became a religion with the hippies."

It also became an instant hit with the listeners. "The next morning the program director called me in and said, 'I see you got a little hit there of a show,'" Steele says. "And I said, 'Yeah, looks real good doesn't it?' And he said, 'Well, now I'm going to tell you how to do it,' and I said, 'Wrong!' And I did it my way. But let me tell you how hard it was. First of all they made me music director for the same money. Then, when the station got chugging, they brought in another man to shorten everybody's shift. But instead of giving me the earlier shift, they buried me at 2 A.M., from 2 to 6 in the morning, an unheard of shift then, though now it's not uncommon. But they paid for a survey and found out, I'm sure much to their surprise, that at 2 in the morning, I was number one in the tri-state area—in New York, New Jersey, and Connecticut—with the colleges. And that's when they first realized that they had something. Finally. And that took a while. They then moved me to 10 P.M. to 2 A.M. where I stayed for years."

Steele's move to an earlier shift also meant she no longer had to serve as music director, a position she describes as "an appendage of the two to six shift, so they could wring you out to the last drop. It was just a fancy title for somebody that would pick records and work harder. But because of it, I learned more about music. I used to take home ten records a night and listen to every note, and pretty soon I knew everything that was there; I brought to that progressive sound something they could never do, and that was a very poetic assessment of the music." This carried little weight with her colleagues, who Steele found disliked taking orders from her. "I had a terrible time with the guys," she says. "They resented it mightily that a woman would be in that position, and they would certainly try to ignore my advice. And management never backed me up, which was so weird. I mean, they hired me to do the job, they would tell me what they wanted me to do, and then when one of the jocks would come screaming into the manager's office saying, 'She can't do this, she can't do that,' they would never back me up and say, 'We told her to do it.' I'll give you an idea of how they treated 'women in rock.' I complained to the station manager that I wanted a requisition to buy a step stool because I couldn't reach the record rows on the top. And he said, 'Tell you what we'll do. We'll get a taller person.' Which was typical."

Steele's *Nightbird* show remained one of the most popular programs at WNEW, where she stayed until 1979. And despite being the first woman to win *Billboard's* "FM Personality of the Year" award in 1978, the scarcity of other women in the radio industry wasn't something she gave a great deal of thought to. "I was totally unaware of this," she says. "I was just doing my job. I was a darling of the age, and I didn't even know it at the time. The thing that was so surprising is that it took other stations a long time to understand what was happening. You would think a month, a year after my success was obvious that somebody would have added a woman, but they didn't. But I didn't think about 'making it as a woman.' I just wanted to make it. And I never used being a woman to achieve anything. When you aren't anything, you've nothing to protect, and you follow instinct, you take chances. I did what I thought was right and it worked."

She also held on long enough to be around to reap her reward, the same year she won her *Billboard* honor. "WNEW was then the hottest station in the country as far as progressive rock was concerned," she remembers. "We were number one in New York. And we would do a certain amount of public appearances; this particular one took place in Madison Square Garden, a charity concert. Part of the ceremony was introducing the air staff to the crowd. They would start with the morning man, and then the next guy would come out until there was a line across the stage. And as the last person at night, I was the last person to be introduced. So they were all on stage when they introduced, 'Alison Steele, the Nightbird.' And they had to stand there while eighteen thousand kids screamed and ranted and raved for ten minutes at the Garden. I got a standing ovation, and the other six guys had to stand there and swallow it. I'm sure if looks could've killed, I'd have had holes in my back, but I didn't care. It was my moment of glory. I worked hard for it. I took a lot of shit over it. And I enjoyed every minute of it."

As the '60s came to an end, it was evident that women had made substantial progress in the music business both on and offstage. Instead of being interchangeable members of a vocal group, they now had names, faces, and personalities. Women were also able to take advantage of the social upheavals of the period to reshape their own roles in the music business, and challenge stereotypical perceptions of what women were "supposed" to do. But there were still limitations as to how far they could stretch the social boundaries. The Supremes were "too white," Joplin was a "bad" girl after all, Cass Elliot was constrained by her "Mama Cass" image, and Steele was a woman with just a little more power than was deemed necessary. Not everyone paid as high a price as Janis Joplin did in challenging accepted mores—but the overall message regarding a woman's "proper" position in the industry was nonetheless clearly received.

Women had been extensively involved in the different social movements of the '60s, and the gains of the civil rights and anti-war movements were reflected in the music of artists like Aretha Franklin and Joan Baez. But societal attitudes toward the treatment of women were rarely even mentioned, let alone questioned. Even the freedom of the so-called "sexual revolution" came with its own proviso, that while women's sexuality had the right to be freely expressed, it was best to express it solely for a man's benefit. Women had begun actively campaigning for their rights as women—the National Organization for Women (NOW) had formed in 1966—but the necessity for a women's movement was something not yet fully understood by the counterculture or mainstream society. But regardless of this lack of interest in women's equality, a modern-day feminist movement was growing behind the youth and civil rights movements that would take a closer look at these issues in the '70s, a movement that would have no hesitancy in fighting for and demanding change. It was also a movement that would ultimately have an impact on the lives of millions of women, bringing about dramatic changes in how the music industry related to women—and how women related to the music industry.

4

Hear Me Roar

"You hear most of the male representatives of culture say the '60s was really when things were happening, and then the '70s and the '80s were dead. But I think that's because women rose to a sense of self-value and appreciation in the '70s, and developed a cultural phenomenon that men weren't in the middle of. So they don't think it happened."
—Holly Near, in the Olivia Records video *The Changer: A Record of the Times*

In December 1972, Helen Reddy's "I Am Woman" hit number I on the *Billboard* charts. It was, as the title of one of her later albums put it, a long hard climb, both for the song and Reddy's career. The song was Reddy's fourth single, and her first Top 10 hit, but its significance went beyond the fact that it established Reddy as a major star. Whereas previous songs such as Lesley Gore's "You Don't Own Me" and Aretha Franklin's "Respect" had addressed the issue of female independence, neither were as explicitly associated with feminism as "I Am Woman" was. The song, co-written by Reddy, had been written as a direct response to the feminist movement of the early '70s and Reddy's own involvement in that movement. The music may have been easy-listening pop, and the lyrics delivered in an equally light-hearted fashion, but the under-lying message was clear: from the opening line, "I am woman, hear me roar," to the chorus, with its repeated assertion, "If I have to, I can do anything/I am strong, I am invincible," "I Am Woman" was a statement of female pride and solidarity articulated with a directness that had never before reached the pop Top 10.

By the early '70s, feminism, or "women's liberation," had emerged as a powerful social, cultural, and political force. This "second wave" of twentieth-century feminism was the result of several contributing factors from the previous decade, such as the publication of Betty Friedan's *The Feminine Mystique* in 1963, the formation of the National Organization for Women (NOW) in 1966, and the anti-war and civil rights movements. Women working for these causes had raised the issue of women's equality in groups like SNCC and SDS (Students for a Democratic Society), but the topic was not necessarily regarded seriously by the men: "Both the new left and the civil rights movement were dominated by men who were, at best, uninterested in challenging sexual inequality," wrote Alice Echols in *Daring to Be Bad: Radical Feminism in America 1967–1975*. As Judy Dlugacz, a founder of Olivia Records, told *New York Newsday*, "I abandoned leftist politics because of the inadequacy of the left's agenda in a *lot* of areas." As a result, women began leaving the "new left," utilizing the organizing skills they'd developed while working in the movement to form their own women's groups.

The first "women's lib" action to capture national attention was a protest at the 1968 Miss America Pageant in Atlantic City (a beauty pageant established in 1920, the same year women received the right to vote). A cheery flyer invited all interested women to participate ("It should be a groovy day on the Boardwalk in the sun with our sisters"), and approximately one hundred women from as far away as Florida arrived to picket and engage in "guerrilla theater": chaining themselves to a Miss America puppet, throwing "instruments of torture"—high heels, copies of *Playboy* and *Cosmopolitan*, and bras (which sparked off the myth of "bra-burning feminists")—into a "Freedom Trash Can," and crowning a live sheep as "Miss America." Inside the hall where the pageant was held, sixteen protesters (five of whom were later arrested) held up a banner reading "Women's Liberation" as the previous year's Miss America read her outgoing speech, while chanting "Freedom for women!" and "No more Miss America!"

This dramatic action brought feminism into the national spotlight, and helped galvanize women into joining the movement, forming their own groups, and staging their own actions. In 1970, NOW joined other women's liberation groups to hold the Women's Strike for Equality, and in the same year over one hundred women invaded the New York offices of the *Ladies' Home Journal* to hold a "sit-in," demanding that the magazine hire more women and change their editorial content to "focus on the real issues facing women today." 1970 also saw the publication of Kate Millett's *Sexual Politics*, Shulamith Firestone's *The Dialectic of Sex*, and the anthology *Sisterhood is Powerful*, edited by Robin Morgan; Germaine Greer's *The Female Eunuch* followed in 1971, and in 1972 *Ms.* magazine was launched, with its first issue of three hundred thousand selling out in eight days.

The reaction to feminism from the mainstream press was not always as positive. Articles ignored the issues feminists were raising and instead focused on their looks ("Ugly women screaming at each other on television," wrote *Commentary*), and in 1970 *The*

Atlantic reported that a male editor at *New York Newsday* assigned a female reporter to write a story about women's liberation with the words, "Get out there and find an authority who'll say this is all a crock of shit." Among the youth culture, reaction to feminism often mirrored the disinterest of the "new left." Others viewed women's liberation as a continuation of sexual liberation: *Sisterhood is Powerful* quoted Black Panther Eldridge Cleaver as saying, "Women? I guess they ought to exercise Pussy Power," while Youth International Party ("Yippie") co-founder Abbie Hoffman stated, "The only alliance I would make with the Women's Liberation Movement is in bed."

But the so-called "sexual revolution" was viewed with skepticism by women who couldn't help but notice that though the "revolution" aimed to liberate all people from outdated attitudes toward sexuality, pervasive ideas of what constituted "proper" sex roles remained steadfastly unchallenged. As Anselma Dell'olio's 1972 article in *Ms.*, "The Sexual Revolution Wasn't Our War," pointed out, "The Sexual Revolution was a battle fought by men for the great good of mankind. Womankind was left holding the double standard." This double standard had been upheld in a wide range of rock songs performed by women, where submissiveness, however debasing, was offered as the ultimate proof of one's femininity. Such "doormat" themes were readily seen in songs like the Crystals' "He Hit Me (And It Felt Like a Kiss)" and Joanie Sommers' "Johnny Get Angry," though not all songs went to such masochistic extremes: Bobbi Martin's 1970 hit "For the Love of Him" merely urged women to make their man the absolute center of their homebound universe. In this kind of atmosphere, a song that openly embraced feminism, as Helen Reddy's "I Am Woman" did, was bound to be a very radical statement indeed.

Helen Reddy was born in 1942 in Melbourne, Australia, into a show business family and had been performing before audiences from the age of four, both with her family and other acting troupes. Originally hoping to become a dancer, Reddy had to switch to singing when her dancing career was curtailed because of a kidney operation. "I more or less was forced into specializing, I guess," she says. "Coming from a family such as I did, we obviously did not want to be competing with each other for jobs, and while I don't think anything was ever said, or perhaps even thought on a conscious level, each of us tended to carve out our own little niche. I went into music and it is, in retrospect, what I am best at."

Although Australia in the 1950s was far removed from the rock & roll boom occurring in the United States, Reddy got an enticing taste of the new music in 1958 when her parents made a trip to the States and brought back every single currently in the U.S. Top 40 as a present for her. "A lot of it was stuff that had not been released in Australia, including what would at that time have been called 'race music,'" she says. "So I was suddenly exposed to Chuck Berry and Ray Charles and a lot of people I really wouldn't have known about. But I was very snobbish because I was coming basically out of a jazz background—although I don't think of myself as a jazz singer by any means. I did in the early days sing with jazz groups, and there was a tremendous snobbishness about these rock upstarts who only played three chords, and every song sounded the same. So I was very hostile on an intellectual level, but on the other hand, when I heard rhythm & blues I wanted to go *whoa!* It moved me!"

By the '60s, Reddy had moved into pop, finding it "a nice middle ground; I always think of pop as your borrowing bits and pieces from this and that." She also had her own radio show, *Helen Reddy Sings*, which aired twice a week on the Australian Broadcasting Commission, but she was looking to move into greener pastures. In 1966, she entered a "Bandstand International" contest (not affiliated with *American Bandstand*), which offered a first prize of a trip to New York and a recording contract with Mercury Records. Reddy won the contest, but found claiming the prize to be a bit more difficult. "It took me four months to pin them down to when I was going," she remembers. "I was in a kind of limbo. I sold all my furniture, because I wasn't planning on coming back. And I didn't want to take any jobs, because I couldn't guarantee that I was going to be there to do them. Finally, after daily phone calls, at the end of four months, they came through with the ticket."

By the time the ticket came through, Reddy's daughter from her first marriage, who could have flown free at the age of two, had turned three, meaning Reddy had to buy a ticket for her, which wiped out the prize money. Things were little better on their arrival in the States, where Reddy found plans for her career amounted to "absolutely nothing" in the eyes of her new record company. "When I got here, somebody from the record company took me to lunch," she says. "I said, 'What's happening about the record deal?' And he said, 'Oh, well, the prize was for an audition, and they sent us a tape, and you sing very nicely, dear, but we were really hoping for a male group; do give us a call before you go back to Australia, and have a nice time while you're here.' So a lunch is what I got. Who said there's no free lunch? Of course, looking back as a businesswoman, I can see where they were coming from: there weren't any female solos on the charts except Petula Clark, and the airwaves were full of male groups."

Nonetheless, Reddy was glad to have arrived in America. "If you were a painter in the 1880s, you wanted to be in Paris," she says. "If you were a musician in the '60s and '70s, you wanted to be in Los Angeles. If you become a star in America, you're automatically an international star. It's the big time! I just wanted to be exposed to all those wonderful musicians." Reddy then tackled the task of earning a living for herself and her daughter, which entailed working almost continually to maintain a hand-to-mouth existence. "I did a lot of going back and forth to Canada," she remembers. "I'd get a booking and work up there for a week or two until I had some money so that I could come back to New York and afford to live for another week or two while I did the rounds of the agents. And some of the agents were willing to overlook the fact that I didn't have a green card and book me in some little spaghetti place where I got fifty bucks for the night or something. Quite honestly, I don't know how I did it, but you just take it a day at a time. That's the thing about show business—it's like winning the lottery. You never think that something's going to take twelve years. You think it's going to happen tomorrow, or maybe next week, or at the very latest, next month! That's what keeps you going. It's just slightly out of reach. It's just around the corner. You *know* it's going to happen."

Helen Reddy
1986 at Genetti's in Hazelton, Pennsylvania, Photo by Mark Reinhart/RFU, courtesy Jim Keaton

While in New York, Reddy met Jeff Wald at a "fundraiser" party her friends threw for her birthday. Wald, who later became Reddy's husband and manager, was then working at the William Morris Agency; he also managed Tiny Tim and George Carlin. The two moved to Chicago, where Reddy worked in a theater revue and Wald was a talent buyer for a local club; in 1968, they moved to Los Angeles. But though she was again living in one of the country's music centers, Reddy initially had trouble finding work. "Basically, nothing at all happened for the first five years I was in America," she explains. "Jeff was managing other people and he was on the road a lot with other acts. I didn't know a lot of people, so I was more or less out of circulation. That was a factor, and also, musically, it was a time when male groups were the dominant sound."

Then, in 1970, Reddy landed a spot on *The Tonight Show* with the help of her friend, comedian Flip Wilson, who was guest-hosting the show. Her spot on the show, her first major television appearance, helped her to secure a contract with Capitol Records for one single. "So we are talking pressure here," Reddy says. "In other words, you've got one chance to have a hit." Reddy had been impressed by a song she saw Mac Davis performing on *The Tonight Show*, "I Believe in Music," and felt it was a good choice for the single's A-side, and the ballad "I Don't Know How to Love Him," from the rock opera *Jesus Christ Superstar*, was suggested for the B-side. Reddy didn't particularly care for the number, but agreed to record it: "They said to me, 'If it's on the B-side, it doesn't matter. No one ever listens to the B-side.'

"So we went into the studio," she continues. "Oh God, I remember that night! I had never in my life felt such pressure. And when I listened to the playback later on, 'I Believe in Music' sounded like 'I Believe in Terror.' It just wasn't there. But all of the emotions I'd been feeling worked perfectly for 'I Don't Know How to Love Him.' It was obvious, even to me, that it was the superior cut, that it had to be the single. And I thought, oh well, that's it, because I really didn't think that it had a chance. I also found out there were other people that recorded it, and some of them had names far better known than me." One of those people was Yvonne Elliman, who had starred in *Superstar* and recorded the original version of the song, but it was Reddy's version, released in 1971, that came out on top, peaking at number 13.

"After that, it was panic time!" says Reddy. "Because record companies make money on albums, and all of a sudden, here I am, a hit artist on their hands, and they don't have any product. So they couldn't wait to rush me into the studio." Reddy was presented with a list of current hits to choose from, but she held out to include songs from the new crop of singer-songwriters who were now rising to prominence, though she did agree to let the album be named *I Don't Know How to Love Him* to tie in with her first single. Reddy released two further singles in 1971, "Crazy Love," and "No Sad Song," and the album *Helen Reddy*, none of which charted in the Top 40.

During this time, Reddy had become involved in the burgeoning feminist movement, welcoming the opportunity to interact with people who shared her feelings about women's inequality in society. "When the women's movement, as we called it, first started to happen, it was like I'd come home," she says. "At long last, there were other people who felt the way I did, that women should be valued. I remember when I was a little girl, I saw a show, and one of the comedy sketches involved a guy who was painting a model, and he wasn't really painting at all; the joke was that he wasn't an artist, he was just a dirty old man. And I was so offended—at the age of four! I wasn't able to articulate why, but it really bothered me, it bothered me so much that here I am forty-four years later, and I still recall it! So whatever it is, whatever the feeling is, it's very deep with me and always has been."

Spurred on by her friend, fellow Australian and rock critic Lillian Roxon, Reddy began holding her own consciousness-raising sessions. "I was living in the Hollywood Hills at the time, and we started a little Hollywood CR group," she says. "I was going to a lot of meetings and getting involved. I was very politically correct at the time—I didn't want to shave under my arms and all that stuff." She was also inspired to include a song about her involvement with the women's movement on her first album. "I wanted at least one song on the album that said something about how I now felt about being a woman," says Reddy, who quickly found that most songs about the "female experience" presented stereotypical "good women" bravely accepting their position of subordination. "Have you heard 'If You're Born a Woman' by Sandy Posey?" she says. "It's all about how her man treats her like absolute shit, but when he comes home he makes me glad and happy that way. It is just a *total* doormat song! And every song I looked at, this was what I was coming up against. I finally realized I was going to have to write the song myself because it simply didn't exist. And that was the genesis of 'I Am Woman.' It was my statement as a feminist."

At the time of its initial release, "I Am Woman," co-written with Ray Burton, was simply another track on *I Don't Know How to Love Him*, and there were no plans to release it as a single. "I certainly didn't hear it as a hit," Reddy admits. "I didn't hear it as an anthem." The song might well have remained an album track, but a year later Reddy was approached by the makers of a feminist documentary, *Stand Up and Be Counted*, who wanted to use the song in the film. "So I agreed, and Capitol said, 'Well, why don't we put it out as a single to coincide with the release of the film,'" says Reddy. "It was too short to be a single because there were only two verses, so I wrote an extra verse and went in and re-recorded it, and that was the version that was put out as the single. So of course the picture came and went in six days, and the song became a hit a year and a half after it was originally released!"

Released in May 1972, "I Am Woman" initially met with resistance from radio stations. "I always got a very strong reaction to the song in person, and fan mail used to mention it, which seemed a little odd because we knew we were getting no airplay whatsoever on the song," says Reddy. "But it was obvious that we were touching some sort of a nerve. So because of the resistance to airplay, I went on television. There were a lot of television variety shows in those days, and I sang 'I Am Woman' on nineteen different shows. Then women started calling up radio stations and requesting the song, so it was women who forced the airplay on it. My son was born the week the song went to number 1. It was a very emotional time in my life. There was a lot going on within and without, so I really felt that the revolution had come, that we were just going to blaze it on down."

As an anthem, "I Am Woman" differed from protest songs of the '60s in that it was so obviously pop-based in melody and was born out of optimism and hope rather than frustration and anger, however righteous. From a musical standpoint, it's difficult to understand what it was about "I Am Woman" that so bothered the press, but the fact that this pleasant pop tune addressed the issue of feminism made it an easy target. Critics found the song "not effective either as propaganda or as schlock," and found Reddy herself "beneath contempt" and a "purveyor of all that is silly in the women's lib movement." "For a lot of men, thinking about the women's movement makes them grab their groins," says Reddy. "What can I say? I didn't say that we were going to cut their dicks off or anything, you know? But one guy told me that he was going to medical school, and he used to play that song every morning just to get him going, so it obviously transferred. It was just a positive statement of self."

Reddy's statement about the nature of God when she accepted the Grammy award for Best Contemporary Female Pop Vocal Performance (for "I Am Woman") also got her into trouble, when she ended her list of thank-you's with God "because She makes everything possible." When the remark prompted angry letters, such as one that began "You skinny, blasphemous bitch," Reddy defended herself in an interview with the comment: "I knew any feminist would understand what I was saying; it seemed like the only thing I could say that summed it up." Ironically, while derided for being a feminist by some, Reddy was also derided for not being feminist enough by others in the women's movement. "As soon as I became popular, I was not politically correct anymore," she says. "This does tend to happen. But people talk about the 'women's movement' like it's all one organization with a party platform, but there are so many different people with so many different points of view. I am first and foremost a singer. That's how I earn my living. I don't earn my living as a feminist. Nobody else speaks for me, and I can't really say that I speak for anybody else. If you relate to what I'm saying, great, but I don't represent X amount of women. I'm a feminist and I always will be, but I will not have my life dictated by somebody who has set themselves up as an authority on what is politically correct."

The criticisms—from whatever side—had little overall impact on Reddy's career, and she had substantial chart successes through 1976, with such Top 10 hits as "Leave Me Alone (Ruby Red Dress)," "You and Me Against the World," "Ain't No Way to Treat a Lady," and two further number 1's, "Delta Dawn" and "Angie Baby," along with seven Top 20 albums. She also was the first host of the rock music television variety program *The Midnight Special* in 1973 and returned to the show in 1975 as the regular host, and in 1977 she made her film debut in the Walt Disney feature *Pete's Dragon*. Though she was never associated with a particular feminist group or organization, and never wrote another song in the vein of "I Am Woman" (though the song "Don't You Mess With a Woman," on *Long Hard Climb*, was a feisty number in celebration of "the sisterhood"), Reddy continued to represent the women's movement to many people and was repeatedly questioned about her views on feminism in interviews. In 1975, declared the International Year of the Woman, the United Nations used "I Am Woman" as its theme song, and while on a world tour that year, Reddy was able to see the feelings generated by her song on an international level. "Even to this day, I'm not somebody who deals in numbers and charts," she says. "That's not how I measure achievement. To see women linking arms and singing outside the stage door in New Zealand, in Japan, in places where you never imagined that they would respond . . . if you can have a positive effect on somebody's life, then you've served a purpose. When somebody comes up to me on an airplane and says, 'I went to law school because of you' or 'I had the courage to leave a battering husband because of you,' this is what 'achievement' means to me. This is what it's all about."

At the same time that Reddy was enjoying her Top 40 successes, there were other women mobilizing on a more grassroots level on behalf of women who wanted to be involved in some aspect of the music industry. The year Reddy accepted her Grammy for "I Am Woman," a group of women in Washington, D.C., formed Olivia Records, a woman-owned-and-operated record company that helped crystallize the musical movement that came to be known as "women's music." It was natural that this movement developed at the same time as the feminist movement. "I think that we were very much paralleling the women's movement," says Judy Dlugacz, who was part of the collective that founded Olivia Records and is today Olivia's president. "The term 'women's music' was an organically developing term, which enabled people to identify that this music spoke about women and to women," she says. "It was really speaking from a woman's point of view about women's lives. At that time it was really a very baby concept, and it also was, whether anybody knew it or not, an extremely wonderful marketing tool, because it let women know right away that this was something they might be interested in. And at that point in time, that was a very significant, revolutionary concept."

Although recording for a major label, Reddy herself shared this viewpoint; asked by the British music weekly *Melody Maker* if she minded the continual questions about feminism, Reddy replied that she didn't, stressing, "I sing songs about women's lives," making the connection that the issue of feminism was also "about women's lives." She also understood the necessity of having women gain control by running their own businesses (a step Reddy would take in the '80s when she started her own production company, Helen Reddy Inc.). "I think small business is the way to go, because trying to advance in the corporate world—there's just no way they're ever going to let you play with the big boys," she says. "That's the way I feel about it. And when you've got your own company, you're playing by your rules. In fact, you're inventing a whole new set of rules."

Olivia Records was also based on this philosophy of giving women opportunities and inventing new rules. "What we were trying to say at Olivia was that women have never really been given the opportunity to participate in this industry, and we would like to create those opportunities," Dlugacz explains. "And if it required us to make loud, clear statements, we would do that; and it did indeed require that! It was such a travesty in terms of women's participation in the music business, both on the musical end and in the main office. And so we said, we're going to try to find out what the possibilities could be of women performing together, and women producing albums, and women being the players. And the structure of Olivia was based upon creating that opportunity."

Dlugacz was twenty years old and living in Washington, D.C., at the time of Olivia's inception. A fan of Motown, late '60s progressive rock, and female singers like Joplin, Laura Nyro, and Joni Mitchell, Dlugacz initially had no interest in the music business; in addition to working with retarded children and becoming involved in the feminist movement, she was planning to attend law school. At the same time, the group of friends Dlugacz was working with in the feminist movement had been looking for a new project to work on. "In the midst of having these discussions, Cris Williamson came through town and did an interview with two people in our group, Meg Christian and Ginny Berson," says Dlugacz. "And they asked Cris what it was like to be in the music industry [Williamson had recorded a solo album for Ampex Records], and she talked about some of the positive things, some of the negative things. And out of that conversation, Cris said, 'Gee, why don't you all start a women's label? A women's record company?'"

The idea gave the group a focus, and, true to the spirit of the times, Olivia began life as a collective of ten people, which quickly became five "as it became clear that this would be a big commitment." After raising four thousand dollars in donations, Olivia's first release was the single "If It Weren't for the Music," performed by Williamson, backed with Carole King's "Lady," performed by Christian. After the single's release, the collective decided to relocate to California's Bay Area and concentrate fully on launching the new label. "The only way we could really do that was to live together and work together twelve to sixteen hours a day," Dlugacz explains. "We were this combination of very hopeful and idealistic; we believed that we could change the world and at the same time really loved the possibility of what we were undertaking. It was very exciting." At the time the collective moved in 1975, Olivia had been preparing for its first album release, Meg Christian's *I Know You Know* (which contained the archetypal song of a teenage crush, "Ode to a Gym Teacher"), and the albums arrived in Olivia's Oakland living room at the same time the new owners did. Sales quickly surpassed even the collective's own expectations, and *I Know You Know* went on to sell more than sev-

June Millington and Cris Williamson, Fall 1974
Courtesy of Olivia Records, Inc.

enty thousand copies. "We thought we'd sell five thousand records over the course of several years, and that would be a nice start," remembers Dlugacz. "We really didn't understand very much about the economics or anything."

1975 also saw the release of Cris Williamson's *The Changer and the Changed*, which became Olivia's most successful album, eventually selling over a quarter of a million copies. Williamson's clear voice and melodic style combined to create a women's music classic, with songs (all but one written or co-written by Williamson, who also produced the album) that addressed passion ("Dream Child" and "Sweet Woman"), female solidarity ("Sister"), and spirituality ("Waterfall" and "Song of the Soul"). As the best-selling women's music album, and one of the best-selling albums on an independent label, *The Changer and the Changed* was actually not far removed from the best-selling commercial album of the time, Carole King's *Tapestry:* both records featured strong vocal performances, flowing, piano-based melodies, and songs clearly written from a woman's perspective.

June Millington was another musician who played on *The Changer and the Changed*, an appearance that served as her introduction to women's music, the women's music community, and feminism. "I always say that women's music was the feminine principle becoming manifest, because it was time for it to manifest," she says. "And it was expressing itself through all these people through music. These songs touched a very, very deep nerve and a deep impulse in a lot of women at the same time who needed to take control of their lives. It was just amazing. It was like the first bloom of an incredible love affair, and it will never be the same again. I just happened to be at the right time, and the right place, where something was exploding."

Before her work on *The Changer and the Changed*, Millington's involvement with the music industry had been in the commercial realm, as lead guitarist with the all-female band Fanny, the first all-female band to have a Top 40 hit. Fanny was part of a wave of all-female and mixed-gender bands—who played their own instruments, unlike the all-female vocal groups—that sprang up in the late '60s and early '70s, including Berkeley's Joy of Cooking and the Deadly Nightshade on the East Coast, who were also signed to major labels. Other groups, such as the New Haven and Chicago Women's Liberation Rock Bands, formed as the result of the feminist movement.

But despite the increase of female musicians in the music scene, women who played instruments other than acoustic guitars were still seen as something of an oddity. About the only women in the rock scene who didn't challenge anyone's preconceptions were the groupies, the young women who hung around bands to provide sexual favors or other services such as cooking or sewing for their idols. This aspect of the rock scene was initially kept carefully under wraps because of the potential controversy, but the "sexual revolution" had resulted in sexual matters being discussed more openly—if sexual mores remained unchallenged. "Status in the groupie world was determined by what stars a woman hung out with, just as the status of her mother, or any woman in straight society, was determined by the man she married," wrote Steve Chapple and Reebee Garofalo in *Rock 'n' Roll is Here to Pay*. Groupies may have felt they were "rebelling against the plastic uptightness of straight American consumer society," but their "rebellion" only reaffirmed a social system in which women were defined by the man they were aligned with.

Such a definition also meant that women did not consider artistic participation in the rock scene as a viable option. "I wanted to express myself creatively . . . [but] I didn't know what to do or how to do it," said Pamela Des Barres, author of *I'm With the Band: Confessions of a Groupie*, in 1989. "The nearest thing was to be with the people who created the music." Des Barres was also a member of groupie contingent the GTO's (Girls Together Outrageously), who were pictured in the center spread of *Rolling Stone* when the magazine did a cover story on the "groupie phenomenon" in 1969 (the fifth issue of the magazine to feature women on the cover). Des Barres eventually found her creative outlet when Frank Zappa produced the GTO's album, *Permanent Damage*, and released it on his Straight Records label. The "songs" were primarily spoken-word pieces, with lyrics written by the GTO's and music provided by Zappa's Mothers of Invention, Jeff Beck, and Rod Stewart. The album is now a highly sought after item among record collectors, but the GTO's appeal at the time remained strictly limited to a cult audience of L.A. scenesters.

The 1970 film *Beyond the Valley of the Dolls*, by sexploitation director Russ Meyer, also found a substantial cult audience. The storyline (co-written by Meyer and film critic Roger Ebert) was drenched with the groupie credo of sex, drugs, and rock & roll, but the film also was (and remains) one of the few rock movies from any period that featured an all-female rock band who were the film's main characters. As the "Carrie Nations," "Kelly," "Casey," and "Pet," become superstars in true rags-to-riches style, while confronting typical expectations regarding their musical abilities. Upon being told her niece "has these friends in a rock group," Kelly's aunt jokes, "Don't tell me you're a groupie!" When Kelly explains, "It's the other way around—it's my group," a male lawyer comments in disbelief, "Now let me be sure I fully understand this—*you* are a rock & roll singer?" (Kelly's wide-eyed reply: "Why? Is that a no-no?") In between dealing with innumerable romantic complications and flouncing around in a state of undress, the group also finds the time to make music not too dissimilar to Fanny's brand of West Coast rock.

The experiences of real-life all-female bands at the time were not that far removed from those of the "Carrie Nations" in some aspects, at least as far as their musical abilities were perceived. "What would happen to us a lot is people would walk into a building where we were playing and start bopping around," remembers the Deadly Nightshade's Pamela Brandt. "Then somebody would come out and say, 'Hey it's a really good band, they're all women.' And the people would go, 'Oh no they're not! No way!' Then they would go in and see that it was all women, but initially they would have thought, 'Gosh, they sound so good, it couldn't possibly be women playing those instruments.' And these guys would always come up and tell me this and mean it as a compliment! I would always smile and be pleasant, and then I would think, 'Here I am, proving myself once again!'"

By the time the Deadly Nightshade was signed by RCA in the mid-'70s, Brandt, who played bass in the group, had been "proving herself" as a rock musician for almost ten years. Born in 1947 in Upper Montclair, New Jersey, Brandt studied piano for ten years before switching to guitar, though her mother insisted on her studying classical guitar "because it was more dignified." A fan of Peter, Paul and Mary and Ronnie Gilbert of the Weavers, Brandt had not considered playing rock & roll until her sophomore year at Mt. Holyoke College, when she was asked to play in an all-female quartet called the Moppets. "At the time I was sort of sneering about the idea of being in a rock & roll band because I just liked pretty folk music and classical music," she says. "But the woman who was the bass player fed me a lot of beer one night, brought me over to the canoe house, sat me down on an amplifier and handed me a lead guitar! And as soon as I realized how loud it was I was really charmed. I decided I was going to make my living as a musician about five minutes after I got into the Moppets."

Now a five-piece group, the Moppets played a mix of original material and cover songs, such as "Louie Louie," "Woolly Bully," and songs by the Beatles and the Supremes, and recorded a single, a cover of the Beau Brummels' "Just a Little" backed with the Supremes' "Come See About Me." Dubbed "America's foremost college ladies of rock," the Moppets received write-ups in the *New York Times*, *Life*, and *Look* magazines, were signed by the William Morris Agency, and attracted the attention of various record companies. But corporate reservations about working with an all-female band meant the group was unable to secure a record contract, and the Moppets eventually broke up in 1967. The following year, three of the Moppets, including Brandt, formed a new group called Ariel, which also included Helen Hooke and Anne Bowen. The band spent a summer practicing together in Vermont, perfecting their "pretentious material," as Brandt describes it. "A lot of the songs were our own, but if they were somebody else's, we would always take them and make them totally inaccessible. If something was in a simple 4/4 time beat we would always make it into 7/4 but only if we couldn't make it into 11/4! We had a touch for that."

After playing a gig at Bill Graham's Fillmore East in New York, Ariel was soon approached by record companies, only to find that the attitude toward all-female bands had not changed appreciably since the days of the Moppets. "Columbia wouldn't even listen to our demo tape, because they said they already had an all-girl band," says Brandt. "And if you say to them, 'But wait a minute—you have forty "all-boy bands" signed to this label. You just don't *call* them that. Why is it that all of us females have to compete for the same novelty slot?' they really don't get it. They *still* don't." The group's encounters with other record companies were in a similar vein. "We were in the office of this person discussing a record contract one day," Brandt says, "and some guy who was the head producer stuck his head in the door and said, 'Eddie, don't sign an all-girl band, you'll only have to pay for their abortions!'"

Discouraged by such attitudes, Ariel broke up in 1970. Brandt and Hooke, who had become romantically involved, spent the next two years in Northampton, Massachusetts, working at various odd jobs (including their own garbage collection agency called the Wrecked Wrecking Company) and playing as a duo. In 1972, Anne Bowen, who had been working at Northampton's women's center, contacted Brandt and Hooke to put together a band for an upcoming women's arts festival, with Bowen and

Hooke on guitars and Brandt on bass (a sound embellished by the use of violin, wash-board, and Brandt's stamping on a plywood board in lieu of a drummer). The response to their set inspired the three to stay together. "We went over remarkably well and people said, 'Hey, you could make some money at this,'" says Brandt. "So we looked at each other and said, 'Well, it sure beats collecting garbage!' And it basically just escalated like that. We kept getting more and more jobs and we never really went after anything."

The name "Deadly Nightshade" was resurrected from the days when Ariel would give out fake band names and phone numbers to promoters they suspected were more interested in the fact that they were women than musicians. Once again, the band hit the club circuit, while their manager (who had also worked with Ariel) tried to land a record contract. Though facing "some of the same old all-girl band kind of reaction" initially, the group was eventually signed by RCA, who released the band's albums on their Phantom Records label. The group also had a clause written in their contract that gave them the right to prohibit sexist advertising on the part of the record company. It was a clause they invoked immediately after RCA ran an ad in Boston which began with

Deadly Nightshade, circa 1975
(left to right): Helen Hooke, Anne Bowen, Pamela Brandt, Photo by Bonnie Unger, courtesy of Pamela Brandt

the statement "The Deadly Nightshade is female dynamite," described their music as "women's lib with a sense of humor," and offered the assurance that "Male chauvinists will not be offended." "We told them that next week they had to run the same ad over again but we were going to cross it all out and change it," says Brandt. As a result, "female dynamite" became "musical dynamite," and "women's lib" became "women's liberation." "And needless to say, in the 'Male chauvinists will not be offended' line we crossed out the 'not,' underlined the 'will' three times, and put a lot of exclamation points after it. After that, the record company seemed to catch on real fast."

The group faced a different set of problems in the recording studio. "We were largely ignored during the making of our albums," says Brandt. "It was not a pleasant experience. The truth is the albums did not sound very much like the band did at all. We were really a dance band, a basic Western Massachusetts very loud boogie band. The record company didn't like our rough edges—they basically wanted to clean us up and make us sound a whole lot more like every other group that was coming out in the '70s. I just can't tell you what it was like to go into that studio and have the chief engineer say, 'I can see little old men from Omaha, Nebraska, really loving this album. I hear it as sounding like "Tie a Yellow Ribbon Round the Ole Oak Tree."' And we thought that they had signed us because they liked us!

"We insisted on playing our own instruments, much to their dismay," Brandt continues. "But still, when there are thirty studio musicians in there with you, that only has a little bit of an effect!" The group also encountered resistance when they tried to use additional female musicians, bringing in the horn section from Isis, Carol MacDonald's latest band, to play on the debut album. "Felix [Cavaliere, the producer] would say to us, 'Okay, we're going to give them two chances. And if they don't cut it, the Brecker brothers [two studio musicians] are going out there and doing it,'" says Brandt. "And we would be trying to keep the horn section from Isis from knowing this kind of stuff was being said, 'cause if you can imagine having to play under circumstances where you know this is going on, you would just clutch." Brandt found herself in this position when the group recorded "Dancing in the Streets" on their second album. "The producer arranged it and I had to read from a chart," she says. "And he pointed to this guy—one of the snazziest studio bass players—in the control room and said, 'Don't worry about it. We have him right out here, so if you can't do it, he'll come in and play it instead.' And I had to sit there and try and read this goddamn stupid chart and get this song down knowing that this guy was hanging over my shoulder."

Though the group felt that their albums were not a true representation of the band's sound, both *The Deadly Nightshade* (released in 1975) and *Funky & Western* (released in 1976) received good reviews: the *Los Angeles Times* hailed them as "a fresh new force in pop," and the *Boston Phoenix*, reviewing their first album, wrote, "They clearly love music and it's their zest as much as their ideology that makes this a success." The band received a Grammy nomination for Best New Group in 1975, and in 1976 had a regional hit with a tongue-in-cheek disco version of the theme song from the TV show *Mary Hartman, Mary Hartman*, which peaked at number 68 nationally. Feminist themes ran throughout their work: the first album included songs like "Dance, Mr. Big, Dance," where a former secretary turns the tables on her old boss when he applies for a job at her company, and "High Flying Woman," an anthem of female strength and pride; in addition to "Mary Hartman, Mary Hartman" and "Dancing in the Streets," *Funky & Western* also included "Ain't I A Woman," based on an 1850s speech by Sojourner Truth, a former slave and African-American activist.

The Deadly Nightshade also backed Florence Ballard in her last live appearance in Detroit in 1975, at a benefit concert for Joann Little, who was charged with murder for killing a prison guard who allegedly raped her. "It was one of the great moments of my whole musical career," says Brandt. "We really idolized the Supremes—we had their picture on our practice room wall!" The group assumed Ballard would be performing a Supremes number and were surprised when Ballard announced she wanted to do "I Am Woman," a song the Deadly Nightshade didn't know. But the group held a quick practice session backstage to learn the song, and Ballard's performance that evening received a standing ovation. "The crowd really really loved her," says Brandt. "It was obvious that she was who they were waiting for. Then she walked off the stage and was standing on the side, and it was obvious that she wanted to come back on, but she was real insecure. So I ran over and said, 'Come on, you have to come back! They're dying for you!' and grabbed her hand and started dragging her back. As soon as she got one foot on the stage the audience erupted anew. She was bowing, and then she straightened her shoulders, got completely secure again, and strutted across the stage in front of us. And as she passed us she threw back her head and whispered, 'By any chance, would you happen to know "Come See About Me"? We said, 'Yes, yes, yes, yes!' She sang lead and we got to do her old parts and Mary Wilson's parts—she was fantastic!"

Two years later, the Deadly Nightshade broke up when Anne Bowen left the group. "She decided she wanted to have a personal life and quit," says Brandt. "And when one person of a three-person band quits . . ." Brandt continues to play in bands in addition to working as a journalist, and in 1991 published her first book, a "gay European Grand Tour" travel guide entitled *Are You Two . . . Together?*", written with her partner, Lindsy Van Gelder; Hooke and Bowen have also worked on musical projects. In 1978, the Smithsonian Institute introduced a display of Deadly Nightshade albums and other memorabilia in their Women's History collection, an indication that the group's impact was more than just musical. "Sometimes we would just sit down and think to ourselves, 'Well, who knows what's going to happen in the future,'" says Brandt in assessing the Deadly Nightshade's career. "Maybe ten years from now whatever we did musically will be totally forgotten and what our contribution will really be is that we brought women a little farther forward. So maybe our main contribution will be political, and that will be fine also."

On the West Coast, the group Fanny made an equally significant contribution to rock history when they became the first all-female band to be signed to a major label. Sisters June and Jean Millington, the core of the group, were born in the Philippines in 1949 and 1950, respectively, and moved to California in 1961. The two had started out on ukuleles as children, later progressing to guitar, and after their move to the States, June and Jean found further inspiration from the West Coast music scene. After seeing an early Grateful Dead show June remembers, "I was riveted. I saw Jerry Garcia's hands flying all over that guitar and I just really freaked out. I realized that people could play like that on electric guitar!" Other musical favorites included the Beatles, folk performers, and girl group songs like "Please Mr. Postman" and "Will You Love Me Tomorrow." The sisters soon became performers themselves when their involvement with the local YWCA led to their playing at the Y's social functions; this activity also enabled them to meet other young women their age with whom they later formed their first band, the Svelts.

"Things just kept snowballing," says June. "There was really kind of a dichotomy there: we were very, very shy young girls who had this thing about playing rock & roll; we were very insecure, straight-A students, and then we'd sneak off with our two girlfriends and rehearse. We'd learn 'Heat Wave' and all those tunes off the radio, and we'd do gigs. We would get all this incredible attention from people that we didn't get at school 'cause we were so shy! And we had boyfriends who were in surf bands, so we would go to their gigs and sing during the breaks, four girls with our four acoustic guitars singing Beatles songs!"

When the group acquired a drummer, they realized they also had to make a switch to electric guitars, and soon after, the boyfriend-girlfriend shows ended when, auditioning for the same gig, the Svelts were chosen over their now ex-boyfriends' band the Psychics (in addition to acquiring the services of the Psychics' manager). But the group faced continual changes in the lineup, which also necessitated occasional name changes—the band also appeared under the name Wild Honey, and the members played in other local groups like the Freudian Slips. "The pressure not to play rock music was unbelievable," explains June. "And of course in those days without any role models, we couldn't say, 'Well, look at so-and-so, they made it!'" These obstacles only made the sisters more determined. "All I can say is, it really fed our spirits," says June. "We really wanted to have an all-girl band. It was like we were obsessed. I can't tell you why. I think we always knew that we were supposed to do something. We didn't know what it was, but there was something beckoning us. I really believe it was our destiny. We were meant to do it."

And if the members' parents weren't too sure about their daughters pursuing a career in rock music, the pressure of being judged as a novelty act provided an additional burden, a focus that was mentioned even when the group was being praised: "People sometimes laugh at the idea of an all-girl band," began an early article on the group, though this opening sentence was followed by, "But when they hear the Svelts, they don't laugh. They listen." Not every critic was as willing to debate the merits of an all-female band, but the group soon learned to take it in stride. "By the time we were playing in Fanny, you've got to remember we'd been playing in bands for at least five years," says June. "So we had heard every comment that you can imagine. We didn't even hear it after a while—it became a point of pride for us. 'Let's just be so fucking good that whatever they say doesn't matter!'" Yet June found that "playing good" was often equated with "playing like men." "You weren't really expressing yourself creatively, past proving to the world that girls could play like guys," she says. "It's kind of hard to realize that now, but believe me, that's exactly the way it was in the late '60s. You had to prove that you could play like a guy, or play as good as a guy. That's really all there was. The whole attitude, what you wore, the way that you projected every note that you played, was male territory."

During June's senior year of high school, the Svelts encountered the harsh realities of the music business when their manager ran off to Hawaii with the money they had earned. After graduation, June considered becoming a surgeon and was taking pre-med classes but continued playing with the band. The group was now making trips to Los Angeles in the hope of attracting major label interest, though with little results. "Linda's [Linda Kavars, the group's new manager] recollection was that she went to every agency, every big manager to talk about us, and everybody just laughed at her," says June. But in 1968, the secretary to Richard Perry, a producer at Warner Bros., caught the band's show at the L.A. club the Troubadour and called her boss the next day. "She had called Richard on a Sunday afternoon and said, 'These girls are great, you've really got to see them,'" says June. An audition was set up the same day, and Perry was impressed. "He was really knocked out, and he got Mo Ostin [Warner Bros.' CEO] to sign us sight unseen," June says. "Nobody in the record company heard us, even for the first year I think they didn't hear a note. But Richard was hot because he had just gotten a mega-hit out of 'Tiptoe Through the Tulips' with Tiny Tim."

Now signed, the band decided to think of a new name. "When we were casting about for names, there was a girl band in L.A. that had a girl's name," says June. "I thought 'God, what a great idea, a person's name!' I remember driving in Hollywood one night and the name Fanny popped in. I said, 'Let's add Fanny to the list,' and it made it." The group received some criticism for the sexual innuendo of the name—which some believed was conceived by Perry ("That's a myth," says June)—exploited in items such as "Get Behind Fanny" bumper stickers, but June says the group's own feelings about the name were far more playful. "We just thought it was funny," she explains. "It was a woman's name, and it was a double-entendre at the same time. We felt it was like a woman's spirit watching over us. We didn't really think of it as a butt, a sexual term! I think we needed to feel like we had a woman guardian angel watching over us, like a Russian grandmother, with kindly eyes and glasses and white hair, going 'I'm your Aunt Fanny, and I'll help you get through this.'"

The band's lineup now featured June on rhythm guitar, Jean on bass, Addie Clement on lead guitar, and Alice De Buhr on drums. A management dispute led to Linda Kavars leaving the group and Clement, who was involved with Kavars, left with her. "I remember when Addie left the group that Jean and Alice looked at me and said, 'Well, now you've got to play lead guitar,'" says June. "And I just freaked out. I literally went for a walk and was talking to myself, I was so scared. And I practiced night and day; I would take records, by Jimi Hendrix or Eric Clapton, and I would slow the solos down and practice. It was hard, but that was the only avenue that I had open."

Jean Millington (bass) and Alice De Buhr (drums) of Fanny
1974 at the Whiskey-A-Go-Go, Los Angeles, Photo by Sherry Rayn Barnett

Though Fanny had been signed in 1969, their first album had been put on hold as they searched for a fourth member. They eventually chose Nicole (Nickey) Barclay as their keyboardist, and their self-titled debut LP (produced by Perry) was released in 1970. The songs (with nine of the eleven songs written by various group members) jump with a driving rock beat, punctuated by occasional whoops from the group when the music heats up, as on Barclay's "Changing Horses." After the album's release the group was immediately sent out on the road to promote it. "But once we got on the road it was nonstop!" says June. "We were really the only all-girl band that was starting to get known, and you didn't have MTV so you had to go on the road. The only way that we could convince people that Fanny could play was to get out in front of audiences!"

Over the next three years, the group released the albums *Charity Ball* (1971), *Fanny Hill* (1972), and *Mothers Pride* (1973), though only the single "Charity Ball" reached the charts, peaking at number 40 (the group also appeared as backing musicians on *Barbra Joan Streisand*). June attributes the failure of the group to break into the mainstream to timing: "I think that we just didn't have the right song at the right time," she says. "I think that is everything, the timing between those two things. And we just didn't have it." Yet the importance of seeing women playing electric instruments in a band was doubtless still making an impact on audiences, even if that impact wasn't being reflected in the charts; in a *Ms.* magazine article on the group in 1974, Lynne Shapiro concluded, "If Fanny had been around when I was 16, I might be a feminist rock 'n' roll musician today."

June herself was ambivalent about the issue of women's liberation, and admits she would feel embarrassed when the members of Fanny would be asked about feminism in interviews. "When the band broke up, I can't say that any of us could say that we were 'feminists' by any stretch of the imagination," she says. "It was such a dirty word! My mindset was like 'Hey man, I have put myself out on the line out here, just holding this fucking electric guitar. Don't put me in any more spots.'" Racism in the music industry was another issue June preferred to be "in denial" about when she was a member of Fanny. "We didn't look at racism a whole lot," she says. "The sexism was more than enough. It was very low on the agenda because everything else was so much to deal with. It's like one step at a time or I'll blow my brains out or something! I know that I didn't start looking into racism until after I had produced Holly Near. By that time, I'd been involved in women's music for six years. I remember having a conversation with Holly and telling her I was just starting to look at it, and she looked at me like 'I can't believe what I'm hearing!' I still was not dealing with it then, and I was thirty-two!"

By 1973, the pressures of being in a rock group had become too much for June, and she quit the band. "I didn't have a personal life, and I fell apart," she explains. June moved to Long Island, and then to Woodstock, New York, where she took a break from music. She eventually regained her confidence and began making demos and playing with bands again, but the additional pressures Fanny had experienced made her reluctant to consider working in an all-female lineup again. Back in L.A., Fanny, with a lineup of Jean, Nickey, Patti Quatro (Suzi Quatro's sister), and Brie Howard (an original member of the Svelts), released their final album, *Rock and Roll Survivors*, in 1974. The group then split, but by early 1975 had their highest charting single when "Butter Ball," a song from the album, reached number 29. Jean, visiting June in Woodstock when she heard the news, persuaded her sister to return to L.A. in order to assemble a band for a three-week tour. "It was me and Jean, and one of the women from Smiles [a band June was then playing with], Brie, and Wendy Haas, who had been in the Freudian Slips. And it was so good! We kicked butt. I started to write material, and all of a sudden *boom!* we had a manager, we started to go for a record deal."

Unfortunately, plans for the band, now called the L.A. All-Stars, fell through. "A record company was going to sign us," says June. "We were literally at [attorney] Michael Lippman's office, about to sign the record contract, and then the guys go, 'Uh, ahem, there's just one thing. We want you to call the band Fanny.' Jean and I just flipped out. 'Cause it was not Fanny. It was not Fanny! And we knew if they made us call it Fanny, we'd go out there and they'd want to hear Fanny material, which we weren't about to do. It was a completely different ball of wax, we were playing more pop-funk going into salsa, R&B. Oh, we were so pissed! So we didn't sign it. Jean and I ended up paying about twelve hundred dollars just for not signing the contract, and when we turned the contract down, the band broke up."

During the same period, June met Cris Williamson, who had been introduced to her by the woman June was then involved with, bass player and cellist Jackie Robbins. "And of course I didn't know who Cris was," June says. "Nobody knew who she was, really. It turned out that Cris was a fan of mine, which I didn't know, and every once in a while she would say, 'Why don't you play with me?' I didn't have the heart to say to her, 'You? You? You play folk music!' I was doing my funk-rock thing." But while in L.A. working with the All-Stars, June did play on *The Changer and the Changed* and wound up joining Williamson, and the women's music movement, after the release of *Ladies on the Stage*, an album she recorded with Jean (and featuring backing vocals from Cris Williamson). Released in 1978, *Ladies on the Stage* also marked June's initial foray into production, as she co-produced the album with her sister Jean and Tom Sellers. The record failed to take off, but it also sparked June into changing her musical direction. "After *Ladies on the*

Stage, I became so discouraged that I decided to just get into working with other women," June says. "I was casting about, sort of at loose ends. So Cris said, 'Well, why don't you do this tour with me?' And I said, 'Okay.'

"Now I count my blessings!" she continues. "That changed my life; it was really a great blessing in disguise because Cris ended up being one of my best friends, and I went out there and really viscerally saw and felt what the women's movement is about in the context of people's lives, real lives. It wasn't just some dumb theory. I think the first thing that really struck me was seeing women out there, of all different ages, just living their lives and struggling in the same way I did with my electric guitar, saying, 'I'm really going to try to have a life of my own.' They could be in their forties, already have raised three children, and all of a sudden they'd realize, 'This is not me. I've got to go back to college and do something else with my life.' And I felt this tremendous surge of pride, just pride. All of a sudden I was proud to be a woman."

June's comments illuminate why the emergence of women's music was an important development for all women, not just musicians. Critics of women's music often focused on the separatism of the movement, which was seen as an "ineffective" way of advancing women's rights in society. In 1984, in an article commenting on Olivia's ten-year anniversary, *Rock & Roll Confidential* found the concept of women's music outdated, saying that the notion of "women isolating themselves from men . . . appeals to only a tiny handful of social hermits." But the point, as Judy Dlugacz repeatedly stated in interviews, was not about finding ways to isolate women from men; it was about finding ways to involve women, to give women the chance to develop skills that were not encouraged by an almost totally male-owned-and-operated industry. "There were questions like, 'Aren't you discriminating against men?'" said Dlugacz in an interview with the *San Francisco Business Times.* "I go, 'No, not if there haven't been any opportunities for women to do this at all.'" "I think separatism was necessary," says June. "Because the male-dominated rock thing was so exclusionary anyway, you needed to form something that you could say, 'Hey, this is ours, we're claiming it. This is our territory, this is our pride, and we're going to provide a safe space for ourselves to be creative and learn how to do it.' It *was* incredibly separatist, but at the same time, the joy that was being expressed I would say far outweighed anything else."

"Anytime you have something where women choose to have it be all women, everybody gets all upset and talks about discrimination," agrees Holly Near, another singer involved with women's music who would have her own problems in dealing with the "discrimination" of presenting shows only open to women. "The most separatist organizations are probably the Senate and the Supreme Court! Women tend to get together not because they are plotting against the rest of society, but because they're trying to offer each other a safe place to work and think clearly where they're not endlessly having to be in a state of defense."

Others have cited the lack of mainstream commercial success of women's labels like Olivia as another sign of their "failure." But such success, beyond basic maintenance of the business, never appeared to be a goal of any of the labels; the importance lies not in the numbers, but in what women's music meant to those involved in it, from both sides of the stage. *Rock & Roll Confidential* applauded the "broad-based success" of such records as "I Am Woman" and Donna Summer's "She Works Hard for the Money" for addressing women's oppression "in a way that a huge audience can embrace," as if the attaining of a huge audience was the only true measure of success. Yet there were those involved in women's music who found the impact of a record that only sold in the thousands, rather than the tens of thousands, to be just as meaningful in their lives.

Separatism also raised the issue of lesbianism, a problematic and sometimes hotly contested issue in both mainstream society and within the feminist movement. When *Time* wrote about Kate Millett's bisexuality in 1970, they noted that the revelation "is bound to discredit her as a spokeswoman for her cause . . . and reinforce the views of those skeptics who routinely dismiss all liberationists as lesbians." The same year, Betty Friedan referred to lesbianism in the women's movement as a "lavender menace," and, Alice Echols wrote, "reportedly spearheaded a successful effort to prevent lesbians from being elected or re-elected to office in the 1970 New York-NOW elections." In 1971, NOW changed their stance and passed a resolution supporting lesbianism, and lesbian-feminists coined the less threatening term "woman-identified woman" ("We were trying to figure out how to tell women about lesbianism without using the word, lesbian," explained Jennifer Woodul—another Olivia founder—in *Daring to Be Bad*), but tensions about the "gay-straight split" in the women's movement remained.

These tensions were also present in the women's music community. In her chapter on women's music in the anthology *Women's Culture: The Women's Renaissance of the Seventies*, Ruth Scovill wrote, "Women's Music reflects a consciousness of *women-identification*. In contrast to popular music's prevalent degradation of women, Women's Music holds the feminist and humanist ideals of self-affirmation and mutual support." But as Pamela Brandt noted in the *Soho News*, "The term *says* 'women's music,' but, if you hadn't guessed, it almost always *means* 'lesbian music.'" It was a distinction that undoubtedly had an impact on the way the commercial music industry perceived women's music— and explains why Carole King's *Tapestry* had ready access to the Top 40 while the equally tuneful songs on Cris Williamson's *The Changer and the Changed* (which contained only one love song specifically directed toward a woman) could only find airplay on alternative radio shows. And distinctions existed within the women's music community as well.

Some women did have direct ties to the lesbian-feminist movement; Olivia co-founders Jennifer Woodul and Ginny Berson had been members of the lesbian-feminist collective the Furies. But the artists on Holly Near's Redwood Records label, a label never as "woman-identified" as other women's music labels (men, including Near's father, were involved with the label from the beginning), found themselves being stocked in the "women's music" bins in record shops even if they were male because of Near's involvement in the women's community.

But if their crossover appeal to the mainstream was limited, lesbians involved in women's music could at least feel freer about expressing their sexuality as opposed to lesbians in the commercial music industry, who were advised to not mention their sexual identity at all. Pamela Brandt would avoid answering questions about her own sexuality when she was a member of the Deadly Nightshade, remembering that when DJ Cousin Brucie (Bruce Morrow) asked her, "What would you say if I asked you if you were gay?" she had replied, "I'd tell you to mind your own business." "That is probably not worse than what a lot of people would do today," she says. "And a lot of people would probably lie about it. We never lied about it or went out with guys or anything, but really, 'Mind your own business' is not what we should have said. We should have said, 'Yes. So what?' I think the majority of people are largely willing to accept gay people, it just makes them uncomfortable. They have to have it presented to them in a way that makes it seem normal and acceptable. And if you're a performer you already have the weapons—your performer's charisma—to make it acceptable to people. So I think performers probably could make it more acceptable than anybody else, and I think they ought to give it a try."

Carol MacDonald had also kept her sexual preferences under wraps during her time with Goldie and the Gingerbreads, and was determined that things would be different when she started Isis, despite being told to keep quiet about the subject. "I had too many years of being in the closet," she says. "I did that with Goldie and the Gingerbreads—it drove me crazy! I hated it." MacDonald, who returned to New York City after her years in England, played with the short-lived all-female group Blithe Spirit before starting Isis in the early '70s. "I wanted to have the first women's band with a horn section," she explains. "I wanted it to be a really hip thing. I always loved horns, and I said, 'Women playing horns? How outrageous—nobody's done it yet.' So we formed Isis."

MacDonald admits her openness about her sexuality may have worked against the band; she wrote much of the band's material, and songs like "She Loves Me" and "Bobbie and Maria" didn't always go over well with radio programmers. "Isis may have made it if I hadn't come out," she says. "Maybe. I don't know that though. And not everybody in the band was gay, and we got that label. The girls that came in the band, they were just about all of 'em gonna get a rep as being gay because of me, and I would tell them that from the beginning, 'You girls are going to have to prove it yourselves if you don't want the image!' because most of them weren't. Basically it got around that the whole band wasn't gay, so of course they gave us leeway then. And God bless the Nightbird [Alison Steele], because she played our album continuously. She loved the band, she really did, and she loved our music."

Isis also served as a sort of training ground for women musicians, going through seventy-three members in seven years. "It was very hard, especially for women horn players, to break in," says MacDonald about New York's music scene. "They'd always give the men the jobs. So Isis became a school, it really did. And I encouraged the women to go out and work in other places because there were so few jobs, and we weren't getting work all the time. So they had a rep; they'd say, 'I played with Isis.' It was like a job reference." After failing to impress Herb Alpert, the "A" in A&M Records (who said, "They're great but I think women look stupid playing horns," according to MacDonald), the group recorded two albums for Buddah Records and one for United Artists (their debut LP was produced by Shadow Morton), and toured as an opening act for Leon Russell and Three Dog Night. But the group failed to break through to a big audience. "A bunch of things in the formula have to be right," MacDonald says. "And I still think they never took us seriously. I really think they were out to make fast money and let it go." Nor did they find ready acceptance in the women's community, to MacDonald's consternation. "I'm writing about women, for Christ's sake!" she says. "But they didn't really get that. They looked at us as an establishment group, because we were doing TV. You'd think they would want you to do that!"

Olivia, which had also started out as a training ground for women, ended up relaxing its standards after a few years. "The point wasn't to do ourselves in," explains Dlugacz. "We were trying to make a strong point, and it was a constant struggle to do that. But it became clear that we were too small, and it was asking too much of ourselves to do both quality work and create that opportunity. I would say that after the first three years that was not the main focus anymore, so then every slot was not filled by a woman. Had we had our own studio and a multimillion-dollar budget, we would have done a lot more training." But even without sufficient resources, Olivia's presence in the music scene was still able to attract women interested in getting involved in some aspect of the music industry. "How do you break into something that you're not wanted in?" says Dlugacz. "How do you become proficient at producing if no one's going to give you the opportunity to do that? The first engineer we worked with, she found us. And that's often what happened: people would find us."

Sometimes even the mere sight of a woman doing non-traditional work was capable of providing inspiration. Boden Sandstrom, owner and co-founder of Woman Sound Inc. in Washington, D.C.—now City Sound Productions—began her career as a sound engineer after seeing Judy Dlugacz behind the mixing board at an Olivia concert in D.C. Born in Rochester, New York, and a D.C. resident since 1972, Sandstrom worked as a librarian but harbored a strong interest in music as well. "I played the French horn for years," she says, "and I very much wanted to get back into music. I actually went to my first women's music concert, which was an Olivia production, here in D.C. before the collective moved to California, and I saw a woman mixing—it was Judy Dlugacz. I thought I would really like to do that, so I talked to her about it, and she told me there was a singer in town who was looking for an engineer and was willing to train the person. That was Casse Culver, and I called her up and sure enough, she agreed to train me."

Sandstrom's work with Culver soon led to her working at a local club, which brought further offers to mix at rallies and benefit concerts, and by 1975 the two decided to start their own business (Sandstrom is now the sole owner), in part for the same reason the Olivia collective had started its label—to provide opportunities. "I started the business because it was quite clear that it was going to be very difficult to get to work for any of the sound companies in town because they were totally male-dominated," says Sandstrom. "In fact, there weren't any women at all, and it was very hard to get hired and get trained. It was also very hard to rent equipment and know the quality of what you were getting, so we really desired to have our own equipment." The launching of Woman Sound Inc. coincided with the beginnings of the women's music festivals, which provided the new company with plenty of work. "I was there pretty much from the beginning," Sandstrom says. "For example I mixed the National Women's Music Festival [originally held in Champaign-Urbana, Illinois, now in Bloomington, Indiana] for at least ten years running. And I did the second Michigan Womyn's Music Festival. I got to see artists start in the beginning, like on the open-mike stage; the first time I saw Tracy Chapman was an open-mike at the National Women's Music Festival."

The company also found work from the political community, who warmed to the difference in sound quality the company offered as well as its politics. Woman Sound provided sound for such events as gay pride and pro-choice rallies and the 1978 rally for the Equal Rights Amendment (Gloria Steinem sent the company a thank-you letter saying "Allowing women to hear each other is the basis of this revolution, and you are doing that, spiritually as well as technically").

The company worked on numerous other events as well, including a tour for Lily Tomlin and such local events as the Mayor's Arts Awards. But the mainstream rock community was not as accepting. "The rock & roll world didn't want to hire Woman

Sound," Sandstrom says. "Sometimes it would be because whoever was producing would be concerned about well, what would all these male rock & roll musicians coming from out of town think about having an all-women's sound company? The producer would worry that the musicians wouldn't think it would be as good, or they wouldn't want to relate to the women that way. It's the Good Old Boy network; wanting to just relate to themselves while they work and not wanting to interface with women. But there were some men in that world who had heard my sound at a festival and thought it was just great. And they were much more supportive. So you had to kind of fight through all that."

Woman Sound soon built up a pool of women sound engineers, engendered in part by the classes Sandstrom held on sound mixing. "In the beginning, the classes were only for women," she says. "I would advertise in the women's newspapers, and then I would say that whoever wanted to work after that class was welcome. Just about everyone who worked for me was trained that way, and the ones who were really into it would stay. It really takes, on a part-time basis that way, three or four years to become a decent sound engineer. There's just so much to learn." After being trained, many women moved to other cities to continue their careers. Sandstrom's classes expanded when she began teaching at D.C.'s American University but she still finds the number of women actually working as sound engineers disappointingly low. "The sound companies are still pretty much all male," she says. "The bigger ones especially, and the guys that run those hire the men that are around before they'll hire the women who are at least equal, if not better."

Women were also able to acquire skills in the recording studio—another male-dominated realm that was difficult to break into—through their involvement with women's music. After co-producing *Ladies on the Stage*, June Millington began to produce records for women's music artists, beginning with Cris Williamson's *Strange Paradise*. "I was nervous, but it was something I wanted to do very badly," she says. "When I quit Fanny I remember telling my mom that I wanted to produce records, which was of course yet another crazy dream—that happened!" Since women's music labels focused on using women in every area as often as possible, June soon found her skills were in demand, and she produced Williamson's *Lumiere* and Mary Watkins's *Something Moving* for Olivia, Holly Near's *Fire in the Rain* for Redwood Records, and her solo albums for her own Fabulous Records label.

Teresa Trull also used her base in the women's music community to move into production, though she didn't produce while she was with Olivia Records herself. Born in Durham, North Carolina, Trull had been singing virtually all of her life. "I started singing right from the very beginning in church," she says. "At first I was forced by my parents, but then I was highly motivated! And when you do music in church, in the South, it's gospel-oriented, and gospel teaches you a lot of different things." Trull began writing songs at sixteen, but regarded her songwriting as more of a "personal outlet" than a potential career. "I sang as a hobby," she says. "I was really an artist—I was dead set on going to college and being an illustrator."

Trull also sang with groups in high school as a "hobby," and while performing in a talent show in 1972 was approached by a professional all-male rock group to sing with them, though her reason for joining them was typically pragmatic. "I thought, 'God, somebody's going to pay me to sing, I guess I'll do it,'" she says. "It was a totally practical gesture. Then when I was in college the band offered me a tour, and I thought, 'I can't believe that people are going to pay me to sing. I really enjoy singing and I think I'll just go!' And I quit college and went on tour with this rock band. The amazing thing was, I got such a response from singing that it literally convinced me to go into music. I was astounded when people started coming up to me and saying 'Don't ever stop singing!' So I was very fortunate. I got a lot of work and a lot of support from audiences."

While on tour with the band, Trull and the group's guitarist appeared on a local radio show, and unknown to Trull, the radio host sent a tape of the program to Olivia, who contacted her. By 1975, Trull had quit the group, frustrated by the sexism in the songs the band performed, and was living in New York "on really no money at all," she says. "So I finally wrote Olivia and told them the kind of troubles I was having, and they hired me immediately to come out and work for them." Trull moved to the Bay Area and served as an A&R rep for Olivia in addition to recording three albums with the label, with her debut album, *The Ways a Woman Can Be*, released in 1977. Produced by Linda Tillery and featuring contributions from Meg Christian on vocals and June Millington on guitar, *The Ways a Woman Can Be* was an excellent showcase of Trull's bluesy, gospel-tinged vocals. Trull wrote six of the album's eight songs, including the rollicking "Woman-Loving Women," which, she explained on the lyric sheet, she wrote "for the women in my hometown lesbian community. I hoped that it would serve for a 'sing along dyke stomper' when the going got tough." Trull's subsequent albums for Olivia included *Let It Be Known*, and *Unexpected*, recorded with Barbara Higbie.

Unexpected, released in 1983, was the first album she produced, though she had been co-producing demos with her songwriting partner, Ray Obiedo, whom she'd met in 1980 and with whom she collaborated for the next several years. "Ray and I spent all these years in the studio cutting albums' and albums' worth of material," she says. "Going to every studio in town, always trying to get a deal, and meeting a million different engineers and a million different players. And over this period of five years or so of recording these tunes, we got an enormous amount of studio experience under our belts. Sometimes not having money is a great teacher. You try every method you ever heard about to get a quality sound without spending the money. So it was producing these song demos that gave me my technical know-how in the studio."

Trull's work on *Unexpected* attracted the attention of other artists who enlisted her as a producer, including Romanovsky and Phillips, the Washington Sisters, and Hunter Davies. Her production work on Deidre McCalla's *Don't Doubt It* resulted in a nomination for Independent Producer of the Year in the 1985 New York Music Awards, a type of recognition she rarely received for her work as a performer. "The most support I've gotten has been for my production work," says Trull. "I've gotten a lot of critical acclaim as an artist, but I've never had the support behind me to accumulate a large amount of sales. I've always fallen in the cracks. I'm a little too commercial for the independent industry—which involves women's music and folk and the independents that initially supported Jane Siberry and people like that—and I'm not commercial enough for the music industry. So I've run across a lot more battles as an artist."

Trull tried to pursue a more "commercial" direction with *A Step Away*, released in 1986 on Redwood Records. "That was a big project for me," says Trull. "My dream was to use musicians that were my idols. I hired people that I'd seen on records all my life, people I really admired." The resulting album was a strong collection of well-crafted pop and netted positive reviews: "Trull has plunged head-first into rock sounds, with delicious results . . . she deserves to be right up there in the Top 10 next to Huey Lewis," wrote Larry Kelp in the Oakland *Tribune.* Trull's connection with Huey Lewis went beyond this comparison, for one song on the album, "Rosalie," had originally been written for Lewis by musician and songwriter Bonnie Hayes, who also played keyboards on the LP.

Hayes later toured as the opening act on a Huey Lewis tour, and offered Trull a place in her band. Trull accepted, curious to see what life was like for a Top 40 musician like Lewis who had found commercial success. "To be honest, I was slightly horrified," she says. "I came face to face with the realization that what I've been trying to attain for all these years might not be the thing that's going to make me happy. What horrified me the most was the way that the people who achieved this amount of success had become a marketable product. They lose that edge, that excitement. And I don't think it's their fault—I think it'd be very hard to avoid it. They're under a certain amount of pressure because you have this phenomenal overhead, like accountants, lawyers, publishing—you see people doing records not because they want to, not because they have a bunch of new material, they're doing records to pay their accountants and to please their management. Because when you become a business, and the people involved are business people, they're not interested in music as much for music's sake as for how much money they can make off of it."

Trull's experience on the Lewis tour also reconfirmed for her the reasons why she'd chosen to work outside the mainstream. "The main reason for my involvement with the women's music industry has more to do with my ethics than it does with my direction," she says. "I'm not willing to compromise. I'm not willing to dress a certain way, I'm not willing to do songs that somebody thinks I should do because they'll sell more. I really think that something that's believable is what works. And you have to be true to yourself. When artists stop being true to themselves, that's when they stop selling records."

Holly Near is another singer who has found the motivations of the commercial mainstream to be limited. "The listeners are denied access to diversity," she says. "There's a whole lot of music out there, but unless money's put behind it, people don't get to hear it. Now that's hard on the artist, but to me the people who suffer the most are the listeners. They're denied access to knowing about all the possibilities. The only ones that get handed to them are the ones the companies decide to put a lot of money behind. And they're only going to do that if they can make money off of it. And I love some of the stuff that's on Top 40 radio, but what if Paul Simon hadn't introduced us to some of the people on his last two records? What if Peter Gabriel hadn't brought Youssou N'Dour over here? We shouldn't, as listeners, have to be dependent on Paul Simon or Peter Gabriel deciding to integrate these people into their acts, we should

Holly Near, 1989
Photo by Irene Young

have access to these great artists. I mean, we live in a high-tech communication society—there is no reason why we shouldn't have access to diversity!"

Near herself has chosen to work outside the commercial mainstream because of the freedom she has found in the alternative music scene, though it was a choice that happened almost by chance. Near started Redwood Records in 1973 after she had visited Vietnam, so she could release an album of political songs and "get it out of my system." "Every record I made for Redwood, I kept thinking, 'This will be the last one and then I'm going to go back to L.A.,'" she says. "'Then I'm going to start doing the real stuff.' Up through the third record—by the fourth I said, 'Who's kidding who? This is where I am.'" As a politically progressive independent label, Redwood shared many of the same concerns other women's music labels did: "Olivia had lesbian feminist priorities and believed in world peace. Redwood had world-peace priorities and believed in lesbian feminism," said Near in her autobiography *Fire in the Rain . . . Singer in the Storm.*

Born in 1949, Near grew up on a ranch in Potter Valley, a small town north of San Francisco. Music was a regular part of the Near household, and Holly took voice lessons as a child. When she was ten, her teacher, who had also taught Johnny Mathis, got her an audition for a Columbia Records A&R rep, who, after complimenting Near on her singing, told her the songs she sang were "pretty grown-up" for her age—to which Near soberly replied, "I'm not as young as you think." Near had also started playing ukulele as a child, later moving to guitar, though she admits, "I wasn't really interested in being an instrumentalist. I loved the Weavers [Near dedicated her second LP, *A Live Album,* to Ronnie Gilbert] and Paul Robeson, but I wasn't really a folkie type; I wasn't interested in sitting quietly on a stool in a dimly lit coffeehouse with long hair playing acoustic guitar singing long, sad Northern European ballads. I wanted to be a Broadway singer, and Broadway singers don't play the guitar. They don't have to. I should have been a singer in the '30s and '40s—that's where my heart was."

Despite her lack of interest in being a "folkie type," Near sang with an all-male folk-styled group in high school called the Freedom Singers, with Near taking on the "Ronnie Gilbert" parts. She also witnessed an early performance by Janis Joplin when Big Brother and the Holding Company played at a school dance. Because Joplin hadn't walked on stage with the band at the start of the show, Near initially thought Joplin was the girlfriend of someone in the band, until she started to sing. "It was great, it was extraordinary," Near remembers. "In fact, when she started singing, people sat down. We didn't dance anymore. It was like the first rock concert where everybody went, 'Oh my God, listen to this.'" In 1967, Near graduated from high school and attended UCLA, where she studied theater and political science, appeared in university productions, and joined the anti-war group Another Mother for Peace.

One of her stage appearances resulted in Near's "discovery" by an agent, who got Near her first film role in *Angel, Angel, Down We Go* in 1969, the story of a young rock singer who wreaks havoc in a wealthy family (Near played the daughter in the family), which also featured songs from Barry Mann and Cynthia Weil. Her next film, *The Magic Garden of Stanley Sweetheart*, addressed the "youth concerns" of tuning in, dropping out, and turning on and co-starred future *Miami Vice* star Don Johnson. After completing *Sweetheart's* filming in New York City, Near finally made it to Broadway, winning a role in the long-running musical *Hair.* Returning to California, Near and her sister Timothy joined another anti-war organization, the Entertainment Industry for Peace and Justice, where she first learned of an anti-war show Jane Fonda had put together under she name FTA for "Free the Army" (also variously known as "Fun, Travel, and Adventure" and "Fuck the Army"). The FTA show had originally been put together to tour Vietnam, but had been denied permission by the Pentagon; the show toured the U.S. instead, playing in venues located near military bases, where the show was also banned.

Near was thrilled to learn of a group that combined her interests in performing with political work, and when she learned that one of the group's members was dropping out, she auditioned and joined the company on a tour of Hawaii, the Philippines, Okinawa, and Japan, which was filmed for theatrical release. Near also joined Fonda and Fonda's future husband Tom Hayden on the similarly styled Indochina Peace Campaign, which put together a show that toured the U.S. twice in 1972 and 1973. Near pursued her "straight" acting career as well, appearing in the film *Slaughterhouse Five* and such TV shows as *The Partridge Family*, *The Mod Squad*, and *All in the Family*, while continuing her singing career by performing in local clubs with a friend from high school, Jeff Langley, who played piano.

Near's club performances generated a lot of interest from record companies, though they weren't always happy with her choice of material. "There would be generalized comments like 'I think you could really make it if you would choose not to be a political singer,'" she says. "Both industry people and friends would say that. They'd say, 'You've got so much talent. Why are you undermining it?' I think on the one hand they were very interested because I was selling out these clubs. But they also felt I needed to change the words, and other people felt there wasn't really enough element of submission in my voice to be a star. I think back then women chose to be the red-hot mama or the help-less waif—there were two images, which is not unlike what it was in literature. You could be the whore or the nun or the virgin. You were the one Mary or the other."

Near remembers how some specific comments about "It Could Have Been Me," her song about the students killed by the National Guard at Ohio's Kent State University, made her examine the differences between a song being seen as "commercial" or "political." "This one guy said, 'God, you just write hook lines and great melodies! That could be a hit song in a minute! It's just you can't have those verses with the political things,'" she says. "If I kept that line and melody and turned it into a love song, I'd have a hit song on my hands. I thought, 'Well, great, I'm glad you think that I can write good hook songs. But I wrote this song for these kids who died at Kent; I can't make that into a love song now.'" Near was also finding her contacts with the mainstream music industry unrewarding, despite the potential for commercial success. "It was hard," she says. "You had to knock on doors and humiliate and humble yourself to get somebody to pay attention to you. But when I went to do political stuff or play in these clubs, I wasn't humiliated or humbled at all. There were people clapping and cheering and saying more, more, more. I have an artist's ego, and I loved being loved. I loved that there was an audience saying 'Yes, we loved the Weavers, we loved Phil Ochs, we loved Judy Collins, we loved Joan Baez, we loved Pete Seeger, we loved Bob Dylan, and now we want some more. And now we want you.' Everybody was saying yes. And it's real hard to turn down yes."

Near's introduction to feminism had come from the women she'd worked with during her FTA days, and she became more involved with the women's movement as the decade progressed. In 1975, she appeared in her first all-women's production, a benefit for the Los Angeles Woman's Building, which also featured Cris Williamson, Meg Christian, and Lily Tomlin, among others. She also appeared with Williamson, Christian, and singer-songwriter Margie Adam in Lynne Littman's television special *Come Out*

Meg Christian and Cris Williamson, November 1982 at Olivia Records 10th Anniversary, Carnegie Hall, New York. Photo by Irene Young

Singing, and the four also performed at the San Diego Women's Music Festival. After her recording debut with *Hang In There* in 1973, Near released *A Live Album* in 1975; by the time she released *You Can Know All I Am* in 1976, she was integrating more feminist numbers into her show—and finding herself caught between audience members who were confused at hearing feminist songs at what they thought was a political event and those who disliked hearing political songs at what they thought was a women's event.

The issues were no easier to solve among the people with whom she was now working. Having sung backup on Williamson's *The Changer and the Changed,* Near invited Williamson to sing on her own album, *You Can Know All I Am.* She also asked Christian, who refused, as she preferred to work only on projects that were all-women. When Near, Williamson, Christian, and Adam began planning a tour they dubbed "Women On Wheels," there were myriad questions to be addressed, such as whether the concert should be women-only, whether the concert could be billed a "women's music tour" if all the participants were white, if the press should be invited, and if so, just the gay press or the straight press, too, what the ticket prices should be, if there would be child care, and who should be allowed to record and/or film the show. Trying to come to terms with the different issues generated tension, and the group, hindered by the fact that the performers recorded for three different labels, could not come to agreement on the last question, meaning the historic tour went unrecorded. Near later commented in her book, "I wish we had asked an outside party to tape it and then put it away in a locked box for twenty years." But the sold-out show, which toured California in 1975, gave Near a clear illustration of the impact women's music was having on its audience; walking onstage for a concert in Sonoma to wild applause and cheering, she thought, "My God, we are the Beatles of the women's movement!"

Music critics have noted that whereas gay male imagery was allowed to creep into the mainstream via performers like David Bowie and Elton John and the rise of disco music from gay bars into the realm of *Saturday Night Fever,* women's music performers were unable to make this same move into the commercial world. But Near points out that there was more involved than simply making music. "Women's music was not just music being done by women," she says. "It was music that was challenging the whole system, a little different from disco, a little different from David Bowie playing with androgyny. Women also don't have money, at least the women who are doing women's music, so there was very low capitalization. Some aspects of the gay men's community have more money, because they have a male income, and they aren't single mothers or getting fifty percent less salary for equal work. So there were a lot of class issues, there were issues around children and family, what to do about crossing race and culture. We were dealing with a lot of issues that David Bowie wasn't dealing with, questions his management wasn't asking. So it was not just the music. It was like taking a whole look at systems and societies and letting a music rise out of those questions."

Near's involvement with women's music intensified when she began a relationship with Meg Christian, which lasted for three years. She celebrated her "coming out" on the album *Imagine My Surprise*, released in 1978, though there were now new tensions between Redwood and Olivia, where Christian's ex-partner Ginny Berson still worked; after beginning their affair, Near had been approached by an Olivia rep who expressed the collective's concerns that the Christian-Near alliance might cause the company to fold. For their part, Redwood wasn't comfortable at being lumped in with other women's music labels as a separatist company. "Sides are funny," says Near. "They're not always clearly delineated. Even in the mainstream, you've got record company presidents who don't like each other. Why would it be any different for women? I guess it's a surprise because we held up a fairly nonconflicting front for a long time. It wasn't anything to fight over if we were just being two different companies in the world. It was the fact that we were thrown together, not necessarily voluntarily. If feminism and lesbian feminism and peace work and all that stuff had been completely accepted in the world, they'd be their company and we'd be ours. But because it wasn't, and there was hostility and conflict and hardship directed toward alternative music, people had to bond together in order to be a force to contend with. A lot of times people were thrown together in coalitions who might not otherwise have chosen to work with each other, but they had to because they needed a unified front."

Olivia eventually became the travel company Olivia Cruises and Resorts. Redwood Records has become a branch of the nonprofit Redwood Cultural Work, a multicultural arts organization that works on concerts and other events in addition to recording. Near also recorded and toured with one of her earliest musical idols, Ronnie Gilbert, during the '80s. The two met after the release of Near's *A Live Album*, the record Near had dedicated to Gilbert, choosing Gilbert's name out of a list that also included Janis Joplin, Odetta, and Aretha Franklin. After appearing together in the film *Wasn't That a Time*, Near and Gilbert toured together and released the live album *Lifeline* in 1984. The following year Near and Gilbert were joined by Arlo Guthrie and Pete Seeger to form HARP (the name taken from the first letter in each performer's name), which toured together briefly and also recorded a live album, and in 1986 Near and Gilbert recorded another LP together, *Singing With You*.

In the early '80s, Olivia launched its Second Wave label in an attempt to diversify their roster. By the time of its ten-year anniversary, Olivia was justifiably proud of its accomplishments in the past decade, but it was also clear the atmosphere in the '80s was going to be considerably different. Being given a women's music bin in record stores in the '70s was a point of pride; by the '80s, the Seattle-based *Women's Music Newsletter* reported that one store manager, after witnessing Lucie Blue Tremblay at Olivia's Fifteenth Anniversary Concert, refiled the album in the "rock" section because "he really wanted to do something for her and the rock bin is where all our best-selling albums are." Ironically, Olivia now found itself trying to break out of the "women's music" genre they had worked so hard to create. In addition, the lack of substantial income kept the label at a disadvantage in an increasingly competitive market.

Dlugacz felt these limitations clearly; she told *Musician* magazine the "problem" with being seen solely as a feminist label was "how the rest of the world deals with terms . . . So I have to look at the term 'feminist' and say, well, what they're doing [by calling us feminists] is trying to limit what I'm doing." But *Musician* concluded, "For a younger generation of music fans, Olivia must seem like an anachronism." This view was shared by some of Olivia's artists as well. "Women's music has got to change. As a concept it is flagging a bit," said Teresa Trull in a 1986 interview after the release of *A Step Away*, though she did return to Olivia to record *Country Blessed* with Cris Williamson, released on the Second Wave label in 1989. June Millington also feels Olivia's identification with women's music will make it hard for them to successfully enter the mainstream. "I feel the weight of their history is against them," she says. "They're so identified as being 'Oh, the women's record label' and immediately you're in a bin. Olivia started as a label that existed for women and by women. The fact is, if they want to make it big time in the big world, they'll have to pretty much do what the other companies have to do, which is to have a mafia mentality, if not mafia connections. That's the tradeoff. You don't make it in the music business by being Mr. Nice Guy."

But if Olivia's artists had not managed to cross over into the commercial mainstream, Dlugacz still had a clear sense of the label's historical importance. "I think that Olivia has done for women what small independent labels in the '50s did for black music," she told the *New York Times* in 1988. "We helped pave the way by identifying the market for music by strong intelligent women." The truth of Dlugacz's claim was readily seen in the female singer-songwriter boom of the late '80s, when a string of performers like Suzanne Vega, Tracy Chapman, and Michelle Shocked clearly benefitted from the inroads labels like Olivia had made. Nor was the concept of "women's music" necessarily outdated. "I find the question, 'Is women's music dead or is it needed now that women have equality?' surprising," said Holly Near in 1991. "We will always need to write songs that remind us to hold fast to our dignity. It's a part of life and will continue to be."

There were some women who managed to move between the alternative and mainstream music realms of women's music and "commercial" music in the offstage sector of the industry. Leslie Ann Jones worked for labels on both ends of the spectrum in her move from musician to artist relations rep to recording engineer. The daughter of madcap musical "rearranger" Spike Jones, Jones credits her parents' work in music with giving her the push to enter the music business. "I don't know if they hadn't been involved in music whether I would have chosen this path, but it sort of seemed inescapable," she says. A California resident, Jones sang in different vocal groups in her teens, such as Nobody's Children, a group she'd formed with her relatives. "It was a sort of a combination Beach Boys–5th Dimension," she says. "We hooked up with a lot of different producers, but it was the classic Hollywood story. Every time we got signed to a label, the A&R person who signed us quit or was fired and we were dropped. So we did nothing but record a lot and nothing ever came out. We were constantly in the studio. I signed more contracts when I was young!"

Despite never releasing any material, Jones enjoyed the experience of working in the studio, especially since her groups were able to work with some of the top session players of the time, such as Glen Campbell, then a session guitarist, and drummer Hal Blaine, who appeared on records for artists like the Beach Boys, the Mamas and the Papas, and Nancy Sinatra. Jones then sang and played guitar with local rock bands and eventually got a job in artists relations at ABC Records in the early '70s. At the same time, she ran a PA company with some friends, having inherited a sound system from one of the rock bands she'd worked with (in 1974 she toured with Fanny as their road manager and sound mixer), and found she enjoyed working with sound more than being a musician.

"ABC had its own recording studio," she says, "and I knew everybody that worked over there, so I asked if I could get transferred." In 1974, following her tour with Fanny, ABC offered her a studio job. "They were a little concerned because there were no women doing what I was doing," she says. "But my boss was pretty honest about it. He said to go ahead and see how the clients liked it. He was more than willing to give it a shot." Jones found her peers in the studio to be equally supportive of her work. "I was always surrounded by guys who were real good at what they did," she explains, "and who, I don't want to say treated me like 'one of the guys,' but they didn't treat me any different because I wasn't. They didn't make me feel stupid because I didn't know everything that they did, and they took a lot of time with me. If I hadn't gotten that attitude from them, I would never have been able to do what I did. But all the way along the line, I've had people like that. But you have to seek that out. That just doesn't show up. You have to be ready to accept people's help."

Ironically, the first time Jones did run into problems being a female engineer, the complaint came from someone not only outside the company, but outside the project she was assisting on as well. Jones had moved up from a tape copy room entry level position to fill in for an assistant who wasn't able to work on a rescheduled project. "I was working with someone whose wife seemed to get a little insecure about the fact that there were not just guys in the studio and asked me to be taken off the project," Jones says. "She just called one day and I answered the phone, and the next thing I knew my boss was calling me into his office, and he said, 'Well, we knew it would just be a matter of time and I'm really sorry, but I have to take you off this project.'" Not all reactions to Jones's presence on a project were so extreme, but there were occasions when Jones would be met in the studio by artists who would ask where the engineer was and be surprised when she responded, "I'm right here."

"That's when I felt I had to prove myself, because they definitely weren't expecting me," she says. "That presumption that you're not it, that's what's hard to get past, because it automatically presumes that you're not talented enough, that there has to be somebody else other than you. So I might pull out a couple of flashy tricks in the first two hours until they calm down, and then we have a great time. But you have to do it without bullying people. There's a real fine line to it, and it's stupid, because I shouldn't have to go through this shit, but I do."

Jones left ABC in 1977, and was then hired by Automat Studios in San Francisco, working for chief engineer Fred Contero, whose credits included work for Janis Joplin, Santana, and Blood, Sweat and Tears. "I was told, 'Well, Fred's the only engineer and we're not really sure whether you're just going to be an assistant or whether you'll be a first engineer, but we'd like you to start,'" Jones remembers. "And I thought, 'Well, all it's going to take is one person calling that doesn't have their own engineer and I'll be it.' And that's exactly what happened. After that, everyone knew that I was, in fact, an engineer, and it just started from there. That's when I first started working in women's music as well. I did an album with Cris Williamson, and then I did the first of nine albums with Holly Near."

Jones's first work with Near was on the *Fire in the Rain* album produced by June Millington; 1982's *Speed of Light* gave Jones her first job as a producer (co-producing with Evie Sands), an area she was eager to move into. "What I wanted to do was to be able to both produce and engineer, and then possibly not be an engineer anymore," she says. "It's a hard line to cross; sometimes it's hard being taken seriously as a producer when you're an engineer because people still look at you as an engineer." Jones worked with other women's music artists, producing records for Margie Adam, and Tret Fure's *Terminal Hold* for Olivia; she also worked for other independents, producing one of Terry Garthwaite's (a member of Joy of Cooking) solo LPs and Jane Fonda's "workout" records along with the music for the accompanying videos. She also moved into management with Jeannie Bradshaw, owner of the San Francisco club the Great American Music Hall, working with Teresa Trull and Linda Tillery for two years. "I really liked it," she says, "and I would have probably continued with that, except I got an offer to be a staff engineer for Capitol and really couldn't pass it up. Back with the big boys! I decided to take it, because I thought that being with a major label again I'd have access to the A&R department and would be able to start doing more of what I wanted to do, which was producing."

Despite Jones's own record of success in the industry, she hasn't seen an increase in the number of women working as engineers. "I think the most disappointing thing to me after all the time I've been doing this is that there aren't more women doing it," she says. "There are some, but certainly not as many as I would have thought. One time at the Automat, we had a staff of six and three were men and three were women, and that's unheard of—I don't think any studio's ever had that. I don't know why there aren't more women engineering. I think part of it is socialization: because you don't grow up thinking that's something you'd do, you don't get interested in it. If I hadn't owned the PA, I probably never would have thought of being a recording engineer, but it's through that I realized I was good at it."

Although women like Leslie Ann Jones and Boden Sandstrom managed to move into technical areas of the industry usually not open to women, and the rise of women's music had helped others get their start, attitudes in society as a whole were slower in changing. The women's music community and other independent labels offered a realm where women were free from dealing with those attitudes, but those who later chose to join the mainstream found they were confronted with the same expectations of what women could—or should—do.

At the same time that Helen Reddy was making her statement as a strong and independent woman—a statement the industry was happy to profit from—the exploitation of the "one Mary or the other" dichotomy continued, at a sometimes tragic cost. The year 1970 saw both the death of rock's archetypal bad girl, Janis Joplin, and the rise of rock's archetypal good girl, Karen Carpenter. The music, and image, of the Carpenters represented a return to "traditional values" in the aftermath of the counterculture explosion and the social upheavals of the '60s as the liner notes on their album *The Singles: 1969–1973* made clear: hits such as "We've Only Just Begun" and "Top of the World" were described as "a refreshing relief in our stormy age of social chaos . . . when the turbulence of the Rolling Stones or Janis Joplin seems more in tempo with the times . . . the songs of the Carpenters fulfill that timeless yearning for escape from the troubles of the world." But this return to "refreshing relief" would offer Karen no escape from her own troubles, and would instead lead her to an ultimately fatal destination.

Karen Carpenter was born in 1950 in New Haven, Connecticut, and moved with her parents and her older brother, Richard, to Downey, California, in 1963. She began her musical career playing drums in the school band, and in 1965 joined her first group, the Carpenter Trio, which included Richard on keyboards and their friend Wes Jacobs on bass. The trio won first place in a "Battle of the Bands" talent contest held at the Hollywood Bowl, winning a recording contract with RCA, but the material they recorded went unreleased (Karen did release a solo single in 1966 on the Magic Lamp label, "I'll Be Yours"/"Looking for Love"). The trio then broke up, and in 1967 Karen and Richard formed a larger group, Spectrum, which played the L.A. clubs. When Spectrum broke up, Karen and Richard decided to work as a duo.

Karen was persuaded to quit playing drums on stage so she could concentrate on her singing, which she reluctantly agreed to do; in a later interview she talked about her custom-designed fiberglass drum kit, one of only three in the world (Hal Blaine and Ringo Starr owned the other two), which she was unable to take on the road "because you can't see me behind them." A Carpenters demo eventually attracted the attention of Herb Alpert, who signed the duo to A&M. In 1969, they released their first album, *Offering*, along with the single "Ticket to Ride," both of which made little impression on the charts. But their next single, Burt Bacharach and Hal David's "(They Long to Be) Close to You" (previously covered by Dionne Warwick and Dusty Springfield and recorded at the suggestion of Alpert) shot to the top of the charts in 1970, the first in a remarkable string of hits: in the next five years, the Carpenters would have fifteen Top 40 singles (eleven in the Top 5), six Top 40 albums (five in the Top 5), and would also win three Grammy awards.

Karen's warm and mellow voice was emphasized on the Carpenters records through continual vocal overdubs, creating full, rich harmonics. The pleasant, laid-back tone of their material was heralded in an early press release as "bringing back the 3 H's—hope, happiness, harmony—that have been missing in the last musical decade of dissonance, cynicism and despair disguised as 'relevance.'" As the Carpenters were clearly not interested in attaining such "relevance" themselves, they were welcomed by the status quo with open arms: President Nixon even gave his stamp of approval by inviting the Carpenters to perform at the White House and lauding them as "young America at its very best." By 1973, a *Billboard* supplement on the group reaffirmed their essential wholesomeness by stating, "Soft rock stars like the Carpenters are proud to belong to the establishment. Their lifestyle as well as their music reflects traditional middle-class American values."

The underside to this relentless optimism and patriotic sentiment told a somewhat different story. The pressures of being Young America's premiere representatives at

Karen and Richard Carpenter
August 1972 at the Greek Theater, Los Angeles, Photo by Sherry Rayn Barnett

home and abroad soon began to take their toll, and in 1975 a thirty-eight-date sold-out British tour was cancelled due to Karen's poor health. In an interview in *Melody Maker*, headlined KAREN: WHY I COLLAPSED, Karen gamely admitted, "I've travelled with bronchitis and fever and everything else" in the best show-must-go-on tradition. But in reality Karen's health problems were rooted in her struggle with anorexia nervosa. Karen's anorexia stemmed from her dieting regime (a leading cause of anorexia), and as her concern about her weight was merely seen as reflecting a woman's (particularly a performer's) "natural" concern about her appearance, Karen's weight loss was not initially viewed with any alarm. "My Lord, I remember she would come in between shows and just flop down," Richard told the *Los Angeles Times*. "She was down to 80 pounds and she'd walk out on stage and her voice was absolutely marvelous. We were in awe at first. But then we had to cancel two tours the following year."

In addition to the physical disorders it causes, anorexia frequently leads to the development of psychological problems. This created a double burden that worked to undermine both Karen's confidence as a performer and her physical ability to be a performer, and the Carpenters career began to suffer as a result. By 1979, the Carpenters had not had a Top 40 hit for two years, and Richard had entered a drug rehab program to fight his own dependence on quaaludes. But while Richard was, as Karen delicately phrased it, "on vacation," she made a rare stab at independence and attempted to launch a solo career. In an atypical move, she left her home base of Downey and went to New York to record her solo debut with producer Phil Ramone. It was a step she regarded with trepidation. "I was scared to death beforehand," she admitted. "I'm not real good at being away from home by myself." But once she started work on the project, she found she enjoyed the experience: "It was fun cutting it and seeing that I could do all that—sing a different type of tune and work with different people," she said in a 1981 interview with Paul Grein that appeared in *Goldmine* after her death.

But back in California, Richard was hurt that Karen had started working without him. When the album was later previewed for Richard, Herb Alpert, and A&M cofounder Jerry Moss (the "M"), they were less than enthusiastic about its release, and Richard in particular made it clear he would prefer to start work on a new Carpenters album. Karen acquiesced, and later shrugged off her solo project by saying, "It didn't mean that much to me. It was just something to keep me busy." Ramone had a markedly different opinion about Karen's feelings. "Karen was frustrated by the goody-two-shoes image," he told *Goldmine*, and while on vacation with Karen in Mexico he observed her distress at the pressure to shelve her record. "I watched this girl disintegrate in front of me," he said. "It was hard for her to express anger, but sometimes she'd be sitting there and she'd say 'Why is this happening? What did I do wrong? Should we listen to the tape?'" The self-titled album was eventually released in 1966.

A short-lived marriage to Tom Burris, whom Karen married in 1980 and divorced shortly before her death, did little to improve her morale. But the Carpenters' 1981 album, *Made in America*, gave them their first Top 40 hit in nearly four years with the single "Touch Me When We're Dancing." Work on the next album commenced, but Karen became too ill to complete it, and, finally facing up to her anorexia, went back east for therapy. She returned to her parents' home on completion of the program, but her heart had been weakened by the years of dieting, and on February 4, 1983, a month before her thirty-third birthday, Karen collapsed and was taken to the hospital, where she died of a heart attack. The "sincere, wholesome, and unpretentious lifestyle" of the Carpenters that had been praised by their record company in 1973 had turned into a farce for a young woman unable to transcend basic societal conceptions of how a female body was "supposed" to look.

Anorexia also has political implications that strike at the very heart of feminism's aims of self-determination, in particular a woman's right to define her own standard of attractiveness as opposed to adhering to a narrow standard of "beauty" set by the dominant culture. But in a grim irony, Karen Carpenter, who had never taken a stance against the dominant culture, had nonetheless perished as a result of those traditional values she was seen to represent. Such values were typically disdained by the rock community. "Janis, on the one hand, was a heroine," wrote Robyn Archer and Diana Simmonds in *A Star is Torn*. "Miss Karen was a joke. Now the joke was dead too." In a parallel that escaped many, Karen Carpenter had been destroyed by the limitations inherent in playing the role of the good girl as Joplin had been destroyed by the limitations in playing the role of the bad.

The women's liberation movement worked to expose and change those kinds of limitations. The movement also gave the women involved in it a collective voice, and those women who pursued careers in the music industry were able to use that voice in carrying the ideas of feminism into the mainstream, as Helen Reddy did with "I Am Woman," or in creating an alternative to the mainstream, as labels like Olivia were able to do. And as the women involved in women's music worked to "try to find out what the possibilities could be" in creating that alternative, they also questioned and explored new definitions of "success." "People say, 'If you'd stayed more commercial you could have made it,'" says Holly Near. "Well, who knows? Lots of people who are good don't make it. But if you do make it, you make it very big, whereas in the alternative world, if you make it, you don't ever make it big in the economic sense, but you do make it big in the spiritual sense. I may not ever have the stature of a famous rock star, but I will probably be able to work all my life, and I don't live with the pressure or the tension that people feel to stay on top."

This view of "success" was not one the commercial realm was particularly interested in exploring, but women's music nonetheless had an impact on the roles of women-in-rock that carried over to that realm. The opportunities women's music labels provided—especially in technical work—enabled women to develop skills they could use elsewhere. Women like June Millington, Leslie Ann Jones, and Teresa Trull all developed second careers as producers through their involvement in women's music, and Boden Sandstrom's sound engineering classes enabled women to find jobs in clubs and theaters across the country. The artists who created the music were also able to explore musical alternatives by speaking to women from a perspective not usually found in the Top 40. The role models these artists provided had an impact on innumerable women, whether or not they went on to play "women's music" themselves. Ultimately, feminism inspired women to create their own opportunities. When Helen Reddy couldn't find a song that expressed her feminist leanings, she wrote one herself. It was a step more women were now willing to take, with the result that more women began finding a place for themselves in the music industry—or were able to create that place themselves.

5

Diverse Directions

"I'm waiting, I'm just waiting for that woman musician to come along like the Messiah. There's gonna be a woman musician in the next three or four years that's just gonna knock everybody's heads off . . . There's gonna be some girl who right now is maybe fourteen, and she's gonna blow everybody's mind. I just can't wait."

—Linda Ronstadt, 1974

I n 1971, Carole King emerged from behind her songwriter shadow and spectacularly rejuvenated her singing career with the release of her album *Tapestry*, which topped the charts, as did its accompanying single, "It's Too Late"/"I Feel the Earth Move." The LP also included her song "You've Got a Friend," a number 1 hit for James Taylor (who also played on *Tapestry*), "So Far Away," which reached number 14, and a new version of "Will You Love Me Tomorrow," an homage to King's girl group past. *Tapestry* was a huge success, remaining on the album charts until 1976, and earning King four Grammy Awards—Album of the Year, Best Female Pop Vocalist, Song of the Year for "You've Got a Friend," and Record of the Year for "It's Too Late." It became one of the biggest selling albums not only of the '70s, but of all time, selling in excess of thirteen million copies by the 1990s.

King's breakthrough as a solo artist coincided with the rise of a number of women singer-songwriters in the early '70s, who brought both softer music and more introspective lyrics to the rock scene. The singer-songwriter movement combined the acoustic instrumentation of the folk acts of the '60s with a pop sensibility, but the key difference between the two movements were the sentiments the music expressed: folk artists worked within an established genre steeped in a historical tradition, whereas the music of the singer-songwriters came from an intensely personal perspective. Some singer-songwriters had roots in folk music, including Joni Mitchell, Judy Collins, Janis Ian (whose first hit at age fifteen, 1967's "Society's Child"—produced by Shadow Morton—concerned an interracial romance), and Carly Simon, who sang in a duo with her sister Lucy in Greenwich Village folk clubs before finding success as a solo artist in the '70s with songs like "You're So Vain" and "Anticipation." Others, like Carole King, came from the pop realm, though until her breakthrough with *Tapestry*, King's greatest success had been as a songwriter.

King had been involved in a number of different musical ventures in the wake of the girl group era before launching her solo career. In the mid-'60s she started the Tomorrow label with her husband Gerry Goffin and columnist Al Aronowitz; the label released records by the Myddle Class, and a solo single from King ("Road to Nowhere"), but then folded. King divorced Goffin and married Charlie Larkey, bass player in the Myddle Class, and the two formed a new group, City. City recorded one album for producer Lou Adler's Ode Records label, *Now That Everything's Been Said*, released in 1969, which included an early version of "You've Got a Friend." But when the album proved to be unsuccessful, City broke up, and King and Larkey moved to Los Angeles.

Carole King
1970 at Queens College, New York (opening for James Taylor), Photo by Sherry Rayn Barnett

After moving to the West Coast, King initially concentrated on session work, playing piano on John Stewart's *Willard* album, James Taylor's *Sweet Baby James* LP, and on two albums for the group Jo Mama. In 1970, she finally released her own solo LP, *Writer: Carole King*, on the Ode label, with Lou Adler producing the album. *Writer*, in addition to featuring new material, also had King digging back into her own songbook, as she would do on her subsequent albums, including a version of "Goin' Back," previously recorded by the Byrds, and "Up on the Roof," recorded by the Drifters. The album made little impression on the charts, but the stage had been set for *Tapestry*, which King recorded with many of the same musicians who had played on *Writer* and with Lou Adler again serving as producer.

Tapestry was released in early 1971, and upon its release King went on the road to promote it, touring as the opening act for James Taylor. But King soon graduated to headliner status when *Tapestry* began storming up the charts, remaining in the Top 40 for over a year. *Tapestry's* twelve songs, all written or co-written by King, combined contemplative lyrics with strong melody lines and King's gentle, expressive vocals. Her interpretation of "Will You Love Me Tomorrow" emphasized the melancholy undercurrents that had been somewhat hidden by the "sha-la-la" vocals of the Shirelles' original version (she also recorded her own version of the Aretha Franklin hit "(You Make Me Feel Like) A Natural Woman"). The album's uptempo numbers, such as the optimistic "Beautiful" and the down-home fun of "Smackwater Jack," added to *Tapestry's* varied mix of romance and realism.

Though King had another seven Top 20 albums in the decade (including the number I LPs *Carole King Music* and *Wrap Around Joy*) and single hits with the songs "Sweet Seasons," "Jazzman," "Nightingale," and, in 1980, a number 12 hit with another of her girl group classics, "One Fine Day," *Tapestry* proved to be the high mark of her solo career. Though King remained active in the recording studio, releasing an album each year throughout the '70s, she rarely toured, and cut back on her live appearances as the decade progressed. By the late '70s, King had moved to Idaho, in part to escape from the pressures of L.A.'s music scene, and primarily limited her live work to appearances at benefits. But though King's subsequent records may not have had the impact of *Tapestry*, that album's phenomenal success helped to pave the way for the female singer-songwriters that followed.

Laura Nyro, like Carole King, also withdrew from the rigors of the music industry in order to avoid being reduced to, in her words, a "commodity." Though Nyro's records did not attain the sales that King's had, she was also an acclaimed songwriter, providing many artists with the Top 10 hits she could not attain herself. Born Laura Nigro in the Bronx in 1947, Nyro began writing songs as a child and was also an avid reader of poetry. She later attended New York's High School of Music and Art and sang in local clubs in her teens. Her first album, *More Than a New Discovery*, was released on Verve in 1966 when she was nineteen, and the following year she performed at the Monterey Pop Festival, though the experience did not pay off for her in the way it had for Janis Joplin. Her performance was low-key in comparison to the high energy offerings of Joplin, Jimi Hendrix, and the Who, and received only polite applause.

But back in New York, Nyro's fortunes in the music industry changed when she met David Geffen, then working as a music agent for the Ashley Famous agency in New

York. Geffen had been impressed with a tape of Nyro's Monterey performance and quit his job to become her manager: "Anyone who sounded that good and had such a public disaster had to have something going for her," he later explained to *Vanity Fair*. Geffen then brought Nyro to Columbia, who signed her; her first album for the label, *Eli and the Thirteenth Confession* (which she co-produced), was released in 1968.

Nyro's records embraced a wide variety of musical styles coupled with lyrics of intense poetic imagery. Her dramatic vocals soared from a bluesy, gospel wail to a whisper, usually at the most unexpected moments. As a result, Nyro's music ultimately proved to be too eccentric to find more than a substantial cult audience: "The fever pitch at which she performed was ultimately as frightening as it was impressive," wrote critic Janet Maslin. Clive Davis, then-president of Columbia, attributed Nyro's reluctance to compromise musically as the reason for her failure to break into the rock mainstream. "When she finished an album, it was clear that one or two changes in a particular song could produce a big single hit," he wrote in his autobiography, *Clive: Inside the Music Business*. "But she refused to let me make them." The number of artists who had hits when they covered her songs clearly demonstrated the commercial potential of Nyro's material: the 5th Dimension had Top 30 hits with "Stoned Soul Picnic," "Sweet Blindness," "Blowing Away," and "Wedding Bell Blues" (which went to number I), Blood, Sweat and Tears had a number 2 hit with "And When I Die," Barbra Streisand had a number 6 hit with "Stoney End," and Three Dog Night had a number 10 hit with "Eli's Coming." But Nyro herself had only one Top 40 entry, when the album *New York Tendaberry* reached 32 in 1969. Her records ultimately became showcases for songs other performers could transform into hits.

New York Tendaberry, released in 1969, was a brilliant fusion of rock and jazz influences primarily held together by Nyro's voice and the piano, occasionally filled out by multi-layered horn arrangements. "I had all this musical energy and I was exploring writing. And song form. And realities," she later told *Musician*. Nyro's next album, 1970's *Christmas and the Beads of Sweat*, utilized a diverse array of musicians, including members of the Rascals and guitarist Duane Allman. *Gonna Take a Miracle*, released in 1971, paid homage to the classic girl group songs of the '60s and was recorded with the newly rechristened Labelle, then in the process of leaving their own "Patti LaBelle and the Bluebelles" girl group days behind. But after the release of *Gonna Take a Miracle*, Nyro "retired" from the music business in 1972, and moved to New England, married (she later divorced), and had a child. Frustrations with the business side of the music industry had precipitated Nyro's "retirement": tensions between Nyro and Geffen regarding his sale of her publishing company to Columbia, and a dispute over whether Nyro would remain with Columbia or move to Geffen's newly-established label Asylum led to a split between the two. Nyro was also uncomfortable with "the whole fame trip" of being a performer. "When I was very young everything happened so quickly for me," she told *Musician*. "I hadn't really contemplated being famous. I was writing music, I was just involved in the art of it at that young age. Then, when it all happened, I did not know how to handle it."

Nyro continued to record sporadically, releasing *Smile* in 1976, *Nested* in 1978, and the live set *Season of Lights* in 1977 before "retiring" again. Nyro released two subsequent albums and died of ovarian cancer on April 18, 1997. While none of these albums achieved great chart success (though Melissa Manchester's version of "Midnight Blue" from *Smile* gave Manchester her first Top 10 hit), they did challenge industry conventions about the necessity of releasing records on a regular basis. In 1965, a top-rated act like the Supremes was releasing five albums and six singles per year, but by the late '60s, artists were taking longer to record albums, and the old constraints were beginning to be stretched. Of course, record companies preferred the resulting album to be a blockbuster success, but artists like Nyro were demonstrating that a core audience— like the audience that continued to buy Nyro's records and attend her infrequent shows—could be cultivated and would remain faithful to a performer despite the lack of a constant flow of product.

Joni Mitchell, who enjoyed her greatest commercial success during the '70s singer-songwriter era, had started out as a folk singer, though as she told *Rolling Stone* in 1979, "I was only a folk singer for about two years, and that was several years before I ever made a record." After the release of her first record in 1968, Mitchell soon moved beyond the singer-songwriter genre (or, as she called them, "art songs, which I liked best") and crossed a variety of musical boundaries throughout her recording career. Born Roberta Joan Anderson in Fort McLeod, Alberta, Canada, in 1943, Mitchell grew up listening to early rock & roll artists like Chuck Berry, Ray Charles, and Elvis Presley, but initially had a greater interest in art, and attended the Alberta College of Art with plans of becoming a commercial artist. But while at college she began playing the ukulele, then moved to guitar, teaching herself with help from a Pete Seeger instruction record. Soon music became more of a priority than art, and after attending the Mariposa Folk Festival in Toronto in 1964, she moved to Toronto and began playing in local clubs and coffeehouses. The next year she married Chuck Mitchell, and the two moved to Detroit, where she continued to build a following. After her divorce in 1966, Mitchell moved to New York, then settled in Laurel Canyon, outside L.A., in 1968.

During her stay in New York, Mitchell had made a number of important contacts, including Elliott Roberts, who became her manager, and David Geffen, who would later sign Mitchell to his Asylum Records label. She also met David Crosby, who produced her self-titled debut LP for Reprise Records in 1968. Initially, Mitchell's success on the singles charts was due to her skill as a songwriter, rather than as a singer: Judy Collins took Mitchell's "Both Sides Now" to number 8 in 1968, and Crosby, Stills, Nash and Young had a Top 20 hit with Mitchell's "Woodstock" in 1970. But Mitchell's second album, *Clouds* (which included her own version of "Both Sides Now"), became her first record to land in the Top 40, and also won that year's Grammy for Best Folk Performance. *Clouds* was also the first album Mitchell produced (she has produced or co-produced all of her subsequent records); most of her albums have also utilized her own artwork and paintings for cover art.

Mitchell's subsequent albums, *Ladies of the Canyon* and *Blue*, released in 1971, each charted progressively higher (with *Blue* becoming Mitchell's first platinum album, selling over a million copies) but at the end of the year she took a break from live performance. Her success had come as a surprise—she told *Rolling Stone* she thought of her music as "a hobby that mushroomed"—and she was displeased with Warner Bros.' marketing of her image, taking exception to an ad for her first album that referred to her as "99% virgin." "A man in the promotion department criticized my music for its lack of masculinity," she complained. "They said I didn't have any balls. Since when do women have balls anyway? Why do I have to be like that?" She was also annoyed when her songs that detailed broken romances became subjects for guessing games; after *Rolling Stone* drew up a diagram tracing Mitchell's alleged love affairs, giving her an award as "Old Lady of the Year," she didn't grant the magazine an interview for eight years.

By the early '70s, Mitchell's music had progressed from her previous acoustic-based work, and with *For the Roses*, released on the Asylum label in 1972, the jazz and rock influences were readily apparent. The album also contained Mitchell's first Top 40 single, "You Turn Me On, I'm a Radio," which reached number 25. Lyrically, Mitchell's songs had always been more literate compared to other singer-songwriters of the time, and they drew favorable comparisons to Bob Dylan's work as early as 1967, when a reviewer wrote, "She plays Yang to Bob Dylan's Yin, equalling him in richness and profusion of imagery and surpassing him in conciseness and direction." *Court and Spark*, released in 1974, continued the integration of rock and jazz and became Mitchell's most successful album, reaching number 2 on the charts and yielding two Top 40 singles, "Help Me" (which reached number 7) and "Free Man in Paris." Mitchell's tour in support of the album, which featured a full band, was met with enthusiastic response and the resulting album, *Miles of Aisles*, reached number 2 on the charts, and a live version of "Big Yellow Taxi" reached the Top 30.

Mitchell's response to the success of *Court and Spark* and *Miles of Aisles* was to pursue—in the opinion of her fans—a radical new direction. *The Hissing of Summer Lawns*, released in 1975, drew even more heavily on jazz rhythms and, lyrically, moved away from the confessional introspection of her previous work. She also experimented with seemingly unlikely juxtapositions: "The Jungle Line" combined the Moog synthesizer with Burundi drumming, years before other pop artists would utilize similar "world beat" rhythms in their work. The album still reached number 4 in the charts, but was critically panned at the time of its release. Mitchell's next albums, *Hejira* (1976), *Don Juan's Reckless Daughter* (1977), and *Mingus* (1979) continued her exploration of jazz until, as she said in 1991, "I started working in a genre that was neither this nor that. People didn't know where I fit in anymore, so they didn't play me at all." *Mingus*, recorded with jazz bassist Charles Mingus (who died shortly before the project was completed), perplexed people in both genres: "I was considered an expatriate from pop music," she told *Rolling Stone*. "Meanwhile, the jazz folks thought, 'Who *is* this white chick?'"

Mitchell's recorded output during the '80s (when she signed with David Geffen's new label, Geffen) was limited to four albums in comparison to the nine she'd released in the '70s, but Mitchell remained more interested in developing as an artist as opposed to blatantly cultivating commercial success. "You have two options," she explained to *Rolling Stone*. "You can stay the same and protect the formula that gave you your initial success. They're going to crucify you for staying the same. If you change, they're going to crucify you for changing. But staying the same is boring. And change is interesting. So of the two options, I'd rather be crucified for changing."

Joni Mitchell
November 1976 at Winterland, San Francisco,
Photo by Peter Stupar

Bonnie Raitt was another performer more interested in maintaining her artistic integrity instead of subduing it for commercial gains. And though not strictly an acoustic-oriented singer-songwriter, she was one of the few female performers of the time who became highly regarded for her ability as an instrumentalist, particularly her skill as a slide guitar player. Raitt had been inspired by folk, and later the blues, gaining her first performing experience on the road by playing with blues legends Buddy Guy and Junior Wells. Born in 1949 in Burbank, California, Raitt came from a strong musical background: her mother, Marjorie, was a pianist, and her father, John, was a Broadway star, who appeared in such productions as *Oklahoma!*, *Carousel*, and *Kiss Me Kate*. After moving between the East and West Coasts, the Raitts settled in Coldwater Canyon outside L.A.

Raitt, who received her first guitar at age eight for Christmas, found her musical inspiration back East, where she went to camp every summer. She taught herself guitar listening to a counselor's Odetta records and later "fell in love" with Joan Baez, longing to become part of the folk scene on the East Coast. "It counteracted the whole beach boy scene in California which I couldn't stand," she said in the book *Baby, Let Me Follow You Down*. Her family later moved back East, where Raitt graduated from high school in Poughkeepsie, New York. She then set her sights on Cambridge, Massachusetts, eager to be a part of the folk community where Baez had gotten her start. "I just couldn't wait," she said. "I was playing guitar, and I was a real folkie. It wasn't that I wanted to play music so much, it's just that I wanted to be around it. I chose Radcliffe because of Cambridge and the Club 47 and went there in the fall of '67."

Unfortunately, Raitt arrived at the tail end of the folk movement in Cambridge, and Club 47 closed after her freshman year. But by that time Raitt had met Dick Waterman, whom she dated and who later became her manager. Waterman also managed the careers of a number of blues artists, and soon Raitt was keeping company with many of her idols: Son House, Fred McDowell, Sippie Wallace, and Muddy Waters. Eventually she began to think more seriously about performing. "One night I was in this club and I saw this girl doing '500 Miles,'" she remembered. "And I said, 'This is 1969. There's better around than this to be doing. If she can get twenty bucks, so can I.'" With Waterman's help, she began playing in clubs. "I was the weird little white girl playing Robert Johnson songs," she remembered in 1991 in *Q* magazine. "They got a big kick out of the fact that a woman was playing slide guitar in the first place, let alone an 18-year-old round-faced redhead!" Raitt was next taken on by Buddy Guy and Junior Wells as part of their act when the two were hired to open for the Rolling Stones. She was twenty years old.

Raitt soon had a record deal with Warner Bros., who released her self-titled debut

Bonnie Raitt (right) and Sippie Wallace
September 1980 at the Universal Amphitheater, Los Angeles, Photo by Sherry Rayn Barnett

LP in 1971, with Raitt covering songs by blues artists Robert Johnson and Sippie Wallace, and featuring instrumental contributions from Junior Wells and A. C. Reed. But Raitt's tastes encompassed more than just the blues, and though she continued releasing albums on a regular basis, she had trouble in fully capturing her sound on record, utilizing a series of producers as she searched for an appropriate "musical translator." "I have very specific taste in what I want and what I like but I don't know how to tell someone to change what they're playing," she said, "whereas a producer does." Her mix of musical styles—blues, rock, and country—also made it hard for her records to generate hit singles through radio exposure. Raitt herself professed little interest in attaining huge commercial success, but she still experienced the frustration of not finding a welcoming place on radio playlists. "Everybody was always saying, 'Gee, I really love your record. Too bad radio won't play it.' That's been my story all along," she told *Rolling Stone.*

In addition to her work as an instrumentalist, Raitt was also one of the few performers of the decade who was consistently outspoken on political issues, a consciousness that sprang in part from her Quaker upbringing: "I was going to save the world from the time I was eleven," she said. Raitt regularly performed (and continues to perform) at a number of benefit concerts each year, and in 1979 helped found Musicians United for Safe Energy (MUSE), an anti-nuclear organization. And while expressing admiration for those who preferred to work at independent labels, such as Holly Near ("She could get a contract with a major company any day"), she didn't see her own choice to work with a major label as selling out. "I represent a political force now," she said in *Melody Maker* in 1976, "whereas if I'd gone with a lesser company I would be artistically true and politically true but this way I've got the best of both. I don't have hit records but I'm successful enough after five years of steady touring to really mean something to the political causes in which I'm involved."

Yet straightforward pop success remained, in the eyes of record companies, the most desirable path to follow. Linda Ronstadt emerged from a folk rock band of the '60s to become the most commercially successful solo female singer of the decade. Born in 1946 in Tucson, Arizona, Ronstadt's first singing experience came as a member of the Three Ronstadts, a folk trio she formed with her sister and brother. In 1964, Ronstadt moved to Los Angeles to further pursue her singing career. There, she helped found the Stone Poneys, a folk rock group styled after Peter, Paul and Mary. The group signed with Capitol in 1966, but their three albums met with little success, and the Poneys split up shortly after their sole chart entry, "Different Drum," a Top 20 hit in 1968. Ronstadt remained with Capitol as a solo artist, though the three albums she recorded for the label made little impression on the charts; only "Long Long Time," from her second solo LP, *Silk Purse*, managed to reach the Top 40.

Ronstadt then signed with Asylum, with her first album for the company, *Don't Cry Now*, released in 1973. But Ronstadt still owed Capitol another record, and *Heart Like a Wheel*, her final album for the label, became a breakthrough smash: released in 1974, the album topped the charts, and the accompanying singles, "You're No Good" and "When Will I Be Loved," did equally well, reaching numbers 1 and 2 respectively. Although not a songwriter herself at the time, Ronstadt was one of the few singers able to cover songs from the past and update them without a trace of nostalgia, and her choice of material covered a wide terrain: '50s rock & roll (Buddy Holly's "That'll Be the Day" and "It's So Easy"), Motown (Martha and the Vandellas' "Heat Wave," the Miracles' "The Tracks of My Tears"), and R&B ("You're No Good," previously an R&B hit for Betty Everett).

Ronstadt's versatility enabled her to find substantial crossover success in both the pop and country fields: her version of Hank Williams's "I Can't Help It" won her the Grammy for Best Female Country Vocal in 1975, and the album *Hasten Down the Wind* won a Grammy for Best Female Pop Vocal Performance in 1976. Ronstadt began writing some of her own material (such as "Lo Siento Mi Vida," co-written with her father and the Stone Poneys' bass player Kenny Edwards), but she remained better known as an interpreter of songs, with the skill to move easily into other areas: in the '80s, she starred on Broadway in the operetta *The Pirates of Penzance*, appeared as "Mimi" in a New York production of the opera *La Boheme*, and recorded a series of highly successful albums of classic ballads with the Nelson Riddle Orchestra. And in spite of the projected image of her as a sweet, vulnerable-looking girl—an image enhanced by the dewy-eyed "cheesecake" shots on her early album covers—Ronstadt remained very much her own person, her determined personality coming through strongly in interviews. "I didn't set out to become a star," she said in *Rolling Stone*. "I set out to become a singer. I would have sung, no matter what. The star part is just something that they made up in Hollywood in 1930."

There was a similar influx of female singer-songwriters in Britain during the early '70s, some of whom came from Britain's own folk tradition, where it had long been acceptable for females to perform, holding their guitars while singing the "sad Northern ballads" that had kept Holly Near from becoming a folk singer. Sandy Denny, widely considered one of Britain's top female vocalists, moved from London's folk club circuit to a brief tenure with the Strawbs in the late '60s, later joining the folk rock group Fairport Convention. She started her own band, the short-lived Fotheringay, in 1970, rejoined Fairport Convention for a period in the mid-'70s, and pursued a solo career until her death in 1978 at age thirty. Judy Collins was among those who covered Denny's work, using "Who Knows Where the Time Goes" as the title track for her 1969 album. Another performer, Maddy Prior, sang in a folk duo with Tim Hart and went on to join Steeleye Span, another long-running traditional group in the mold of Fairport Convention; she later released solo albums and teamed up with folk singer June Tabor to record *Silly Sisters* in 1976 and *No More to the Dance* in 1989.

Mary Hopkin was more well known to American audiences than Denny and Prior because of the international success of her debut single on the Beatles' Apple Records label, "Those Were the Days," released in 1968. Hopkin, a fan of Joan Baez and Judy Collins, began singing with a folk rock band in her native Wales in her teens. When the band folded, Hopkin continued to perform as a solo artist, recording traditional songs in Welsh and English for a local label. An appearance on *Opportunity Knocks*, a British television talent show, brought her to the attention of Paul McCartney, who decided to have her record "Those Were the Days." The song was recorded in a variety of languages, and became a chart-topper around the world, but Hopkin's success quickly soured for her. Unlike the more acquiescent girl groups of the '60s, Hopkin chafed at both her image and the songs she was made to sing. "It was bad enough that I was straight from school . . . but then [Apple] proceeded to exaggerate all that," she told *Record Collector*. "They took great pains over creating a ghastly sugary image for me . . . then I became an embarrassment to them, because I wasn't hip."

Hopkin became increasingly disillusioned with the music business and the efforts to preserve her "sweet Welsh lass" image: "Hell, I've been swearing since I was six!" she said. An offer of a role in *Hair* was turned down by Apple, and she wasn't even allowed to be photographed holding a wine glass. Nor was she happy with the progress of her recording career. Hopkin's early records were produced by Paul McCartney, but she found working on later records with producer Mickie Most an unrewarding experience: "He came to visit me," she told *Record Collector*, "and he came to ask me what key I would like to sing in, then he'd record the whole thing without me and add my voice at the end. There was no way I would put up with that treatment, so he thought me extremely difficult." Her appearance at the 1970 Eurovision Song Contest was an equally demoralizing experience: Hopkin later referred to the song she performed, "Knock, Knock, Who's There," as "one of the most appalling songs of all time . . . really, it was quite awful."

Her frustrations at not being offered songs she wanted to sing, coupled with the over-protectiveness of her father, who managed her, led Hopkin to abandon her solo career in 1972, though she continued to record, providing backup vocals for the acts her then-husband, Tony Visconti, was producing, such as David Bowie and Thin Lizzy. In the '80s, when she sang with the groups Sundance and Oasis, her determination to avoid manipulation was just as strong: "They wanted [Sundance] to do support on a Shirley Bassey tour," she recalled. "I immediately turned that down and was sacked on the spot!" Hopkin might not have found consistent commercial success, but she was not about to compromise her independence again to achieve that success, something that hadn't even been considered in the girl group era.

Joan Armatrading, who released her first album in 1972, emerged as one of Britain's most highly acclaimed singer-songwriters, and despite being unable to find substantial commercial success in America, she has developed a solid core audience over the length of her career. Born in the West Indies in 1950, Armatrading moved with her family to Birmingham, England, in 1958. Though Armatrading's father was a musician, he did not encourage his daughter's own musical ambitions and would hide his guitar from her at home. But Armatrading taught herself to play the family piano and eventually acquired her own guitar, which she also taught herself to play. When she was fourteen, Armatrading was inspired by a television appearance by Marianne Faithfull to write her own material, and though she soon began playing in local clubs, she was initially more interested in developing her skills as a songwriter, rather than a singer.

When she was eighteen, Armatrading landed a role in the London production of *Hair*. She then began a musical collaboration with Pam Nestor, who had also been a member of the *Hair* company, and the two were signed to Cube Records. Their debut album, *Whatever's For Us*, was released in 1972, but Cube, intending to push Armatrading as the "star" of the duo, credited the album solely to her. As a result, Armatrading and

Nestor split up, and Armatrading spent the next few years in limbo, trying to extricate herself from various record and management contracts, eventually signing with A&M. Armatrading's first release with the label was a reissue of *Whatever's for Us*, with her solo debut LP, *Back to the Night*, released in 1975.

Back to the Night sparked further interest in Armatrading and she was soon working on her next record. A&M planned a major promotional push for the new album and decided to play up her individuality in its advertising, since black singer-songwriters were virtually nonexistent in the genre. "*Joan Armatrading* is one of the most original albums of 1976," ran A&M's full-page ad for the LP in *Melody Maker*. "But will you listen? She's not the next anybody. She's just a brave black lady who won't accept compromise." The album was an immediate success in Britain, giving Armatrading her first U.K. Top 10 hit with "Love and Affection" and winning fans over with its mix of musical styles, well-crafted lyrics, and the rich, mellow tones of Armatrading's voice. The British weekly *Sounds* wrote, "We need Joan Armatrading like we need Bob Dylan and the Beatles. You'll play this record once in a while forever."

Her success established, Armatrading soon faced the obligatory questions about being a woman-in-rock. She side-stepped the issue of feminism by saying in 1977, "I think there's a way of helping without waving a banner. A woman succeeding helps other women." Yet she also found that her success hadn't been able to help change preconceived notions about her own ability as an instrumentalist. "I'm used to people thinking it's a guy playing guitar on my albums when it's actually me," she said. "I suppose a lot of girls think they're

Joan Armatrading
Photo by Ian Astle, courtesy of A&M Records

expected to just strum along—to get by—but it annoys me that people should automatically think that's the extreme of my capabilities, too." Armatrading was also reluctant to discuss her private life in interviews, preferring to keep the focus on her music—though that didn't mean she was especially interested in analyzing her work either: "I wish people would just listen to the songs and leave me alone," she told the British feminist magazine *Spare Rib*.

Another source of frustration was her lack of success in America, where she received good reviews but poor sales, and by the end of the '70s, she had switched producers in search of a more commercial sound. Richard Gottehrer, who produced Blondie's first two albums, was taken on to produce 1980's *Me Myself I*, which also featured the instrumental talents of Chris Spedding and Clarence Clemons and resulted in Armatrading's most powerful pop performance yet. The title track was a particularly bright statement of independence, picturing a newly self-empowered woman of the '80s boldly stepping out to enjoy a blissful life of solitude six days a week—a punchy successor to Helen Reddy's "I Am Woman."

Armatrading pushed up the pop quotient in her subsequent albums *Walk Under Ladders* (1981) and *The Key* (1985), produced by Steve Lillywhite, the latter album featuring the cheeky song "(I Love It When You) Call Me Names." Initially, Armatrading's move to a more commercial sound worked, for her album sales in America grew and both *Me Myself I* and *The Key* reached the Top 40. But substantial commercial success in the U.S. still eluded her.

Joan Armatrading's career provides a ready illustration of the difficulties black performers still faced in crossing over to a white audience; her material was clearly not R&B, yet it could find no place on the pop charts either. Armatrading's music could have easily sat on the charts among the other singer-songwriters of the '70s who found commercial success but perhaps American audiences were not ready to hear a black woman who performed such "white" music. Ironically, when Tracy Chapman broke through to massive critical acclaim in 1988, she was heralded as "the new Joan Armatrading," arguably giving Armatrading more attention than she received for her own work, either in the '80s or the '70s.

Black female performers in other musical genres also had difficulty in achieving consistent pop chart success; most managed only a few hits before disappearing for good. But black performers in the '70s did have a greater autonomy than their '60s counterparts and so were better able to challenge stereotypical images, as Patti LaBelle and the Bluebelles did when they shed their girl group image and re-invented themselves as Labelle in the '70s. By the late '60s, the group had become a trio, with the departure of Cindy Birdsong, who left in 1967 to replace Florence Ballard in the Supremes. "We realized that there was never a four-part harmony in our group," Patti explained to *Rolling Stone.* "Cindy had been doubling up a note. So we really didn't need another voice. And we found our own sound with three voices." The group was still a popular live draw, but their recording career had been less successful, and when the Bluebelles finally extricated themselves from their contract with Atlantic Records they contacted *Ready, Steady, Go!* producer Vicki Wickham, who had expressed an interest in producing the group.

Wickham had remained friends with the group since their appearance on *RSG* in the mid-'60s and she agreed to help revamp the Bluebelles. Wickham also became the group's manager, in spite of her own reservations. "I told them, 'I know nothing about managing. I don't know that much about America. This is silly, you need a real person,'" she says. "And they said, 'Well, our last real person was a thug who's now in jail, so you've got to be better than he was.'" For their part, the Bluebelles felt the time was right to try something new. "We had the talent and the ability and the possibility of changing and moving into the '70s, rather than carrying the '60s into the '70s," explains Nona Hendryx. "And I think we all felt like we needed a change—otherwise we'd still be doing 'Over the Rainbow.'"

Along with shortening the group's name to "Labelle," the group, and Wickham, also agreed that a new visual identity was in order. "I really thought that it was time, having come from the Supremes and the Shirelles, that there was a new day," Wickham explains. "Why couldn't black girls just be a group in the same way that the Animals

Labelle, 1970s
Courtesy of Vicki Wickham

were, or the Who?" Sarah Dash, at the 1990 New Music Seminar, further explained the group's reasons for wanting to establish a new image for themselves: "When we were Patti LaBelle and the Bluebelles, we all wore the same wigs, the same dresses, and the same heels," she said. "Then we came together saying it is time to break this mold. Why do black women all have to look alike because they're singing together? And of course, the Supremes were the reigning queens at the time—and they had three wigs, three dresses, and three pairs of shoes that all matched! I'm not putting that down, but we wanted to change the whole image and the whole mentality of how black women were supposed to represent themselves in this industry."

In their first attempt to "break the mold," Labelle was pictured in denim jeans on the cover of their self-titled debut album, produced by Wickham, and released on Warner Bros. in 1971. But they soon realized that the "dressing down" didn't suit their personalities. "They weren't comfortable," Wickham admits. "But luckily, a marvelous guy who was a fan, Larry LeGaspi, started saying, 'Please let me make some clothes; I've really got some great ideas.' And he came up with the whole silver concept; later he did stuff for Kiss and George Clinton, but he really conceived the whole Labelle look. And then it suddenly struck me that I was totally wrong in playing them down, that actually they were three great-looking girls, so let's go the other way—be totally outrageous. Let's really have fun with it and do a theatrical show, but with some relevance, trying to say something as well. So that's how that all came about."

The ornate, futuristic outfits gave Labelle a strong visual identity well suited to the

Nona Hendryx, 1970s
Courtesy of Vicki Wickham

"glam rock" era of the early-mid-'70s, when performers like David Bowie, Elton John, and Alice Cooper dressed in outrageous, glitter-festooned costumes, and staged elaborate shows. As virtually the only all-female group that was as flamboyant as the male glam performers, Labelle should have been exceptional for that very reason. And the group's extravagant live shows did win Labelle a devoted following, as *Rolling Stone* noted in 1974: "Labelle owns New York. The city which is supposed to be the performer's ultimate conquest bows in unashamed surrender any time the group takes the stage." They also became the first black rock group to perform at the New York Metropolitan Opera House. But their records, which now included *Gonna Take a Miracle*, the album recorded with Laura Nyro, *Moonshadow*, released in 1972 on Warner Bros., and *Pressure Cookin'*, released in 1973 on RCA, made little impression on the charts.

Finally, in 1974, the group had substantial hits with the album *Nightbirds*, produced by Allen Toussaint, which reached number 7, and the accompanying single, the dance-oriented "Lady Marmalade," which hit number 1. Half of the album's ten songs were written by Nona Hendryx, including the title track, "Nightbird," a ballad written as a tribute to Janis Joplin. But instead of opening the door to further opportunities for Labelle, the success of *Nightbirds* was the group's high mark. The stratification of black and white performers on radio playlists left Labelle little room for maneuvering: white radio wouldn't play them because they were black, and black radio wouldn't play them because rock was white music. Black artists who played rock music—or, as in the case of Joan Armatrading, any musical style identified as "white"—were faced with a contradiction that could not easily be resolved.

At first, the lack of radio exposure was not much of a problem, for Labelle was well established as a strong live act. "It was frustrating," says Hendryx, "but we had, luckily, been a group that didn't primarily need radio play to sell records or to perform. Yes, airplay did bring us a wider audience, but it wasn't like we couldn't exist without it. Our audience was always there; they came, and they said that they loved us. And we would sell a certain amount of records, so we had a core basis." But when Labelle's next albums, *Phoenix* (1975) and *Chameleon* (1976), failed to build on the success of *Nightbirds*, the group, who had now been together close to fifteen years, decided it was time to disband. "This was really not fun anymore," Hendryx explains. "And we had this argument about everything. We'd known each other for so long we had lots of arguing to get out, we had a lot to argue about! And it was just best we split up." Growing musical differences also played a role. "There just came a point where musically nobody really was in agreement," says Wickham. "There was a point where it was time for every-body to go do their own thing. Everybody grew up. It was really that simple."

Each member of Labelle has pursued a solo career since the breakup. In addition to her recording work, Patti LaBelle starred on Broadway in *Your Arms Too Short to Box with God* in the early '80s, and appeared in such films as *A Soldier's Story*. She also had hits with the songs "New Attitude" (from the film *Beverly Hills Cop*), a Top 20 hit in 1985, and the album *Winner in You*, which topped the charts

Labelle backstage
(left to right): Sarah Dash, manager Vicki Wickham, Patti LaBelle, Nona Hendryx, Photo by Wendi Lombard, courtesy Vicki Wickham

in 1986; a single from the album, "On My Own" (a duet with Michael McDonald), also topped the charts. Sarah Dash released her own albums and sang backup vocals for a number of performers, including the Rolling Stones and Keith Richards, and on the records of her former bandmates.

Vicki Wickham chose to continue managing Nona Hendryx. "I would have loved to have managed Pat and there was the opportunity," she says, "but I knew what she was going to do, and I knew what she should do—go to Vegas. Whereas with Nona, I felt that Nona had that edge, and wasn't going to do the conventional, so I decided to remain friends with Pat and manage Nona." Hendryx's solo albums (which she also co-produced) were primarily oriented toward dance rock and featured guest appearances from artists as varied as Peter Gabriel, George Clinton, and Keith Richards. The lineup on "Design for Living" (a track on 1983's *Nona Hendryx*) was particularly impressive, featuring Heart's Nancy Wilson on guitar, Talking Heads' Tina Weymouth on bass, the Go-Go's' Gina Schock on drums, Laurie Anderson on violin, Valerie Simpson on piano, and backing vocals from Patti LaBelle. Hendryx also began producing other artists, including Britain's Sophia Jones. In 1991, LaBelle, Hendryx, and Dash sang together for the first time since Labelle's breakup on the track "Release Yourself" (co-written by Hendryx) on Patti LaBelle's album *Burnin'*.

The Pointer Sisters were another all-female vocal group that challenged the established visual "mold" for black performers in the '70s. Ruth, Anita, Bonnie, and June Pointer were born between 1946 and 1954 in Oakland, California, to parents who were ministers at the West Oakland Church of God. The sisters began their singing careers in the church choir, and by the late '60s had decided to pursue a career in popular music. Their introduction to show biz was a rocky one: after arriving in Houston for their first out-of-town shows, they were left stranded when their prospective bookings didn't pan out. They put in an emergency call to a producer they knew in California, David Robinson, who forwarded the group money to return home and then found them work as backup singers for such performers as Grace Slick, Esther Phillips, Boz Scaggs, Dave Mason, and Taj Mahal.

In the early '70s, the Pointer Sisters began recording under their own name, releasing their first two singles on Atlantic. When the singles were unsuccessful, the sisters signed with Blue Thumb, who released their self-titled debut LP in 1973. By this time, the sisters had fashioned a distinctive look for themselves through the use of '40s-styled dresses embellished with such accessories as feather boas. The combination proved to be a winning one: both the group's album and the accompanying single, Allen Toussaint's "Yes We Can Can," reached the Top 20, and after an acclaimed show at L.A.'s Troubadour club, offers of live work and television appearances came pouring in.

1973 was also the year Bette Midler had a Top 10 hit with her version of the Andrews Sisters' "Boogie Woogie Bugle Boy," which momentarily typed the Pointer Sisters and Midler as revamped nostalgia acts. But the Pointer Sisters' versatility encompassed more than the jazzy scat singing that mirrored their '40s image. "Fairytale" (written by Anita and Bonnie) not only reached the pop Top 20 in 1974, it also crossed over to the country field, winning that year's Grammy for Best Country Vocal Performance by a Duo or Group. Their second album, *That's a Plenty*, covered a wide musical territory, with the sisters' trademark scat singing on "Salt Peanuts," Bonnie's soulful "Shaky Flat Blues," and a sassy rendition of "Steam Heat," from the musical *The Pajama Game.* The group had further hits with their 1975 album *Steppin*, which reached number 22, and the single "How Long (Betcha' Got a Chick on the Side)," another original composition, which reached number 20. But the sisters soon faltered under the strain of constant touring, and they began to feel hampered by their image. "We weren't growing as singers," explained June. "We didn't really know what our voices could do."

After the release of *Steppin*, Bonnie left the Pointer Sisters (she later signed with Motown as a solo artist), and in 1977, following the release of *Having a Party*, the group disbanded briefly. But the breakup didn't last long—Ruth, June, and Anita soon regrouped and signed with Richard Perry's Planet Records label, becoming more successful as a trio than they had been as a quartet. They had their biggest hit to date in 1979 with "Fire," written by Bruce Springsteen, which went to number 2, followed by another number 2 hit in 1981, "Slow Hand." 1983's *Break Out* did just that, reaching number 8 in the charts, kicking off a run of four Top 10 single hits in a row, and winning them two further Grammy awards. The Pointer Sisters' skills as singers, songwriters, and performers had helped them to find a new direction when their "nostalgia" image had grown stale for both themselves and their audience.

But Motown, the label that had helped innumerable black artists find commercial success in the '60s, would have more trouble in finding a new direction for their artists in the '70s, in spite of a promising beginning. By the early '70s, Motown had permanently relocated to Los Angeles and planned to expand into other areas of the entertainment business. Initially, it appeared the company would maintain the influence it had had on the industry in the '60s: it produced a number of successful television specials for Motown artists, invested in the Tony award-winning Broadway musical *Pippin*, and made its first foray into film in 1972 with *Lady Sings the Blues*, for which Diana Ross received an Oscar nomination for her performance as Billie Holiday. But by the end of the '70s, the situation had changed considerably and a number of major Motown acts, including Diana Ross, had left the company.

The Supremes, Motown's flagship group, finally disbanded in 1977, seven years after

Ross's departure from the group. Though there had been speculation that the group could not survive without Ross, the "new" Supremes—Mary Wilson, Cindy Birdsong, and Jean Terrell—managed to hold their own in the early '70s. Their first post-Ross single, "Up the Ladder to the Roof," was a Top 10 hit and through 1972 the group had six further singles in the Top 40 and a Top 30 album (1970's *Right On*). But in 1973, the Supremes began having trouble maintaining a stable lineup. Cindy Birdsong was the first to leave and was replaced by Lynda Laurence (later Lawrence). But the Wilson-Terrell-Lawrence lineup soon felt frustrated by the lack of attention they received from Motown, which they felt was uninterested in promoting them in the U.S., although the group continued to have hits overseas, where they remained an in-demand live act. They considered signing with another label, but Wilson was reluctant to leave the only company she'd ever been with, so Terrell and Lawrence ended up quitting. Birdsong returned, along with a new member, Scherrie Payne, but Birdsong ended up leaving again in '76 and was replaced by Susaye Greene. The constantly changing lineup made it difficult for the group to maintain continuity, and the Supremes' final Top 40 entry came in '76 with "I'm Gonna Let My Heart Do the Walking." After the group finally split, Wilson spent another several years battling Motown over the rights to the name "Supremes" (a suit she ultimately lost).

Meanwhile, Diana Ross's career, though it got off to a slow start in the '70s, gradually rose from strength to strength as she blossomed into an all-round entertainer. Her first solo single, "Reach Out and Touch (Somebody's Hand)," reached the Top 20 in 1970, and her next, a cover of the Gaye-Terrell hit "Ain't No Mountain High Enough," topped the charts, but she didn't have another Top 10 hit until 1973 when "Touch Me in the Morning" went to number 1. The hits were more readily forthcoming for the rest of the decade, and included two more number 1s, "Theme from *Mahogany* (Do You Know Where You're Going To)" and the disco-flavored "Love Hangover." Her work in film was less notable: *Mahogany*, her second film, was not as acclaimed as *Lady Sings the Blues*, and *The Wiz* (an all-black version of *The Wizard of Oz* that starred Ross as "Dorothy") was an outright box office failure, despite being a Tony award-winning smash on Broadway (with Stephanie Mills, in her first professional role, as Dorothy). But Ross ended the decade on a high note: her 1980 LP *Diana* reached number 2 and spawned three Top 10 singles, and her final hit on Motown was a duet with Lionel Richie, the theme song from the film *Endless Love*, which reached number 1. She then departed for RCA in 1981, though she returned to Motown in the late '80s and eventually acquired a two percent interest in the company. Her latest album, *Gift of Love*, was released in 2000. But a Supremes reunion tour that year, featuring Ross, Laurence, and Payne, was cancelled after a few shows due to poor ticket sales.

Gladys Knight, unlike the Supremes, had not been hesitant about leaving Motown in the '70s when she became frustrated with the lack of attention she felt she and her group, the Pips, were receiving. Knight, born in 1944 in Atlanta, Georgia, had started singing in church as a child, and toured Alabama and Florida with the Morris Brown Choir at age four. After winning first place on the television program *Ted Mack's Amateur Talent Hour*, she was approached with numerous offers for TV appearances, commercials, and live work. By the end of the '50s, Knight, her brother Merald, sister Brenda, and cousins William and Elenor Guest formed Gladys Knight and the Pips, and quickly became a popular live act. During the early '60s, the group recorded for a number of small labels, having Top 40 hits with the songs "Every Beat of My Heart," "Letter Full of Tears," and "Giving Up." Brenda and Elenor quit the group during this period, and were replaced by another cousin, Edward Patten. Knight herself also quit the group briefly when she gave birth to two children, but rejoined in 1963.

In 1965, the group signed with Motown, though Knight herself was opposed to the decision; she felt that by not coming from Detroit, they would be at a disadvantage compared to the locally based acts. But Knight was outvoted, and the group signed with the label, recording for the Motown subsidiary Soul. The group had a fair measure of success during their years with Motown, including three Top 10 singles, two of which, "I Heard It Through the Grapevine" (1967) and "Neither One of Us (Wants to Be the First to Say Good-bye)" (1972) reached number 2 in the charts. But Knight felt the group was being seen as more of an R&B act than a pop act; her version of "Grapevine" had crossed over from black radio, whereas Marvin Gaye's version (released in 1968) was a straight-ahead pop hit and stayed at number 1 for seven weeks. She was also disappointed the group was not able to work with Motown's songwriting/producing team Holland-Dozier-Holland.

In 1973, the group moved over to Buddah Records, and for a time it did seem as if they'd finally found the consistent pop chart success Knight wanted: "Midnight Train to Georgia" became the group's first number 1, and the first in a series of four subsequent Top 10 hits. They also won two Grammy awards, Best Pop Vocal Performance for "Neither One of Us" and Best R&B Vocal Performance for "Midnight Train." But by 1975, the group had their last Top 40 single of the decade, and as they disappeared from the charts, their live work began to fall off as well. There were additional problems when the group became involved in a royalty dispute with Buddah, during which time they were banned from performing, and Knight's debut film venture, *Pipe Dreams* (which used the unlikely setting of the Alaska Pipeline as the backdrop for a love story), was a commercial failure. But Knight and company were persistent, and in 1980 they signed with CBS, and, in 1985, MCA, where in 1988 the group had their first Top 20 hit in almost thirteen years with "Love Overboard." In an interview with *Rolling Stone* that year, Knight again complained about the segregation of rock and R&B radio airplay. "It's a need to keep black people, no matter what they do, in their place," she said. "I still have to go Top 10 R&B before I can cross over to pop. I resent that."

In the early '70s, the Detroit-based Hot Wax and Invictus labels briefly managed to bridge the gap between rock and R&B and released records by a number of black artists who landed on both the pop and R&B charts, including Honey Cone, Freda Payne (Scherrie Payne's sister), and Laura Lee. That the music on Hot Wax and Invictus had such crossover appeal was no surprise, given that the two labels were founded and operated by Holland-Dozier-Holland, the team that had helped create Motown's success. H-D-H had left Motown in 1968, frustrated by the lack of financial compensation they had received for their work at the company, and started Hot Wax and Invictus the following year. By that time, H-D-H was involved in a lawsuit with Motown (eventually settled out of court), and they were barred from producing their acts. But the labels still managed to get off to a good start, with the first release on Hot Wax, Honey Cone's "While You're Out Looking for Sugar," reaching the Top 30 in the R&B charts.

Honey Cone had been formed by Edna Wright, who had been asked to put together a vocal group for an Andy Williams TV special. Wright was Darlene Love's sister, had recorded a single under the name Sandy Wynns, and appeared as one of Ray Charles's "Raelettes." The two women Wright asked to join the group, Carolyn Willis and Shellie Clark, had equally diverse backgrounds. Willis was a former member of Bob B. Soxx and the Blue Jeans, and had been a backup singer for such artists as Barbra Streisand and Lou Rawls. Shellie Clark was a former Ikette with the Ike and Tina Turner Revue and had also performed with Little Richard and as a member of Cab Calloway's Cotton Club Revue. After seeing the group perform on the Andy Williams special, Eddie Holland signed the trio to Hot Wax and named them "Honey Cone."

Honey Cone's first three singles were written by the songwriting team of Edith Wayne and Ronald Dunbar, and all three reached the Top 30 in the R&B charts. The group's breakthrough into the pop Top 40 came in 1971 with their fourth single, "Want Ads," which topped both the pop and R&B charts. "Want Ads" was a playful number in which the trio took the matters of love and romance into their own hands through the medium of advertising after discovering their man has been unfaithful. In Honey Cone's next song, "Stick Up" (a number 11 pop chart hit and the group's second R&B number 1), the trio fell back on a more conventional use of feminine wiles by setting a "tender trap" for their man to ensure an "unexpected" pregnancy and subsequent marriage, but the following single, "One Monkey Don't Stop No Show" (a Top 20 pop hit, number 5 R&B) had the group coolly dismissing a failed love affair with little regret. "The Day I Found Myself," the group's last Top 40 pop hit, was a frank heart-to-heart talk about developing one's independence in the aftermath of a breakup.

Freda Payne also enjoyed a run of crossover success on H-D-H's Invictus label beginning with "Band of Gold," which reached number 3 in the Top 40 charts in 1970. Born in Detroit in 1945, Payne had attended school with Brian Holland, who introduced her to his brother Eddie. Eddie in turn introduced Payne to Berry Gordy when he was starting to build his Motown empire, but Payne's mother felt she was too young to pursue professional work. Payne eventually moved to New York, where she acquired extensive musical experience by singing in the touring bands of such artists as Pearl Bailey, Duke Ellington, and Quincy Jones. She also recorded a single for the Impulse label, and, as a member of Bob Crosby's Bobcats, two albums for MGM. While visiting Detroit in 1969, Payne saw Brian Holland at a party, and Holland, on learning Payne was without a record contract, offered to sign her to his new label. Payne accepted.

"The Unhooked Generation," written by Edith Wayne and Ronald Dunbar, was Payne's first single, released in 1969. Payne joyfully celebrated her status as a single ("unhooked") woman in the song, but the record made little impression on the charts, a situation that changed dramatically with the release of Payne's second single, "Band of Gold." The song's subject matter illustrated how far H-D-H had come from the stylized "cool" of the Supremes' turf: "Band of Gold" had Payne coping with her husband's impotence on their wedding night. Payne had been initially reluctant to record the song, but nonetheless gave a convincing performance as the distraught wife, and "Band of Gold" not only reached the Top 5 in the pop charts (number 20 R&B), it went on to sell over five million copies. Payne's next Top 40 entry was "Deeper and Deeper," which reached number 24 in 1970, but her next notable single, and her final Top 40 entry, was 1971's "Bring the Boys Home." The song was a direct attack on the war in Vietnam, which Payne decried as a "senseless war," demanding that the government "bring them back alive." Payne's heartfelt pleas were readily accepted by the record-buying public; "Bring the Boys Home" reached number 12 on the pop charts, number 3 on the R&B charts, and was awarded a gold record.

Laura Lee did not enjoy the same degree of crossover success as Freda Payne or Honey Cone, but her singles for Hot Wax, such as "Women's Love Rights" and "Wedlock is a Padlock," reflected some of the impact feminism had made in popular song outside of the realm of women's music. Born in Chicago in 1945, Lee was adopted by the Rundless family, who lived in Detroit, when she was nine. She began her singing career as a member of her mother Ernestine's gospel group, the Meditation Singers, making her first recording with the group in 1954 (her father, Ernest, was also a gospel singer who performed with the Soul Stirrers). In 1966, she recorded her first pop single for Detroit's Ric-Tic label, and made further recordings for Chess and Cotillion before being signed to Hot Wax.

"Women's Love Rights," released in 1971, was the only single of Lee's to reach the Top 40 on both the pop and R&B charts (reaching numbers 36 and 11, respectively). After announcing to "women liberators and men sympathizers" that she was forming her own organization to stand up and fight for "women's love rights," Lee urged women to search for love as aggressively as men did. "Wedlock is a Padlock," also released in 1971, starts off with a brief excerpt of "The Wedding March" played on an organ before Lee's voice kicks in, though despite its title, "Wedlock" bemoans marriage to the wrong man, not the state of matrimony itself. The song reached number 37 on the R&B charts. Lee's biggest R&B success came in 1972 with "Rip Off." Lee sounded positively gleeful in the song as she detailed her plans to give her man the brush-off, smiling and greeting him at the door with slippers in hand while arranging her escape, which involved confiscating all their "joint" possessions, including *both* television sets. But despite the bold assertions of independence in her songs, Lee denied any affiliation with "the women's lib thing." "That's not really me at all," she said during the same year that "Rip Off" reached number 3 in the R&B charts. "I believe that a woman should basically be a woman, but I think a man should accept a woman and treat her right. One partner in a romance should never dominate the other."

But after their initial years of success, Hot Wax and Invictus began to falter. The company began experiencing cash flow problems, complicated by lawsuits and counter-lawsuits with the artists on their roster (including Freda Payne). After the demise of Hot Wax and Invictus, Honey Cone disbanded, Laura Lee returned to the gospel field, and Freda Payne pursued acting and hosted a syndicated talk show, *For You, Black Woman*, in the early '80s. Hot Wax and Invictus might not have made the lasting impression in music that the Motown labels did, but the songs of Honey Cone, Freda Payne, and Laura Lee made a different kind of statement: though not overtly "political" (with the obvious exception of "Bring the Boys Home"), their songs expressed pride in being able to stand up for one's self, and cheerfully informed women about the benefits of attaining such independence for themselves. When matched with a sprightly pop production, such "radical" sentiments had little difficulty in finding commercial acceptance.

In the late '70s, a new musical form with roots in both the black and gay communities would cross over to the mainstream with spectacular success, and come to symbolize the '70s credo of flamboyant narcissism and willful excess: disco. In the '60s, a discotheque had been a club that played recorded, as opposed to live, music, but by the '70s "disco" had become a musical genre of its own, whose only intention was to get its audience to dance. A pair of turntables and DJ patter had long been a fixture at black parties, and by the early '70s DJs at gay clubs in Manhattan and gay haunts such as nearby Fire Island also began playing disco records which remixed songs into extended dance numbers. Eventually, through the efforts of such radio DJs as Frankie Crocker at New York station WBLS, disco mixes began receiving radio play and interest in disco began to grow. In late 1977, the film *Saturday Night Fever*, the story of a working-class youth who dances away his frustrations on the weekend at the neighborhood disco, introduced the disco phenomenon to a nationwide audience and became a smash hit. The following year, A Taste of Honey, a quartet that featured Janice Marie Johnson on guitar and vocals and Hazel Payne on bass and vocals, topped the charts with the disco hit "Boogie Oogie Oogie," and became the first black group to receive the Grammy for Best New Artist.

But as it grew in popularity, disco also faced a strong backlash, not only from the conservative elements of society who opposed the sensuous rhythms and lyrics of the music, but also the rock community itself. White rock fans alienated by disco's elitism (exemplified by "celebrity discos" like New York's Studio 54) and its association with black and gay communities responded with hostility: "anti-disco" rallies were held, at which disco records were burned and smashed, and during a performance in Chicago the gay-themed group the Village People was pelted with marshmallows thrown by attendees planted in the audience by a homophobic DJ. Numerous music critics charged that disco had no musical value due to its "mindless" and "monotonous" beat, and that the genre was unable to produce any notable stars because it was primarily a producer's medium.

There was some truth to the latter charge: a producer could assemble a group of faceless musicians and vocalists to churn out dance music, such as the German group Silver Convention, whose hits "Fly, Robin, Fly" and "Get Up and Boogie (That's Right)" would surely be more recognizable to their audience than the singers' faces or names—Penny McLean, Ramona Wolf, and Linda Thompson—would be. But other performers, such as Sister Sledge, did manage to transcend disco's built-in anonymity factor and establish themselves as a recognizable group. Before their move into more pop-oriented music, Sister Sledge—sisters Debra, Joan, Kim, and Kathie Sledge— scored a number 2 disco hit in 1979 with "We Are Family," written for the group by Bernard Edwards and Nile Rodgers (who, as members of the group Chic, had their own disco hits with the songs "Dance, Dance, Dance (Yowsah, Yowsah, Yowsah)" and "Le Freak"). Like Aretha Franklin's "Respect," "We Are Family's" call for solidarity came to be seen as an anthem for both the black community and the women's movement (in the documentary *Lily Tomlin*, Tomlin and her stage crew are shown singing "We Are

Family" together backstage to psyche themselves up for the evening's performance). The song's celebration of "sisterhood" was further underscored by the sisters' own status as a family.

But the undisputed Queen of Disco was Donna Summer, who had thirteen dance hits during the disco era, including ten in the Top 5, and nine albums in the Top 40. Born Adrian Donna Gaines in Boston in 1948, Summer was a fan of Mahalia Jackson and first sang in church before developing an interest in rock music, joining a local rock group, Crow, in her teens. In 1967, Summer moved to New York, and then to Germany when she won a role in a German production of *Hair*. Summer spent the next several years in Europe, appearing in German productions of *Godspell* and *The Me Nobody Knows*, and the Vienna Folk Opera's productions of *Porgy and Bess* and *Showboat*. She also married (and later divorced) an Austrian actor named Sommer and gave birth to a daughter, Mimi.

While living in Munich, Summer also began working as a backup singer, eventually meeting Giorgio Moroder and Pete Bellotte, a songwriting/producing team. The two signed her as a solo artist, changed "Sommer" to Summer, and began releasing a series of singles which were highly successful in Europe. In 1975, Moroder took a song he and Bellotte had written with Summer, "Love to Love You Baby," to the U.S. in the hopes of finding a record deal. Neil Bogart agreed to sign Summer to his Casablanca Records label, and, after observing the excitement a tape of "Love to Love You Baby" generated at a party he was hosting, asked Moroder to remix an extended version for the dance clubs.

"Love to Love You Baby," released in 1975, was wildly successful on both the dance floor and the radio, where it reached number 2 in early 1976. The song, with its standard disco formula that combined an incessant rhythmic pulse with lyrics that amounted to little more than endless repetitions of the song's title, gained further notoriety from Summer's orgasmic moaning throughout the number, which created the expected controversy—copies of the "demonic" single were burned in Florida and the song was also banned by the BBC. Summer's next single, 1977's "I Feel Love," repeated the formula and reached number 6. She had further hits with the songs "Heaven Knows," "MacArthur Park," and "Last Dance" from the 1978 film *Thank God It's Friday*, which won both the Oscar for Best Film Song and a Grammy for Best Female R&B Vocal Performance. In 1980, Summer became the first female singer ever to have three number 1 singles in a year with "Hot Stuff," "Bad Girls," and "No More Tears (Enough Is Enough)," the latter a duet with Barbra Streisand.

As the disco sound began to decline in popularity, Summer worked to overcome her "Queen of Disco" title. In a 1978 article in *Rolling Stone* entitled "Donna Summer: Is

There Life After Disco?" she referred to "I Feel Love" as a "popcorn track," and further pointed out the discrepancies in her perceived image by adding, "I couldn't go on singing those soft songs. I've sung gospel and Broadway musicals all my life and you have to have a belting voice for that. And because my skin is black they categorize me as a black act, which is not the truth. I'm not even a soul singer. I'm more a pop singer." She was also feeling increasingly suspicious about the management of her finances. When Summer had returned to the States for the launching of "Love to Love You Baby," she had no manager, and Neil Bogart was more than happy to recommend one— his wife, Joyce. But despite the lavishness of Casablanca's promotional events for Summer (the label once arranged for a life-size cake sculpted in Summer's image to be flown in from New York to Los Angeles for a party, met at the airport by a freezer ambulance to "escort" the confection to the event), she remained uneasy about the close alliance of her management with her record company and later alleged that all her lawyers had been chosen—and approved—by the Bogarts. She finally hired a lawyer with no ties to the label and sued Casablanca for fraud; they countersued for breach of contract (Bogart died of cancer before the suit was settled).

Summer then began varying the material she recorded and performed: the album *Bad Girls*, released in 1980, mixed in ballads and slower-tempo songs in addition to the disco tracks. Summer also moved into production, co-producing an album for the group the Brooklyn Dreams (who had appeared with Summer on the single "Heaven Knows"). After leaving Casablanca, Summer became the first artist signed to David Geffen's new label, Geffen, and, after becoming a born-again Christian, began including gospel material on her albums (winning two Grammy awards in the '80s for Best Inspirational Performance). But Summer still found success recording pop material: her biggest single hit after leaving Casablanca came in 1983 with "She Works Hard for the Money," which was accompanied by an impressive video detailing a day in the life of a single mother, alternately a waitress, a cleaning woman, and a sweatshop garment worker. Summer's track record with Geffen has not been as impressive as her years with Casablanca were, but her determination to maintain control over her career not only kept her a viable recording artist after the disco era, but also helped her avoid "being a commodity." "It can be pretty frightening when you realize you're a part of the machine," she told *Rolling Stone*, "but you can always change that."

The gains of the feminist movement throughout the '70s had enabled women working in all areas of the music industry to assume more control over their careers. Though there were still fewer women working in non-traditional jobs in the commercial side of the industry as opposed to the alternative realm, there were women who had worked their way up from clerical jobs in the '60s to more important positions in the

'70s, in part because the industry hadn't yet locked itself into a rigidly corporate structure. "At that time there was no way to 'learn' the industry," says Ivy Bauer, who learned the industry herself through hands-on experience, moving up from secretarial/assistant positions to become a road manager, concert promoter, and manager. "There were no schools, no courses at New York University. So people who ended up as recording engineers started as gofers, bringing coffee and learning how to do the board in their spare time. That's really how the majority of the people learned in those days."

Bauer had grown up in Brooklyn, and in the late '60s, at age eighteen, she moved to Greenwich Village, where she worked in a showroom in New York's garment district and faithfully listened to Alison Steele's "Nightbird" radio show in the evenings. "I got into the music business by accident," she says. "My roommate Beverly came home one day and said, 'You're not going to believe this, but I have a job in a recording studio, and I can go to work at ten o'clock in the morning and I can wear jeans!' And I thought 'Boy, that's fabulous!' To make a long story short, Beverly ran off with a guy, quit her job, and I took it. The studio recorded Jimi Hendrix and they did the voices for Mattel dolls, so it was an interesting learning experience on what goes into booking a studio! And as soon as I got that first job, it never occurred to me to do anything else. I didn't know what specifically I wanted to do in the industry, but I wanted to learn as many aspects of it as I could."

Bauer's desire to learn led her to work in a variety of areas, first learning about publishing and copyrights by working for Kama Sutra Music, the publishing arm of Buddah Records, and then moving into management, eventually working for Larry Goldblatt in the early '70s, who was at that time managing Blood, Sweat and Tears. "I started out there as an assistant," says Bauer. "Larry was an entrepreneur; he taught me how to book the band, work with promoters, negotiate deals, go out on the road, settle shows. His attitude was, the more you learn, the more I can be on my boat on the Hudson River and not worry about it. So I really lucked out on having an opportunity where somebody recognized my brightness and was willing to say, 'If you're willing to learn, I'll show you everything there is.'"

Goldblatt's willingness to have Bauer take on as much as she could handle led to her becoming one of the few—if not the only—female road managers of the time, at the age of twenty-two. "It was scary," she remembers of her early sojourns on the road. "I was overwhelmed, because there were no women! It never occurred to me to wonder where women were in the industry, why they weren't executives at corporations, why they weren't presidents of record labels. I didn't think in terms of women in business at that time in my life, I didn't think about discrimination. I didn't think about any of those things until I was in my mid-thirties."

Bauer eventually found her freedom had its limitations, and she became frustrated at the lack of progression in the company, which was now also managing Mott the Hoople and Lou Reed. She began doing more work out of her home, and then decided to move to Seattle, marrying John Bauer, a promoter she'd met during her touring days with Blood, Sweat and Tears. She suggested to her husband that they go into business as promoters together, merging her skills in the industry with his knowledge of the Northwest market. John agreed, and their company was formed as the John Bauer Concert Company, despite the fact that John and Ivy were partners. "My attitude was, again, still not conscious of women's issues, 'What do I care? It all goes in the same pocket,'" Bauer explains, adding, "Of course, in retrospect, I would never think like that again! But at that time, it didn't make a hell of a difference to me."

The differences would become very apparent to Bauer when she and John divorced in 1984: Ivy ended up losing all of her stock in the company (which had now branched out into management), in addition to being restricted from working in the concert promotion business west of the Mississippi. She also lost the male "protection" she'd received as a married woman. "People don't attack a woman as quickly when she has a partner as when she doesn't," she says. "Attorneys would never say the same kinds of things to me when I was married to John that they would say to me alone. Actually, it's been quite insulting. When I went through the divorce, the attorney looked at me and said, 'You know, I don't see what your problem is. Why don't you just take the money, stay home, and raise your child?' I flipped on the guy. I said, 'If you think that's so hot, why don't you stay home and raise your four-year-old?' I'm not sure that was such a hot negotiating point! And when I was doing management, I ran into a tremendous amount of chauvinism being on the road: 'You should be home with your baby. What are you doing on the road when you have a year-old baby?' Nobody asks a salesman what he's doing on the road when he has a baby."

In England, Gail Colson had faced similar attitudes during her career in the music business. Like Bauer, Colson worked in numerous areas of the industry, eventually ending up in management, and she too landed her first job in the music industry by "accident." "I always liked music, though not necessarily thinking that's what I wanted to go into," she says. Colson had entered the music business in 1965 when a friend told her of a secretarial job available at a PR firm, Jonathan Rowlands Associates, whose clients included Tom Jones and Engelbert Humperdinck. "I worked for Jonathan for about six months," she says. "He used to share an office with an American record producer called Shel Talmy, and it turned out that Jonathan actually had no money and Shel had been paying my wages all the time. So when Jonathan left, I stayed and worked for Shel."

Talmy was one of the first independent record producers in England, who worked with the Kinks, the Who (at the time they were called the High Numbers), and also produced records for Goldie and the Gingerbreads. Because Talmy's eyesight was failing, Colson found herself serving as his "eyes," giving her a unique perspective from which to learn the business. "Shel taught me everything," she says. "I had to read his contracts and learn them because he couldn't read them himself; I had to make sure they were absolutely right." During the same period, Colson had also been working for Tony Stratton-Smith, a manager then working with the Nice and the Bonzo Dog Doo-Dah Band. "We used to sit and drink together and bemoan the music business," she says. "By this time, I'd left Shel and I was doing nothing, didn't know what I was going to do, and Tony said, 'Will you come into partnership with me?' And I said, 'What do you mean, partnership? You've got no money!'" But Colson eventually changed her mind after observing the non-working relationships Stratton-Smith's bands had with their record companies when they toured the States. "We sent the Nice to America, and Immediate [their record company] was on answer-phone the whole time they were there," she says. "They were actually on answer-phone for the three weeks of the tour. So we used to sit together in the evenings saying we could do better than this, and we started a record company called Charisma."

Though Colson and Stratton-Smith had each been working in the music industry for several years, neither had had much experience with record labels before. "We were enthusiastic amateurs," Colson admits. "In those days we were the manager, the agent, and the record company, and it grew from there. It grew from two people to four people to a company." Charisma's first single, released in December 1969, was "Sympathy" by Rare Bird. The label went on to develop an eclectic roster, releasing albums by the Nice, Van Der Graaf Generator, Lindisfarne, comedy albums by Dame Edna Everidge and the Monty Python troupe, three albums of poetry from poet laureate Sir John Betjeman, and Genesis.

Genesis went on to be Charisma's biggest selling act, and as the label's fortunes grew, Colson's position grew with it. She was appointed managing director of the label in 1974, and though she was the first female managing director of a label in Britain, it was a distinction she didn't think about much at first. "I didn't actually feel that different," she says. "Going from label manager to general manager to managing director actually was no different because the company grew and somebody had to be in charge of all this. I knew I was the only woman, but Charisma was also a very independent company. We liked being an indie. It was us against EMI and CBS, and we never dealt with those companies because we were on our own. We dealt with Polygram, who used to distribute us, and they thought we were a bunch of hippies and weirdos anyway, so it made no difference that there was a woman in charge of all this chaos."

But outside of the independent realm, the reaction to Colson's position in the company fell back on established perceptions about how women "advanced" in the music industry, as she found out when she was interviewed for the British edition of *Cosmopolitan*. "A guy phoned me up and asked to interview me because I was the only female managing director of a record label," she remembers. "He came to interview me, and the first thing he said was, 'What's your relationship with Tony Stratton-Smith?' I said, 'What do you mean? I've worked with him for years and we started the company together.' And he said, 'Do you sleep with him?' This was the second question. And I said, 'I beg your pardon?' And he said, 'Do you sleep with him?' And I said, 'No, I don't sleep with him,' and he said, 'Is he gay, then?' I should have got up and said, 'Fuck off!' But I didn't handle it properly, I went shy. I couldn't believe it afterwards, and from then on I said, 'That's it. Never again do I do an interview!'"

Colson ran up against similar attitudes in America, which came as a surprise to her. "I assumed, the way Shel talked, that America was much more advanced than we were," she says. "I always thought American men were much more pro-women until I got to America and found nothing. It's exactly the same as in England. I can remember going to Atlantic and I used to deliberately dress down, so I'd walk in in jeans and no makeup. I remember going in with Tony Smith [no relation to Tony Stratton-Smith] and the men bowing to him because he's Genesis's manager, and they assume I'm his secretary. And he says, 'Well, actually, no, this is Gail Colson and she's the president of the record company in England that we license your records through.' And suddenly they'd start taking notice.

"Over the years I got so used to it, it's like water off a duck's back," she continues. "I remember this A&R man in America, sitting playing this tape to me, and he turned off the tape halfway through and said, 'What perfume are you wearing?' And I said, 'I beg your pardon, I'm here to play the tape. What do you mean what perfume am I wearing? If I were a man, would you be sitting here asking me what aftershave am I wearing?' And this same person actually sat looking at my breasts. I said to him, 'Look, if I sat looking at your crotch for a whole meeting, how would you feel?' And he actually apologized."

Both Bauer and Colson still work as managers in the business, though they feel that changes in attitudes regarding women's positions in the industry have not been substantial. Colson, when accompanying Terence Trent D'Arby (one of her clients) to a festival in Brazil in the '80s was told by her interpreter that a man at the local branch of D'Arby's record company had assumed that Colson was D'Arby's girlfriend, not his manager. Bauer admits her own perspective on sexism in the industry only changed when it became a personal issue for her. "Until discrimination hit me, I never really knew it was discrimination," she says. "Then I looked around the industry at some point in my thirties and realized there were very few women in really high-powered executive positions—they were all in publicity. I think it's taken a long time for women to be able to demand their own respect for what they're doing. And it has evolved a lot. There are a lot of successful women in the business, but I think there could be many more—in any business, not just the music industry."

The examples set by women working in the music industry like Gail Colson and Ivy Bauer in the 1970s indicated that greater career prospects were increasingly becoming available for women. On the performance side, artists like Joan Armatrading and Labelle, who challenged racial stereotypes, illustrated the possibilities that existed outside the established "mold" for black artists. And by the mid-'70s, white female performers were looking beyond the singer-songwriter image to establish themselves as rock artists, a genre where women were still primarily relegated to being singers, not instrumentalists.

Suzi Quatro was one of the first such performers to present a radically different way for women rockers to look. Not content with challenging conventional notions of femininity by adopting a laid-back wardrobe of jeans and t-shirts, Quatro chose to wrap her diminutive self in the form-fitting leather outfits usually associated with avid motorcyclists, boldly telling *Melody Maker*, "I feel funny in dresses and skirts." Though critics in both the U.S. and U.K. dismissed Quatro as a novelty—England's music weekly *New Musical Express* wrote that Quatro was "Really just punk *Penthouse* fodder— all lip-smacking hard-on leather," and *Rolling Stone* called her a "pop tart"—there was greater resistance to Quatro's image in the States, with the result that only one of her singles made it into the Top 40 (1979's duet with Chris Norman, "Stumblin' In," which reached number 5). Quatro's status in the U.S. as a cartoon parody of a male rocker was sealed by her characterization of "Leather Tuscadero," the sister of an ex-girlfriend of "The Fonz" on the TV series *Happy Days*—itself little more than a cartoon parody of '50s life.

Yet Quatro was a genuine performer, not the calculated media dream some of the press tagged her for, and she had been playing in bands for nearly ten years before her breakthrough in England. Born in Detroit in 1950, Quatro came from a musical family and got her first taste of performance at age eight in her father's jazz band. After witnessing a Beatles show in 1964, Quatro was inspired enough to pick up a bass guitar and form her own band with her sisters, the Pleasure Seekers. The band became regulars at the Detroit club The Hideout and cut a single for the club's label, Hideout Records, in late 1966, "Never Thought You'd Leave Me"/"What a Way to Die." The band eventually moved beyond the Detroit area, touring neighboring states and U.S.

Army bases in Vietnam and cutting a single for Mercury Records, "Good Kind of Hurt"/"Light of Love."

By 1968, the band had become more of a progressive rock group and changed their name to Cradle: it was this incarnation that was seen by producer Mickie Most, who was in Detroit recording Jeff Beck in 1971. Most was especially taken with Quatro and offered to help launch her as a solo artist in England, an offer Quatro initially declined. But Cradle disbanded shortly thereafter, leading Quatro to contact Most and move to London that October. Most signed her to his RAK Records label, and Quatro's first single, "Rolling Stone" (written by Phil Denny, Errol Brown, and Quatro) was released in 1972 to little interest. Most then pulled in the hit songwriting team Nicky Chinn and Mike Chapman, purveyors of the bubblegum-glam rock churned out by such hit-makers as Sweet, Mud, and Smokie. Their touch worked for Quatro too, with "Can the Can" hitting the top of the British charts in 1973, soon followed by "48 Crash" (number 3) and "Daytona Demon" (number 14) that same year, and further Top 20 hits in 1974.

But by 1975, Quatro's run on the charts was coming to an end, and success itself seemed to have become somewhat tarnished for the singer, who told *Melody Maker*, "The dream is always better than living it. Unfortunately." In the '80s *Greatest Hits* magazine would assert that "Suzi Quatro made a welcome change from the wimpy, folksy girls who were rock's only other female representatives at the time," but the reception during Quatro's heyday had been somewhat different. Her "tough chick" appeal came in for attack from critics who saw her look, not her music, as the act. Others undercut the potential subversiveness by digging out the heart of gold under the "trash." "On the surface at least, this is a girl no anxious parent would be sad to see her son taking up the aisle," claimed the same *Melody Maker* piece, thus taming the hellcat by putting her in her proper place—under his thumb (and properly wed). At a time when male performers such as David Bowie, Elton John, and Queen's Freddie Mercury were toying with personae that freely questioned acceptable "masculine" and "feminine" behavior, such freedom for women came at a high price.

Still, Quatro's example would serve as an inspiration for future female performers. Joan Larkin, for one, was impressed enough with Quatro that she picked up a guitar herself and, as "Joan Jett," went on to establish the Runaways in the mid-'70s. The actual genesis of the Runaways has become mired in the conflicting reports offered by the band members and their manager, Kim Fowley. Fowley claims he had the idea of enlisting teens for an all-female rock group some years before he met Joan Jett, but Jett maintains that Fowley merely helped her realize her own dream of starting a band. But both Jett and Fowley agree that they met in Los Angeles in 1975 and decided to work together in developing a group, first drafting in Sandy West, who had been a drummer from the age of nine, and Michael (Micki) Steele as vocalist. But Steele's tenure as vocalist did not last, for reasons variously attributed to her "sweetness" and/or the fact that Fowley wanted a blonde to front the group for more visual impact. Steele was eventually replaced by Cherie Currie, but she later resurfaced in the '80s pop band the Bangles.

The group was rounded out by Jackie Fox (Fuchs) on bass (after an original audition on guitar) and Lita Ford, who had been playing guitar since the age of ten, as lead guitarist. The group hit the club circuit, and their self-titled debut album was released in May 1976 by Mercury Records, who signed the band after witnessing a rehearsal session. Tensions already present in the group (Ford had initially quit the group three days after joining because of Fowley: "He was rude and disgusting. I thought he was a pig," she later told BAM) were magnified by the album's cover photograph, a solo shot of vocalist Currie. "The album was the Runaways, but the cover wasn't," grumbled Fox to Craig Rosen. "That really started it." There was also continual tension over who really "controlled" the group, with Fowley, who produced and wrote some of the band's music in addition to serving as their manager, staking his claim only to be contradicted by the members: "He should get a lot of credit, but we weren't puppets," insisted Jett in an interview, stressing the group's own contributions to the Runaways' music.

But although the group enjoyed success as a live act, particularly in Japan, their raucous material never translated into mainstream success. Part of this no doubt lay in the presentation of the group itself: the name of the group, coupled with the tough-chick stance of the members, conveyed an image of young teenage hustlers on the run, an easy image for the media to trivialize ("Ninety percent of the rock crits in America used the Runaways for target practice," wrote *Creem* magazine in 1984). Being treated by some elements of the press as little more than a joke didn't counteract the tensions percolating in the band, and following a 1977 Japan tour (captured on the album *Live in Japan*), Currie and Fox left the group. Fox was replaced by Vicki Blue, and Jett, who had already been splitting vocal duties with Currie, became lead vocalist. But by 1979, the group split for good; Jett and Ford continued working as solo performers, Currie pursued acting and wrote her autobiography, *Neon Angel: The Cherie Currie Story*, and Fox became a music attorney.

At the time the Runaways disbanded, punk was the new musical movement on the scene, a movement that offered a more egalitarian arena for female musicians to work in. Punk also raised the opportunity to comment on social and political issues, something which had been dormant in much of the music of the early '70s. Nor were the performers themselves necessarily outspoken on such topics. Both Quatro and the Runaways distanced themselves from feminism: "I really don't agree with having a group of women's libbers all thinking the same," Quatro told *Melody Maker* in 1975, and the Runaways adopted an ignorance-is-bliss stance, stating, "We are far too young to understand what women's lib is all about." When they were old enough, Jett dismissed feminism in a 1981 interview with the comment, "I don't need a movement like that to make me a worthwhile person." But while disparaging feminism, the performers had no hesitation about expressing their frustrations at dealing with sexist attitudes in the music industry. "If you have one good record, they try to get you to put on an evening gown and become middle-of-the-road," Quatro complained, and Jett, talking of the group's experience with interviews, remembered, "The first question would be, 'I heard you girls are all sluts, right?' It was torture."

Though Suzi Quatro and the Runaways made little headway in changing perceptions regarding female rock musicians in the mainstream, a mixed-gender band like Heart was able to find greater success, and sisters Ann and Nancy Wilson were not critiqued as harshly in the media for their roles as, respectively, lead singer and guitarist in the band. By working to avoid being presented as women first, and performers second, the Wilsons were more readily able to be seen as simply two members of the five-member group. Bands like Fleetwood Mac and Abba also had female/male lineups, but not only

Ann Wilson of Heart
1970s, backstage, Courtesy of Lou Wilson

did Heart's hard rock approach differentiate them from their contemporaries musically, the Wilsons' position in the band was more important creatively, with the sisters writing or co-writing the bulk of the group's material.

The Wilsons' integration in Heart was also a key point, and Ann repeatedly stressed in interviews that Heart was a *band*—that she was not a singer fronting an anonymous backing group. It was a balance the sisters also strove to maintain in their role as women-in-rock. Asked in 1976 about the failure of previous women rockers to be accepted by the public on a large scale, Ann told *Melody Maker*, "They've either tried to be rockers in the sense that they're male, like Suzi Quatro being as male as they come, or they became super-sexual, so sexual that the normal person can't relate to them." Conversely, Ann told the *Los Angeles Times*, she and Nancy tried to project an image of being "real" women: "We don't try to be like men and we don't go in for the heavy feminine bit either."

The Wilson sisters had shared an interest in music from childhood and began their career with the advantage of coming from a musically inclined environment. "We had a real musical family," says Nancy. "We were from a military family, so we were always driving across the country singing songs in the car. And we didn't run into any discouragement—we were lucky enough to be encouraged. Really lucky, because a lot of people we've played with since had families where it was not sanctioned to be a musician at all." Further musical inspiration arrived via the British Invasion in the '60s, and after the arrival of the Beatles in America, the sisters decided to pick up instruments themselves. "I, in particular, just flipped for the Beatles," remembers Nancy. "We just had to get guitars right away and be as much like them as we could." The two then began assembling their own groups, drafting in other girls as prospective members. "We come from a family that had no brothers, so we didn't really relate to boys at all," says Nancy. "So we would get these girlfriends and teach them how to be in our band: 'Here. Here's a guitar, here's how you play it, go be in our band.' We had quite a few different bands, folk rock bands, playing all kinds of Simon and Garfunkel and Beatles songs, at churches, schools, and living rooms. We did a *lot* of living rooms—including our own!"

The family had by this time settled in Bellevue, a neighboring city of Seattle, Washington, where Ann made her first records in 1968, two singles recorded with the group Daybreak: "I'm Gonna Drink My Hurt Away"/"Through Eyes and Glass" (the latter a Wilson sisters composition, though Nancy was uncredited) and "Wonder How I Managed"/"Standin' Watchin' You." Eventually, the age difference between the two led to a temporary split. "I was still in high school," says Nancy, "and being four years younger, I couldn't really follow in Ann's footsteps, since she was starting up with bands with electric guitars and drums, guys, all that stuff." Even after Nancy's graduation from high school, she delayed the musical reunion with her sister. "We always knew we would end up together," Nancy explains. "I had a standing invitation to join Heart all along, and I actually put it off because I wanted to explore my own career. I'd been the little sister forever and I needed to explore myself as an individual before I got on the wagon."

Nancy ended up spending two years attending college and performing in local coffeehouses and lounges with her acoustic guitar; in the meantime, Ann had joined a band called White Heart, which would form the nucleus of Heart when the group relocated to Vancouver, British Columbia, in the early '70s to avoid the draft. Nancy then joined the group as guitarist and vocalist, and the two struck up romantic liaisons with two brothers working for the band, Nancy with Roger Fisher, another of Heart's guitarists, and

Nancy Wilson of Heart
1970s tour, Courtesy of Lou Wilson

Ann with Roger's brother Mike, the road manager. Steve Fossen served as the group's bass player, and the group was later joined by Michael Derosier on drums and Howard Leese as lead guitarist during the recording of their first album. Ann's role as lead vocalist was embellished by her work on guitar, keyboards, and flute.

The group hit the local club circuit, began recording material, and looked for that elusive record deal, running into opposition and confusion because of the band's composition. Ann's position as lead vocalist was hardly a new concept, but the unified front of the band, and Ann's alliance with her guitarist sister, presented a different kind of image. "Heart was really a new kind of configuration," says Nancy, "with women fronting the band and men playing in it too. It was like, 'Well, we're not sure where to put these females . . . what category do you lump that into?' We got turned down by every major record label in the States. But we kept looking and kept looking and just kept plugging and plugging and plugging away like a fly on a window, looking for some response from somewhere."

They finally found a response in their adopted city, Vancouver, when Mushroom Records signed the group. Heart's debut album, *Dreamboat Annie*, was initially released in Canada with its U.S. release following in 1976. The album was an enticing mix of ballads and hard rock, undercut by the softer image conveyed on the cover, which featured head-and-bare-shoulders shots of the sisters on either side of a red heart, rightly leading Ann to complain that the depiction of them as "cute, pink, lacy girls" could only lead the public to assume they made cute, pink, lacy music. The fact that no other band members were pictured on the cover also focused attention on "the chicks in the band," instead of presenting the group as a unit of equals, and drew the expected innuendos, even from the band's own label: one full-page ad was set up as a *National Enquirer* parody that carried the headline "Heart's Wilson Sisters Confess: 'It Was Only Our First Time!'" Ann in particular found such portrayals "vulgarizing," and these attitudes did not endear them to Mushroom over the long run. The focus on the women in the band was also highlighted on original copies of the debut single, "Magic Man," which was credited to "Heart Featuring Ann Wilson," a distinction that was later dropped. Nonetheless, Nancy admits the "novelty" aspect of having women in a rock band had its advantages. "Being a woman in rock, largely you don't get taken seriously; that's the downside," she says. "Nobody believes that you're an artist or that you can play that well or that you are legitimate to begin with. But you prove them wrong! But being a woman in rock also, especially when we came along, sold albums. Because nobody else was doing it and it was really 'interesting.' So even if it seemed like a novelty at the time, it definitely got us noticed when we got out there."

But in addition to being "interesting," Heart's music was also able to make a substantial commercial impression. *Dreamboat Annie* was an immediate success in Canada, with Heart winning two Juno Awards (the Canadian Grammy) in 1976 for Best Group, and Michael Flicker winning Best Group Producer for his work on the album. The band then concentrated on breaking the group in the U.S. market. "We took it region by region," says Nancy. "We basically toured the album across the United States and went to every radio station and met everybody in every record store across America. It was really all due to the fact that there was one guy at Mushroom that believed in us so much that he pushed us and said, 'This'll happen, if we just do this and this and this.' So we figured what do we have to lose, we'll do everything we can, whatever it takes. So we did it . . . and it worked!"

Dreamboat Annie went on to sell more than four million copies, with the singles "Magic Man" hitting number 9 and "Crazy On You" reaching number 35, and the album itself reaching number 7. The sales firmly established the group as a Top 40 success, cemented by a major label deal with Portrait Records, a CBS subsidiary. It was a move that also embroiled the group in legal difficulties with Mushroom, who had now lost one of its biggest successes. In 1977, just as Heart released their major label debut, *Little Queen*, Mushroom threw its own Heart product on the market, the album *Magazine*, compiled from partially completed tracks and live tapes from a club gig. The group retaliated by obtaining a court order which allowed them to withdraw the album from the market and remix and re-record tracks themselves before Mushroom was able to reissue it, after which the band officially ended their association with the label.

But as the group was busily scoring Top 20 hits with songs like "Barracuda" and "Straight On," they were also being confronted with media perusal that tended to stress the obvious: Ann and Nancy's gender. It was a focus that put a strain on all members of the group. "How do I put this graciously?" says Nancy. "It's hard for any male to be in a band where the focal points are females who automatically get all the attention. It's nothing we have any power over, really, it's just the way it is with some people. So the more people want to talk to Ann and I than they do the guys in the band, the harder it is for them to swallow. We do talk about it quite a lot because it's nothing that Ann and I have in mind; we do make a special effort because we are a band and we want to be acknowledged as a band. But you just can't help it. Even an all-guy band, like Led Zeppelin, it's always been Jimmy and Robert. It's the same in most bands, but the fact that we're women probably makes it a little bit worse."

Such tensions were underscored by the Wilsons' involvement with the Fisher brothers. "We just weren't equipped for the load we were under," says Nancy. "It is bigger than people might imagine. All the little in-group things, all the jealousies and politics can really get heavy. You have to be a group of really strong, clear-thinking people to find your way through it. All that stuff really helped break up that particular lineup. But if you love playing and you do have the right people on your side and you have a chemistry within the team, then there's nothing that can stop you. Having survived that as a band—we deserve medals after that! We're still here."

The sisters' way of dealing with these issues in the '70s had them playing down the female-male difference in the band by avoiding extremes—and not surprisingly, these "extremes" included avoiding linking themselves to the feminist movement. Even the press release for the band's 1980 LP *Bebe Le Strange*, an album directly inspired by female fans who had written to Ann and Nancy over the years about the inspiration they'd received from the group, made this distinction clear, with Ann quoted as saying "*Bebe*

Le Strange is a kind of collective name for all the young people who have contacted us; it's a name like 'Johnny B. Goode'—it stands for much more than a 'feminist statement' about rock. It goes beyond that."

But Heart's generally apolitical stance of the '70s would shift during the next decade and the Wilson sisters' attitudes toward women-in-rock would also change. In the '70s, Ann told *Melody Maker*, "I've found that there is this void where female rockers should be . . . But the more women come into rock, the more people will understand women in rock." But in the '80s, the sisters became aware that the reality for women, still viewed as variations from the norm in the rock world, was quite different. "It still seems to be a big deal," says Nancy. "It's almost like it's set aside into a whole different category than music itself. We expected it to be more of an accepted thing than it even now seems to be. Especially in rock & roll—in rock bands, in real rock music, driving, kick-ass rock music, you don't find a lot of women. They're maybe just now starting to scratch the surface."

The '70s has become a decade much maligned by contemporary rock critics for its supposed lack of musical innovation. This supposition is supported in part by the lack of an identifiable "youth culture": when the counterculture movement of the '60s split into different factions in the '70s, the music scene also diversified in innumerable directions. As a result, the degree of change in such a fragmented musical climate appeared to be small. But in fact, women involved in the music industry were exploring more avenues than ever before. Singer-songwriters like Carole King and Joni Mitchell helped bring a decidedly female perspective to the pop charts in a substantial way for the first time since the girl group era. Performers like Labelle and Joan Armatrading continued to break down the racial barriers that divided music into "white" and "black" categories, and Suzi Quatro, the Runaways, and Heart tackled the gender stereotypes regarding women instrumentalists. Most importantly, performers were taking more control of their work through writing and production, and women working on the business side were also continuing to progress, moving into areas previously thought to be "closed" to women. The overall impact the inroads women were making would have on the music industry would not become apparent until well into the next decade. And with the arrival of punk, which momentarily turned the industry upside down, these inroads would become greater than ever.

6

Punk Revolution

"Anything went during punk."
—June Miles-Kingston (Mo-Dettes), in *Q*

976 is cited as the starting date for the "punk revolution," which began in Britain and soon crossed the Atlantic to the States, but in fact the definition of "punk" has always been somewhat problematic. The term "punk rock" had originally been used to describe music of American origin, specifically the garage rock that emanated from countless U.S. bands in the wake of the '60s British Invasion, including such bands as the Kingsmen, the Seeds, the Thirteenth Floor Elevators, the Trashmen, the Sonics, and innumerable others. When the term resurfaced in the '70s, it was haphazardly applied to many up-and-coming bands simply because they were new, young, sounded different, or were some combination of the above. A magazine cover headline even referred to Blondie as a "punk rock group," which probably seemed as ridiculous at the time as it does now (even the scruffy appeal of the group's debut LP in 1977 was tempered by the music's pure power pop overtones). The Jam was also initially labeled "punk," despite a look and sound that reflected the mod styles and rock sounds of the '60s.

In 1976, the music industry appeared to be going about business as usual on the surface. Donna Summer was riding high on the charts with "Love to Love You Baby" and disco was passing from the next big thing to fad to novelty status (Rick Dees's "Disco Duck" would top the U.S. charts that fall), all while generating plenty of money. Rock bands infatuated with technology were swamping their concerts with bank upon bank of instruments, for technique and skill were now more highly regarded than raw emotion among the rock elite. But not every music fan was enamored of boogie-ing down to a disco beat or grooving to the sounds of arena rock groups derisively referred to as "dinosaur bands." There was a new, younger generation coming up that was anxious to drag rock & roll back to its three-chord roots that everyone could understand (and, more important, play) and was intent on wresting the game away from the hands of the major record companies by starting their own independent labels and publishing their own magazines, such as the inexpensively xeroxed publications called "fanzines." In the wake of bands like the Sex Pistols, who helped make punk a household word, countless young people built upon the prevailing "if they can do it, so can I" attitude, and punk bands began springing up in abundance. Punk, and later new wave, a less frenzied, more melodic off-shoot of punk, emphasized initiative over technique; musical skills weren't important, but the desire to make music was. And with all the rules being broken, even if sometimes only for the sake of breaking them, women for the first time found it easy to join in the new movement from the start and be just as involved as their male counterparts. Why not? There was literally nothing to lose.

In addition to their musical legacy, the spirit of the mid-'60s garage rock bands and their successors, such as the Velvet Underground and the MC5, is readily seen in '70s punk. The music of Yoko Ono would also find its reflection in punk, though, unlike the Velvet Underground, Ono would rarely see herself listed as an influence in rock histories. This undoubtedly stems from her association with John Lennon, whom she met in 1966 and married in 1969. Given the reverence accorded to the Beatles, it was not surprising that Ono's liaison with Lennon placed her directly in the firing line for near-universal condemnation and scorn, especially when it became obvious that Ono was not afraid to speak her mind and refused to remain in the background as had the other Beatle wives. Linda Eastman, who married Paul McCartney eight days before Ono married Lennon, shared the burden of being "the women who broke up the Beatles," and the two women also experienced problems with obtaining songwriting credits on songs they later co-wrote with their husbands; EMI just didn't believe Ono and Eastman were capable of composing with Lennon or McCartney.

Ono also faced outright racism, evident in such headlines as "John Rennon's Excrusive Gloupie" in *Esquire*, though this was not a new experience: the Ono family had lived in the U.S. prior to World War II, but returned to their native Japan when tensions arose between the two countries as the conflict escalated. Ono was born in Tokyo in 1933 into a wealthy household; her mother's family was in banking, and her father had given up a career as a pianist to work as a banker in Japan, and later in branch offices in San

Francisco and New York. Ono was tutored in classical piano as a child, and in her teens began keeping notebooks of her writings. In 1953, after two terms as a university student in Japan, Ono moved with her family to join her father, now working in New York again. She lived in Scarsdale and attended the nearby Sarah Lawrence College (where Linda Eastman would later be a student), where she continued writing, though without finding much support in her new environment. "Whenever I wrote a poem, they said it was too long, it was like a short story," she said later. "And a short story was like a poem. I felt that I was like a misfit in every medium."

She also discovered avant-garde composers such as Arnold Schoenberg and Anton Von Webern and began seeing a Julliard student, Toshi Ichiyanagi, who shared her interest in the work of these composers and newer figures like John Cage. In 1956, she married Ichiyanagi against her parents' wishes, and the two moved to New York City. Ono later set up a loft on Chambers Street on the Lower West Side of Manhattan, eking out a meager living while pursuing her interest in the arts. In the early '60s, Ono's loft became the site of a series of performance events called "happenings," which presented any number of activities going on at once: music, poetry readings, and other types of "performance," such as Ono, dubbed "the High Priestess of the Happening," throwing dried peas at the audience while whirling her long hair to provide "musical accompaniment." Audiences were invited, and often encouraged, to participate during the "happenings."

By the mid-'60s, Ono was an established figure in the underground art scene; she had begun performing musical pieces, presented "events" with a loosely affiliated group of artists who worked under the name Fluxus, published a book of "instructional poems" entitled *Grapefruit* ("Hammer a nail in the center of a piece of glass. Send each fragment to an arbitrary address"), and was making films. But her work came in for frequent critical derision; when she performed in Japan as a solo artist in 1962, one American reviewer said she stole her ideas from John Cage. While in Japan Ono also divorced her first husband and married Tony Cox, a former art student; their child, Kyoko, was born in 1963. In 1966, she was invited to London to participate in a "Destruction in Art" symposium, where, among other works, she performed her now-famous "Cut Piece," in which she knelt on stage and invited the audience to cut off her clothing with a pair of scissors. Her appearance was a success, and she was then invited to hold her own exhibition at London's Indica Gallery. It was at a preview for her show, on November 9, 1966, that she first met John Lennon.

The two later admitted they shared a mutual attraction, but they would not become romantically involved until the spring of 1968, though Lennon would finance her "Half a Wind" show (which featured everyday objects such as cups and tables painted white and cut in half), which opened in October 1967. In the meantime, Ono remained in London, producing and directing the film *Bottoms*, which featured a series of 365 human bottoms (initially refused a certificate from the British Board of Film Censors as being "not suitable for public exhibition"); staging an "event" in which she wrapped the lions at the base of Nelson's statue in Trafalgar Square in white cloth; and performing in concert with Ornette Coleman at the Royal Albert Hall. Finally, in May 1968, Lennon invited Ono over to his house, and the two spent the night recording the bizarre tapes that would later become *Unfinished Music No. 1: Two Virgins*, released that November. The album's contents, avant-garde "noise" and spoken word snippets from the two, mystified the public, but the cover, which featured front and rear shots of Ono and Lennon in the nude, created an uproar. Though pressed on the Beatles' Apple Records label, neither EMI nor Capitol in America, who distributed Apple product, would carry it, so the record was distributed in a plain brown wrapper by two smaller companies; it was later claimed that the LP was technically a Top 20 hit in the U.S., but sales figures had not been reported because of the cover.

Ono and Lennon then unleashed a series of performances, recordings, and "events" on a public that alternated between incomprehension and outrage. Few seemed to appreciate the underlying humor in the couple's events, such as their public appearances in which they remained hidden in bags as a protest against judging by appearance. They also began holding "Bed-Ins" and on announcing their first, a "Bed-In for Peace" held in their honeymoon suite at the Amsterdam Hilton Hotel in March 1969, the press had fought to get in, thinking that the two would be having sex for the cameras; what they found was a pair of newlyweds, sitting in bed, wearing pajamas, and eager to talk about world peace. Another "Bed-In" in May 1969, this time in Montreal, resulted in the recording of their first single, "Give Peace a Chance," a Top 20 hit for the newly christened "Plastic Ono Band." The two also made films together, and continued their musical experimentations, making their first public performance together at Cambridge University in March shortly before their marriage. It was a show that demonstrated the schism between their respective audiences; the art crowd in attendance couldn't understand why Ono was working with a rock & roller, while the Beatles fans present hesitated to call Ono's material music.

Though their musical collaboration confounded many, it was a rejuvenating experience for Lennon, who had tired of the Beatles' conventional image but was at a loss as to how to find a new direction for his music. Playing with Ono freed him, and he enthusiastically praised her own perception of music in interviews. "If somebody with a rock oriented mind can possibly listen to her stuff you'll see what she's doing," he told *Rolling Stone*. "It's fantastic. She makes music like you've never heard on earth. It's like 20 years ahead of its time." The two released their first proper solo albums, *Yoko Ono/Plastic Ono Band* and *John Lennon/Plastic Ono Band* in 1970. These were records of more conventional material, as opposed to their experimental LPs, which by now included *Unfinished Music No. 2: Life with the Lions* and *The Wedding Album*, a lavish box set documenting their marriage, with a booklet of press clippings, photographs, and a cardboard slice of wedding cake. A live album, which documented their appearance at the 1969 Toronto Rock 'n' Roll Revival Show, gave a clue as to what the solo albums would sound like, with Side Two being an extended jam on Ono's numbers, "Don't Worry Kyoko (Mummy's Only Looking for Her Hand in the Snow)," and "John, John (Let's Hope for Peace)." The latter was the group's closing number; it went on for twelve minutes,

with Ono's voice and Lennon's guitar culminating in a neverending howl of feedback, during which the musicians left the stage.

Yoko Ono/Plastic Ono Band did not merely define the roots of what punk rock would become, it *was* punk rock, a harsh, confrontational barrage of noise in which the instrumentation and vocals were just barely restrained from tumbling over into complete chaos. Over a solid core of drums, played by Ringo Starr, a pumpedup bass played by longtime associate and artist Klaus Voormann, and Lennon's frenzied, scratching guitar, Ono's vocals consisted of little more than repeated, reverberating, ululating screams, with lyrics distilled to their primal essence. "Why?" was not just a song title, it was also the only word in the song. The album would probably have been hailed as innovative and exciting had it been released five years later, and

Yoko Ono in performance (John Lennon looks on) January 1972 at Alice Tully Hall, Lincoln Center, New York, Photo by Sherry Rayn Barnett

had Ono never had an association with any of the Beatles, but critics in the early '70s, trying to evaluate the record as a rock album, were bound to be confused, having absolutely no frame of reference in which to place Ono's music. The material on Ono's second solo album, *Fly* (released in 1971), was in a similar vein, including such numbers as the rock & roll parody "Midsummer New York" and the soundtrack to her short film *Fly*. But not all of Ono's songs were "primal screams"; her material also encompassed quiet ballads, such as the gentle "Listen the Snow Is Falling," and the haunting "Mrs. Lennon."

Ono was also an outspoken feminist, and during the early '70s many of her songs addressed the issue of women's equality. Her first explicitly feminist song was "Sisters O Sisters," a reggae-flavored anthem of unity first performed at a 1971 rally to free imprisoned writer/manager John Sinclair. Ono also introduced Lennon to the concept of feminism and co-wrote "Woman Is the Nigger of the World" with him, based on a line from one of Ono's interviews. The song (which Lennon sang) appeared on the Ono/Lennon LP *Some Time in New York City*, released in 1972, which also featured "Sisters O Sisters" and a cataclysmic live rendition of "Don't Worry Kyoko" recorded at a charity concert in 1969, when Ono and Lennon fronted a "Plastic Ono Supergroup" that included George Harrison, Eric Clapton, and Keith Moon, among others.

Ono's 1973 albums, *Approximately Infinite Universe* and *Feeling the Space*, were both her most accessible records of the decade and the most feminist-oriented. On *Approximately Infinite Universe* songs like "What a Bastard the World Is" focused on the inequality of female/male relationships, "I Want My Man to Rest Tonight" addressed the problems men have in coming to terms with their own sexism, and "I Have a Woman Inside My Soul" and "Death of Samantha" were moving portrayals of women who have repressed all feelings for the sake of outward appearance. In June 1973 Ono and Lennon attended an international feminist conference (sponsored by NOW) in Cambridge, Massachusetts, where the conference attendees stood up to join them in singing the chorus of "Woman Power" from *Feeling the Space* (released that November). The album also contained the songs "Woman of Salem," about the witch trials in colonial America and "Angry Young Woman," based on the life story of a woman Ono had met at the NOW conference. But none of Ono's work appeared in the charts, save for the *New York City* LP, which reached number 48; Ono also released solo singles, and her songs appeared on the B-side of most of Lennon's singles.

Ono and Lennon experienced a wealth of problems in their personal life during their early years together. Lennon in particular had been lambasted by the British public for divorcing his wife; Ono was awarded custody of her daughter following her divorce from Cox, but lost her when Cox kidnapped the girl and vanished. Ono and Lennon eventually moved to New York, where Lennon immediately became embroiled in a legal battle to remain in the U.S. that lasted for five years, during which time Ono and Lennon separated and then reconciled. Ono also had a number of miscarriages before giving birth to Sean Taro Ono Lennon on John's birthday in October 1975, and both Ono and Lennon had problems with drugs. These repeated crises were detailed far more in the press than Ono's—or even Lennon's—music ever was, and, expectedly, when the two put their musical work on hold after Sean's birth to deal with family business, it was Lennon's disappearance from the rock scene, and not Ono's, that was mourned in the press. Even when Onoesque vocalizations resurfaced in punk bands during the late '70s, her influence was scarcely acknowledged until the two returned to the music scene in 1980 and Lennon began pointing it out. A full reassessment of her music has yet to be done.

1975, when Ono and Lennon "retired," was the same year Patti Smith released her first album, building on the combination of rock and poetry that Ono had experimented with. It was around the same time that Ono was first working with Lennon that Patti Smith arrived in New York to immerse herself in the city's avant-garde arts scene, where, unencumbered by the media derision Ono faced, her impact on rock was both more immediate and more evident. Born in Chicago in 1946, Smith grew up in Pitman, New Jersey, under the spell of myriad influences: her love of '60s icons like Jim Morrison, Bob Dylan, Jimi Hendrix, and the Rolling Stones went hand in hand with the writings of such poets as William Blake, William Burroughs, Charles Baudelaire, and Arthur Rimbaud. Dropping out of college after becoming pregnant (and giving the baby up for adoption), Smith took a job in a New Jersey factory, saving enough money to finance her eventual move to New York City in the late '60s. Smith quickly fell in with the city's downtown art scene, where she met photographer Robert Mapplethorpe; after a trip to Paris in 1969, she shared a room with him at the Chelsea Hotel, a base for many in New York's art community.

While working as a clerk in a bookstore, Smith pursued writing, encompassing rock journalism (for the magazines *Creem* and *Rock*), plays (the loosely autobiographical *Cowboy Mouth*, which she co-wrote and performed with playwright Sam Shepard), and poetry. Smith also gave readings of her poetry, and in 1971 drafted guitarist and rock journalist Lenny Kaye to provide musical accompaniment. At the time, the music scene in Manhattan was changing directions from the progressive rock of the late '60s, and young, up-and-coming bands playing original music were searching the Lower East Side for places to play, spearheaded by the New York Dolls, a punky glam-rock group. One such venue was the Mercer Arts Center, a haven not only for rock bands playing original rock, but for other types of artistic endeavors as well; the performance space The

Patti Smith
November 1974 at the Whiskey-A-Go-Go, Los Angeles, Photo by Sherry Rayn Barnett

Kitchen was initially located at the Center, in, appropriately enough, the old kitchen of the space. When the Arts Center was forced to close in 1974, a narrow bar in the Bowery, CBGB and OMFUG (which stood for "Country, Bluegrass, and Blues and Other Music for Urban Gourmets") became the new headquarters for the growing music scene, along with another club, Max's Kansas City. In 1973, Smith added pianist Richard Sohl to what was becoming a full-fledged group, and met publicist Jane Friedman. Friedman suggested that Smith try singing, not just reciting, her poetry, then booked the group into the Mercer Arts Center and became Smith's manager. In 1974, the group, with the addition of Television's Tom Verlaine on guitar, recorded their first single, "Hey Joe (Version)"/"Piss Factory." "Hey Joe" was a garage rock cover that featured a monologue written by Smith for Patty Hearst; Smith's own "Piss Factory" was a spoken-word piece about her experiences on the New Jersey factory production line.

The single's first run of sixteen hundred copies sold out quickly, adding to Smith's growing reputation; the group, feeling it was outgrowing a trio format, next added Ivan Kral on guitar and bass, and Jay Dee Daugherty on drums. In 1975, the group played CBGB's and became the first of the new breed of rock bands emerging from Manhattan to be signed to a major label, when Clive Davis, who had signed Laura Nyro and Janis Joplin while president of Columbia Records, signed Smith to his new label, Arista. In late 1975, her debut album, *Horses*, was released, produced by the Velvet Underground's John Cale, and made a powerful impression in the rock scene. The cover itself (photographed by Mapplethorpe) made it clear Smith was no ordinary female singer: skinny, dressed in jeans and a white shirt with a tie draped around her neck, Smith faced the camera with a defiant, uncompromising stare. Her commanding, androgynous presence presented a view of a female performer that hadn't been seen on a record cover before, and the music on the record was just as striking. Opening with Smith's raw voice stating

"Jesus died for somebody's sins but not mine" before launching into a cover of Van Morrison's "Gloria," *Horses* freely mixed rock and poetry, a reflection of Smith's apparent disinterest in conventional song structures. "I'm not into writing songs," she told *Melody Maker*. "I find that real boring." Smith's biting delivery was something new for a female singer, but her music nonetheless began finding wide acceptance among rock audiences.

Her strong stance naturally provoked equally strong reactions. In Britain, the *New Musical Express* (*NME*) announced that *Horses* was a better first album than those of the Beatles, Rolling Stones, and Bob Dylan, but *Melody Maker* was not amused, huffing, "There's no way that the contrived and affected 'amateurism' of *Horses* constitutes good rock & roll." Smith further intrigued and/or irritated the press by refusing to play by the rules, such as not answering questions if she found them boring. Her frequent references to the French poets and rock heroes who inspired her also labeled her as pretentious to some, but her audiences were fanatically devoted, and members of the press were sometimes caught up in the spirit as well. "When I first sat down at my typewriter all I wanted to do was type 'It was great' over and over until I fell asleep," wrote a reviewer in *Sounds* of Smith's first appearances in Britain in 1976; London's *Evening Standard* more matter-of-factly observed, "She is the only girl singer I have ever seen spit onstage."

Smith's second album, *Radio Ethiopia*, was released in 1976, but it did not generate the critical excitement *Horses* had. Her career suffered a more serious setback in January 1977, when she fell off the stage during a performance in Tampa, Florida, and broke her neck. With all musical activities put on hold, Smith spent the next year undergoing physical therapy, in addition to writing *Babel*, another book of poetry. In 1978, Smith returned to live performance with a special Easter "resurrection" concert at CBGB's, with new keyboardist Bruce Brady, followed by the release of her third album, also entitled *Easter*. The show, and album, marked a triumphant return to form, with *Easter* giving Smith her first Top 40 hits; both *Easter* and "Because the Night," co-written with Bruce Springsteen during their respective recording sessions for *Easter* and *Darkness on the Edge of Town* at the same recording studio, reached the Top 20. If Smith's return was a welcome surprise, having a record in the Top 20 was an added bonus, one that pleased Smith immensely. "I think it's great that I have a hit single," she told *Rolling Stone*. "People say to me, 'Do you think you sold out?' They should be saying 'Oh wow, you're on AM radio.' To me, the place for us would be right out on the front line." For in spite of the derision Smith and her music sometimes received, she took rock & roll very seriously and viewed it as being capable of nothing less than salvation. "It's the only religion I got," Cavale, Smith's alter-ego in *Cowboy Mouth* explains to Slim

(Shepard), her would-be "rock-and-roll Jesus with a cowboy mouth." "Any great motherfucker rock-'n'-roll song can raise me higher than all of Revelations. We created rock-'n'-roll from our own image, it's our child . . . a child that's gotta burst in the mouth of a savior."

In addition to stretching the limits of what counted as valid artistic expression in rock, Smith's defiant stance as an outsider also hit home with her audience, as she noted in *Rolling Stone*. "I toured Europe more than America," she explained. "Those kids that bought *Horses* or 'Piss Factory' or heard about CBGB's became the Clash, became the Sex Pistols, became a million other bands—some that will make it and some that won't. But the important thing is that they became." Smith's arrival in the U.K. in 1976 coincided with the increasing notoriety of the Sex Pistols, and the growing momentum influenced any number of kids to waste little time in "becoming." But Smith herself was about to momentarily leave the rock arena. After the 1979 release of *Wave*, produced by Todd Rundgren, the Patti Smith Group embarked on their final tour. In March 1980, she married Fred "Sonic" Smith, guitarist with the MC5, and moved with him to the suburbs of Detroit, retiring from music to raise a family until the release of 1988's *Dream of Life*. Smith had little problem in leaving her career once she'd made her point, a perspective shared by some of the group. "I think what happened is that we'd done everything we'd set out to do," Kaye explained in a *Goldmine* interview. "Our first show was in February of 1971 in front of 200 people at St. Mark's Church, and our last show in Florence, Italy, in September 1979 was in front of 70,000 kids. Our story has a kind of completeness to it." After her husband's death in 1994, Smith returned to performing and has released three additional albums.

Other groups were now busily joining in the growing punk explosion, and the general public, as well as the rock establishment, was being suitably shocked. In Britain in particular, the Sex Pistols were synonymous with the term "punk rock" and its attendant scandal. Initially an underground phenomenon, the Sex Pistols emerged in late 1975 with the aid of their manager, professional *provocateur* Malcolm McLaren. McLaren had long been seeking ways of outraging the public; the clothing shop he ran on London's King's Road with his partner Vivienne Westwood had moved from selling Teddy Boy clothes (the drape jackets and crepe-soled shoes favored by British rock & roll fans in the '50s) to leather biker gear to bondage wear (and was now suitably called "Sex"), and he'd also tried his hand at management, having managed the New York Dolls in their final months. After turning his attention to the Sex Pistols, consisting of Johnny Rotten (John Lydon), Steve Jones, Paul Cook, and Glen Matlock (later replaced by Sid Vicious [John Simon Ritchie]), McLaren was hardly reticent about his motivations: "Rock and Roll is not just music. You're selling an attitude," he told *Rolling Stone* in 1977. In another interview he said that selling records was not the point ("That was the icing on the cake"); the point was "creating havoc" and "getting money from an industry which sorely wanted the Sex Pistols as part of their tame machine. That was the excitement of it all."

Certainly it was the Sex Pistols' "attitude," more than their music, that eventually granted them household name status. On December 1, 1976, prodded by Bill Grundy, host of the British television show *Today* to "say something outrageous," Jones obligingly responded with "you dirty fucker." THE FILTH AND THE FURY! screamed the next day's headline in *The Daily Mirror*, and the Pistols were well on their way to becoming, as Greater London Council member Bernard Brooke Partridge stated in the Pistols' "docu-drama" *The Great Rock 'n' Roll Swindle*, Public Enemy Number One. But the Pistols' reign was actually short-lived. After spending a further year outraging the British Isles, the group collapsed amid the disarray of their U.S. tour in early 1978, a tour that needled American sensibilities by eschewing metropolitan centers like New York or Los Angeles for appearances in such Bible Belt hot-spots as Memphis, Atlanta, and Dallas. But the reverberations of punk were to linger on, both as a music style and an "attitude."

This was especially true in Britain, which was seen as the birthplace of '70s punk despite the influence of U.S. '60s garage rock bands, later performers like the Velvet Underground, Yoko Ono, the New York Dolls, Patti Smith, the Ramones, and Richard Hell of the Voidoids, said to have invented the torn t-shirt look so associated with punk; even filmmaker John Waters (*Pink Flamingos, Female Trouble, et al.*) dressed his stars, particu-larly the flamboyant Divine, in clothes now easily recognizeable as punk fashion. But whereas punk influences took their time spreading throughout America, in Britain it was a whole different ball game. Because the U.K. was a good deal smaller than the U.S., new trends and fashions took hold faster. The music scene was also helped along by a fleet of music weeklies (*NME, Melody Maker, Sounds, Record Mirror*), whose frequency meant they were always on the lookout for new material, ensuring bands a greater chance of getting media coverage once they'd arrived on the club scene or released a record; even American groups frequently found it easier to get press coverage overseas than in their own country. Women at the music weeklies used the punk explosion to forge identities for themselves. Caroline Coon, a staff writer with *Melody Maker*, carved out her own niche as a champion of punk, and even managed the Clash for a brief period, though she found her gender caused problems ("Whatever I did was sabotaged by the fact that I had tits"). Other writers, such as Julie Burchill, who wrote the acidic examination of the punk scene *The Boy Looked at Johnny* with Tony Parsons (the title from a line in "Land" on Patti Smith's *Horses* LP), developed their own highly individualistic styles.

In Britain, the punk scene also had a political aspect that was not a part of the scene in the States. As Dierdre Rockmaker pointed out in an article on the Sex Pistols in *Gold-*

mine, the working-class roots of many of the bands made punk "a class movement disguised as a youth movement." The Pistols' "God Save the Queen," released in 1977 as a vitriolic commentary on the Queen's Silver Jubilee celebrations (commemorating the twenty-fifth anniversary of her coronation), not only attacked the monarchy but also the British class system. With unemployment on the rise in the U.K. throughout the decade, a growing number of young people were finding themselves with few options on leaving school other than immediately signing on the dole. The Sex Pistols expressed the anger and frustration of having "no future" in such songs as "Anarchy in the U.K." and "Pretty Vacant." Other groups, like X-Ray Spex, utilized a satiric edge in their work that was just as critical in its examination of contemporary society.

X-Ray Spex, one of the first punk bands to feature a dynamic female front person, was formed by Marion Elliot, who renamed herself "Poly Styrene" when she started the group. By not being thin, white, or conventionally "feminine," Styrene's mere presence in a rock band was enough to challenge convention, and her songs, which cheerfully attacked the materialism of the modern world, added to that challenge. Born in London to an interracial couple, Styrene had been writing songs since age twelve, and briefly worked behind the candy counter at Woolworth's while training as a clothes buyer before deciding to pursue a less traditional lifestyle. After a sojourn around Britain, Styrene ran her own clothing stall, named "X-Ray Spex," at Beaufort Market on King's Road, and soon decided to start a band. "I don't know how—I just did!" she said in *The Boy Looked at Johnny.* "It was just that time when anybody could form a band." She advertised for members; the resulting initial lineup also included Susan Whitby, a fifteen-year-old saxophone player, who, inspired by Styrene, promptly changed her name to Lora Logic.

The band made their first record appearance on the 1977 compilation *Live at The Roxy, London WC2,* performing the song that would become their first, and best, single, the explosive "Oh Bondage, Up Yours!" released in October 1977 on Virgin Records. Opening with a veritable battle cry as Styrene shrieked the title with glee, "Bondage" eagerly steamrolled over the idea of objectifying women by confronting the notion head on, though the intended irony of the verses was misunderstood by some and the single was banned by the BBC. "The way the frightened press deliberately misconstrued the anti-oppression song into a pro-repression message was reflected in the attitude to Poly herself," wrote Burchill and Parsons in *The Boy Looked at Johnny.* "Pretty, personable but determinedly asexual onstage, Poly was attacked by threatened male critics for having a brace [braces], a brain and no visible boyfriend." The single did not chart, but quickly became an essential item that found its way into every self-respecting punk record collection of the time.

The band's next singles, released by EMI, addressed such topics as "The Day the

World Turned Day-Glo," the crisis of "Identity" (both of which reached the Top 30), and Styrene's past in "Warrior in Woolworths." The band's sole album, *Germ Free Adolescents*, was released in 1978 and peaked at number 30, but Styrene soon succumbed to the pressures of feeling "owned" by the public and broke up the group in 1979. She released a solo album (*Translucence*) in 1980 before leaving the music business to become a Hari Krishna, and in 1986 released an EP, *Gods and Goddesses* (recorded in the Krishna's own recording studio, donated by Krishna devotee George Harrison). X-Ray Spex also reunited for a few shows in the '90s and released the album *Conscious Consumer* in 1995. Logic, who left X-Ray Spex after the release of "Oh Bondage," formed her own band, Essential Logic, and pursued a solo career; like Styrene, she also became a Krishna follower. X-Ray Spex's tenure may have been short-lived (in keeping with the life span of many punk groups at the time), but the band provided a ready inspiration for the groups that followed, and Styrene's rough and ragged singing style further established frenetic, idiosyncratic vocals as being the norm, leaving the door open for, and in fact encouraging, further experimentation.

A number of women performers sprang up in the wake of X-Ray Spex. Siouxsie and the Banshees released their first single on Polydor in August 1978, and Lene Lovich released her first single with Stiff Records in February 1979, though Siouxsie Sioux and Lovich, like Styrene, were primarily vocalists. In the energized atmosphere, bands also frequently swapped members. The original lineup of the all-female band the Slits had featured Arianna Forster (Ari Up) on vocals, Suzi Gutsy on bass, Kate Korus, formerly of the all-female Castrators, on guitar, and Palmolive, who played in the Flowers of Romance with Sid Vicious, on drums; Gutsy was replaced by another member of the Castrators, Tessa Pollitt, and Korus, who left to join the all-female Mo-dettes, was replaced by Viv Albertine, who'd also played in the Flowers of Romance. Like Fanny before them, the Slits caught some flack for their double-entendre name ("No one liked it," said Albertine. "It was obscene to everybody"). Their live debut came when they were invited to open for the Clash in 1977 on their "White Riot" tour, though by the time they recorded their first album, *Cut*, on Island Records in 1979, their music had changed dramatically from their earlier rock approach, and exhibited a definite reggae influence. The album's cover generated its own controversy, with the group pictured topless, wearing loincloths and slathered in mud; "Nobody could see the strength, the joke, the little twist that we were all a bit fat," explained Albertine. Other performers of the time included the all-female Raincoats (the group Palmolive joined after leaving the Slits in 1978), the Adverts, with Gaye Advert on bass, Penetration, with lead singer Pauline Murray (who later formed the Invisible Girls), the Delta 5, the Au Pairs, Toyah Willcox, and many others.

Women in the later bands were quick to acknowledge their debt to the earlier trailblazers: the Raincoats cited both the Slits and Patti Smith as inspirations, the Au Pairs' Lesley Woods pointed to Styrene and Sioux. Sioux herself extended a helping hand to the Scottish band Altered Images when lead singer Clare Grogan sent Sioux a tape along with a request to be the Banshees' opening act when they played Glasgow. Altered Images not only got the gig, they were invited to join the Banshees on their 1980 summer tour, and Banshees bassist Steve Severin had a hand in producing Altered Images' first album.

The Banshees became one of the few bands from the punk period to develop a long-running career. Siouxsie Sioux (Susan Ballion) had been a member of the "Bromley Contingent," a group of fans that followed the Sex Pistols from gig to gig, and she had also been on the set when the Pistols made their infamous appearance on the *Today* show, bantering with Grundy (his suggestion to Sioux "We'll meet again afterwards, shall we?" prompted Pistol Steve Jones to label Grundy a "dirty old man"). Given the do-it-yourself spirit of the punk movement, it was only a matter of time before Sioux decided to take the stage herself, which she did in September 1976 as part of the 100 Club Punk Festival, held at London's 100 Club. The short set, performed by an early lineup of Sioux, Marco Pirroni, Sid Vicious, and Steve Severin (whom she'd met in 1975 at a Roxy Music show), consisted of a medley of "The Lord's Prayer," "Twist and Shout," and "Knocking on Heaven's Door." An A&R rep from Island Records was quoted as saying "God, it was awful" and the Banshees were initially passed over by the major labels in the initial rush to sign punk bands after the success of the Sex Pistols. They finally secured a contract with Polydor in Britain in 1978, though their records were not released in America until the '80s.

"Hong Kong Garden," released in August 1978, made the British Top 10, and was followed by the Banshees' debut album, *The Scream*, in October. Sioux's cool, piercing vocal style was embellished through her highly theatrical and stylized use of make-up and costumes; while still part of the Bromley Contingent, she'd gained notoriety for her appropriation of such fascist paraphernalia as swastika armbands, in addition to leather bondage wear and "peek-a-boo" bras. But as a member of the Banshees, she tried to circumvent the media focus on the female lead singer that so frequently adds unwanted tension to a band, insisting that the group be interviewed together, though Sioux later admitted it was difficult to change people's preconceptions of the proper way to deal with a group. "We used to go to tremendous lengths to get the band idea across," she said in *New Women in Rock*. "But it was impossible to have four people at an interview and it was a waste of time anyway, because they just put all the quotes down to me."

But despite the egalitarian *Zeitgeist*, the new guard was just as capable of employing the same tricks as the old. Gaye Advert found that she had posed "naked" for publicity photos, when Stiff Records superimposed her head on a nude woman's body and offered Gaye as the prize to the sales rep who sold the most Adverts records. And despite the gains punk had made in opening doors for women, the only ones to find substantial commercial success were those in the mainstream who adhered to the tradition of woman-as-singer, like Debbie Harry or Kate Bush. Still, the comparative freedom available to performers on indie labels allowed women to investigate new options as musicians, and offered a potential platform to express one's views on social and political issues. Even if a group's lyrics were not outspoken politically, the performers felt freer to express views that showed a social awareness. "I didn't want to believe that it was any big deal being a girl, but I'm not exempt from discrimination," said Siouxsie Sioux in an interview, with a casualness that had been noticeably absent when performers discussed the issue of sexism earlier in the decade. "Even the words for women are horrible. Like spinster when she's not married. It sounds all shrivelled up. But the word for man is bachelor, and that sounds so carefree."

Some groups were explicitly political, both in their make-up and in their music. The Coventry-based indie label 2-Tone, founded in 1979, boasted a roster of racially integrated acts, including the all-female Bodysnatchers (who later became the Belle Stars), and the Selecter, with lead singer Pauline Black, who rocketed into the U.K. charts with a series of infectious songs about the racism, rioting, and youth unrest that had become a part of daily life in modern-day Britain. The rise in racial tensions had led to the formation of organizations like Rock Against Racism (RAR), which promoted concerts with the aim of bringing black and white bands and their audiences together (RAR's feminist counterpart was Rock Against Sexism). The subsequent mix of reggae and punk influences was expertly captured by 2-Tone, and songs like the Specials' "Ghost Town," released in 1981 as race riots were breaking out in London and Liverpool, were a clear reflection of the times. In 1982, one of the final 2-Tone singles, "The Boiler," addressed the issue of date rape (well before the term had come into popular usage) in an especially harrowing fashion. As performed by ex-Bodysnatcher Rhoda Dakar with a light, jazz-flavored backing from the Special A.K.A., the song's narrator related her story in a near deadpan voice, building to the climactic terror of her horrifying screams when she is unable to fight off her attacker. The single's subject matter resulted in its being banned by British radio, though it nonetheless reached number 35 in the British charts.

Feminist concerns were addressed by groups like the Raincoats, who recorded for the indie label Rough Trade, while bands such as the Delta 5 (who also recorded for Rough Trade) and the Au Pairs demonstrated new ways male and female musicians could work together. The Au Pairs, who were introduced to London audiences through RAR shows, were particularly uncompromising in their outlook, though gui-

tarist Lesley Woods (the group also included Paul Foad, June Munro, and Pete Hammond) stated the band hadn't deliberately intended to use the stage "as a political platform." *Playing With a Different Sex*, released in 1981 on Human Records, came on with
a sharp instrumental attack, the guitar-bass-drums base honed to a fine point, and
matched by equally pointed lyrics. Sex roles came under frequent scrutiny: "We're So
Cool" cynically reducing the freedom of open relationships to a refrain that only re-
establishes each partner's possessiveness, "Repetition" exploring the constraints of an
abusive marriage, and Woods and Foad sharing vocals in "Come Again," about a tepid
sexual encounter.

1982's *Sense and Sensuality* was musically subdued but maintained the lyrical intensity.
"Stepping Out of Line" neatly encapsulated the ideas that reduced women to sexual
nonentities:

> *You're a frivolous female*
> *A femme fatale with an evil intention*
> *You're a neo-hysteric*
> *A neurotic with a problem it's better not to mention . . .*
> *We've got you summed up, we've got you defined*
> *And you're stepping out of line. . . .*

Other topics that came under attack included Armagh Prison on *Different Sex* and President Reagan's administration on *Sensuality*. But in the wake of their second album, the
group split up because of "a lack of money, nervous breakdowns and drugs . . . the
usual rock 'n' roll story," Woods admitted in 1990. Like many groups of the time, the
Au Pairs' life span was brief, but their musical output was potent: the taut rhythms and
aggressive lyrics of *Different Sex* make it a classic example of how the influence of punk
could steer rock into exciting new areas.

In contrast to the political territory being explored by some of their contemporaries, the vocals of performers like Nina Hagen and Lene Lovich were more obviously indebted to the avant-garde approach set by Yoko Ono, a comparison Lovich
had experienced before she was a musician. "I was certainly aware of what she and
John were doing," she says, "because she was in the media, and she was a woman who
was doing her own artistic activity. Before I was even involved with music, people
would shout out to me on the street as if I was trying to copy her. I mean, anyone
who looks slightly different is either John or Yoko!" Others were quick to spot the
similarity between Hagen and Lovich, particularly in their topsy-turvy vocal gymnastics,
with musician/actor Ann Magnuson going so far as to merge their styles, sounds, and

names in creating a mock video for a singer dubbed "Lene Haagendaasovich."

Hagen, born in East Berlin in 1955, had moved to West Germany in 1976. Already a professional singer, she signed a contract with CBS Germany on arrival in the West, after which she traveled to London, where she met the Slits and collaborated on material with them. In 1977 she formed the Nina Hagen Band and recorded her initial albums in German, displaying her frenetic, guttural voice on such inventive covers as "TV Glotzer" (a reworking of the Tubes' "White Punks on Dope") and "Gott Im Himmel" (a cover of Norman Greenbaum's Top 10 hit "Spirit in the Sky"). Lovich and Hagen met in 1979 when both appeared in the film *Cha Cha*, and they have since maintained a personal and professional relationship. "We just had this good feeling about

Nina Hagen
January 1984 at Skoochies, Seattle, Photo by Cam Garrett

each other," says Lovich of their meeting. "It's like when you recognize somebody from the same planet, a kind of homey feeling." Hagen included a German-language version of Lovich's new wave hit "Lucky Number" on her 1980 LP *Unbehagan* and the two later sang together on "Don't Kill the Animals," an animal rights song that has appeared on various compilations.

Lovich, born Marlene Premilovich in Detroit to a British mother and Yugoslavian father, had little interest in music as a child though she did have a sense of civic pride in the accomplishments of Motown Records. "Every kid on the street in Detroit was really proud of the Motown success," she says. "It just seemed like a miracle that ordinary kids could be making music that would be successful. Stevie Wonder was about the same age as me, and having a hit at such an early age was really exciting for children, you know? We loved it! It seemed suddenly something better to do in life, although I never thought of myself ever being a singer."

At age thirteen, Lovich's parents divorced, and her mother returned to England with Lovich, her two sisters, and brother. In 1968, Lovich moved to London to attend art school, and from 1970 to 1973, she studied sculpture at London's Central School of Art. Unfortunately, Lovich found what she hoped would be a free-form environment of creativity to be limited in its approach. "Only certain kinds of art were accepted," she says. "In the sculpture department it was either heavy metal welded sculptures painted in bright colors—abstract, of course—or conceptual works where you all sat around and had a conference about it." But Lovich's years at art school were not a complete loss, for she met her future collaborator and partner, Les Chappell, with whom she has worked ever since. She also began meeting people involved in theater and music and eventually decided to try her own hand at music. "Music was exciting because it was more direct," she explains, "and it didn't seem to be such a small world. Music had so many different categories, and all were accepted. You could do anything you liked."

But initially, Lovich discovered that her voice wasn't necessarily something that would be accepted, or liked. "Singing was something that everyone could do," she says, "so I thought, 'I can open my mouth, I can make a sound, I can be in a band.' But it wasn't as simple as that. The sorts of bands I would've liked to have been in didn't want me, because there was nobody singing in the way I was singing. So I had to go away and work for about five years to learn more, be in other people's bands, learn an instrument, all these things to help me be more certain, to give me a bit more confidence." Lovich's experiences took her to the Continent, where her seemingly unconventional voice soon learned to adapt to a wide variety of mainstream material. "I worked in hotel bands, where you work for five hours a night," she explains. "We'd do everything, bossa novas, waltzes, Abba numbers . . . it was a marvelous education."

Lovich also experimented with playing different instruments. "I started out playing the guitar," she remembers. "I learned quite a few chords and I did play it in the band, but they said the look of concentration on my face was upsetting the audience!" Lovich then moved to violin, and eventually the saxophone. She also worked on material with French disco star Cerrone, and found work dubbing screams for horror films. When she returned to London, she began writing songs with Chappell, initially working in a group called the Diversions, who released singles on the Gull and Polydor labels. By 1978, Lovich had begun working as a solo artist, and Radio London DJ Charlie Gillett took a demo version of Lovich's "I Think We're Alone Now" to Dave Robinson, who ran the indie label Stiff Records. Robinson promptly signed her and released the song, backed with an early version of "Lucky Number," as a mail-order-only single.

Stiff, founded in 1976 by Robinson and Jake Riviera, was not a completely punk-oriented label, but did benefit from the interest punk generated; its slogans such as "If it ain't Stiff, it ain't worth a fuck" were very much in tune with the punk attitude. Lovich remembers the period as an exciting era of freedom. "It was really wonderful because all the record companies were totally confused," she says. "They didn't know what was going on. For the first time in a long time, the audiences were deciding what they wanted, instead of having to put up with what they were given. Of course, very quickly it became a kind of cliché, and even now you can go down Carnaby Street and buy punk stuff. But the whole idea of it in the first place was to do your own thing, which was really exciting, and people who couldn't play were getting up and playing because they really wanted to play. There was that good gut reaction. So the record companies left their doors open because they had to. And then as soon as they could, they shut them. It was really a short period of time."

But Lovich also observed that attitudes toward women frequently remained steadfastly the same. Once she was thrown offstage after being invited to jam with a band because the road crew "thought I was just some groupie or something. And I had my saxophone around my neck!" she exclaims. "I was aware that women can be noticed because they are a novelty. But to be taken seriously, to be given some sort of credibility, is much more difficult. I think it's because music is part of society, and you have to wait for society to catch up for things to change. I think many women would have liked to have done music, but you had to be willing to be completely manipulated, you know, 'Wear this dress, don't play the trumpet, play either guitar or piano, you can move as long as you shake your titties'—it was very confining. Stereotypes, really. I think the stereotypes are fairly strongly stamped in people's brains, especially people who run record companies.

"That's still the case, but you can go your own way now," she continues. "You're not guaranteed a lot of success, but you can go your own way because there have been a few precedents at least. Successful pop or rock music is very traditional. Think of all the bands that are in the charts now; they are playing traditional music from a traditional style. It's difficult for women to compete in that tradition because they haven't been there from the beginning. I think it'll be quite a long time before it becomes perfectly normal. Women still look awkward playing guitars and things like that because there's not that length of tradition; it's still a bit of a novelty."

Lovich was able to change some perceptions of female musicians when she was asked to audition for the film *Breaking Glass*, released in Britain in 1980. By that time, Lovich had released two albums, *Stateless* and *Flex*, and a number of singles, with "Lucky Number" reaching number 3 in the British charts in 1979, and she had successfully toured in both Britain and the U.S. (where, strangely, her quirky new wave pop drew comparisons with the more confrontational music of Patti Smith). *Breaking Glass* was the story of a punk rocker's rise to national success, with the lead role originally written for a man. Urged on by Charlie Gillett, Lovich met with the producers, who later came to see one of her performances. "They told me that after seeing my show, they thought the lead should be female," she says. "They picked my brains a lot and asked what I thought the future of music was going to be in the next five years, and that sort of thing." But when offered the part, Lovich decided against taking it. "They modeled the whole starring role on me and they really wanted me to play it," she says. "But I thought the role was too close to me, yet it really wasn't me. People would think it was my life story and yet it wasn't my life story. And there wasn't enough fantasy in it for me. I really don't like films that are about everyday life. It doesn't interest me. I never go see films about divorces."

In the end, singer Hazel O'Connor was chosen to play the role of "Kate" in *Breaking Glass*; she also wrote and sang all the songs in the film, netting three U.K. Top 40 hits for herself in the process. Though successful in Britain, *Breaking Glass* was derided in some corners for being too obviously corny in the *A Star is Born* tradition. More disturbingly, the film reflected none of the progression women had made in the realm of punk and new wave, for "Kate" turns out to be just as easily manipulated as any stereotypical female musician; despite her protestations that she doesn't want/need a manager or record contract she winds up with both, in addition to becoming just the sort of musician her character is supposed to despise—a blatantly packaged "image" constructed by the predatory executives who work for a record company prophetically titled "Overlord." Kate eventually suffers a drug overdose that nearly kills her, but is given the will to go on when her erstwhile manager/boyfriend "Danny" (Phil Daniels, star of *Quadrophenia*), visits her in the hospital and brings along her trusty portable keyboard (the overdose/recovery ending was cut from U.S. prints of the film).

But *Breaking Glass* was at least truer in spirit to the realities of the street than such British productions as the television series *Rock Follies*, which followed the adventures of a vocal trio called the "Little Ladies." Shown at the height of the punk era in the U.K., the "Little Ladies" didn't even play any instruments, and the short haircut of Julie Covington's character was the only acknowledgment of punk's existence. In comparison, Derek Jarman's film *Jubilee*, originally released in Britain in 1978, and one of the first nondocumentary features to deal with the phenomenon of punk, offered a radically different perspective of women in rock. Set in Britain at an undetermined future date, *Jubilee*'s London setting is unrelentingly grim: the city streets deserted save for roaming gangs, the Queen assassinated, and Buckingham Palace turned into a recording studio. The loosely knit storyline follows the adventures of a group of friends living in a ramshackle loft, with the female characters clearly the dominant—and lethal—force, going on murderous rampages out of revenge or simply boredom. Many of the women involved in *Jubilee* also had direct ties to the punk community: Little Nell appeared in the musical *The Rocky Horror Show*, a campy update of horror films which offered the perfect do-it-yourself punk credo in the song lyric "Don't dream it, be it" (she also released solo singles and appeared in *Rock Follies*); Toyah Willcox, who performs with an all-female band called the Maneaters in *Jubilee*, later released her own records and appeared in *Quadrophenia*; and Jordan, a legendary punk personality, had worked in Malcolm McLaren's clothing shop, managed Adam Ant (who was also in *Jubilee*) and shocked people simply by going around London wearing outlandish clothes. The Slits and Siouxsie and the Banshees also put in brief appearances in the film.

When *Jubilee* was released in the States in 1979, it made little sense due to the fact that a number of scenes were cut. That same year Jarman had a new project in release, three shorts he'd directed set to the music of Marianne Faithfull, who had resurfaced in 1979 with *Broken English*, a collection of songs that surprised everybody with their immediacy and power. Since her days as a '60s icon, Faithfull's life had gone from bad to worse, and to most people she was just another name from the past. Her liaison with Mick Jagger had led to an unending series of problems; at the famous drug bust at Keith Richards's house in 1967, she arguably gained more notoriety than Richards or Jagger (who actually faced the drug charges) by simply being present wearing nothing but a fur rug, and she was condemned by churches across Britain for openly living with Jagger and refusing to marry him even after becoming pregnant (she later miscarried). Following a suicide attempt in 1969, she eventually split with Jagger in 1970 and was on her own.

Faithfull's recording career had also suffered during her involvement with Jagger. "I didn't understand then that it was very important for me to work, whatever happened in my life," she later admitted. In 1967, she released her final album of the '60s, *Love in a Mist*, and in 1969 released her final single, Goffin and King's "Something Better," backed with her own "Sister Morphine," which she later referred to as "really my first song." Later covered by the Rolling Stones (Jagger had primarily written the music, and later difficulties with the Stones kept Faithfull from receiving royalties for many years), Faithfull's version sounds a sad, despairing note atypical of the '60s good vibrations, but indicative of Faithfull's own growing involvement with drugs. Faithfull had also pursued acting, appearing in London theater productions of Chekhov's *Three Sisters* with Glenda Jackson, *Early Morning, Hamlet*, a film version of *Hamlet*, and as a leather-clad biker in *Girl on a Motorcycle*, but her dramatic career was also curtailed by her drug use.

In 1974, David Bowie asked Faithfull to appear in his television special, *1980-Floor*

Show, in which she sang three numbers. "Bowie was the first person who came along and started to try to haul me back," she said in a radio interview. "I didn't want to do it. And now, when I look back, I can see that it was crucial. He planted something; self-respect." In 1975, she released a single, "Dreamin' My Dreams," followed in 1978 by the country-flavored LP *Faithless*, which included a cover of Jackie DeShannon's "Vanilla O'Lay." "Dreams" gave her a number 1 hit in Ireland, but Faithfull saw the records more as a way for her to start working again. "[Country music] wasn't what I really wanted to do," she later explained. "I was still looking around for how I could express what I wanted to say." When punk came along, she realized she'd found her answer. "I liked it because it was unstudied and unpretentious," she said. "And it was very angry too, and I could identify with that. It just made me feel that this was probably an arena I could work in." She recorded demos of "Broken English" and "Why D'ya Do It?" which play-wright Heathcote Williams had written hoping Tina Turner might perform it. "I just laughed," Faithfull remembered in *Interview*. "'You think Tina Turner would do this? You're out of your mind. You won't get anyone else to do this, so let me have it.'" The demos attracted the attention of Chris Blackwell, who signed Faithfull to his label, Island Records, and released *Broken English* in 1979.

To those who had missed *Faithless*, Faithfull's vocals on *Broken English* appeared to have gone through an incredible transformation from her sweet schoolgirl lilt of the "As Tears Go By" days; her raw, cracked voice painted a vivid picture of the hard life she'd lived. The songs on the album, three of the eight co-written by Faithfull, were equally stunning, making *Broken English* one of those rare LPs in which virtually every song is a classic. The title track opens the album on a haunting note, while "Why D'ya Do It?" the final track, seethes with the anger Faithfull admired in punk; "Guilt" jumps with an underlying, unresolved tension, and her powerful covers include evocative versions of John Lennon's "Working Class Hero" and Shel Silverstein's "The Ballad of Lucy Jordan," the story of a housewife who winds up being driven mad by the boredom of domesticity (later used in the film *Thelma & Louise*). Though failing to find a place on the charts, *Broken English* was a highly acclaimed work and represents Faithfull's true musical coming-of-age, establishing her once and for all as a serious artist who would never be solely remembered as "the girlfriend" again; over the subsequent decade she released the albums *Dangerous Acquaintances*, *A Child's Adventure*, and *Strange Weather* (which included a newly recorded version of "As Tears Go By"). 1990 saw the release of the powerful live recording *Blazing Away*, recorded at St. Anne's Cathedral in Brooklyn. Faithful has released five albums since, and also returned to acting.

In contrast to the U.K., the U.S. had relatively few women involved in its punk music scene, despite the seeds of inspiration laid by Yoko Ono and Patti Smith. But the few women who were present were often integrated into their bands as apparent equals, with little attention given to the fact that they were female, such as Poison Ivy Rorschach, guitarist for the Cramps, and Tina Weymouth, bass player for Talking Heads. The music was also grounded more in artistic experimentation, or in a revamping of rock & roll's roots, without the political perspective that was a part of the British music scene.

The Cramps in particular created an incendiary blend of '50s rockabilly and '70s punk (dubbed "psychobilly" by the group "to whip people up into coming to our shows"), tossing in an abundance of references to the tackier side of American culture, such as grade-B sci-fi and horror films and comic books. It was a combination that made the Cramps critical favorites, in addition to winning them a substantial cult audience. The band was formed in the mid-'70s by Ivy (Kristy Wallace) and her "partner in crime" Lux Interior (Erick Purkhiser), who shared a mutual fascination for grade-B Americana and '50s rock & roll, but found the options for doing anything interesting limited in Cleveland, their home at the time. "There was no place in Ohio where you could have an original band," Ivy told *Guitar Player*. "We knew that CBGB's was starting to happen . . . we loved the New York Dolls . . . we had boring jobs, we were taking speed, and with the combination of those things we ended up going to New York." With an early lineup that featured Lux on vocals, Ivy and Bryan Gregory on guitars, and Miriam Linna on drums (soon replaced by Nick Knox [Stephanoff]), the Cramps debuted at CBGB's in 1976, and released their first single, "The Way I Walk"/"Surfin' Bird," on Vengeance Records in April 1978.

With Lux as the lead singer, less attention was focused on Ivy, though her form-fitting outfits sometimes drew more comment than her musical abilities. Other critics missed the humor in the group's raunchy lyrics, which Ivy attributed to "people confusing sexism with sexy." "Our band's been accused of being sexist," she says, "which is really absurd, because the women in our band are doing something totally original [a number of women have played with the band in various lineups]. They're not mimicking something men have done or that other women have done. I haven't tried to think up a particular female role to be. What I'm doing is, I'm totally dedicated to playing rock & roll. I love it. It's what I've listened to all my life." She dismissed her own encounters with sexism as "pretty trivial" ("I go into a guitar store and they call me sweetheart"), but admitted she found remarks like "you play as tough as a guy" irritating. "That's insulting," she told *Guitar Player*. "No guy taught me to play. I taught myself . . . I'm sure that there's even something about being a girl that has an original flare to it, and women should try to allow that to come out in their playing."

In comparison to Ivy, who has gone on to become the Cramps' manager and their sole producer, Tina Weymouth's role in Talking Heads has remained low-key. The band was an off-shoot of the Artistics (occasionally billed as the "Autistics"), a group founded by guitarist David Byrne and drummer Chris Frantz while both were students at the Rhode Island School of Design in the early '70s. Like Lene Lovich, the two had become disenchanted with art school and drifted into music. They later asked another student, Martina Weymouth, to join them, though Byrne later admitted he was hesitant to have a woman in the group ("Rock 'n' roll is thought of as a male music. I wasn't sure how it would be received," he told Caroline Coon in *Melody Maker*) and when the band was signed to Sire Records, Byrne made Weymouth audition again to keep her place in the group. For her part, Weymouth tended to admit the existence of sexism while denying it was a problem for her. "Women musicians tend to be treated by critics like women drivers," she said. "If they aren't much good, well what can you expect? And if they're hot stuff, it is despite the fact that they are women," adding "I simply can't be bothered with this [Women's] Lib analysis." But a 1981 interview in *The Face* showed she was well aware of her image as a role model and saw her choice to downplay her gender as a positive thing. "One thing I did that I'm glad about in retrospect is that I never talked about the problems of being a woman," she said. "I didn't want to discourage anyone who had the same idea. I didn't want to make it look like an uphill trek, which it was."

The Artistics eventually moved to New York and became Talking Heads in 1975 with the addition of guitarist/keyboard player Jerry Harrison, formerly a member of Jonathan Richman's Modern Lovers. The band quickly found a place in the growing Manhattan scene, playing CBGB's, and sharing bills with bands like the Ramones and Blondie. By 1977, they were signed to Sire Records, with their first single, "Love Goes to a Building on Fire," and the album *Talking Heads: '77* released that same year. The group's songs, primarily written by Byrne, were more satirical and less abrasive than those of their punk contemporaries and were accordingly dubbed "literate rock" by the critics; ironically, it was a cover of Al Green's "Take Me to the River," from their second LP, *More Songs About Buildings and Food*, that gave Talking Heads their first Top 40 hit in 1978.

Weymouth's own role in the group, since she was not projecting any sort of extreme persona that could be readily categorized (tough chick, snarling punk, mainstream feminine singer), was read as being asexual. "She exudes chaste self-assurance," wrote an *NME* writer; another British journalist saw her as "a kind of friendly Mother Superior." But the attention placed on Weymouth as "the woman in the band" still produced tension, adding to the uneasiness developing between Byrne and the other members as the band's popularity continued to grow. "David assumed credit for everything that ever happened in Talking Heads," Weymouth later explained to *Rolling Stone*. "And we allowed that to happen." After the release of 1980's *Remain in Light* (which featured a guest appearance from Nona Hendryx), Weymouth and Frantz, who had married in 1977, decided to re-establish their independence and formed the Tom Tom Club. The group, which included two of Weymouth's sisters as vocalists, released their first single, "Wordy Rappinghood," in 1981, followed that year by a self-titled debut LP and a further single, "Genius of Love," which reached the Top 40. Building on Talking Heads' growing interest in African polyrhythms, evident on *Remain in Light*, the music of the Tom Tom Club explored equally rhythmic and danceable terrain, with "Wordy Rappinghood" giving white audiences an early taste of rap, a musical movement developing in New York's black communities. The group also provided a musical outlet for Weymouth and Frantz during the times when Talking Heads were inactive. Talking Heads disbanded in 1991; Tom Tom Club's latest album, *The Good the Bad and the Funky*, was released in 2000.

The B-52's had an easier time of being seen as a complete band, for though the two women in the group, Cindy Wilson and Kate Pierson, were the primary vocalists, Fred Schneider was also a vocalist, and the band's eccentric image was equally played up by all members. The five members, including Wilson's brother Ricky and Keith Strickland, formed the group in 1976 in Athens, Georgia, where the Wilsons and Strickland were born. Though their musical experience varied greatly—Pierson had performed in a folk group, the Sun Donuts, Schneider had played in local bands, and Strickland was a drummer in rock groups during high school—the five friends were inspired to start their own group over drinks at a Chinese restaurant. They made their debut at a party on Valentine's Day in 1977, with vocalist Cindy Wilson on guitar and percussion, Pierson and Schneider on guitar and keyboards in addition to their vocal duties, Ricky Wilson on guitar, and Strickland on drums. The group's wacky tongue-in-cheek image included the copious use of thrift store clothing, and, in the case of Wilson and Pierson, towering bouffant wigs, hairstyles known colloquially in the South as "B-52's." Later that year the B-52's traveled to New York with another Athens group, the Fans, and left a tape at Max's Kansas City, which later brought the group back for their New York debut in December; Pierson later recalled the audience thought she and Wilson were drag queens because of their wigs.

By 1978, the group had released their first single on the Boo-Fant label, the classic "Rock Lobster." In many ways still the quintessential B-52's song, "Rock Lobster" offered a perfect illustration of the primary ingredients of the group mixed to their ultimate potency, at once quirky, off-beat, experimental, and highly danceable. The frenetic warblings of Wilson and Pierson would not have been out of place on Yoko Ono's

"Why?" and indeed John Lennon was said to have been musically inspired by hearing the song while in a Bermuda disco, saying, "Grab the axe and call mother!" and later telling Ono, "They're ready for you this time" (the B-52's later covered Ono's "Don't Worry Kyoko"). In 1979, the group signed with Warner Bros. and released their self-titled debut album, produced by Chris Blackwell, whose Island Records released the B-52's material overseas. The B-52's kitschy appeal won them an instant audience, particularly in Britain. The group's second album, *Wild Planet*, released in 1980, became their first Top 40 hit, though their big commercial breakthrough would not arrive until 1989, when their album *Cosmic Thing* hit the Top 10 along with two Top 10 singles.

But the woman who was probably most identified with the rise of punk and new wave in America was undoubtedly Debbie Harry, the lead singer of Blondie, who simultaneously updated and poked fun at the conventions of '60s pop and the girl group persona, though the group's breakthrough hit in America was the disco-oriented single "Heart of Glass." Born in 1946 in Miami, Florida, Harry grew up in New Jersey and arrived in New York City in the late '60s with the intention of making a living as a performer. Her first gig was as a singer with the folk group the Wind in the Willows, though Harry saw singing as only one facet of what she might do. "I think what drew me to singing at first was that I was a natural singer," she says, "so that made it very easy. But I was very interested in the performance value. I was more of a performer than a technician, although I've become a better technician over the years."

Wind in the Willows released one album in 1968 before disbanding, and Harry worked numerous odd jobs (Playboy bunny, waitress at Max's Kansas City) while waiting for her next break. By 1974, she was singing with the all-female trio the Stilettos, and had tried her hand at songwriting, including the Stilettos' signature tune "I Want to Be a Platinum Blonde." Chris Stein, a former art student, eventually joined the group on guitar, and soon Harry and Stein decided to form a new group, taking on bassist Gary Valentine, James Destri on keyboards, and Clement Burke on drums to form Blondie, who struggled to find a place for themselves in Manhattan's music scene. "It was an exciting period," Harry remembers. "I was influenced by the spirit of the times and the fact that there was a renaissance of sorts between painters and photographers and musicians. I was real lucky to be involved in it, glad I was in the right place at the right time."

In 1976, the group signed with Private Stock, which released the group's self-titled debut album, produced by girl group veteran Richard Gottehrer, that year. Ellie Greenwich provided backing vocals, despite having been unimpressed with the band's demo tape, which she'd heard when the group was looking for a record deal. "They really weren't very good, and I was looking for more of a voice," she admitted in *Will You Still*

Love Me Tomorrow? "But little did I know!" The bristling powerpop edge of Blondie's music had little in common with the brashness of punk, but Harry viewed it as being just as radical. "Musically it was a reversal to the pop thing that existed in the '60s," she says. "And at that time in the mid-'70s, it really wasn't so accessible, it wasn't available on records that much. And it was a new version of that, so it was sort of shocking in that respect." She also notes how her own role in the band challenged convention. "It was a pop that was very aggressive, and with a female front person," she explains, "and an aggressive female front person had never really been done in pop. It was very difficult to be in that position at the time—it's hard to be a groundbreaker."

The band broke little ground in America at first, though *Blondie* was well received overseas and the single "In the Flesh" reached number 2 in Australia. But in the States, Blondie wasn't even able to get radio airplay, something Harry attributes to a "boycott." "I think with new things there's always a certain amount of reluctance," she says. "You have to build up credibility. In a way, that in itself is good, because it makes you work harder and do it right." Blondie, minus Gary Valentine, then moved to Chrysalis, who released *Plastic Letters* (again produced by Gottehrer) in 1977. Though not as distinctive as its predecessor, *Plastic Letters* gave the group further hits overseas, including a cover of "Denis," a hit for Randy and the Rainbows in the early '60s, chosen as a single by Harry against the group's opposition, and "(I'm Always Touched by Your) Presence, Dear," both of which reached the Top 10 in Britain; the album also reached number 10. And again, America remained disinterested. That would change dramatically in 1978 with the release of *Parallel Lines*, produced by Suzi Quatro's producer Mike Chapman, whose penchant for slickness Harry viewed with some wryness: "I think he thought it was a comedy album and it turned out to be music," she says. But Chapman's touch worked well with Blondie's material, the group had additional musical talent with two new members, Nigel Harrison and Frank Infante, and the album reached number 6 in the states in 1979, with "Heart of Glass" becoming an international smash and the group's first number 1 single in the U.S.

As Blondie's lead singer and the group's only female member, Harry naturally came in for the most scrutiny by the media. Chrysalis had already played up this angle overseas, using the title of "Rip Her to Shreds" from *Blondie* to caption a promotional poster of Harry "Wouldn't You Like To Rip Her To Shreds?" For her part, Harry felt that the slogan "Blondie Is A Group," coined by their first manager, actually drew more attention to the fact that she was female: "He built that into a problem because it really wasn't a problem until he made that statement," she contends. She also found that her work as one of the band's primary songwriters (responsible for much of the group's best work, like "X Offender," "One Way or Another," "Heart of Glass," "Call Me," and

Debbie Harry of Blondie
October 1989 at the Moore Theater, Seattle, Photo by Cam Garrett

"Dreaming") was being overshadowed by her role as the group's sex symbol. "In the early days there weren't a lot of serious music articles written about us," she says. "Those came a little bit later. I think that Patti Smith, because of her intellectual nature and her identity as a poet, was taken very seriously and was praised for her work as a writer, and because I approached my work as a pop figure, it was overlooked at first."

Harry also admits that the exclusive focus on her had a detrimental impact on the group. "We tried to focus on the group image, and it was so difficult," she says. "It's automatic that the vocalist whether it's a man or a woman, is singled out and is more often than not the spokesperson for the band. I think if we had been an all-girl band or an all-male band it would have been a little bit simpler. But obviously we didn't handle it too well since the band isn't together!" Blondie also had problems maintaining their momentum into the '80s, though this was not immediately apparent. 1979's *Eat to the Beat* did not match the success of *Parallel Lines*, nor did the singles from the album, "Dreaming" and "Atomic" (both of which also featured backing vocals from Ellie Greenwich), the chart as highly, but "Call Me," theme song from the film *American Gigolo*, gave the group another number 1, followed by two more number 1's with the reggae-flavored "The Tide Is High" and "Rapture," both taken from the 1980 LP *AutoAmerican*.

"Rapture" was one of the first songs to introduce rap to a mainstream audience, in the year after the Sugarhill Gang's "Rapper's Delight" had reached number 36 in the charts. The extended rap in the middle of "Rapture" was inspired by Harry's and

Stein's interest in New York's graffiti/breakdance subculture and a meeting with graffiti artist Fab 5 Freddie (who receives a special mention in the rap, along with DJ Grandmaster Flash). But *AutoAmerican* proved to be the last hurrah for the band, who foundered in the wake of 1982's *The Hunter* and its accompanying single "Island of Lost Souls," neither of which fared well on the charts; the situation was additionally complicated by Stein's three-year battle with pemphigus. "Everyone in a way outgrew the band," Harry explains. "We actually did become a pop phenomenon, and that was what the goal was. So once you've achieved that and you have a bunch of people that are creative and not just stagnant, you want to do independent projects. Jimmy did a solo record, I did a solo record [1981's *KooKoo*], and everybody started playing on other people's records, and Chris started his own label and was producing. I think it was partially that, partially business, and partially personality." But though Blondie had split (the group would reform in 1998), there was already an influx of new wave/post-punk bands capitalizing on the group's power pop sound, carrying the band's influence into the next decade.

Punk had made its mark on the West Coast, too, though the music there was harder and faster (hence the name "hardcore"), and without the artistic elements of the East Coast scene. There was also a notable lack of women involved, though one woman would prove to be invaluable in documenting the West Coast punk scene during its heyday—Penelope Spheeris. Born in New Orleans, Spheeris had a strong interest in music from childhood. "I listened to music to take my mind off my troubles, as an escape," she says. "And I think still, today, that's why kids listen to music." Her interest intensified when she discovered her "ultimate get-off" while a film student at the University of California in Los Angeles. "I love putting music to film—that's my drug, since the first time I did it," she says. "I was in school, and I put Traffic together with my sister riding a motorcycle. A Harley. It was bitchin'. And I went, 'Ah, this is my calling in life, putting music to film.' I still love it. I'm here to pave the way for all the other women who might get off on the same thing later!"

Spheeris and film director Donna Deitch (who later directed the film *Desert Hearts*) were among the few female students at UCLA's film school, and Spheeris herself was the first woman to work in the school's technical office, which loaned equipment to the students. The lack of women as role models kept Spheeris from labelling herself a "director" despite her work in film. "I never really said I was going to be a film director because there weren't women film directors back then," she explains. "The only women film directors were Lina Wertmuller and Leni Riefenstahl. And I didn't have a German name, so I figured well, I must not be a film director. It took me years to call myself a film director." After college, Spheeris worked as an assistant editor on various educational films and started her own company, Rock 'n' Reel, which produced films for the music industry, including promotional films (forerunners of videos) for such artists as the Doobie Brothers, Fleetwood Mac, Kenny Rogers, and David Essex.

An association with Albert Brooks led to her producing his short films for *Saturday Night Live* in the mid-'70s and his feature-length work, including 1979's *Real Life*. "The logical, practical person would have gone on to produce other feature films," she says, "because I had my foot in the door with the establishment-type people. But no, I have to be the rebel as usual. I have to go off and make a documentary about punk rock music." The documentary was *The Decline . . . of Western Civilization*, and behind its inception lay a dual fascination with the documentary format and the punk movement. "I'd never seen anything like that," she says of her trips to the punk clubs. "It was a movement I was just astounded by. I realized somebody had to document it. The whole scene was like a total anarchy carnival."

As a fan of the music, Spheeris was less intimidated by the critical attitudes of many of the L.A. punks. "They generally were pretty intelligent people," she says. "They were making new trends, they were breaking tradition. They were into something new." She also observed a sexual "equality" that seemed due more to a denial, rather than a challenging, of sex roles. "In the punk rock days, the girls cut their hair and wore big boots and got tattoos and wore big belts like the boys. I think generally when you're a teenager you're looking, desperately searching, for identity. And part of that search has to do with sexual identity. But in the punk rock days, they sort of liked to deny that sex existed, which is really funny now, 'cause they all have babies." Spheeris would later update her look at the L.A. music scene in *The Decline of Western Civilization Part 2: The Metal Years* (in addition to directing a more tongue-in-cheek representation of the metal scene in the 1992 hit *Wayne's World*), but the reception of the first *Decline*, released in 1980, disappointed her. "It was looked at like some street level rebellion movie," she remembers. "Now, ten years later, it's acquired a sort of classic status, and everyone's got the respect for it they certainly did not have when it was first released. But it was good for me as a filmmaker to have been through that experience, because whenever I run up against negative criticism now I just think, 'Well, who knows? Maybe what I'm doing will be a classic in ten years.'"

One of the bands Spheeris documented was X, a high-energy outfit that featured Exene Cervenka sharing vocals with her then-husband John Doe. Born in Chicago in 1956, Christine Cervenka later moved to Florida and left for Los Angeles in 1976. A poet, Cervenka initially had no desire to go into music, especially at a time when she found no women to look up to as role models except Patti Smith and having no idea she would come to be seen as her generation's Patti Smith. In 1977, Cervenka met John

Exene Cervenka of X (John Doe, left)
October 1982 at the Showbox, Seattle, Photo by Pete Kuhns

Doe at a poetry workshop held at the small press library where she worked. Doe, a bass player, was playing with two friends, guitarist Billy Zoom and drummer Mick Basher in a band, and he invited Cervenka to join the group as a vocalist, though the other members later admitted they were initially less than enthusiastic about working with a woman they regarded more as "John's girlfriend" than a musician. The songwriting and atonal harmonies Cervenka and Doe created soon changed their minds, and the band took their name, X, from her newly adopted first name, Exene.

X quickly established a local following by playing in such punk venues as the legendary Masque, a hole in the wall located in the basement of a porno theater, embellished with such graffiti as "Hippies Go Home!" In 1978, D. J. Bonebrake replaced Basher on drums and the group released their first single, "Adult Books"/"We're Desperate" on the Dangerhouse label. In 1979, after being turned down by the majors, X signed with the indie label Slash, and their first album, *Los Angeles*, was released in 1980, produced by the Doors' Ray Manzarek, who also produced the group's next three LPs. *Los Angeles* burned with a fierce energy as the band dissected the city they viewed with a caustic eye: "You just feel everyone's insane there," Cervenka told *Rolling Stone*. Musically the group drew on such diverse influences as rockabilly, the blues, and country in addition to the barreling hardcore beat, and, with a nod to their producer, covered the Doors' "Soul Kitchen."

The album was a critical favorite and after the release of *Wild Gift* in 1981, X was able to make the move to a major label (Elektra) for their subsequent releases. Cervenka also continued writing poetry: the book *Adulterers Anonymous* featured her work along with that of New York performer/poet Lydia Lunch. X also exhibited their social awareness by performing at benefits, which Cervenka says later inspired her to form the acoustic country group the Knitters (named after the Weavers) with Doe, with the idea that the band would perform primarily at benefits.

1985 saw the long-awaited release of the documentary film on the band, *The Unheard Music* (directed by Christopher Blakely and Everett Greaton) and the group also released their fifth album, *Ain't Love Grand*, a title which assumed some irony due to the fact that Cervenka and Doe divorced at the end of the year. Though the band continued working together, Cervenka noticed that attitudes toward her had changed. "I didn't really experience a lot of sexism in X because of one main reason—I was married to John," she says. "And I think people treated us more as a couple than individuals. But when John and I split up, I did notice that a lot of people went holding me responsible for things about X that they no longer liked. People who liked John's voice a lot, because it was a lot more pleasing in a commercial, classic way, thought that that was the time they could say what they had really thought all the time—'I really don't like Exene. I've always liked John, I wish he'd make a solo record.'" "There is a lot of sexism [in the music industry]," she concludes. "But I try to surround myself with people who aren't like that. Sexism is a pervasive thing in our society, and I think everybody, every woman especially, has to do their best to make sure that people realize that no, it's not okay." Despite periods of non-activity, X continued releasing albums into the '90s. Cervenka also formed the band Aunti Christ.

But although punk's stab of independence had dealt an unexpected blow to the established music industry, there was never any real danger of its toppling. "It was a nice outburst," says Vicki Wickham, who was managing Nona Hendryx's solo career. "I liked the fact that people were yelling and screaming and putting down the Queen. That was quite amusing. But it didn't really last and I didn't think it would." Once the major labels saw that despite their brashness punk groups could still turn a profit, they wasted no time in scooping them up. Outside of punk, it was business as usual for the majors, who carried on signing and grooming acts following well-established routes. Sheena Easton and Kate Bush, both with EMI in Britain, were two performers who followed this path during the punk era, Bush signing with the company during the first frenzied year of punk in 1976, and Easton signing in 1979. Though both were initially marketed as much for their looks as for their material, Bush was able to overcome earlier media perceptions of her as little more than an attractive body with a high-pitched voice, eventually attaining complete control over the direction of her career. Easton would have a harder time rising above her image as a carefully packaged product.

Part of the difficulty was the manner in which Easton's career was launched. Born in Glasgow, Scotland, in 1959, Easton had been inspired by classic vocalists like Barbra Streisand and had sung with local rock groups while attending the Royal Scottish Academy of Music and Drama. After graduation, she was chosen as the subject for a BBC television documentary, *The Big Time*, which chronicled her efforts to become a successful singer, showing her auditioning for EMI executives (performing "You Light Up My Life," "I Got the Music in Me," and "Feelings"), recording her first single, "Modern Girl," visiting established managers and artists (such as Dusty Springfield) for advice, and undergoing a complete makeover. The idea of marketing Easton as a product, not a singer, was a strong undercurrent throughout the proceedings—in one instance, noting how difficult it can be to generate interest in an unknown act, a comparison was drawn not between Easton and other established singers, but between food items like baked beans and margarine.

Despite this insight on how to break a singer in the pop market, initial attempts to sell this item were not successful: "Modern Girl" was released in England in February 1980, rose into the Top 60, and disappeared. But following the airing of the *The Big Time* that summer, "Modern Girl" was re-released and this time made it into the Top 10, quickly followed by her second single, "Nine to Five," making Easton the first British female vocalist to have two singles in the Top 10 chart simultaneously. "Modern Girl," an admittedly catchy tune, was somewhat daring in its story of a young woman who's liberated enough to sleep with her boyfriend one night and turn him down the next for the pleasure of her own company. But priorities were quickly put back in their proper order with the release of "Nine to Five" ("Morning Train" in the U.S.), with Easton quite happy to remain at home waiting for the arrival of her man after his eight-hour workday. In 1981, Easton repeated her success in the States, with "Morning Train" reaching number 1, and "Modern Girl" and the theme from the latest James Bond film, *For Your Eyes Only*, reaching the Top 10; she also received the Grammy for Best New Artist. Successfully established as a middle-of-the-road chanteuse, Easton eventually displayed an unexpected musical versatility, including forays into country, Latino, and black music: "Me Gustas Tal Como Eres," a duet with Mexican singer Luis Miguel, won a Grammy for Best Mexican/American Performance in 1984, while "Sugar Walls," co-produced by Prince, went to number 3 in the black music charts.

EMI may well have been happy if Kate Bush had turned out to be such a performer, but her determination to have a say in decisions affecting her work and her willingness to challenge decisions with which she did not feel comfortable ensured that she would not become just another pop product. Bush also had the advantage of being a musician and songwriter in addition to being a performer. Born in 1958 in Kent, England, Bush grew up in an artistic household: her father played piano, her mother had been a folk dancer, and her older brothers were involved in poetry, photography, and music. Bush first took up the violin as a child, and later taught herself piano at age eleven. She soon began writing songs, something she was careful to hide from her friends at first, although her family encouraged her musical development. When a friend of her brother gave a demo tape Bush had recorded to David Gilmour of Pink Floyd, Gilmour arranged for and financed a professional demo tape for Bush; the recording was produced by Andrew Powell, who would go on to produce her first two albums. On the strength of this demo and Gilmour's recommendation, Bush was signed to EMI at age seventeen.

Because of her age, EMI agreed to allow Bush to spend a few years further developing her singing, songwriting, and dancing, and during this period Bush formed the KT Bush Band to gain live experience, performing such covers as "I Heard It Through the Grapevine" and "Come Together" in local pubs. In the summer of 1977, Bush started recording her first album, *The Kick Inside* (which included two of the demos she'd recorded with Gilmour), and on its completion felt confident enough to insist that "Wuthering Heights" be released as the first single. EMI had preferred the more rock-oriented "James and the Cold Gun," but while label executives and Bush were discussing the situation, another executive walked in and casually announced, "Hi Kate, loved the album! 'Wuthering Heights' definitely the first single, eh?" "It was so well-timed it was almost as if I'd paid the guy to do it," Bush recalled in an interview with *Q*. "They obviously thought of me as just a strong-willed girl, but they trusted his opinion." She was equally insistent about her choice for the album's cover art, and again prevailed, though it meant the LP's release was delayed. *The Kick Inside* was finally released in February 1978 and peaked at number 3. Bush's intuition about the lead-off single proved to be correct when "Wuthering Heights," released in January 1978, topped the charts by March. Clearly, the combination of Bush's high-pitched, ethereal delivery of the Cathy and Heathcliff story and her striking looks were irresistible to the British public.

EMI capitalized on Bush's appearance through the conspicuous use of a promotional poster featuring the picture the label wanted to use for *Kick Inside*'s cover (and which did appear on the Japanese version of the LP), which pictured Bush in a tight sleeveless shirt that emphasized her breasts. Bush appeared seemingly unaware of the effect of such promotion at the time, telling *Melody Maker* in 1978, "The sex symbol thing didn't really occur to me until I noticed that in nearly every interview people were asking 'Do you feel like a sex symbol?'" She was far more outspoken in later interviews, showing a clear understanding of how she was marketed in the late '70s, pointing out that the same techniques were used with Debbie Harry. "We were both being promoted on the basis of being female bodies as well as singers," she told *NME* in 1982. "I wasn't looked at as being a female singer-songwriter. People weren't even generally aware that I wrote my own songs or played the piano. The media just promoted me as a female body. It's like I've had to prove that I'm an artist in a female body."

Bush also admitted that she herself fell prey to traditional perceptions of women in rock. "When I'm at the piano I hate to think that I'm a female because I automatically get a preconception," she told *Melody Maker* in 1977. "Every female you see at the piano is either Lynsey DePaul, Carole King. And most male music—not all of it but the good stuff—really lays it on you. It really puts you against the wall and that's what I'd like to do. I'd like my music to intrude. Not many females succeed with that. I identify more with male musicians than female musicians because I tend to think of female musicians as . . . ah . . . females." During the recording of her second album, *Lionheart*, she soon found her own musical output was being affected by such preconceptions about female musicians, when she ran into problems with producer Andrew Powell. "If you are an artist who's young [Bush was twenty at the time of recording *Lionheart*], and if you're a female, a lot of what you say is not taken very seriously," she explained on the British radio program *Small Beginnings*. "And so a lot of the points that I would have liked to have pushed, I would have maybe just suggested, and would have been told that it wouldn't work, and so I wouldn't push it. But now I would push it all the way! Which is really the way I am."

There were further problems with the work on *Lionheart*, which was released in December 1978. The two to three year period Bush used to prepare for *Kick Inside* was compressed into two to three months for *Lionheart*. She was equally frustrated by the constant interruptions imposed on the sessions to do promotional work. Unsurprisingly, the resulting album came across as a paler copy of *Kick Inside* and Bush herself was displeased with it. As a result, she stepped up efforts to have more control over her career, forming her own publishing and management companies (Kate Bush Music and Novercia), with herself as managing director and her family on the board of directors. For Bush, the route to independence was obtained by gradually distancing herself from the business people in the music industry, either having family members assuming their roles or taking them on herself. Her next project was the planning of her first tour. With typical attention to detail, Bush was involved in every aspect of the production, designing the sets and costumes, choreographing the numbers, and hiring the musicians and crew. But although the twenty-eight-date tour, held in the spring of 1979, was lauded as a critical and commercial success, the preparation had proved to be so exhausting Bush would not consider touring again for over ten years.

In 1980, she began work on her third album, *Never for Ever*, handling co-production for the first time. Her work as a backup vocalist for Peter Gabriel on his third album had introduced her to rhythm boxes and the Fairlight, a computer synthesizer and sampler that figured prominently on *Never for Ever*, her first number I album. *The Dreaming*, released in 1982, was the first album she produced completely and marked a dramatic change in her musical approach. Though hardly the naive romantic "suburban princess" she was sometimes called—her previous work had dealt with such subjects as incest, adultery, murder, and nuclear war—*The Dreaming* largely abandoned her previous richly melodic style for something more percussive and altogether harsher. There were hints of what was in store when a preview single, "Sat in Your Lap," was released in June 1981. Suddenly, the fresh-faced nineteen-year-old who had warbled optimistically about spiritual growth in "Them Heavy People" in 1978 was now a rather jaded-sounding twenty-four-year-old lamenting her realization that one's quest for knowledge is irrevocably doomed to failure with a cry of frustration.

The rest of the album was equally fraught with a wilder, angrier emotion than Bush had revealed before, as she metamorphosed into a Vietcong soldier or the wife of illusionist Harry Houdini, mourned the vanishing Aborigine, and ended the affair with a particularly vigorous door slam in "Get Out of My House." The album was a puzzle to the British public, selling less than any previous Bush LP, though it still reached number 3 in the British charts. "That was my 'She's gone mad' album," Bush told *Q*. Interestingly, the LP was hailed as a "masterpiece" and a "musical tour de force" in America, where the response to *Kick Inside* had been so tepid that EMI/America hadn't even bothered to release Bush's *Lionheart* and *Never for Ever*. But back in Britain, EMI was not happy, and Bush's response was, as usual, a retreat into greater self-sufficiency, as Gail Colson, who met Bush when Colson managed Peter Gabriel, explains: "Kate told me after *The Dreaming* they sat her down at EMI and said they wanted her to have a producer, that she couldn't produce herself. And she was so angry that she went home and built a studio and made *Hounds of Love*."

Building her own studio not only gave Bush complete control over her work, but also allowed her to take as much time as she needed to complete a project; as result, there was a three-year gap between *The Dreaming* and 1985's *Hounds of Love*, a four-year gap until the release of 1989's *The Sensual World*, and another four-year gap before 1993's *The Red Shoes*. Though Kate Bush would never be associated with the realm of punk rock, she turned out to be one of the performers who would take its do-it-yourself ethic to its logical conclusion, maintaining her ties with a major label while adopting a thoroughly independent approach to her work. The emergence of punk had brought more changes with it than just a momentary infusion of energy; it had given performers a chance to call the shots themselves. And for the women who were able to avail themselves of the opportunities punk offered, it was a profoundly liberating experience.

7

Post-Punk Waves

"WHY BITCH?
Because lots of what gets written about women in rock is ALL THE SAME.
I'm bored with sexist 'Chicks ain't rockers' articles.
I'm bored with mainstream 'Wow, chicks can play rock' articles.
Especially since they all seem to mention the same ten women over and over again,
creating the impression that no other women in rock exist."
—Lori Twersky, *Bitch* debut issue, August 1985

In 1982, the Go-Go's became the first all-female band in rock history to have a number 1 album, with *Beauty and the Beat*. It had taken seven months for the LP to climb to the top of the charts, the culmination of the band's "overnight" success. The album was supported by two Top 20 singles, "Our Lips Are Sealed" and "We Got the Beat." The latter, which reached number 2 in early 1982, was an '80s equivalent of "Rock Around the Clock"—but it had taken women over twenty-five years to get into the Top 10 and call the tune themselves. The Go-Go's had formed in the late '70s as the direct result of the punk explosion and for the same reason that many punk bands were created: anyone could do it, despite the lack of experience. And unlike most of their contemporaries, the Go-Go's were able to cross over to the pop mainstream from their punk beginnings, as the B-52's and Blondie had done. But the Go-Go's success also had different implications because the group was an all-female band. There had never been an all-female band—as opposed to vocal group—who achieved the commercial success that the Go-Go's did, an accomplishment that was a turning point in rock history for female musicians.

The Go-Go's achievement provided a clear illustration of the impact both the feminist and punk movements had had on the music industry, even though the Go-Go's themselves were not identified as feminists, nor would their music be classified as punk. If feminism had inspired women to create their own opportunities, punk offered women a specific realm in which to create their own opportunities as musicians. And though virtually no female performers from the women's music era crossed over to the commercial mainstream, and few punk bands lasted more than a few years—if that long—female performers during the '80s were able to use the gains of feminism and punk to forge increasingly successful careers. And if the Go-Go's inadvertently established a new stereotype for women in rock, it was also a stereotype that hadn't existed before. Prior to the Go-Go's, all-female bands were generally not considered to be commercially viable—as all-female vocal groups like the Chantels had not been considered "saleable" in the '50s. The Go-Go's shattered that myth once and for all, meaning that all-female bands would never be seen as complete anomalies again.

The sparkling, effervescent pop that would eventually give the Go-Go's three Top 20 albums was far removed from their punk roots in the late '70s. Belinda Carlisle, who grew up just north of Los Angeles, was a cheerleader at her high school during the week but haunted L.A.'s punk clubs like the Masque and the Starwood on weekends. She eventually met up with another club regular, Jane Wiedlin, and the two traveled to San Francisco to see the Sex Pistols' final performance. On returning, they were inspired to form their own band, with Carlisle as lead singer, Wiedlin on guitar, Margot Olaverra on bass, and Elissa Bello on drums, and adopted the name Go-Go's from Wiedlin's suggestion. Two months later, in May 1978 they asked another friend, guitarist Charlotte Caffey, to join. "They asked me to be in the band because they thought I had all this experience," says Caffey, who had previously played in a number of different bands, including the Eyes with X's D. J. Bonebrake. "I was in other bands, but the other girls thought, 'Well, if all our friends can do it, we can do it too,'" Caffey explains of the band's inception. "It was basically on a whim. It was fun. When we first had rehearsals, they didn't even know how to plug in their equipment."

Caffey agreed to join the band, but a tour of England with another local band, the Dickies, kept her from becoming a full-time member until July 1978, so the Go-Go's made their debut without her at a party at the Masque. But the group soon found that the supposed freedom of the era did not necessarily extend to female musicians. "Basically no one wanted to know about us, and they literally laughed at the idea of an all-female band," says Caffey. "There had been Fanny and there had been the Runaways, but I guess 'cause we formed our own band, wrote all our own material, and played all the instruments, maybe they thought it would never work. There were immense obstacles, but the more obstacles there were, the harder we worked and the more we were determined."

Charlotte Caffey (guitar), Belinda Carlisle, and Kathy Valentine (bass) of the Go-Go's
May 1982 at the Greek Theater, Los Angeles, Photo by Sherry Rayn Barnett

In spite of their determination, the band was on the verge of breaking up in 1979, but their fortunes began to change when Gina Schock replaced Elissa Bello on drums. Schock, a native of Baltimore who had played in bands there before moving to the West Coast, was skeptical of the band's abilities, but felt they had potential. The group also acquired a manager, Ginger Canzoneri, and a booking at the Whiskey a-Go-Go, where they opened for the ska band Madness, impressing the British group enough that the Go-Go's were invited to join Madness on a 1980 tour of England. The group's sound was now moving away from punk to pop, and while in the U.K., the Go-Go's recorded "We Got the Beat" on Madness's label, Stiff. But back in the U.S., the Go-Go's still found it hard to attract attention from the record companies, despite the fact that the group was now a strong audience draw; a special showcase at the Starwood, set up specifically so A&R personnel could see the group, did not generate a single offer.

At the end of 1980, the group also took on a new bassist, Kathy Valentine (previously a member of Britain's all-female heavy metal band Girlschool, and L.A.'s Textones), who filled in for Margot Oliverra when she was ill and eventually replaced her in the band. Finally, Miles Copeland signed the group to his I.R.S. Records label on April Fool's Day, 1981: "He was the only one willing to take a chance on us," says

Caffey. Richard Gottehrer, who produced Blondie's first two albums, was hired as producer, along with Rob Freeman, and *Beauty and the Beat* was released in late summer. The album's eleven songs were all written by the group, with Caffey writing or co-writing eight, including "We Got the Beat."

The group worked hard to promote *Beauty and the Beat* (which eventually sold over two million copies) through constant touring, but the LP's ultimate success still caught the group, and their label, by surprise. "We really had no idea we were going to do what we did," says Caffey. "We thought, 'God, if we could only sell one hundred thousand albums, we'd be so happy.' We were just naive, we didn't know. And when it happened, it was a lot of pressure. It was our first experience, and it was I.R.S.'s first experience with such a success, so we did every single thing we could possibly do. And they kept saying, 'Well, I guess we're on a roll, so we better do this-this-this.' So within a two-year period we made two albums, and we really felt burned out."

The group had also not considered the impact they would have as the first successful all-female band. "We just happened to be the first ones," said Caffey in 1990. "I think it's just that there's not a lot of female bands. Once there's more, people won't make such a big deal out of it." Heart's Ann Wilson had made a similar statement herself in an interview—thirteen years previously. And in spite of the gains the group had made, the Go-Go's discovered that some people still found it difficult to take the idea of an all-female group seriously. The group continued to take knocks, especially regarding their musical abilities, from various factions of the music press, and the group's playful presentation of themselves—pictured in towels and facial masks on the cover of *Beauty and the Beat*, in their underwear on the cover of *Rolling Stone*, and as a waterskiing team wearing tutus on the cover of *Vacation*—also alienated them from some feminists not yet ready for girls who just wanted to have fun. Other articles, such as the Go-Go's first *Rolling Stone* cover story, inadvertently pointed out the balancing act an all-female band was required to maintain for the sake of being "natural": "You won't see them flaunting their sexiness à la the Runaways or ignoring it like Fanny did; they're simply comfortable being female," wrote Steve Pond, who further emphasized the lack of any visible threat by concluding, "The Go-Go's are safe, wholesome and proudly commercial."

Ironically, once the Go-Go's managed their breakthrough, they found that their success had only led to the creation of a new mold for female performers. Perceptions about women shifted enough to embrace the idea of female musicians—but only if they fit the mold of the Go-Go's. Instead of opening up more possibilities for female performers, the success of the Go-Go's had in some ways narrowed the field: all-female bands that emerged in the wake of the Go-Go's (especially if they came from California) automatically ended up being compared to them, even if it was only to say that despite the fact band *X* was composed entirely of women, they still sounded nothing like America's Number One All-Female Band.

The group's reactions to the pressures of their success played themselves out in the time-honored show-biz fashion of drug and alcohol abuse: "In the late '70s and early '80s, coke, in the industry, was so prevalent . . . people were shoving it in your face because they wanted you to like them," remembered Jane Wiedlin in 1988. There were further problems when the band claimed that I.R.S. was withholding royalties from them, a dispute eventually settled out of court. The Go-Go's subsequent albums, *Vacation* and *Talk Show*, were not as highly acclaimed as their debut LP, though they yielded the Top 40 hits "Vacation," "Head Over Heels," and "Turn to You." But by 1984, the group had lost their enthusiasm for playing together. Wiedlin left the group to pursue a solo career at the year's end, and Caffey and Carlisle broke up the band the following year, though not without hard feelings from the other members.

After the split, each member of the band pursued a solo career, with Carlisle attaining the most success; Kathy Valentine reunited with her former Girlschool band-mate Kelly Johnson and formed the World's Cutest Killers. Caffey, who had worked with Carlisle on her solo albums, formed her own band, the Graces, in the late '80s, with Meredith Brooks and Gia Ciambotti, though she had initially resisted working with another "all-girl band," "I was scared of working with women again," she explained to the *Los Angeles Times*. "I didn't want to face the problems women bands have to go through. Things are a lot better for women bands now." She also found herself benefiting from the inroads the Go-Go's had made in challenging the perception of "female musician" as being a contradiction in terms. "People still distinguish the Graces as an all-female band," she says. "They don't say U2 is an all-male band. But I think the Go-Go's paved the way for the Graces, so I feel like stuff that happened back then is helping us now. I think people are much more open-minded now." The Go-Go's eventually overcame the acrimony of their split and re-formed in the '90s, releasing the album *God Bless the Go-Go's* in 2001.

The early '80s saw the commercial breakthrough of a number of female performers, including Chrissie Hynde of the Pretenders, whose debut LP topped the U.K. charts in 1980, as did the single "Brass in Pocket" (in the U.S., the album hit number 9 and "Brass in Pocket" reached the Top 20). Hynde, born in Akron, Ohio, in 1951, had grown up on a musical diet of "anything that a kid in Ohio with a transistor radio could pick up on"; after starting out on the ukulele, she eventually learned guitar. In 1973, after three years of college, Hynde fled life in middle America for London, working as a waitress, a journalist for *NME*, and in Malcolm McLaren and Vivienne Westwood's King's Road clothing shop. She also played in a combo in Paris called the

Frenchies and returned briefly to the States to play with the Cleveland R&B band Jack Rabbit.

On returning to London, Hynde continued working with different bands, playing with Mick Jones, who later joined the Clash, future Damned members Dave Vanian and Rat Scabies, and singing backup vocals for artists like ex–New York Doll Johnny Thunders. In 1978, Hynde met Dave Hill, a former A&R man who was starting his own label, Real Records. Hill became Hynde's manager, and by the summer Hynde had formed the Pretenders (a name she'd chosen), with James Honeyman-Scott on guitar, Pete Farndon on bass, Jerry McIeduff on drums, and Hynde on rhythm guitar. The Pretenders got off to a good start, with their first single, a cover of the Kinks "Stop Your Sobbing" released on Hill's label in January 1979, reaching the U.K. Top 30. The group built on this success through constant live work and the release of two further singles, "Kid," which also reached the U.K. Top 30, and "Brass in Pocket"; Martin Chambers also replaced McIeduff on drums.

The group's debut album *The Pretenders* (on Real Records in the U.K., Sire Records in the U.S.) was released to almost universal acclaim: the Pretenders' powerhouse rock & roll was fresh enough to be different, and yet not too heavy to alienate those put off by the abrasiveness of punk. The album's twelve songs, all but two written or co-written by Hynde, ranged from the moderate pop tempo of the previously released singles to the bracing, no-holds-barred rock attack of songs like "Tattooed Love Boys" and "Precious." There was also Hynde's compelling presence as the group's lead singer, commanding attention and inviting the listener to "fuck off" (in "Precious") if they couldn't take it. The Pretenders were also clearly a group, not just a backing band for Hynde, as *Rolling Stone* noted in their review of the band's debut LP: "The rest of the Pretenders are neither subservient to Hynde nor condescending to her; the Pretenders are a group and unlike certain other bands that make that claim, there is never any doubt about it."

Hynde updated the "tough chick" image in rock previously established by Suzi Quatro and the Runaways, but this time there was no doubt that she was the one in charge, especially as the decade progressed and Hynde was able to endure the departures, firings, and deaths of various band members and still manage to keep the act going. And at a time when few women maintained the dual role of lead singer and instrumentalist in a rock band (and certainly not in a band as commercially successful as the Pretenders), Hynde served as an inspiration to many who weren't used to seeing a woman in such a position before. Nor were most people in the music business used to seeing a female performer take her children on the road as Hynde did when she became a mother, demonstrating that motherhood and a performing career in rock & roll didn't necessarily have to be incompatible.

But Hynde made it clear that feminism was not one of her causes, which was seen as another point in her favor by some: "Chrissie Hynde's never allied herself to any sort of female militancy except by example. In that, she really is special," wrote Giovanni Dadomo in *New Women in Rock* with a noticeable sigh of relief. The irony was that whereas the stereotype of a "feminist" was an aggressive "man-hater"—a stereotype someone might see reflected in Hynde's tough, leather-jacketed demeanor—the only woman in the rock mainstream who had openly identified herself as a feminist was Helen Reddy, hardly anyone's idea of a threatening personality. Hynde herself expressed more traditional views regarding the position of women in rock. In a 1990 interview in *Pulse*, Hynde cited the lack of the birth control pill, not sexism, as a reason for the smaller number of women musicians in the rock scene, adding, "It's not sexist to say that a woman's place is in the home looking after children." Yet Hynde was able to be a mother, and eventually a single parent, without sacrificing her life as a rock musician.

But to the female audience inspired to pick up guitars themselves in the wake of Hynde's arrival on the music scene, it was her presence as a musician that carried more weight than her views on feminism. And in addition to the records Hynde released through the '80s (landing five albums in the Top 30 and including such hit singles as "Back on the Chain Gang" and "Don't Get Me Wrong"), Hynde maintained a strong sense of independence, refusing to be caught up in the rock star "cult of celebrity": "I'm just not concerned with my popability profile," she told Tom Hibbert in *Q* magazine, who also noted, "The word 'pop' is always hissed from her mouth like some foul curse." She also became an increasingly vocal advocate for animal rights and vegetarianism, subjects about which she developed a passion that seemed to surpass her feelings for rock & roll. "You can say what you like about my music," she said in 1990, "but *no one* takes the piss out of my causes."

Pat Benatar presented another version of the "tough chick" singer, but one that was more palatable (and, in the U.S., more commercially successful) than Chrissie Hynde's, for despite Benatar's musical preference for "the hard, fast stuff," her image was more conventionally feminine. Born in Lindenhurst, Long Island, in 1953, Patricia Andrzejewski was the daughter of an opera singer and studied opera herself; other musical favorites included Judy Garland and the Beatles. In her late teens Pat married Dennis Benatar and moved with him to Virginia, where he was stationed with the army. Benatar spent the next two and a half years working as a bank teller, but eventually quit to return to music, singing in local bars and lounges.

In 1975, Benatar moved to New York to pursue a singing career. One of her early appearances was at an open audition night at the club Catch a Rising Star, where her rendition of Judy Garland's "Rockabye Your Baby" resulted in a regular spot at the club. The club's owner, Rick Newman, also became Benatar's manager. The next few years were spent in trying to secure a major label deal, with little luck, an experience that Benatar said helped define her forthright demeanor on stage. "Everyone told me I was a great kid with talent. Period," she said. "Being sweet doesn't pay the bills. I became defensive. That's how my stage presence emerged."

Finally, in 1978, Benatar got a deal with Chrysalis and her debut LP, *In the Heat of the Night*, was released the following year; by 1980, the album had reached the Top 20, accompanied by two Top 30 hits, "Heartbreaker" and "We Live for Love" (during this period Benatar also divorced her husband and married Neil Giraldo, a guitarist in her band). Benatar's next album, *Crimes of Passion* (released the same year), did even better, reaching number 2, with the singles "Treat Me Right" reaching the Top 20 and "Hit Me with Your Best Shot" reaching number 9. The album also won Benatar the first of four consecutive Grammy awards for Best Female Rock Vocal Performance, and the following years brought further success: eleven further Top 40 singles, and six Top 30 albums, with 1981's *Precious Time* reaching number 1.

Benatar was the kind of hard-rocking female that the mainstream could easily accommodate; unlike Chrissie Hynde, Benatar was not the type to spit out a contemptuous "fuck off" in a song lyric. But her very success also enabled some critics to write her off for what they saw as an attempt to pander to commercial tastes. "Her musical and performing stance is original only in that she *is* female," reads the entry in the 1988 edition of *The Harmony Illustrated Encyclopedia of Rock*. "Whether the power-chord clichés and humorless posturing of heavy metal are rendered any more interesting when performed by a tiny, spandex-clad redhead (even with natural talent) rather than by the usual macho howlers is questionable."

In fact, Benatar's impressive vocal range was backed by a hard-edged delivery that made her, along with Ann Wilson and Chrissie Hynde, a gutsier female singer than most in the Top 40. She also had a hand in writing or co-writing much of her material, addressing such issues as child abuse in "Hell is for Children" on *Crimes*, eight years before Suzanne Vega would cover the same topic in her Top 5 hit "Luka." And she enjoyed the power of her stage persona. "I like being tough on stage," she told the *Los Angeles Times*. "I don't like being sweet. I can't sing about love in the afternoon among the flowers and sunshine. I like to sing about things that make me mad, like bad relationships. People might think I've been treated like some of the women in some of those songs. No way. If I was treated that way, I'd inflict serious injury on the guy."

But the media focus on Benatar as a sex symbol led to her other strengths being overlooked. It was not a focus Benatar was happy with. "I used to think I could be real sexless onstage," she told *Rolling Stone*. "It doesn't work. You're a female, and it comes out no matter what you do." She also admitted she found the promotional efforts of her record company that played up her image as a sex symbol "embarrassing." "I came back from the last tour and found out they'd made a cardboard cutout of me in my little tights. What has that got to do with anything? They also took out an ad in *Billboard* and airbrushed part of my top off . . . If *that* is gonna sell records, then it's a real sorry thing." In response to such attitudes, Benatar stopped wearing tights on stage, and cut her hair short. Benatar maintained a continuous schedule of touring and recording, and after a decade of releasing hard rock/pop records switched direction in the '90s with the release of *True Love*, a "jump blues" album in which she covered songs by Big Maybelle and B. B. King, among others.

Though performers like the Go-Go's, Chrissie Hynde, and Pat Benatar were not all associated with punk in the beginning of their careers, it was clear each had benefited from the punk explosion, for if they had launched their careers a decade earlier, chances are they would not have found the success they did in the '80s. Whereas performers like Fanny, the Deadly Nightshade, Suzi Quatro, and the Runaways had found it difficult to achieve commercial success, female performers in the '80s—particularly those who played instruments—were now more readily accepted and less likely to be written off as novelties. But not every performer used the realm of punk, or as it would eventually be called, "alternative music," as a springboard into the Top 40. Punk's do-it-yourself credo also inspired artists working in non-musical areas to begin introducing music into their work. Some artists, like Karen Finley, only used music as another aspect of their work; others, like Laurie Anderson, developed secondary careers as musicians.

Yoko Ono, whose innovative musical endeavors had predated the punk era, resurfaced in the early '80s after taking a five-year break from any artistic activity, during which time John Lennon raised their son, Sean, and Ono took care of the family's finances and made profitable investments. Then, in the summer of 1980, it was announced that Ono and Lennon were returning to the recording studio, and in October, the single "(Just Like) Starting Over"/"Kiss Kiss Kiss," was released, following the pattern of previous Lennon A-side/Ono B-side single releases. Within a month the single was followed by the release of the album *Double Fantasy*.

Double Fantasy had Ono and Lennon trading off songs as they had on their 1972 LP *Some Time in New York City*, with far more effective results. This time the subject matter was their relationship, and for the first time the praise for Ono's work outweighed that for Lennon's. "All the most interesting material on *Double Fantasy* is Yoko's," said Charles Shaar Murray in an *NME* review, adding, "in the '80s—post-Slits etc.—her music sounds vastly modern and considerably more interesting than Lennon's." But this spate of critical reassessment ended when Lennon was assassinated on December 8, 1980. Whereas Ono's musical career had previously stood in the shadow of Lennon's physical presence, it now seemed destined to remain in the shadow of his ghost.

This was evident with the release in February 1981 of Ono's first solo single in seven years, "Walking on Thin Ice," which the couple had been remixing on the night that Lennon was killed. Realizing the chances for showing the public how "ready" they were for Ono's work would be limited as long as her songs were paired with Lennon's, a "Yoko Only" single featuring "Thin Ice," backed with the glowing ballad "It Happened," was planned for release in the wake of *Double Fantasy*, along with a twelve-inch single for club DJs. But instead of being a showcase for Ono, the single now became something of a tribute record to Lennon, being the first new material released since his death (Lennon played an appropriately scratchy guitar on the track). The cover was subtitled "For John," with a "Finishing Note" on the back that read, in part, "Getting this together after what happened was hard. But I knew John would not rest his mind if I hadn't. I hope you like it, John. I did my best." The song is among Ono's best, with a driving beat that made it a natural for the dance clubs and haunting, enigmatic lyrics underscored by the recent tragedy. It reached number 58 in the charts, number 13 on *Billboard*'s Disco chart and was later nominated for a Grammy.

In interviews immediately following Lennon's death, Ono maintained a dignified calm, but her next solo album, *Season of Glass*, released in June 1981 and co-produced by Ono and Phil Spector, revealed the extent of her sorrow and her rage, beginning with the cover, which prominently displayed Lennon's blood-stained glasses. Side One was relatively low-key, beginning with the bittersweet ballad "Goodbye Sadness" and interspersed with brief spoken-word passages from Ono and Sean, then five years old. Side Two told a very different story, with Ono unleashing her anger with a fierce directness. The lurching roll of the opening track, "I Don't Know Why," gives way to Ono's fury at the song's conclusion as she shouts, "You *bastards!* Hate us, hate me! We had *everything!*" The edgy "Extension 33" follows, leading straight into the four gun shots that open "No, No, No" while Ono screams "No!" *Season of Glass* was also the first solo Ono LP to hit the upper reaches of the *Billboard* charts, reaching number 49, though Ono viewed her new-found acceptance by the public with some wryness: "If it brought John back, I'd rather remain hated," she told Ray Coleman in his book *Lennon*.

Ono released four further albums before temporarily retiring into her role, as she describes it, of "Keeper of the Wishing Well," two Ono-Lennon collaborations (1984's *Milk and Honey* and 1986's *John Lennon Live in New York City*) and two solo LPs, 1982's *It's Alright* and 1985's *Starpeace*. The latter LP contained the song "Hell in Paradise," a powerful dance rock number that featured Nona Hendryx on backing vocals. The song also became Ono's biggest commercial success when it was released as a twelve-inch single, charting at number 16 on *Billboard*'s Disco Sales chart and number 13 on the Club Play charts. Following the release of *Starpeace* Ono embarked on a brief European tour (she had previously appeared as a solo performer in a weeklong residency at the New York club Kenny's Castaways in 1973 and on a tour of Japan in 1974), but the often harsh critical reception she received caused her to curtail her own musical activities. "After [the tour] I just thought, 'OK, forget it for a while. Let's give it a rest,'" she told *Goldmine*. "And that was good to give it a rest. When things are totally against you that way you don't want to go on and on."

Ono revived her music career in the '90s beginning with an appearance on a re-recorded version of "Give Peace a Chance," released on the eve of the Persian Gulf conflict between the U.S. and Iraq in 1991, with new lyrics written by her son Sean. The following year saw the release of *Onobox*, a lavish box set of her work released on the Rykodisc label. The set was comprised of six compact discs which drew on material from each of Ono's solo albums, along with unreleased material (*Walking on Thin Ice*, a single CD of highlights from the set, was also released). Critics, who had previously scorned Ono's work on its original release twenty years ago, were now generous in their praise. *Billboard* hailed the songs as "musically years ahead of their time," while *Entertainment Weekly* stated, "The way she invents what others took for granted . . . turns this collision of rock's primitive energy and performance art's self-dramatization into a preview of musical hybrids." The publication of John G. Hanhardt and Barbara Haskell's book *Yoko Ono: Arias and Objects* (an examination of Ono's artwork) in the same year suggests that Ono's work is now receiving the long overdue attention it deserves. Two subsequent albums, *Rising* (1995) and *Blueprint for a Sunrise* (2001), also received critical acclaim.

In the same year that Yoko Ono and John Lennon recorded and released *Double Fantasy*, Danielle Dax, in the U.K., was moving from visual art to rock music with the release of *We Buy a Hammer for Daddy*, her first recorded effort with her new band the Lemon Kittens. Born in Southend, England, Dax had leaned toward visual self-expression from childhood and had initially considered working in television because of her involvement in plays at school. "I wanted to be a director when I was young," she remembers. "That's really what I wanted to go into. But when I was fourteen or fifteen I suddenly realized that I couldn't get a job with the BBC because I was a girl and they wouldn't employ trainee girls. That really put me off, so I sort of lost interest." Dax moved to Reading in her late teens, where she continued her work in visual art by painting and staging her own solo "events." "I remember I went through an alien phase where I used to dress up in completely one color," she says. "It was almost like performance art. I used to do it totally on my own, dress up in the most bizarre clothing possible and walk around Reading in a very stylized, slow way and see what would happen. Eventually I'd get followed by a crowd of kids and have to seek refuge in a shop or something. I just used to enjoy it. I always enjoy creating something quite out of the ordinary just to make people stop and take stock of the situation."

Dax did not have an equal interest in music at the time ("It was just a series of abstract sounds"), but a chance encounter with another musician showed her its potential as a creative medium. After being approached by Karl Blake to design a record cover for his band the Lemon Kittens, Dax visited Blake a few days later and became entranced with his improvised home recording studio. "I found it very inspiring," she says. "It was love at first sight. Something just clicked inside, and I felt like suddenly I had some sort of purpose." Dax ended up joining Blake's band, though her previous musical experience had been limited to a few brief encounters with the saxophone ("I could actually get a sound out of it, so I figured it was probably an omen") and she initially suffered from a near-paralyzing stage fright. "I was terrified," she says of her first performance. "Almost to the point of not being able to go out and do anything. But the very nature of the performance, the fact that I was totally disguised from head to foot so no one would realize it was me, that helped quite considerably. It's always kind of been chucking yourself in at the deep end—if I thought about it too much I wouldn't have gone ahead with it."

Undaunted by her lack of familiarity with different instruments, Dax set about recording the first Kittens album, *We Buy a Hammer for Daddy*, soon after joining the band, securing a studio through an ad in *Melody Maker* that offered free studio time at Guildford University. "We used to record from eleven at night to six in the morning," Dax remembers, "and there would just be Karl and I. It was in the middle of winter. We'd have to take two trains from Reading, which used to take ages, with all our equipment, walk up a really bleak hill through what is one of the most disgusting architectural eyesores of the British landscape, and record in this huge room made for orchestras, with tympani lying around and music stands everywhere. And we literally didn't know anything. We just used to each go into this great big empty room and play what we wanted. I really didn't understand music when I started. I didn't understand how harmonies worked, why something sounds in tune, why it doesn't sound in tune. I couldn't even hear bass guitar or bass drum on records when I started."

The resulting album, released in 1980, was neither mainstream rock nor much like the punk/new wave music of the time. The lyrics and song titles might have been inspired, as Dax says, by children's books, but when matched to the fractured, clattering music, the overall effect was something more cryptic. The band, who had by this time relocated to London, next released a single and contributed to various compilations before releasing their second album, *The Big Dentist*, in 1982. But soon after, the group fell apart because of internal friction, and Dax decided it was time to strike out on her own. "I got enough experience out of the situation to have confidence to leave the musical nest," she explains, and she began work on her first solo effort, *Pop Eyes*, which was released in 1983. Undertaking all aspects of the record—writing and performing all the material (playing more than ten instruments, ranging from guitar and trumpet to "toys"), in addition to producing—presented little problem. "There was no one else to do it, so I did it," says Dax. "At the time I knew nothing about the music business at all. I didn't realize the control and the responsibilities of producers or separate mixing people or what cutting involved. It was just a case of that was normal to me. It was just a step away from doing it at home in Karl's bedroom. I didn't use anybody else, I didn't get lazy, I wanted to do it, so I set about learning how to do it and achieved the goal that I'd set up. It didn't seem like such a big deal. It never really has."

But while Dax's manner of working was not a "big deal" to her, she did recognize the implications it had for other female performers in the music industry. "I think it was quite an important statement for that period, the way I went about doing it," she says of the album. "I mean literally, there weren't any other women working like that at the time, going into areas that were predominantly in the male domain, especially in terms of engineering and the technical side of things, and not just being front singers or backing singers or always being backed up by a whole bastion of male musicians or businessmen or whatever. Just going ahead and doing what they wanted. And if it was going to be hard for women to work with men, then just fuck 'em, do it on their own. I think they do more now. A lot's changed since I first started, a hell of a lot."

The music on *Pop Eyes* had a greater cohesiveness than the Kittens' work, but Dax's ideas were just as disturbing, especially on the cover, which she also designed, a gruesome mosaic of body parts that formed a horrific face; the album was later repackaged in a less provocative sleeve after record distributors refused to carry the album in its original cover. But Dax herself was pleased with her work. "I was able to do things that were quite pure," she says. "It only seemed odd when everybody kept saying it was odd. I think it was a good album. I think it was a very naive album, but I'm proud of it." Her next album, *Jesus Egg That Wept*, released in 1984, demonstrated considerable growth from the sparse, harsh instrumentation of *Pop Eyes*. "Evil Honky Stomp," an attack on bigotry, lurches along with a hideous warp, with guitars and piano built on top of a tape loop taken from an old blues track, "Jukebox Boogie." "Pariah," a chilling depiction of a lynch mob, utilizes lush banks of synthesizers to provide a bed for its malevolent scenario. And by the release of her twelve-inch single, "Yummer Yummer Man"/"Bad Miss

'M'"/"Fizzing Human Bomb" in late 1985, Dax's vision was increasingly clear: taking conventional styles of music and twisting them into startling new shapes, as "Fizzing Human Bomb" did with dance rock, and "Bad Miss 'M'" did with country & western, setting its commentary on then-prime minister Margaret Thatcher to a giddy beat.

Dax attributes some of this development to an upgrading of her equipment. She also increased her self-sufficiency beyond the creation of her music (though she was now collaborating with her guitarist, David Knight) by setting up her own label and taking charge of the rest of her career, as much out of necessity as for the sake of having control. "I wanted a manager, but no one wanted to do it at the time," she explains. "They thought the music was too odd. So I tour managed, I arranged press, I got the bands together. I didn't really think about it, I was too busy getting on with all the work. The only reason to have a manager would have been to get a bigger deal, because the rest I could more or less do anyway."

Even with the onset of punk, it was rare for any performer, female or male, to handle virtually all the responsibilities of their careers. Dax also experienced prejudices female performers often face simply because they are female, which she says inspired the song, "Flashback" (on the album *Inky Bloaters*, released in 1987). "It's just about wanting things and going for things," she says. "Being a woman doing this, doing it the way I do it, it's hard for people to take. It's so hard to get the respect and the coverage that would be given to males doing the same thing. That puts people off. A lot of people give up the struggle quite early on because it's like banging your head against a brick wall at times. But the women that do get through are really tough and really good because of that. They've probably done twice as much sweating and working to achieve the same ends."

Dax released two further sin-

Danielle Dax
1990 in New York City, Photo by Michele Taylor

gles and the album *Inky Bloaters* before her perseverance paid off and she finally secured a major label contract with Sire in the U.S., who released *Dark Adapted Eye*, a collection of early material, in 1988, and *Blast the Human Flower* in 1990. "It's a relief, but it's a bit like instead of playing around with a vicious cat I feel I've stuck my head in the lion's mouth!" she says of her move to the majors, but she readily welcomed the greater exposure that comes with being on a major label. "I don't have this big art trip where I want to be some obscurist asshole playing for two hundred people forever," she says. "I think that's pointless. I believe that what I do is important. It's important to me, but I believe it's important generally, because I think I have levels of taste and integrity that aren't always there in music, music that gets through to the mainstream. So I think it's important for me to try and make it work so that there are things available, just so people have a choice." But equally significant was Dax's own determination to succeed, a determination fueled by "total, almost unswerving belief in what I was doing," she says. "I don't believe in failure. I never have. I've always believed that if you do something for long enough and try hard enough eventually it pays off. You have to believe that. The alternatives are inconceivable."

Laurie Anderson, who also began her career as a visual artist before working with music, had spent most of the '70s exhibiting her work in galleries or performing in New York venues like the Kitchen. Though music was usually an accompaniment to her work, it was never the main focus. "When I was making a lot of films, which was how I got into this, I'd go to a 'film festival,' which was basically eight people in a loft," she remembers. "I was always late, and I never had time to do the soundtrack, so I'd stand in front of the film and play the violin and tell stories. And that was how music got into it—really as soundtrack songs." Yet in 1981, Anderson had a surprise hit with "O Superman," initially released independently, which went to number 2 in the British charts. "It was very odd," she recalls. "The singles were basically stacked up in my loft, about a thousand of them. We were selling them by mail order and I thought, 'We'll never get rid of these things.' Then I started getting calls from England—'Yes, we'd like to order forty thousand of these records.' So I looked over at the stack—'Oh, no problem! Right away, I'll get back to you.' And actually Warner Bros. had been talking to me about doing records but I really didn't want to work with a record company, so I hadn't picked up on that. But now I called them and said, 'Listen, can you just do this? 'Cause I really can't lick this many stamps.'"

Born in 1947 in Chicago, Anderson studied classical violin as a child, and later attended Barnard College and Columbia University, where she received an M.F.A. (Master of Fine Arts) in sculpture in 1972. That same year she staged her first performance, *Automotive*, in Rochester, Vermont, conducting an "orchestra" of car horns played by local residents. She continued her work in New York, living in Soho and finding herself part of the growing "performance art" movement, an extension of the "events" and "happenings" of the '60s, but which now featured even greater explorations into multimedia, especially film and video. Though the term confused the public, Anderson saw herself as part of a long-running tradition. "I don't think of myself as working in a new art form at all," she says. "People think that performance art is some kind of new thing when it's actually been around for—well, Bauhaus, they were doing it. But it's just that there aren't any companies, like opera companies, that represent things. So people think that they're being invented all the time. But I'm not really a professional anything. Well, maybe a professional storyteller, but all the music and the pictures are just ways to tell the stories."

In 1978, Anderson's view of herself as a "storyteller" underwent a change when she realized there was room for her work outside the narrow confines of the art community. "It's very hard to be an artist in the United States," she says. "And the art world and the avant-garde are about protecting that in a way. And I really benefited from that attitude, but ultimately it's quite a snobbish attitude; it's like anything that's not in the avant-garde is ridiculous, and pop culture is garbage. And that's a little extreme. But my own realization of what I could see my role being was doing this concert in Houston. It was supposed to be in a museum, but we had it in a country & western bar instead because there wasn't enough room. So a lot of the regulars came, and they stood around the bar, and the art crowd was milling around elsewhere, and in the middle of the show I understood that the regulars got this perfectly well. 'Cause it was also advertised as a country fiddling thing, which was a little odd, but I was playing the violin and telling stories, and the stories were a little bit weird, but Texas stories are extremely weird, too. So I realized 'Wait a second! These people get the hang of this! I don't really have to do it the way I've been doing it.' That taught me a lot."

As Anderson was establishing herself in New York's art community, her future producer, Roma Baran, was developing her own skills. Originally born in Poland in 1947, Baran moved to Montreal, Quebec, Canada, with her family when she was five and began playing guitar in high school partly as a rebellion against her parents' wishes that she play piano and partly because of a romantic interest in a fellow student. "I think the incentive to learn guitar was this guy named Tommy Pendon, and I had a crush on him," she says. "I think I got a guitar to somehow bring me closer to Tommy's aura. But my parents wouldn't pay for guitar lessons, so I taught myself, and I taught myself to play really weird—I invented a tuning, and I learned to play in my lap, kind of lap style; it took me a while to unlearn that! Then I joined a band; the guys wore powder blue dinner jackets with black satin lapels, and I wore a powder blue strapless thing, my hair in a big teased French twist. I played in a couple of bands, and then my first year in college I played in this folk trio."

It was another romantic liaison that pushed Baran into regarding music as more than just a "hobby." "I fell in love with a woman who was playing in a band, the Penny Lang Band," she says. "Same thing, different gender! So I just hung around this club near McGill University till all hours of the night. Eventually I did join the band, and after that the priorities shifted a little. I thought of myself more as a musician than as someone who was going to grow up and go to college to be something else. But I still went to college off and on whenever I couldn't think of what else to do." Baran eventually moved to California to study music at the San Francisco Music Conservatory, then attended the University of New Hampshire for her masters degree, and finally ended up in New York in 1976, completing her Ph.D. course work at New York University.

She continued her involvement in music by playing with a variety of different artists, including folk singer Rosalie Sorrels and fellow Canadians Kate and Anna McGarrigle. It was her work with the McGarrigles that led to her first job as a producer, when the folk trio Huxtable, Christensen, and Hood asked her to produce their album for Philo Records in 1977. "They had seen me play a number of times with Kate and Anna," Baran says. "I rarely say no to anything, often much to my dismay. So I said, 'Yes, sure,' and went up to Burlington, and I was horrified by everything I didn't know. I guess I have this sort of megalomaniac fantasy that I'll see it, I'll get it. I'll somehow figure it out on the spot, but of course it's not like that, ever. The engineer was very sweet. He tried to sort of hold me up, but it was very difficult to plan for things. So that was wonderful fun, and I loved the album, and it all turned out fine, but I right away was very hungry for that knowledge."

During the same period, Baran first saw Laurie Anderson perform in New York and later got to know her while working as a staff producer/engineer at ZBS Media, a studio Anderson was also working in, located in upstate New York. "I think it originally stood for 'Zero Bullshit,' but then everybody was sort of embarrassed about that and would never admit it," Baran says. "The studio had a government-funded artist-in-residence program, so everybody went through there: Phil Glass, Meredith Monk, Laurie Anderson, everybody who eventually became better known in avant-garde and performance art. I met Laurie socially that way, although I didn't work with her there." Baran soon approached Anderson with the idea of working on a record, but on finding that Anderson was not interested at the time, she began working with her on her live shows. "I ended up touring with her, doing her live sound mixing, playing keyboards, hanging around at her house," she says. "And all of that really is not that far from the job definition of production anyway. It's a way of getting to know her and her work."

In late 1980, Baran again tried to convince Anderson to make a record after hearing "O Superman" at a sound check. "The first time I heard it I flipped," she remembers. "And I rarely have that feeling about an artist or a piece of music. I just thought it was wonderful. And I said to myself, 'Okay, now, that's it, I'm going to grab her and do this now!' She actually was starting on a record project, she had gotten a small grant to do a spoken-word or poetry record for a very small label, and she was having trouble finishing it. So I think I caught her at a good moment, when she was frustrated with the other project. So I said, 'Let's just take that one song and do a single.' And Laurie was, 'Well, let's see, after Christmas I'll get a studio and I'll raise some money . . .' And I said, 'How about right this moment?' I think it was Saturday and the stores were closed so we just did it on her home equipment with secondhand tape right then. I basically finished it pretty quickly. I think I went home a couple of times to get clean underwear— it was very intense!"

Recorded for four hundred dollars, "O Superman" was released in 1981 privately on the 110 Records label, backed with another Anderson composition, "Walk the Dog." "O Superman" was a delicately painted portrait of technology and power, encompassing traditional authority figures (the military, mom) and household appliances (answering machines), over a tape loop of steady "ah-ah-ah's" from Anderson. After its release, Baran, who apparently had more faith in the song than Anderson did, began taking "O Superman" to different record labels. "I had that kind of moment of blindness: I knew what the industry was and what they usually thought and bought, but I just believed in it," she explains. "I took it to every major label, and I got the same response pretty much everywhere. People would say, 'I absolutely love this. This is the most wonderful thing I've ever heard, but how can we market this? How can I make my boss think I haven't gone mad?' To her credit, Karin Berg at Warners was right away very interested, and she said, 'Now, we just have to think about how to ram this through.' She came to a performance of Laurie's and cried, she was very moved by it. Laurie had her reputation, too, and I think Warners was interested in that part of it, the cachet that her art legitimacy brought the label. So after a long negotiation, Warners signed her."

Anderson's first project for Warner Bros. was the album *Big Science*, which featured selections from her eight-hour multimedia show *United States*, co-produced by Baran, and Anderson, whose previous production experience had been limited to "O Superman." Fortunately, the unique nature of Anderson's work tended to keep the record company away while she was working. "I know that sometimes they hang around," Anderson says, "but, especially in the early time when I was working with them, they didn't know what to do. They couldn't come by and say 'more bass' because there wasn't any bass on it anyway. So they left me alone, and I really appreciated that a lot." Anderson also found another aspect she liked about being on a major label. "It was actually a big relief, getting out of the art world," she says, "because the economics of the art world was never something I felt comfortable with at all. You know, you have a painter selling a work for five hundred thousand dollars, and then it just goes into somebody's stock portfolio for an investment and hangs in their living room. And pretty soon the artist has to go, 'Wait a second! Who is this for? What am I making this for?' I really love records 'cause they're cheap. And concerts too, comparatively. So I really like the directness of the economics."

Big Science, released in 1982, was a concise condensation of the *United States* show. The "songs" were more a series of surreal stories, with Anderson's well-modulated voice making cool observations about American society—its isolation, its fascination with development (in the title song, the narrator gives directions by using buildings that aren't even constructed as landmarks), and its technology going awry. Anderson's own image, which she describes as "sort of a generic New York artist!" was also something different for the rock audiences her work was starting to attract, and a number of articles commented on her "androgyny." "I don't think that was calculated," she says. "I never was a really fluffy type of person, pink dresses and puffy sleeves. I just dressed like I do. As someone who told stories, I wanted to tell them from different points of view." Anderson's white shirts, plain suits, and cropped thatch of hair not only made her gender ambiguous, they made it irrelevant, as her persona switched from female to male, storyteller to authority figure to backup group, with help from her battery of microphones. Her songs also made subtle comments on relations between the sexes, as in "Let X=X," where a woman's attempt to start a conversation is met with the repeated comment "Isn't it just like a woman?" from her male partner.

Though none of Anderson's records have made a substantial impact on the record charts, she has been able to maintain her position as a prestige artist for her label, an artist who may not leap into the Top 10, but who can hold onto enough of a core following to make it worthwhile to release her records. "I think they keep me around because people there like what I'm doing," she says, "but I'm not a million seller, which is fine with me. And as long as it's fine with them, it's okay. I'm very uninterested in the numbers. If I thought that the more people that liked the music, the better it was, I'd be more interested, but if I thought that, then I would think that Guns n' Roses and Bon Jovi are making the finest music of our time. Which I don't think it is. I mean, it's okay music, but the equation doesn't work for me—the more popular the better."

For her part, Baran continued working with Anderson on her subsequent albums, *Mr. Heartbreak, United States Live, Home of the Brave,* and *Strange Angels*. She also produced records for other performers in New York's art community, such as percussionist David

Laurie Anderson
May 1984 in Chicago, Photo by David Tulsky

Van Tieghem (who had played drums on Anderson's albums). She later branched into film, serving as music producer or sound designer for such films as Anderson's concert film *Home of the Brave*, *Swimming to Cambodia*, a documentary of Spaulding Gray's one-man show, Lizzie Borden's *Working Girls*, and *Bloodhounds of Broadway* (which also featured Madonna). In the '90s, she also returned to school once again, this time as a law student.

Karen Finley was another visual/multimedia artist who began experimenting with music in the early '80s as a result of her involvement in New York's downtown art/club scene, though she is primarily known for her performance work. "I wanted to appropriate music lyrics to advance music because I think it's really backwards," Finley explains. "I feel like music is behind all the other art forms, by, I would say, at least seventy years. One, because of the FCC, and because people are really making music for the money, and the idea that you have to have it on the radio. And music is all censored and the other art forms aren't; if you use a four-letter word in music, forget it, it's forbidden. But if you use a four-letter word in literature, it's all right, or in movies, plays. I felt I wanted to challenge that. So my involvement wasn't necessarily for a musical reason, but for a political reason."

Finley was born in Chicago and studied performance and video at the San Francisco Art Institute, receiving her M.F.A. in 1981. She subsequently moved to New York. "I moved there to get press," she says, "and I got it. I wanted performance to be taken as seriously as painting or other art forms, and I felt like I could only do that being in

New York." It was at one of her early shows at performance space P.S. 122 that Finley met Lori Seid who, as Baran had done with Anderson, offered to help Finley with the technical aspects of her performances. "Her piece moved me so much I went to her after the show and said, 'Look, I don't know a lot, but I'll do anything for you'" remembers Seid. "And we not only struck up a friendship, I still work for her. She said I was the first person to ever offer to help her do anything."

Seid's career as a tech worker (handling lights, sound, stage management, and other duties) began as a result of her girlfriend's involvement in New York's underground art scene of the early '80s, which was replacing the music scene of the late '70s. "Quite honestly, I was working in a xerox shop, and I met this woman I fell in love with," she says. "We were having this wonderful affair, but every day she'd disappear for six hours, and it was starting to get on my nerves. She was going to rehearsals for Tim Miller's *Democracy in America*, so I started to hang out to see what this was about, and started helping—running errands, getting people food, stuff like that. Before I knew it, I was—*bam!*—assistant stage manager at the Next Wave Festival in November. That was the first thing I ever did." Seid's first job soon led to others, and eventually she was working for a variety of avant-garde performers in the city. "I worked with all of them!" she remembers. "Tim Miller, Eric Bogosian, Ethyl Eichelberger, Holly Hughes— people who are now the front-runners. Everybody at this point was up-and-coming. I still had my full-time job, but at night people would hire me to work, and the deal was that I would work for free if they would teach me. I would do anything anybody would teach me to do for free."

While working to establish herself as a performer, Karen Finley also worked as a bartender at Danceteria, one of New York's hipper dance clubs, where she met her second husband, Michael Overn, one of the club's VJs ("video jockeys"). Overn's access to videos led to the creation of "Bad Music Video," a mixed-media collaboration between Overn, Finley, Seid, and another friend, that combined the presentation of "bad" videos ("The *worst* videos," says Seid. "George Michael Thomas of *Miami Vice*, Jermaine Jackson and Pia Zadora's, and we did a whole series on royalty—Elvis and Princess Stephanie") with live performance. Finley's experiences working at the club also provided her with the incentive to make records herself. "I heard a lot of dance music lyrics," she says, "and I was fed up with the one-dimensionality, which I thought was really aggressive toward female sexuality, putting women as sexual objects rather than having a sexual voice. So I just went in and did it."

Finley's first single was "Tales of Taboo," produced by another Danceteria connection, DJ Mark Kamins, who also produced Madonna's early records. The song, in which Finley demanded sexual satisfaction in harsh, confrontational language, was aptly described by her as being "extremely radical. I think that in terms of music history it was really the most aggressive in terms of changing the position of the female to a dominant sexual position." Confronting attitudes toward sexuality was also a theme evident in her performance work, which quickly gained notoriety. One piece in which Finley smeared canned yams on her bottom sparked a debate between *Village Voice* writers C. Carr, who praised Finley's performances, and Pete Hamill, who denounced her. Finley contends that her detractors missed the point of her work: "They didn't ever talk about the fact that I talk about rape, child abuse, oppression of women," she says. "They never really would talk about that. They were never interested in my intellectual abilities."

Finley later jokingly referred to the situation in her song "Gringo" from *The Truth is Hard to Swallow*, in which different men list the sexual activities they enjoy, one of them gleefully announcing, "In the butthole go the yams!" But Finley, like Anderson, also feels her work is part of an established history of performance. "I come from a strong tradition of performance that's been going on for years," she says. "There are other people like me that have been doing work on the edge and doing things with their bodies for years." Finley also feels her use of strong language has had an effect on music lyrics, though her records are primarily played in dance clubs (her duet with Sinéad O'Connor on the latter's "Jump in the River" was limited to dance club play because of Finley's "controversial" reputation). "The general public doesn't know much about me," she admits, "but a lot of DJs in dance clubs and people in the music industry know about me, and I think that is good. I see that lyrics are opening up more. Songs use a lot more words that people wouldn't use before."

Nor does Finley see her records as the only way of posing a challenge to the music industry. "I eventually would like to take the FCC to court," she says. "I think that has to happen. I think music gets the raw end of the deal in terms of accessibility because you can buy a record for eight dollars. And more people can be hearing it at the same time. You can have a very subconscious effect with music, and I believe that governments know music can really influence and challenge governments and society."

During the '80s, Finley and other people involved in the alternative music scene, would find a new platform from which to discuss their views at New York's annual music convention, the New Music Seminar. The first Seminar had been held in 1980 as a way to bring people working in the music industry together to address the changes the punk explosion had brought about in the alternative music scene in general—changes that were being ignored by the major labels and the commercial mainstream. The first Seminar drew two hundred people; it would eventually attract several times that number and become the largest music industry convention in the country. It also provided a common meeting ground for people working in New York's alternative art community; Michael Overn worked for the Seminar as exhibits manager and video consultant in the mid-'80s, and hired Lori Seid as his assistant, while Finley put in regular appearances as a panelist.

Although Seid found the people who ran the Seminar "very good people, very hardworking," her initial encounters with the Seminar's exhibitors gave her a different perspective of the music business. "This was, of course, my first big-time dealing with the music industry," she says. "And I found it very sexist. The first year I worked it, when I went up to people at the booths and said, 'Can I get anything for you?' sex was mostly discussed. Blow jobs, in fact. That really blew my head off. I'm just an outsider that can only see so much, but the first two years I worked the Seminar it struck me very strongly that in the music industry women are still second-rate."

Despite the sexism Seid has encountered from attendees, woman have been actively involved in helping to organize the Seminar since its inception, such as Una Johnston, who began working for the Seminar in its second year, then moved into a full-time staff position in 1986 and eventually served as managing director and international director. Johnston was born in Ireland and grew up in a family where her musical interests were encouraged—as long as they were not something she pursued as a career. "My father did his best to deter us from actually committing to music as a line of work, because it's not something that one would imagine would have any kind of stability," she says. She also received a solid education in feminism as her mother was a founding member of the Irish Women's Liberation Movement. "My background was just totally immersed in feminism," she says. "I was reading Betty Friedan when I was fifteen, Kate Millett, all those women." As a result, Johnston was able to see the freedom women were allocated during the punk era as a logical extension of the achievements of the civil rights and women's liberation movements. "I think that the civil rights movement and the women's movement were laying the groundwork for the young adults of the '80s," she says. "It all had a part to play. I think any woman my age in the music industry has to have been influenced by the civil rights movement and the feminist movement and the punk rebellion."

In 1977, Johnston moved from Ireland to New York, and after working as a booking agent for local clubs, set up a production company with her boyfriend, a sound engineer, which ran for four years. During that time, she witnessed the change-over from music to art in the downtown Manhattan scene. "I was very involved in the club scene and in the performance scene in the early '80s," she says. "It was really dynamic at that time. I lived in the East Village, and that was the place to be: clubs were crowded, after-hours clubs were crowded, new wave was happening; there was a whole kind of energy that was all part of the New Music Seminar, too. And when I sort of side-stepped from that in 1984, in a very short time it became obvious the art scene had taken over in the East Village. Clubs were being run out of business by cabaret laws, and the after-hours clubs were being closed down. The scene had this big strangulation at its grassroots level. And at the same time, the art scene and the galleries were starting to take over and then the performance art scene. Those two scenes seemed to rise out of the ashes of what was the club scene."

Johnston's production company folded when she and her boyfriend split up in 1984, and she spent the next few years working on shows for Latin and African musicians, and for Irish musicians she'd kept in touch with from home, before joining the Seminar as full-time office manager in 1986. And like Lori Seid, Johnston has sometimes found it difficult to work with people outside of the core Seminar staff. "I have come across sexism, there's no doubt about it," she says. "But I think that if you're sure of what you're doing, if you have that confidence within yourself, you're competing on equal terms, you don't have to be afraid of going into their turf. I don't think one should pander to the attitude that you should be more thorough because you're a woman. If you believe in doing your job well, that speaks for itself. I think that personal responsibility should be everybody's motto."

A frequent criticism of the Seminar is the lack of women on the panels in proportion to men, a critique the attendees are not hesitant about expressing even during a panel: during a rock critics panel in 1987, someone called out, "Is rock journalism as white male-dominated as this panel is?" and after a pause the panelists conceded that it was. "Believe me, there is an ongoing awareness on the part of the directors of the need to have balanced panels," Johnston says. "And it's not just women, it's other minorities and different points of view that need to be represented—it's also U.S. views balanced with international perspectives. That's the goal of the panel: to have plenty of representation, not to have affirmative action programs that have token women on panels. But I think because on a mid-to-high management level there is a smaller percentage of women in those jobs, it unfortunately happens that there is a smaller percentage of women on the panels." She also acknowledges the absence of women keynote speakers. "The keynote speaker is a very difficult position to fill," she says, "and all the reasons why it's difficult make it just that much more of a challenge to find the right person regardless. I don't doubt that it will happen someday though." And in 1990, at the eleventh New Music Seminar, it did happen: the keynote speaker was a woman who had begun exploring her career as a musician at the same time the Seminar itself was getting off the ground—Laurie Anderson.

Performers were not the only people to take advantage of the "training ground" punk offered as an entry into the music business. The punk years had inspired women who were not musicians to publish their own fanzines and magazines, become managers, or set up their own record labels. As with the punk bands of the time, many of these enterprises were short-lived, but the acquired experience could then be used to further a later career in the music industry. During the '80s, an increasing number of women would be able to establish long-lasting careers as a result of their utilizing the do-it-yourself ethic of punk to lay the necessary groundwork.

Lisa Fancher, who began her career writing about the Los Angeles music scene for local fanzines, eventually started her own label, Frontier Records, in 1980, which, unlike other indie labels that sprang up during the punk/new wave years, is still operating in the '90s. "Ever since I was a whelp I was into music," says Fancher, whose musical education as a child was helped along by the tastes of her older sisters. "They liked completely different stuff, which was good," she says. "One of them was real tough, so she just liked soul music, 'cause all the tough girls liked soul music; one just liked British Invasion stuff; one was into the L.A. scene, so she liked Love and the Byrds. I got their cast-offs, so I had a pretty well-rounded view, which was good for being a rock critic. And my mom, of course, hated all rock music. Even the Beatles she hated."

Fancher began writing in her teens, moving up from fanzines to daily papers, including the *Los Angeles Times* and the *Herald Examiner*, while following L.A.'s burgeoning punk scene. "I really liked the hardcore scene," she says. "I was checking out bands like Redd Kross and Circle Jerks and Black Flag, all those kind of people when punk was young in L.A. They really sped things up; the Pistols sounded like plodding heavy metal next to the Circle Jerks, who were like ninety miles an hour. Same thing with Black Flag. And the early days of Fear were pretty amusing, because all they did was tell hideously racist, sexist jokes, and the audience spit on them and they spit back, and they threw bottles and you threw bottles back. It was pretty interesting. Even though everybody laughed about L.A. being a punk town, saying, 'Oh, all you guys are just in chaise lounges drinking margaritas.'"

Fancher soon began thinking about how she could become more involved with the music scene. "It'd been brewing in my head that I wanted to get into the business somehow," she says, "and be more than a writer, because writing—I didn't find it that effective in terms of actually changing people's minds outside of L.A. or bringing things to their attention." She decided to start a record label, and chose the name Frontier, releasing her first record, a single by the Fly Boys, in 1980. "That was pretty much of an abject disaster," she admits. "It took me about six or eight months to get the record out, and then they broke up about the same time. I sold the ones that I had but I decided that maybe being a record label owner wasn't that groovy of an idea."

Nonetheless, by the summer she'd decided to try again. "I heard that the Circle Jerks had a tape," she remembers. "So I called them up and said I was interested. The drummer was the one who was handling their business at the time, and he said, and I quote, 'No girl's going to be putting out my record.' For somebody who was going to be a lawyer—he was going to law school—I thought that was remarkably sexist. But I didn't cuss him out or anything, I just went 'Oh well, okay.' Anyway, they investigated me from other local sources and decided that I was okay and then called back about a week later and said that they'd changed their mind—some girl could put out their record!"

The Jerks' "Group Sex," released in November 1980, was an immediate hit, selling nearly one hundred thousand copies, which convinced Fancher to keep Frontier going, though she continued to hold down jobs in record stores for about five years and ran the label out of her apartment. "As I'd roped one band, the most popular band in L.A., it was easier to get other people," she says. And she took perceptions about her position at the label in stride: after hyping Frontier on the phone to people, Fancher would sometimes hear, "Your label sounds interesting—can I talk to the president?" "People are just like that, and it didn't really bother me," she says. "I honestly haven't found people being unbelievably sexist or mauling me or anything else—but of course nobody would dare do that! Unless they wanna die!"

Frontier initially specialized in hardcore acts like the Jerks, Suicidal Tendencies, and Christian Death, but eventually shifted to the '60s-influenced pop of bands like the Long Ryders, Three O'Clock, the Pontiac Brothers, Thin White Rope, EIEIO, and the Young Fresh Fellows. Fancher attributes the change to both her own tastes and the nature of the L.A. scene. "Your tastes change when you get older," she says. "And it was also the shift of the scene, which went from a punkish thing into a melodic pop band thing." But Fancher found that marketing melodic pop bands was not as easy as selling the hardcore acts. And as the decade progressed, she also began facing competition from the major labels, who had finally picked up on the commercial potential of alternative music. "Everything accelerated when major labels became more involved in the alternative world," she says. "Suddenly major labels built their own alternative departments, because a lot of their bands couldn't get any airplay but college radio, and they started working the same marketplace that was our livelihood. And it began to dawn on me that we couldn't stay indie; we'd either have to put out more antisocial records, which is what young kids want to buy, which is going backwards in time, or try to get a major label deal."

After talking with a number of different labels, Fancher struck a deal with BMG, who licensed records of two Frontier acts (Thin White Rope and American Music

Club) through its RCA label; another deal provided production-and-distribution for other Frontier acts. "It's definitely a low-priced deal with RCA, but it doesn't bother me 'cause I don't want to spend two hundred thousand dollars making records," Fancher says. "I would rather try to help bands out with the major label's money, and keep the creative control and the close personal ties that we have, where they can always get me on the phone and they're not dealing with some horrible corporation."

By the end of the decade, Fancher's "horrible corporations"—major labels—would dominate the music industry to the point where six main companies would control ninety percent of the record market. Though indie labels were far from diminishing in number, few of them had the identity and impact indies like Sun and Motown had enjoyed; larger "indies," such as A&M, Chrysalis, and Virgin, were being sold to the majors (Motown would finally be sold to MCA in 1988). As in the '50s, major labels were moving in to capitalize on a musical trend originally discovered and promoted by indie labels. It was the logical conclusion of a familiar cycle in the music industry, and as the schism between majors and indies widened, indie labels were left with fewer distribution outlets and major labels appeared to be increasingly shifting their emphasis from an interest in music to an interest in business at the expense of music—best illustrated by the growing tendency to refer to an artist's work as "product."

It was not only people working in the indie realm who disliked the creeping corporate feel of the music industry. Holly Knight, a songwriter who has written material for such major label acts as Pat Benatar, Heart, Tina Turner, Aerosmith, and Bon Jovi, also has strong feelings about the increasingly rigid corporate structure that developed in the music industry throughout the '80s. "The whole business right now to me has become very corporate and very businesslike," she says. "Although I'm really happy to be in this business, I have a strong dislike at the moment for certain facets of it. It's happened over the last few years more than ever. The labels always want the perfect package. They want the perfect tune, the perfect look, the perfect image. And it ends up that they're manufacturing product."

Knight, who grew up on the East Coast, studied classical music as a child while also listening to a wide range of music from Broadway musicals to Motown. "The Stones were always my favorite though; I thought they epitomized rock & roll," she says. In her teens, she began playing with local bands, and in 1978 became the keyboardist for Spider, with whom she recorded two albums. She also began writing her own material. "It wasn't like I had been dreaming about it all my life," she explains. "It's just that everybody else was writing. They weren't writing great tunes, so I figured I might as well try. And that's how I became a songwriter!" It was around this time that Knight met Mike Chapman, then working with Blondie and considering a move to California.

When Knight quit Spider in 1981, Chapman offered her a publishing deal and the opportunity of collaborating with him if she'd move to L.A. Knight, then in her mid-twenties and living in New York, agreed and soon discovered that she'd found a very compatible songwriting partner in Chapman. "I was lucky to have met up with Chapman because it turned out to be a very fruitful relationship," she says. "Chapman was like my mentor, and I gained a lot of experience and knowledge through him that would have maybe taken twice as long on my own."

Knight's first collaboration with Chapman was on "Better Be Good to Me," later recorded by Tina Turner, but she remembers a Pat Benatar song as being a particular turning point in her career. "Pat Benatar called up and asked Chapman to write her a song for her next album," Knight recalls (Chapman had first worked with Benatar when he produced songs on her debut album). "And he asked me if I wanted to do it with him. So we ended up writing a song called 'Love Is a Battlefield' [a number 5 hit for Benatar], and then all of a sudden people started calling, and it kind of took off." Knight also continued her career as a musician, though songwriting remained her major focus. "Every time I would pursue my recording, my writing would suffer," she explains. "And I felt like I was competing in an arena where there's so many people that just being a talented player wasn't enough. Because there's a lot of talented players. I felt I had more to offer as a writer."

Knight also felt that as a performer she was perceived as a "female musician," a tag that wasn't attributed to her as a songwriter. "People never say, 'She's a great woman writer,'" she says. "I've never gotten that distinction, ever, as a songwriter. I may have gotten it once or twice as a player, and it was always the people I worked with. I had to work with Rod Stewart on a tune [Knight co-wrote 'Love Touch' for Stewart, a Top 10 hit in 1986], and they were going to take me on tour for three weeks. These guys were from Scotland and England and were really chauvinistic, pompous, vain guys. Working with them was hard. Not so much Rod; Rod was open to it. I think his mates, though, were highly intimidated that there was a woman dealing with them."

Knight has also experienced difficulties in dealing with men in her business relationships. "I know how I want to do things, and I'm not going to be manipulated or muscled into doing it a certain way," she says. "That's pretty much how it's always been with me. You end up getting a reputation for being difficult or bitchy—but my attitude is if you still want a hit tune from me you're going to call me up. And they do." Knight's tendency to speak her mind led to friction in her partnership with Chapman and the two eventually parted ways. But by the time she stopped working with Chapman, Knight was successfully writing on her own (Tina Turner took Knight's "One of the Living," from the film *Mad Max Beyond Thunderdome*, to number 15 in 1985), and was also making plans to move into production. "I found out Chapman became a producer because he was a songwriter," she explains, "and he was tired of giving songs to other producers and having them mess up the tune or interpret it in a way that wasn't how he heard it. And I can understand that now, and that's why I want to produce records."

Knight is aware of the lack of women working as producers. "You won't find one that's full-time who does all sorts of different acts," she says. "I'm hoping to change that." Nor does she plan to let her dismay at dealing with the corporate aspects of the industry chase her away. "Don't get me wrong," she says. "I'm thrilled to be a part of the business because I'm able to make money doing what I really like to do. But I know some writers that are really successful because they schmooze all the time and they just play the game. And I don't play that game too well. Fortunately I don't have to deal with it too much. I have a studio in my house, and I only deal with the people that I really like to work with. I guess that's the only way around it, really. I mean, if you just say the hell with it and stop, then they're kind of getting the best of you, aren't they?"

Though it was not yet apparent in the early '80s, the growing number of women becoming involved in the music industry would have a sizeable impact by the end of the decade. And while the contributions of the women working on the business side were generally overlooked, media coverage of women performers was encompassing an increasingly wide range of singers and musicians in stories about women-in-rock. Books also began to appear on the subject, though they usually limited themselves to a particular period: Alan Betrock's *Girl Groups: The Story of a Sound* presented a detailed look at the girl group era, while two books, each entitled *New Women in Rock*, focused mainly on the punk/new wave years, with some coverage of forerunners like Joan Armatrading, Patti Smith, and Heart.

In 1985, a fresh new voice approached the subject of women in rock from a dramatically different perspective in the form of *Bitch* magazine. Subtitled "The Women's Rock Newsletter [later 'Mag'] With Bite," *Bitch* was launched in August 1985 with the intention of providing coverage for female performers overlooked by a media the *Bitch* staffers saw as primarily interested in perpetrating the accepted stereotypes of women in rock. "It's a sort of permanent novelty position," Lori Twersky, one of the magazine's founders, says about traditional perceptions of women's roles in the rock industry. "There's already a problem with the way the history is presented. Women keep being left out of the histories, so if you've grown up on the rock magazines, then you always think that women are a new big deal because they don't bother reporting that there were women before. There are dozens of bands out there, but there just isn't the motivation to cover them. There seems to be a very big conviction that, 'Well, nobody would be interested.'"

The challenge for *Bitch* was not only to provide coverage for female musicians but also to analyze how and why the accepted perceptions about women in rock worked to keep women out of histories. "The prevailing attitude was that female bands are a novelty," Twersky explains. "When the Go-Go's split up, it was only then, you'll look back, that the Bangles got publicity; they were just picked up and dropped straight into the slot that the Go-Go's had vacated. The extent to which women have to prove themselves over and over and over—it's like they have to start from scratch with each album if they're doing anything a little bit different. If you fall into the singer-songwriter niche, that will carry you for a while, because the media will go, 'Well, we know this stereotype.' But if you're at all breaking out of that stereotype, you have to prove yourself again and again."

Born in Palo Alto, California, in 1954, Lori Twersky began writing in her teens in the early '70s; she was also an active street performer and sang briefly with a rock band. "I actually sang, when I was about fourteen, with a semi-psychedelic band in San Jose," she says. "We performed at some place near San Jose State that was the size of a closet that was a lunch counter during the day. At night the shades were pulled down, and it was kind of a private music club. I used to sneak out of the house to do that; I would tell my parents I was going to bed early and then climb out the bedroom window."

But despite her start in performing, it was writing Twersky ended up pursuing. After dropping out of college, she joined the staff of the Santa Clara–based *Good Times*, starting out as the art and theater critic and inheriting other columns—women's sports, restaurants, and cooking—when their respective writers left the staff. "I had a sort of punkish food column," she remembers. "I got a death threat once for recommending using orange peels in a recipe. This guy called me up and asked if I didn't know that orange peel had Red Dye Number Two and fascists like me should pay for recommending that innocent children be given this. It was probably the most exciting time to be a food critic than at any other point. It wouldn't have been something I thought was a very controversial area when I started doing it."

Twersky eventually moved back to San Jose, continuing her food critic antics at another local paper, *Metro* ("This is how most people think of me, actually. I'm probably best known as a food writer!"), and also writing about rock music. She found that her interest in music didn't always coincide with the interests of the rock press, though a piece for *Trouser Press*, "Devils or Angels? The Female Teenage Audience Examined," attracted a lot of attention for its revelations on the subject of teenage fans. "The going stereotype was that the only reason women were interested in rock music was because of sex, period," she says. "All women musicians were glorified groupies. And if people really believed that, and a lot of people really did, then what I was saying *was* a new idea: gee, maybe women just like music." Not all magazines were as receptive, which led to the conception of *Bitch*. "At one point, there were a bunch of female bands I really liked that it was almost impossible to get information on, of which Girlschool and the Pandoras were the two big ones," says Twersky. "*Bitch* grew in part out of being unable to find any information about them."

Bitch also inadvertently grew out of plans Twersky and a group of writers had to start another magazine. "We wanted to start a regional paper in San Jose similar to *Good Times* but with more news," Twersky explains, and after working on the business plan for the proposed weekly one day, the writers decided to have a little fun assembling a magazine about women rock musicians. "It was a 'what if' thing," says Twersky. "'Wouldn't it be great to have a magazine called *Bitch*?' But we didn't really expect it to become one; we ran off fifty photocopies of the first issue and only gave about half of them away. I had originally thought *Bitch* would probably be ten issues mailed among friends." But to the surprise of the staff, *Bitch* became an instant hit, especially after *Musician* magazine ran a short item on the magazine. The sixteen-page debut issue managed to cover a wide range of territory, including a news column, record and book reviews (including a review of a comic book about the adventures of the all-female band Josie and the Pussycats), a debate about the Live Aid charity concert, an article on Janet Gambino, drummer with a New Jersey band called the Bluesettes in the late '60s, and a feature on Girlschool ("Not Metal Mamas, But The Real Thing," ran the headline).

"We just got flooded with mail," says Twersky. "We had put in this subscription ad, almost as a joke, and then suddenly there we were with money in hand. And we thought, 'My God, we can't rip these people off. We better do this.' I kept expecting it to settle at some level; I thought we'd wait until it settled, then see about going on with the weekly. *Bitch* just kept growing and growing and we were totally unprepared for it, totally understaffed." *Bitch*'s circulation eventually "settled" at around seven thousand, and quickly developed into a resource for musicians, providing free classified ads, ready-made posters bands could use to advertise gigs, and offering tips on the technical aspects of putting out fanzines. *Bitch* also ran lengthy essays ("Are Female Fans the Same as Groupies? Give the Right Answer or Die. A Symposium") and invited audience response, with debates continuing in successive issues. Twersky was also committed to addressing other aspects of the music business. "The job issues are really more important to me," she says. "On the one hand, I think rock writing on the whole is now much, much better about presenting women as legitimate musicians rather than as groupies. On the other hand, I look at the masthead of *Rolling Stone*, and I can see that the choicer, better-paying editorial jobs seem to have gone to men.

"It really pisses me off when some white male rock critic will get up on a soapbox complaining about MTV not giving enough space to black musicians or female musicians," she continues. "And I'll go, 'Well, what about your job? How many black writers or female writers does your paper have? How many editors do they have? How many of them are associate editors as opposed to editorial assistants?' That, I think, is one of those things people tend not to look at because so much of the business is involved in image, and ultimately I'm less interested in image than in what's going on behind the scenes. We have a bunch of female artists at the top of the charts now, but I don't know what their contracts look like. I don't know if they're going to get royalties next year. I don't know if they're ever going to get paid their royalties. I don't know whether they signed away the rights to their name. And that's more important than whether or not they're topping the charts. What good does it do you to top the charts if you're never going to see any royalties?"

In 1989, *Bitch* was put on hold so the staff could work on an encyclopedia of female rock performers, tentatively entitled *Who's That Girl: The Bitch Guide to Women in Rock & Pop.* (The book remains unpublished.) Sadly, Lori Twersky would not live to see the results of her years of hard work. On November 3, 1991, she died of complications arising from eclampsia, a convulsive disorder, after a two-year struggle with lupus. She was thirty-seven. Twersky's legacy would be the twenty-five issues of *Bitch* she helped produce, which proved there was an audience—both female and male—very much interested in reading about female musicians from a different perspective than was offered in mainstream music publications, in addition to learning about the innumerable performers whose stories had been "lost" or unacknowledged in previous rock histories.

After the turbulence of the punk years, the early '80s were a time of transition that women were able to use to their advantage. Women who started out in the punk arena were able to use their experience to continue their careers on a more successful level when the punk era had ended, as the Go-Go's and Chrissie Hynde were able to do as performers, and as Lisa Fancher did with her record label, Frontier. Other performers, like Laurie Anderson and Karen Finley, were inspired by the energy generated by punk to introduce musical elements into their own work. And by the time alternative music was recognized as being "commercial" by the major record companies, women were well positioned to move up the corporate ladder in greater numbers than ever before. The arrival of MTV, which sparked the growth of music videos as a marketing tool would offer another avenue for exploration and innovation. And now women were able to use the credo of self-sufficiency put forth by both feminism and punk to play a greater role in running the show themselves.

8

Smile for the Camera

"I may be dressing like the typical bimbo, but I'm in charge . . . people don't think of me as a person who's not in charge of my career or my life. And isn't that what feminism is all about? Aren't I in charge of my life, doing the things I want to do, making my own decisions?"
—Madonna, on ABC's *Nightline*, December 3, 1990

At midnight on August 1, 1981, Music Television, better known as MTV, made its debut with a video clip by the British group the Buggles, "Video Killed the Radio Star." Initially broadcast to a mere two million households in the U.S., within ten years the audience would have expanded to 249 million households in forty-one countries (an exposure "unmatched by any American institution short of government itself," the *Village Voice* would note). If the medium of video had not entirely eliminated the "radio star," it had nonetheless become a powerful social and cultural phenomenon, which in turn further emphasized the important role a performer's visual identity had always had in rock.

Film clips of performers lip-synching to their latest hits were hardly a new development in the music industry. In the '40s, musicians like Louis Armstrong performed in "Soundies," which were shown on specially designed jukeboxes, an innovation replaced in the '60s by "Scopitones," film clips also screened on jukeboxes, which featured such performers as the Exciters and Nancy Sinatra. By the early 1960's, clips of rock performers were being used on television variety shows and had established how effective a link between rock music and a strong visual image could be—who can hear the Supremes' "Stop! In the Name of Love" without seeing the three singers holding up their hands in the "stop" pose? And as rock became a bigger and bigger business, aspiring directors, like Penelope Spheeris and her Rock 'n' Reel company, took advantage of the chance to gain directing experience working on such clips. "'Long about 1974, the record companies figured out by some brilliant deduction that they didn't have to send a whole band to Australia—they could just send a piece of film," Spheeris explains of her company's work in producing clips then called "promotional films" as opposed to "videos," which were produced on videotape.

But initially, promotional films had few outlets except variety shows, and there was certainly no channel, or even program, that had considered showing nothing but promo films; music shows like *American Bandstand* and *Midnight Special* used such clips but kept the focus on in-studio performances. But with the advent of cable television, which opened up the possibilities for myriad channels that could accommodate every conceivable taste, the idea of a twenty-four-hour video channel became a viable prospect and, for the record companies, a potentially powerful marketing tool. The power of this tool was demonstrated almost immediately when bands receiving extensive MTV airtime saw their record sales rise in direct proportion. The surprise was that these bands were heretofore little-known groups, primarily from Britain and Europe, where videos had been a part of the music scene for some years. With twenty-four hours to fill, MTV's programmers were forced to look overseas for material until U.S. record companies began arranging for videos to be churned out by their artists.

As a result, MTV's early years exhibited a musical diversity missing from mainstream radio, though as more major label artists leapt aboard the video bandwagon, this diversity was inevitably homogenized. But the downside to achieving the wide exposure available from MTV was that an act had to be visually impressive in order to make an impact. For female artists who had been trying to question the focus on a musician's—particularly a woman's—appearance as opposed to her performance, the rise of MTV signaled a return to convention. Women who stressed substance over style were virtually nonexistent, or at best under-represented, in the realm of video, in contrast to similarly styled male performers such as Bruce Springsteen, John Cougar Mellencamp, and Sting.

But for female performers with imagination and a sense of humor, there was another option: appropriating the traditional images of femininity and, through blatant exaggeration, subverting them. The visual medium of video offered an excellent opportunity to explore, comment on, and question gender roles, and a number of performers were well positioned to take advantage of this opportunity and exploit it on a mass scale that had been previously unavailable in rock. Eurythmics' vocalist Annie Lennox and Cyndi Lauper were among the first women who benefited from the exposure MTV offered them, Eurythmics having their first Top 40 hit in the U.S. in 1983, Lauper in 1984.

Lennox also played with androgyny in a manner no female performer had really explored before, a trend dubbed "gender bending," and popularized by other performers, such as Culture Club's Boy George and the cross-dressing singer "Marilyn."

Lennox, born in 1954 in Aberdeen, Scotland, studied piano and flute as a child, and was an avid fan of Motown artists like the Supremes and Marvin Gaye. At seventeen, she was accepted at the Royal Academy of Music in London, where she moved in 1972. But she found the Academy stifling and after three years she left to pursue her developing interest in singing and songwriting. She first joined a folk rock group, Dragon's Playground, next appeared with the jazz rock outfit Redbrass, with

Annie Lennox of the Eurythmics July 1983 at the Palace, Hollywood, Photo by Sherry Rayn Barnett

whom she recorded one album (*Silence's Consent*), and briefly sang in a vocal duo with another woman, Joy Dey, called the Stocking Tops. In between gigs, Lennox supported herself by waitressing. It was while working as a waitress at a health-food restaurant, Pippins, that she met David Stewart, a guitarist who'd previously played in the band Longdancer. Stewart's first words to Lennox were reportedly, "Will you marry me?"— an offer she declined, though she did move in with him.

Their first group, the Catch, was formed with a guitarist friend of Stewart's, Peet Coombes. The Catch released the single "Black Blood"/"Borderline" (the former written by Stewart and Coombes and the latter written by Lennox though both songs were credited to Lennox-Stewart-Coombes) on Logo Records in the fall of 1977, then added Jim Toomey on drums and Eddie Chin on bass and renamed themselves the Tourists. The Tourists released their first single (also on Logo), "Blind Among the Flowers"/"He Who Laughs Last" in May 1979, with their self-titled debut LP released the following month. In contrast to the punk/new wave of the time, the Tourists played fairly straightforward '60s-influenced rock; Lennox's voice, later a powerful asset to Eurythmics' sound, was strong but undeveloped, and curiously devoid of emotion.

The group released two subsequent albums, *Reality Effect* in 1979 and *Luminous Basement* in 1980 (a compilation album, *Tourists*, was released in 1981), and had four hits in the British Top 40, including a cover of Dusty Springfield's "I Only Want to Be with

You," released in October 1979, and which reached number 4—the same position Springfield's version had reached in 1963. In 1980, the group played a forty-date tour in America (where the group's second and third albums were released on Epic) and signed with RCA, but by 1981 problems within the band led to their eventual breakup. Lennox and Stewart's romantic involvement also ended, but the two decided to continue working together under a new name, Eurythmics, a name taken from a Greek dance movement called "eurhythmics." "It described what we wanted to be," said Stewart, "European and rhythmical."

Lennox and Stewart also decided to maintain a revolving lineup of musicians instead of forming another band, which they felt would be too restrictive. Lennox was also determined to maintain a greater degree of involvement in her new venture as opposed to what she viewed as her limited position in the Tourists as "girl singer." "I'm not only a singer, I'm also a songwriter, I'm also part of an actress, part of a designer, part of a clothes designer," she said in the book *Sweet Dreams*. The first Eurythmics album, *In the Garden*, was recorded in Germany with a wide range of musicians, including Marcus Stockhausen (son of composer Karlheiz Stockhausen), Blondie drummer Clement Burke, and members of the German cult band Can, and was produced by Conny Plank, with whom Lennox had co-produced an album for Italian singer Gianna Nannini. Released on RCA in 1981, the album's experimental electronic approach was a dramatic departure from the Tourists' material. Although the album and the accompanying singles made little impression on the charts and were not released in America, they did inspire interest in the duo's future work.

During this time, Lennox stumbled upon a striking visual image, something she'd been playing with since the days of the Tourists, when the press was already writing that "Annie's day-glo clothes and bleached white hair make her pop's freakiest pin-up." While performing in a club one night, a member of the audience pulled off Lennox's wig and revealed her cropped, slicked-back hair to favorable audience reaction. Lennox then began embellishing her appearance by wearing men's suits, unleashing her new look to the public at large in the video (written and directed by Stewart) for "Sweet Dreams (Are Made of This)," the title track of their second album, both released in January 1983. Lennox's commanding presence underscored the song's cynical commentary on the nature of motivation, with Lennox sporting a bright orange crew cut and wielding a riding crop in a manner both teasing and threatening, intercut with surreal images of Lennox and Stewart playing cellos in a cow pasture or sitting in an RCA board room while a cow walked around them. Matched with a hypnotic Europop beat, "Sweet Dreams" proved to be irresistible to American record buyers, and hit number 1, while the album reached number 15 (the song and album reached numbers 3 and 2 respectively in Britain).

After the success of "Sweet Dreams," the group reissued "Love Is a Stranger," previously released in Britain to little notice. This time, the song jumped into both the U.K. and U.S. charts with the boost from another eye-catching video. On this outing, Lennox adopted a variety of guises, including a long-haired, glamorous blonde; a leather-clad, brunette dominatrix; and, briefly, a man in a suit. When initially shown in America, MTV blacked out the shots of Lennox "changing" from a woman to a man (she pulls off her wig), assuming the singer was a male transvestite; Lennox was forced to submit legal documentation proving that she portrayed the character.

In the wake of the success other British groups were finding on the U.S. charts following video exposure on MTV, *Newsweek*'s January 23, 1984, issue, featured a story entitled "Britain Rocks America—Again," with Lennox and Boy George paired on the cover as the prime gender benders of their generation. Lennox took her own gender bending to new heights when Eurythmics appeared on the Grammy Awards in 1984 to sing "Sweet Dreams," flaunting an Elvis-styled hairdo complete with sideburns, in part to overcome their own hesitancy about appearing on the show. "We were very reticent about it," Lennox explained to the *Los Angeles Times*. "We felt our stance was not in the bosom of the conventional music scene . . . we wanted to find a way to present ourselves that would satisfy the record company and satisfy our own feelings."

Eurythmics' next album, *Touch*, built on the group's cool techno-pop with strong instrumental arrangements encompassing everything from torch ballads to calypso, and was the band's highest charting album in the U.S., reaching number 7. Lennox's playing with sexual ambiguity was still apparent, most notably on the album's cover, a dramatic shot of a bare-armed Lennox flexing her muscles while staring out from behind a leather mask—and in the high jinks of the video for "Who's That Girl" (a Top 30 single is America). Cast as a nightclub singer, the blonde-wigged Lennox bemoans the loss of her man while being silently appraised by a dark-haired man in the audience—also played by Lennox; meanwhile, Stewart cavorts in another club in the company of various "dates," including members of Bananarama (Stewart would late marry Bananarama's Siobhan Fahey), Hazel O'Connor, a Debbie Harry look-alike, and "Marilyn." Lennox eventually ends up with her male alter ego and kisses herself at the video's conclusion.

After releasing their proposed soundtrack for a film remake of *1984* (their music was ultimately not used in the film, and some radio stations banned the song "Sexcrime" because of its "controversial" title), the duo entered more soulful territory with *Be Yourself Tonight*, released in 1985, a lively collection of songs backed with fiery horn arrangements. In addition to the singles "Would I Lie to You," which reached number 5, and "There Must Be an Angel," a Top 30 hit that featured Stevie Wonder on harmonica, Lennox traded vocals in a duet with Aretha Franklin, "Sisters Are Doing It for Themselves," a Top 20 hit. The song also appeared on Franklin's own *Who's Zoomin' Who* album, her highest charting LP in over 10 years, which put Franklin back in the Top 20, and gave her Top 10 single hits with the title track (which she co-wrote) and "Freeway of Love" in addition to "Sisters." "Sisters" forthrightly championed female strength but typically avoided a direct advocacy of feminism, which no doubt added to its commercial appeal—though Tina Turner, who had originally been approached to sing with Lennox, reportedly turned down the offer because she felt the song was "too feminist."

Eurythmics released another three albums in the '80s, with their final LP, *We Too Are One*, released in 1989 after the group moved from RCA to Arista. *We Too Are One*, like *Be Yourself Tonight*, emphasized Lennox and Stewart's love of soul, in sharp contrast to their earlier synth-pop work. But though entering the U.K. charts at number 1, the album was far less successful in the States, only reaching number 34; their previous LP, *Savage*, hadn't even entered the U.S. Top 40. The group was still highly regarded despite their lack of record sales—a concert review in the *Hollywood Reporter* in 1989 hailed Lennox as "the best white soul singer alive"—but by the end of the decade Lennox and Stewart put Eurythmics on hold to work on solo projects Lennox released her solo debut, *Diva*, in 1992, followed by *Medusa* in 1995. Eurythmics reformed in the late '90s and released the album *Peace*.

As the first major female MTV star, Lennox had demonstrated how visual imagery could be used to challenge traditional images of women in rock. Lennox was well aware of the tendency to stereotype performers by their appearance. "When I had blonde hair [during the Tourists days] you have no idea how many comparisons I had with Debbie Harry!" she said in *Sweet Dreams*, explaining the development of her own gender bending image. "One of the main reasons I wear the clothes I do and have an androgynous image, is because I didn't want to be seen as a 'girlie' singer wearing pretty dresses. I don't want to change sexual labels—I want to sidestep them, and to confound people a little bit with something fresher and less clichéd." Instead of seeing videos as just another promotional tool, Eurythmics used the medium as another avenue of artistic expression, learning to manipulate their image instead of being manipulated *by* their image.

Cyndi Lauper, who also used the medium of video to help launch her career, made a strong feminist statement in her video for "Girls Just Want to Have Fun," an anthem of female solidarity. Born in Queens, New York, in 1953, Lauper spent her early years in Brooklyn and later returned to Queens when her parents divorced. A fan of Brenda Lee, and later the Beatles, Lauper learned to play guitar from her older sister and began writing songs at age eleven. She quit college to pursue her work in music and in 1974 started out singing backup vocals for the dance band Doc West, performing songs by Labelle and Janis Joplin. Lauper then formed another cover band, Flyer, but after three years on the club circuit, she came perilously close to permanently damaging her singing voice and had to enlist the help of a vocal coach before she could resume her career.

In 1978, Lauper met saxophone/keyboard player John Turi; the two began writing songs together and eventually formed the band Blue Angel, which quickly became a favorite on the New York club scene with their new wave/rock & roll mix: "If you can imagine the Crystals with punk hair and Fender guitars, you've got the picture," said *Rolling Stone*. The band signed with Polydor in 1979 and released their first (and only) album the following year, but despite good reviews *Blue Angel* did not sell up to expectations, and musical disagreements among the band members led to the band's breakup in 1982. Lauper then acquired a new manager, David Wolff (whom she married and later divorced), got a job performing at a Japanese piano bar, and worked at a used-clothing shop called Screaming Mimi's while looking for a new record deal. She was eventually offered a contract with Portrait (a subsidiary of CBS), who released her first solo album, *She's So Unusual*, in late 1983.

The album's first single, "Girls Just Want to Have Fun," was a playful romp celebrating female camaraderie. The accompanying video cast Lauper as every teenage girl's potential best friend, decked out in thrift-shop finery and surrounded by a lively female street gang that danced with her down the city streets; Lauper's mother was also featured in a role. The original version of the song, written by Robert Hazard, had been quite different, and as explained in the magazine *Jump Cut*, Lauper had initially turned down a suggestion from her producer, Rick Chertoff, that she consider the song for *She's So Unusual*. "It was basically a very chauvinistic song," Lauper remembered. "[Chertoff] said, 'But wait, think about what it COULD mean . . . forget all this other stuff, and think about what it could mean.'" So Lauper did think, and ended up changing the song's male orientation to a female one.

Her decision paid off, for "Girls" went all the way to number 2 and Lauper thanked Hazard in the album's credits "for letting me change your song." The album itself, which reached number 4 and sold more than four and a half million copies, featured four songs written or co-written by Lauper, backup vocals from Ellie Greenwich, and a record number of hits from a debut LP—all four of the follow-up singles to "Girls" landed in the Top 40, three of them in the Top 5. Each single also displayed a different side to Lauper's musical makeup: "Time After Time" (a number 1 hit) and "All Through the Night" were ballads, the cover of the Brains' "Money Changes Everything" was more straightforward rock, and "She-Bop" was a tongue-in-cheek number celebrating the joys of masturbation.

Cyndi Lauper
January 1985 at the American Music Awards,
Los Angeles, Photo by Sherry Rayn Barnett

Lauper's frank approach to girl talk, as well as her humorous approach, readily won over her audience: she was as likely to carry the banner for her favorite sport, pro-wrestling (she also managed a wrestler, World Wrestling Federation female champion Wendi Richter), as to be honored by *Ms.* magazine in its January 1985 "Women of the Year" issue (along with Holly Near, Vice Presidential candidate Geraldine Ferraro, and nine other women). Unlike Annie Lennox, who shied away from feminist interpretations of "Sisters Are Doin' It for Themselves," Lauper had no hesitation about aligning herself with the feminist movement, citing the church, the family, and the government as "the three biggest oppressors of women that will ever come along." "If Helen Reddy's recording of 'I Am Woman' was about anger and a new-found collective pride," wrote *Ms.*, "'Girls Just Want to Have Fun' is about a newer, defiant joy and the celebration of our strength."

Unfortunately, Lauper's campy sensibilities, embodied in everything from her wardrobe to her squeaky Betty Boop–styled voice, give her an image as a wacky novelty figure, an image she later found hard to shake, and she was unable to equal the successes she'd enjoyed in 1984 (which included winning the Grammy for Best New Artist). *True Colors*, released in 1986, was generally considered a weaker effort than her debut, though it still spawned two Top 5 hits (including the title track, which went to number 1) and reached number 4 in the album charts; it was also the first of her albums that Lauper co-produced. But the three-year lapse between *True Colors* and Lauper's next album, *A Night to Remember*, resulted in a sharp drop in momentum for the singer, and though the single "I Drove All Night" made it into the Top 10, the album itself barely cracked the Top 40. Nor did a planned film career come off when *Vibes*, her film debut in 1988, was critically panned. Lauper continued to release albums in the '90s.

But the performer—female or male—who turned out to be the most skillful at capitalizing on the potential of video, especially its capacity to comment on and challenge conventional perceptions of sex and sexuality, was undoubtedly Madonna. Madonna dove head-first into the arena of sexuality, cultivating the image of a modern-day

Marilyn Monroe in one of her many .incarnations—though aside from looks, there were few other similarities between the two. Whereas Monroe's sexuality had only increased her vulnerability and insecurity, sexuality represented the core of Madonna's strength. Her initial street urchin look, with torn jeans, lingerie worn as "outer wear," dangling jewelry, a belt buckle that read "Boy Toy," and bare midriff (an appearance as rag-tag as Lauper's thrift-store chic, though Lauper was seen as the friendly "good" girl while Madonna embodied the raunchy "bad" girl) was adopted by "Madonna Wannabes" across the country. The mainstream press wasted no time taking potshots at her appearance ("Around her famous navel the MTVenus packed a little mound of tummy blub," noted *Entertainment Weekly*), and feminists were either drawn to or repelled by the image of a woman in power who had resorted to her sexuality to get that power and was now influencing an army of preteens to do the same.

To female artists trying to escape being regarded as sexual objects first and performers second, Madonna's tactics were seen as reactionary and regressive. "The thing about her that people think is so great is that she's made it in a man's world and is now a multimillion dollar corporation," said Exene Cervenka in *Option*. "So she's successful and that's supposed to be great for women. But what made her successful was keeping her pants unzipped." Karen Finley also expressed the problems some women had in admiring Madonna's undeniable strength, while feeling uncomfortable with what they perceived as her underlying message. "I think she's really powerful and I like her," says Finley, "but I find her politics extremely offensive. She really doesn't know how to present herself publicly unless she is presenting herself as being sexually desirable. And record companies love that."

For her part, Madonna claimed to take her role less seriously. "I never set out to be a role model for girls or women," she said in *Cosmopolitan*, answering charges about her "regressive" image by saying, "They didn't get the joke. The whole point is that I'm *not* anybody's toy. People take everything so literally." She also pointed out the double standard she felt lay behind the attacks on her utilization of sexuality in her work. "When someone like Prince, Elvis or Jagger does the same thing, they are being honest, sensual human beings," she told *Newsweek* in a 1985 article on "Rock's New Women" (which featured Cyndi Lauper on the cover). "But when I do it: 'Oh, please. Madonna, you're setting the women's movement back a million years.'"

Born Madonna Louise Veronica Ciccone in 1958 in Bay City, Michigan, Madonna grew up in a family of five brothers and two sisters. She began performing at a young age and later appeared in plays while attending Catholic school. She persuaded her father to let her study dance instead of the piano, and eventually set herself up as a dance instructor to the neighborhood children. After high school she won a dance scholarship to the University of Michigan, but left for New York in 1978, training first at Alvin Ailey's American Dance Center, and later with the Center's co-founder, Pearl Lang, in Lang's own dance company. But she felt the opportunities in the dance world were limited, and landed a job in a disco revue in Paris, singing backup for French singer Patrick Hernandez and so impressing the producers they wrote her a specialty number, "She's a Real Disco Queen."

Back in New York, Madonna began performing with bands, starting out as a drummer in a group called the Breakfast Club in 1979. But she soon stepped out from behind the drums as a singer, fronting her own bands. In the early '80s, one of her bands signed a management contract, but musical differences soon arose between Madonna and the rest of the group, leading to an eventual split. Madonna then began writing and recording more dance-oriented material with Stephen Bray, a friend from college, and hanging out at the Danceteria club, where Karen Finley was waitressing. She eventually met DJ Mark Kamins, who played a demo of her first single, "Everybody," at the club, and, noting the favorable response, helped Madonna get a record deal with Sire Records.

"Everybody," produced by Kamins, was released in April 1982 and proved to be a strong dance club favorite, as did her follow-up 12-inch single "Burning Up"/"Physical Attraction," though neither appeared on the Top 40 charts. In 1983 Madonna released her self-titled debut album, which also became a dance club favorite but had little impact in the charts until the release of the single "Holiday" toward the end of the year. By early 1984, the single peaked at number 16, followed in the spring and fall by two Top 10 hits, "Borderline" and "Lucky Star"; the album itself reached number 8 and sold over nine million copies, its success delaying the release of *Like a Virgin* until 1985.

If 1984 had provided Madonna with a solid introduction to the pop mainstream, her accomplishments in 1985 solidified that success and firmly established the performer as a full-fledged pop star. *Like a Virgin* became her first number 1 album (all of Madonna's LPs have reached the Top 10, except for an album of single remixes, which reached number 14), along with four Top 5 single hits, including the title track, which reached number 1, and went on to sell eleven million copies. Produced by Chic's Nile Rodgers, *Like a Virgin* was a more polished effort than its predecessor and featured five songs written or co-written by Madonna. She also branched out into film (having made her debut in the low-budget soft core film *A Certain Sacrifice* in 1980): her role in Susan Seidelman's *Desperately Seeking Susan* received good reviews even from critics who were not Madonna fans, and her appearance in *Vision Quest* resulted in another number 1, "Crazy for You." She also embarked on her first concert tour, which was unsurprisingly an instant sellout.

The excitement and attention Madonna's work elicited was matched by incessant coverage in the media (including a *Time* cover story in 1985), which found the performer's heady mix of sexuality and success both irresistible and saleable. Whereas sex had always been a part of rock, few understood how to use it as an instrument of provocation as well as Madonna, who appeared to delight in her ability to use her sexuality to extract what she wanted from men, disposing of them with efficiency when finished—as vividly illustrated in the video for "Material Girl," where Madonna accepts jewels from a chorus line of adoring men, along with their wallets and money, and then kicks them down the stairs. It was a stance traditionally taken by men, rather than women, and Madonna's co-opting of the pose flew in the face of both conservatives, who found such tactics "obscene" when carried out by a woman, and some feminists, who found Madonna's apparent celebration of female duplicity offensive. Madonna freely admitted to the commercial potential of her public image and again contended that people on both sides of the debate missed the underlying irony. "I know the aspect of my personality, being the vixen, the heart-breaker and the incredibly provocative girl is a very marketable image," she told *People*. "But it's not insincere. You just can't take it seriously."

But if the characterizations she presented in videos and onstage were delivered with a wink, Madonna's ambitions regarding her work were deadly serious, an aspect of her

Madonna
July 1987 at the Kingdome, Seattle, Photo by Pete Kuhns

personality that was at first overlooked in favor of topics the media found more worthy of investigation, such as the publication of nude photos taken of Madonna before her recording success or the state of her turbulent marriage to actor Sean Penn (married in 1985, the couple divorced in 1989). Donna Russo, vice president of publicity at Warner Bros., was among those who admired Madonna's handling of her own career. "She's very much a businesswoman," says Russo. "She's incredibly disciplined, she knows exactly what she's doing, exactly where she's headed, she knows exactly how she likes things. She keeps track of all her money, she keeps track of all her business deals. No one's going to rob Madonna! She's a perfectionist of the first order. And I admire that, because it's so hard to be that disciplined. It's like she's been in a Buddhist temple in her past life or something."

With the release of *True Blue* in 1986, Madonna began co-producing her work. More pop-oriented than its predecessors, *True Blue* hit the top of the charts, produced five Top 5 singles, and sold seventeen million copies. In 1989, Madonna released her most accomplished album yet, *Like a Prayer*. Along with such jubilant numbers as "Express Yourself," "Keep It Together," and a collaboration with Prince on the track "Love Song," the album (which again topped the charts) also took an autobiographical look at Madonna's life—her troubled marriage, her mother's death, and her relationship with her father. She followed up this ambitious project with *I'm Breathless: Songs From and Inspired by the Film Dick Tracy*, a film in which she also starred. *Breathless*, which reached number 2 on the charts, also revealed how far her voice had developed from her early dance rock days, as she tackled material ranging from Broadway composer Stephen Sondheim's intricate work to her own tribute to nightclub *poseurs*, "Vogue" (a number 1 hit). In 1992, Madonna announced the formation of her own entertainment company, Maverick, in partnership with Time Warner, in a deal that was reported to advance her as much as sixty million dollars. As her career progressed, Madonna would continue to use her media platform to confront attitudes regarding sexuality, a topic that would take on entirely different meanings in light of the AIDS epidemic.

While Madonna's rise put the solo female singer firmly in the spotlight (launching a series of solo female singers—including Debbie Gibson and Tiffany, among others—into the pop marketplace) other female performers were presenting updated versions of tried and true roles for women in rock and finding substantial success. Joan Jett resumed her "tough chick" role as a solo artist, the Bangles emerged as the latest all-female band, and Whitney Houston found long-lasting success as rock's new diva. A key difference between these performers and their predecessors was the degree of involvement they had in the creation of their music, a situation that was becoming the norm for a growing number of female artists in the rock mainstream. Most were writing their own material; some, like Joan Jett, Cyndi Lauper, and Madonna, also began producing their records. Even Whitney Houston, primarily regarded as a singer, moved into production on her third album, 1991's *I'm Your Baby Tonight*.

Jett's breakthrough as a solo artist came in 1982 when "I Love Rock 'n' Roll" topped the charts. Jett had been despondent after the breakup of the Runaways, but she continued to work, traveling to England, where she recorded material with ex–Sex Pistols Steve Jones and Paul Cook, and produced the Germs' album *GI* in L.A. She also found new managers in Kenny and Meryl Laguna, though Kenny later admitted he had been slow to see Jett as a serious instrumentalist, recommending she use an outside guitarist on her early demos, a suggestion Jett refused to consider. Jett began her solo career with the European release of a

Joan Jett
1980 at the Showbox, Seattle, Photo by Cam Garrett

self-titled LP in 1980. Unable to find a record deal in the U.S., Jett released the album, now titled *Bad Reputation*, on her own Blackheart Records label, selling copies at her live shows; the album was eventually picked up by Neil Bogart, and released on his Boardwalk Records label in 1981.

Jett recorded her first album for Boardwalk that same year with her new band, the Blackhearts, and *I Love Rock 'n' Roll* not only produced a hit with the title track, but also yielded two additional Top 20 hits, covers of "Crimson and Clover" and "Do You Wanna Touch Me (Oh Yeah)," while the album itself reached number 2. Jett was one of the few female performers who played straight-ahead rock with no concession to prevailing musical trends. Although 1982 marked Jett's biggest year in terms of chart placings, she had three subsequent Top 40 albums and six Top 40 singles, including the Top 20 hit "Light of Day," the title song from the 1987 film in which she co-starred with Michael J. Fox. Jett continues to be a strong concert draw today, leaving the "novelty" tag behind because of the longevity of her career.

Unfortunately, the same would not be said of the Bangles, who broke up within three years of cracking the Top 40 in 1986. The group was the only other commercially successful all-female band to come along after the Go-Go's, but in some ways the Bangles never really emerged from the Go-Go's shadow, being almost relentlessly compared to them because of their perceived similarities: both bands played pop-flavored rock music, both came from Southern California, both had recorded for the I.R.S. label, and both were all-female outfits who also played their own instruments.

But such comparisons failed to present a complete picture. Though the Bangles were part of L.A.'s club scene in the early '80s, they showed a decided preference for '60s pop in contrast to the Go-Go's original punk leanings; their vocal harmonies had more in common with the Beatles, one of the band's favorite groups and most obvious influences. The Bangles were formed in 1981 when guitarist Susanna Hoffs answered a musicians-wanted ad placed by a woman who'd previously played with sisters Vicki and Debbi Peterson in a group; on meeting the women, who shared a house together, Hoffs elected to join the Petersons' group instead. Hoffs had studied acting and dancing in addition to music, and the Petersons had been playing in bands since their teens, Vicki on guitar, and Debbi on drums (purchased for her by Vicki).

Annette Zalinskas on bass was the next to join, and the band hit the L.A. club circuit as the Colours, the Supersonic Bangs, and finally just the Bangs. After recording the single "Getting Out of Hand" on their own label, the Bangs were approached by Miles Copeland to release a record on his Faulty Products label. The group was at first suspicious of his connection with the Go-Go's ("I thought, 'Oh, here it is: he wants to make us the poor man's Go-Go's,'" Vicki told *Rolling Stone*), but eventually signed a contract and released an EP on I.R.S. in 1982, which sold forty thousand copies. On the strength of the EP's sales, the group was signed to Columbia the following year and changed their name to the Bangles after learning there was a New Jersey band working under the name the Bangs. Zalinskas left the group and was replaced by Michael (Micki) Steele, a veteran of innumerable L.A. bands, including a brief stint with the Runaways.

All Over the Place, released in 1984, was a vivid illustration of the band's love of '60s pop. Starting with the opening song, "Hero Takes a Fall," the album was awash with harmonies and catchy hooks, even evoking the '60s British Invasion in song titles like "Going Down to Liverpool." Though only reaching number 80 in the charts, *All Over the Place* received good reviews, and the band continued to build their following, touring as the opening act for Cyndi Lauper. In late 1985, *Different Light* was released, and by February 1986 the group had their first success in the singles charts with "Manic Monday" (written by Prince under the pseudonym "Christopher"), which reached number 2; the album also reached number 2, accompanied by two further Top 40 singles, including the number 1 hit "Walk Like an Egyptian."

But the Bangles' success was undermined by a dissatisfaction with their work on the album, which had been rushed into production after the months they'd spent on the road. The band had been forced into using more outside material, and Debbi, who had repeatedly clashed with producer David Kahne in the studio, was unhappy about the songwriting credits he received on her songs and particularly disappointed that she neither played drums nor sang on "Walk Like an Egyptian." "'Walk' to me is a nice little novelty song . . . but I don't feel like it's us," she told *Rolling Stone*. Vicki's attitude toward the album expressed an equal dissatisfaction: "I feel very detached from the record in a lot of ways," she admitted. A focus on Hoffs, who sang lead on "Manic Monday" (and whose mother had directed two of the band's videos and also directed her daughter in the 1987 film *The Allnighter*), also generated some tension as the group had no permanent lead singer (lead vocals were shared among the members who provided harmonizing vocals as well). The group took their time in releasing a follow-up album, 1988's *Everything*, which reached number 15 and gave them two more Top 5 hits, including the number 1 song "Eternal Flame," but within a year the underlying pressures caused the band to split. "The Bangles were becoming a prison, weighed down by all these rules and restrictions," Hoffs said in *The Rocket*, explaining how the early spirit of camaraderie had disappeared: "Everyone would go into the studio at separate times and work on *their* songs." After the breakup, Hoffs launched her solo career in 1991 with the release of the album *When You're a Boy*, followed by a self-titled album in 1996. The Bangles reformed in 1999.

Unlike female performers like Joan Jett and the Bangles, Whitney Houston was never obliged to disprove a "novelty" tag as a performer, partially because she did not play a rock instrument like the guitar or drums, and partially because of her own sterling musical pedigree. Born in 1963 in New Jersey, Houston grew up singing in the choir her mother, Cissy, directed for the New Hope Baptist Church and accompanied her to sessions where her mother's backup group, the Sweet Inspirations, sang for artists like Aretha Franklin or Dionne Warwick, the Houstons' cousin. By age fifteen Houston began singing backup vocals at sessions for Chaka Khan and Lou Rawls, and it seemed inevitable that she would pursue a musical career of her own. She signed a management contract while still in her teens, but Houston, along with her family and her manager,

Gene Harvey, elected to let her talent develop for a few more years. "When she had just turned eighteen, two major labels wanted to sign her, but I felt it was too early," Harvey told the *Los Angeles Times*. "I didn't want her to have to deal with those kinds of pressures at that point."

Houston spent the next two years working as a model and backup singer (continuing to perform with her mother's choir and taking solo spots during her mother's own shows), until Clive Davis signed her to his Arista label in 1983, though it was another two years before her self-titled debut LP was released. *Whitney Houston* offered a range of material meant to cater to every taste, and the release of the album's singles were planned accordingly. Davis told the *Los Angeles Times* that "You Give Good Love," a smooth ballad that displayed Houston's vocal range to good effect, was specifically chosen as the debut single because "We wanted to establish her in the black marketplace first. Otherwise you fall between cracks, where Top 40 won't play you and R&B won't consider you their own." But the Top 40 was more than willing to play "You Give Good Love," which reached number 3, opening the way for the subsequent number 1s: "Saving All My Love for You" (which won a Grammy award for Best Female Pop Vocal Performance), "How Will I Know," and "Greatest Love of All." The album also reached number 1, where it stayed for fourteen weeks and remained in the Top 40 for over a year, becoming one of the best-selling debut albums by a solo singer.

People magazine predicted, "It will take an act of Congress to keep this woman from becoming a megastar," and 1987's *Whitney* proved this conclusively, debuting at number 1—the first album by a female artist to do so—in the company of the number 1 singles "So Emotional," "Didn't We Almost Have It All," and "I Wanna Dance with Somebody (Who Loves Me)," which won that year's Grammy for Best Female Pop Vocal Performance. 1990's *I'm Your Baby Tonight* reached number 2 (number 1 on the R&B charts) and had two chart-topping singles, "All the Man that I Need" and the title track. Houston's success was all the more welcome to the commercial mainstream because of her image as a fresh-faced, wholesome, girl-next-door, one who was not about to challenge perceptions regarding traditional female behavior as Madonna did. She was a consummately "safe" artist, the type record companies are most comfortable and happiest in dealing with: someone without controversy who shifts plenty of units. She later moved into acting, appearing in *The Bodyguard* (the soundtrack featured the number 1 hit "I Will Always Love You") and *Waiting to Exhale*, among other films.

Houston was also one of the few young black women who maintained a high profile in the pop mainstream and thus was also welcomed on MTV. The network was no doubt glad to find a black artist to feature, considering the frequent charges of racism MTV faced in the early '80s because of the noticeable lack of videos by black artists that were screened on the channel. As Ed Steinberg, who worked with the video pool RockAmerica, said in *The Rolling Stone Book on Rock Video*, "There are three ways to guarantee MTV rotation, no black faces, pretty women, and athletic guitar solos." MTV countered by claiming that most black artists did not play "rock" music, but those endeavoring to create acceptable fare for the channel sometimes had a different story to relate. *Rock & Roll Confidential* reported in 1983 that Keith Williams, who had written the script for the Donna Summer video "She Works Hard for the Money," had been told to focus on a white family in the video "for MTV." MTV's racial barrier was finally cracked to some extent following the release of Michael Jackson's *Thriller* album in 1982, though the station had initially resisted airing the videos accompanying the record by again arguing that Jackson's music was not "rock"—until the enormous popularity of Jackson's material caused them to capitulate (Jackson's label, Epic, also reportedly had to force MTV's hand by threatening to pull videos of its other acts if MTV didn't air Jackson's work).

Other artists also found it difficult to fit into the restrictive niches of the MTV playlists and Top 40 charts. Though the momentary upheaval provided by punk and new wave was over, a continual influx of new artists entered the music scene, and independent labels were once again well-placed to pick up on new trends ignored by the majors. With indie support, a band could keep going for some time, achieving some measure of exposure, and operating with the hope that they might eventually graduate to a major label and larger audiences. It was a setup that could provide a band with the motivation to continue for years with minimal compromise, though the inevitable burnout brought on by the grind of the club circuit led to innumerable casualties among acts.

Uncle Bonsai was an example of such a group. Formed in Seattle in 1981, the group consisted of two women, Arni Adler and Ashley Eichrodt, and one man, Andrew Ratshin. The group used a single acoustic guitar to provide musical backing, along with occasional percussion, but the humorous, aggressive content of their songs went beyond the realm of typical singer-songwriter fare. Despite being approached by major labels a number of times over their eight-year existence, Uncle Bonsai never found a contract. Adler attributes this failure, in part, to problems record companies had in dealing with the Bonsai image. "There's a certain image that I think record labels might be looking for that's an easy one for them to sell," she says. "I wouldn't be so bold as to say what the image is for Suzanne [Vega] or Tracy [Chapman], but it's an easy one to read, and it was harder for us. I think it takes one bold person in a record company to say, 'Hey, let's take a chance. Here's something different—I think this could catch on.'"

Uncle Bonsai came together when Eichrodt placed an ad in a Seattle paper, looking for people to form a folk group, and Adler and Ratshin responded. In an interesting coincidence, the three had attended Bennington College in Vermont at the same time, though they had not known each other well, and following college, they had each made their way to Seattle. Adler, a theater major, hadn't considered singing in a group before and joined Bonsai partly because she wasn't doing anything else at the time. "I didn't have anything lined up," she explains. "I didn't have a job, I didn't have any money, and I loved to sing! We all really loved to sing, and the harmonies sounded so great, it was something to go on for a while. None of us thought we were going to stay in it for eight years. I think we all just figured this would be a nice thing to do until we knew our real thing."

The group initially relied on singing cover songs, adding off-beat touches to make the arrangements more distinctive, such as performing "Wild Thing" while banging on toy xylophones, or singing cartoon songs after distorting their voices by inhaling helium. But Ratshin, already a veteran club performer, proved to be a prolific songwriter, and mixed in with conventional material like "Suzy" (about a frustrated office worker) were tunes with more pointed observations on modern society, such as "Billboard Love," "Cheerleaders on Drugs," and "Penis Envy" (the latter two co-written with Adler). "Penis Envy" quickly gained notoriety when it was committed to vinyl on the group's first independently released album in 1984, *A Lonely Grain of Corn*. The lyrics were a humorous listing of how the lives of the female members of Bonsai would change if they possessed the valued item, closing with the line, "If I had a penis I'd still be a girl/But I'd make much more money and conquer the world." The song was condemned by some critics for its "revolting lyrics," and in 1989 was cited in obscenity charges filed by the FCC against Florida radio stations WIOD and WZTA. Adler countered the "revolting" charge by stating in an interview, "It's better to be revolting than insipid. But I think it's playful. And after all, that's the prevailing Bonsai attitude."

By the time Uncle Bonsai released their second album, *Boys Want Sex in the Morning*, recorded live in 1986, they'd established themselves as a standing room–only draw in the Pacific Northwest and were expanding that base through constant touring, including regular appearances at New York's Bottom Line. But despite the consistent audience turnout and critical praise they received (including glowing write-ups from *New York Times* critic Stephen Holden), the one thing Bonsai couldn't get was a major label contract. "We had a lot of interest from a lot of different labels," Adler says. "But since our format was so strange, nobody quite knew what to do with us. We knew we were marketable, because we went from this group who nobody knew to a group that could draw full houses in Seattle, and after being in a city once or twice start to have a significant following. And we knew that once we got radio play, that significantly changed the amount of people who came to see us. So we knew."

In 1988, it seemed like Bonsai's fortunes were on the verge of changing: Joel Webber, then an A&R rep at Island Records (and also one of the founders of the New Music Seminar), decided to sign the group. But four days before the contract was due to be signed, Webber was fired and soon after died of a congenital heart condition. Since Webber had been Bonsai's primary contact at Island, the group then found themselves without a supporter. "When he left Island a lot of the groups he was promoting were also dropped," says Adler. Within a year, Bonsai decided to disband. "I think we really started getting bored," Adler says. "We'd basically just run the thing out of juice." By this time, a new stream of singer-songwriters had captured the industry's attention, but though Bonsai had frequently been paired with some of these acts in performance (like Suzanne Vega and Tracy Chapman), they were unable to find a record company that felt able to handle a seriously funny acoustic group. "Tracy Chapman was on *Saturday Night Live* just with her guitar and that's what we were—the three of us with a guitar," explains Adler. "It's just that there was humor in our music, and I think sometimes people don't know what to do with that."

Even young bands that had the support of a record company could become victims of burnout, especially if they were unhappy with the niche they felt their record companies tried to fit them into. Wednesday Week, an L.A.-based outfit with a standard rock band setup—lead guitar, rhythm guitar, bass, and drums—found themselves continually being compared to the Go-Go's and the Bangles, despite having a three women to one man ratio. "It was always these girl group comparisons," remembers Kristi Callan, the group's rhythm guitarist and lead singer. "They'd always say 'girl band, sounds like the Bangles'—gee, don't we sound a bit like R.E.M. or something? Now I understand—in this business you're looking for a gimmick, an angle, something to classify a band, and that's all the record company was trying to do. But I didn't understand it then. I felt like we didn't have a chance to stand on our own."

Wednesday Week was formed by Kristi and her sister, Kelly, both of whom had been interested in music since they were children; while growing up in Oklahoma, Kristi had been "the singer in the family," and Kristi, Kelly, and their brother had all played guitar. Following their parents' divorce, the siblings moved with their mother to Los Angeles in 1976, just in time for the punk explosion, and the sisters were soon going to clubs as often as they could. "We just loved it," says Callan. "We went out five nights a week, and Kelly and I had fake IDs, always, because so many clubs were twenty-one-and-over."

Eventually, the Callans decided to form their own band. "Since I was five I wanted to be a singer," says Callan. "I'd seen singers on TV, on variety shows, and I thought, 'Oh, okay. That's what I'll do.' Then when we started seeing bands, it was so exciting because it was the bridge between me and what I'd seen on TV. This showed you the way. And, of course, the whole punk thing, a lot of the attitude was anybody can do this, so that was very encouraging." With Kristi on guitar and Kelly on drums, the two sisters set up a practice space in Kelly's bedroom, though the initial results were not very encouraging. "I'll never forget the first day I dragged my amp into Kelly's room so we could play," remembers Callan. "It was so depressing—it was so awful that I took my amp back to my room and didn't try again for months!"

By 1981, the two had advanced to the point where they made their debut, with another friend, in their mother's living room, under the name Goat Deity. In the fall, under the name Narrow Adventure, the band began playing on the club circuit, and by 1982 they recorded their first songs as Wednesday Week for a local compilation. A variety of male musicians came and went until 1983 when Heidi Rodewald joined on bass, though the Callans were at first reluctant to accept her, not wanting to be stuck with the tag of being a "girl band." "Who were the all-girl bands right then? The Go-Go's?" says Callan. "I mean, I really did like the Go-Go's—the first time I saw them I thought they were wonderful—but we just weren't going for this cutey thing, and we thought it would be perceived as such."

But Rodewald managed to convince the sisters to let her in the band, and the group remained a trio, occasionally taking on a fourth member to play lead guitar, contributing songs to various compilations, and releasing an EP in 1983, *Betsy's House*. Callan found her apprehension about being perceived as a girl band, in that order— girls first, musicians second—was not unfounded. "After we got Heidi we were on all these all-girl bills, all the time," she says. "If any band even had a girl in it, like a girl bass player or a girl lead singer, they'd put us on the bill, even if we didn't have anything to do with them. At first I got mad, and then I said, hey, it's a show—it was easier to get shows." Ironically, by the time David Nolte joined the group in 1985, the group faced a backlash from people who were upset the band had disrupted the all-female makeup. As a joke, the band said Nolte was Rodewald's brother. "Somebody said they looked alike, and so we thought, 'Yeah, brother and sister,'" Callan says. "Then it was okay. I swear to God, then they would accept it."

At the time Nolte joined, the band was on the verge of signing with Enigma Records, who released *What We Had* in late 1986. Produced by Don Dixon, the album's melancholy pop rock found a receptive welcome from the critics: *Goldmine* said, "If this is any indication of the direction pop is heading, there's good reason for optimism," and *Stereo Review* wrote, "One of the best debut albums we've heard lately." But the expected, and dreaded (at least by the band), "girl band" comparisons were also present in abundance: *Rockpool* wrote, "This isn't the Go-Go's or the Bangles. This is real rock/pop," the *New Paper* wrote, "I'm sure Wednesday Week is tired of hearing the 'B-word' and the 'G-

G-word,' so I won't use either of 'em here," the *Boston Globe* wrote, "They're bound to get compared to the Bangles. So here goes: *What We Had* isn't as tuneful as the Bangles' last album, but they have a tougher guitar sound . . . with frontwoman Kristi Callan an arguably better, more passionate singer than the Bangles' Susanna Hoffs," and *Melody Maker* killed several birds with one stone by stating, "Wednesday Week are the Bangles with balls. The Runaways with toons. The Go-Go's on speed and Debbie Harry finally forced to record in a garage."

But despite the acclaim, album sales lagged behind the record company's expectations, and Enigma was reluctant to work with the band again. "I remember, the president said, 'If you're going to make a record like the last record, we don't want to do it,'" says Callan. "He said, 'Everybody really tried hard and it didn't sell that well, so how am I going to get them to push another record that's very similar when they worked hard and it didn't happen?'" Callan feels the pressure to have a big success straight away may have hurt the band. "I think things just got too big too fast," she says. "They didn't seem to build gradually."

By mid-1987, Rodewald quit the band, tired of the stresses of constant touring. For the next three years, a number of people joined the band, though no permanent lineup was established. Callan was able to observe the difference in the inner functioning of the band when the female-male ratio went from three-one to two-two: "I find it's really hard working with guys," she says. "Maybe that's why there aren't that many bands with both girls and guys, except for a Blondie thing or where you have Edie Brickell as girl lead singer. But you don't find so many three girls and one guy or two and two." The problems intensified when two male musicians split their time between Wednesday Week and their own band the Stingrays for a period in 1988. "We had a real problem when those guys were playing with us," Callan says. "One of them was the singer in the Stingrays, but we didn't need him to sing because I was the singer. He kept saying over and over, 'I like to think of us as like Fleetwood Mac, merging into this one great band, and I want to sing and I want to write.' And I said, 'Well, you have your own band. This is Wednesday Week, and I sing and Kelly and I write.'" Despite being dropped by Enigma, Wednesday Week continued to release EPs through their fan club, releasing a final cassette, *No Going Back*, before breaking up in 1990. And though the band may never have found a place for itself, the core members continue to be active in their local music scene.

But some artists were able to find a place for themselves on major labels in spite of being difficult to pigeonhole in a readily identifiable category, such as Jane Siberry. Siberry, like Laurie Anderson, with whom she shares a record company (Siberry is on the Warner Bros. subsidiary Reprise), has never had a major chart success in the U.S., but maintains a strong and loyal cult following. Born in Etobicoke, Canada (near Toronto), Siberry started making music as a child. "I've played piano since I could climb onto one," she says. "I played by ear. I didn't write any songs until I was seventeen, so it was always just free music, just playing whatever I felt." When she moved to Toronto in the late '70s to attend college, she took up guitar, which led to writing songs. "It was sort of the punk period, and the end of folk music being popular," Siberry remembers. "It was in that funny limbo period, where folk clubs couldn't get audiences. But I liked punk. I liked more angry stuff, things that were direct; I loved the energy of it. But I just couldn't play like that. And I wrote songs alone, I had never worked within a band situation, which is often more of a collaborative thing."

When Siberry eventually did move into a "band situation," she found the interaction with other musicians had a positive effect on her own music. "The biggest thing when I started working with other musicians was I could write what I could hear, as opposed to writing what I could play," she explains. "And that was a completely freeing thing. And as I became a better musician, and worked with people who were also getting better all the time, it was exciting because I could get even closer to what I heard." That difference was evident in the music on Siberry's first and second albums. Her self-titled debut was released in 1981 on the independent Street Records label, financed by money Siberry earned from waitressing (an experience she later detailed in the song "Waitress"). Siberry co-produced the folk-flavored LP along with David Bradstreet and Carl Keesee. "I didn't want to be 'produced,' " she says. "I wanted to go for what I wanted, and so I ended up producing. And they [the label] were independent, so there was no pressure."

For her second album, *No Borders Here*, Siberry formed her co-production partnership with her bassist John Switzer, with whom she worked on her subsequent albums. Released in 1984, *No Borders Here* was originally set to be an EP, but Siberry's signing to Open Air Records, a subsidiary of Windham Hill Records, gave her the money to expand the project to album length. In contrast to her first album, the music on *No Borders Here* was far more keyboard-based and introduced the use of the Fairlight synthesizer; the song content ranged from a satiric look at "Extra Executives" to surreal encounters at the shore ("Mimi on the Beach"). Her next album, *The Speckless Sky*, released in 1985, was driven by a more obvious pop beat, but was still heavily keyboard-based.

Siberry then signed with Reprise, and made her U.S. major label debut in 1987 with *The Walking*. Siberry's enigmatic, quirky folk-pop music drew favorable comparisons to Laurie Anderson's work, and like Anderson, Siberry appreciated being left alone by her record company. "I stay away from the record company while I'm writing and recording," she says. "People seem pretty respectful of what I'm trying to do. I often feel they'll eventually get what they want if they let me get what I want." Nonetheless, Siberry was aware of the economic necessity of turning a profit with her work. "I feel badly if people are disappointed with the album, or if they don't know what to do with it," she says, "but I try to keep things pretty cheap, too! So it's not a disproportionate amount of money being spent on something that isn't going to make back a lot of money."

Even so, *The Walking* did not meet record company expectations in terms of sales. Roberta Peterson, a vice president of A&R at Warners who had been responsible for signing Siberry to the company, says that the album was a commercial disappointment. "Jane wanted to be accessible, and there's no way in the world this record could've been accessible. I just put that album out of my mind because I knew going in that it just wasn't going to connect. There were some beautiful things on it, but you talk about selling records, we knew we weren't going to sell zip." Certainly, the record was an atypical release when stacked up against the Top 40 successes of the day: more of an extended tone poem or symphony than a straightforward collection of songs, only three of the album's eight tracks ran less than five minutes, and one of them was more than ten.

But Siberry herself was pleased with her work. "I felt like *The Walking* was a definitive album for me," she says. "It was all about sound and searching out ways to capture an ambience, capture feelings that are difficult to describe—that kind of an album." Siberry also didn't see chart success as a priority: "It would be nice, but the bottom line is if I feel proud of it." But she was willing to talk with the label about her next album, and for its part, Reprise refrained from strong-arming the artist (unlike EMI, which had alienated Kate Bush after *The Dreaming* by telling her she had to bring in an outside producer). "We had this very serious conversation with Jane," says Peterson, "and I said, 'There's not much of a sense of humor, which has always been there before,' and she said, 'Okay, next time I'll make you a comedy record!'"

Bound by the Beauty, released in 1989, did not turn out to be a comedy record, but it did reflect Siberry's determination—and perhaps obligation—to make an album "really fun and different and distinct from the last record." She brought in new musicians and recorded the entire album at the studio she used to make her demos, giving the music a looser, freer feel—the original demos for "Hockey" and the title track were even selected for the final album. "I went for people who were more stylized, which I've never done, I've always gone in the opposite direction," Siberry says. "I loved all the people I worked with on the last record, but this time I wanted a different chemistry. So there were very little arrangement directions. I just gave them the chords, and they went off with that and did it." From this perspective, *Bound by the Beauty* was an undoubted success in creating a new sound that allowed Siberry's quirkiness to shine through—though the record was still not one that would sit any more comfortably on the Top 40 charts than *The Walking* did. After releaseing two further albums on Reprise, Siberry formed her own label, Sheeba.

A younger generation of women, who, like Siberry, had been inspired by punk even if they weren't directly involved with the movement, was also moving into different areas of the music industry, bringing along a whole new set of attitudes. Most significantly, women were consistently moving from alternative realms of the industry into main-stream strongholds, such as the media. Celia Farber made her move into rock journalism in the mid-1980s, starting out as an intern at *Spin* magazine, eventually moving up to senior editor. Farber had spent her teenage years in Sweden, originally a Who fan, and later inspired by punk to play in a band herself. The "scene" in the town where she lived revolved around a venue that served as a vegetarian restaurant by day and a punk club at night. "I started hanging out there," Farber recalls, "and I met this guy who was a phenomenal drummer—he used to play until his hands bled! I used to watch him all the time and finally I mustered up the courage to ask him if he would teach me how to play. And he did. And the government—this says a lot about the Swedish govern-ment—the government bought us the drum set to practice on! It wasn't even really like lessons; I was an angry fifteen-year-old who had to get her aggressions out on some-thing, so he said, 'Take these sticks and just bash. You'll get the idea. Just listen to the drums on Iggy Pop's "Lust for Life"—and play like that.'"

Farber's next step was starting her own band, the town's first predominantly female band (it included one male), though she says, "It was such a small town, anything you did you were the only female to do it. But the scene was such that anyone could play whatever they wanted, and nobody was going to start remarking, 'Oh, you're a girl.'" Farber found this sense of equality was absent from American society when she returned to the States to attend college. "I thought America was really backward, really frustrating," she says. "As soon as I moved here it was, 'Oh, you're really good for a girl; you hit the drums like a guy.' No, I hit the drums hard because I think that's what you should do in rock & roll.

"When I came to this country it had never occurred to me that there would be a problem with sexism," she continues. "This culture is in many ways unsophisticated. But on the other hand, I see that in a sense as the price you pay for what is great about this country, and that is that there is a kind of chaotic wonderfulness about it. So I finally learned to not take things too seriously." It was an attitude that not only helped her in dealing with the new environment in America but also with situations at *Spin*.

"There's sexism at *Spin*, sure, in the obvious ways—women as objects and all that," she says. "But I think the more insidious brand of sexism comes from those who seem the least sexist on the surface. The worst kind are the ones who are *afraid* of women. They're the ones who will put you down whatever way they find. They may not pinch you in the butt but they'll also never tell you if you did a good job, or had a good idea. They'll just sit there cold and aloof and politically correct, quietly demeaning you."

Farber's internship led to a job as a research assistant when the internship ended, and she moved further up the ladder in 1987 when she began writing a monthly column on AIDS for the magazine, despite some initial opposition from the staff. "It was kind of a stain on the magazine in a sense," Farber explains. "We're supposed to be hip and happening and fun and entertaining and all of sudden—*ba-dom!*—there's this AIDS column. But Guccione [Bob Guccione, Jr., *Spin's* publisher/editor] was very adamant all the time that AIDS is one of the most important issues we face and that people need to know about it." Farber has found Guccione a supporter of all her work, not just her AIDS columns. "He believed in me," she says. "When I said, 'I don't know if I can write this AIDS article,' he would say, 'Of course you can. Just do it.'"

Rachel Felder, who began her career in the music industry as a rock journalist (she has gone on to work as an A&R rep and artists' manager) was also inspired by punk and new wave during her teens: "When I was thirteen and fourteen years old, the Jam and the Clash were all I lived for!" she says. Felder was originally interested in pursuing a career in film, but while studying for an English degree at Columbia University in New York, a job working on a popular culture column for NBC radio turned her interest toward writing. She has since written for *Alternative Press*, *DV8*, and *Gig*, hosted her own cable television show, *Slews of Reviews*, and served as managing editor of a paper put out during the New Music Seminar for attendees, *NMS Today*.

But along with the steady progression in her career, Felder has also encountered less enlightened attitudes toward women working in journalism. "I don't feel sexism in my job a lot, but I feel it occasionally," she says. "I feel it at things like industry luncheons, at press conferences. And at concerts I don't like going alone; it's easier for a guy to know what to wear to a concert than a girl. People look at me funny sometimes. I'm this young chick, I have the wild clothes, will I be taken seriously?" The difference in attitude over something as relatively insignificant as female and male dress may appear trivial on the surface, but such attitudes also reflect deeper feelings regarding "appropriate" behavior for women and men. "I think that there's a lot of things you have to do in journalism that if a man does it, no one bats an eyelash, but if a woman does it, people say, 'Oh, she's such a bitch. Who does she think she is?'" says Felder. "I know one woman who's a gossip columnist. She's very serious about what she does, and I would call her tough. She's very hard-working, she sees a job, she does it, she does it real well. And so many people have said to me, 'She's so bitchy, she's so catty, she's so awful.' And they wouldn't say that about a guy who's a tough editor."

Both Farber and Felder feel such attitudes influence the way women are written about in the rock press. "I think one of the reasons it's harder for females to come through the way men do in rock is because it is in many ways a masculine art form," Farber says. "A lot of it has to do with raw aggression, qualities that are predominantly male, like anger and sexual aggressiveness. A lot of it isn't about things like compassion. Somebody wrote in *Spin*, 'I was standing behind Patti Smith in line. She's the most unattractive woman I've ever seen in my life.' Would a woman write that? How many rock stars aren't totally unattractive men? With men it's like a shock if a woman isn't attractive."

Felder agrees: "You don't see overweight women rockers," she says. "I think unless you did a very specific kind of folkie music, if you went to a record company and they loved your tape but you were one hundred pounds overweight, they'd make you lose weight before they signed you. I don't know that for a fact, but I bet you they would! I think there's a lot of ugly men rock stars out there, that if they were the female counterpart, wouldn't get signed."

The prevalence of these attitudes in rock journalism is no doubt because most rock journalists are men—and virtually all of the top editorial positions at national rock magazines are also held by men (a notable exception being *B-Side*, now defunct, based in Burlington, New Jersey, run by Sandra Garcia, Sandra Davis, and Carol Schutzbank). "The powerful rock writers are men," says Lisa Shively, who deals regularly with the press as the head of her own independent PR firm, the Press Network. "But I also think that hardcore group of writers is being infiltrated by a lot of young writers, men and women. I do think there's more women freelancers out there, so they're starting to go up the ladder, but in editorial positions, it's still mainly men."

But although men outnumber women as rock journalists, the reverse is true in the field of publicity work, whether at publicity departments at record labels or PR firms. Shively's Press Network, which she founded in 1984, was part of a growing number of independent PR firms that sprang up on the East and West Coasts during the '80s. Some firms, like Shively's, were started by women just entering the field of publicity. Others, like Susan Blond's company Susan Blond Inc., were started by women who had moved as far up the corporate ladder as the company would allow and found self-employment was the only avenue left for them to advance their careers. Shively also feels the fact that the publicity field is dominated by women has led to a tendency to downgrade the importance of publicity work. "I remember being on one publicity panel, and the moderator said that until he and a few other men got into publicity, it was basically considered a glorified secretary's job," she says.

Women working in publicity departments at major labels confronted similar perceptions. Veterans like Donna Russo, vice president of publicity at Warner Bros., are well aware that PR work wasn't always highly regarded. "Publicity wasn't really thought of as a very vital department fifteen or twenty years ago," she says. "Most record companies didn't have a publicity department. If you wanted any publicity on an act, you hired a publicist. When you didn't want him anymore, you stopped paying him. I think that [radio] promotion is the lifeline for a record company, because if you can't get the record played on the radio you're not going to sell records. But publicity was always thought of as a luxury, it was never thought of as a necessity." She attributes the overwhelmingly female-male ratio in publicity departments to the perception that patience and understanding are traditionally viewed as "female" traits. "Publicity has always been a female-dominated area," she says. "I personally think it's because women's tolerance is so much higher. Women can deal with artists much better than men can. I think women are better with people, period."

Originally an actress, Russo worked as a contract employee for Warner Bros. in New York for three years before being hired to work for the company on a full-time basis in the mid-1970s, when the New York office then employed around eight people. "Warners always had this very small family feel to it," she says. "They really are very supportive: nobody here points their finger and says, 'You fucked up.' Mo Ostin [Warner Bros.' CEO] always knew my name . . . and he still knows my name, thank God." One of Russo's first projects was compiling *The Book of the Road*, a guide for touring bands; she then began working in Artists Relations, a new area set up to help artists negotiate their way through aspects of touring that didn't necessarily involve performing—"teaching them why it was important to go meet the retail people who stock their records, and the radio people who were playing their records," a new type of marketing concept at the time. Over the years she has worked with such performers as Mark Knopfler, U2, Peter Gabriel, and Madonna, not only coordinating press interviews, but also dealing with personal needs that can range from setting up doctor appointments to accompanying an artist on a shopping trip.

In 1987, Russo finally became a vice president, and though she notes that the number of female executives at the company has increased, she admits progress has been slow. "It's not a drastic change, to be quite honest," she says. "It never happens quick enough—it should have happened a long time ago! But years ago at Warner Bros., there were no female vice presidents, there were no female executives, really. And now there are a number of us. There's not a lot of us, but there's a smattering of female vice presidents. And each year there's more. I think things are changing now. But a woman in the music industry can still be very intimidating, especially an executive. And we have our fair share of chauvinists, but I just let it roll off my back. I have been anything but a shy, quiet flower in my position at Warner Bros. over the last fifteen years. And I can stand up to, if not surpass, any loud-mouthed chauvinistic guy in the music industry. I just don't accept it, and I have very few men who pull it on me because they know better.

"The other problem is that as a woman, most of us came up through the ranks, as secretaries," she continues. "A lot of men are brought in in an executive position, or in a managerial position at least. And I think we have to work a lot harder because as females we have to prove that we're as good or better. Women have to be perfect; you have to be the perfect mother, the perfect wife, the perfect executive, you have to be perfect at everything, and then they say, 'Gee, isn't she great.' Meanwhile you're ready to collapse, but you do it. You do it because you have to. You almost feel like you owe it to womankind. 'I'm going to show these bastards that I can do it better than them, and juggle every ball at the same time.' Each one of us has to do what we can as individuals. Not make revolution and disrupt an entire corporation, but do what I can as Donna Russo, vice president at Warner Bros. Records."

At the same time women who had been working for many years on the business side of the music industry were moving into the upper echelons of corporations, female artists who had also been performing for years and enduring periods of little commercial success began to resurface in the '80s, reviving careers long written off as dead, receiving greater recognition for their previous accomplishments and going on to achieve even greater success. Tina Turner returned in 1984 with a flourish, netting three Top 40 singles, a number 1 album, and winning three Grammy awards, the culmination of eight years spent rebuilding her career since leaving Ike Turner in 1976. Tina had finally found the strength to leave her abusive husband, walking out at the start of yet another tour as he slept in their Dallas hotel room and calling her lawyer for a return ticket to L.A. Their divorce was final in 1978, with Tina forgoing alimony and her share of their joint publishing royalties in order to break with Ike once and for all. She then embarked on a solo career, touring extensively with a nightclub act. In 1981, she appeared with Rod Stewart on the television comedy/variety show *Saturday Night Live* and then opened for the Rolling Stones at three of the shows on their U.S. tour that fall.

In 1982, Martyn Ware and Ian Craig Marsh, members of the group Heaven 17, asked Turner to contribute to a project their spin-off group, B.E.F. (British Electrical Foundation), was compiling, an album of their favorite songs performed by their favorite artists. Turner agreed, performing the Temptations' hit "Ball of Confusion" on

Tina Turner
August 1984 at the Forum, Los Angeles, Photo by Sherry Rayn Barnett

B.E.F.'s compilation LP *Music of Quality and Distinction*. The song attracted favorable attention overseas (it was not released in the U.S.), and after initial indifference, Capitol signed Turner. She then recorded her next single, "Let's Stay Together" (previously a number 1 hit for Al Green) with B.E.F., though Capitol, unconvinced of B.E.F.'s skill in producing, did not initially release the single in the U.S. "Let's Stay Together" went on to be a massive hit overseas, topping the charts in the U.K. and was equally successful in Europe. As a result the single was released in the U.S. in 1984, where it reached the pop Top 30 and hit number 5 on the black music charts.

Capitol was now eager to have Turner record an album, and *Private Dancer* was recorded in two weeks and released later that year. *Private Dancer* reintroduced Turner to American audiences, and despite her hard years, Turner's voice was better than ever. "What's Love Got to Do with It," a number 1 hit, rang out with a world-weary sigh, and the rest of the album's material was equally strong—she had further Top 40 hits with such assertive numbers as "Better Be Good to Me" (co-written by Holly Knight), "Show Some Respect," and the slower-tempoed title song, written by Mark Knopfler of Dire Straits, which hit the Top 10. The singles underscored Turner's strength as a rock vocalist. "We wanted to highlight her voice," explained Rupert Hine, one of the album's producers. "Tina had been a screamer so long, people didn't realize what a great *singer* she is." Another highlight was the album's melancholy opening track, "I Might Have Been Queen," based on Turner's life story and her interest in reincarnation. It also contained a line that seemed to sum up the essence of her personality: "I'm a soul survivor."

Private Dancer reached number 3 and sold more than ten million copies. Turner won three Grammy awards for her "Pop" performance on "What's Love. . . ," her "Rock" performance on "Better Be Good to Me," and for Record of the Year with "What's Love. . . ." Her success continued in 1985 with an appearance in the film *Mad Max Beyond Thunderdome* and a number 2 hit with a song from the film, "We Don't Need Another Hero (Thunderdome)." And while her follow-up to *Private Dancer*, 1986's *Break Every Ride*, did not match the success of the previous LP, it still yielded the number 2 hit "Typical Male," with the LP itself reaching number 4. Turner's autobiography, *I, Tina*, written with rock journalist Kurt Loder and published in 1986, also became a bestseller. Turner's re-emergence in the rock world at the age of forty-six effectively shattered another preconception about the inability of an "older" person to be a rock performer. "A lot of people seem to think that anybody that age [forty-six] ought to be looking around for a place to lie down and die," she said in *I, Tina*. "Why is that? Wilson Pickett came backstage after one of my shows . . . and asked if I thought I was strong enough to 'hold up' under this new success I was having. I said, 'What do you mean? I'm not sick.'" As an increasing number of rock performers in their forties—and fifties—continued to have viable careers as recording artists and live acts, age "limits" for performers would continue to be crossed. And though all performers would benefit from this type of re-evaluation, it was a particularly important development for female performers, who had traditionally borne a greater burden from "aging" than male performers had.

Heart also returned with a bang in the mid-'80s, following a slump after the release of their *Greatest Hits/Live* album in 1980. "Heart had been around for a few years and the average lifespan of any rock band, they say, is three to five years," explains Nancy Wilson. "And so after five years the record company was like 'Oh yeah, these guys . . . let's sign the new groups!' So we got lost in the shuffle. It was a really scary time, 'cause we not only didn't have any support from the label, the management company was not working out, and there was a lot of inner-group turmoil at the same time, and so everything was wrong."

The inner tensions within the group led to the departure of Roger Fisher, Steve Fossen, and Mike Derosier. The situation was complicated by the Wilsons' involvement with the Fisher brothers, a subject which the sisters quickly tired of dealing with in interviews. "It got ridiculous for a while," says Wilson. "It was just 'Let's talk about the [romantic] breakup!' for so long . . . well, what about the new music? Nobody wanted to know about that. We were kind of licking our wounds for a little while. But it was a good thing, because we had to stop and really decide if we wanted to go on and why. And we did decide we wanted to go on and the reason was that we loved to play. We also had to regroup as far as business stuff and know how to have more control over our careers and our lives so that this wouldn't happen to us again."

After recording a final album for Epic, 1983's *Passionworks*, the Wilsons, guitarist Howard Leese, and Heart's two new members, bassist Mark Andes and drummer Denny Carmassi, changed their management and record company, signing with Capitol and giving serious thought to the approach they'd take on their next album. "We rallied all of our energy and said, 'Okay! Whatever it takes!'" says Wilson. "'It's either this or be a guitar teacher in Bellevue!' So if it looks better to do rock videos and be sexy a little bit more than we might have chosen for ourselves, we did it. We put on the jewelry and made a big splash, and it worked." Their Capitol debut, simply titled *Heart* and released in 1985, became the group's biggest selling album and put the band back on top of the album and singles charts, with "These Dreams" reaching number 1, and three other singles becoming Top 10 hits. 1987's *Bad Animals* gave Heart a second number 1 hit with "Alone," while the album itself reached number 2.

The band's new albums aimed for a more commercial direction—which the music critics were quick to pick up on—but the group also worked to hang on to their hard rock edge. "We have a personality that wasn't really represented on the last two albums, although there was some really great stuff on them," Wilson says. "But we didn't rock as hard as we can. We like to play loud and hard sometimes. This time [during the recording of 1990's *Brigade*] we said, 'Okay, we gotta have fun too, we gotta be a little more experimental.'" Their efforts were rewarded with a number 3 album and the number 2 single "All I Wanna Do is Make Love to You." The band has since released one and two live albums.

Ann and Nancy also returned to the club setting of their earlier days by forming the Lovemongers in 1991, a group which also included Frank Cox and their longtime songwriter Sue Ennis. "I think anyone who's played the monster venues simply yearns for the atmosphere of the smaller venues," Nancy explains. "It brings you back to your roots and to the reasons you started performing to begin with—for the love of it." The Lovemongers, who primarily appeared in the Seattle area, performed acoustic renditions of Heart songs and a variety of cover material that would have been out of place at Heart's stadium shows, ranging from the Beatles, to the B-52's "Love Shack," to Tina Turner's "River Deep, Mountain High." Following the release of the EP *Battle of Evermore* in 1992, the Lovemongers released the album *Whirlygig* and *Here Is Christmas* in 1998. The Wilson sisters also became co-owners of Seattle's Bad Animals recording studio, which opened in 1992.

Like Heart and Tina Turner, Bonnie Raitt had also faced her share of commercially slow periods since her earlier success in the '70s. While a strong concert draw, she had never been a prominent figure on the record charts, though in 1977 her version of the Del Shannon hit "Runaway" just missed the Top 40. But her two subsequent albums, *The Glow* and *Green Light*, did not bring the breakthrough hit that Warner Bros. hoped for, and a day after completing her next album, *Nine Lives*, Raitt was informed she was being dropped by the label. Warner Bros. eventually released *Nine Lives* in 1986, and Raitt tried to keep herself going by drawing on her own savings in order to continue touring. She also wrestled with alcohol and drug problems. The turning point came in late '86, when she considered the possibility of working with Prince. "I knew that if it were a successful collaboration, I would probably do a video with him," she told *Rolling Stone*. "And frankly that was the thing that made me have enough self-respect to slap me into wanting to do something about it." Raitt quit drinking and adopted a healthier lifestyle, and though the collaboration with Prince never came off, she soon had a new record deal with Capitol, who released *Nick of Time* (which Raitt referred to as "my first sober album") in 1989.

Nick of Time went on to be one of the most commercially successful records of Raitt's career; selling over three million copies, it was her first Top 40 entry in seven years, and her first album to reach number 1. Featuring two songs written by Raitt, *Nick of Time* was a warm, rich album that combined a range of musical styles from the bluesy pop swing of John Hiatt's "Thing Called Love" to the reggae lilt of Bonnie Hayes's "Have a Heart" to the playful drawl of "Real Man" and Raitt's own "The Road's My Middle Name" (Leslie Ann Jones, Holly Near's former producer, also worked on the album as a recording assistant). Raitt won three Grammy awards for *Nick of Time*, including Album of the Year, Best Female Pop Vocal Performance, and Best Female Rock Vocal Performance; she also won a fourth Grammy for the duet "I'm in the Mood" with John Lee Hooker on his album *The Healer*.

Raitt's next album, *Luck of the Draw* (released in 1991), repeated the successful formula of *Nick of Time*, reaching number 2 on the charts and selling over three million copies. Co-produced by Raitt and featuring four of her own songs (including "One Part Be My Lover," co-written with her husband Michael O'Keefe), the album also won Grammy awards for Best Female Pop Vocal Performance, Best Female Rock Vocal Performance, and Best Rock Performance by a Duo or Group for the song "Good Man, Good Woman," which Raitt performed with Delbert McClinton. 1994's *Longing in Their Hearts* topped the charts, and Raitt has released two albums since. Along with enjoying her reappearance on the charts, Raitt has continued her work on behalf of different political causes and continues to make appearances on albums for lesser-known artists today. Two recent appearances have included her work as backup vocalist on "Rosie Strike Back," Eliza Gilkyson's song about wife-battering, on her 1989 *Legends of Rainmaker* LP, and on Holly Near's 1987 *Don't Hold Back* LP.

In the late 1980s, Raitt began serving on the Board of Trustees of the Rhythm & Blues Foundation, an organization founded by Ruth Brown. Based in the Smithsonian Institution's National Museum of American History, the Rhythm and Blues Foundation is involved in establishing an R&B archive in the museum, awards money and recognition to R&B artists through its Pioneer Awards Program, and offers grants to R&B performers in need of financial assistance. Brown started the Foundation with assistance from her lawyer, Howell Begle, and then approached Raitt, among others, about being involved in the organization.

"Bonnie had gone around with me a number of times, she also being a great lover of blues," explains Brown. "And we had talked about the needs of the R&B artists that are still living and out of that came the idea for this Foundation. Each year we select at least eight persons who have given to this music and they've been awarded grants. We're paying for funerals, paying for hospitals, paying for living. A lot of the things we do, we don't talk about in print. That's not why we're doing it. And if the people we assist want that to be known, good, but I know that when I was having difficulty, I did the best I could to keep it out of the press, because that was my dignity I was trying to keep intact."

Brown's "difficulty" in her career started while she was still with Atlantic Records and her record sales began to decline. She eventually left the label in 1960 and spent the next few years recording for a number of different companies with little success: "Each time I'd go in, the label would go under," she says. Brown eventually left the music business completely and worked as a domestic and bus driver until 1976, when she decided to try and revive her career again, singing and working in theater. She also found a powerful supporter in Howell Begle, whom she met when he came to see one of her shows. Begle was a music fan as well as an attorney, and after meeting Brown, he helped recover her "lost" record royalties from Atlantic in addition to helping her start up the Rhythm & Blues Foundation.

Before long, Brown's career was taking off in a number of directions. While she was appearing in a New Orleans workshop production of Allen Toussaint's *Staggerlee*, Brown was called to New York to audition for another show, *Black and Blue*, winning a role and traveling to Paris in 1984, where the show ran for eight months. On her return to the U.S., *Staggerlee* had moved off-Broadway, and Brown rejoined the cast; she also became the host of the national radio program *Harlem Hit Parade* (now called *BluesStage*). Her next project was an appearance in John Waters's 1988 film *Hairspray*, where she was chosen for the role of "Motormouth Mabel," an R&B record store owner and DJ, by a casting director who had seen Brown's performance in *Staggerlee*. Set in Baltimore in the early '60s, *Hairspray* was a satire of earlier teen flicks in which the competition for the title of "Miss Auto Show" on the *American Bandstand*–styled *The Corny Collins Show* is matched with a push to integrate the program (which only allows blacks in the television studio once a month for "Negro Day"); the film also featured Debbie Harry in the role of "Velma Von Tussle," a white supremacist housewife who urges her daughter to plug Shelley Fabares records on the show instead of "that colored music."

It was a period Brown could easily relate to, but she admits she had some problems in accepting certain aspects of her role at first. "I didn't want to wear a blonde wig and the crazy costumes that Motormouth Mabel wore," she explains. "I felt kind of stereotyped or something. John had to convince me. He and Divine sat me down one day and said, 'But that's not Ruth Brown out there. That's Motormouth Mabel.' And when we started to talk about it, I realized that the story he was telling in *Hairspray* was indeed a true story, but he was smart enough to do it in a way that would make people laugh—like he said, it was a funny story about a serious situation. That role was very possibly one of the luckiest things that ever happened to me, because I really got a whole new audience of young people. I walk the streets sometimes and I see the kids staring, and they'll walk up and say, 'I saw you. Weren't you in that movie *Hairspray*?' And I say, 'You mean I don't even look any different?'"

Brown rejoined the cast of *Black and Blue* when the show opened on Broadway in early 1989, winning a Tony award for her performance (when she left the show, she was replaced by another R&B legend, LaVern Baker). Brown subsequently won a Grammy award for her album *Blues on Broadway*, a recognition that demonstrated the

Ruth Brown, late 1980s
Courtesy of Ruth Brown

value of perseverance to her. "What it proved mostly to me is that if you hold on to what you know you've got, it's always there," she says. "So I'm having a lot of fun now. It's physically kind of exhausting, but basically it's good." But although enjoying her newfound success, she points out that the changes she's lived to see in the music industry are not yet universal. "There are still white acts that can play places that I can't get into," she says. "I would never be asked to play in them. There are some changes, but not so much that it has stretched to me. I really have no complaint, though. The changes have been for the better, for this young generation, for the Whitney Houstons, the Anita Bakers, the Janet Jacksons—all good, all good. For them, I'm glad. But all of that had to have a foundation, a base upon which to build. There were other folks that went out front and kind of took the blows a little bit."

Throughout the 1980s, women working in all areas of the music industry had maintained a greater degree of control over the development of their careers than their counterparts in the '50s and '60s. Because of this control, performers like Annie Lennox, Cyndi Lauper, and Madonna were able to use the medium of video to their advantage, further enhancing a career they were in charge of. Women in the business side of the industry were also helping to change perceptions by bringing in new attitudes and proving their self-sufficiency by starting their own companies if the corporate environment turned out to be too restrictive. But along with the gains women were making, there was also an increasing focus on and growing respect for the achievements women had made in the past. It was a recognition that not only helped renew the careers of a number of female performers, but also helped all women working in the industry gain a sense of their own history. And by the end of the '80s, the gains women had made in the music business in the past and in the present would be acknowledged on a scale that had never been experienced before.

9

Step Into the Future

"I'd rather fight a lot now so that my daughter and my friends' daughters won't have
to fight so hard next time."
—Alannah Currie (The Thompson Twins), in Stephanie Bennett's video
Women in Rock

In the summer of 1987, Suzanne Vega's single "Luka" hit the Top 10, peaking at number 3. It was an event that surprised everyone, including Vega's record label, A&M, and Vega herself, for Vega was considered a "folk" musician and folk was no longer considered a commercial musical style. Because the folk era of the '60s (when albums by artists like Joan Baez and Peter, Paul and Mary had been consistent sellers) had long since passed, Vega had found it hard to attract the interest of a label in the early '80s because of her perceived "folkie" roots. But despite her use of an acoustic guitar and her apprenticeship in the traditional folk spawning ground of Greenwich Village clubs, Vega's introspective lyrics were actually closer to the work of early '70s singer-songwriters than '60s folkies. Even so, A&M had been reluctant to sign her, but were eventually won over by the persistence of Vega and her manager, Ron Fierstein. "We went after A&M specifically because we had heard that they were interested in artists for the long run," Vega explained in *Musician*. Nancy Jeffries, then an A&R rep for A&M, related the label's concerns in the same article. "We all had some doubts because you're scared of signing a folk singer in 1985," she said. "But then I go down to see her, and before she's through with three lines, I'm in love. Everyone [at A&M] went through the same cycle with me: 'Oh my God, it's a folk singer—what are you doing?' Then they'd see her and instantly it was, 'Okay, let's make this work.'"

The *Musician* article on Vega appeared in their June 1988 issue, with a cover that featured a picture of Sinéad O'Connor and the headline: WHY THE BEST NEW ARTISTS OF *1988* ARE WOMEN: THE MAJOR LABELS CHANGE THEIR TUNE. The approach itself was not unique; women performers had routinely been asked about the female perspective of working in a male-dominated field, with the equally obligatory questions about feminism tagged on in the '70s. The number of articles and books that focused on female performers was increasing, but unlike the *Musician* piece, they profiled the women as individual performers, not as a specific development within the industry. But the *Musician* cover story, which featured profiles of O'Connor, Tracy Chapman, Michelle Shocked, and Toni Childs, also discussed why these women had emerged at approximately the same time. The new question asked of female performers was how they felt about being part of an apparently new genre of "women-in-rock," not the sole woman performer in a group of men, but part of their own musical "movement."

Many—though not all—of the women lumped into the women-in-rock "trend" were, like Vega, singer-songwriters: solo performers who played acoustic guitars who had been overlooked during the first half of the '80s, as the rise of MTV and other video outlets played up the importance of a performer's appearance. Annie Lennox, Cyndi Lauper, and especially Madonna had been able to exploit the necessity of an extravagant look to their advantage, but women who were not interested in or willing to play that game found it harder to compete in the marketplace. Vega's success changed that attitude when she proved that a "serious" female performer could make money. Thirty years earlier, George Goldner had questioned whether the Chantels were "saleable" because he doubted anyone would be interested in listening to a group of teenage girls; in the early '80s it was obvious this type of reasoning was still being applied to performers who fell outside the boundaries of what was believed to be commercial music. "Since when did the industry that insisted its strongest women play cartoon characters such as rock's Tina Turner, Cyndi Lauper and Annie Lennox allow a serious, powerful, flesh-and-blood female to stand firm on a concert stage?" wrote Susan Wilson in an article about the women-in-rock "trend" in the *Boston Sunday Globe*. "Since when did the folks who brought us Tiffany and Pebbles care about female singing or songwriting talent? Since when did the corporations that gave us Sheila E. and Madonna allow a female performer to sell social conscience instead of sex?" Finally, because of Suzanne Vega's success, a number of female performers were able to stretch those "commercial" boundaries with a vengeance, introducing a wealth of fresh, new musical talent into the music scene.

Born in 1959 and raised in New York City, Vega had grown up thinking she was half–Puerto Rican until her father, writer Ed Vega, told her he was really her stepfather and that her biological father lived in California and was white, a revelation that set off something of an identity crisis for Vega. "I was really confused because I had this really strong identity as a half-Puerto Rican girl," she told *Musician*. "I had all these really weird ideas about white people. So to realize that I was in fact white was obviously a big shock. It was hard for me to accept that I had this other *thing* that seemed to mark me as being different from my family." When Vega finally met her "other" father, after her success with "Luka," she learned that both of her parents had musical backgrounds: not only was her mother a jazz guitarist, her biological father's mother had been a drummer who played with the Merry Makers Ladies Orchestra in the '20s and '30s.

Vega's own interest in the arts had been encouraged as a child: "Both of my parents thought that being an artist was the only reasonable thing in this society that a person could do," she said. Vega initially pursued dancing, which she studied while attending New York's High School for the Performing Arts, but she also wrote songs, sang, and played guitar; she later recalled one of her first singing experiences was in a show sponsored by the Alliance of Latin Arts ("I was the only white girl"). By the time she attended her first rock concert, a Lou Reed show, at age nineteen, she had given up her dream of being a dancer, was attending Barnard College, and was trying to get booked in Greenwich Village clubs. When her efforts to find work in the Village proved unsuccessful, she sought out gigs on the college coffeehouse circuit and began building a following, keeping a notebook diary evaluating every show. By the early '80s, she managed to move into the Greenwich Village scene, at last finding a welcoming atmosphere for her work from people who didn't consider her to be a '60s throwback. "That five years I spent there was like finding my own tribe of people," she said in *Musician* in 1990. "I felt accepted. I was popular. I'd stay out and drink all night, and I had a lot of fun."

After being turned down by A&M twice, Vega's manager submitted a demo to A&M's then-president Gil Friesen, who then gave the tape to Nancy Jeffries; Vega was signed to the label in the mid-'80s. Her self-titled debut LP, released in 1985, kept the focus on Vega and her acoustic guitar despite the use of electric instruments. Co-produced by former Patti Smith Group guitarist Lenny Kaye and Steve Addabbo, the album's songs, all written by Vega, combined poetic imagery with a cool delivery to create a subdued, but intense atmosphere. Although the album had little impact on the charts, it generated good reviews in the press, and her subsequent tours met with a positive response from audiences, particularly in Britain, where Vega played the Royal Albert Hall and was one of the few Americans on the bill at the annual Prince's Trust charity concert in 1987 (her "Marlene on the Wall" was included on the album of highlights from the show). Back in the States, the song "Left of Center," included on the soundtrack of the John Hughes film *Pretty in Pink*, became an alternative radio hit. By 1987, the stage was set for the release of Vega's second album, *Solitude Standing*, which, if all went according to plan, would build upon Vega's previous success and expose her to a larger audience. What was not expected was that the album would be a Top 20 hit (reaching number 11 and selling over one million copies) or that "Luka" would be a breakthrough smash.

Produced by the Kaye-Addabbo team, *Solitude Standing* had lusher instrumentation than its predecessor, though Vega's concise delivery still took center stage. But there was no obvious single on the album, which made "Luka" a surprise hit. Songs about child abuse were not unheard of in rock music (Pat Benatar's "Hell Is for Children" being an obvious example), but the issue was rarely addressed, even in the realm of political songs, and no song on the subject had ever made it into the Top 40 before. But "Luka's" story, narrated in a calm, near-expressionless voice by the abused victim, struck a responsive chord in the public, and Vega received awards from child abuse organizations for the recognition her single had brought to the issue. Many of the album's other songs had equally disquieting themes: the narrator in the a cappella "Tom's Diner" is cast as an eternal observer even when reflecting on a failed love affair, "In the Eye" depicts a potentially violent confrontation that could be either an argument or an assault, and the title track depicts "solitude" as an eternally present, enigmatic visitor.

Vega's next album, *Days of Open Hand* (which she co-produced), was released in 1990. In contrast to the personalized focus of her previous work, the majority of the songs on *Days of Open Hand* were observations of the outside world, with Vega, the omnipresent narrator, maintaining a detached perspective, even in situations where she is a participant, such as "Institution Green," where Vega waits to cast her vote in an anonymous bureaucratic building. "Fifty-Fifty Chance," the story of a suicide attempt, features a taut undercurrent of strings, arranged by Philip Glass, "Men in a War" contemplates physical and emotional loss, and the opening track, "Tired of Sleeping," has Vega trapped in a dream-like haze. In comparison to the success of *Solitude Standing, Days of Open Hand* did poorly, only selling around 350,000 copies. Vega admitted in *Rolling Stone* she was disappointed in A&M's handling of the album: "They [A&M] had forgotten what I represented, what I stood for . . . I never started making songs in order to get played on the radio—that was just a nice bonus." Her penchant for experimentation continued the following year when the British duo DNA released a bootleg record called "Oh Suzanne" that reworked "Tom's Diner" into a dance-rock track. A&M apprehended the duo for their unauthorized use of Vega's vocal track (which had been extensively sampled for DNA's record), but Vega suggested releasing DNA's imaginative "cover" as a legitimate record. The song became a number 2 hit in the British dance charts, and in 1991 Vega produced the compilation *Tom's Album,* a collection of widely varying cover versions of "Tom's Diner." Vega has since released four albums.

When Tracy Chapman, another solo performer who played an acoustic guitar, rose to prominence in 1988, she readily acknowledged the role Suzanne Vega had played in her own success, telling *Musician,* "She opened the minds and ears of radio programmers to a kind of music that had gone ignored for quite a while." Born in 1964 in Cleveland, Ohio, Chapman and her older sister were raised by their mother after their parents' divorce. Growing up listening to a musical diet that ranged from Barbra Streisand and Gladys Knight to Cher and Mahalia Jackson, Chapman's own musical career began with the ukulele and later included stints with the clarinet, organ, and finally, the guitar. She spent her high school years at the Wooster School in Danbury, Connecticut, after winning a scholarship, and regularly performed her own songs at school functions; in recognition of her talent, a collection was held among students and faculty to buy Chapman a new guitar during her sophomore year, and in her senior year the yearbook predicted "Tracy Chapman will marry her guitar and live happily ever after." After graduating in 1982, Chapman attended Tufts University in Boston, majoring in anthropology. She also played guitar on the folk circuit that still buzzed in the Boston-Cambridge community and opened for out-of-town acts.

Though Chapman was interested in a pursuing a musical career, she doubted that her socially conscious material would be of much interest to the general public. "I didn't think there was any indication that record people would find the kind of music that I did marketable," she admitted to *Rolling Stone.* But a fellow Tufts classmate recommended Chapman to his father, Charles Koppelman, who had worked alongside Carole King at Aldon Music and had become her boss when he was promoted to head of the publishing company; now he was the "K" in SBK (at that time a music publishing house). Koppelman liked Chapman's work, and signed her to SBK after she graduated from Tufts in 1986; he also helped her get a record deal with Elektra later that year. By the time Chapman finished recording her debut album, she had also taken on Elliott Roberts (who had previously worked with Joni Mitchell) as her manager.

Chapman's self-titled debut LP was released in the spring of 1988 and she toured extensively to promote it. Prior to the LP's release, Chapman was given the opening slot on a tour with Elektra labelmates 10,000 Maniacs, a folk rock outfit whose 1987 album *In My Tribe* was finally putting in an appearance in the Top 40 nearly a year after its release. Natalie Merchant, the Maniacs' lead singer, also opened for Chapman when she made her debut in London, as a way of introducing her to an overseas audience—

and the media. In June, Chapman appeared at the Nelson Mandela 70th Birthday Tribute Concert (held at Wembley Stadium in London) and then joined Peter Gabriel, Youssou N'Dour, Sting, and Bruce Springsteen on the 1988 Amnesty International world tour.

Meanwhile, her album was generating its own excitement, and during the summer of 1988 it seemed to be playing everywhere. Women's coffeehouses played it endlessly, while Top 40 airplay helped push it to the top of the charts; the single "Fast Car" made it to number 6. Musically, it harkened back to the '60s era of protest singers in a much clearer fashion than Vega's work did, for aside from "Luka," Vega's songs more often addressed personal, relationship-oriented concerns. Chapman's album (produced by David Kershenbaum, who'd previously worked with Joan Baez) began with the forthright "Talkin' 'Bout a Revolution," which sang of a future uprising by the disenfranchised members of society, "Behind the Wall" addressed the issue of domestic violence, and "Fast Car" derailed a couple's attempts to escape the grind of poverty. The hope for a better future was an appropriate sentiment for a presidential election year, and the success of the album was no doubt due in part to Chapman's willingness to address issues the United States government had found easy enough to dismiss during the '80s: the growing ranks of the homeless, an ever-rising crime rate, and a failing education system.

With the music industry's reluctance to vary from a proven commercially successful formula (the kind of reluctance that had hindered Suzanne Vega's search for a record contract), a song as stark as "Fast Car" not only stood out in comparison to most songs receiving airplay on the radio, it was also capable of inducing outright shock—reviewers recounted being frozen in their tracks the first time they heard the song. Even Chapman's love songs were tinged with a haunting melancholy, from the nervy "For My Lover" to the resignation of the one-sided relationships in "Baby Can I Hold You" and "If Not Now . . . ." Chapman won two Grammy awards, for Best New Artist and Best Contemporary Female Pop Vocal Performance for "Fast Car," and in 1989 she released her follow-up LP, *Crossroads*. The album adhered to the sparse instrumentation of her debut LP, but the political commentary was more outspoken: in both "Material World" and "Subcity" she attacked the corporate greed that was creating a widening gap between the rich and poor classes in America, "Freedom Now" is a song of support for the then-imprisoned anti-apartheid activist Nelson Mandela, and in "Born to Fight" Chapman announces her refusal to be beaten into "a white man's drone." She also addressed the price of fame in the title song and "All That You Have is Your Soul" (which also featured Neil Young on guitar and piano). Though the songs were perhaps too stark to produce any Top 40 single hits, the album reached number 9 and, like her debut, was another platinum seller. In the spring of 1992 she released her third album,

Matters of the Heart, which peaked at number 53. But 1995's *New Beginning* reached the Top 5, and 2000's *Telling Stories* also reached the Top 40.

After Tracy Chapman's success, it seemed that a plethora of female singer-songwriters —such as Michelle Shocked, Melissa Etheridge, and the Indigo Girls—arrived to leap on the bandwagon, though in reality their mutual appearance was more a matter of fortuitous timing than strategic planning. Chapman had been signed in 1986, a year before Vega hit with "Luka," and 1986 was the same year Michelle Shocked's first album was released on Cooking Vinyl, an independent label in Britain. The following year, both Melissa Etheridge and the Indigo Girls were signed to major labels.

The Indigo Girls' self-titled debut LP, released in 1989, was actually the fourth record for the duo, who had previously released a single, an EP, and an LP on their own label and had built up a strong regional following in the Atlanta area. Amy Ray and Emily Saliers had grown up together in neighboring Decatur, but did not begin playing music together until high school. Ray had taken up guitar at the urging of her older sister, and Saliers had sung with her sisters and taken guitar lessons at the YMCA. The two joined forces while students at Shamrock High "kind of on a whim," Saliers later recalled in *The Rocket*. "It was just for fun, because we both knew that we played guitar and sang songs."

After high school, the two initially attended separate colleges but kept playing together in local clubs during college breaks as Saliers and Ray. Both later transferred to Emory University in Atlanta (Saliers majoring in English, Ray in religion) and continued to hit the club circuit as the Indigo Girls, a name chosen by Ray by looking through the dictionary. But Saliers remained ambivalent about pursuing a musical career and was considering going to graduate school until Ray gave her an "ultimatum" during their senior year. After considering Ray's request, Saliers agreed to abandon her grad school plans and the two began pursuing their musical career in earnest.

Although the Indigos' sound was grounded by the interplay of their acoustic guitars, Saliers and Ray did not think of themselves as folk musicians initially; the underlying passion and drive in their songs gave them too much of an edge to be easily slipped into that category. "I was scared of being called 'folk,'" Ray later admitted in *Spin*, "because I didn't want us to be classed with that era of folk-pop." The Indigos' mix was also flavored by their different musical tastes, Ray admiring artists like the Replacements and Patti Smith, and Saliers leaning toward singer-songwriters like Joni Mitchell (whom she thanked for "inspiration" on the liner notes of the duo's major label debut) and James Taylor.

But after discovering Bob Dylan, the two felt freer to let their folk influences come to the fore ("We became Bob Dylan fanatics and it became important again to recognize that we were folk players," Ray told *Spin*) and released the single "Crazy Game"/"Someone to Come Home" in 1985. Their EP followed in 1986, and *Strange Fire*, a full-length LP comprised mostly of originals that featured the Indigos' trademark soaring harmonics and vibrant guitars, was released in 1987. The album attracted the attention of Epic, and after an A&R rep caught one of their shows, they were offered a contract.

The Indigos' Epic debut, *Indigo Girls*, was a far stronger release than *Strange Fire*, exhibiting an undeniable confidence. The ten songs explored the terrain of personal and spiritual salvation, freely drawing on religious imagery in both the titles ("Land of Canaan," "Prince of Darkness") and lyrics; there were also musical contributions from fellow Georgians R.E.M. (whose lead singer Michael Stipe sang on "Kid Fears") and Ireland's Hothouse Flowers. The duo made their national television debut on *The David Letterman Show* performing the album's first single, "Closer to Fine." The album itself reached number 22 in the charts and won the Grammy in Best Contemporary Folk Recording. 1990's *Nomads*Indians*Saints* album netted the duo a Grammy nomination for the song "Hammer and a Nail," and was followed by the release of an eight-song live EP, *Back on the Bus, Y'all*, in 1991, and the album *Rites of Passage* in 1992. They have released four albums since. The Indigo Girls, unlike some other female singer-songwriters, took the women-in-rock media focus in stride, though Ray was quick to point out that attitudes toward women performers lagged behind the media's renewed interest in female performers. "I think every woman musician has had to put up with being condescended to," she said in the *Illinois Entertainer*, "but it's something that happens to women in every field that's still male-dominated."

Melissa Etheridge's instrument of choice was also acoustic guitar, but her first Grammy nomination came in the Best Female Rock Vocal category for "Bring Me Some Water." Etheridge's raw voice and impassioned delivery set her apart from the other female singer-songwriters of the time as a true rocker in the gutsy manner of Janis Joplin, whose songs she performed. In her autobiography, Holly Near remembered her impression of first seeing Etheridge perform a Joplin song: "At first I thought, *Oh, no, another girl with a guitar*. But she was tearing them up. She ended with a Janis Joplin classic and did it no discredit." Etheridge was born in Leavenworth, Kansas, and at age twelve was fronting a country band. She later moved to Boston, studying guitar at the Berklee College of Music while playing coffeehouses and lounges at night. "I knew there were lots of compromises to be made if I wanted to work five nights a week and not have a day job," she told *Outlines*. "I knew I had to play other people's songs. I knew I had to sing the Barbra Streisand medley. But I would be making a living at music." She later relocated to Los Angeles at the beginning of the '80s, though she was dismayed by the abundance of heavy metal in the club scene.

Despite her initial qualms, Etheridge did find room in the clubs around L.A., where she played for five years. At the end of 1986, while playing at the Que Sera Sera club in Long Beach, she was approached by Chris Blackwell, who made the decision to sign her to his Island Records label after hearing only twenty minutes of her set. Etheridge's first album was recorded in one month, though both Etheridge and Blackwell felt the initial production buried the heart and soul of her music under too many synthesizers and had the album reworked before its release in 1988. Described by the *Los Angeles Times* as having "the most electrifying rock phrasing of any record this year," *Melissa Etheridge* was a passionate debut, right down to the album's cover, which had the singer in a dramatic pose, her head tilted back, eyes shut, and fists clenched. In Etheridge's songs, love

became an exercise in pain, a soul-searing experience that left one either unfulfilled or forsaken by the longed-for object of desire. Etheridge ultimately lost the Grammy for Best Female Rock Vocal Performance to Tina Turner (for her *Live in Europe* album), but she performed "Bring Me Some Water" at the awards presentation. Her album eventually reached number 22, as did the follow-up, 1989's *Brave and Crazy*. Her third release, *Never Enough*, came out in 1992.

The most consistently politically outspoken of the emerging wave of female singer-songwriters was undoubtedly the iconoclastic Michelle Shocked. Shocked's performances regularly included lengthy anecdotes that outlined her political agenda. It was a stance that sometimes rubbed Shocked's critics the wrong way ("I know that with Shocked you can't separate the singer from the

Michelle Shocked
The 1990 Bumbershoot Festival, Seattle, Photo by Mark Van S

politics, but if she had left out the preaching she might have more time to let her voice ring out in song," wrote a Seattle reviewer in 1989), but Shocked viewed her unexpected position as a singer in the mainstream as an opportunity too good to waste. She also viewed her sudden rise to success with a good deal of irony: when her major label debut, *Short Sharp Shocked*, was nominated for a Grammy for Best Contemporary Folk LP in the same year as Chapman's, she found the honor "Amusing. I stated my intentions to destroy the system from within and I get an award for it!"

Born in Texas, Shocked's parents divorced when she was a child, and her mother's second husband, who was in the military, took the family around the country from army base to army base before returning to East Texas. Shocked also maintained contact with her father, who lived in Dallas, visiting him during the summer, noting the sharp contrast between her two parents. "My mother's such an orthodox fundamentalist," she says, "and there was such a striking difference, my father being a fairly atheistic, liberal hippie. I mean, there were two versions of reality that most kids don't have an opportunity to experience that early on. You know that no matter what you believe, there's always an opposing point of view, but to have that from your own mother and father was pretty dramatic, and it gave me a lot of food for thought."

Shocked's father also provided musical inspiration, introducing his daughter to the music in his extensive record collection—including Doc Watson, Big Bill Broonzy, Guy Clark, and one of Janis Joplin's early influences, Leadbelly—and giving her the incentive to start making music herself. "Really, as far as getting my hands on a music instrument, that credit's due to my father," she says. "Because when he was maybe thirty-five, he went to the store and bought a book on how to play mandolin and just started teaching himself. He couldn't even carry a tune in a bucket, but he just enjoyed it, and he had a lot of good reasons for doing it. It was very stimulating. You could travel. You could get attention. It was a good way to meet people. Lots of advantages." By the time she was sixteen, Shocked ran away from her mother's home to live with her father permanently. She later attended the University of Texas in Austin in 1981, but she ultimately found college to be a limiting experience: "I was just taking basic courses and I was so blown by the idea that I was supposed to decide what I wanted to be when I grew up," she says. "But I had a pretty clear idea that I wanted a very interesting life. So it was real hard for me to knuckle under and say, 'Oh, I want to be an accountant. I want to be a this. I want to be a that.'"

After two years at the university, a phone call from a friend prompted Shocked to move out west, as Joplin had done two decades earlier, to San Francisco. "My friend was living there in a house in exchange for doing the dishes," Shocked explains, "and she was making beaded jewelry and selling it on the street for cash and playing her fiddle. So she invited me to join her, I think pretty much in the spirit of a big sister or something." But Shocked's first trip to San Francisco ended badly. "I was fresh off the boat from Texas," she explains, "not only leaving Texas, but also having just gotten out of school. What it basically meant was that I'd been in one institution or another all my life, and this was freedom staring me in the face, and I didn't adjust very well at first. A month after I arrived I was picked up by the police in Santa Cruz and taken to a psychiatric hospital just for walking around disoriented. My dad came and got me and brought me back to Texas, and I tried to work with him—he's a carpenter—but unfortunately they had given me a prescription for a drug called haldol and they didn't explain that one of the side effects was the equivalent of wearing a mental straitjacket. It was physically impossible to work. I'd pick up a hammer, but I could not conceive of making it meet a nail."

Shocked's father eventually threw her out of the house, and she ultimately returned to San Francisco. It was during her second stay in the city that Shocked's political awakening occurred. "Living in the closet across from my friend was a fellow who was a political activist working out of a book collective on Haight Street," she says. "He took me around and showed me the squatting scene, so that when I went back in 1984, I ended up living in a squat, and from there I traveled and engaged in political activism during the Republican and Democratic conventions." Shocked later referred to her time in San Francisco as "homelessness with a very political edge," as the squatters freely mixed music and politics together, playing in hardcore bands while working for nuclear disarmament, running their own soup kitchen, and putting on shows under the banner of Rock Against Racism.

Shocked next returned to Austin and was living in the basement of a bookstore, when her mother made a dramatic reappearance in her life. Concerned about her daughter's "immoral" lifestyle, she had Shocked committed to a psychiatric hospital. The experience of being committed, along with additional incarcerations in jail when she was arrested at political rallies, inspired the last name of "Shocked," which readily conveyed her feeling of being "shell shocked" by a system she viewed as corrupt and apathetic. After being released from the hospital, which deemed Shocked as "cured" when her mother's insurance ran out, Shocked made her way to New York, and eventually Europe, where her distance from the States added to her disillusionment with the country in the wake of Ronald Reagan's re-election as president. "I saw America in the worst possible light," she recalled in *The Rocket*. "I realized how little optimism there is in this country. That led me to quite strong dissident politics."

On her return to the U.S. in 1986, she turned up at the Kerrville Folk Festival in Texas. Shocked paid her way to the event by working for the eight-dollar-a-day stipend and participated in the informal sing-alongs held around campfires in the evening. As she was playing her songs, Peter Lawrence, a record producer from Britain, asked if he could record her impromptu set on his Sony Walkman; Shocked agreed. Later that year, Lawrence contacted her, asking for permission to release the songs officially on his record label, Cooking Vinyl. Shocked was initially hesitant about the project ("I was so anti-establishment, anything that resembled business deals I would have burned"), but finally agreed because Lawrence's label was an independent. *The Texas Campfire Tapes* was released in the U.K. in late 1986, and Lawrence brought Shocked to Britain for a tour in January 1987; by February the album had hit the top of the independent charts.

The *Campfire Tapes* album was eventually released in the U.S. in 1988 (an accompanying press release jokingly noted, "It holds the distinction of being the only major label LP that cost less to make than it does to buy"), by which time Shocked had signed with PolyGram and was working on her first major label LP, *Short Sharp Shocked*. She was well aware of the contradictions she would face in moving up to a major label. "I could look at it politically and say that I want . . . to be more idealistic and not get involved with corporations," she explained to *New Music*, "[but] then again a lot of people would like this opportunity that never get it. So when the opportunity came to me then I said, 'Yeah, I'll see what I can do with it.'" Shocked had tried to turn down her advance from the label completely, saying all she needed was complete artistic control and PolyGram had to insist she accept at least fifty thousand dollars.

Short Sharp Shocked was released in 1988 and fully exhibited Shocked's skills as a consummate storyteller-reporter with a wry outlook on life. Her warm, mellow voice was equally effective whether relating memories of her childhood ("V.F.D.," "Run to Gladewater") or offering political commentary, as on "Graffiti Limbo," which told the story of graffiti artist Michael Stewart, murdered while in police custody; she also tagged on a remake of "Fogtown" from *Campfire Tapes*, with instrumental assistance from hardcore band M.D.C. The album's cover was striking, showing Shocked held in a chokehold by a police officer while being arrested at a rally, not for blocking the sidewalk—only a misdemeanor—but conspiring to block the sidewalk—a felony. PolyGram was nervous about the picture ("The marketing department was quite sure that it was going to be the doom of an otherwise brilliant record," she said in the *Los Angeles Daily News*) and took the added precaution of air-brushing the officer's badge number out of the shot.

Navigating the demands of an industry that she saw as a "realm of contradiction" became easier for Shocked when she found she was able to turn situations to her advantage. "What usually happens is whatever compromises you're called upon to make, you're never painted into a corner so absolutely that you can't say, 'Well, wait a minute.

I'll make this work for me,'" she says. "I have a real strong political philosophy against video, yet if I have to do a video, I'm going to give them something that I feel is fairly subversive." She also stated that if the contradictions of working "within the system" became too great, she would not be afraid to leave. But after the release of her second major label LP in 1989, the big-band-styled *Captain Swing*, her observations about how music is marketed left her feeling uneasy. "You know, there's a real kind of wisdom in the industry that a debut artist is supposed to go as high as they can because it's all downhill from there," she says. "What does that say about artistic growth? It's basically saying you're supposed to be better when you're one than when you're ten. That is insane. That is a way to kill artistic growth. When too many people know about you for one thing, you can't defeat those kinds of expectations."

She was equally wary about the women-in-rock trend. "I just felt like what [the media] were giving with one hand, they were taking away with the other," she explains. "That when I started being compared not on the basis of music, but on the basis of image, I felt like they were winning the game. Because one of the things that I've tried to do in my involvement inside the system is to say, 'Let's stop consuming so many things that are just based on someone's selling us an image,' whether that's politics or commodities or music. And to realize that I was being marketed the same way just gave me plenty of fuel for my fire. Because when really pressed to it, beyond image and style, there weren't many musical similarities between myself and Tracy Chapman."

By 1990, the "phenomenon" of women-in-rock had disappeared from both the media and the charts, as the follow-up albums by many of the key artists—such as Suzanne Vega's *Days of Open Hand* and the Indigo Girls' *Nomads*Indians*Saints*—failed to reach the Top 40. This made little difference to the artists themselves, who had grown tired of being depicted as women first and musicians second. Their previous commercial successes also meant that they were still able to record for major labels and the fact that they wrote their own material gave them an additional measure of control. Vega's *Days of Open Hand* was a bold step away from her previous musical style, and Michelle Shocked, none of whose albums have reached the Top 40, freely experimented with different musical forms on her records; for 1992's *Arkansas Traveler*, the singer traveled around the world, recording with artists as varied as blues guitarist/fiddler Clarence "Gatemouth" Brown, the Hothouse Flowers, and former members of the Band.

But forgotten in the rush to chronicle, in *Musician*'s words, "the women's movement of 1988," was an acknowledgment of the role the performers and labels involved in the women's music movement of the '70s had played in laying the groundwork for the women-in-rock trend of the '80s. Nor were those still involved with women's music reaping the financial benefits from an industry that had decided it was okay for women to be serious again. The leading women's music label, Olivia, had been unable to expand their roster because of their dwindling resources; in fact, both Tracy Chapman and Melissa Etheridge had sent demos to the label and both had been turned down because Olivia simply hadn't had the funds to produce new artists. Holly Near's label Redwood had put in a bid for Chapman, but had been unable to match the offer Elektra made. Nor had women's music attracted a substantial new audience from younger generations, who were more interested in rock and found a greater inspiration to make music from the punk scene. Meanwhile, the women's music core audience of the '70s had begun to drift away from the movement as they'd grown older.

The fact that the earlier trailblazers were not reaping rewards for their efforts was a point that was not lost on those still actively involved in women's music. "We've made the world safe for androgyny in the charts, but a few women musicians in the forefront is not what we wanted," said Olivia recording artist Deidre McCalla in *Outlook* in 1990, while Cris Williamson reflected on the gains her hard work had brought: "There I am, hacking with my machete making my way through the jungle," she told the *Boston Sunday Globe*. "And I look behind me and Tracy's striding down the path. Part of me is a bit jealous of that success. And in my rational mind I say, 'Cris . . . this is why you did it.'"

The ties women's music had with the lesbian community had helped keep women's music and its performers on the fringes of a conservative industry that not only wanted its artists to deny any allegations of unorthodox sexuality, it preferred the subject not be mentioned at all. Etheridge and Chapman had each played at women's music festivals before landing their major label contracts (and Etheridge continued to play at such events), a fact never mentioned in the mainstream press. For some in the women's music community, the opportunity to be open about their lifestyle was an issue just as important as the opportunity to make music, and the new female singer-songwriters who remained ambiguous about their sexuality, both in their music (relying on "you and I" pronouns in love songs, waggishly dubbed NGRs for "non-specific gender references") and in their interviews, were disdainfully regarded as "passing" and thus helping to maintain the invisibility of gay culture in the mainstream.

In her autobiography, Holly Near pointed out the difficulties in maintaining an allegiance with her lesbian audience while holding on to her right to have a private life: "I figured I was a grown-up now. I could decide when and with whom to make love without asking the permission of ten thousand dykes." Yet she felt uncomfortable about being seen as "straight" if she chose to go out with a man: "I couldn't bear the idea of hurting lesbians, and I couldn't stand the thought of heterosexuals celebrating my relationship with a man as if somehow they had won," she wrote. Michelle Shocked also addressed this conflict in an interview in *Outlines*, a gay paper in Chicago. "I felt like I was put in a position where I was damned if I did 'come out' and I was damned if I didn't," she said. "There would be a lot of straight media that would really like to know that I was *not* gay as much as there would be a lot of gay press that would like to know that I *was* gay . . . for me I've never really been able to fit into square holes *or* round holes. So for my part, I just leave the question open." (Shocked has since married.) Unfortunately, women performers who chose to be open about their lesbianism invariably lost the chance to reach a broader audience. In the '70s, women's music had sought to minimize that loss by creating their own audience, only to find that attaining a "women's music" bin in the record shops brought its own limitations (a sticker on the cover of *Short Sharp Shocked* instructed record stockers to "Place In Pop/Rock Section"). In the '80s, performers like Ferron, Two Nice Girls, and Phranc worked to eliminate that marginalization by recording for (primarily independent) labels outside the women's music community.

Born in 1952 in Toronto, Ontario, Ferron Foisy, the oldest of seven children, later moved with her family at age seven to Richmond, a suburb of Vancouver, British Columbia. She had started playing guitar and writing songs at age eleven, finding musical inspiration from fellow Canadian Joni Mitchell, in addition to Joan Baez and Judy Collins. At fifteen she left home, supporting herself with a series of blue-collar jobs, and in 1976 made her public debut performing at a benefit for Press Gang, a women's printing collective. She soon found other gigs in women's coffeehouses, and in 1977 released her first album, *Ferron*, followed by *Ferron Backed Up* in 1978, both of which she recorded in a TV studio and distributed out of her basement (she later referred to the records as "the basement tapes"). In 1978, she met Gayle Scott, an American freelance photographer. "She asked me if I wanted to sing for a living," Ferron later recalled in a press release promoting her 1990 album *Phantom Center*. "Nobody had ever asked me that. I didn't know you could do that. I thought maybe you were born into it. Who had time to think about it?"

Scott persuaded Ferron it could be done and became her manager and business partner; together they formed their own label, Lucy Records/Penknife Productions Ltd. In 1980, Ferron released her first studio album, *Testimony*, which was licensed by Redwood Records, and she began to tour Canada and the U.S. In 1984, she released the highly acclaimed *Shadows on a Dime*, produced by Terry Garthwaite, formerly of Joy of Cooking. Ferron's songs dealt with the same tortured terrain of relationships that Melissa Etheridge would later explore, with an expressive delivery that made the societal change she sang about in "It Won't Take Long" seem like it was just around the corner. *Shadows* was lauded by the critics, receiving a four-star rating in *Rolling Stone*, while the *Boston Globe* stated, "Someday they will call Dylan the Ferron of the '60s." Yet at the moment when she had the greatest potential of breaking through to a larger audience, the increased pressures of touring and performing caused Ferron to put her career on hold. "I took a back seat to my own life for a while," she told the *Georgia Straight*. "I had to re-evaluate where the passion comes from."

Ferron's period of re-evaluation meant there was a six-year gap between *Shadows* and 1990's *Phantom Center*, released on Chameleon Records, a label started in 1985 as the outgrowth of a record importing business. While the accompanying press release noted her ties to the women's music community, it also stated that "even though Ferron is deeply appreciative of the support she receives within that peer group, and remains connected to its issues and values, she's leery of being straightjacketed by a label." The magazine *Hot Wire* was not as cautious about such terminology, headlining their interview with the singer in their January 1991 issue "The Return of Ferron to Women's Music"; in the interview Ferron stated, "Women's music is not only about women opening up, it's about all people opening up to women." Attendance at her concerts also shows that Ferron's audience is still overwhelmingly composed of women.

Elsewhere, the Austin, Texas-based group Two Nice Girls was also trying to show that openly lesbian performers could find an audience beyond the genre of women's music without compromising their integrity. Gretchen Phillips, guitarist for the group, told *Pulse* magazine, "We don't want to be branded feminists or lesbians. We'd like to be thought of as songwriters and musicians." The group worked hard to have their feminism and lesbianism recognized as part of the group's makeup, while keeping the music the primary focus. Not that they shied away from discussing either subject: "I don't want to cave in to any sort of notion of being palatable in order to be successful," Kathy Korniloff, the group's other guitarist, told *Hot Wire*.

Two Nice Girls was founded in 1985, in the wake of both the women's music scene and the punk movement, giving the group a wide range of influences they eagerly cited in the liner notes for their 1989 self-titled debut album—influences ranging from Joan Armatrading to the Shaggs to Led Zeppelin to Joni Mitchell to the Slits. The members' experiences matched their influences. Gretchen Phillips grew up watching her parents playing in a lounge band called the Orphans, and attended Houston's High School for the Performing and Visual Arts; prior to Two Nice Girls, she played in the bands Meat Joy and Girls in the Nose. Kathy Korniloff studied violin as a child before discovering the guitar, Jethro Tull, and Joni Mitchell at age twelve. After graduating from the University of Texas with a degree in film, she founded Litris Media, which sponsors the annual Third Wave International Women's Film & Video Festival in Austin. Bassist Meg Hentges had previously played in the all-female punk band the Neo-Boys in Portland, Oregon, before moving to Austin and joining Two Nice Girls after the release of their first album. Drummer Pam Barger, who replaced the group's original drummer Laurie Freelove, had played with Phillips in Girls in the Nose in addition to the band Child Bearing Hips, and listed Karen Carpenter, Maureen Tucker, John Bonham, and Keith Moon among her drum heroes.

The group's debut album, released in 1989 on Rough Trade, was punctuated with a gentle humor, and featured an inventive medley of Lou Reed's "Sweet Jane" and Joan Armatrading's "Love and Affection," and a cover of Jane Siberry's "Follow Me." But the song that gained the band the most notoriety was "I Spent My Last $10.00 (On Birth Control & Beer)," a country & western "tale of woe" about a lesbian who unexpectedly finds love in the arms of a "strong hairy man" following a breakup with her girlfriend, climaxing in an audience sing-along on the chorus. The song's humorous take on homosexual "conversion" made it an alternative radio hit, though one critic who failed to get the joke referred to it as a "stridently anti-male diatribe." The group's tongue-in-cheek approach was elaborated on in their next release, the EP *Like a Version* (released in 1990), which included another inspired medley, "I Feel (Like Makin') Love" (which combined Bad Company's "Feel Like Makin' Love" with Donna Summer's "I Feel Love"), covers of "Cotton Crown" (from New York's Sonic Youth), "Bang, Bang" (first recorded by Janis Martin), the theme song from the cartoon series *Speed Racer*, the Carpenters' "Top of the World," and "$10.00." 1991's *Chloe Liked Olivia* (a line taken from Virginia Woolf's *A Room of One's Own*) was a more ambitious work, adding a variety of instruments to the group's acoustic base, and offering lyrics that ran the gamut from a eulogy to gay life in "The Queer Song" to a scathing look at President Bush, who only offers "a kinder and gentler fuck" in "For the Inauguration."

On the West Coast, singer-songwriter Phranc was also offering witty commentary in her songs and working to keep the focus on her music while being upfront about her lesbianism. Like Two Nice Girls, Phranc also recorded for labels not associated with women's music, releasing her first record on Rhino, and then signing with Island. "You gotta keep pushing," she says. "Two Nice Girls and I come up against the same stuff a lot of the time. People focus on our sexuality more than our music, and I hate that. I hate that! But I'm not going to shut up about it either." As virtually the only self-proclaimed "all-American Jewish lesbian folksinger," Phranc, with her snappy flattop hairstyle, was a category unto herself, but she was quick to point out it was also a category with universal appeal. "My songs speak to everybody," she says. "I have some songs that deal with the issue of lesbians, and there's an identification of me being a lesbian, but my sexuality is not the biggest part of me—it's part of me like my haircut and my shoes; it's not the biggest part and it's not the smallest part. But when I was growing up, there were so few examples of people that were out as lesbians, I felt like I was the only one! I'm not the only one. Young people need to know that they're not the only one. They should have the right to grow up and be whoever they are. That's the point I'm making."

Born Susie Gottlieb and raised in Los Angeles, Phranc began playing music at age five, progressing from piano to violin to guitar by age ten. "I grew up listening to Pete Seeger records, Broadway show tunes like *South Pacific*, and Allan Sherman, one of my bigger influences—especially his 'My Son, The Folk Singer' [a number 1 hit for Sherman in 1962]. So that's how I started." By her teens, Phranc started attending women's music concerts and began playing at coffeehouses; she left home in the mid-'70s, at age seventeen "because I couldn't be queer at home. It was that time when women's music was brand new, and in Los Angeles there was a strong lesbian feminist community. I grew up there." As a "radical junior lesbian separatist," Phranc continued playing her guitar and writing songs while working for publications such as the *Lesbian Tide* and *Sister*, eventually moving to San Francisco to investigate its women's community; as Michelle Shocked would be in the '80s, Phranc was soon caught up in the city's punk and hardcore scene.

"What took me to the punk thing was it was the first time I really felt like I fit in with my peer group," Phranc explains. "I met people my age that were angry and tired of not being taken seriously because they were younger. The women's community wasn't especially all-inclusive. I was really young, and at that time there weren't a lot of young lesbians [in the movement]; there were two other young women that I knew that were sixteen and seventeen and that was it. Everyone else was at least ten years older than us." She also found she enjoyed her renewed contact with the "outside world." "I came from a place of being completely politically separatist, and all of a sudden I joined the huge world again, with all different kinds of people, and men, and it was just a very different life," she says. "But it was very exciting for me because I identified in a major way with other people that were my age who were angry and excited and creative and political."

Phranc carried her interest in punk back to L.A., where she played with the bands Nervous Gender ("I didn't sing with them," she said later, "I screamed") and Catholic Discipline, who were featured in Penelope Spheeris's *The Decline . . . of Western Civilization*. By the early '80s, she'd also moved back into acoustic performing as a result of writing the song "Take Off Your Swastika," an attack on punks who adopted the fascist symbol as a fashion accessory. "That's how I came back to playing folk again," she explains. "Because for that particular song I really wanted the words to be heard. The format of the ballad is the perfect way to tell the story through song, and it works really well for me. Punk rock was great. It's so much like folk music. It was so simple and so strong, lots of messages, real political, but the focus was never on the lyric. So much good stuff came out of punk, so many good lyrics and great songs, but a lot of them were lost because of that."

Unable to attract the interest of a record company, Phranc saved the money she earned from teaching swimming and recorded her first album for fifteen hundred dollars. Rhino then offered her a deal, and *Folksinger*, co-produced by Phranc, Ethan James, and Craig Lee, was released in 1985. The album's songs addressed a variety of topics, from female mud-wrestling (complete with sing-along chorus), to the Pope's immortalization in a comic book ("Caped Crusader"), to her experiences as a swimming instructor ("One o' the Girls"), in which her students try to get her to shave her legs (a suggestion met with a resounding "No way!"). *Folksinger* received good reviews, but poor distribution meant there were few sales, and Phranc was dropped from the label. She toured extensively for the next few years, opening for such acts as the Smiths, X, and the Violent Femmes, before heading back into the studio on her own. "Once again I got tired of waiting for someone to make my record, so I went and made it myself," she recalls. Phranc took on the Violent Femmes' drummer Victor DeLorenzo as her producer, recording the album at his Milwaukee studio. "I came back home with the tape, and then there was a lot of interest," she says. "So I had lunch with all the majors. And you know, they love you when they have lunch with you, and they say how great you are and start talking about what your album's going to be like and how much you can spend and all this stuff, and then the next week they pass. Emotionally it's very devastating to go through the record deal process. Pick yourself up out of the gutter and go and smile and sell yourself to the next Joe Schmo. I did that for a long time, and it was very discouraging, very frustrating."

Phranc admits her "all-American Jewish lesbian" tag might have put some record companies off, but adds, "Nobody will say it. Nobody comes right out and says that, you just don't get a record deal!" But Island Records ultimately signed her and released *I Enjoy Being a Girl* in 1989. "Island is setting an example by signing me and loving me just the way I am," she maintains. "I don't have to do anything except be creative and make the music. I'm not pressured to change my hair or the way I look or what I say or who I am. It feels really good after all this time to feel like the label is behind me and can put that support behind me. There's a quote from the *L.A. Times*, when they did an interview with me, they also interviewed, unbeknownst to me, the head of marketing at Island, and he said, 'There's no Jewish lesbian folksinger record bin in record stores. The fact that Phranc is a lesbian is not important at all except for the fact that it's part of her.' To see that in the paper from the head of marketing at a major label is pretty exciting. It was just such a kick in the pants to all those people in the industry that had stood in my way."

Her Island debut featured songs on serious issues ("Take Off Your Swastika," and

"Bloodbath," which addressed apartheid) along with humorous numbers about her obsessions (toy stores and female tennis star Martina Navratilova), and her own look at the singer-songwriter trend in "Folksinger," which wryly noted, "Androgyny's the ticket/at least it seems to be/Just don't wear a flattop/and mention sexuality/and girl you'll go far." There were also inspired covers of the title track (by Rodgers and Hammerstein) and "Moonlight Becomes You." The album's cover was equally tongue-in-cheek, a glowing portrait of a dreamy-eyed Phranc in a red turtleneck, leaning on a bank of fake grass and holding a glass of milk. Island then re-released *Folksinger* in 1990 with the additional track "Everywhere I Go (I Hear the Go-Go's)," in which Phranc laments how people prefer to emulate Belinda Carlisle's looks instead of her own. It was followed in 1991 by *Positively Phranc!* The release was Phranc's most accomplished work yet, with Two Nice Girls providing vocal backups on two songs, including the rockabilly-infused "64 Ford"; a collaboration with the Blasters' Dave Alvin on "Hitchcock," about the female stars in Hitchcock films; a hilarious rewrite of Jonathan Richman's "Pablo Picasso," which she renames "Gertrude Stein"; a song about the life of Billy Tipton, the jazz musician who "passed" as a man for fifty years, and another inventive cover, an a cappella duet with Syd Straw on the Beach Boys' "Surfer Girl."

Though Phranc, Two Nice Girls, and Ferron were eager to serve as a bridge from their so-called "alternative" camps into mainstream culture by working with larger independent labels (or in Phranc's case, a major label) that had more financial clout than underfinanced women's music labels, the recording careers of both Two Nice Girls and Ferron were stalled by difficulties with their respective labels (Ferron remains an active live performer, but Two Nice Girls broke up after a final tour in 1992). Rough Trade declared bankruptcy in 1991 and Chameleon (who had also released Holly Near's 1990 album *Singer in the Storm*) drastically scaled back their operations, which left Ferron's *Phantom Center* out of print. Phranc also found herself without a label once again when Island dropped her after the release of *Positively Phranc!*

But there were other groups, like Casselberry/DuPreé, who weren't especially concerned with entering the mainstream at all, finding regular work at women's music festivals, ethnic and cultural festivals, and political events. Consisting of Judith (Jay) Casselberry on vocals and rhythm guitar, Jaqué DuPreé on vocals and hand percussion, Toshi Reagon (Bernice Reagon's daughter) on bass, and Annette Aguilar on percussion, the group played a blend of music that encompasses ethnic rhythms and strong vocal harmonizing. And like many an American act before them, they sometimes received greater recognition abroad than at home. "We were like rock stars over there," says Annette Aguilar about their tour of Spain in the late '80s. "It was very successful. We were on the news right before Bruce Springsteen!"

Casselberry-DuPreé Band
(left to right): Toshi Reagon, Judith Casselberry, Annette Aguilar, Jaqué DuPreé, Courtesy of
Annette Aguilar

Aguilar had joined "the girls," as she refers to Casselberry/DuPreé, in 1981, having met the two in 1979 when they performed on the same bill at San Francisco's Gay Pride Day festivities. Aguilar's parents had come from Nicaragua to San Francisco, where Aguilar was born in 1957. After seeing the Beatles on television, she became interested in playing the drums and began playing in the school band in sixth grade. She later acquired a conga drum and began playing Latin rhythms, and soon embarked on a deliberately well-rounded musical education, playing with an all-female Latin-Brazilian jazz group and the Bay Area Women's Philharmonic while studying for her bachelor's degree in music at San Francisco State University (she later received a master's degree from the Manhattan School of Music).

Aguilar played her first gig with Casselberry/DuPreé while still in college, but she remained in San Francisco to finish her degree before joining the two when they moved to New York in 1983. Aguilar arrived in New York two years later, in time to play on the group's 1986 album *City Down*. Produced by Linda Tillery, *City Down* went on to win an award from the National Association for Independent Record Distributors (NAIRD) for Best Reggae Album of the year. The group then began touring extensively, and found that although the music regularly won over audiences, the reaction to the group's racial mix wasn't always as warm. "It's like you got four women up there," says Aguilar, "three black and one Hispanic. One time they didn't want to let us through the border! And these girls are so clean—they don't do drugs, they're wholesome! But when we walk into the airport, forget it! But they're very humorous, the girls, and they can jive with any kind of person. I mean, I've seen Jay Casselberry talk to the

Annette Aguilar of Casselberry-DuPreé
Photo by Leigh H. Mosley, courtesy of
Annette Aguilar

most bigoted white men with a smile. We don't have too much of a problem with hotels, just a lot of stares, but when we go in there, we're smiling and saying 'How are you?' and Jay has a very nice, long smile."

The group also encountered their share of sexist reactions in addition to racism, though these attitudes changed dramatically once the "girls" had proved they were "real" musicians. "We had one gig in Boston," remembers Aguilar. "And we went to do our sound check, and there's these white boys, these guys that do the rockers. They looked at us like, look at these dreadlock bitches, man, these black girls and that white girl . . . what are you going to do, play a couple of Go-Go's songs? It's like we don't know nothing about sound. We don't know nothing about mikes. And they do. And then we start playing and they all flip out. All of a sudden they want to be nice to us!" But Aguilar noticed the changes in perceptions about female performers once artists like Tracy Chapman, a friend of Toshi Reagon, began to appear on the music scene.

"Finally the record companies are looking at how powerful women artists are and how talented they are," Aguilar says, remembering the reaction to Chapman's album when it arrived at the CD shop where she was then working in New York. "People need to know what the hell is going on in this world, and that's why people like Tracy Chapman," she says. "People need to be educated. When my boss first got Tracy Chapman's album in, I said, 'Oh, you ordering Tracy Chapman? That's Toshi's friend. She's played in Michigan, she played a gig with the girls, Tracy's cool. She came to our gig last January at the Strand in Boston, and Toshi told me she was coming out with an album. You'll like that stuff. You put it on.' And he's looking at me like yeah, yeah, yeah, and he puts on this goddamn thing, man, and everybody's blown away. And all of a sudden she was on the cover of *Rolling Stone*, she's on the Amnesty tour with Sting, and it's like, look at this black girl with the dreadlocks and t-shirt and the jeans, man, singing. That's education, man."

In addition to overlooking the contributions women's music had made in establishing a path for the '80s women-in-rock, the music industry also tended to overlook women who did not fit into the singer-songwriter mold, or who made less obviously commercial music. "If we believe the A&R men, Kate Bush will never make it in America," says Gail Colson. "Because her voice 'isn't right for American radio.' Which is a terrible thing. What does that mean, if her voice isn't right for American radio?" In spite of these predictions, Kate Bush finally did crack the U.S. Top 40 in 1985 with *Hounds of Love*, which reached number 30, and the accompanying single "Running Up That Hill (A Deal With God)," which also reached number 30. But aside from these two hits, Bush's music has been unable to penetrate the U.S. market successfully. After the release of *Hounds*, Bush moved from EMI America to Columbia in the U.S. in an effort to gain greater exposure in the American market. But her Columbia debut, *The Sensual World* (released in 1989) just missed the Top 40, and the accompanying single, "Love and Anger," also failed to register prominently on the charts. 1991 saw the release of the box set *This Woman's Work*, a compilation of Bush's previous albums and singles, which was not released in the U.S., but 1993's *The Red Shoes* did reach the U.S. Top 40. Bush has maintained her status as a strong cult artist in America, and she remains an alternative/college radio favorite.

Commercial radio had an equally difficult time with k. d. lang's music, which combined country and rock in a manner that flew in the face of established conventions in both genres. When lang's fourth album, *Absolute Torch and Twang*, went gold in 1990, she quipped, "Me and Metallica . . . gold with no radio!" in a press release. For despite her lack of airplay, lang was able to carve out her own niche and gain a strong following, proving that there was a place for artists who didn't fit into a readily definable slot. Lang's success was a reflection of her own determination: "As long as you're willing to work for something, I believe that you get what you want," she told *Goldmine*.

Born in 1961, Kathy Dawn Lang grew up in Consort, Alberta, Canada, a town with a population of 650. After studying classical piano for three years, lang switched to guitar at age ten; the previous year, she had written a song entitled "Hoping All My Dreams Come True," which she sent to Canadian singer Anne Murray. After high school, she studied music at Red Deer College in Alberta, and at the age of nineteen fell under the spell of country & western music. Lang's tastes in music had always been broad—in addition to citing inspiration "by everyone from Julie Andrews to Yoko Ono," she was also a fan of Peggy Lee and Joni Mitchell—and through her role in a stage show called *Country Chorale* she was introduced to the music of Patsy Cline, who would provide further inspiration. There had been resistance to casting lang as Cline in the show, which was based on Cline's life, because of her tomboy appearance, foreshadowing problems she'd have in the future, but once cast, lang threw herself into her role and into her discovery of country music.

After *Country Chorale* she answered an ad for a singer placed by a western swing band based in Edmonton, called Dance Party, in 1982, and following the band's breakup in 1983, formed her own group, the reclines. The band quickly earned a strong local following and soon issued their first single, "Friday Dance Promenade," followed by the release of *A Truly Western Experience* in 1984 on Bumstead, an independent label based in Vancouver, British Columbia. Co-produced by lang, who also wrote or co-wrote three of the album's nine songs, *A Truly Western Experience* displayed all sides of the group, getting off to a rousing start with "Bopalena," a country & western rocker made for the dance floor, giving a nod to Cline on "Stop, Look and Listen," and closing with "Hooked on Junk," a remarkable piece that rambled on for six minutes, delivered by lang with a suitably downbeat, scraped raw vocal, unlike anything she has recorded since. The album was successful in generating further exposure for lang and the reclines, who signed to Sire Records by the end of the year, with lang winning a Juno award for Most Promising Female Vocalist in 1985. Her major label debut, 1987's *Angel With a Lariat*, which focused on upbeat material, attracted good critical notices, but was a slow seller, a reception her future recordings would also face.

Although lang's records and live shows proved to be popular with critics and audiences, radio lagged behind in accepting her blend of country and rock, and her flamboyant, theatrical appearance. For if her music was a hybrid of conventional styles, her stage dress was far removed from the traditional country look of flowing lacy gowns, or pastel fringed jackets. Lang was not adverse to gowns or fringe (she once wore a wedding gown to an awards ceremony), but she dressed up her wardrobe with thrift-shop chic and such accessories as sawed-off cowboy boots to give a spin on conventional country fashion, while her spiky haircut emulated the classic 'dos of '50s male rockers (after seeing one of lang's performances Madonna commented, "I've seen Elvis—and she's gorgeous!"), a look that made her a great favorite for television work. Alternative radio made room for lang, but her gender bending met with resistance from the more conservative country music industry, and even a liberal audience could miss the tongue-in-cheek aspect of her work. "I received a

k. d. lang
December 1987 on *Top of the Pops*, Photo by Sherry Rayn Barnett

letter just the other day from a feminist saying 'I'm really upset by you doing "Johnny Get Angry" because I can't figure out whether you're condemning or condoning it,'" she said in *Ms.*, adding, "I would assume that a woman who looks and acts like me, well, it would be pretty obvious what I felt about it." Lang countered such opposition by arguing it was more important for people to change their minds about her. "Most people haven't tried to understand where I'm coming from," she said in *Goldmine*. "They think on the surface I'm a novelty act, and I agree that novelty is certainly a part of my approach to life. But I think that those are the people who are afraid to explore the different dimensions of k. d. lang, though they *will*, eventually, if they want to."

Lang's next project directly challenged the country music industry's perceptions of her work. *Shadowland* was not only recorded in Nashville, using session musicians instead of the reclines, but was also produced by Owen Bradley, Patsy Cline's former producer. Bradley was introduced to lang's work by a mutual friend who worked for RCA in Nashville, and after seeing lang perform Cline's "Three Cigarettes (In an Ashtray)" on *The Tonight Show*, he came out of a ten-year retirement to work with her. Released in 1988, *Shadowland* slowed the pace down with a selection of bluesy, jazz-tinted crooners and also had veteran country stars Brenda Lee, Kitty Wells, and Loretta Lynn sharing vocals with lang on "The Honky Tonk Angels Medley." The same year, lang won a Grammy for Best Vocal Collaboration for her duet with Roy Orbison on "Crying." The reclines came back on board in 1989 for *Absolute Torch and Twang*, again co-produced by lang, who wrote or co-wrote the bulk of the album's material. In addition to being her first album to go gold in the U.S., it also won lang her first Grammy award as a solo artist, for Best Country Female Vocalist. In the '90s, lang's versatility as a performer expanded into film work. She made her film debut in Percy Aldon's 1991 feature *Salmonberries*, and in 1992, a duet with Jane Siberry, "Calling All Angels," was included in the soundtrack for Wim Wenders' film *Until the End of the World*. 1992 also saw the release of her fifth album, *Ingénue*, a series of ballads about the pain of love, described by critics as "torch without the twang."

Sinéad O'Connor was another performer perceived as being "too odd" for American audiences, which made her eventual breakthrough even more unexpected than Vega's had been. And although O'Connor was chosen for the cover of *Musician*'s women-in-rock trend issue, she was also the least inclined to associate herself with that trend: "I also hate being asked, 'How do I feel being a *woman* in rock,'" she said in a *Musician* sidebar entitled "Questions Sinéad O'Connor Hates." It was all part of O'Connor's overall displeasure at being seen as part of any category, whether the focus was on women or being Irish. Born in Dublin, Ireland, in 1966, O'Connor grew up in a troubled, abusive household; her parents separated when she was eight, and O'Connor lived with her mother for a few years before deciding to live with her father when she was thirteen. Her mother was later killed in a car accident in 1985. In this unhappy atmosphere, O'Connor found a refuge in music, remembering later that she made up songs while out walking. "It wasn't that I wanted to be a singer," she said in *Rolling Stone*, "it was just that I could actually *express* the pain that I felt with my voice."

O'Connor also took ballet and voice lessons, but was unhappy at school and began cutting classes to go shoplifting. When she was caught trying to steal a pair of shoes, she was sent to a series of boarding schools, where she concentrated further on her music, playing guitar (purchased for her by a volunteer teacher) in her room and writing songs. Performing at the volunteer teacher's wedding in 1982 (she sang "Evergreen"), she attracted the attention of the teacher's brother, a member of a local band, In Tau Nua; she eventually ended up co-writing the band's first single, "Take My Hand." After this experience, O'Connor began performing in a folk duo in local clubs, mixing in her originals with Bob Dylan covers and developing her distinctive vocal style in part to make herself heard above noisy pub audiences. "I used to get really annoyed when people would talk while I was singing so I used to just shout," she told *Musician*. "It used to really frighten them, which I enjoyed." In 1984, O'Connor formed the band Ton Ton Macoute, and briefly attended Dublin's College of Music. The following year, Nigel Grainge and Chris Hill from Ensign Records saw the band while in Dublin and invited O'Connor to keep in touch. Six weeks later O'Connor wrote Grainge and Hill to say she'd left the band, and the two brought her to London, where she recorded a four-song demo produced by Karl Wallinger of the Waterboys, on the strength of which she was signed to the company.

While working on her first album, she also co-wrote and sang on the song "Heroine" with U2's guitarist the Edge (Dave Evans), featured on the soundtrack for the film *Captive*. But work on her own record, *The Lion and the Cobra*, did not progress as smoothly. Tensions between O'Connor and producer Mick Glossop marred the sessions: "He wanted to make a Grace Slick sort of album," O'Connor complained. Neither O'Connor nor the record company was happy with the results, so O'Connor took over as producer, though tensions still ran high, especially when O'Connor became pregnant and the record company advised her to have an abortion. "They thought I was jeopardizing my career," she explained in *Rolling Stone*. "My attitude was that if I had been a man, and my wife or girlfriend was pregnant, they wouldn't be telling me that I couldn't have it." O'Connor did consider abortion, but decided to have her child, giving birth to her son, Jake, two weeks after finishing work on *Cobra*. It was clear that Ensign had underestimated O'Connor's determination to be in charge of her own life and not be manipulated, whether dealing with her music, childbearing, or appearance. When discussing O'Connor's shaved head in *Rolling Stone*, Grainge saw it as little more than the result of her "always playing with her hair . . . she walked in, and she had shaved herself bald. We thought, 'Well, *there's* a statement.'" O'Connor, in a later *Rolling Stone*, saw her motivations in different terms. "Years ago, Chris Hill and Nigel Grainge wanted me to wear high-heel boots and tight jeans and grow my hair," she remembered. "And I decided that they were so pathetic that I shaved my head so there couldn't be any further discussion. I also did it for other reasons, but that told them."

The Lion and the Cobra was released in late 1987, and was an arresting debut. O'Connor's steely vocals, which could go from a whisper to a wail to a shout with remarkable fluidity, were combined with music whose only common denominator was its intensity. Though far removed from typical dance rock Top 40 fare, *Cobra* was neither overly esoteric nor inaccessible; the catchy intro to "Mandinka" in particular seemed tailor-made for radio play. The song did reach number 17 in the U.K., but in America the album wasn't expected to sell, and Mike Bone, then-president of Chrysalis Records, O'Connor's U.S. label, said if *Cobra* sold more than 50,000 copies in the U.S., he'd shave his head. But college and alternative radio stations began playing the album, particularly "Mandinka," and *Cobra* began to sell, eventually edging into the Top 40 in the spring of 1988, reaching number 36; O'Connor herself shaved Bone's head while in the States that March. In Britain, O'Connor was already seen as a controversial performer because of her looks and her candor, though she stressed to *Q* magazine, "I might speak my

MC Lyte and Sinéad O'Connor
1987 at the Beacon Theater, New York, Photo by Dorothy Low/Exile Pictures

mind but I'm not aggressive. A lot of it is that [the press] can't handle what they see to be the histrionics of a little woman with a shaved head. They can't understand why I don't just shut up and get a bust job." America got a taste of her frankness in the *Musician* story, in which she castigated Chrysalis for changing the cover of her album (which featured a pensive O'Connor gazing down with her mouth shut, in contrast to the original cover, which had her in a similar pose but screaming) and promoting her by sending out a photo of their staff wearing skull caps. "It's a stupid thing to do," she said. "If they have ever even listened to the record then they would know that I'm not concerned . . . with trying to be a fucking pop star. . . . That's just proof as far as I'm concerned that they have no clue what I'm about and that they probably never listened to the record in the first place."

Two years later this same scenario would be repeated on a larger scale in the wake of O'Connor's success with her second album, *I Do Not Want What I Haven't Got*. The album was recorded at a time of emotional upheaval for the singer, who had parted with her son's father, John Reynolds (who also played drums on her records), split from her manager, with whom she had also been romantically involved, then reconciled with and married Reynolds (they have since separated), all under the scrutiny of the media. The album reflected this inner turmoil, opening with O'Connor's reading of Reinhold Niebuhr's "Serenity Prayer" ("God grant me the serenity to accept the things I can't change, the courage to change the things I can, and the wisdom to know the difference"—a statement also found on the cover of Whitney Houston's debut album) before heading off into its harrowing terrain of shattered relationships and O'Connor's reflections on her newfound fame. "It is simply a record about a twenty-three-year-old human being and what she makes of her experiences," she told *Rolling Stone*, keying in on the very aspect that made Ensign reluctant to release the album, which the label found "too personal." But O'Connor held firm ("I said, 'People that like me, like me *because* of that. That's what I do'") and was ultimately vindicated by the success of the album, which topped the U.S. charts, as did the single "Nothing Compares 2 U," written by Prince, with an accompanying video that heightened the song's emotional content by focusing entirely on O'Connor's anguished face.

Her subsequent tour that summer was an expected sellout, but she also became embroiled in a new series of controversies. She refused to appear on the television program *Saturday Night Live* in protest over the choice of "hate comic" Andrew Dice Clay as the evening's host (she later appeared on the opening episode of the show's 1990–1991 season). Next, she refused to have the American national anthem played before a concert at New Jersey's Garden State Arts Center, a demand the venue's management agreed to—though they then announced they would ban her from returning to the hall. Some radio stations suggested a boycott of O'Connor's music, and even Frank Sinatra joined in, stating he'd like to "kick her in the ass." But O'Connor was ready with her responses, dismissing Sinatra's threat by saying "If you believe everything you read, I wouldn't be the first woman he's threatened to do that to," and further explaining her motivations in *Q*: "I'm not sorry and I'd do it again in a second . . . I will not go on stage after the national anthem of a country which imposes censorship on artists. It's hypocritical and racist."

She also gave another lengthy interview to *Musician*, in which she railed against record company treatment of artists ("They're just abused, treated like shit, packaged and turned into products in order for those people who work at record companies to make a whole lot of money and buy a big house in Antigua") and the difficulties in dealing with "the whole *fame* aspect" of being a star. O'Connor's candor in the face of opposition was refreshing, especially at a time when clampdowns on all manners of artistic expression made honesty seem an increasingly risky—and uncommercial—stance to take. "Artists are afraid that speaking out will hurt their careers," O'Connor explained in *Newsweek*. "I want to prove that there is nothing that can harm you when you speak the truth." O'Connor continued to air her concerns, boycotting the Grammy Awards in 1991 partly in protest of the Persian Gulf War. And the need to maintain control over her career was a recurring theme. "Now I feel like I'm sitting at the helm, where I'm supposed to be sitting," she told *Rolling Stone* after her breakthrough with *I Do Not Want What I Haven't Got*. "Now I'm the captain of my own ship."

While the singer-songwriters of the '80s were offering a new musical and visual option for female performers, solo singers in the pop mainstream were more than holding their own. In 1986, after the release of two lackluster albums, Janet Jackson finally broke through with *Control*, a number 1 smash which sold over eight million copies, and yielded five Top 5 singles, a record Madonna would equal with the release of her 1986 effort, *True Blue*, and that Jackson herself would beat with 1989's *Rhythm Nation 1814*, which produced a record-breaking seven Top 5 singles and sold over seven million copies. Jackson, the youngest member of the performing Jackson family, was born in 1966 in Gary, Indiana, and moved at age four to Los Angeles, where the family relocated in preparation for the launching of the Jackson 5, Janet's brothers' group that rode to pop success with Motown in the early '70s. Jackson made her professional debut at age seven during a Jackson 5 engagement at Las Vegas, duetting with her brother Randy (not yet a member of the group) on Sonny and Cher songs and Mickey and Sylvia's 1957 hit "Love Is Strange." Jackson wrote her first song, "Fantasy," at age eight, and appeared with her brothers in their television specials, but at age ten she began pursuing an acting career, landing a role on the TV series *Good Times* and later appearing in the programs *A New Kind of Family*, *Diff'rent Strokes*, and *Fame*.

In her teens, her father, who also managed her brothers' careers, persuaded Jackson to revive her singing career when he got her a contract with A&M; her self-titled debut LP was released in 1982. *Rolling Stone* wrote off the album as "forgettable," but it still made an appearance in the lower reaches of the pop charts, reaching number 63. 1984 saw the release of *Dream Street*, which only reached number 147, though the song "Don't Stand Another Chance" did hit number 9 in the black singles charts. Jackson also made a brief stab at rebellion by marrying James DeBarge, a singer with his own family group, in 1984, but pressure from her family led to an annulment within a year. Her *Control* album would make a far more lasting statement when it was released two years later. In addition to co-writing seven of the album's nine songs, Jackson was also involved in the production and arranging, working with the production team of Jimmy "Jam" Harris and Terry Lewis, members of the Time, the funk group formed by Prince (*Dream Street*

Janet Jackson
June 1990 at the Tacoma Dome, Tacoma, Washington,
Photo by Cam Garrett

had been produced by another member of the Time, guitarist Jesse Johnson). Although crossover success to the pop charts was a hoped-for goal, the team's first priorities were to Jackson's core black audience. "We wanted to do an album that would be in every black home in America," Harris told *Rolling Stone*. "We were going for *the* black album of all time."

On the opening and title track, Jackson announced her intentions by coolly stating, "This is a story about control," and went on to relate an autobiographical tale about life with her parents, her first marriage, and breaking free. In "Nasty" she informed the listener that her name was no longer "baby," and, urged on by her friend Melanie Andrews, she demanded "What Have You Done for Me Lately" of an inattentive boyfriend. The taut dance rhythms made *Control* an invigorating statement of independence. The videos from the album, assembled in two collections, were also successful, selling over a million copies each. At the same time, Jackson was asserting more control in other areas of her career, taking over from her father as manager and beginning work on *Control's* follow-up release.

If *Control* symbolized Jackson's venture out into the world as an adult, *Rhythm Nation 1814* chronicled her reaction to that world. "I feel that most socially conscious artists—like Tracy Chapman, U2—I love their music, but I feel their audience is already socially conscious," she said in *Rolling Stone*. "I feel that I could reach a different audience, let them know what's going on and that you have to be a little wiser than you are and watch yourself." Nonetheless, Jackson had no hesitation in delivering her own State of the Union address on *Rhythm Nation 1814* (with the "1814" part of the title taken from the year Francis Scott Key wrote the U.S. national anthem, "The Star-Spangled Banner") in songs that addressed racism, homelessness, and drugs, with the title track envisioning a future "rid of color-lines," celebrated by the "Rhythm Nation" in dance. Also mixed in with songs like "State of the World," "The Knowledge," and "Livin' in a World (They Didn't Make)," were romantically themed numbers such as "Miss You Much" and "Come Back to Me." Jackson also wrote or co-wrote seven of the album's songs and was again credited with co-production.

Jackson later revealed that she had been advised that her use of "socially conscious themes" in her material would have a negative impact on *Rhythm Nation's* sales—a prediction soon proved wrong when the album was certified multi-platinum and went on to top the pop, black, and dance charts. Jackson also released a thirty-minute film based on the album, featuring choreography by Jackson and Anthony Thomas, which won a Grammy (Jackson's first) for Best Long Form Video. Jackson and Thomas also choreographed the dance routines for her sellout world tour in 1990; the following year, Jackson moved from A&M to Virgin Records in a deal estimated at anywhere from thirty-two to sixty million dollars. Her next three albums all topped the charts.

By the time *Rhythm Nation* had hit the top of the charts, Jackson's former choreographer, Paula Abdul, had launched a successful recording career of her own. Abdul, the daughter of Syrian-Brazilian and French-Canadian parents, was born in 1962 and grew up in North Hollywood, finding her career inspiration not from music, but from films, especially lavish Hollywood musicals. By age eight, she was taking dance lessons, studying tap, ballet, and modern, though when she graduated from high school, she chose to pursue her show business ambitions at California State University at Northridge, majoring in television and radio with the intention of becoming a sports broadcaster. But during her freshman year of college, the former high school cheerleader landed a job on the cheerleading squad for the Los Angeles basketball team, the Lakers, becoming the choreographer and eventually the squad's leader. Abdul soon decided she wanted to make the squad something more than a cheering section. "I wasn't into pom-poms or yelling," she told *Melody Maker*. "But I *did* want to build a dance-group and it was the first time anyone had tried to do that with a sports entertainment team."

The squad's dance routines soon attracted the attention of the media and eventually the interest of the Jackson brothers (now called the Jacksons), who approached the nineteen-year-old Abdul to choreograph the video for "Torture," the first single from their 1984 album *Victory*. Abdul's next assignment was working with Janet Jackson, whom she trained for a year before choreographing the videos for Jackson's *Control*. In the wake of her success with Jackson, Abdul's career took off, and she worked with artists as varied as the Pointer Sisters, Debbie Gibson, and George Michael, provided choreography for the films *Coming to America*, *Bull Durham*, and *The Doors*, won an Emmy for her work on *The Tracey Ullman Show*, and was seen plugging tennis shoes and soft drinks in television commercials. She made her own bid for pop success with *Forever Your Girl*, released in June 1988 on Virgin Records, though at first it appeared the album might be a rare failure for Abdul when the first two singles failed to reach the Top 40. But six months later the third single, "Straight Up," took off, reaching number 1, as did "Cold Hearted," "Opposites Attract," the album's title track, and the album itself; a seventh single, "(It's Just) The Way That You Love Me" reached number 3. *Shut Up and Dance*, an album of dance remixes of Abdul's hits, reached the Top 10 in 1990; 1991's *Spellbound* topped the charts, and 1995's *Head Over Heels* reached the Top 20.

Abdul's material, primarily concerned with romance, was more pop-oriented than Jackson's, and was set to a nonstop dance beat; in her videos, Abdul's dancing was as important as the song content. Whereas the singer-songwriters had adopted a "natural" look that kept the focus on their music instead of their appearance, the reverse was true for the new dance-rock divas like Abdul, Jackson, and Gloria Estefan; their image was a very important aspect of the overall package. Abdul's athletic moves kept the viewers' attention on the body, necessitating a sleek, smooth look to match the sleek, smooth music. But there was no development of unsightly musculature; only Madonna, who embarked on a workout regime in the interest of eliminating her "little mound of tummy blub," appeared onstage in outfits emphasizing her newly pumped-up shoulders. Abdul, as a lifelong dancer, already had an appropriately athletic figure, but Jackson and Estefan, both described as "pudgy" in the media, worked to lose weight in order to complement their burgeoning pop success. Jackson maintained a sense of individuality by her preference for comfortable clothing as opposed to the revealing outfits other female dance-rock artists wore. But in Estefan's case, the singer dropped forty pounds, underwent a make-over (called a "polish" by her hairdresser), and was pulled out front to become the visual focal point of her band, the Miami Sound Machine, which then received second billing to the singer.

The Miami Sound Machine had started as the Miami Latin Boys in 1974. Founded by Emilio Estefan, a Cuban immigrant and the group's accordion player, the group played weddings and parties for Miami's Latin community. In 1975, Gloria Fajardo saw the group at a wedding and later auditioned for them with her cousin, Merci. Estefan, thinking of the additional appeal female singers would bring to the group, hired them. Fajardo, born in 1957, had emigrated from Cuba to Miami with her family when she was two. Her father, a former bodyguard to President Fulgencio Batista, later served in Vietnam, where he contracted multiple sclerosis as a result of being exposed to Agent Orange; looking after her father as a teenager, Fajardo turned to music for comfort. "I'd lock myself up in my room with my guitar," she explained to *Rolling Stone*. "It was my release from everything, my escape." When she joined the Miami Latin Boys, now renamed the Miami Sound Machine, in 1975, Fajardo was also studying psychology and communications at the University of Miami; she graduated in 1978, the same year she married Emilio Estefan.

By the late '70s, the Miami Sound Machine began making records, eventually winning a contract with Discos CBS International, the Hispanic division of CBS. The group's first seven albums, recorded in Spanish, presented a mix of disco and ballads and quickly found success in Central and South America, Mexico, and Puerto Rico, where they regularly topped the charts. In 1984, the group released their first English-language LP, *Eyes of Innocence*, which indicated the Miami Sound Machine was ready for crossover success when the song "Dr. Beat" became a dance chart hit in Europe. The following year, *Primitive Love* was released, and the Latin-flavored disco song "Conga" became the first single to hit the pop, black, Latin, and dance charts in the U.S. at the same time; two more Top 10 hits, "Bad Boy" and "Words Get in the Way," followed in 1986. *Let It Loose*, released in 1987, and *Cuts Both Ways*, released in 1989, were equally successful, both reaching the Top 10, *Loose* accompanied by four Top 10 singles, and *Cuts Both Ways* with two. After being waylaid in 1990 by an accident in which the band's tour bus was hit by a truck and Gloria cracked a vertebra, the group returned to the music scene with the release of *Coming Out of the Dark* in 1991, followed by a world tour.

But along the way to the pop charts, the group was slowly being restructured. Although Gloria was the only member of the band pictured on the cover of *Primitive Love*, the record was still credited to the Miami Sound Machine. On *Let It Loose* the band was listed as "Gloria Estefan and the Miami Sound Machine," and on *Cuts Both Ways*, Gloria Estefan's name was the only one on the cover, the Miami Sound Machine having been relegated to the cover's spine and the accompanying sleeve credits. Emilio Estefan had quit the band in 1986, taking over as the group's manager and producer, and the other members were slowly being replaced by younger musicians; in 1988, the last original member, drummer Enrique "Kiki" Garcia, left the group. "There is no Miami Sound Machine," he later told *Rolling Stone*. "There is Gloria and Emilio telling a bunch of hired musicians what to do." The article contended that by the release of *Primitive Love* there were two "Miami Sound Machines," the studio group and the road group. The group's music was also moving away from Latin rhythms in favor of ballads, Gloria's specialty as a singer and songwriter (she wrote eight of the songs on *Cuts Both Ways*). The end result was a make-over for the whole group, who had now become, in *Rolling Stone*'s words, "a familiar music-industry package: a beautiful, talented female singer-songwriter backed by skilled pros."

The increased prevalence of such packaging made it questionable whether the "natural" look of the women-in-rock trend had made any dents at all. Furthermore, the reliance on style over substance also left performers open to criticism. "If it seems like there's no spontaneity involved in this process, it's best to remind yourself that this isn't rock-and-roll," wrote Simon Reynolds in his review of Paula Abdul's third album, *Spellbound*, for the *New York Times*, echoing the comments of those who noted that Abdul's "package" appeared to be rather obviously modeled on that of Janet Jackson, adding, "the crucial difference was that Ms. Abdul replaced Ms. Jackson's soft-core feminism with a more traditional female persona." Shortly before *Spellbound*'s release, singer Yvette Marine sued Virgin Records, contending that her "guide vocals" had been used to enhance Abdul's voice on *Forever Your Girl* and that she had not been properly credited. Abdul and Virgin denied the charge, saying Marine had been used as a backup singer only, but skepticism about Abdul's vocal abilities remained.

The logical extension of such techniques put the power back in the hands of producers, who were behind the creation of a series of girl groups who emerged in the late '80s, such as Seduction, Exposé, the Cover Girls, Sweet Sensation, Pajama Party, and myriad others, a boom that initially drew comparisons to the girl group era of the early '60s. But most of the girl groups in the '60s had come into existence on their own before meeting up with the producers and songwriters who worked together creating the hits. The new producers of the '80s viewed the contributions of their "girls" as far more negligible. "What you need is a talented production source and a hit song," said Bob Gordon, Seduction's manager and Pajama Party's producer. "Then you can match the faces and voices to that." "Groups" were sometimes not formed until a single recorded by session singers under a group name had become a hit; then the appropriate "faces" would be recruited to perform "their" hit in dance clubs, as in the case of Seduction. In other instances, session singers would be used to test the waters. Miami producer Lewis Martineé wrote and produced the song "Point of No Return" in 1985 with three session singers, releasing it under the name Exposé; when the song became a local hit, Martineé brought the original members back to recut the song and record an album, but when one member quit, the other two were fired, and Ann Curless, Jeanette Jurado, and Gioia Carmen were brought in to become the "new" Exposé. "Point of No Return" eventually reached the Top 10 in 1987, along with three additional singles (including "Seasons Change," which topped the charts) from their 1987 album *Exposure*, which reached number 16 and sold over two million copies. The group's next release, 1989's *What You Don't Know*, was also successful, spinning off three more Top 10 hits.

In a bid for maximum crossover appeal, a racial mix within the groups was seen as an effective marketing tool; when producers Robert Clivilles and David Cole were putting together Seduction, they had wanted four women—one black, one white, one Hispanic, and one Asian. They were unable to find a suitable Asian singer and the group remained a trio: Idalis Leon, April Harris, and Michelle Visage. Seduction had a number 2 hit with "Two to Make it Right," while their album *Nothing Matters Without Love* gave the group their first gold record and reached number 36. Leon left the group after the release of the record and was replaced by Sinoa Loren. But the change in singers made little difference, for the tendency of the producers to regard their singers as interchangeable parts of the machine resulted in a steady stream of soundalike dance-rock singles. Girl groups of the early '60s had experienced such changes in their lineups, but they had also developed their own identities; you could not mistake the Shangri-Las for the Ronettes, for example. But the lineup changes among the "new" girl groups confused even their fans. "People ask us if we're the Good Girls or 'Sweet Seduction' all the time," said Seduction's Visage. Cole and Clivilles then released their own album, *Gonna Make You Sweat*, credited to the C + C Music Factory, which went to number 2 in the charts, though one of the singers on the release, Martha Wash, sued the producers for improperly crediting her on the record and for not being included in a video because she was deemed overweight (nor was she pictured on the album's front cover).

Women working within the music industry were at a good vantage point to observe the persistence of traditional perceptions of how female performers were "supposed" to present themselves—especially if they wanted to reach the broadest possible audience. "The media and labels and the world in general—besides Madonna, who is an exception to almost every rule—don't seem to be ready to launch a band made up of women into rock stardom and let them be beautiful *and* musically great," says Rachel Matthews, vice president of A&R at Hollywood Records. "Singer-songwriters don't need to have a huge image to get them across; they write good songs, and they can get by on that. They don't have to get by on being marketed to mass America, which isn't sure it can accept a female being a Bon Jovi unless she shows her tits and ass, which most of them unfortunately are still too willing to do."

But neither Matthews nor Roberta Peterson, vice president and general manager of A&R at Warner Bros. Records, were surprised by the development of the women-in-rock trend of the '80s. "There have always been women in rock," Peterson points out, adding that the trend was naturally helped along by its success in the marketplace. "When Tracy Chapman happened, every girl went out and bought a guitar and thought, 'I'm gonna try this!'" she says. "So a certain amount of them are going to surface." Peterson herself was among those who readily understood the appeal of artists like Suzanne Vega or Sinéad O'Connor, and had tried to get Warner Bros. to sign Vega, "but they wouldn't have any part of it," she says. Peterson had a history of signing acts that were not seen as being obviously commercial; one of her first signings on being made general manager was avant-garde "robotic pop" band Devo ("Nobody got Devo. They thought that was weird"), and she got the same reaction when she was involved with signing k. d. lang. Peterson had also urged the company to sign Jane Siberry, at a time when she had taken a leave of absence from the music business but continued to work for Warner Bros. as a consultant; she eventually signed Siberry herself when she returned to the company on a full-time basis.

Peterson's appointment as a general manager in 1975 had also broken with the "obvious" perceptions about women's roles in record companies. "It was very unusual at the time," she agrees. "There weren't a lot of women in A&R—Warner Bros. just had Mary Martin on the East Coast. It was a man's business. The women were all secretaries, or in publicity." Peterson acknowledges that her length of time with Warner Bros. (whom she had worked for since 1971) and her close ties to the people at the company (including her brother, a member of Harpers Bizarre and a producer for the label) played a role in helping her overlook chauvinism. "This was a pretty chauvinistic company," she says. "But because I knew the people who ran the company so very well, it was just something that I was used to, so it never bothered me. But I realized it existed. And it took a long time for them to have a woman VP here, a long time— but the other thing about Warner Bros. is that people don't leave here! A lot of people have been here at least twenty years. I wish there were more opportunities, but there just aren't."

Rachel Matthews, who began working in A&R for Capitol Records more than fifteen years after Peterson had started working for Warner Bros., also found that women—including herself—were still regularly passed over for promotions. "You have to be tougher," she says. "You have to work harder. You have to go out more nights. You have to do more than any male would do, because that's the only way you're going to get noticed. Otherwise, because they're male, they're going to end up with the promotion. I believe that. That happens, I think, in the business world as a whole. Instead of seeing it as who's the best qualified, it still comes down to a sex issue, which it shouldn't, but it does." But Matthews also sees the increase of women in all aspects of the business as a mirror of similar growth in the world at large. "It's just part of the whole evolution of women becoming a more integral part of society," she says. "It's like—women priests. How long did it take for that? How many thousands of years—certainly long before we were worrying about record companies! There are still more men than women in A&R, but there are a lot of women coming in, so that's better."

The increase of women working in the music business has varied greatly across the industry, particularly in the executive suite. Michael Greene, head of the National Association of Recording Arts and Sciences, revealed during a panel on sexism at the 1989 New Music Seminar that although more women were receiving promotions at record labels (comprising thirty-two percent of all promotions in the '80s compared with ten percent in the '70s), the percentage of women in vice-president positions at major labels had dropped from fifteen percent to eleven percent during the previous two years.

But there were also women making their own opportunities in other areas of the industry such as management. Gail Colson, for example, left her position as managing director at Charisma and formed her own management company, Gailforce, and after taking on Peter Gabriel as her first client, went on to manage Chrissie Hynde and Jesus Jones, among others. Other women had also gone into management after working a variety of jobs in the music business. When Linda Clark began managing Los Lobos in 1984, she had fourteen years of experience in the industry, having started as a college radio DJ in San Diego in 1970. She went on to work for commercial radio stations, record labels (including United Artists), a radio tip sheet, and handled promotion and publicity for Mismanagement, the firm that managed such artists as Supertramp and Chris DeBurgh. But Clark did not consider being a manager until she was laid off from her job as promotion director for Slash Records in 1984.

"I said to myself, 'I am tired of working for other people only to be shown the door,'" Clark remembers. "And I was toying with the management thing. I didn't want to work for another record company large or small—I was just burned out on it." Clark knew Los Lobos through her work at Slash (the band's label), and after she left the label the band approached her for advice. "Slash was putting a lot of pressure on the band to get a manager," she explains. "So they asked me, 'Do you have any good ideas?' And half joking, half serious, I said, 'What about me?' And they said, 'That's perfect. You know us, our families know you. Great. Okay, you're our manager.' I had done just about everything else, so I figured I might as well do the management thing. Lord knows I've dealt with enough bad managers in my life. So I figured, well, I'd give it a try."

Susan Silver, whose first major label signing was with the metal/punk band Soundgarden, had a diverse apprenticeship in the Seattle music scene, having helped launch an all-ages club, worked as a promoter, and briefly managed a few local bands throughout the '80s. In the mid-'80s, the band Soundgarden, who were building a substantial underground following, began getting calls from major labels and turned to Silver, who had booked them as an opening act on her shows, for assistance. "I tried to help them find a manager, or somebody to field the phone calls," she says. "And nobody came to the table. So I just started doing the work and have been doing it ever since!" Unlike Clark, who had her years of experience to draw on, Silver found herself in a completely new situation. "It was really intimidating," she remembers. "Everything the labels talked to us about we figured was some spook story we'd heard before—how they were going to steal the band's music and put their lives on hold for five years until they were too old to do anything. We were very paranoid and very skeptical, very suspicious, very intimidated!"

Silver's attitude changed when she began meeting A&R reps who flew up to Seattle to see the band. "I realized the more I got into this, that there wasn't any formula to it," she says. "There weren't any secrets about it. It was just relating to people and using common sense and not bending people and researching enough to get the strongest people around the band, a really strong support system." Linda Clark also relies on common sense in her management work. "A lot of times I wish I was a hell of a lot smarter and had this grand marketing plan," she says. "But it's just basically trusting your gut instinct. I was on the receiving end for so many years of screaming tirades, I figured there's got to be a way to develop a management style of getting things done without screaming, and if it got to the point that I was screaming they would take me very seriously. I'm not a screamer. God help me if I get to that point! Someone described me as being tough but sensitive. And I think having—I hate to use the cliché 'a woman's touch'—but having sensitivity to people rather than being a bull in a china shop helps."

During her years in the business, Clark, who also manages such artists as the Violent Femmes and Bob Mould from Hüsker Dü, has seen some changes for the better for women in the music industry, particularly regarding the pay discrepancy between male and female employees at radio stations in the early '70s. "I was bringing home $152.80 every two weeks," she says. "I will never forget that figure as long as I live! People said I should have sued, but there was no recourse in those days, and you didn't want to get yourself blacklisted on your first or second job in the business. Basically you just grinned and bore it. It's gotten a little bit better, but it's still very much a boys' club mentality in the music business. The fact that I've been around and survived this long—and thank God that I've had some success with my artists—I'm listened to and respected."

Silver, being younger, has sometimes run up against attitudes similar to those Frontier Records owner Lisa Fancher experienced in misperceptions. "When people in the good old boy administrative network meet me for the first time, they might make a couple of comments: 'You don't look like a rock band manager!' And I'll go, 'Well, you know, what can I say? You don't look like Santa Claus!' I think that women definitely have to work harder at getting past a stereotype than men do, but it's no different in this industry than it would be in any executive position or any managerial position in any sort of business." Silver, who formed Silver Management when Soundgarden signed with A&M and released their first major label LP in 1989, also had to deal with perceptions about her romantic involvement with Soundgarden's lead singer, Chris Cornell, whom she later married. "I'm sure I would have been a paranoid wreck if I'd really let myself think how many times I was referred to as 'just the girlfriend,'" she says. "At first, I'm sure, that was the perception, and maybe people that knew about it on the administrative level thought I would fall away. But I hope they are able to see now that I'm doing this because it is what I love to do, and I really want to be good at it."

Michele Anthony, a former music attorney who worked with many of the acts Silver manages, has been one of the few women to make the climb into the executive suite. Her progression from legal work for some of the top entertainment firms in the country to her current position as a senior vice president at Sony Music, the new name for CBS Records as of January 1, 1991, was rooted in her virtually lifelong involvement in the music business. Her father, Dee Anthony, was a manager who worked with a variety of British acts, including Traffic, Joe Cocker, Jethro Tull, Emerson, Lake and Palmer, Humble Pie, and Peter Frampton, and Michele's own eventual employment in the industry was taken for granted. "I literally grew up on the road from the time I was about eight or nine," she says. "It was a unique childhood that really gave me an education in the music industry. When I was about fourteen I went on the road with Joe Cocker and Mad Dogs and Englishmen and I sang backup; there were eight hundred people on stage, and I was one of about seven or eight people singing backup with my little 'Cocker Power' button on! So I spent a lot of time with artists, and spent summers working at my dad's management company."

Because of her work with her father, it was assumed that Anthony would also become a manager, an idea she resisted. "I came from a house where you'd wake up and there'd be artists there, there were always artists' problems, and I thought, 'I want a little bit more distance, I want to be more academic and more professional,'" she explains.

"And when I was in college a friend of the family who was a music lawyer said, 'You should be a music lawyer, it's the perfect synthesis of the academic world and the music business. At the time I was a philosophy major at George Washington University, and I thought I'd maybe do a dissertation in philosophy, but the idea of law school sounded intriguing. In my naive mind I thought if I was a music lawyer as opposed to a manager I would have more limits in my life. And of course it winds up being the exact same thing—clients call at four in the morning, and it's even worse! It's like being a doctor; you're on call a lot."

Anthony moved to Los Angeles to attend law school, and when her studies were completed in 1980, she joined the firm Mitchell, Silverg & Knapp. She moved a year and a half later to the firm Rosenfeld, Gasoy & Krauss, working with such acts as Stevie Nicks, Carly Simon, Carole King, and the Eagles, and in the mid-'80s moved to Manatt, Phelps, Rothenberg & Phillips, becoming a partner in the music department, where her client roster ran the gamut from Lita Ford and Guns n' Roses, to Toni Childs and the Sugarcubes. Though she had been accustomed to being one of the few female lawyers in her field, she was pleased to find that three of the seven lawyers in the music department at her new firm were women. "There aren't that many women lawyers compared to the amount of male lawyers in the music business," she says. "But there are more and more. And you are starting to see more women in the business affairs and legal affairs departments of record companies, which you never used to see."

In 1989, Anthony was offered a position as senior vice president at CBS and she joined the company in 1990, though it meant leaving her private practice. "I thought it was a really wonderful opportunity for me to learn more about the record industry," she explains. "One of the big philosophical issues that I grappled with when I was making my decision was that at the end of the day the thing that made my job personally gratifying as an artist's attorney was that I was truly affecting human lives—whether it was taking a young bewildered band and helping them put their entire business life into place or helping a particular client through a divorce—those were the things that made my job very gratifying. And in deciding to come inside a record company, what was gratifying for me was the ability to help make this company into an artist-oriented company—and so I could also affect lives here."

If the upper echelons of the industry were slowly being cracked, the same was happening at the technical end of the spectrum, among the road and technical crews that worked with touring bands. The realm of "roadies" was, and still is, male-dominated, but Carol Dodds, a video director and lighting designer who has worked in the field since the early '70s, has seen attitudes toward women working on crews change considerably over the years. "Originally when I started to get involved with lighting, I'd say I'd like to work with this person or that person and people would say, 'Oh, well, they don't use women on their crew,'" she recalls. "And so, of course, immediately it was a challenge: What do you mean they don't use women on their crew? It wasn't a verbal challenge so much as thinking to myself, 'Well, it's never held me back before, and obviously these people haven't met me yet.' It was kind of naive. Now I find that as many or more people say they want to work with me because I'm a woman. The last job I got was specifically because I was a woman. It was for a woman artist and they were concerned about having somebody that could work with her, and that was one of the reasons they called me. But as far as the actual working relationship, that's changed not because I'm a woman or a man, but because my role has changed. Now I'm not the third or fourth man on the totem pole. I'm the head guy, or head woman, whatever you want to call it!"

Dodds, who grew up on the East Coast, got her start in tech work while she was an acting-directing major at a college in West Virginia, which involved working on and off stage. "I decided that I should know how to do everything," she explains. "And that's why I got involved with lighting, to get a real solid grip on all the technical aspects." She moved to New York after graduating in the mid-'70s and took on part-time lighting work to support herself while pursuing an acting career. Eventually, her involvement with lighting became more of a priority than performing. "I went back to college and worked on the master program in lighting," she says. "And on a summer break from the program I went ahead and started working. Then I just kept working and never went back." Her work encompassed theater work off-Broadway and off-off-Broadway, and rock shows; her first stint on the road was a summer festival, and she was soon touring with Blue Oyster Cult, Aerosmith, and Kiss. "I was third or fourth electrician," she says. "I hung cable, I climbed ladders, I plugged in dimmers, I just did all the grunt work. It was a very basic, starting-at-the-bottom kind of learning experience."

It was also a learning experience for the crews she toured with, and for the in-house crews at the concert halls. "Many people were shocked that I was there," she says of her presence as virtually the only female member of a crew. "A lot of people were shocked that I could do the work, because I was smaller than a man doing it. The stagehands were definitely shocked, because there weren't women working in the stagehand industry at that point either." At times, being the only woman worked to her advantage. "The stagehands would take me under their wing when we would get to a venue, and these were guys who had worked in the theater for years and years," she says. "And they'd show me the old transformers where you'd have to use your hands and legs and feet and sticks and teeth and whatever you could grab to make the cue happen. And it was a wonderful experience, all these men that had knowledge about how to do things and were teaching me and enjoying the fact that I was interested. They were very open.

People would also watch how I did something, because they knew I wasn't as strong as them and would use mechanical advantage to move a box or to get something lifted."

But not everyone reacted as favorably to the thought of working with a woman. "I know at one point, there were some people who were very interested in having me do a particular act as the lighting designer," she remembers. "And the person who was the leader of the act said, 'No, I can't use her because she'll come here and she'll tell my wife that I'm off on the road seeing other women.'" She also contends that such incidents happened infrequently, and her methods of dealing with such situations were decidedly nonconfrontational. "We played this one hall where one of the stagehands was quite fresh," she recalls. "At the time I thought, 'I really want to deck this guy, but we still have to load this show out tonight.' So I just swallowed it. And the next time I walked into that venue, the guy just couldn't believe that I would walk back in there—he was so shocked to see me that he never tried anything again."

Dodds was working as a lighting designer within six months of getting her first job, and by the late '70s, she had started her own company, Morgan Barret, Inc. In 1982 she moved to Los Angeles. The acts she has worked for cover the rock spectrum and include Talking Heads, the Go-Go's, Cyndi Lauper, Peter Gabriel, Ted Nugent, and Barry Manilow, among others. She also began exploring work in video, working with Todd Rundgren and directing Bruce Springsteen's "Tunnel of Love" video—as well as live directing for shows that used video screens, including the 1988 Amnesty International tour that featured Tracy Chapman, and David Bowie's "Sound and Vision" tour in 1990. And Dodds found new challenges as "head woman" on a crew. "I noticed an amazing change," she says. "All these guys on the crew that would take me under their wing and teach me stuff now backed off when I had to tell them what to do. It was surprising to me when it first happened, but I've grown to realize that in the same way that they had respected me and I responded to that, as long as I respect them, they'll respond to that."

Like Carol Dodds, Lisa Macek got her start in theater tech work while attending college; she also worked as a stagehand at rock shows and was involved with college radio. Her internship for a company working with independent bands landed her a job in the company's New York office after she graduated from college in 1986—though three weeks later she was laid off because of the company's financial difficulties. Macek then interviewed at the production company C-Factor and was hired the next day: "So I went from doing normal industry work back to being a technician within a month!" Three months later she was out on a Lou Reed tour as an assistant to the lighting designer, and later worked on tours for Ashford and Simpson, Squeeze, and Bryan Ferry.

Macek, like Dodds, also preferred to handle volatile situations in a nonconfrontational manner, partially to keep her job. "I kept my mouth shut because you can complain, but you pretty much end up losing your job if it gets to be too much of a hassle," she explains. She also found she could rely on support from her own crew in such situations and was not afraid to speak up herself when a situation became too uncomfortable. But she felt more uncomfortable when she was in charge of a crew. "I guess it's one of my weak points," she admits. "I think I could handle being a designer, but in shows that we did in New York, I'd have to take new guys out from the shop and be the master electrician. I didn't particularly care for it; I'm pretty young and I was dealing with these old union guys who could have been my grandfather. I felt uncomfortable giving orders to guys. Maybe it's just me, or maybe it's the fact that guys are inclined to think twice when some girl asks them to do something. That's part of the reason I quit, because I knew I was going to have to do that all the time."

But though Macek left C-Factor in the fall of 1988, she didn't leave the music world entirely; she worked for Production Arts, a lighting company that concentrates on theatrical work. She also takes on the occasional freelance music job and agrees that there are more women working in tech areas, particularly in the smaller, independent realm. "From what I see in New York, I see more women working in clubs than touring," she says. "Though I have a girlfriend who works for Sonic Youth, and they take her just about everywhere they go. And there's a girl who was working at CBGB's for a long time, and she's on the road now with Living Colour. Other than that, all of the women I've come into contact with are just working at little clubs and hoping for their break." And though Macek feels progress is slow, she also hopes that as more women enter the field perceptions regarding women working on road crews will also change.

As women continued to challenge perceptions regarding their work in all areas of the music industry during the '80s, they also made noticeable headway in the overwhelmingly male-dominated genres of heavy metal and rap music. Metal and rap, which both rose to prominence in the '80s, were as loathsome to parents, religious leaders, and elected officials as rock & roll had been in the '50s, and when censorship groups began attacking rock music in the late '80s, it was no coincidence that their initial targets were metal and rap. The genres were also seen as being the voice for less powerful groups in society, poor white teenagers (metal) and poor black teenagers (rap)—though women's involvement in both genres as either creators of the music or as a part of its audience was generally overlooked or ignored.

This was especially true in the realm of metal. In contrast to her first *Decline* film, Penelope Spheeris's *The Decline of Western Civilization Part 2: The Metal Years*, a documentary about the metal scene in Los Angeles released in 1985, featured very few women as musicians—women in the film were primarily contestants in swimsuit competitions held at rock clubs or fans (and, in one memorable interview, a probation officer). According to Spheeris's observations, dismissive attitudes toward women were an intrinsic part of the metal scene and apparently accepted by females and males alike. "They've worked out a man-woman relationship that puts the woman in a very medieval, submissive role," she says. "And it's not just the guys that think of women that way, the girls act stupid on purpose to turn the guys on. I have a term for this—I call it 'Marilyn Monroe Damage.' It's just a search for love and attention, but it's kind of pathetic."

Spheeris's non-judgmental approach drew remarkably revealing answers from her interviewees, illustrating the motivations underlying such behavior. Spheeris also feels the lack of female metal bands is due in part to economics. "There are female heavy metal bands, you just don't know about them because the record companies haven't signed them yet," she says. "It all goes back to money. As soon as a girl band starts making mega-millions, then they're gonna sign a bunch of girl bands. It's just the way it works."

Of the female hard rock bands or performers that were signed to major labels, only Joan Jett made consistent appearances on the charts in the '80s. Others managed to build substantial cult followings with an eye to breaking through to mainstream success, such as Girlschool, a British all-female metal band. The band released albums throughout the '80s, and managed to break into the U.K. charts with relative ease, but success in America eluded them, probably due in part to the group's continually changing lineup. Girlschool, originally known as Painted Lady, was formed in London in 1977 by Enid Williams, who played bass, along with Kim McAuliffe on rhythm guitar, and original lead guitarist Kathy Valentine, who would later play bass guitar for the Go-Go's. When Valentine returned to the States, she was replaced by Kelly Johnson; drummer Denise Dufort was drafted from a punk band, and the group changed their name to Girlschool.

The band's first single, "Take It All Away"/"It Could Be Better," was released in 1979. On hearing the single, Doug Smith, the manager of Motorhead, a rising metal band, booked Girlschool as the opening act on Motorhead's next tour and helped them acquire a record deal with Motorhead's label, Bronze. Girlschool's debut album, *Demolition*, released in 1980, reached the U.K. Top 30, and the following year's *Hit and Run* did even better, reaching the Top 5; an EP recorded with Motorhead, *St. Valentine's Day Massacre*, also reached number 5. Not that everyone was convinced of their abilities; in a 1989 interview in *Traffic*, McAuliffe recalled guitarist Jeff Beck's reaction to hearing their latest single, "Race for the Devil" on a British television show: "He turned around and said, 'There's no way that's a girl playing!' So we invited him down to a gig and watched him eat his words." The rough and tumble swagger of the band's music was also tempered by doses of humor, as in the 1980 single "Yeah, Right," where a parent's continual demands are met with the response "yeah, right," initially delivered with disinterest and eventually screamed out with gusto.

But in spite of their chart success, Girlschool was handled somewhat cautiously by their American label, Stiff, who released a single album combining tracks from *Demolition* and *Hit and Run*. Internal tensions were also beginning to surface, with Enid Williams leaving the band in 1982, replaced by Gil Weston-Jones. Kelly Johnson left in 1984, forming a new band, the World's Cutest Killers, with Kathy Valentine. Johnson was replaced by Chris Bonnacci from another all-female hard rock band, She; Jackie Bodimead, also from She, joined the group as keyboardist for one album. The band continued releasing albums, but by now interest in the group in the U.K. had faded, and interest in the U.S. failed to take off. Nonetheless, the group continued recording and touring, primarily in Europe. The group's most recent album, 1989's *Take a Bite*, had a new lineup (Tracey Lamb replaced Weston-Jones in 1987), but managed to retain the band's hard-driving high spirits, with a brash cover of Sweet's "Fox on the Run" and the cheeky "Girls on Top." Unfortunately, their lack of commercial success in the U.S. meant that Girlschool's groundbreaking role as female performers in what is still a heavily male-dominated musical genre has been overlooked.

Conversely, ex-Runaway Lita Ford managed to find some of the mainstream success Girlschool had been unable to attain when two singles from her 1988 platinum album *Lita* hit the Top 40, after a decade of work as a solo artist. Ford released her first album, *Out for Blood* in 1983, a year after Jett had her success with "I Love Rock 'n' Roll" and followed it with *Dancin' on the Edge* in 1984. When her label, PolyGram, declined to release her third album, *The Bride Wore Black*, Ford, who had been with the label since her Runaways days, decided it was time for a change; in 1985, she took on a new manager, Sharon Osbourne (who also manages Ozzy Osbourne, her husband), and moved to RCA. "I wanted to work with a female manager at the time," she says. "I really had trouble relating to the management company I had before Sharon and I wanted to work with a woman. I felt that a woman could understand me better—understand my needs and help me get what I wanted. And she did." She appreciated this same attitude on the part of her producer, Mike Chapman, who produced both *Lita*, released in 1988, and *Stiletto*, released in 1990; "He allowed me to do what I always wanted to do, instead of trying to change me," she told *Guitar World*.

Ford's first success from *Lita* was the single, "Close My Eyes Forever." Co-written by Ford with Ozzy Osbourne (who also shared vocals with her), the song reached number 8. Ford also collaborated with Mötley Crüe's Nikki Sixx and Motörhead's Lemmy

Kilminster on material for the album, which eventually reached number 29. *Stiletto* was less successful in the charts, but received good reviews, and included a moving tribute to Ford's mother, the ballad "Lisa"; the title song was co-written by Ford and Holly Knight. Ford herself looked optimistically to the future. "Now I'm thirty and I feel like I'm just starting to kick in," she told *Bam*. In 1991, Ford returned with a new album, *Dangerous Curves*, another mix of ballads ("Bad Love") and out-and-out shouters ("Hellbound Train"). This was followed by *Black*, released in 1995.

By the late '80s, L.A.'s music scene had switched from punk to metal, a music style described in the book *Rock of Ages* as the aural equivalent of a horror movie: "Loud, exaggerated, rude, out for thrills only." In contrast to punk's down-at-heel look, the metal scene relied heavily on the glam rock tradition of the '70s, the standard accoutrements being make-up, Spandex and "big hair." "What happened in the punk rock days was that the girls looked very much like the boys," says Penelope Spheeris. "In the metal scene, the boys looked more like the girls, with the big poofy hair and the make-up and the plucked eyebrows." Real women were welcome to adopt the look, but still found it hard to be accepted as musicians, as Vixen's guitarist Jan Kuehnemund joked in *Guitar World*: "We kept thinking, why are we having such a tough time where there's lots of guys out there that are looking really feminine and wearing make-up? We've been doing that all along!" Kuehnemund's joke addressed a bitter truth the band had encountered during their early years together, when the band members' looks had landed them film and television work (including the film *Hardbodies* and such TV shows as *Cagney and Lacey*), but a potential record deal was nonexistent. The group was also given the nickname "Bimbo Monkees." "You gotta realize that when Vixen came out, the rock scene was filled with the likes of Bon Jovi, Cinderella, Def Leppard, and Mötley Crüe," explained drummer Roxy Petrucci in a press release. "Everyone, and I seriously mean everyone, was waiting for us to make even one little mistake because no one believed that women could really rock."

Kuehnemund was Vixen's founder, having started the band in her native St. Paul, Minnesota, in 1981. The band eventually headed for Los Angeles, though Kuehnemund was the only original member to arrive; undeterred, she assembled a new lineup with Petrucci, bassist Share Pederson (who, like Melissa Etheridge, had studied at the Berklee College of Music), and rhythm guitarist Janet Gardner, who also handled lead vocals (this lineup was interviewed for *The Metal Years*). Working hard to overcome their "Bimbo Monkees" tag, Vixen were finally offered a contract with EMI (who was nonetheless initially skeptical about whether the group were really playing their own instruments on their demo), and their self-titled debut album was released in 1987. The album's high-powered music, topped by Gardner's gutsy vocals, found a ready audience, and *Vixen* went on to sell over a million copies. Kuehnemund later told *Guitar World* she felt the album was "a little too safe in areas," something she attributed to the lack of songs written by the band—a situation rectified on their next album, 1990's *Rev It Up*, on which ten of the eleven songs were written by the group. The band was then dropped by EMI, but eventually released another album, *Tangerine*, in 1998.

With most major labels shying away from female metal and hard rock bands (rock that was equally loud, but not as "exaggerated" as metal) because they weren't perceived as being "saleable," Vixen's deal with EMI was a step forward. But the band also represented the tip of the iceberg as far as the number of female metal and hard rock bands that were in existence, not only in L.A.'s club scene, but across the country. Some were on indie labels (the Lunachicks, Dickless, the Clams) while working to build an audience. Precious Metal, based in L.A., recorded their first album for Mercury, former home to the Runaways, but then signed with Chameleon (their subsequent self-titled album featured background vocals from former Runaway Cherie Currie and included a song co-written by Ann and Nancy Wilson, "Real Trouble," which also featured guitar contributions from Nancy). The more garage rock–oriented Pandoras, another L.A. band who, like Precious Metal, had formed in 1984, recorded for Rhino and Elektra (though the tracks from their Elektra sessions were never released), before signing with Restless (the group's career was brought to an abrupt end by the death of founding member Paula Pierce in 1991).

The increase in the number of female instrumentalists should have had a positive effect on attitudes about women's roles in rock bands. But it was apparent that attitudes about female performers still remained unchanged in some quarters. Like Vixen, the women in Precious Metal—guitarists Janet Robin and Mara Fox, bassist Julia Farey, singer Leslie Knauer, and drummer Carol Control—had heard doubts expressed about their abilities as players, even when performing live. Control recounted to *Music Connection* how the band had been asked, "Are your boyfriends playing behind a curtain?" when performing onstage at a club that had no curtain—only a brick wall. Women's ability to rock was still seen as something that needed "proving." "On Tour At Last, Lita Ford Proves Women Can Rock Hard," ran a headline in *Circus*, while *Cashbox* reviewed Vixen's debut album with the comment *"Vixen* proves that women can rock and rock hard." Sexuality was another problematic area for women in metal, a realm where tight-fitting clothes indicated stud appeal in a man and slut appeal in a woman. Though Lita Ford had stated, "Sex is not for men only" in an interview, others regarded the matter differently. "Lita Ford has always been mislabeled a wanton slut because of a sweaty pose or two," said *Music Connection*, helpfully adding, "when, in fact, there's much more depth to her emotions," and even Ford's label couldn't necessarily be counted on to provide support. Recalling an RCA party, where a fan had been turned on to cool the room down, Ford told *Traffic*, "When I walked by, it blew the little mini skirt I was wearing up in the air. One of the women who worked at the label said 'That's right, Lita. Sell another 40,000 more records.'"

Female rappers faced the same sort of chauvinistic and sexist attitudes when they began appearing in the midst of a male-dominated genre, particularly when dealing with issues of sexuality. Rap had evolved during the '70s in New York, at clubs and block parties, when DJs mixing records began improvising rhymes as they spun. Eventually, the roles of DJ and MC—the record mixer and the "rapper"—split, making the rapper/MC the focal point down front. Rap then began moving beyond the black community into New York's music/art communities through the efforts of people like graffiti artist Fab 5 Freddie, who organized rap shows in downtown venues like the Mudd Club, and went on to host the television program *Yo! MTV Raps*. New wave acts like Blondie and Talking Heads also began utilizing rap rhythms in some of their material.

One of the first people to pick up on the commercial potential of rap was Sylvia Robinson, a woman with an extensive history in the music business. In the '50s, Sylvia Vanderpool was one half of the duo Mickey and Sylvia with guitarist McHouston "Mickey" Baker. Baker taught Vanderpool to play guitar, and the two co-wrote "Love is Strange," a Top 20 hit in 1957, with Bo Diddley. Vanderpool also released records as a solo artist and played guitar on Ike and Tina Turner's 1961 R&B hit "It's Gonna Work Out Fine." Vanderpool then married Joe Robinson, and the two started their own label, All Platinum. In 1973, Robinson had a hit as a solo artist with "Pillow Talk," which topped the R&B charts and reached number 3 in the Top 40. In 1975, the Robinsons shut down their All Platinum label and started a new one, Sugar Hill, and in 1979, Sylvia heard a trio from Harlem rapping at her niece's birthday party. She signed the group, dubbed them the Sugarhill Gang, and introduced rap to the Top 40 in 1980 with "Rapper's Delight," which reached number 36. Robinson later produced the Grandmaster Flash and the Furious Five hit "The Message" and celebrated her own success in "It's Good to Be the Queen," released in 1982. Her son Joey was in another Sugar Hill act, West St. Mob, and her nephew, Spoonie Gee, also recorded for the label and was backed by an all-woman crew, the Sequence, that went on to make their own records. The Sequence—Blondie, Cheryl the Pearl, and Angle B—were originally a trio from Columbia, South Carolina, and were among the first female rappers to match male sexual boasting with their own and "dis" (disrespect) their opponents, on such tracks as "Funk You Up."

Though rap continued to make inroads in the pop charts throughout the '80s, it was not reported on as a cultural phenomenon until the end of the decade, by which time the focus was on the violence and misogyny in the lyrics of some of the male rappers. *Newsweek's* cover story on rap, in their March 19, 1990, issue, dubbed rap part of the "Culture of Attitude . . . It is the culture of American males frozen in various stages of adolescence: their streetwise music, their ugly macho boasting and joking about anyone who hangs out on a different block—cops, other races, women and homosexuals," closing by soothing the reader with the consolation that, "if we learned one thing from the '60s, it's how *little* power rock and roll has to change the world." The article drew a flurry of angry responses for its patronizing tone, as Janine McAdams pointed out in her *Billboard* column "The Rhythm and the Blues": "Most objectionable: The article's notion that rap's most visible contribution has been 'the disinterment of the word nigger' (what of the Stop The Violence Movement? What of the whole school of social consciousness? What of the emergence of female rappers?)."

While a number of female rappers had emerged by the end of the '80s, women rappers had actually been a part of the growing hip hop culture (which encompassed break-dancing and graffiti art as well as rap) throughout the decade. In 1979, Lisa Lee formed Us Girls, one of the first all-female rap crews, with Sha Rock from the Funky Four Plus One More (Sha Rock was the "One More") and Debbie Dee (aka Sparky Dee); the crew later appeared in the 1984 film *Beat Street*. In the mid-'80s female rappers found a way of joining in the rap scene through the popular ploy of the answer record. In 1985, fourteen-year-old Lolita Shanté Gooden released "Roxanne's Revenge," under the name Roxanne Shanté, an answer to UTFO's previous record "Roxanne, Roxanne," in which the crew had unsuccessfully tried to pick up their new female neighbor. After initially circulating as a tape, "Roxanne's Revenge" was released on the Pop Art label and proved to be hugely successful. "Oh God! They played it on the radio so much, I just turned the radio off," Shanté told *Soul Underground*. "My mom said, 'We're rich!' and we were. I turned fifteen and I bought my first cadillac. I wanted the best car, and I didn't know about Mercedes then." A threatened lawsuit by UTFO, annoyed that Shanté had freely sampled the instrumental track from their own "Roxanne," led to Shanté's re-recording the song with a new backing track.

The success of "Roxanne's Revenge" sparked the release of innumerable answer records (including "Roxanne's a Virgin," "Roxanne's a Man," and "No More Roxanne (Please)"). UTFO joined in and found their own female rapper, dubbed the Real Roxanne (Joanne Martinez), "the lady devastator," whose claim "I'll make you feel hotter than it is in Grenada" was not so far removed from Wanda Jackson's comparisons of herself to the atom bomb in 1957's "Fujiyama Mama." The arrival of the "Real" Roxanne also generated a running duel between Martinez and Shanté, Shanté priding herself on the fact that she wrote some of her own material instead of relying on the song-writing skills of the male UTFO production team Full Force, as the Real Roxanne did. Shanté's raps also packed a harsher punch, as in "Brothers Ain't Shit," her scathing indictment of sexual harassment, and "Fatal Attraction" (included on her 1989 LP *Bad Sister*), in which the married man who plays around with Shanté but ultimately refuses to leave his wife is rewarded with castration. The Real Roxanne adopted a more light-hearted approach in her work. Her best-known number, "Bang Zoom (Let's Go-Go)," released in 1986, boasted of her skill as a rapper while mixing in sound-bites from Warner Bros. cartoon characters; it eventually crossed over to alternative radio airplay. By the time she released her self-titled debut LP in 1988 she was also co-writing her material, and along with such assertive raps as "Roxanne's on a Roll" and "Look But Don't Touch" was a number called "Respect," which drew on both the Aretha Franklin song of the same name and Helen Reddy's "I Am Woman."

By the time "Bang Zoom" was released, a new all-female crew was coming together that would be the first female rappers to hit the Top 40 charts. In 1985, Cheryl James and Sandy Denton. two friends from Queens who worked together at Sears and Roe-buck while attending community college, were drafted by their manager, Hurby Azor, to make a record. Azor, who billed himself as "Hurby Luv Bug," had been a member of a crew called the Super Rappers, and the record he worked on with James and Denton was a project for his studies at the Center for Media Arts. The two were not especially interested in rap, but as Denton explained in *Will You Still Love Me Tomorrow*, "It wasn't that difficult to do. If you're born and raised on the streets of New York, there's always rap at your block party, in your neighborhood, and you kinda get to know how it goes." Azor's "The Showstoppa" was an answer record to Dougie Fresh's "The Show," and when the demo tape began receiving airplay on local radio stations, the group, then called Supernature, won a record contract on Pop Art Records, and "Showstoppa" went on to sell over a quarter of a million copies and reached the Top 20 in *Billboard*'s black singles chart. James and Denton then changed their name to Salt-N-Pepa (James being "Salt" and Denton being "Pepa") and released "I'll Take Your Man" (backed with a reworking of the Pointer Sisters' hit "How Long (Betcha Got a Chick on the Side)") on Next Plateau Records. They also added a DJ, Latoyah, called "Spinderella," though Latoyah was soon replaced by Dee Dee Roper.

The group released their debut album, *Hot, Cool & Vicious*, in 1986, accompanied by the singles "My Mike Sounds Nice" and "Tramp," their label for promiscuous men. Two years later, *Hot, Cool & Vicious* became the first female rap album to crack the Top 40 (reaching number 26) and to go platinum when "Push It," a playfully suggestive dance number that was originally the B-side of "Tramp," was remixed and released as a single. "Push It" also went platinum and received a Grammy Award nomination for Best Rap Performance, but when the group learned the presentation of the award would not be televised, they boycotted the ceremony, along with other rap acts. The group's second album, *A Salt With a Deadly Pepa*, also hit the Top 40 when it was released in 1988. In addition to such instructive numbers as "Spinderella's Not a Fella (But a Girl DJ)," the platinum-selling album also featured a number of covers, including Joe Tex's "I Gotcha" and the Isley Brothers' "Twist and Shout."

By the release of *Black's Magic* in 1990 (which reached number 38), Salt-N-Pepa had become the most popular female crew in the country and were also assuming more control over their career. Their early material had been written and produced mainly by Azor, but by *Black's Magic* they were writing their own material and Salt had stepped in as producer on a number of tracks, proudly announcing this accomplishment in the album's lead-off single, "Expression." "[Producing is] something I've been wanting to try for a long time," Salt told *Billboard*, adding that the role had given her a new outlook on the future. "Salt-N-Pepa, the way it is now, will not last forever," she said matter of factly. "It'll probably be over within the next three or four years. When it ends, I intend

Salt-N-Pepa
(left to right): Spinderella, Salt, Pepa, 1988, Photo by Dorothy Low/Exile Pictures

Queen Latifah
1991 at the Black Women in Rap performance, Los Angeles Sports Arena, Photo by Malcolm
Payne Sr.

to work full time as a producer." Indeed, her next project after completion of *Black's Magic* was with Next Plateau labelmates 4-Play as writer and producer. *Black's Magic* celebrated the group's African-American heritage in numbers like "Negro Wit' an Ego" and the title track (co-produced by Spinderella), and the cover, which pictured the group reading in a study surrounded by the spirits of Billie Holiday, Minnie Ripperton, Louis Armstrong, and Jimi Hendrix. "Expression," a strong statement of self, was certified gold and set a record when it topped *Billboard's* rap charts for eight weeks. The group followed this success with the release of *A Blitz of Salt-N-Pepa Hits*, a collection of dance remixes of their earlier work. 1993's *Very Necessary* reached number 4, and 1997's *Brand New* reached number 37.

Queen Latifah (Dana Owens), the self-proclaimed "Queen of Royal Badness," also crossed over to the pop mainstream when she rapped on David Bowie's "Fame '90" remix of his earlier hit "Fame," though she had already released her debut album, *All Hail the Queen*, a year before on Tommy Boy Records. Born in Newark, New Jersey, Owens grew up in nearby East Orange; in high school she made her first appearance as a performer in the trio Ladies Fresh. In 1988, she released her first single, "Wrath of My Madness," under the name "Queen Latifah" (an Arabic word meaning "delicate and sensitive"), followed by a second single, "Dance With Me," and *All Hail the Queen* in 1989. "With the possible exception of Neneh Cherry's *Raw Like Sushi*, this was the strongest debut LP created by a woman in the history of hip hop," wrote Havelock Nelson and Michael A. Gonzales in *Bring the Noise: A Guide to Rap Music and Hip-Hop Culture*. The album reached number 6 on the R&B charts and sold over a million copies.

The topics of Latifah's material soon moved her to the forefront of rap's socially aware performers. If her first two singles focused on her skills as a "microphone commando," *All Hail the Queen* also addressed inner urban decay in America's cities in "Evil That Men Do" (produced by KRS-One, the creator of equally progressive raps) and brought in Britain's Monie Love (Simone Johnson) to announce it was time to do away with stereotypes in "Ladies First," an anthem of female pride. *Nature of a Sista'*, released in 1991, saw Latifah playing a greater role in the production of her work, and in addition to the no-nonsense delivery of "Latifah's Had It Up 2 Here" (in which she castigates rumor-mongers) and "Fly Girl," she also worked in a wider range of musical styles, including the reggae-flavored "Sexy Fancy," and the slower, soulful tempos of "Give Me Your Love" and "How Do I Love Thee." She has since released two further albums. Latifah also branched out into film and television, making appearances in the movies *Jungle Fever*, *House Party 2*, and *Juice*, and a pilot for a proposed television comedy series co-starring Monie Love called *Out of My Face*.

By the end of the '80s, women-in-rap were becoming as much of a "trend" as women-in-rock. Again, articles on female rappers tended to put the focus on gender first, musicianship second—as seen in the headlines "Not for Men Only" (*Time*) and "I Am Woman, Hear Me Rap" (the *New Times*)—but they did give greater exposure to a variety of female rappers, such as MC Lyte (Lana Morer), who began her career at her father's label, First Priority, and addressed social issues like crack addiction in "I Cram to Understand U (Sam)" and safe sex in "I'm Not Having It." Lyte also collaborated with Sinéad O'Connor on a single remix of O'Connor's "I Want Your (Hands on Me)." Yo-Yo (Yolanda Whitaker) dared to match wits with Ice Cube on "It's a Man's World," a track on Cube's *AmeriKKKa's Most Wanted* LP; Cube then co-produced Yo-Yo's debut album, *Make Way for the Motherlode*. Yo-Yo went on to form the Intelligent Black Women's Coalition, which, a press release stated, is "devoted to increasing the self-esteem of *all* women." The daughters of black activist Malcolm X, Gamilah-Lamumba and Ilyasah Shabazz, formed Shabazz by Birth. Britain was also the home to a growing movement of female rappers, including Neneh Cherry, formerly a member of pop-jazz group Rip, Rig and Panic, as well as a club DJ, who mixed pop and hip hop together in her 1987 album *Raw Like Sushi*; Monie Love, who released her debut album, *Down to Earth*, in 1990; the Cookie Crew; and the Wee Papa Girl Rappers.

Because rap was perceived as a highly sexist genre, female rappers were expected to retaliate with progressive messages while presenting a positive female image, which, of

Yo-Yo
1991 at the Black Women in Rap performance, Los Angeles Sports Arena, Photo by Malcolm Payne Sr.

course, translated to being feminist. It was a tag the female rappers wore with caution. When asked in *Interview* about the "great pride in feminism" expressed in their song "Let Me Speak," Gamilah-Lamumba substituted the word "womanhood" for "feminism," explaining "I don't put a title to my views." Queen Latifah dealt with the matter in a similar fashion. "I'm not a feminist," she said in *Mother Jones*. "I'm not making my records for girls . . . I'm just a proud black woman. I don't need to be labeled." But other female rappers were not as defensive about the issue. "As for being called feminist, it never dawned on me," said Monie Love in *Option*. "It's obviously easy for me to see things from a woman's point of view, so I guess that maybe I am." Salt was even more outspoken in *People* magazine. "We're feminists," she said in 1988. "We're doing something that only guys are expected to do and doin' it RIGHT!"

Female rappers who competed with male rappers using the same techniques were a different matter. Women had observed the double standard in the rap arena and were careful in knowing where to draw the line. Salt, discussing her views on how sexual boasting would be perceived coming from a woman, told Charlotte Greig: "If a woman wanted to do that kind of bragging, I'd just say go ahead. But I know what she'd have to deal with after." Soon, there were women who did do that kind of bragging, Hoes Wit Attitude and Bytches With Problems, who had plenty to deal with when their debut albums, *Livin' in a Hoe House* and *The Bytches*, were released in the early '90s. Critics and other female rappers attacked the two groups; Salt called their explicit lyrics "a gimmick," while another female rapper, Harmony, dissed them on *Let There Be Harmony*.

As a result of such hostility, and wary of provoking further controversy, the groups withdrew from a panel addressing the topic of explicit female rappers that was part of a hip hop conference at Howard University in 1991. "There were people who came to curse these sisters out," one of the conference's student organizers told *The Wall Street Journal*. "With all the other problems of the black community, we don't need these negative women disrespecting themselves. Other panelists told fans at the conference, 'Don't buy this stuff.'" The groups themselves remained unrepentant. "We talk about women's problems and almost all women can relate to something on that album," explained Bytche Tanisha Michelle in *Pulse*, with her partner Lyndah McCaskill adding, "It's not really a turning-the-tables type thing; it's just coming from the perspective of the woman." Michelle also stated that their name was chosen to take back some of the implied power they saw in the word "bitch": "Take that title and wear it as a medal of honor," she said in the *New Times*. The songs on *The Bytches* (released in 1991) did work at cutting the male ego down to size; "Two-Minute Brother" scornfully dismissed male boasts of sexual prowess, "Coming Back Strapped" was a warning to men who liked to verbally harass women walking down the street, and "Is the Pussy Still Good" detailed a humorous sexual encounter where a would-be two-timer gets thrown out of the bedroom after satisfying his partner. Bytches With Problems also addressed such serious issues as date rape in "No Means No" and police brutality in "Wanted." In spite of their provocative stance, Bytches claimed to be trying to work beyond being seen as a foul-mouthed "gimmick"—and, as *Rolling Stone* pointed out, the vulgarity was closer to the bawdy raps of Millie Jackson than the vitriol of comparable male rap groups like 2 Live Crew or N.W.A.

But as musical styles like rap and metal worked their way into the mainstream, major labels once again crowded the independent labels, who had helped popularize the genres initially, out of the market. The encroaching corporatization had its effect on the music, a situation Michele Anthony particularly decried in explaining how her role as an attorney had changed over the years. "It's ridiculous that artists can't shop tapes to certain record companies unless they're represented by a lawyer or a reputable manager," she says. "That's the policy of most record companies, so that certainly has put a huge responsibility on us. In my opinion, we aren't the ones who should be determining the tastes of future America; that should be left to A&R people and managers. But we are put in the middle more and more. It didn't used to be that way; lawyers were used in a much more limited role. Today we're involved in a lot more of the business because everything is business! The industry is small enough so that a lot of things turn on relationships, but lawyers are still involved in almost every aspect of the process, and there is a corporateness to making the music and signing the bands that didn't used to exist so much. The result is that the music business has lost some of its creativity and personality."

A potentially greater threat to the rock industry was the growing censorship movement, in particular the formation of the Parents Music Resource Center (PMRC) in 1985—ironically, the same year the rock mainstream rediscovered their political consciousness in the wake of Live Aid, the daylong charity concerts for African famine relief organized by rock musician Bob Geldof. The PMRC was co-founded by Tipper Gore, who had been alarmed at the lyric content of Prince's *Purple Rain* album, which she had bought for her daughter, particularly the song "Darling Nikki" with its reference to "masturbating with a magazine." Gore and co-founder Susan Baker launched the organization in May 1985; its first action, on May 31, was to send a letter of complaint to the Recording Industry Association of America (RIAA), accusing the record companies of making records that glorified indulgence in sex, drugs, and violence and making those records freely available to minors. The twenty women who signed the letter were more than just "concerned parents"; the majority of them were married to elected officials, including the PMRC's founders, Gore being the wife of then-Senator Gore, and Baker the wife of then Secretary of State James Baker. As a result, the complaints of the "Washington Wives" were not judged lightly, and the group received a letter from the RIAA two months later, agreeing to place warning labels on recordings with potentially objectionable lyrics.

On September 19, 1985, the Senate Commerce Committee—which included five husbands of PMRC members—held a hearing on the subject of "pornography in rock," which gave artists the chance to air their views alongside members of the PMRC. Artists as varied as Frank Zappa, Dee Snider of Twisted Sister, and John Denver appeared, but Michele Anthony was among those disappointed at the lack of response from most artists. "When the PMRC first started, I attended several meetings held by the California Copyright Society," she says. "And there were groups that emerged from those meetings that went to Washington, and Frank Zappa was wonderful; he really spearheaded that whole movement and at least told the other side of the story. But I was dismayed at artists for not taking a stronger stand. I guess if their rights were threatened more severely maybe we'd see a better reaction."

On November 1, 1985, at a joint press conference held by the PMRC, the RIAA, and the PTA (Parent Teacher Association), the RIAA formally announced they would place warning stickers on their releases, but it was an uneasy compromise for all parties. The RIAA only represented forty-four companies (primarily major labels), meaning that most independent labels were not bound to adopt the RIAA's "voluntary" agreement. There was also no standardized definition as to what material should be considered "explicit." As a result, the PMRC contended that "offensive" material was still being released and pushed for more stringent regulations. And although the PMRC insisted they were not advocating censorship in their demands for warning stickers, retailers and record chains, nervous about the possibility of prosecution, began refusing to stock recordings with such stickers. The anti-censorship organizations who weren't afraid to speak up, such as the monthly newsletter *Rock & Roll Confidential*, were quick to point out that stickering amounted to little more than selective enforcement, since most releases with stickers were heavy metal, rap, or comedy records, while country and opera, which dealt with many of the themes the PMRC supposedly decried, were overlooked. In an interview in *Goldmine*, PMRC member Jennifer Norwood put forth that country should be stickered, though adding, "I don't see the point in stickering opera because I don't know anyone under the age of eighteen who listens to opera."

By 1990, it appeared that an all-out war on popular culture, including, but not limited to rock music, had been declared. Mandatory stickering bills, which would have made it illegal to sell "offensive" recordings to minors without a warning label, were introduced in a number of states; one actually passed in Louisiana, but was vetoed by Governor Buddy Roemer. Rap group N.W.A. (Niggers With Attitude), who included a song entitled "Fuck Tha Police" in their act, received a warning letter from F.B.I. public relations director Milt Ahlerich, stating the song "encourages violence against and disrespect for the law enforcement officer . . . Music plays a significant role in society, and I wanted you to be aware of the F.B.I.'s position relative to this song and its message"; the group faced repeated harassment from police while on tour that year (but, in a surreal twist, a group member had lunch with George Bush at the White House the following year). In Florida, members of the rap group 2 Live Crew were arrested for performing songs from their album *As Nasty as They Wanna Be* in a twenty-one-and-over nightclub after the record had been declared obscene by a U.S. District Court judge in Fort Lauderdale; a record retailer was also arrested for selling the album (the group was acquitted, the record retailer was found guilty). In Nevada, metal group Judas Priest faced accusations that "subliminal messages" in their album *Stained Class* had led to a teen suicide and an attempted suicide (the group was acquitted). At Cincinnati's Contemporary Art Center, an exhibition of photographs by Robert Mapplethorpe was declared obscene and the museum's director taken to court (he was later acquitted). And four artists who had been awarded grants from the National Endowment for the Arts (N.E.A.), including Karen Finley, had their grants revoked by the Endowment's then-chair, John Frohnmayer, because of, in his words, the "political realities" of the times—that is, the potentially controversial nature of the artists' work (the four sued the N.E.A. in response).

Female performers rarely experienced the attacks that groups like N.W.A., 2 Live Crew, or Judas Priest did, though their work was scrutinized by organizations like the PMRC, who, in analyzing sexism on MTV, gave Pat Benatar's "Love Is a Battlefield" video a negative rating, citing: "one performer fights with her ornery parents then leaves home to become a hooker." Sometimes a performer's promotion of non-musical issues did result in censorship of their work: after making a commercial urging people to consider a vegetarian lifestyle, k. d. lang's music was dropped from the playlists of radio stations in cattle farming areas—though given the fact that lang was routinely overlooked for radio play, the "banning" probably had little impact.

The most notable exception in this area was Madonna, who was accused by PMRC member Pam Hower of teaching her fans "how to be a porn queen in heat." Ironically, in 1986, Tipper Gore praised Madonna's "Papa Don't Preach" video (in which Madonna plays an unwed mother-to-be who decides to keep her child) for its "sensitivity" (conversely, the executive director of Planned Parenthood disparaged what he saw as the video's message—"that getting pregnant is cool"). Madonna would face harsher criticism later in the decade. In 1989, a protest launched by the American Family Association, a Christian "watchdog" group, caused Pepsi to withdraw a commercial Madonna had made for the company that tied in with her latest single and video, the title track from her album, *Like a Prayer*. The AFA's complaints were not directed at the commercial (which was screened only once), but the video, in which Christian imagery was juxtaposed with scenes in which Madonna prays to a black saint and kisses a black man whom she later rescues when he is wrongfully arrested. The loss was more Pepsi's than Madonna's, for both the album (which sold eleven million copies) and the single went to number 1, and three further singles from the album also hit the Top 10.

Madonna's 1990 Blonde Ambition tour also provoked controversy for its use of sexual imagery. When the show played two nights in Toronto, police arrived backstage and relayed the message that the show either be toned down or the singer would face arrest. Madonna refused, telling her manager Freddy DeMann, "Freddy, I ain't changing my fuckin' act," and the show went ahead as scheduled; she later added, "I would rather have canceled the show than let anybody dictate how I can or can't express myself. This is certainly a cause for which I am willing to be arrested." Initially, the police tried to deny they'd taken such heavy-handed action against the singer. A *People* magazine report stated that officers attended the show "but found no infringement of the law," and that it was the record company, "sensing a publicity windfall," that built up the situation by issuing a press release stating that Madonna had been threatened with arrest, a story the police dismissed as "silly . . . not worthy of discussion." But the film documenting the tour, *Truth or Dare*, released in 1991, caught the story as it happened, capping its scenes of the police in tense conversation with DeMann—and DeMann relaying messages to Madonna—with coverage of a news broadcast relating the police version of the event.

No sooner had the tour finished when Madonna found herself embroiled in yet another controversy over her "Justify My Love" video, which had been banned by MTV because of its content and "overall tone." The video, shot in a Paris hotel room in grainy black and white, had the singer and an assortment of women and men in various stages of dress engaged in a variety of erotic couplings, and ended with a shot of the quote "Poor is the man whose pleasures depend on the permission of another." After being banned, the clip was released as a "video single" and sold over a quarter of a million copies; the single itself would top the charts.

Madonna was given a chance to convey her thoughts on censorship in December 1990 on the late-night television program *Nightline*, in which she and host Forrest Sawyer discussed the furor over her "Justify My Love" video. After Madonna had stated that she drew the line at depicting "violence and humiliation and degradation; that's what I don't want to see," Sawyer questioned her about the scenes in which she was chained in her "Express Yourself" video. "There wasn't a man that put that chain on me," she explained. "I did it myself. I was chained to my desires. I do everything by my own volition." She also pointed out the schism between the censoring of sexuality on television and the censoring of violence. "Why is it okay for ten-year-olds to see someone's body being ripped to shreds or Sam Kinison spitting on Jessica Hahn?" she asked. "Why do parents not have a problem with that? But why do they have a problem with two consenting adults displaying affection for each other regardless of their sex?" She then wryly suggested that if MTV would provide a special viewing time for adult-themed material, such as her videos, they could also offer a "violence hour" and a "degradation to women hour." Madonna also discussed how she urged her audience to use birth control, and provided AIDS information with her records, and when Sawyer commented that some parents might feel it was their job to teach their children about sex, she defended herself by saying, "Guess what? They're not doing their job."

AIDS was another controversial issue Madonna frequently addressed in interviews. The virus, which surfaced in the early '80s, was initially considered a "gay disease" by mainstream America since the overwhelming majority of early AIDS cases in the U.S. were gay or bisexual men, followed by intravenous drug users, groups at the bottom of the rung as far as civil liberties were concerned, and so seen by some as "deserving" of the fatal disease. When heterosexuals, and particularly children, began contracting the disease, they were described as "innocents" by the media, as in the *USA Today* headlines discussing the persons who contracted AIDS as a result of organ transplants from an AIDS-infected donor (in fact, on a worldwide basis, seventy-five percent of all persons with AIDS are heterosexual). AIDS was (and continues to be) particularly devastating to the arts community. Madonna regularly championed AIDS causes, doing a number of benefits; she was also one of the few performers to speak freely about her gay following, telling *The Advocate*, "They know that I'm completely compassionate about their choice in life, their life-style, and I support it. To have a person like me saying that is helpful to them. They appreciate that."

Diamanda Galás
April 1992 at the Doghouse Restaurant, Seattle,
Photo by Cam Garrett

Diamanda Galás, the avant-garde "sonic vivisectionist" who appeared on the music scene in the early '80s, made the AIDS epidemic the central focus of her work, beginning with the release of *The Divine Punishment* in 1986. Initially conceiving the work, *Masque of the Red Death*, as a trilogy, she released *Saint of the Pit* in 1987 (after which her brother died of AIDS) and *You Must Be Certain of the Devil* in 1989. By the time she performed selections from all three releases in 1990, she billed the work as *Plague Mass*, added a new section, *There Are No More Tickets to the Funeral*, and announced her plan to continue adding to the work until "the end of the Epidemic." *Plague Mass* was one of the most powerful responses to the AIDS epidemic from any artist and drew on Biblical references, the work of French poets like Charles Baudelaire and Gerard de Nerval, and gospel music. It also introduced the singer to a larger audience beyond the avant-garde arts community, though she pointed out in an interview, "I don't think of my work as avant-garde or bizarre, I think of it as a natural expression. When you come from a place like San Diego you don't know about avant-garde."

Galás was raised in a strict Greek Orthodox household in San Diego, where she was forbidden to listen to the radio, but did play piano with her father, who played in jazz bands and ran a gospel choir; she also played with the San Diego Symphony. Singing was not a part of her musical education. "My father told me that singers were tone-deaf and had no sense of time, and they were complete morons," she told *Rockpool*. "I wouldn't say that's altogether untrue. He also said, as far as women singers were concerned, they were a bunch of whores. So as a Greek Orthodox, singing wasn't one of the things I was encouraged to do." Nonetheless, Galás eventually took singing lessons and developed a particularly harrowing vocal style of wails and shrieks. After her initial experience performing in mental institutions ("I had a lot in common with the people . . . I guess the only difference is that they were locked up and I wasn't"), avant-garde composer Vinko Globokar brought her to Europe to appear in the lead role in his opera *Un Jour Comme Une Autre*. When she returned to the U.S., a performance at the Kitchen in New York in 1982 won her high critical praise (Gregory Sandow wrote in the *Village Voice*, "She's by far the most powerful new music singer alive . . . As long as I live, I'll never forget her"). She released her first album, *Litanies of Satan*, based on Baudelaire's *Les Litanies de Satan*, the same year ("The first album terrified my family," she later told *Sounds*), followed by *Diamanda Galás* in 1984, before beginning work on her *Plague Mass* project.

Galás experienced run-ins with right-wing censors, who were able to force the cancellation of her shows because of the supposed "satanic" influences in her work; the subject of her *Plague Mass* also met with criticism. "My so-called 'peers in the music world,'" she told *Alternative Press*, "they were all like, 'You don't want to be associated with that! You're going to ruin your career.' Well, I've already been associated with the devil for so many years, it can't get much worse." Galás also joined the AIDS activist group ACT-UP (AIDS Coalition to Unleash Power) and was arrested in December 1989 when the group staged a "Die-In" at St. Patrick's Cathedral in New York. In 1992, she released *The Singer*, an album of gospel and blues songs, including "Were You There When They Crucified My Lord?" and "Let My People Go" (both of which had been included in *Plague Mass*) and Screamin' Jay Hawkins' "I Put a Spell on You," performed with a hair-raising intensity. "I separated my work from a safe and useless concept of 'music' back in 1974," she said, assessing her work in the *Angry Women* volume of Re/Search Publications. "Music that is truly meaningful contains a distillation of reality—and usually that's *tragedy*. . . . Most pop music is descriptive; it's *about* the thing, not the thing *itself*. Whereas my work *is* the thing itself . . . Fuckin' cocktail drinkers have music that expresses what they supposedly go through; why can't people who experience *deeper* emotions have the same?"

By not being afraid of the "stigma" of association with the "gay disease" ("People always ask me why I'm singing to a special interest group," Galás told *Sounds*. "I tell them I am the special interest group, *we all are*"), Galás's work no doubt helped pave the way for other artists' involvement with AIDS causes, and by the beginning of the '90s, a variety of other artists were contributing their talents to AIDS benefits. Dionne Warwick was one of the first to organize a charity single to benefit AIDS groups: "That's What Friends Are For," which also featured Gladys Knight, Elton John, and Stevie Wonder, and topped the charts in 1986. Ann and Nancy Wilson, Paula Abdul, and Pat Benatar all contributed a track to *For Our Children*, released in 1991, which benefited the Pediatric AIDS Foundation. In December 1990, the television special *Red, Hot and Blue* an AIDS-awareness show hosted by celebrities like Whoopi Goldberg and Richard Gere, featured videos of artists interpreting Cole Porter songs; among others, Sinéad O'Connor, in a flowing blonde wig, performed "You Do Something to Me," k.d. lang took on "So in Love," Annie Lennox did "Ev'ry Time We Say Goodbye," Deborah Harry duetted with Iggy Pop on "Well, Did You Evah!" and Neneh Cherry included a topical rap on AIDS in her version of "I've Got You Under My Skin."

The issue of AIDS also prodded artists into examining other social issues of the time. Laurie Anderson, who admitted, "Like everybody else, during the Reagan years I was taking a nap," pointed to the AIDS epidemic as the motivating factor behind her new politicized stance. "I've been to too many funerals," she told the *San Francisco Examiner*. "I miss so many people who have died." A photo session she held with Robert Mapplethorpe shortly before he died of AIDS was also a moving experience for her. "He was very weak during the session," she wrote in *Exposure*. "He could walk a little bit, but there was no way you could ignore his condition." She used Mapplethorpe's portraits of her for the cover of her 1989 album *Strange Angels*. In contrast to the spoken-word delivery of her previous work, Anderson sang most of the material on *Strange Angels*. The album also featured "Beautiful Red Dress," an explicitly feminist song that shrugged off that notion that women were not qualified to hold the office of president because of premenstrual tension with the light-hearted threat "Well, push my button, baby, here I come," and made reference to the disparity between women's and men's wages.

Anderson then added censorship to her agenda, a topic which she made the focus of her keynote address at the 1990 New Music Seminar. After stating, "Censorship silences the extreme, but it also makes way for a culture that's totally bland," she then discussed the 2 Live Crew arrests. Anderson admitted that after listening to *As Nasty as They Wanna Be*, "I was having a really hard time thinking of this as an anthem for freedom," but added, "For me, this has never really been a First Amendment issue. 2 Live Crew can sing about pussy all they want . . . This is a battle of competing ideas, and I consider it part of my job as an artist to make art that competes."

She also examined the tolerance for violence in American society ("One of the reasons violence doesn't get that much attention is that this government respects violence. It uses violence, and censoring violence would mean censoring itself") and the claim that censorship groups wanted to ban "harmful" materials in the name of protecting women and children from the violent crime that rock music was alleged to promote. "We make a really big deal here in America about how much we love kids," Anderson said. "Disneyland, Pampers—industries are built around how much we love kids. In fact, in the United States, we have the worst record for child abuse of any country in the Western world. We abandon them, sexually abuse them, and starve them. We hate kids. We hate women. We hate black people, gay people, and don't forget the old people. We don't have that much use for them either. There are laws that protect the rights of some of these groups . . . in reality, of course, these laws are hard to enforce, and it's much easier to attack artists who point out these painful realities, especially if these artists are black, female, gay, or all of the above." She concluded, "Censorship is only effective if we can't make something that dwarfs it. And I'm looking forward to the role that music can play in the creation of that aggressive alternative to the mainstream and to the creation of a new American left that can champion free speech, lobby effectively in Washington, protect the rights of gay people, blacks, and women, and stand up for diversity in American culture." In 1991, her anger at the Persian Gulf War led to Anderson's undertaking a speaking tour of college campuses, presenting a revised and updated version of the NMS speech.

By the 1990s, artists as varied as Laurie Anderson, Diamanda Galás, Madonna, Queen Latifah, Janet Jackson, Sinéad O'Connor, and Tracy Chapman were addressing a wide variety of issues in their work, including sexism, racism, homophobia, substance abuse, homelessness, AIDS, censorship, and government oppression. It was a far cry from the 1950s, when racism would have prevented some of these artists from appearing in the Top 40 at all, let alone singing about any subject deemed controversial. But in the '90s, such songs were a potent fusion of artistic and political ideas made all the more powerful by the international exposure given to rock music. And female artists were now not only writing their own material on a more frequent basis, they were also involved in the production and marketing of their music, enabling them to attain greater control of their work and express the ideas they wanted to convey. Women involved on the business side of the music industry were also making substantial gains in virtually every area—except in attaining the position of president at any major record company.

Women in all areas of the music industry have consistently faced opposition from both the outside world and the music industry itself as they have questioned and challenged assumptions regarding a woman's "proper" position in the industry. But women who have dared to stand up and have persevered to maintain a career in their chosen field have managed to change some of the negatives into positives. While sexism remains an intrinsic part of the music industry, as it is in society, it is also being continually challenged by an increasing number of women in every level of the industry, from the practice room to the board room. The gains may be slow, but they are constant, and as women continue to challenge sexist attitudes in the industry, the resulting changes will be felt in society.

Music is an art form capable of eliciting a highly emotional response from its audience, which is a primary reason it is so frequently attacked by conservative forces who fear a power that is capable of bringing the possibility of change to established societal attitudes revolving around entertainment, sexuality, and politics. For women in the music industry, this power can also be used to contribute to their involvement in rock's present and the development of the future roles they will have in the realm of rock & roll.

Note for the Nineties

"A lot of people think feminism is a dirty word. They'd rather call themselves humanists. But the word humanist doesn't recognize that women aren't yet treated equally . . . The truth is that a feminist is any-one—male or female—who believes that women are equal to men and deserve the same opportunities and respect."

—Jodie Hargus, teenage guest editor, *Sassy*, December, 1991

In 1991, the issue of feminism resurfaced in the mainstream media on a broad scale, from the release of the film *Thelma & Louise* to the publication of such books as Naomi Wolf's *The Beauty Myth*, Susan Faludi's *Backlash*, and Gloria Steinem's *The Revolution Within: A Book of Self-Esteem*, to the attention given to the issue of sexual harassment in the wake of the Anita Hill/Clarence Thomas hearings. Two years previously, in a poll conducted for a December 4, 1989, cover story in *Time* magazine entitled "Onward, Women!" the majority of the women surveyed (fifty-eight percent) did not consider themselves feminists, though, conversely, a similar majority (sixty-two percent) felt that feminism had been helpful to women. Since then, the increasing threat to women's reproductive freedom is the U.S. has mobilized a growing number of women to reawaken from a state of "post-feminist" complacency and recognize that the fight for equality has not yet been won.

Though the battle over abortion rights caused women to recognize the underlying fragility of the gains the feminist movement had made, the media focus on other "women's issues" further illuminated the struggles women continue to face in society. Shortly after the Hill/Thomas hearings brought the issue of sexual harassment into the public eye, the music industry was rocked by the announcement of allegations of sexual harassment involving executives at three major record companies and an attorney at a leading L.A. law firm. A November 3, 1991, story in the *Los Angeles Times* not only discussed the specific allegations, it also examined sexual harassment in the record industry as a whole, and revealed the "put up or shut up" bind women who experience harassment are placed in: forced to either learn to adjust to an uncomfortable situation, or file suit knowing that whatever the outcome of the case, they will be unlikely to get a job working in the music industry again. As a result, instead of going through the legal system, women working in the industry have been driven to create an informal grapevine to pass on information about companies deemed "safe havens" from sexual harassment and to warn each other about the "bimbo hounds" in different record company departments. Fred Goodman and Ira Robbins, after discussing the harassment allegations in a "Rockbeat" column in the *Village Voice*, offered a pungent summary of the lack of respect women receive in the music industry by wryly observing, "We'd be willing to bet a woman will be president of the United States before one runs Sony Music or Warner Bros. Records."

Attitudes toward a female presence in the workplace showed few signs of change in other areas of the music industry as well. An article in *Billboard* on March 2, 1991, noted that though almost half of the sales positions in radio were held by women, there were far fewer women working in programming or on-air positions. Phyllis Stark, the article's author, made the observation that "Many women say they simply are not taken seriously" in assessing why women felt their advancement in the radio industry was hindered—a perception that has a disturbingly familiar ring. In the same article, Lisa Lyons, a program director at Dayton, Ohio, station WAZU, related a story about the necessity of "dressing down" (a tactic similar to the one Gail Colson had adopted when she was managing director at Charisma Records in the '70s) that also sounds depressingly familiar: "I always make it a point to look like a slob. It's a little humiliating and degrading when an artist shakes your MD's [music director's] hand and asks you to sleep with him."

Even the Rock & Roll Hall of Fame, established in the mid-'80s to recognize the contributions of those involved in the music business, has been criticized for overlooking women's contributions to the industry. Mary Wilson noted this discrepancy in *Supreme Faith* when she wrote about the Supremes' induction into the Hall of Fame in 1988, and her participation in the all-star jam that traditionally occurs after the ceremonies: "It seemed so symbolic of the record industry, and rock and roll in general, that the only two women onstage were Yoko Ono, there to accept her late husband John Lennon's award [the Beatles were inducted into the Hall of Fame in the same year], and me." Out of the nearly one hundred performers, songwriters, label executives, and promoters now in the Hall of Fame, the only female inductees to date are the Supremes, Aretha Franklin and LaVern Baker, inducted as performers, Carole King (with Gerry Goffin), inducted as a non-performer, and Bessie Smith and Ma Rainey, inducted as "Forefathers" (since changed to "Early Influences"). Though women's visibility in the music industry did not increase substantially until the '70s (and to be eligible for the Hall's yearly nomination process, a performer must have released a record commercially at least twenty-five years before), the number of female inductees is nonetheless pitifully small: where are Ruth Brown, Brenda Lee, Connie Francis, the Chantels, the Shirelles, Ellie Greenwich, Mary Wells, Gladys Knight, Darlene Love, or Big Mama Thornton—to mention a few? (Since this book's original publication, Brown, Lee, the Shirelles, and Knight have been inducted, along with other women.)

Censorship is an issue that continues to exert pressure on the freedom of artistic expression in the music industry, and after many failed attempts in other states, the first bill to make the sale of "erotic" recordings illegal to minors was passed in the state of Washington in 1992 (ironically, Governor Booth Gardner signed the bill into law during the same week he signed a proclamation in recognition of "Northwest Music Week"). Though obviously affecting performers of both genders, censoring the work of women artists reflects a continued desire on the part of the dominant culture to suppress the views of women and other "minority" groups who "don't know their place." Ann Wilson, in discussing MTV's rejection of Heart's "You're the Voice" video, which featured footage of anti-war and pro-choice demonstrations and had the Wilsons abandoning their flashy stage wear for street clothes, told *Billboard*, "We see now exactly what is expected out of females in the rock industry and it hasn't changed in the 15 years we've been in the business."

But at the same time, there have also been indications of positive changes that have benefited women in the music industry. In the alternative rock scene, female performers have been integrated into bands with an ease noticeably absent in the mainstream rock scene, continuing the egalitarian ethic that is the punk movement's most notable legacy. Some bands, such as New York's Sonic Youth, have also managed to cross over from indie to major label companies. Sonic Youth emerged from New York's underground music scene in the early '80s, and like Poison Ivy in the Cramps and Tina Weymouth in Talking Heads, bassist Kim Gordon was simply another member of the group (though unlike Ivy and Weymouth in their bands, Gordon shared vocals with guitarist Thurston Moore). Over the course of the decade, mixed gender bands would become commonplace in alternative rock, including such groups as the Pixies, Throwing Muses, Mary's Danish, Lush, My Bloody Valentine, and others. Performers in the alternative rock scene have also readily collaborated with each other on various projects: Kim Gordon appeared on Maureen Tucker's 1989 album *Life in Exile After Abdication*, and Kim Deal from the Pixies, Tanya Donelly from Throwing Muses, and Josephine Wiggs from the Perfect Disaster joined forces to create their own group, the Breeders, who released their debut album *Pod* in 1990.

The independent realm has also been quicker to abandon stereotypical perceptions about female musicians. An article in the Spring/Summer 1992 edition of the Seattle-based C/Z Records newsletter wrote of one of their acts: "For those of you who are excited about Seven Year Bitch's debut release merely because they're an all 'girl band,' get a fucking life! . . . By now you'd think that there's been enough women in music that you'd get over the 'novelty' of it and realize that they're just musicians, and mighty good ones at that." Women have also found it easier to advance into high-level positions in the independent scene—or were able to create their own business opportunities. Suzanne de Passe, hired as Berry Gordy's creative assistant in the late '60s (at a time when Motown was moving its center of operations from Detroit to Los Angeles), eventually worked her way into an executive position and is today the president of Gordy/de Passe Productions (formerly Motown Productions), a television production company. Monica Lynch, after being hired as a "Gal Friday" at New York's Tommy Boy Records in 1981, went on to become the label's president. After leaving the major label arena in the early '80s, Helen Reddy decided to start her own company, Helen Reddy Inc., partially as a means of attaining a firm grip on her career. "Artistically, opening up my own label gives me total artistic control," she says. "I don't have to worry that fifteen years from now somebody's going to repackage something and put an old picture on the cover and I won't have any say in the matter."

Women have been forming coalitions on other levels as well. June Millington, who has continued her career as a producer in addition to recording as a solo artist, founded the Institute for the Musical Arts in the '80s for the purpose of providing information, training, and support to women interested in pursuing careers in music; Roma Baran was a member of the founding board of directors, and Leslie Ann Jones, Teresa Trull, Bonnie Raitt, and Cris Williamson all have served on the Advisory Board. Women In Music, a networking organization for women in the music industry (though men are also invited to be members), was formed in 1985, and held their first meeting at the New Music Seminar; Margo Lewis, from Goldie and the Gingerbreads, served as vice president in 1990. There are now branches of Women In Music in Los Angeles, Chicago, and the Bay Area as well as New York.

In addition to furthering their careers in the industry, women in the music business have also been addressing the issues they face as women, particularly around the issue of abortion rights. In 1991, artists as varied as Debbie Harry, Queen Latifah, Kate

Pierson, MC Lyte, Tina Weymouth, and Kim Gordon all participated in a public service announcement geared toward a youth audience in support of abortion rights—though due to its controversial nature, the PSA was ultimately rejected by MTV and was only screened on a few cable networks. Bands such as L7 and the Lunachicks were among those that played benefit shows for the pro-choice organization Rock For Choice—an organization founded by L7. Laurie Anderson, discussing the formation of the Women's Action Coalition in the March 1992 issue of *The Wire*, noted, "There were a lot of cross-the-board artists, painters, sculptors, film makers, and it was very thrilling to see the same kind of rage." Anderson strove to tap into this energy while on the lecture circuit. "My real subject is the membrane between the personal and the political," she told *The Wire*. "And now politics are getting extremely personal because, especially for women, it's a question of getting crushed. And silenced."

Over the course of rock & roll's forty-plus years, women have worked hard to overcome the dismissive "novelty" tag they have so often been saddled with. Given that the music industry is already highly competitive, the additional burden of sexism has served to further undercut women working in the industry on every level. "Everybody in the music business has to play games," observed Nona Hendryx at the 1984 New Music Seminar, adding, "but women have to play them a lot harder . . . Production, arranging, the business side are all predominantly male and deliberately so. My whole career has been dedicated to changing that."

But in spite of these obstacles, women's involvement in the rock industry has helped them to not only find their own voices as entertainers, but to also find how to use their voices as a force for creating positive social and political change. While such changes will be particularly meaningful for women, they will also benefit society as a whole. Currently, a younger generation is emerging that has moved well beyond debates about the necessity of equality for all women to challenging all societal structures. In the May/June 1992 issue of *Option*, Kathleen Hanna, of Bikini Kill, described all-female bands who, in author Gina Arnold's words "tried to integrate their presence as women into classic rock 'n' roll forms," as being "assimilationist . . . they just want to be allowed to join the world as it is; whereas I'm into revolution and radicalism and changing the whole structure. What I'm into is making the world different for me to live in." The hope of making such a difference is what keeps rock & roll such an enlivening art form. And for women, the opportunities for determining the direction of rock & roll's future are virtually unlimited.

10

Enjoy Being a Grrrl

"I think part of what made people so venomous in their attacks on Riot Grrrl in the underground and mainstream press, and to my face, was the fact that it was not cohesive and easily consumable. We didn't have a mission statement we could pass out, we didn't have a sentence that encapsulated it, we didn't have one unified goal, we didn't have one way to dress or look."
—Kathleen Hanna, in *Angry Women in Rock, Volume One*

I f 1991 was, as filmmaker Dave Markey called it, "The year punk broke" (the title of his documentary about Sonic Youth's 1991 European summer tour), 1992 was the year the impact of that explosion began to be felt. On September 24, 1991, Nirvana released their landmark album *Nevermind*. Less than four months later, it hit the top of the charts, sparking an immediate interest in alternative bands around the country.

This time, as opposed to the search to find the "next Sex Pistols" during the punk era, the search for the "next Nirvana" included primarily or all-female alternative bands. Some, like Babes in Toyland, L7, and Hole, were happy to align themselves with major labels, even as they challenged mainstream expectations with their aggressive music. But there was also a new, loosely knit musical and political movement known as "riot grrrl," young women committed to a DIY ethic that was staunchly opposed to conventional ideas of "success."

And because riot grrrl bands accepted the presumed limitations of working exclusively within the indie music scene, they avoided scrutiny by the media for most of 1992, as mainstream female performers remained in the spotlight. In the June 16, 1992, issue of *The Advocate*, k. d. lang ended years of speculation about her sexuality by coming out. Melissa Etheridge followed her out of the closet in January 1993, when, at the gay rights–themed Triangle Ball celebrating the inauguration of President Bill Clinton, she unexpectedly announced to the crowd, "I'm proud to say I've been a lesbian all my life." Madonna caused a sensation with the October 1992 publication of *Sex,* a book of sexual fantasies as relayed by the fictional "Dita," illustrated with provocative pictures of the performer in sexually explicit poses with men and women (it became an instant bestseller). Sinéad O'Connor created an even bigger sensation with her October 3, 1992, appearance on *Saturday Night Live,* where she recited Bob Marley's "War," after which she ripped up a picture of the Pope, shouting "Fight the real enemy!" The stunt got her banned from the program for life, and at protest rallies her albums were destroyed.

Nearly lost was the fact that each woman was also promoting a new album. *Ingénue* became lang's highest charting album to date, accompanied by the Top 40 single "Constant Craving," which won a Grammy for Best Female Pop Vocal Performance. *Erotica,* Madonna's aural companion to *Sex,* reached number 2 and produced the hit singles "Deeper and Deeper" and "Bad Girl." O'Connor's *Am I Not Your Girl?,* a collection of jazz and showbiz standards, reached the Top 30. Far from hurting Etheridge's career, coming out preceded her 1993 album *Yes I Am,* her first to crack the Top 20, with sales of over six million (her biggest to date); her song "Come to My Window" also would win a Grammy for Best Female Rock Vocal Performance.

But for a younger generation of women, female performers their own age were making the most exciting music at the time. And the riot grrrl movement in particular empowered aspiring female musicians in ways not felt since the punk years. While the movement had roots in both the feminist consciousness-raising sessions and the punk movement of the '70s, the rise of the indie rock scene in the '80s—and the roles of women in that scene—had a major impact as well. As Michael Azerrad noted in his book *Our Band Could Be Your Life,* a "cultural underground railroad" developed during the decade that would inspire not just riot grrrls, but others involved in the '90s alternative music scene.

Some of the most influential rock bands of the '80s never would cross over to mainstream chart success—at least not in the U.S. But the musical innovation of groups like Throwing Muses, the Pixies, and Sonic Youth blazed a trail for those who wanted to explore their own idiosyncratic musical visions. This movement took courage at a time when the word "alternative" was not a description of an acceptable genre but a signifier of outsider status. "We had always been called alternative," Throwing Muses lead singer and guitarist Kristin Hersh told *Rolling Stone,* "but it meant that we were an alternative to real music."

Hersh was born in 1966 in Georgia and grew up listening to what she calls "mountain songs": "real whiny and minor key, with bad grammar." At age six she moved to Newport, Rhode Island; her parents separated when she was eleven. By then Hersh was playing guitar and writing songs, having picked up the instrument at nine after watching her father play around the house. At fourteen, Hersh persuaded her friend Tanya Donelly to form a band with her. Like Hersh, Donelly, born in 1966, had an unconventional upbringing, which included living in communal households; Donelly also became Hersh's stepsister when her father married Hersh's mother. The group, originally called the Muses, began as an acoustic, all-female band (Elaine Adamedes was the third member), and they hoped to find another female friend to play drums. But when the search proved unsuccessful, they invited David Narcizo, a school friend, to be the drummer.

The band's name was then amended to Throwing Muses. "It should mean thrown around by inspiration, instead of being the inspiration," Narcizo later explained. The group's first record was a self-titled EP, released in 1984, followed by *The Doghouse Cassette* in 1985. The music was strikingly original; Hersh's voice swooped and stuttered around the scale to an alarming degree, and the musical turns were just as dramatic, going from taut, edgy rhythms to shimmering pop—frequently during the same song. British label 4AD was impressed enough to make Throwing Muses the first American act it signed. By the time they released their self-titled debut album on 4AD in 1986, the band had a new bassist, Leslie Langston (born in 1964), and had relocated to Boston.

The album featured newly recorded versions of many songs on *Doghouse*, and the underlying mood remained unsettling. "Delicate Cutters" begins in typical singer-songwriter fashion with Hersh singing almost sweetly, backed by an acoustic guitar, but becomes progressively harsher as the song unfolds into a frightening portrait of madness. At the time, no one knew of Hersh's own struggles with mental illness. In her teens she began experiencing songs as "forces" visiting her; diagnosed as schizophrenic (later re-diagnosed as bipolar), she also suffered seizures. When she finally began talking publicly about her illness in the '90s, she noted with some wryness that she had been written off as "crazy" for years because of the nonlinear structure of the band's songs. "And I was totally unprepared for being branded as a psycho-depressive chick," she told writer Liz Evans. "I didn't know how to get beyond it."

The Muses released one more EP on 4AD (1987's *Chains Changed*), then signed with Sire in the U.S., releasing the EP *The Fat Skier* the same year. If mainstream success eluded the band, they found a welcoming home on the burgeoning college radio circuit, and the Muses' audience grew with the release of *House Tornado* (1988) and *Hunkpapa*

(1989), records that saw the band gradually moving toward a more pop-oriented sound, though retaining some of the melancholic intensity of their earlier work.

Langston left after *Hunkpapa*, and the band nearly collapsed because of a welter of crises. Hersh split with her boyfriend, the father of her first son, who then sued for, and won, custody of the child. (Hersh eventually married Billy O'Connell, a label manager at Sire, and had two more children.) Business problems erupted with the band's manager and the IRS. Donelly had joined forces with the Pixies bassist, Kim Deal, forming a side project band, the Breeders, and was becoming increasingly interested in recording songs on her own. And at the end of 1990, Hersh checked herself into a mental hospital. Though the band's next album, 1991's *The Real Ramona*, had already been recorded (with Fred Abong on bass), the band members assumed the record would be their last.

Instead, Hersh and Narcizo reunited with Langston for *Red Heaven* (1992) and, with Langston replaced by Bernard Georges, recorded two more albums, *University* (1995) and *Limbo* (1996), before breaking up for good. Hersh had launched a solo career with 1994's largely acoustic album, *Hips and Makers*, an experience she said made her think about sexism in the music industry for the first time. "I thought I could bypass it by not being a bimbo, by making either gender-free music or music that's real, instead of dip-shitty music they usually pass off as feminine," she said in *Grrrls: Viva Rock Divas*. "But if you do that, I think they disappear you; they really cannot market three-dimensional women." *Hips and Makers* reached number 7 in the U.K. and failed to chart in the U.S.; Hersh has released three subsequent albums. In May 2000, Hersh, Narcizo, and Georges came together for what they insisted would be a one time Throwing Muses reunion show.

While the Muses had an especially strong female presence, an increasing number of bands included female musicians in their ranks, even though they did not hold the common position of lead singer. One example is Gillian Gilbert, keyboardist in the British group New Order, formed by members of Joy Division in the wake of the suicide of their lead singer, Ian Curtis. More influential in the rise of the alternative rock scene in America were the Pixies, whose bassist, Kim Deal, also sang and co-wrote songs for the group, further enhancing her status as a role model. As *Spin* observed, "For women too young to idolize Patti Smith and tired of Chrissie Hynde, Kim Deal was the coolest girl to play in one of the '80s coolest bands."

Born in 1961, Kim and her twin sister, Kelley, grew up in a suburb of Dayton, Ohio. Kim began writing songs in high school and learned to play guitar in college; she and Kelley later briefly performed in a country duo together. Kim then married and moved with her husband to Boston in 1986, where she answered a "musicians wanted" ad placed by guitarists Joey Santiago and Charles Thompson IV (soon to assume the stage name "Black Francis"), who were looking for a bass player; they cited Hüsker Dü and Peter, Paul and Mary as influences. Kim passed the audition, and Kelley was invited to join on drums. When she declined, Kim brought her friend David Lovering into the group, now called the Pixies.

By the fall of 1986, the group was opening for Throwing Muses, a connection that brought the band to the attention of the Muses' label, 4AD, who released the Pixies' debut EP, *Come on Pilgrim*, in 1987; the album *Surfer Rosa* followed the next year. (Deal, still married, was credited as "Mrs. John Murphy" on both records.) The band's mix of punishing rock tempered by solid pop hooks (mirrored by Francis's wildly off-kilter vocals and Deal's more measured delivery) meant the Pixies were far too risky for mainstream radio. But *Surfer Rosa* became a college radio favorite, as did 1989's *Doolittle*, the same year the group was lauded as Best New American Band in the *Rolling Stone* critics' poll. And though, the group never cracked the Top 40 in the U.S., in the U.K., *Doolittle* hit the Top 10, as would the Pixies' next two albums.

But by the time of *Bossanova*'s release in 1990, Deal was beginning to explore other musical outlets. Neither *Bossanova* nor 1991's *Trompe le Monde* featured any of her songs, and she was at a loss to explain why she did not push her own material more. "I never went in and said, 'I have this song that means a lot to me, I really want you guys to enjoy this, and I want you guys to play it,'" she later told *Spin*. "I would never dream of doing that."

Instead, Deal formed the Breeders, originally meant as a side project, in 1989. The group featured Deal and Tanya Donelly on guitar, Josephine Wiggs of Perfect Disaster on bass, and Britt Walford (credited as Shannon Doughton) on drums. On the group's first album, *Pod*, released in the U.K. in 1990 (1992 in the U.S.), Deal wrote or co-wrote all the songs (including one with Donelly and one with Wiggs), aside from a forceful cover of the Beatles' "Happiness Is a Warm Gun," and provided the lead vocals. The music was more subdued than the thrashings of the Pixies, an indication of the stronger pop direction the group would pursue. The group's next record, the EP *Safari*, was released in 1992, and the Breeders became Deal's full-time band the following year when Francis informed the other Pixies—by fax—that the band had broken up. But the Breeders would soon be having hits of their own.

Sonic Youth's bassist, Kim Gordon, was another influential female musician of the '80s. Indeed, subsequent generations frequently cite Gordon as a "godmother" of riot grrrl, though Sonic Youth's trademark wall of sound shares little musically with riot grrrl bands, whose sound is clearly reminiscent of earlier punk outfits like X-Ray Spex; riot grrrl's politics are also far more direct than Sonic Youth's wry irony. Nonetheless,

Kim Gordon of Sonic Youth
At the 1997 Bumbershoot festival, Seattle, Photo by Gillian G. Gaar

Gordon's highly individual persona, and her involvement in a variety of projects in addition to her work with Sonic Youth, made her a role model to young women, who, Amy Raphael noted in *Grrrls: Viva Rock Divas*, would approach Gordon after shows with the request "Will you be our mother?"

Gordon was born in 1953 in Rochester, New York, and raised in Los Angeles. She grew up listening to music from her father's jazz collection and her brother's Beatles and Rolling Stones records. She formed her first band while attending York University in Toronto, a one-off group that performed at the Ann Arbor Film Festival. Though the band had the plug pulled on them before they had finished their set, Gordon discovered she enjoyed the visceral energy of live performance. After graduating from L.A.'s Otis College of Art and Design with a degree in fine art, Gordon moved to New York City in 1980.

Gordon quickly became involved in SoHo's art scene, curating occasional shows and writing for art magazines. She also played guitar in another one-off band called CKM, a name taken from the letters of the members' names. One night the "M"—Stanton Miranda—took Kim to see a band called Coachmen and introduced her to the group's guitarist, Thurston Moore. The two soon became a couple, married in 1984, and had a daughter in 1994. The Coachmen broke up shortly after Gordon and Moore met, but Moore had also been playing in a trio with Miranda, which Gordon joined after Miranda's departure. Members and names came and went over the next six months; the band first played under the name Sonic Youth in June 1981 as part of a nine-day event called the Noise Festival, which Gordon and Moore organized.

After the festival, Moore's friend Lee Ranaldo joined the band on guitar; the group went through numerous drummers until Steve Shelley joined in 1985. Moore and Ranaldo's unusual guitar techniques relied on various tunings, distortion, and feedback and strings as likely to be manipulated by screwdrivers or drumsticks as guitar picks. This experimentation freed Gordon to develop her own style. "I never wanted to learn to play the bass in a conventional way, or the guitar," she told Liz Evans. "There was never any reason for me to learn because in Sonic Youth, we always made music by listening to each other." Vocally she ranged from the deadpan monotone that echoed the spoken-word segments of the Shangri-Las' songs to the fierce declamatory menace heard on her cover of Iggy Pop's "I Wanna Be Your Dog."

An early press release aptly described Sonic Youth's music: "Crashing mashing intensified dense rhythms juxtaposed with filmic mood pieces. Evoking an atmosphere that could only be described as expressive fucked-up modernism. And so forth." Early records, like their 1982 self-titled EP and *Confusion Is Sex* and *Kill Yr. Idols* (both 1983, on Neutral and Zensor, respectively), were harsh and uncompromising, though despite the band's reputation as lovers of noise, as many songs were subdued and brooding as featured wildly distorted guitars. By the time of *Bad Moon Rising* (Homestead, 1985), more comparably conventional song structures were developing, as on "Death Valley '69," which conjured up the horror of the Manson "family" murders that year in an atonal duet between Moore and Lydia Lunch. And though sometimes dismissed because of a perceived air of superiority ("revoltingly elitist," in *Melody Maker*'s words), the group's dry—if occasionally arch—sense of humor was evident in both their own work and innumerable side projects. *The Whitey Album* (Enigma, 1988) had the band reinventing themselves as the band "Ciccone Youth" and featured a bizarre cover of Madonna's "Into the Groove"—here named "Into the Groovey"—as well as Gordon's coolly detached rendition of Robert Palmer's "Addicted to Love," recorded in a karaoke booth. (The song's video was put together in a similar fashion, at a video karaoke booth at Macy's department store, which had Gordon dancing in front of war footage.)

After *EVOL* (SST, 1986) and *Sister* (SST, 1987) came the album regarded as one of the group's strongest efforts, *Daydream Nation* (Enigma, 1988). The raging guitars had enough hooks to cast a pop sheen over much of the album, but a core intensity kept the music on the edge. Gordon's contributions were particularly striking. "Kissability" is a take on the hey-baby-I-can-make-you-a-star scenario, but here lust seems to provoke disgust and fright as much as desire. Even more disturbing is the album's closing track, "Trilogy: Eliminator Jr." inspired by "Preppy Murderer" Robert Chambers, who strangled his girlfriend, Jennifer Levin, to death in Central Park while having sex. The slashing guitars coupled with Gordon's moans and gasps seem to evoke the act itself.

Then, in a move that surprised many of their followers, the group decided to sign with a major label, DGC. Though seen by some as a betrayal of their indie roots, it was a natural progression for a band that had outgrown their original music scene. "When you've been working so long outside the mainstream, it becomes more challenging to work within the mainstream," Gordon told Alec Foege in his biography of the band, *Confusion Is Next: The Sonic Youth Story*. Being with a major label also ensured better distribution, a welcome change for a band dependent on the often erratic distribution indie labels could provide.

But it also meant the group was suddenly interacting with a corporate entity for the first time, something that would be reflected on the band's next album, *Goo* (1990). Visiting the company, Gordon noted how female office workers received flowers on Secretary's Day but were not able to advance in their jobs. The experience inspired "Kool Thing," in which Gordon addresses the power imbalance between men and women, taking on both the role of the male "master" and the disinterested object of his desire, who brushes off his advances and mockingly suggests he help smash "male, white corporate oppression" instead (the song also features a guest appearance by Public Enemy's Chuck D, who urges Gordon to "Tell it like it is!"). The album offers a poignant tribute to Karen Carpenter, "Tunic (Song for Karen)," which visualizes Carpenter in heaven, back behind the drum kit and happy at last. Sonic Youth's cover of the Carpenters' "Superstar" would later appear on the tribute album *If I Were a Carpenter*.

Gordon was not unfamiliar with sexism in the music industry; describing the reaction to her presence on the group's early British tours, she told *Rolling Stone* that "They didn't know how to deal with you unless you were an outrageous character or persona like a Siouxsie Sioux." But now that the band was working within more conventional environments, such behavior became more blatant. On the band's first arena tour in 1991, opening for Neil Young, Gordon observed, "Every time it was somebody's birthday, there'd be strippers hanging around." The crew also expected women backstage to know their place. "Because I was a woman onstage . . . they always thought I was going to get hurt," Gordon told *Rolling Stone*, adding she had been told not to watch the show from the side of the stage because she was "distracting Neil."

But Gordon also told Foege that she liked aspects of performing for Young's "redneck, conservative" audience: "It felt really good that we could actually shock people." And she continued to address sexism on songs like "Swimsuit Issue" (from 1992's *Dirty*), a searing indictment of sexual harassment. Still, the band's capacity to "shock" undoubtedly helped keep them off the airwaves; only 1994's *Experimental Jet Set, Trash and*

No Star would reach the U.S. Top 40, while every album from *Goo* on hit the U.K. Top 40. Throughout the decade that saw the release of *Washing Machine* (1995), *A Thousand Leaves* (1998), *NYC Ghosts & Flowers* (2000), and *Murray Street* (2002), the members increasingly used Sonic Youth as their home base while pursuing other ventures, even launching their own label, Sonic Youth Records, to release recordings deemed too extreme for a major label. Gordon's side projects included the bands Harry Crews (formed with Lydia Lunch) and Free Kitten (a "trashy blues" outfit) and her clothing line, X-Girl. "Kim says we're not goal-oriented—we're interested in the journey itself," Moore told *Rolling Stone* while explaining the secret of Sonic Youth's longevity. "That's what keeps us going. That's the best mind-set to have."

Bands like Throwing Muses, the Pixies, and Sonic Youth helped push adventurous fans into creating their own music scene, at a time when MTV and Top 40 radio were championing artists like Madonna, Bruce Springsteen, Whitney Houston, and Prince. Instead of merely listening to and consuming music, people were encouraged to be as active as the bands: starting record labels, operating clubs, publishing their own magazines and cheaply produced xeroxed fanzines (the latter eventually referred to simply as "zines," in part to drop the "fan" connotation), and taking to the airwaves as DJs at college radio stations, where volunteer positions were sometimes available to non-students as well.

Vancouver, B.C.–based Mecca Normal has used just such a DIY ethic throughout their career, founding and running their own label (Smarten Up!), in addition to handling their own booking, management, and publicity. Jean Smith, the group's singer, has also been tagged a forerunner of riot grrrl, though she dislikes having her influence seen in terms of being a "mother." "I cringe when I hear the terms 'Riot Granny' or 'Godmother of Riot Grrrl,'" she says. "I chose not to have children—I'm not the mother of anyone. For the most part, those terms spring to the minds of journalists, who, lacking imagination, rely on clichés. In my mind, one of the key elements of the riot grrrl agenda was *rejecting* simplistic labels and stereotypical limitations."

Smith's rejection of stereotypical limitations made possible her own move into music. In 1981, Smith was working in the graphics department of the newspaper *The West Ender*, where she met guitarist David Lester. The two went to local shows together and eventually decided to try doing something musical themselves. Smith, married at the time, also was becoming interested in finding an outlet to express her growing interest in women's issues and "the real condescending attitudes that men have [toward women]," she explains. "And as I became introduced to feminist 'rhetoric,' let's call it, I found support for things I already felt that were not finding an avenue of expression. Anyway, I left the marriage and started a punk rock band!"

Mecca Normal, (left to right): Jean Smith, David Lester July 1994 at the first Yoyo A Go Go festival, Capitol Theatre, Olympia, Washington, Photo by Jeff Smith, courtesy of Jean Smith

Mecca Normal challenged perceptions of what could constitute a "band" by their very setup; the only members were Smith and Lester, and the sole instrumentation for a number of years was Lester's guitar. "I also like that I work with a man that I'm not involved with," Smith adds. "I think it defies a whole other set of stereotypes. There was a lot of resistance when we first started doing shows. We were grilled as to what the hell were we doing—this wasn't really going anywhere within that male, four-guys-on-stage kind of scene. And we did not really have this plan of attack, like, 'I know how we can drive people crazy!' We just had a really good time making music. And Dave was totally supportive and into me being really loud and dynamic, and I must say he shares my views about feminism. But we're not negative people. I think we're pretty humorous, and there is, I think, a fair amount of humor to Mecca Normal."

The group's first self-titled album was released in 1986, with a cover Smith designed. People expecting a one-instrument group to sound fairly quiet were surprised to find Lester an abrasive player, and Smith's confrontational performing style, which had her lunging back and forth on her heels like a prize fighter, matched the aggressiveness of her lyrics. "I Walk Alone," a song from their first album that they still perform live, has Smith fiercely proclaiming her right to walk wherever she wants, whenever she likes, and a subsequent song, "Man Thinks Woman," pointed out the tendency to see a woman as a female first, a person second (a frequent complaint made by the subjects of just about every women-in-rock piece). Not everyone welcomed such sentiments; one early critic suggested Lester shoot Smith and find a new singer.

In 1987, Mecca Normal helped organize what they called the "Black Wedge" tours, inspired by Britain's "Red Wedge" music tours of the mid-'80s in support of the Labour party, which featured artists like Billy Bragg and the Style Council. "We were addressing housing concerns, militarism, racism, sexism," says Smith. "We were all total unknowns. We just got in the school bus and drove, and set up weird meetings in soup kitchens, on the street, and at parties and art galleries and nightclub-type places. It was this whole package of trying to get socially relevant poetry back into the fore of the culture, because at that time it simply was nonexistent, as far as we knew." There would eventually be five Black Wedge tours.

One stop on the first tour was Olympia, Washington, the state capital and home to the progressive Evergreen State College. While in town, Smith and Lester met a key figure in the town's burgeoning music scene, Calvin Johnson, a member of Beat Happening and the founder of K Records. Mecca Normal swapped one of their albums for a Beat Happening record, and soon Smith and Lester had a new home for Mecca Normal. The group also would record for Matador (as would Smith's band 2 Foot Flame), and Smith's self-titled solo album was released in 2000 by another Olympia-based label, Kill Rock Stars. Over the course of nine albums, the two gradually introduced other instruments into their lineup; Smith also began to play guitar and played all the instruments on her solo album.

But Smith (and Lester) never lost the desire to work "outside the system." Asked if she would ever consider working with a major label, her priorities are clear. "Absolutely not," she says. "This is just too damn much fun. That would totally kill it for me, if I had to collaborate with somebody who saw dollar signs—and what likelihood of that is there anyway? Let's be real here! A lot of the rock & roll industry, it may as well be car sales to me; it's fairly foreign to what my concerns are. People do send you form letters: 'We understand that you are a band. Please submit your material to this department of our corporation.' Oh, sure, I'm so flattered! I guess some people want that, or they have to follow that path. But I feel like my life is totally complete and full and I do what I want to do.

"I don't mean to sound pompous or pious, but there is a reason why I do this," Smith continues. "And it's not to climb the social ladder of success in the world of rock & roll. I have a lot of ideas that I think are useful to other people, and I'm sure other people have a lot of ideas that are useful to me. And by communicating in this form, I get to travel a lot, meet people, and hopefully strengthen my community, my friendships, and contribute something to other communities. People can take something from what I do and utilize it to make some element of their lives either happier or maybe a little more open to something that kind of felt like a risk before."

Finding one's community—or creating one's own—was always a key element of the alternative music scene. Evergreen student Bruce Pavitt inadvertently created one when he began spotlighting alternative bands in his fanzine, *Sub Pop*, which later became the name of a monthly music column, and then a record label, co-founded with Jonathan Poneman, a former college radio DJ, promoter, and musician, in 1986. Some of the early *Sub Pop* zines were released as cassettes, which gave Calvin Johnson the idea of starting his own label. Johnson, like Pavitt, had been a DJ at Evergreen's college radio station, KAOS, and wrote for *Op* magazine (the forerunner of the now-defunct *Option*). Realizing that cassettes provided an inexpensive way to document and distribute overlooked music, Johnson launched the K label in 1982 with its first cassette, *Survival of the Coolest,* featuring a live session by Olympia's Supreme Cool Beings on Johnson's radio show.

The Supreme Cool Beings' drummer was Evergreen student Heather Lewis, who had just started playing that year. "When I was in high school [in New York's Westchester County], a girl growing up in the suburbs didn't think about being in a band," she explained in Michael Azerrad's *Our Band Could Be Your Life.* Lewis later performed with Johnson and Laura Carter in the trio Laura, Heather, and Calvin; when Carter moved to Seattle, Johnson invited his friend Bret Lunsford to join him and Lewis in a new band they planned to call Beat Happening.

In many ways the archetypal K band, Beat Happening would be the first group on K to attract international attention, chiefly in the U.K. music press. The band had a two-guitar/drums lineup (the members swapped instruments during their sets, though Lewis most often played drums, Lunsford played guitar, and Johnson sang), a combination that gave the music a stripped-down sound, but one that was freewheeling and playful as well. The group's first recording, a five-song cassette, was released in 1984, followed by a full-length self-titled album the next year.

Lewis soon became a role model to younger women, both because of her position as a drummer and because of Beat Happening's studied amateurism, which readily communicated the idea that the listener could just as easily be making the music. "We were in total awe of [Heather's] tough girl, no nonsense style and musical approach," said Tobi Vail, Bikini Kill's drummer, in the liner notes of Beat Happening's 2002 box set, *Crashing Through.* "Her contributions to our scene, via her art, style and attitude inspired the teenage girls to create our own music, poetry and personas on our own terms."

Another local fan, Candice Pederson, eventually became K's co-owner. Pederson was born in California in 1965, and her family moved to Olympia in 1971. In 1983, she became an Evergreen student and quickly involved herself in Olympia's music community (beginning with an informal internship at KAOS when she was still in high school), largely through attending shows. In the winter of 1985–86, she began an internship at K after a friend of hers decided not to take the position. "And I was like, 'Maybe I'll do it,' 'cause I was pretty bored with formal study," Pederson says. "It was just good timing. It wasn't that my mission was to be in the music business, but it was definitely an interest of mine, and once I started going to shows I realized how much I loved it. And I just kept going down this path, somewhat accidentally, somewhat on purpose. And the thing about K was, we never had a big formalized plan and a five-year schedule, so it was really easy to go along and be like, 'Doo-de-doo, I wonder what's next.'"

Releases were sparse in K's initial years and largely limited to cassette (including the first domestic release of Japan's all-female pop combo Shonen Knife, whom Johnson had discovered during Beat Happening's first visit to Japan. At first, Pederson and Johnson took care of all the business; Pederson's jobs included answering the mail, making phone calls to record stores and distributors, and setting up a database when the label finally got a computer. Eventually, they could hire more staff (including Donna Dresch, a key figure in the scene who was in numerous bands, put out her own zines, ran a record label, and in charge of K's mail-order department), and Pederson's responsibilities grew, eventually encompassing the label's business management.

The indie community has been criticized for its insularity and tendency to view anything associated with an independent label as good and anything associated with a major label as inherently bad. It was a notion Pederson did not subscribe to. "I don't think [being an indie] is what makes you superior," she says. "I think it's how you conduct your business. Because it was not like we were solving any world problems; we were bringing some pleasure to people's lives, but we were not doing anything great. When you begin to think you're doing something great, then you're not doing it for the music anyway, you're doing it for yourself. You can't assume that simply because something's indie the people have better motives or ethics."

This observation extended to how the allegedly more progressive realm of alternative music viewed women. Pederson agrees that women formed an integral part of the Olympia music scene. "It seemed like every show you saw, there was at least one female-oriented band," she says. "You saw so many females onstage, it was not a big deal. Then I spent some time in [Washington,] D.C., and that was a real shock to the system, 'cause it was a boys' town. And great boys, but it was new to me. I really thought every place was like Olympia, like the Northwest." But sexism in the indie scene was about to be challenged by the rise of riot grrrl, a movement that grew out of the music scenes in both Olympia and D.C. Chief among the riot grrrl bands was Bikini Kill, whose members were often wrongly assumed to be the movement's "leaders." In fact, Bikini Kill, and others involved in riot grrrl, repeatedly stressed the non-hierarchical philosophy of the movement. But as Bikini Kill became the bestknown of the riot grrrl groups, they remained the definitive riot grrrl group in the eyes of the mainstream audience.

Kathleen Hanna, born in 1969, grew up in D.C. and moved to Portland, Oregon, during high school. "I was really super into my relationships with men until I was 17 or 18," she said in *Dance of Days: Two Decades of Punk in the Nation's Capital.* "I was really fucked over by this guy and I started thinking 'I can't give all this control [to another person].' . . . I had a lot of issues to do with sexual abuse and domestic violence that I hadn't grappled with. I wasn't going to shut it out." Experiences such as working at a domestic violence shelter and as a stripper (an occupation she described as less exploitative than "getting paid $4.25 an hour as a waitress") fueled her work as a spoken-word performer and musician. Hanna eventually moved to Olympia to attend Evergreen, formed the band Viva Knievel, and met Tobi Vail.

Vail, born in 1969, began her performing career at age fifteen in Olympia's Go Team, whose various members also included Johnson, Lois Maffeo (a recording artist and radio DJ with her own zine, *Koo Koo*), and future Bikini Kill guitarist Billy Karren (born 1965); she later played with the all-female band Doris. Both Hanna and Vail also published zines to give voice to their own feminist thinking, reach out to like-minded women, and inspire women to do something creative themselves. "I was on a mission to, like, make feminism cool for younger girls," Hanna later explained.

By 1990, Vail was playing with Evergreen film student Kathi Wilcox (born 1969). When Hanna, who had been reading Vail's zine *Jigsaw*, wrote and suggested that they start a band together, she was invited to join the two women. Though swapping instruments during their shows as Beat Happening had done, the band's primary lineup had Hanna on vocals, Wilcox on bass, and Vail on drums; when the group was unable to find another woman, they asked Karren to be the band's guitarist. The group called themselves Bikini Kill, a name taken from a one-off performance of the same name by Maffeo and her friend Margaret Doherty, that was itself inspired by the 1967 low-budget film *The Million Eyes of Su-Muru*, in which the title character plots to conquer the world with her female army.

Another band coming together at the same time was Bratmobile, founded by Allison Wolfe and Molly Neuman. Wolfe, born in 1969 in Memphis, Tennessee, moved to Mount Vernon, Washington, as a child, and then to Olympia in 1977, following her parents' divorce. Raised by a mother who came out as a lesbian and founded the first women's health clinic in the area operated by women, Wolfe and her two sisters grew up immersed in feminist thought. "We were definitely 'raised by two moms,'" she says. "It was a very outspoken feminist household, not a whole lot of rules and stuff. It was pretty cool. When I look back, I'm thankful."

Wolfe's feminist consciousness was further raised after an incident in high school. One evening, while her mother was out, Wolfe broke up with her boyfriend, who stormed out of the house, then returned to hear Wolfe, her sister, and a friend nervously giggling about the incident upstairs. "And he was like, 'Allison get down here right now!'" she recalls. "Like he was my dad or something. So I went down, and he said, 'Don't you ever laugh at me!' and picked me up by the collar and held me up against the wall, yelling. And then he threw a frying pan against the wall.

"And something in me snapped," she continues. "I couldn't articulate it then, but I just knew I couldn't have anything to do with this. I think a lot of that came from growing up in a violent household where my dad was violent with my mother and witnessing that. So that Monday at school, I instantly started dressing different, wearing long underwear, my collars buttoned all the way up, a big crucifix, I chopped off one side of my hair, and I started to hang out with the random rejects. That was my way of rebelling. In a feminist way, actually, because it was this sexist event that caused me to have a more alternative lifestyle."

After graduation, Wolfe enrolled at Eugene's University of Oregon in 1989, where she struck up a friendship with her dorm neighbor, Molly Neuman, born in 1971 in D.C. A shared interest in music brought the two together. Wolfe had gone through a new wave phase in junior high ("The Go-Go's and Bow Wow Wow were very influential because they were women; their songs were catchy and fun, and I could identify with a girl who's doing cool things and having fun"), then discovered Olympia's rich music scene, seeing shows by groups like Beat Happening and the all-female Calamity Jane. She brought tapes of her favorite bands to college, and Neuman, who had just bought her first guitar, was taken by the sounds she heard emanating from Wolfe's room.

"I was like, 'What the hell is this?'" she recalls. "I was into R.E.M. and New Order. I knew about Black Flag and D.C. punk, but I didn't know how to connect with it. I was intimidated. But this was totally accessible. Like Beat Happening; it's like anybody could do it. They had the most basic elements and they made incredible songs out of them." Further inspiration came when the two caught an Olympia show in January 1990 featuring Beat Happening, Nirvana, and the Melvins. "It was my first real punk rock show," Neuman says. "It was awesome. It was amazing; it totally changed my life. And I met Calvin over the weekend, and Candice too."

It was not long before Neuman and Wolfe began toying with the idea of doing something musical themselves. They first considered starting a radio show featuring female artists, but the university had no radio station. Next came the idea of starting a band, though Wolfe admits it initially existed more as a "concept" and was largely limited to the two singing a cappella songs during breaks at parties. But the ad hoc group nonetheless gained a name—Bratmobile.

In addition to visiting Olympia regularly to see shows, the two corresponded with Tobi Vail and Donna Dresch, which helped word spread about their "band." Even so, they were surprised to get a call from Calvin Johnson inviting them to perform at a Valentine's Day show in 1991, along with Bikini Kill and Olympia's Some Velvet Sidewalk. "We were like, 'We're not a band, we can't play,'" says Wolfe. "But he wasn't going to let us say no." Nor did the two have many songs, though they had made a demo tape, with guitarist Aaron Stauffer from the Tacoma, Washington–based band Seaweed.

In preparation for their show, Neuman, who had been taking guitar lessons, upgraded from her acoustic guitar to an electric. The two then solicited help from Some Velvet Sidewalk's Robert Christie. "We went to his house and said, 'What do we do? Calvin said we have to play this show, and we don't have songs and we don't have a practice space,'" says Wolfe. "He just laughed and said, 'I'll loan you my practice space and you can use our equipment. And it's easy to write songs, just get out some Ramones records and listen to those.' And in my riot grrrl rebellious way, I was like, 'Well, if some guy tells me that's the way to have a band, I'm going to do the opposite.' So from that day on I refused to listen to the Ramones. Because I was like, 'If everybody who wants to be in a punk band gets a Ramones record, then all the bands are going to sound like the Ramones. And we don't want to sound like all the other bands.'"

The show was held at Olympia's North Shore Surf Club, the same venue where Wolfe had seen bands play as a teenager. Neuman switched between drums and guitar while Wolfe sang (and played guitar on one song). Bratmobile's brash sing-along songs (one number, "Girl Germs," was based around the playground chant "girl germs, no returns") struck an immediate chord with the audience. "I don't know if it was just the sheer support of our friends or what," says Wolfe. "It was pretty crazy. Corin Tucker [who founded the bands Heavens to Betsy and Sleater-Kinney] was there; she had some school film project documenting girls in music and asked if she could videotape the show. And Slim Moon [who founded Olympia label Kill Rock Stars] came up and said, 'I'm going to put out a compilation and I really want your song "Girl Germs" to be on it.' And Pat Maley [who founded Olympia label Yoyo Recordings] was there, and he was like, 'I really want to record you guys.' So we recorded right away, I think that weekend."

As the band practiced, Bikini Kill's members continued to publish what Vail was calling "angry grrrl zines" (including *Bikini Kill* and Hanna's *Girl Power*), the spelling of "grrrl" both parodying the way some '70s-era feminists spelled "womyn" and conveying a playful energy. Bratmobile also began working on a zine, *Girl Germs*. The first issue was completed at the end of 1990, when Neuman returned to D.C. for Christmas break and xeroxed the zine in the office of a congressman for whom she had worked. "I had a credential to get in the building, so I went in after hours," she says. "There was this massive snowstorm, and everything was on recess, so there was no one around, and I got snowed in. It was fun, roaming the halls of Congress; I'd go down and get candy bars, potato chips, and Coke and work on my zine, and rip off the government by xeroxing it there."

Neuman would also meet Bratmobile's third member during her trip—Erin Smith. Smith had discovered Beat Happening in the late '80s and had been sufficiently inspired by Heather Lewis to pick up the electric guitar. She and her brother also published the zine *Teenage Gang Debs*, which was more a critique of pop culture, especially the TV sitcom *The Brady Bunch*, than a feminist zine. Calvin Johnson, also in D.C. during Neuman's December 1990 trip, introduced Smith and Neuman at a Nation of Ulysses show. Wolfe met Smith when she accompanied Neuman on her next visit to D.C., over spring break in 1991, and, with Smith and other musicians sitting in, an ad hoc Bratmobile played two shows.

Back in Eugene, Wolfe and Neuman continued to perform as Bratmobile with temporary "special guests" sitting in. By then, Bikini Kill had decided to relocate to D.C., and Wolfe and Neuman planned to spend the summer there as well. Bratmobile was also working on a new zine, along with Hanna, Vail, and Jen Smith (no relation to Erin) called *Riot Grrrl*. The name's inspiration was two-fold. In May 1991, following the shooting of a man by a police officer, D.C.'s Mount Pleasant neighborhood had erupted in riots. Jen Smith (who had sung with Bratmobile during Wolfe and Neuman's spring break visit), wrote them about the incident, noting, "We need to have a girl riot!" After considering *Girl Riot* as the zine's name, they switched it around to *Riot Grrrl*, using Vail's spelling of "grrrl."

Riot Grrrl's third issue announced an "all girl meeting to discuss the status of punk rock and revolution," the first of what would come to be known as "riot grrrl meetings." In essence, the meetings were an updated version of the '70s-era consciousness-raising sessions. Topics might include sexual abuse, sexual harassment at concerts, and how to help female attendees at shows claim "safe space" in front of the stage by asking men to step to the back of the hall. Women circulated ideas further at shows by passing out flyers and other zines. The zines covered music but also featured articles on sexism and racism and suggestions on how to achieve "Revolution Girl Style Now" (the name of Bikini Kill's first release, a self-released cassette they sold at shows): "ENCOURAGE IN THE FACE OF INSECURITY"; "MAKE PORNOGRAPHY that includes more than just hetero sex." Another suggested writing messages on one's body as a means of identifying other "pro-revolution girls"; both bands and audience members wrote words like "slut" and "whore" on themselves as a means of reclaiming slurs traditionally used against women.

The culminating event of the summer took everyone back to Olympia, for the K Records-organized International Pop Underground convention (IPU). The idea was sparked both by a large party K had thrown in summer 1990 and by the idea of creating an alternative to the traditional music convention. "It was a way to combine music and dancing and fun without the pseudo-business stuff," says Pederson. "Unlike most conventions that I'm aware of, everybody got paid fairly. We tried to keep passes as low as possible, thirty-five dollars for five days, just enough to make sure the bands and venues got paid. It was really very community-oriented, the community being whoever had thirty-five dollars. Or not—a lot of people came and didn't pay and just hung out. And that was totally encouraged; if you wanted to be there, you were part of the community. It was that simple."

IPU was held August 20-25; word of mouth sold 450 passes. IPU's events included not only music shows, but also poetry readings, a cake walk, and a *Planet of the Apes* film festival. In keeping with the fiercely independent ethic, the event's program announced, "No lackeys to the corporate ogre allowed," and indeed all of the bands recorded on indie labels, save for L.A.'s L7, which had recently signed to the Slash label, distributed by Warner Bros.

Kicking off IPU was an all-female bill called "Love Rock Revolution Girl Style Now," featuring, among others, Bratmobile, Jean Smith, Tobi Vail, and Seattle's 7 Year Bitch. Coinciding with IPU was the release of the first album from Kill Rock Stars, a label launched that spring with a single featuring spoken-word pieces by Hanna on one side and KRS founder Slim Moon on the other. The *Kill Rock Stars* album compiled music from Olympia artists and included the first vinyl appearances of Bratmobile ("Girl Germs") and Bikini Kill ("Feels Blind"). A later CD version included artists who had appeared at IPU and featured liner notes by Pederson: "KILL ROCK STARS is a collection of people who believe that rules are for squares only. . . . The weak need not apply. Long after the fads, KILL ROCK STARS will stand out as the stellar example for punk rock of the 90's. Fuck alternative."

But the underground scene quietly building throughout the '80s was about to be pushed firmly into the light. In the wake of the success of Nirvana's *Nevermind*, "alternative" had become the new buzz word in the music industry, with most of the attention focused on the Pacific Northwest, Nirvana's home. In a move unimaginable six months earlier, the dreaded "corporate ogre" was pounding on the door, demanding admittance.

Some were simply not interested in any association with the corporate side of the music industry, however lucrative the payoff. Pederson found herself in the unique position of turning down DGC (Nirvana's label) when they called K with an offer. "It was like, 'So-and-so wants to set up a meeting about buying K,'" she remembers. "And I'm like, 'We don't want to sell.' 'You don't get it, we're talking a lot of money.' 'We're not going to sell.' And he was so flummoxed, he called a friend of mine who also worked for DGC, and was like, 'Do you think I got a real person there? Do you think this was true?' And my friend was like, 'Yeah. In fact you could've saved yourself the time and just asked me; I would've told you they weren't going to sell.' There was this half-hour hoopla, and then it was over.

"I've certainly been asked in retrospect, do I regret that decision," Pederson continues. "And, no, I'm as sure of it today as I was then. And I'm sure Calvin feels the same way. You can just say no. Because once you say yes, that's the last part of the decision you actually get to make. From then on somebody else is making all the decisions. I couldn't imagine selling it just for the money. It didn't make sense. And it wasn't fair to the bands; most of them had joined us because of how we did business, and to make a decision like that would've upset the equilibrium that we had in place. It's not what they signed on for."

Bands associated with riot grrrl would soon be fending off such attention from major labels themselves as they began touring outside the Olympia–D.C. circuit. But the tours also put them in touch with their fans around the country for the first time. In the spring of 1992, Bratmobile, with its final lineup of Wolfe on vocals, Smith on guitar, and Neuman on drums, toured across the country with Heavens to Betsy. "There was a real excitement in these young girls seeing us," says Neuman. "There was real inspiration happening, and we still get that. Girls who come to our shows now are like, 'We're in a band,' and they're so nervous to tell us about it, and we're like, 'That's rad, what are you guys called?' It's the coolest thing—they have an idea to be a band! When we were fifteen, we never had that. Tobi had it, but Olympia's different."

The tour ended in D.C. in time for the first Riot Grrrl Conference, held over the last weekend of July. The conference presented performances and workshops on such subjects as sexual abuse, racism, and fat oppression. But this time media were trying to crash the party, to the participants' distress. The mainstream media's first coverage of the riot grrrl movement probably came when Erin Smith, as an intern, brought riot grrrl zines to *Sassy* in 1991 for review. Further interest was generated when Seattle-based writer Emily White published the first substantial look at the movement in the July 10, 1992, *LA Weekly*; publications around the U.S. subsequently picked up the piece.

The media presence at the Riot Grrrl Conference was problematic because of the fear that workshop attendees might not feel comfortable sharing highly personal stories in front of reporters. "So reporters and media were barred from the workshops," Corin Tucker says. "But this *USA Today* woman snuck in and wrote about it afterwards, and used parts of people's personal stories. And it was really terrifying. It was really scary that we were being watched under a microscope. It seemed kind of unreal. And that's when things started getting really out of hand."

By the fall of 1992, virtually every magazine, from music publications to women's journals to news weeklies, had an opinion about riot grrrl. Some revolved around predictable debates that the bands' "primitive" sounds surely didn't constitute real music. Even music magazines split on the question; one reviewer wrote that Bikini Kill "couldn't play a memorable three-chord riff if the first two chords were already constructed," while another praised the band's performance on their 1993 U.K. tour with Huggy Bear: "Any doubts about whether these 'grrrls' can play their instruments or not is inconsequential. They can, and, yes, they have songs too."

While articles in the mainstream occasionally smacked of condescension, the indie press was not necessarily more supportive. "The punk zine editors' use of 'bitches,' 'cunts,' 'man-haters,' and 'dykes' [in writing about Bikini Kill] was proof positive that sexism was still strong in the punk scene," wrote Daniel Sinker in *We*

Bikini Kill, (left to right): Tobi Vail, Kathleen Hanna
April 1992, Rock for Choice benefit, Washington, D.C.,
Photo by Pat Graham

Owe You Nothing: Punk Planet: The Collected Interviews. One *Melody Maker* writer even asserted that "One of the biggest ironies surrounding Riot Grrrl is that it's sprung from the grotesquely male grunge underground"—missing the point that riot grrrl had formed as a direct response to that "grotesque" underground. Nor was the criticism limited to print; Bikini Kill, and Hanna in particular, were often physically attacked by male audience members during shows.

The fact that the outside world was even interested in examining the activities of riot grrrl bands surprised those involved. "You do feel like you're taking over the world, but you still think about it as your small little world," says Wolfe. "So it's weird to start hearing about yourself in third person, or your friends, in some mainstream format, a magazine or newspaper. And it still is weird. Like in interviews I've consented to, when you read them, it's never right, it's never exactly what you said—you just have to accept that. But at the time, I wasn't ready to accept it. And we didn't know what kinds of things you should or shouldn't say to avoid the weirdness. But a lot of times, it didn't matter what we said, 'cause they were going to get the story no matter what. They would just write whatever they wanted."

By early 1993, some riot grrrls suggested an interview boycott. This hardly kept the press from writing about the subject, nor did everyone agree with the boycott. "I never had a problem talking to people, because I grew up in a media-centered world," says Neuman. "I watched the news and read the paper every day. To me, [the media coverage] legitimized what I was doing, what I was putting all my heart and soul into. So I wasn't part of the media blackout thing, because I wasn't freaked out about talking, and I wasn't freaked out about being misinterpreted. Because I didn't trust people to tell my story accurately anyway. So I didn't get that bummed when they didn't." Wolfe, who did agree with the boycott, still saw the elitist aspect of the decision. "You have to acknowledge that you're privileged to have access to alternative culture," she says, "and it might be kind of snobby to deny that access to kids in rural areas who couldn't get it otherwise. There were people who said, 'I heard about you in *Seventeen*,' and it made me realize some good did come out of it."

Much of the media attention focused on the riot grrrls in bands. "The girls who were in it for political reasons ended up feeling like they got a raw deal," Wolfe says. "'Cause the press didn't really help everyone involved—it really only helped the bands. Not to say that we didn't have our own flaws and that it wasn't a flawed movement from the beginning. You could say it was mostly serving white middle-class girls, and the focus was too narrow. But we were just young, and we didn't know what we were doing; it was our first time being really politicized. But in the end it became a weird contest between people—who is more oppressed than who. People just started getting nasty with each other."

There was also the occasional offer Wolfe regretted turning down. "I got a post-card and it said, 'I am Kim Fowley, producer of the Runaways. I want to work with you—call me,'" remembers Wolfe. "And I never did, but I met him later when we were on tour with the Donnas; he came up to me and said, 'I heard you recorded one of my songs.' 'Cause we did a cover of 'Cherry Bomb.' We also got an offer from [TV host] Sally Jesse Raphael to have riot grrrls be on her talk show and battle David Lee Roth [of Van Halen]. Now I wonder why didn't we do that, but at the time we were like, 'No way!'"

The logistical problem of having members living around the country meant that Bratmobile's early releases were limited to singles and compilation tracks; the band would not release a full-length album until 1993's *Pottymouth*. The record might have had the primitive sound of lo-fi (low fidelity) recording, but the exuberance was unmistakable—"Cool Schmool" is a feisty statement of independence, while "Panik" celebrates a crush on a girl who is "the Joanest Jett around"—and the overall effect is one of crackling energy.

But Bratmobile would not be able to further develop their music at the time, for their breakup was imminent. "Things were really tense with riot grrrl," Wolfe remembers.

Bratmobile, (left to right): Allison Wolfe, Erin Smith, Molly Neuman
Circa 1999, Washington, D.C., Photo by Pat Graham

"There was a lot of weird infighting, a lot of people blaming the bands for all the downfalls of riot grrrl. And I felt a lot of pressure from that to live up to some ideal—that I was supposed to be some sort of special person just 'cause the magazines said so. I was having a really hard time with that, and I just buckled under it all instead of standing up for myself. But also I think the weak link in our band was that we weren't agreeing on anything and we weren't communicating."

The meltdown came at a May 1994 show in New York City. The band had not practiced in many months, and everyone was feeling the pressure of playing a high-profile gig in front of such notables as Joan Jett. "I just couldn't keep it together, and everything just fell apart right on stage," says Wolfe. "These girls who had been giving me a lot of grief were at the show harassing me, and also trying to stop the show, I think because they had been assaulted [by an audience member]. All of a sudden not only was I supposed to serve as talent that night, I was also supposed to serve as club manager and security! And the whole show just kind of stopped and everybody was screaming at each other. It was like slapstick comedy or some kind of crazy performance art, and we just broke up onstage. And I guess that was that." *The Real Janelle* EP was released the same year, but Bratmobile was over—until their unexpected re-formation in 1999.

Bikini Kill left behind a more substantial musical chronicle of the period. After their self-released tape, their appearances were limited to spots on compilation albums until their six-track, self-titled EP was released in 1992. Even on record, Hanna's charisma comes across like a bracing gust of fresh air; in performance, songs like "Double Dare Ya" and "Suck My Left One" (the latter the ultimate riposte to a would-be molester) became veritable battle cries. But *Our Troubled Youth / Yeah, Yeah, Yeah, Yeah*, a 1993 split EP with Huggy Bear, suffers from a muddy mix; the band's invigorating punk rock sounds muted.

But the EP also marked the first appearance of "Rebel Girl," which would reappear on a stunning 1993 single along with "New Radio" and "Demirep." The single was produced by Joan Jett, who had offered to work with the group after seeing a New York show; she also played guitar and sang on the record (Hanna returned the favor, co-writing three songs and singing on Jett's 1994 album *Pure and Simple*). The single answered the question of how the band would sound if they left the realm of lo-fi behind, as Jett helped them develop their musical muscle. Both "New Radio" and "Rebel Girl" depict bratty youngsters who exude an irresistible confidence, but most impressive is the commanding drive of the music; never before had the band sounded so authoritative.

Yet another version of "Rebel Girl" appeared on Bikini Kill's first full-length album, *Pussywhipped*, also released in 1993, which returned to the raw thrash of the band's earlier records. Two more singles appeared in 1995, by which time media interest in riot grrrl had waned, which did not displease the group (the press release issued with the "Anti-Pleasure Dissertation" single stated, "Remember that Bikini Kill don't call themselves Riot Grrrls or consider their music Riot Grrrl and never claimed leadership to such a movement," though reviewers also were invited to call the label for more information: "With Bikini Kill fact checking is pretty essential, given the mega-misinformation trend"). And a *Rolling Stone* review of the band's 1996 album *Reject All American* (a well-polished effort that also drew out the band's pop sensibilities on the surprisingly melodic "False Start" and "For Only") speculated that the group was "ripe for rock stardom" and perhaps ready for a major label deal.

But the album would be Bikini Kill's last, though the group would not announce their split until 1998. The band members had already been playing in other groups (Hanna in Suture and the Fakes, Karren, Vail, and Wilcox joining Molly Neuman in the Frumpies, among others), and following Bikini Kill's split, Hanna released an album under the name "Julie Ruin," adopting another persona to sidestep the musical expectations placed on Bikini Kill. Though much has been made about how riot grrrl was never allowed to flower fully before being co-opted by the mainstream, Bikini Kill held together against sometimes substantial odds for around six years (before the break following *Reject All American*'s release hiatus)—plenty of time for their message of empowerment to reach beyond the media onslaught into the hearts and minds of untold numbers of young women.

Other bands from the underground music community were not as hostile to the idea of working with a major label. Babes in Toyland, L7, and Hole were alternative bands that formed in the late '80s and signed to the majors in the early '90s. Yet because their emergence on the national scene coincided with the discovery of riot grrrl by the media, and their music was seen as equally "angry," each band was at some point linked with the movement. When Thurston Moore jokingly dubbed the influx of loud and aggressive female-led bands "foxcore," the term stuck, though most articles failed to grasp Moore's underlying humor. In fact, while each band recognized that being a female rock band, as opposed to a pop group, flew in the face of rock tradition, they were less politically driven than the riot grrrl bands. Still, as female musicians, they all faced obligatory questions about feminism and what it meant to be a woman-in-rock.

Babes in Toyland's bleached-blonde lead singer and guitarist, Kathy Bjelland, was born in 1963 and raised by her stepparents in Oregon; she later said her upbringing was physically and emotionally abusive. Though ostensibly a conventional student—a cheerleader, basketball player, and reporter for the school paper—at home she lived a more reclusive existence. "[I'd] listen to Billie Holiday, read Sylvia Plath, drink Kahlua from my dad's liquor cabinet, and fantasize how I was going to get the fuck out of here," she told Neal Karlen in his biography of the group, *Babes in Toyland.*

After high school, Bjelland briefly attended the University of Oregon. She also joined her uncle's surf band, the Neurotics, on rhythm guitar. Bjelland had received an acoustic guitar in the second grade, but its big neck made it hard for her to play; at nineteen, she moved to electric guitar, after experimenting with her boyfriend's model. She then formed an all-female band, the Venarays, and moved to Portland.

Bjelland worked as a stripper to avoid having a regular day job. A self-described "total small-town metal head person" who had been impressed by Girlschool ("I saw Girlschool and thought, 'Shit! I didn't know girls could do that!'"), she began discovering underground music in the Portland club scene. She also met a like-minded soul, Courtney Love, who, like Bjelland, worked as a stripper and wanted to have a band of her own. The two later moved to San Francisco, and Love invited Jennifer Finch, a pen pal she had met through the magazine *Maximumrocknroll,* to join them. After witnessing a performance by the hard rock all-female band Frightwig, the three decided to form their own group.

The band, called Sugar Baby Doll, featured Love on vocals, Bjelland on guitar, and Finch on bass. Accounts differ as to whether the band played any live shows or merely practiced together, but the project was short-lived (though two songs from the period were later revived: "The Quiet Room" turned up on two Babes in Toyland records and "Best Sunday Dress" was featured in Hole's live set). After the group split, Finch returned to L.A., soon followed by Love, and Bjelland moved to Minneapolis in 1987.

Bjelland soon met Lori Barbero, born in 1960, a dreadlocked, half-Filipina University of Minnesota dropout who worked as a waitress at local clubs and shared Bjelland's interest in Billie Holiday. Outgoing and exuberant, Barbero's love of the music scene extended to hosting touring musicians at her home (the house would eventually be listed in at least two rock travel guides as a historic landmark). Bjelland wanted Barbero's "tribal" energy and approached her about forming a new band.

Barbero had never played an instrument but had considered drums. "I talked about it forever," she says. "For probably seven years—'I'm going to buy drums. I'm going to play drums.' And I got so sick of listening to myself say it, I just bought drums and started playing." Babes in Toyland's original lineup featured Bjelland on guitar, Barbero on drums, Cindy Russell on vocals, and Chris Holetz on bass, though Russell and Holetz soon dropped out. Courtney Love moved to Minneapolis and briefly worked with Bjelland and Barbero, but that lineup fell apart as well. Eventually, Michelle Leon (born 1969) joined on bass, and Bjelland became the vocalist.

The "Babes" in the group's name was meant to refer to babies, not women. "Boys and girls are all babes in the universe," Bjelland was fond of saying. But the band was not unaware of their impact on women. "It's so great when women stand at the front of the stage and rock with us," Barbero told Karlen. "Nothing . . . feels better than seeing girls realize for the first time that rock & roll can be for them too." Nor did the group want traditional perceptions of rock bands placed on them. "I don't think I'm trying to prove anything," Bjelland told *Option*. "Like, 'I can rock just as hard as the guys.' That's just a bunch of shit. It's like, 'No, I'm just trying to play some music here, thanks.'" This attitude came across in their performances. "[Bjelland] was like Linda Blair in the *The Exorcist*, playing the craziest, most inventive guitar chords and wearing a dress," Kathleen Hanna told *Spin*. "She wasn't assimilating into the rock-dude thing— she had her own thing going. That band influenced so many people."

The group released their first single, "Dust Cake Boy," in 1989, and then signed with Minneapolis indie label Twin/Tone, which released *Spanking Machine* (recorded in one day) in 1990. Bjelland's vocals already were proving to be the band's most arresting feature; on "Fleshcrawl" (which appeared on an EP of all-female bands including Frightwig, L7, and Seattle-based Dickless), she snarls with withering contempt about the weakness of the flesh, and her delivery would become even more furious on future recordings. A European tour in the fall of 1990, opening for Sonic Youth, helped break the group overseas. When their EP *To Mother* (with a picture of Bjelland's mother on the cover) was released in 1991, it topped the U.K. indie charts.

Nonetheless, the band did not necessarily feel their style of music could escape the indie ghetto. "You think, 'Oh, I'd love to get a record out, that's what I want to do,'" says Bjelland. "But in the back of your mind you have a safety valve going, 'But that will never happen.' I always thought you had to play nicer, different kind of music to get a record out." Still, the group attracted the attention of Reprise, who signed the band in 1991. But in early 1992, Leon quit, tired of the rigorous touring schedule and shaken by the recent death of her boyfriend, Black Flag roadie Joe Cole, who had been murdered when he and Black Flag lead singer Henry Rollins were mugged in L.A. To replace Leon, Bjelland and Barbero quickly tapped their friend, Maureen Herman (born 1966), who had lived in Minneapolis and was in Chicago playing with the band Cherry Rodriguez. Herman agreed and joined in time for the recording of *Fontanelle*, released in August.

The album title referred to the soft spot on a newborn baby's skull, and the cover art also featured a baby—albeit an unsmiling, naked, anatomically correct one in a photo taken by noted art photographer Cindy Sherman. "This may be the rawest performance ever released by a major label, and also one of the most necessary," wrote the *Los Angeles Times* of the album, which, although containing the melodic instrumental

"Quiet Room," essentially hinged on the strength of Bjelland's coruscating vocals and Barbero's propulsive drumming (Barbero also sang lead vocals on a song she had written, "Magick Flute"). "I think I mainly write about my nightmares," Bjelland said, explaining the frightening imagery in the band's songs. But she explained to Liz Evans that "Just because I'm screaming doesn't mean I'm screaming out of anger. I could be screaming out of passion or frustration. I've always said our songs aren't angry songs, they're just passionate."

But the most notorious song was the album's lead-off track, "Bruise Violet," ostensibly directed toward Courtney Love. Both Bjelland and Love had taken to wearing babydoll dresses, a look reportedly inspired by Carroll Baker's child bride character in the 1956 film *Baby Doll*. On Bjelland and Love, the look was dubbed "kinderwhore" for its mix of innocence and knowing sexuality—and each lay claim to creating it, in a minor feud dubbed "the war of the dress" in the press. The song's lyrics were indeed an angry rejoinder to a nameless rival, while the video featured a host of extras in blonde wigs and babydoll dresses stage-diving at a Babes in Toyland show. Even Cindy Sherman appeared, in blonde wig and babydoll dress, eventually strangled by Bjelland. The video, Bjelland later explained to *Entertainment Weekly*, "is about doppelgängers. People trying to be like you. [Sherman's] like your ghost chasing you, and you have to kill it."

But despite the controversy, which attracted some attention in music and entertainment publications, "Bruise Violet" and the band's subsequent videos received little airplay. "I think the problem is that we write our own songs and we wear clothes," said Barbero in 1993. "And they think the videos are too arty or something," added Bjelland. "They don't look enough like a jeans ad. I would like to see the panel that judges these videos! How can they show that 2 Live Crew video, the one with five million butts shaking, and not show our video? We should make a video where we just show our three butts for the whole video."

In 1993, "Bruise Violet" won a spot on MTV's cartoon show *Beavis and Butt-head*. The fictional characters were deemed "the most powerful critics in rock & roll" in *Rolling Stone* and gave Babes in Toyland their seal of approval (Butt-head: "These chicks rock!"). The same year the band was the only female presence on the mainstage of Lollapalooza, a touring alternative rock festival, and it released the album *Painkillers*, which featured five new tracks and a live set from a 1992 CBGB's gig.

But the band would not release a full album of new material until 1995's *Nemesisters* (though they did appear on compilations, and Bjelland co-wrote a song and appeared on Joan Jett's *Pure and Simple* album). Much of the band's earlier rawness and fire was missing on *Nemesisters*, and even the group's core audience seemed disinterested. Though *Fontanelle* had reached the U.K. Top 30, *Nemesisters* failed to chart (the band's

Suzi Gardner of L7
At the 1997 Bumbershoot festival, Seattle, Photo by Gillian G. Gaar

records never made the charts in the U.S.). Herman then quit the group, and, though another bassist was recruited for touring, the band, in Bjelland's words, "just dwindled off." Babes in Toyland has re-formed on a few occasions since; in 1997, Michelle Leon even joined them briefly. A handful of live albums have also been released. Bjelland subsequently wrote music for the 1998 film *Witchblade* (Barbero performed on the soundtrack) and formed a new band, Katastrophy Wife; Barbero ran her own label, Spanish Fly.

L7 was another hard rock all-female band that captured some national attention during the early '90s but failed to cross over to a larger audience. In their efforts to be seen primarily as musicians, they also generally declined commenting on, or being a part of, articles on women-in-rock. "To create genre out of gender is just horrible to me," bassist Jennifer Finch told *Rolling Stone.* "There's uniqueness in being a woman, but not that much."

L7 was formed in L.A. in the mid-'80s. Guitarist Donita Sparks, born in 1963 and raised in Chicago, had moved to California after high school because of her love of the Beach Boys and Dick Dale. "I went with the intention of being a surfer, actually," she says. "I was obsessed with California and beach movies and surfing. I thought surfing was the coolest fucking thing on earth." A year and a half after her arrival, Sparks finally worked up the nerve to join a rock band; the aspiring guitarist could play, "but I was afraid of my own capabilities," she explains. After a few years playing with local bands Sparks met fellow guitarist Suzi Gardner (born 1960). "That was one of the happiest days of my life," she recalls. "She played me a tape of music that she was working on, and that was exactly what I wanted to play. So we just got together from there."

The two were not especially interested in forming an all-female band. "We were lookin' for anybody who would play with two chick fuckin' guitar player/songwriters," Sparks later told *BAM*. "And that was hard enough." Eventually Jennifer Finch (born 1966), back in L.A. after her brief tenure in Sugar Baby Doll in San Francisco, joined L7 (slang for a square) on bass. The group also had a female drummer, Ann Anderson, replaced by Roy Koutsky for their 1988 self-titled debut, released on Epitaph. After Koutsky's departure, Dee Plakas (born 1960) became the group's permanent drummer.

Though the band's brand of hard rock had the requisite chugging guitar riffs (with an occasional stinging guitar lead), pounding drums, and tough vocals, the songs also had the catchy pull of surf rock. And the band's lyrics frequently depicted the potency of female anger turned outward. "Ms. 45," on the band's first album, echoed the 1981 film of the same name, in which a woman who has been raped picks up a gun and seeks revenge. "Shove," on the band's powerful 1991 album *Smell the Magic*, is the group's one word answer to overcoming any obstacle. "Fast and Frightening" puts a twist on the scenario of many a girl group song; the singer is captivated by the neighborhood bad girl, not the boy, who smokes pot, rides a motorcycle, terrifies parents, and has "so much clit she don't need no balls."

The band eventually landed a major label contract with Slash, which released *Bricks Are Heavy* in 1992. The album was co-produced by Butch Vig, who also produced Nirvana's *Nevermind*, and *Bricks Are Heavy* had a similar surface polish. But the music was just as forceful as ever, with biting lyrics that attacked consumerism ("Pretend We're Dead") and pointedly described where the band's enemies ended up ("Shitlist"). The brilliantly sarcastic anti-war "Wargasm," written by Sparks, was inspired by the John Lennon/Yoko Ono politically themed album *Some Time in New York City*. "I was so blown away by their lyrics and how they just didn't give a shit about who they supported or gave shit to," she explains. "So when it was time to record 'Wargasm,' I was like, God, I'd love to sample Yoko Ono from *Live Peace in Toronto*, some insane scream."

After finding a suitably twisted scream, Sparks talked to Ono to secure her permission for using the sample. "Getting a call from Yoko Ono in my little dive apartment in Los Angeles was amazing!" she recalls. "I was actually at a loss for words, which is very rare for me. And you know what she said? 'I have my fingers crossed for you. It's about time that music like yours got popular.' I was like, 'Oh my God! Yoko Ono has her fingers crossed for us! Awesome!'"

Bricks are Heavy received good reviews and later made *Rolling Stone*'s "100 Essential Recordings of the '90s" list. The band's notoriety rose overseas when Sparks dropped her pants while performing on the British television show *The Word*; the band's appearance at that year's Reading Festival, a weekend rock event, generated further attention when Sparks threw her tampon into the crowd (it was tossed back). "It was just an impromptu thing that she did," Gardner says. "It was very frustrating up there, dodging these big mud clods [thrown by the audience]. It was a knee-jerk reaction to what was going on, and I thought it was an awesome thing. But when everything's said and done, and that's what we're going to go down in history for . . . I just thought, 'Oh, come on. What about our songs?'"

If the band was reluctant to be pinned down on women-in-rock questions, they firmly established their feminist credentials by co-founding the abortion rights organization Rock for Choice. The band had wanted to play an abortion rights benefit, but the feminist groups they contacted were not sure how to work with rock bands. So L7, along with *LA Weekly* editor Sue Cummings, set up Rock for Choice, which then became a project of the Feminist Majority Foundation; Plakas posed for the group's logo, a silhouette of a woman smashing a guitar. The group's first show was held October 25, 1991, at the Palace in L.A., with L7, Hole, Sister Double Happiness, and Nirvana on the bill. Afterward, the band sent information on how to set up a concert to friends in other cities to help the organization stand on its own.

But L7 never managed to transcend fully the alternative scene from which they came. Though both *Bricks Are Heavy* and 1994's *Hungry for Stink* reached the U.K. Top 30, the band never cracked the charts in the U.S. The year 1994 also saw the group appearing in John Waters's *Serial Mom* and on that summer's Lollapalooza tour, and they continued to be regarded as a strong live act (Finch and Sparks also performed on Joan Jett's 1994 album *Pure and Simple*, and Sparks co-wrote the B-side "Hostility" from the sessions). But Jennifer Finch left during the recording of *The Beauty Process: Triple Platinum*, released in 1997, and the band was then dropped by Slash (Finch subsequently played in the bands Lyme and OtherStarPeople). The group founded their own label, Wax Tadpole, to release 1999's *Slap-Happy* (a joint release with Bong Load), but the album was the group's last.

The decidedly pop sound of the Breeders and Belly proved far more palatable to a mass audience. The Breeders' *Pod* had been well received, and when the Pixies went on hiatus in 1992 Kim Deal asked her sister, Kelley, to join the Breeders when they recorded their second record. Kelley agreed on condition that she play lead guitar—an instrument she had never played before. Jim MacPherson was added on drums, and in 1992 the group released the EP *Safari* (with MacPherson billed as "Mike Hunt" on the record). Following *Safari*'s release, Tanya Donelly left the Breeders to form her own group, Belly. The remaining members then released their breakthrough album, *Last Splash*, in 1993.

Last Splash was buoyed by shimmering pop melodies (along with the country & western toe-tapper "Drivin' on 9") and the Deal sisters' coolly confident vocals (Josephine Wiggs also provided vocals). The album reached number 33; the single "Cannonball" reached number 44; the video for "Cannonball" became an MTV staple (both the "Cannonball" and "Divine Hammer" videos were co-directed by Kim Gordon); and suddenly Kim's side project band had ended up outselling her entire catalogue with the Pixies. The group was poised for even greater success, but work ground to a sudden halt when Kelley was arrested in November 1994 for heroin possession.

While Kelley was sent to rehab, the other band members pursued different projects. Kim, MacPherson, and other Dayton-area musicians recorded an album, *Pacer*, released under the name the Amps (originally Tammy and the Amps) in 1995. Wiggs released a solo album, *Bon Bon Life*, in 1996. Her romantic involvement with Luscious Jackson drummer Kate Schellenbach led to her appearing on the group's *Electric Honey* album and co-producing *Klassics with a K* by the Kostars (a Luscious Jackson side project); she also worked with Luscious Jackson's Vivian Trimble in the group Dusty Trails.

But when Kelley left rehab, the Breeders did not re-form; instead, Kelley began releasing her own albums under the name the Kelley Deal 6000 (1996's *Go to the Sugar Altar* and 1997's *Boom! Boom! Boom!*). But Kim still hoped the Breeders could be revived, and continued working on her own, learning to play drums when she could not find a suitable drummer. The song "Collage," credited to the group, appeared on the soundtrack of the 1999 film *The Mod Squad*, and the following year the Breeders finally were relaunched with Kelley back on board, in addition to guitarist Richard Presley, bassist Mando Lopez (both from the L.A. punk band Fear), and drummer Jose Medeles. Still, an album was a long time coming, and it was not until 2002 that it finally appeared. Though not as joyfully celebratory as *Last Splash*, Kim's pop sensibilities were still firmly in place (Kim again serving as the primary songwriter, writing or co-writing each song), and the band once again had possibilities.

Tanya Donelly's Belly also enjoyed a measure of success before she launched a solo career. Donelly's desire to perform her own material had led to her leaving both Throwing Muses and the Breeders, though in the latter instance she told *Record Collector* her departure "wasn't anything dramatic." Belly also included brothers Tom and Chris Gorman, on guitar and drums, respectively, and former Throwing Muse Fred Abong on bass. The group's first EP, *Slow Dust*, was released only in the U.K. in 1992; their debut album, *Star*, was released in 1993.

Star entered the U.K. charts at number 2 and reached number 59 in the U.S. The songs wed sparkling pop melodies to often cryptic lyrics. "If you're not sure about one of my songs, just assume death, not sex," Donelly told *Pulse*. But she was surprised at the media's response to her, now that she was fronting a band. Throwing Muses had been three women and one man; with no other women in Belly, Donelly felt the group was seen more as a "'Tanya and the boys' kind of thing." "I want to get to the point where women aren't treated like . . . giraffes," she told Amy Raphael. "It shouldn't even be interesting at this point that I'm female and do this. It shouldn't even be a point of contention. But it is." She was equally frustrated by being called a "doll" or "childlike" in interviews, which resulted in her cultivating a stronger vocal style for *King*, released in 1995.

By that time, Abong had quit, replaced by Gail Greenwood in part to restore the group's gender balance. But in the wake of *King*'s relative failure in America (though hitting the Top 10 in the U.K., it stalled at number 57 in the U.S.), the group broke up (Greenwood would join L7 after Jennifer Finch's departure). Donelly later acknowledged the group had been having personal difficulties all along: "We were falling apart even before *King* came out. We would have broken up no matter what." In late 1996, Donelly returned as a solo artist with the EP *Sliding and Diving*, followed by *Lovesongs for Underdogs* (1997) and *Beautysleep* (2002).

But the female-led band from the underground that would attain the highest profile was Hole, whose founder, Courtney Love, would become the most polarizing woman in '90s rock—though, typically, much of the debate surrounding her has centered on her image and behavior, not her music. Love was born Love Michelle Harrison in San Francisco in 1965. Love's parents divorced when she was a child, and she was shuttled between her mother, a series of stepfathers, and family friends in Eugene and New Zealand. Love's mother ran a progressive household with an emphasis on a gender-free environment, meaning Love was denied conventionally feminine attire and toys; not surprisingly, gender issues and visual representations of girlishness (dolls, barrettes, baby-doll dresses) would later figure as the centerpieces of her work.

Despite the progressive atmosphere, Love found other ways to rebel, engaging in petty theft and being sent through a continual round of therapists and reform schools, where she discovered punk rock. In her late teens, a trust fund enabled Love to live on her own, and by the early '80s she began thinking of forming her own band. Her first attempt was a group formed with two friends in Portland called Sugar Babylon, though the band's sole output was a photo session, arranged by Love.

When the trust fund ran out, Love worked as a stripper and continued the nomadic existence of her childhood, living in England, Japan, Taiwan, Alaska, Portland, and San Francisco. During one stay in San Francisco, Love sang in an early incarnation of Faith No More, though accounts vary as to how long she was with group. Returning to Portland, she met Kathy Bjelland, but following the demise of their band Sugar Baby Doll, Love put her musical ambitions on hold, moved to L.A., and pursued acting. After working as a "punk rock extra," she eventually won a bit part as Nancy Spungen's friend in Alex Cox's *Sid and Nancy* and a co-starring role in Cox's follow-up film, *Straight to Hell.* When her second attempt to work with Bjelland in Minneapolis did not work out, Love returned to L.A. in 1989, determined to start her own band.

Her ad in a local paper citing Big Black, Sonic Youth, and Fleetwood Mac as influences attracted the attention of Eric Erlandson, who became the group's guitarist; the eventual lineup featured Erlandson, Jill Emery on bass, Caroline Rue on drums, and Love on rhythm guitar and vocals. Love chose the name "Hole" from a quotation in Euripides's *Medea*, though she was not unaware of the name's sexual connotations. Hole's first single, "Retard Girl," came out in 1990, and their 1991 debut album, *Pretty on the Inside*, was released on Caroline (co-produced by Kim Gordon and Don Fleming of Gumball). The music was harsh, with heavy, grinding guitars providing the backdrop for the band's tales of abuse, rape, prostitution, and incest; in a nod to her hippie upbringing, there was also a cover of "Both Sides Now."

But while "Retard Girl" depicts the cruelty of the schoolyard and the fear of being tagged with the hated label of "retard," by the time of "Teenage Whore," *Pretty's* opening track, the fear of being the outsider had become the rage of being the outsider—a rage clearly evident in Love's howling vocals. Yet those who exist outside societal bounds can attain their own power: the power of freedom, the power to do as they please. Love instinctively recognized this fact, wielding her outsider status a weapon, while also projecting an image of powerlessness due to her "kinderwhore" look. Hole's songs expressed pain, sorrow, and anger, but the underlying message was of survival, particularly survival in the face of overwhelming circumstances.

Pretty received raves from the British music press (and reached number 59 in the U.K. charts) and praise in the U.S. as well; Elizabeth Wurtzel called the record "probably the most compelling album to have been released in 1991" in *The New Yorker.* But Hole's momentum was stalled when Love became pregnant and married Nirvana's lead singer, Kurt Cobain, in February 1992; the band was put on hold, and Emery and Rue eventually quit. Love then dealt with a more serious crisis when a profile in the September *Vanity Fair* claimed she knowingly had done heroin while pregnant.

The backlash was immediate and fierce. "I knew that my world was over. I was dead," she said later. "Not only was I going to walk around with a big black mark, but any happiness that I had known, I was going to have to fight for, for the rest of my life." Love repeatedly insisted that she had stopped using drugs when she learned of her pregnancy, and her daughter, Frances Bean Cobain, was born in perfect health, but the couple nonetheless lost custody of their daughter for a few months following the *Vanity Fair* story.

The following year, Love began putting her band back together. Patty Schemel became Hole's new drummer, and the group released a European single, "Beautiful Son," which pointed to a new, pop-influenced direction. Leslie Hardy was briefly the band's bassist, but was soon replaced by Kristen Pfaff, from Minneapolis band Janitor Joe. Now signed to DGC, Hole recorded *Live Through This* in fall 1993, with release set for the following spring.

The album's cover plainly staked out the musical territory within: a beauty queen caught in mid-scream on the front, and a young Love in flannel shirt and jeans on the back. The process by which the girl on the back can be transformed into the woman on the front is explored throughout the album, most specifically on "Miss World," whose very title alludes to beauty pageants. But the song's protagonist is a construction of artifice, trapped on a diet of pills with no chance of rescue. References to eating disorders are prevalent, along with stark depictions of motherhood and domesticity; in "Plump," the narrator dumps the dirty dishes in the crib. "Doll Parts" touches on Love's desire for power and the personal toll such a desire can take; "Softer, Softest" revisits the "retard girl," coupled with a reference to the classic outsider, the witch; on "Rock Star," the one-time riot grrrl supporter castigates the movement for what she perceives as its elitism. But, overall, Love's anger is balanced by solid music—compelling alternative rock with a hint of pop—luring the listener into a potent depiction of the dichotomy between femininity and feminism.

Early reviews of the album and profiles of the group persisted in describing Love in terms of "bad girl" archetypes, as *Spin* did: "Junkie. Star-fucker. Gold Digger." But an admitted dose of irony was present, and the articles invariably went on to lavish praise on the album. But the album's release was overshadowed by Cobain's suicide; his body was found at the couple's home on April 8, 1994, a mere four days before *Live Through This* was set to be released. Articles on the group now focused on the ironies of the album's title, and lyrics that seemed to portend doom ("I'm not psychic, but my lyrics are," Love told MTV); the tragedy was compounded when Kristen Pfaff died two months later of a drug overdose.

In August, Hole finally went on the road to promote their album, with new bass player Melissa Auf Der Maur, previously with the Canadian band Tinker. Yet the band's momentum had been curtailed; *Live Through This* would only reach number 52 in the charts (though it eventually went platinum), and the single "Doll Parts" reached number 58 (in the U.K., both the album and single were Top 20 hits). Aside from the compilations *Ask for It* (1995) and *My Body, The Hand Grenade* (1997), there would be no new music from Hole for another four years.

During the intervening period, Love revived her film career, moving from small parts in *Feeling Minnesota* and *Basquiat* to co-starring roles in Milos Forman's *The People vs. Larry Flynt* and *Man in the Moon*. Yet her credibility was questioned in both realms; despite the acclaim *Live Through This* received, unsubstantiated rumors surfaced that Cobain had helped substantially with the album, and the lack of new material was regarded as "proof" that Love was not capable of writing a song on her own. As for films, it was argued that her role as a drug addict in *Larry Flynt* (Love portrayed Flynt's wife, Althea) was not much of a stretch for someone who acknowledged her own problems with addiction. Finally, some saw her move from kinderwhore dresses to Versace gowns as indicative of her lack of commitment to music in the first place.

Additional controversy surrounded Love's behavior—she was embroiled in a seemingly never-ending series of lawsuits and received a one-year suspended sentence after punching Kathleen Hanna during the 1995 Lollapalooza tour, which featured Hole and Sonic Youth. Her outspokenness also extended to frequent online postings. "Courtney Love has been acting out again," wrote Karen Schoemer in a *Newsweek* article whose subheadline was "Courtney Love's bad-girl image threatens to overshadow her music."

Courtney Love
March 1999 at the Spokane Arena, Spokane, Washington,
Photo by Diana Adams

Finally, in 1998, *Celebrity Skin* was released. The music was far removed from the abrasive sounds on *Pretty on the Inside*. *Celebrity Skin* was an album unabashedly drenched in California sunshine, both in song titles ("Malibu") and the has-been Hollywood world of the title track; the emotive "Northern Star" was interpreted as a tribute to her late husband. Though the critical reception was not as strong as that for *Live Through This*, *Celebrity Skin* fared better in the charts, hitting the Top 10. But more upheaval was to come. Schemel left Hole at the time of *Celebrity Skin*'s release and was replaced by Samantha Maloney. In 2000, Universal sued the band for breach of contract, with Love promptly filing a countersuit the next year. The suit led to her championing recording artists' rights, contending that the contracts major labels offered were "unlawful" and "oppressive."

All the legal activity began to take a toll on Love's musical career, and, after touring in 1999, Hole's output was limited to the occasional single. In 2001, Love attempted to form a side project band, Bastard, with an all-female lineup that included Schemel, Louise Post of Veruca Salt, and Gina Crosley from Rockit Girl (Bjelland was asked to join but declined). The group fell apart before they could record what Love hoped would be "a South of France, AC/DC, fuck-off record." Nor did she revive Hole, announcing in May 2002 that the band was splitting up. She has since announced she is working with Schemel and Linda Perry (of 4 Non Blondes) on a new venture.

Like the punk explosion at the end of the '70s, riot grrrl added a welcome dose of energy to the music scene. Even articles that lumped different groups into one "angry grrrl bands" category nonetheless made it clear just how many female musicians were out there. Many who found the media attention intrusive later agreed that there had been some benefit. "Sure, it's really awful and frustrating when people who don't even know you are saying all this shit about you," Kathleen Hanna said in *Angry Women in Rock*. "But at the same time, people bought the record and paid attention to us. I feel really lucky that people listened to what I had to say." Revolution girl-style not only motivated another generation of young women musically, but it stressed the idea of self-sufficiency—unlike the Sex Pistols or the Clash, neither Bikini Kill nor Bratmobile signed to a major label. This message would reverberate even more strongly later in the decade.

11

New Perspectives

"Being a female musician gets easier year to year and then it falls back for a while. . . . I know every woman in the world has those days where they just sit and shudder because they know power can be taken away."
—Liz Phair, in *Grrrls: Viva Rock Divas*

On May 26, 1993, Liz Phair's debut album, *Exile in Guyville*, was released on the independent Matador label. The initial run was three thousand copies. But word quickly spread about the album, and the singer, whose frank depictions of love, sex, and relationships were delivered in a droll everywoman voice. Without tour support or much radio play (not too surprising since a number of the songs featured explicit language), sales eventually passed the half million mark. Critics adored Phair's audacity as much as her obvious musical strengths, while they tried to avoid sounding overly titillated. As *Billboard* loftily proclaimed, "Sexual awakening as both fact and poetic effigy has stoked the arts since the twinkling of human self-awareness." *Sassy* put it more simply: "Liz Phair is a total diva."

Phair was one of many female performers whose outspokenness, presented in a less confrontational fashion than that of the riot grrrl bands (and lacking the riot grrrls' more obvious feminist component), led to commercial success. Tori Amos and Alanis Morissette explored similar—if not as graphic—terrain in their music. Sarah McLachlan's outspokenness about the unfair treatment women performers received in comparison to men led her to create a festival that emphasized how unwarranted such treatment was. What was common to these, and other, performers was that women were increasingly giving voice to thoughts and ideas they would previously have kept to themselves.

Phair was born in 1967, in New Haven, Connecticut, and was raised by her adoptive parents in the Chicago suburb of Winnetka. She played piano as a child and took up the guitar in seventh grade, listening to music ranging from Joni Mitchell to the Beatles to the *Jesus Christ Superstar* soundtrack. Though she had (in her words) been "making up" songs since she was a child, she began seriously pursuing songwriting while studying art at Ohio's Oberlin College. Back in Chicago, after being encouraged by a friend, she recorded her songs at home and released them on a series of cassettes under the name *Girly Sound*. One such tape eventually made its way to Gerard Cosley, head of Matador. He signed Phair to the label in 1992.

Liz Phair
August 1999 at Pine Knob, Clarkston, Michigan,
Photo by Jennifer Jeffery

Phair set up the tracks on *Guyville* as a response to the Rolling Stones' 1972 album *Exile on Main Street*; as she explained to the *LA Weekly*, she went through the album writing each song from the perspective of the woman in the situation. Rarely had a female performer put her heart and soul on the line to the extent that Phair did on *Guyville*. But while hearing a woman detail her lust with unprecedented bluntness—few female singers offered themselves up as a "blow-job queen"—was indeed a barrier breaking move, Phair's depiction of desire was never one-sided. Coupled with the braggadocio of being available for rent "by the hour" was a recognition of the price women could pay for such "freedom." In "Fuck and Run," the narrator seemingly admits a lack of respect for *herself* the morning after a one-night stand; what had seemed a straightforward expression of desire only led to more complicated questions.

Guyville would go on to top several critics' polls, including *Village Voice*'s "Pazz & Jop" poll—the first time a woman had won the poll since 1974 (when Joni Mitchell was the winner). But Phair professed surprise that *Guyville* was considered so remarkable. "When people were exclaiming over my album, I thought, you've got to be kidding," she told *Harper's Bazaar*. "If this was the greatest thing that ever happened to a female, where *is* everybody?" She also seemed uneasy with the focus on the more sensational aspects of her work. "The only thing they care about is what it's like to be an upper-middle-class cute girl with smart parents singing dirty words," she told *Option*. "There's more pressure for me to be gregarious, social, cute, and fun than for me to be a great musician. I think that's sexism." And she was puzzled by the criticism she received for her cover shot on *Rolling Stone*'s October 6, 1994, "Women in Rock" issue, in which a vulnerable-looking Phair was pictured crouching down wearing a slip (quickly parodied on the cover of "Reverb," the music section of the *LA Weekly*, with Jon Spencer in a similar pose illustrating a "Men in Rock" feature). "No one was getting the point. . . . That's what I thought I looked pretty in," Phair later explained in an article that ran, with unintentional irony, in *Rolling Stone*'s next "Women in Rock" issue (November 13, 1997).

By the time Phair began recording her second album, Matador had signed a distribution deal with Atlantic, guaranteeing greater record distribution. But there were more profound changes in her personal life. She began a relationship with Jim Staskausas, a film editor who had worked on her videos; the two married in 1995 and had a son the following year. Perhaps as a result, *Whip-Smart*, released in 1994, had more romantic undertones than her previous album; instead of wondering how to get a relationship started, songs like "Jealousy" wondered how to keep one going.

Whip-Smart reached number 27 in the charts, but the reviews were not as strong as *Guyville*'s. Already there were suggestions she had "sold out." The backlash sent Phair into retreat. "I used to be a loud-mouthed girl on the scene," she said later. "Now I keep a really low profile and pretend to be nice and demure." Chronic stage fright kept Phair from performing extensively, and, in lieu of a new album, 1996 saw the release of the *Juvenilia* EP, consisting of songs from the *Girly Sound* tapes. *Whitechocolatespaceegg* was finally released in 1998, to more mixed reviews. It was a decidedly subdued work from someone who had previously worn her passion on her sleeve (even when giving in to her masochistic tendencies in "Johnny Feelgood," Phair seems somewhat detached) and only reached number 35 in the charts.

By the time of *Whitechocolatespaceegg*'s release, other female performers had pushed discussion of female sexuality to a new level in song. Tori Amos presented a sensual image not only in her music but also in the provocative way she played the piano. "Through Tori, the piano has become the weapon of power and passion that the electric guitar was for a previous generation," said Kalen Rogers in Amos's authorized biography. Amos herself said playing the piano was one of few ways she could express "passion without guilt."

Amos was born Myra Ellen Amos in North Carolina in 1963 and was raised in Maryland, the daughter of a Methodist minister. Her musical development was extremely precocious: she began playing piano at two and a half, was composing her own pieces by four, and at five won a scholarship to the Peabody Conservatory, part of Baltimore's Johns Hopkins University. But she also had an independent streak, and at eleven her scholarship to Peabody was not renewed; her teachers took exception to Amos's preference for playing by ear instead of learning to read music properly.

But Amos continued in music, singing in the church choir and later performing at clubs and lounges in the D.C./Baltimore area. Before leaving high school, she released her first single, "Baltimore"/"Walking with You," on her own MEA label (her initials). The A-side, co-written with her brother Mike, was a tribute to the Baltimore Orioles baseball team. At twenty-one, she moved to L.A. in search of a record deal. She also changed her first name to Tori, after a friend's date jokingly rechristened her.

Amos found work in L.A. clubs (and in a Kellogg's Corn Flakes commercial) and eventually signed with Atlantic Records in 1987. She agreed to submerge her unique style in favor of an allegedly more marketable "metal chick" image, becoming the lead singer for a faceless pseudo-metal band named Y Kant Tori Read. The band released one self-titled album in 1988 (produced by Joe Chiccarelli, who had recently worked with Pat Benatar), along with two singles. None made any commercial impact (Amos estimated the album sold a mere seven thousand copies). Critics added insult to injury in not only writing off the music but also taking potshots at the cover, which had Amos in typical metal babe garb and frizzed-out hairdo.

Disillusioned by the band's failure, Amos worked as a backing vocalist on such projects as Sandra Bernhard's live album *Without You I'm Nothing* and Ferron's *Phantom Center*. She also continued writing new material, and in February 1991 Atlantic sent her to England to work with their British office, East West Records. That summer, the film *Thelma & Louise* inspired Amos to write about her own rape in L.A. six years earlier. She performed the song, "Me and a Gun," the same day she wrote it, and it would become her first solo single, released that fall. The stark a cappella number made a strong impression. In *Melody Maker*, Billy Bragg chose it as Single of the Week, stating, "It's a great song and she delivers it perfectly. That sort of song is all about how you deliver it. Especially live, if you do it right you can silence an audience" (as Amos's live performances of the song invariably did). In 1994, Amos would co-found the organization RAINN (the Rape, Abuse and Incest National Network).

Little Earthquakes, released in 1992, initially drew comparisons to Kate Bush's work, due to Amos's high-pitched voice, introspective lyrics, and cover art echoing the U.S. cover of Bush's *Kick Inside* album (both featured the women crouched inside wooden boxes). But Amos soon developed her own rabidly devoted following. The pretty, melodic sound of her songs was often at odds with the lyrical sentiments, which explored troubled relationships, the search for identity, and the conflict between sexuality and Christian spirituality (on "Precious Things" she tells a lover who brings her to orgasm that it "don't make you Jesus"). Not every song dealt with weighty issues; "Happy Phantom" presented a breezy look at the afterlife.

Though *Little Earthquakes* received good critical notices, it only reached number 54 in the charts. Amos's U.S. breakthrough would not come until the release of *Under the Pink* in 1994, which reached number 12 in the charts and was more musically adventurous than its predecessor. "*Little Earthquakes* was the romance phase between me and the listeners," Amos told Kalen Rogers. "I knew I had to change direction because it was like,

Tori Amos
April 1998 at St. Andrews Hall, Detroit, Photo by Jennifer Jeffery

'Yeah, we've already seen you naked.' . . . So with *Under the Pink*, I put some clothes on."

But she continued to bare her feelings about the oppressiveness of religion. "God" dealt with "patriarchal religion and how it's just fucked the whole thing up" and featured a scratchy guitar line that threw some radio programmers who were not expecting such discordant sounds on a Tori Amos record. "Icicle" effortlessly conveyed a feeling of winter with its tinkling piano, while the lyrics captured a perfect image of the division between the sacred and the "profane": as the family prays downstairs, the narrator is in her bedroom masturbating.

Amos's playing style also raised eyebrows, due to her rhythmic undulations when she sat at the piano bench. "I don't play the piano, the piano plays me," she told *Q*. In *Women, Sex and Rock 'n' Roll* she expressed some irritation with people—especially women—who took offense at her performance style, "because I was making myself an object. But I didn't see myself as an object, this was how I felt good playing. . . . it is a very passionate thing."

On Amos's subsequent albums, she stretched herself musically. *Boys for Pele*, released in 1996, stripped away much of the orchestral backing on her previous records, with Amos playing harpsichord on a number of tracks; it became her highest charting album, reaching number 2. Though her personal life experienced some upheaval—the *Pele* tour exhausted her, she suffered a miscarriage, and she married her sound engineer—she nonetheless released two albums in close succession, *From the Choirgirl Hotel* (number 5) in 1998 and *To Venus and Back* (number 12) in 1999 (the latter a double album, one disc featuring studio recordings, the other a live album).

The next release, 2001's *Strange Little Girls*, was a covers album with a twist. Amos chose twelve songs, written by men, that she felt "could hold a different character, a female," as she explained to *Q*. The Boomtown Rats' "I Don't Like Mondays," based on a real life school shooting, became a poignant lullaby; Neil Young's "Heart of Gold" was transformed into a swirling squall of noise. But the album's most stunning track was "'97 Bonnie & Clyde," rapper Eminem's revenge fantasy about a man disposing of his murdered wife's body. In Amos's chilling rendition, she near-whispers the dark-humored lyrics over a subdued musical backing, and the track ends with the brutal finality of a coffin lid slamming down.

Alanis Morissette, whose commercial breakthrough came with the 1995 release of *Jagged Little Pill*, also raised the bar as far as expressing emotional angst was concerned. Morissette was born in 1974 in Ottawa, Canada, began playing the piano at age six, and at nine was writing songs. At ten, she landed a spot on the children's TV variety show *You Can't Do That on Television* and used the money she earned to record her first single, "Fate Stay with Me"/"Find the Right Man"—both Morissette originals. She eventually was signed by MCA Canada and in 1991 released her first album, *Alanis*. The album, ten tracks of upbeat dance-pop (Morissette co-writing all the songs), went on to sell over one hundred thousand copies, produced a Top 5 single, "Too Hot," and led to her winning a Juno Award for Most Promising Female Artist. The follow-up album, *Now Is the Time*, released in 1992, retread the same musical territory but did not fare as well, selling half as much as *Alanis* did.

Morissette had spent her entire professional life dealing with older people, a situation she began to find confining. "I had no real self-esteem because of being in an industry so immersed in what others thought I should be," she told *Billboard's* Timothy White. In order to develop her own identity she lived alone in Toronto and then moved to L.A. in 1994. There, MCA Publishing arranged a meeting with songwriter/producer Glen Ballard, who had worked with such artists as Aretha Franklin, Michael Jackson, and Paula Abdul. Despite the difference in age (Morissette was nineteen, Ballard forty-one), the two hit it off, and by the end of their first meeting they had written the song "Perfect." That summer, Morissette was signed by Madonna's label, Maverick.

Jagged Little Pill, Morissette's Maverick debut, was released in 1995, twelve days after her twenty-first birthday. The searing "You Oughta Know," the album's first single, introduced Morissette with a bang. In a bitter diatribe to a former lover, Morissette's vocal burned with rage, and the reference to oral sex attracted as much comment as Phair's brutally honest lyrics had. But for the first time in her career Morissette felt free to express her own feelings in her own way. "The focus for me [had been] entertaining people as opposed to sharing any revelations I had," she told *Rolling Stone*. Now it was time for Morissette to have her say. Songs like "Perfect" and "Right Through You" detailed the pressures of living up to other people's expectations, while "Forgiven" touched on the double standard, particularly as upheld in religion (Morissette was raised Catholic).

Jagged Little Pill went to number 1 and eventually sold twenty-eight million copies worldwide, making it the best-selling album by a solo female artist at the time, and the singles "Ironic" and "You Learn" followed the album into the Top 10. The album would also be nominated for six Grammys, winning four: Album of the Year, Best Rock Album, Best Rock Song, and Best Female Rock Vocal Performance (for "You Oughta Know"). Morissette would win five Juno Awards as well: Album of the Year, Rock Album of the Year, Female Vocalist of the Year, Songwriter of the Year (shared with Ballard), and Single of the Year (for "You Oughta Know").

At the same time, there were quibbles about Morissette's authenticity, especially when her "disco queen" days were rediscovered. *Entertainment Weekly* wrote that *Jagged Little Pill* came across as if it had been "pieced together with the help of a focus group." But critic Gina Arnold pointed out that many such criticisms came from male critics who perhaps felt threatened by Morissette's lyrics and therefore tried to dismiss her.

Morissette herself appeared to be wryly commenting on her angst-ridden reputation in the title of her next album, *Supposed Former Infatuation Junkie*, released in 1998. The songs again focused on the nature of unequal relationships—seemingly impossible to exist in Morissette's world without power struggles—but were set at a pitch less fraught with tension than in *Jagged Little Pill*. The sometimes brash rock on the former album was replaced by a musical richness and experimentation (on one song Morissette played the flute), with a heavy accent on Eastern-flavored rhythms and melodies.

The album again reached number 1, but with only a fraction of the sales of *Pill*. "I

think I might have been the only person who didn't care," she told *Q*. And though Morissette would release the album *Alanis Unplugged* in 1999, there would be no new material until 2002. The intervening years were taken up with touring (in 1999 she shared a bill with Tori Amos) and a return to acting: as "God" in a small role in 1999's *Dogma*, as one of many celebrity performers in the off-Broadway hit *The Vagina Monologues*, and as a guest star on the TV show *Sex in the City*.

Under Rug Swept, released in 2002, returned Morissette to the top of the charts; it was also the first album where she was the sole writer and producer. The album marked a return to the more straight-ahead rock sound of *Pill*, with the recurrent theme of being drawn to (or used by) the wrong man. Nowhere was this clearer than on "Hands Clean" (a Top 20 hit), which Morissette said was

Alanis Morissette
June 2000 at the opening of the Experience Music Project museum, Seattle, Photo by Gillian G. Gaar

based on a relationship she had had with an older man during her teens, who tried to pressure her into an experience in exchange for helping to further her career. "I felt at the time I had only two choices—I pick either working with this person or not doing music at all," she explained to *Newsweek*. Though the song lacks the knockout punch of "You Oughta Know," the bitterness is evident in verses sung from the man's point of view, dangling marriage as a possibility if the protégé can keep her weight down. Morissette might have achieved control over the direction of her career, but her music remained caught up in working through the troubling emotional circumstances of her past.

Sheryl Crow's persona was less tortured, and her more commercially oriented music made her a consistent hit-maker. Crow was born in 1962 in rural Missouri: "Farmland. Three stop lights and a McDonald's," as she told *Q*. Her parents performed in an amateur swing band (her father played trumpet, her mother sang), and Crow also listened to artists ranging from the Rolling Stones and Rod Stewart to Billie Holiday and Bessie Smith. She began singing in rock bands in her teens, playing synthesizer and guitar. After graduating from the University of Missouri with a degree in classical piano, Crow taught music at an elementary school in St. Louis and played with bands in the evening. But when her fiancé pressured her to give up music, Crow broke off the engagement. She used the money she had earned singing on a McDonald's commercial to move to L.A. in 1986, and decided to pursue a career as a musician.

In L.A., Crow sang on commercial jingles while working as a waitress. She then won a spot as a backup singer on Michael's Jackson's 1987-89 *Bad* tour, not only singing backup but also singing a duet with Jackson on his hit "I Just Can't Stop Loving You." She also learned firsthand about the hazards of celebrity life when the tabloid *Globe* incorrectly reported that Crow was Jackson's girlfriend and had given birth to his child.

Back in L.A., Crow continued working as a backup singer for a wide range of artists, including Joe Cocker, Rod Stewart, and Don Henley. In 1991, Crow met producer Hugh Padgham at a party and later sent him a demo. Padgham, then working at A&M, helped Crow get signed to the label; the two of them worked together on her first album. But the tracks proved too slick for Crow's liking, and the entire album was scrapped.

A new direction came in the form of a request asking Crow to join a weekly jam session, dubbed the Tuesday Night Music Club, held at producer Bill Bottrell's house. Crow's then-boyfriend, Kevin Gilbert, was part of the all-male group and suggested they invite Crow to add some "female energy." Crow turned up, and the jams evolved into sessions for what would become Crow's debut, *Tuesday Night Music Club*, released in fall 1993.

The album's down-home style was decidedly appealing—the music encyclopedia

Rock: The Rough Guide giving it the bizarre compliment "So laid-back you could do your ironing on it"—and best captured on "All I Wanna Do," a jovial, relaxed number celebrating the joys of late-night (or early-morning) drinking. But there was a darker side to the good spirits as well; "What I Can Do For You" depicts sexual harassment that was not hard to imagine Crow experiencing as an aspiring musician. But she never elaborated on the song's inspiration (though "The Na-Na Song," also on the album, did name a high-profile manager), simply telling *Request*, "Anybody who's in the position of having a carrot dangled in front of them by somebody who's in a position of power in one way or another has to deal with the prospect of being threatened into doing something they don't want to do."

But the album was not an immediate success, so Crow hit the road for the better part of two years. An opening slot on the Eagles' reunion tour and an appearance at the 1994 Woodstock as one of the few female acts won her greater exposure, and the album began to climb the charts, eventually peaking at number 3 and selling over nine million copies worldwide. She also had two Top 5 hits with "All I Wanna Do" and "Strong Enough" ("Can't Cry Anymore" also hit the Top 40), and won three Grammy awards: for Best New Artist and Record of the Year and Best Female Pop Vocal Performance (for "All I Wanna Do").

Unfortunately, the album's success led to Crow having a falling out with her musicians, who felt they had not received enough credit for their contributions to the album and were irritated that Crow chose not to use them in her touring band. Though Crow attributed the musicians' complaints to jealousy, feelings were further strained by the suicide of friend John O'Brien, whose book *Leaving Las Vegas* had inspired the song on *Tuesday Night Music Club* of the same name, and the death of Kevin Gilbert due to auto-erotic asphyxiation. Though Crow began work on her second album with Bottrell, an argument on the second day led to his quitting the sessions.

Crow ended up producing the entire album herself (and writing or co-writing all the songs, as she had on the first album), in part as a response to "questions out there about my credibility." And there was no doubt who the creative force was behind the album simply titled *Sheryl Crow*, released in 1996. The album had a tougher sound, and there was a greater depth to the material. "If It Makes You Happy" catches a relationship on an off day, and despite the freedom implied in the title "Everyday Is a Winding Road," an uncertainty about the journey lurked underneath.

Both songs were Top 20 hits, and the album reached number 6 (though it ended up being banned by Wal-Mart for the song "Love Is a Good Thing," which had a line about children committing murder with guns bought at the chainstore). But the album still sold over three million copies, and Crow won two more Grammys: for Best Rock

Album and Best Female Rock Vocal Performance (for "If It Makes You Happy"). *The Globe Sessions*, released in 1998, continued her Grammy winning streak, netting her an award for Best Rock Album. The polished work featured a wider range of instrumentation (primarily strings), a song by Bob Dylan, "Mississippi," and a cover of Guns n' Roses' "Sweet Child o' Mine."

Sheryl Crow and Friends: Live from Central Park followed in 1999 (her "friends" included the Dixie Chicks, Chrissie Hynde, Eric Clapton, and Keith Richards). But the making of her next studio album proved to be a struggle, with Crow once again working on material she eventually abandoned as being too slick. Following what she described as a "meltdown," due in part to the breakup of her relationship with actor Owen Wilson (with whom she appeared in the 1999 film *The Minus Man*), Crow became determined to make the kind of record she would enjoy.

Her desire to stay true to herself paid off when *C'mon, C'mon*, released in 2002, became her highest charting album, debuting at number 2. The album was widely acclaimed as one of her strongest and attracted additional attention for its guest performers, including Stevie Nicks, Liz Phair, and actress Gwyneth Paltrow. Even so, a hint of double standard remained in some critics' awe that a forty-year-old woman was still capable of rocking. (As Kim Gordon had pointed out to Liz Evans, "No one bases Neil Young's music on his age, they just say he's getting better.") Crow herself admitted to *Entertainment Weekly* that she had previously avoided wearing revealing outfits "because of not wanting people to perceive me as less than credible." But after "getting into the fact that that *is* a side of my personality," *C'mon, C'mon*'s artwork (and accompanying videos) featured Crow in a bikini. Crow has also become involved in the fight for performing artists' rights, testifying in May 2000 before the House Judiciary Subcommittee on Courts, the Internet and Intellectual Property on copyright issues.

Sarah McLachlan trod an even more conventional path than Crow's good-time-girl one, carrying on the melodic singer-songwriter tradition. But she would have a decidedly unconventional impact on the music industry when she launched the all-female Lilith Fair music festival in 1997, proving to the skeptical that not only would audiences pay to see a show with more than one female act on the bill, but that such a bill could also be extremely commercially successful.

McLachlan was born in Halifax, Nova Scotia, in 1968; her mother, in college at the time, gave her up for adoption (the two later met when McLachlan was a teenager). McLachlan took piano, guitar, and voice lessons as a child. "I always sang," she later told *Us*. "It was my security blanket." While in high school, she began singing with the band October Game, and when she was seventeen the Vancouver, B.C., label Nettwerk offered her a solo deal. Her parents, concerned about the presumed "wildness" of the rock & roll lifestyle, initially said no ("The only thing they'd ever heard about rock & roll was when someone OD'd," McLachlan explained to *Rolling Stone*). But two years later the label approached her again, and this time McLachlan accepted. She moved to Vancouver in late 1987, and her debut album, *Touch*, was released the following year.

Though guitar was her primary instrument onstage, McLachlan played piano on her debut and revealed an impressive vocal range. The album went gold in Canada and was picked up for distribution by Arista, which reissued it the following year. *Solace*, released in 1991, displayed a growing confidence, and McLachlan credited her producer, Pierre Marchand, with helping her develop her musical vision (though the fact that the two were romantically involved for a time did add its share of difficulties).

McLachlan's breakthrough to a larger audience began with the release of *Fumbling Towards Ecstasy* in 1993. Prior to recording the album, McLachlan had traveled to Cambodia and Thailand to work on a documentary about poverty and child prostitution in the area, and the experience inspired a number of the songs and, perhaps, colored the album with a wash of melancholy. *Fumbling* reached number 50 in the U.S. and eventually sold over three million copies.

The single "Possession," which peaked at number 73, would raise McLachlan's profile for non-musical reasons as well. The intense, sweeping love song was based on McLachlan's real life experiences with Uwe Vandrei, a computer programmer from Ottawa who had sent McLachlan hundreds of letters over the previous years. When "Possession" was released, he filed suit against McLachlan, saying the song's lyrics had been taken from his letters and asking for a co-writing credit and $250,000 in damages. Before the suit could come to trial, Vandrei killed himself (in September 1994). McLachlan never elaborated on her own feelings about the situation but did say that after *Fumbling*'s release she suffered an extreme case of writer's block. It would be almost four years before she released a new album. *The Freedom Sessions* in 1995 contained alternate versions of tracks from *Fumbling*, and *Rarities, B-Sides, and Other Stuff*, released in 1996, was another collection of previously released material.

But *Fumbling*'s release also brought home something she later admitted she never had thought much about: the bias against women in the music industry. *Fumbling* was released at the same time as Tori Amos's *Under the Pink*, and, McLachlan told *Newsweek*, she was surprised to find herself "constantly getting pitted against her. Radio said, 'We added Tori this week, so we can't add you.' They never said 'We added Pearl Jam, so we can't add Nirvana.'" She was further surprised when her suggestion that she tour with singer-songwriter Paula Cole was discouraged. No one, a promoter told her, would pay to see two women on the same bill.

"I think a lot of people were living by these old rules that didn't really apply anymore," she said later, "without really questioning what was coming out of their mouth, and how ludicrous it was to say, 'Oh, you don't want to put two women on the same bill.' What the hell does that mean? It just doesn't make any sense." Ultimately, McLachlan was able to get Cole on her tour, but the confrontation inspired her to take the idea one step further: presenting an entire day of female artists. What McLachlan first jokingly referred to as "girlapalooza" eventually became Lilith Fair.

The first Lilith Fair shows were held in summer 1996, limited to four to test the concept. In addition to McLachlan, they also featured artists like Patti Smith, Suzanne Vega, Lisa Loeb, and Aimee Mann. The shows were sellouts, and McLachlan announced Lilith Fair would launch a full-scale tour the following summer. Opening day was set for July 5, 1997, at the Gorge, a venue outside the small town of George, Washington.

McLachlan headlined all of Lilith's thirty-two dates, the rest of the bill changing throughout the tour. The first year featured Jewel, Tracy Chapman, Suzanne Vega, Emmylou Harris, the Indigo Girls, Fiona Apple, Juliana Hatfield, Jill Sobule, and Kinnie Starr, among others. Two smaller stages featured local and lesser-known artists (with over 700 vying for 250 slots). "Five years ago, if we'd tried to do something like this, the promoters would've laughed at us," McLachlan said at Lilith's first press conference. "And there were a few promoters at the beginning of this tour who were a bit hesitant to become involved. But they actually, a few months in, phoned up my agent and apologized for their hesitance!"

While an all-day festival of women artists was not a new idea, Lilith Fair did mark the first time such an event toured—and drew such widespread mainstream attention. From the beginning, McLachlan found herself placed in a defensive position for having the "courage" to put on an all-female show. Two decades earlier, the Deadly Nightshade's Pamela Brandt had written that "women's music" meant "lesbian music" in most people's minds, and, if few of Lilith's detractors dared broach the "l-word," there was still a perception—even among some of the performers—that a tour so supportive of women must be anti-male. "'Women's music' suggests singers who hate men," Mary Chapin Carpenter told the *New York Times*. "The last thing I wanted to be associated with is a festival that is perceived as man bashing." McLachlan herself was pushed to say on more than one occasion "I'm not a man hater."

The "anti-male" charge was a curious one, as most Lilith artists were backed by all-male bands. But McLachlan also caught flak for not being feminist enough. Though the tour took its name from the woman who, according to Jewish tradition, had been Adam's wife before Eve and left because she refused to be subservient to him (McLachlan referred to her as "perhaps the world's first feminist!"), McLachlan told

Natalie Merchant, Sarah McLachlan, Sinéad O'Connor
June 1998 at Lilith Fair, Civic Stadium, Portland, Oregon, Photo by Diana Adams

Billboard the tour was "not a feminist platform." And her comment in *Elle* that "Some radical feminist groups are so far out there, they would love to chop every man's dick off" drew criticism from *Ms.* that she was reinforcing "narrow, negative assumptions about what feminism means." "Absolutely, I'm a feminist," she responded in the book *From Lilith to Lilith Fair*. "Yet many people still equate feminism with man-hating. I tried to diffuse that thinking . . . but I can't escape what many people still believe it to be."

Others found fault with the artists on the bill, who, especially in the first year, tended to be melodic singer-songwriters. The critics asserted that by keeping to a neo-folkie acoustic format Lilith was reaffirming stereotypes about women-in-rock, not breaking them. McLachlan said she had extended offers to "harder-edged artists" and had not been able to get everyone she wanted (subsequent years would present a more diverse array of performers). The nitpicking made little difference to the general public. Most Lilith shows sold out, and the tour was the most popular of the summer, grossing over fifteen million dollars (a dollar from each ticket sale was donated to charity).

McLachlan timed the first Lilith tour to coincide with the release of her new album, *Surfacing*. It became her highest charting album to date, debuting at number 2 and selling over seven million copies. The album also produced four Top 40 hits (including the

Top 5 "Adia" and "Angel"). The haunting "Building a Mystery" and "Last Dance" would win Grammys for Best Female Pop Vocal Performance and Best Pop Instrumental Performance, respectively. McLachlan's next release was the live album *Mirrorball* in 1999; the album reached number 3, and the track "I Will Remember You" won a Grammy for Best Female Pop Vocal Performance. McLachlan then took a break from performing, giving birth to a daughter in 2002.

Lilith Fair raised the profile of other artists as well. When *Time* magazine did a cover story on the first Lilith Fair, Jewel's picture was chosen for the cover, with the headline "Jewel and the Gang" (McLachlan appeared on the cover of *Time*'s Canadian edition). Jewel's first album, *Pieces of You*, released in 1995, had taken a while to catch on. Only her constant touring led to the single "Who Will Save Your Soul" finally reaching number 11 on the charts, followed by two more singles and the album itself hitting the Top 10. By then, the country was charmed by the life story Jewel joked had become a "cartoon": GIRL RAISED BY WOLVES IN ALASKAN MUD HUT MOVES INTO CAR, ROCKETS OVERNIGHT TO FREAKISH STAR STATUS!

Jewel was born Jewel Kilcher in 1974 in Utah and raised in Homer, Alaska, in a log cabin with no running water. She began performing as a child in local villages with her parents and, after her parents' divorce, with her father, an experience that helped her learn how to both perfect her yodel and deal with hecklers. She won a partial scholarship to Michigan's prestigious Interlochen Fine Arts Academy (earning the rest of the tuition by putting on a benefit show in Homer). At Interlochen she learned to play guitar, and began writing songs, including "Who Will Save Your Soul." After graduation, she moved to San Diego, working at various low-paying jobs while living in her van.

She eventually landed a regular spot at the Innerchange coffeehouse, where word of mouth spread, and at nineteen she signed with Atlantic. The songs on *Pieces of You*, partially recorded at the Innerchange, revealed an artist with an astonishingly mature voice for her age, and one brave enough to actually perform a song called "I'm Sensitive." A brief romance with actor Sean Penn, who saw Jewel perform on *Late Night with Conan O'Brien*, heightened her profile; endless touring led to her breakthrough. *Pieces of You* eventually sold eleven million copies.

Along the way, Jewel found herself "typified as this Pollyanna neohippie" because of her wide-ranging discussions in interviews that touched upon everything from the natural beauty of Alaska to the importance of optimism. But she was not starry-eyed about her own work, going so far as to dismiss *Pieces of You* as "embarrassing." In 1998, she published a book of poetry, *A Night Without Armor*, and released the album *Spirit*, which was indeed a richer record than its predecessor, featuring the touching duet "This Little Bird," with Jewel harmonizing to her mother's lead vocal. After the release of *Joy: A Holiday Collection* in 1999, the work stresses of the previous year led Jewel to consider not recording again, and her next projects were not music-related. She made her film debut in *Ride With the Devil* in 1999, and her autobiography, *Chasing Down the Dawn*, was published in 2000. But she eventually returned to recording and released *This Way* in 2001.

In previous decades, women-in-rock articles had tended to surface every few years. But in the '90s, they were published consistently. After the rise of riot grrrl and "angry girl bands" in the early '90s, the media would find some category into which to push female performers, from the sexually outspoken camp (including Liz Phair and Alanis Morissette) to the so-called "quiet grrrls" of Lilith Fair.

Some performers were caught between trends but were nonetheless described as indicative of the new generation of women-in-rock. Mixed-gender bands like Veruca Salt (named after the spoiled rich girl in Roald Dahl's children's book *Charlie and the Chocolate Factory*) and Britain's Echobelly and Elastica enjoyed a brief popularity with their updated brand of power-pop (the latter two were far more successful in the U.K.). The all-female, New York–based Luscious Jackson were one of the first groups signed to the Beastie Boys' Grand Royal label (drummer Kate Schellenbach had played drums in the Beastie's original lineup), and they released four albums of rock-tinged hip hop that garnered critical praise on both sides of the Atlantic.

The music of PJ Harvey and Björk was more idiosyncratic, and neither artist rested easily in a women-in-rock story. Harvey in particular shied away from labels of any kind, projecting a fierce individuality as she toyed with the visual expectations a female artist faced. Born Polly Jean Harvey in 1969, Harvey was raised on a sheep farm near Yeovil, a small town of six hundred in Dorset, England. Harvey's mother, a sculptor, booked bands for the local pub; she bought Harvey a saxophone and encouraged her to play with the visiting musicians. Harvey also learned guitar and grew up absorbing the music from her parents' record collection—blues, classic artists like the Rolling Stones, Jimi Hendrix, and Bob Dylan and Captain Beefheart, crediting the latter two as her strongest influences.

Harvey joined her first band, an eight-member instrumental group called Boulogne, at fifteen. She then formed the folk trio Polekats, joined Automatic Dlamini (on guitar, sax, and backing vocals) in July 1988, and sang on recordings by Grape and Family Cat as well. Harvey had also been writing her own material and was anxious to have her own outlet; by 1991, she had joined forces with bassist Ian Olliver and drummer Rob Ellis, both Automatic Dlamini members, and formed the trio PJ Harvey. A demo tape got the group a deal with Too Pure Records in London, and their first single, "Dress," was released in the fall of 1991.

The single shot up the U.K. indie charts to number 3. Though the lyrics had Harvey ostensibly considering how to dress to please her man, never had donning a piece of clothing sounded so menacing, the rolling drums, insistent rhythms, and savagely played strings (including Harvey on violin) conjuring up a sound the *New Musical Express* referred to as "Sex and bile and rock and roll." The follow-up single, "Sheela-Na-Gig" (with Olliver replaced by Stephen Vaughan), released in February 1992, added to Harvey's acclaim, topping the indie charts and edging into the national charts at number 69. Both songs appeared on Harvey's debut album, *Dry*, which entered the U.K. charts at number 11.

The provocative nature of Harvey's songs and her confrontational appearance (either severely dressed in black or naked, as on the back cover of *Dry* and the cover of *NME*) led people to wonder if she was making a "feminist statement." It was a term she rejected. "I don't think of myself as a feminist and I don't like that word. I'm not conscious of doing anything as a *woman*, it's just me, it's not because I'm female," she told *Melody Maker*. That she professed to be unaware of "doing anything as a woman" was a somewhat disingenuous remark, as a quotation from the same article makes clear: "The things I'm singing—I can't think of any man singing an equivalent." Undoubtedly part of the reason she pulled away from such labeling was her desire to not be pigeonholed.

She used this rationale to explain the creation of her second album, *Rid of Me*, released in 1993. "I didn't want to be packaged into some neat category by my record label," she told *Q*. "I wanted to show them that I had very strong opinions of what I wanted to do and this was the way I was going to do it." Island had hoped for a radio-friendly single to help break Harvey in America, but *Rid of Me*, produced by Steve Albini (Harvey had liked his work with the Pixies), was altogether too harsh to receive much airplay. The title track presented a nightmare scenario, with the narrator literally binding her lover to her, making a vow of undying love a frightening threat, and the rest of the album (as evidenced in titles like "Rub 'Til It Bleeds") was equally abrasive. On "Man-Size Sextet," Harvey whispered about her prowess against a musical backing of violins that could have been drawn from a horror film; her "50 Ft. Queenie" stomps around the countryside with glee. Harvey's original versions of the songs were released later that year on the album *4-Track Demos*.

Rid of Me did not break Harvey in America (the album peaked at number 158 U.S., number 3 U.K.), but it did help build her audience, and she continued to receive great critical acclaim. Having gone as far as she felt she could go with a trio, Harvey broke up her band (though as a solo artist she would continue to be billed as PJ Harvey) and stepped up to co-producing her next album, *To Bring You My Love*, released in 1995. On much of the album Harvey growled like the blues singers she listened to as a child, and

PJ Harvey
October 1998 at the Showbox, Seattle,
Photo by Diana Adams

her new look was just as striking. The black-and-white cover of *Rid of Me* was replaced by a full color shot of Harvey lying in a pool of water in a red dress, hair swirling around her. Her stage outfits—black clothes and boots exchanged for slinky gowns, heels, and feather boas—seemed to both parody and celebrate the allure of glamour. A photo spread in *Q* from this period has Harvey mixing and matching male and female attire—a black bra, heels, and heavy eye make-up with a man's undershirt (a pack of Marlboros tucked in the sleeve), jockey shorts, and baseball cap—creating a look that was both disturbing and sexy.

Harvey would later rein in the more outlandish aspects of her appearance, feeling the look was overshadowing her music. Before the release of her next album, Harvey took time out to work with other artists, including Nick Cave, with whom she was also romantically involved, and Tricky. She also worked with John Parish (another Automatic Dlamini alum who had appeared on *To Bring You My Love*) on *Dance Hall at Louse Point* (1996), credited to both musicians and featuring Harvey's interpretation of Peggy Lee's "Is That All There Is?" But personal problems, including the end of her relationship with Cave, led Harvey to stop work on her fifth album for over a year. She even considered giving up music; "I was so confused that I didn't want to deal with anything anymore. I wanted to abandon everything," she later told *Q*. But she eventually returned to the studio, and her subsequent albums showed her continuing to experiment musically. *Is This Desire?*, released in 1998, was, in places, more subdued than her previous albums, while *Stories from the City, Stories from the Sea,* released in 2000, was her most straight-ahead rock album to date.

Björk similarly resisted easy categorization. She was born Björk Gumundsdóttir (dropping her last name when she joined the Sugarcubes in the mid-'80s) in 1965 in Reykjavik, Iceland, and was raised in a communal household, where the bohemian atmosphere was enlivened by music (her stepfather played guitar, and her mother was an artist). Björk's mother later said Björk started singing when she was seven months old; when she enrolled in music school, she studied piano, flute, and recorder. In 1977, her teachers submitted a tape of Björk singing "I Love to Love" (a number 1 U.K. hit for Tina Charles in 1976) to Iceland's Radio 1, where the song not only aired but led to a record deal with Iceland label Falkkin. *Björk* was subsequently released in December 1977, its cover designed by Björk's mother and featuring her stepfather on guitar. Along with covers of the Beatles' "Fool on the Hill," Stevie Wonder's "Your Kiss Is Sweet," and Melanie's "Christopher Robin," the album also featured a Björk original, "Jóhannes Kjarval" (an Icelandic painter).

Two years later, Björk joined her first band, the all-female Spit & Snot, playing drums. Throughout the '80s, Björk performed with numerous groups (some, like Jam 80, lasting for one gig), in roles ranging from backing vocalist to drummer and clarinet player. Tappi Tikarrass made a more lasting impression by releasing two albums and appearing on various compilations. Björk and two of the band's members then formed Kukl ("Witch"), described by Björk as "punk and literature, with a surrealist sprinkle on it." The group released two albums before splitting in 1986, the same year Björk gave birth to her son (she and her husband later divorced).

After Kukl's split, Björk and some of the band's members then formed the Sugarcubes, who released their first single, "Birthday," in Iceland in October 1986. When released in the U.K. the following year, the mix of cool rock and Björk's high-pitched vocals (which trilled and growled in equal measure) received rave reviews, as did the band's snappy, sharp first album, *Life's Too Good,* released in 1988, which peaked at number 54. But though the Sugarcubes were a critical success in the U.S. (where they were released on Elektra), commercially the group fared better overseas. All three of the band's albums (including 1989's *Here Today, Tomorrow, Next Week!* and 1992's *Stick Around for Joy*) would reach the Top 20 in the U.K., while in the U.S. no album charted higher than *Life's Too Good.* The group would eventually disband after the release of *Stick Around for Joy.*

By then, Björk was already working on side projects, recording an album with Icelandic jazz group Trio Gudmundar Ingolfssonar, *Gling-Gló,* released in 1990. She was also increasingly anxious to record her own material. "I wrote a lot by myself in the

Sugarcubes," she told *Mojo Collections*, "working on [the songs] outside the band but never bringing them to rehearsals because that was not part of the punk ethic."

Björk saw the Sugarcubes' split as an opportunity to start with a clean slate, and she moved to London and immersed herself in the city's vibrant dance culture. She sang on two tracks on the 1991 album *Ex:El* by acid-house pioneers 808 State, and then hooked up with Nellee Hooper (of dance music bands Massive Attack and Soul II Soul), who produced *Debut*, released in 1993. The album entered the U.K. charts at number 3 and received many accolades; *NME* named it Album of the Year, and Björk would win Best Newcomer and Best International Female Solo artist (an award she would win the next two years as well) at the BRIT Awards, the U.K. equivalent of the Grammys.

Björk's singles did equally well in the U.K., while stateside only "Big Time Sensuality" reached the Top 100 (*Debut* peaked at number 61). But her records would do well on the U.S. club and dance charts, not surprising given her penchant for offering remixes of her work (1997's *Telegram* solely featured remixes of songs on the previous album, 1995's *Post*). Subsequent records featured collaborations with Tricky, Mark Bell of techno act LFO, and electronic-dance duo Matmos, with Björk herself becoming one of the few women involved in electronic music.

Björk seemed to view the disparity as something "natural." "Doing [dance] beats, I think, it's quite a male thing," she told *URB*. "I'm not surprised if that's related to gender. . . . I think there's a biological reason why guys provide beats and girls provide soul." Yet Björk apparently transcended the very limitations she described, writing or co-writing all the original songs on her albums and graduating from co-producer to sole producer on 2001's *Vespertine*. And though she disparaged what she called "modern feminism" in interviews, she also acknowledged the need for women to become empowered. Asked if she agreed with women-only shows, she told *Melody Maker*, "I think that's very stupid. But it's something you have to go through. I remember a period in my life when I only wanted to be around women. . . . But that *should* only be the beginning. It should lead you to something else."

Björk's other albums have included 1997's *Homogenic* (which reached number 28) and 2000's *Selmasongs*, her soundtrack for the film *Dancer in the Dark*, in which she also starred (her character's name being "Selma"). Björk won Best Actress honors at the Cannes Film Festival in 2000 for her stunning performance as a Czech immigrant in early '60s rural America, slowly going blind, who occasionally escapes the grimness of her life by reimagining her circumstances in lavish musical terms. Yet she found the experience so stressful she afterward announced she would never act in a film again (her previous film appearances included the dark fairytale *The Juniper Tree* (1987) and a cameo in *Ready to Wear* [1994]). She had also disliked some critics' perception of her as being as guileless in real life as "Selma" was in the film, an extension of the "elfin" tag she had been given since emerging as a solo star in her own right. "People see the kid in me," she told *Rolling Stone.* "They think I'm innocent and naïve and all those things, but being organized and hardworking is completely second nature to me."

An increasing number of black female artists were also finding great success during the decade, both breaking new ground musically and achieving sales in record numbers. Mary J. Blige's mix of smooth vocals over a bed of dance beats gave her a broad appeal; she was eventually dubbed "the queen of hip-hop soul." Though her initial sales were stronger on the R&B charts, she soon crossed over to more widespread success.

Blige was born in the Bronx in 1971 and spent a few years in Georgia before returning with her mother and sister to Yonkers, New York. Blige had begun singing in church and recorded her first demo, a cover of Anita Baker's "Caught Up in the Rapture," at a karaoke studio in a shopping mall at age sixteen. Blige's stepfather passed on the tape to Andre Harrell at Uptown Records, an MCA subsidiary, who signed her to the label. She began working with producer Sean "Puffy" Combs on her debut album, *What's the 411?*, released in 1992.

The album's first single, the love song "You Remind Me" (also featured in the film *Strictly Business*), featured a warm, crooning vocal from Blige, while the underlying beat kept toes tapping—a mix featured on the rest of the album's tracks. The song and album both topped the R&B charts (the single reached the Top 30 on the pop charts, the album number 6), and album sales would surpass three million copies. A remixed version of the album was released in 1993.

Blige later said the sudden success hit her hard. As a result, Angelo Ellerbee, president of Blige's PR firm Double XXposure, had her attend an artist development course that, she told *VIBE*, "gave me a totally new kind of light." Her new attitude was seemingly reflected on 1994's *My Life* (number 1 R&B, number 7 pop) due to tracks with names like "Be Happy" and a number of love songs. But she later referred to the record as a "cry for help," reflecting the turbulence in her life: the end of her relationship with Jodeci's K-Ci, the subject of *My Life's* love songs, and the end of her professional relationship with Combs.

But there were positive developments as well. She appeared with Method Man on the Ashford and Simpson medley "I'll Be There for You"–"You're All I Need to Get By," which won a Grammy for Best Rap Performance by a Duo or Group. In 1997, *Share My World*, her first collaboration with producers Jimmy Jam and Terry Lewis (who had also worked with Janet Jackson), topped the pop and R&B charts. Her next album of new material, 1999's *Mary* (following a live album released in 1998), moved even closer to pop and saw Blige working with such diverse performers as Lauryn Hill (who wrote, produced, and sang backup on "All That I Can Say"), Aretha Franklin, Sir Elton John, and Eric Clapton. She returned to her earlier hip-hop style on 2001's *No More Drama*, crediting her Christian faith with keeping her grounded, along with a newfound faith in herself. "You'll never survive being weak as a woman in this business," she told *VIBE*. "Because it's dominated by men."

The success of En Vogue and TLC showed that the girl group tradition established in the late '50s was still very commercially viable. En Vogue was assembled by producers Denzil Foster and Thomas McElroy, who worked with acts like Tony! Toni! Toné! and the Timex Social Club and were themselves former members of Club Nouveau. The group, chosen through auditions in 1988, included Terry Ellis (born 1966), Cindy Herron (an actor and a former Miss Black California, born 1965), Maxine Jones (born 1966), and Dawn Robinson (born 1968). The group was originally called For You but was credited as Vogue when they performed two songs on Foster and McElroy's 1988 concept album *FM2*. After the album's release, the name was changed to En Vogue. And as Janine Coveney observed in the liner notes of a greatest hits collection, "En Vogue was genetically engineered to win."

The group's first album, *Born to Sing*, was released in 1990 and only reached number 21 on the pop charts (number 3 R&B). But the success of the singles "Hold On" and "Lies," which both topped the R&B charts (and reached number 2 and number 38, respectively, on the pop charts) helped push the album to platinum status. The group's blend of R&B and pop was bolstered by rich harmonies, with a little dash of sass— "Lies" drew a comparison between lying politicians and husbands. En Vogue's big breakthrough came in 1992 with *Funky Divas*, which reached number 8, spawned three Top 10 singles, and sold over three million copies. As the album's title suggested, the music had a tougher sound. In particular, "Free Your Mind" (a Top 10 pop hit) was a feisty, aggressive attack on discrimination set to a solid rock beat.

In 1993, the group released *Runaway Love* (with half of its tracks remixes of songs from *Divas*) and provided backup vocals on Salt-N-Pepa's Top 10 hit "Whatta Man." Robinson left the group as they were recording their third album, but the remaining members continued as a trio with 1997's *EV3*, another Top 10 platinum seller that produced three more Top 40 singles, including the number 2 hit "Don't Let Go (Love)." But the group's fortunes sagged after Robinson's departure; 2000's *Masterpiece Theater* peaked at number 67.

TLC was another group put together by a producer with an eye toward the charts. But unlike the sophisticated En Vogue with their sleek designer wear, TLC initially dressed in baggy trousers and t-shirts, "accessorized" with pinned-on condom packets, the group's way of promoting safe sex (Lisa Lopes's nickname—"Left Eye"—came from her habit of taping a condom over the left eye of her glasses). The members were also more involved in their career (En Vogue rarely made any songwriting contributions to their material), and record sales of over twenty-eight million made TLC one of the best-selling female groups of all time.

TLC was formed in 1991 by producer/singer/songwriter Perri "Pebbles" McKissack, who was looking for artists to sign to LaFace Records, the Atlanta-based label run by her then-husband, L. A. Reid. Tionne Watkins (born 1970) and Lopes (born 1971) were already friends (having met at an audition for another girl group) when they met McKissack outside an Atlanta hair salon. The trio was rounded out by Crystal Jones, who was later dropped in favor of Rozonda "Chilli" Thomas (born 1971).

The group worked with several producers on their first album, *Oooooohhh . . . On the TLC Tip*, released in 1992, but made their own contributions as well. Lopes was credited as co-writer on more than half of the album's tracks, the group had jointly written "Das Da Way We Like 'Em," and Watkins helped choreograph the group's early videos. She also put together the group's original spunky homegirl look. "We made it okay to dress baggy and be respected as a woman and still be feminine," she told *VIBE*. But they also poked fun at their look on the opening track of *Oooooohhh*, in which a male voiceover writes off their fashion sense as "just one of those black things . . . they don't really look like women."

After the spoken intro, *Oooooohhh* kicks off in fine style with "Ain't 2 Proud 2 Beg," which, despite the submissive connotations of the title, was actually a fierce demand for satisfaction (with a subtle allusion to oral sex). The song was also the album's first single and reached number 6. "Baby-Baby-Baby," the album's next single (and a number 2 hit), was equally forthright in its expectations of a lover, if the musical mood was mellower. The third single (and another Top 10 hit), "What About Your Friends," was a more contemplative number that had the group wondering if their friends would remain loyal now that the group's financial status had changed—a bold claim for a debut album.

But it was a claim that would prove true soon enough. *Oooooohhh* was an immediate success, reaching number 14 in the charts and selling over four million copies. TLC's second album, *CrazySexyCool*, released in 1994, was even more successful, reaching number 3, producing four Top 10 singles, and selling over ten million copies. The title referred to different aspects of the female personality (an idea conceived by Lopes), and the musical style was much more soulful in comparison to the playful spirits of *Oooooohhh* (even the cover shots had the group in plain burlap dresses). But "Creep" (a number 1 single) addressed the problem of a cheating boyfriend in typical TLC fashion—they cheat in retaliation—and "Waterfalls" (another number 1), the group's biggest hit, was a moving look at the harsh realities of urban life. The album would receive six Grammy nominations, winning awards for Best R&B Album and Best R&B Performance by a Duo or Group (for "Creep").

But at this key juncture, TLC's career would become mired in a range of controversies. Prior to *CrazySexyCool*'s release, Lopes was convicted of burning down the house of her boyfriend, Atlanta Falcons' football player Andre Rison. She was sentenced to five years' probation, a ten-thousand-dollar fine, and a stay in an alcohol rehab center. In July 1995, the group filed for bankruptcy, stating that despite record sales in the millions, each member was only taking home fifty thousand dollars a year (Rison, having forgiven Lopes, lent the group money to hire a bankruptcy lawyer). The dispute culminated when TLC stormed the office of Arista president Clive Davis (Arista being LaFace's parent label) in early 1996, insisting that their complaints be taken seriously and taking TLC memorabilia from Arista's walls when they left. Despite Watkins' statement to *VIBE*, "I ain't into feminism, that black power stuff and all that, whatever," the group clearly had no problem asserting themselves.

But problems continued to surface even before the group began recording their third album. McKissack, no longer TLC's manager, demanded they pay her for the rights to the group's name. TLC's primary producer and songwriter (and Thomas's boyfriend) also requested a higher fee before he would work on the record. By the time *Fanmail* was released in 1999, Watkins and Thomas were complaining that Lopes was more interested in working on her solo projects than TLC business. For her part, Lopes told *VIBE*, "I cannot stand one hundred percent behind this TLC project."

Fanmail was nonetheless another success, entering the charts at number 1. The album was another smooth and seductive release, which featured two more number 1 singles, "No Scrubs" (a "scrub" being a good-for-nothing male) and "Unpretty," which attacked unrealistic beauty expectations for women and produced a surprisingly graphic video. *Fanmail* would win another Grammy for Best Rap Album, but the group's career again stalled, as arguments grew over TLC's future direction. After the *Fanmail* tour, the members went their separate ways, though a breakup was

TLC, (left to right): Lisa "Left Eye" Lopes, Tionne "T-Boz" Watkins, Rozonda "Chilli" Thomas
January 2000 at Madison Square Garden,
Photo by Leo Sorel/Retna Ltd.

never officially announced and a fourth TLC album was never completely ruled out. Lopes finally released a solo album, *Supernova*, in 2001 (though she was said to be irritated it was only released internationally) and signed a solo deal with Suge Knight's label Tha Row. Thomas, who had been hospitalized due to her lifelong struggle with sickle cell anemia, began working on her own solo album; the group's members had also been involved in a wide number of projects individually. But hopes that the group would reunite were dashed when Lopes was killed in a car accident in Honduras on April 25, 2002.

An increasing number of artists were also redefining what success in the music industry could mean, with sales less important than simply earning enough to make a decent living and having more control over one's career. Ani (pronounced AH-nee) DiFranco shunned both major and indie labels in favor of overseeing every aspect of her career, and was eventually lauded in *Forbes* magazine and the *Wall Street Journal* for her business savvy.

DiFranco was born in 1970 in Buffalo, New York, where her business office is still based. She later described her turbulent childhood to Jonathan Van Meter as "one scary scene after another," and her parents would separate when she was eleven. By then, DiFranco was playing guitar in local clubs, having picked up the instrument at nine. At fifteen, she began writing songs, and, when her mother decided to move to Connecticut, she declared herself an emancipated minor and remained in Buffalo, graduating from high school early in order to pursue a career in music.

DiFranco's first release was a tape she put together to help land gigs; she later began selling the self-titled recording at shows, and in 1990 started Righteous Records, now amended to Righteous Babe Records, after her publishing company. She initially considered signing with a larger label, but after meeting with one indie company and finding their contract "an exploitative little document," she realized she would be better off on her own. Her first proper album, *Not So Soft*, was released in 1991.

DiFranco would release an album a year throughout the '90s. By the end of the decade she would have sold over two million records, a remarkable achievement for an artist largely working outside the system. DiFranco would build her audience the old-fashioned way; since she didn't get much exposure through radio or MTV, she toured constantly, at one point giving up the lease on her apartment in favor of living on the road in her car.

DiFranco initially attracted a female following. Irritated at "guys coming to hear me play because I was cute," she shaved her head, got a nose ring, and wore heavy black boots; "See who'll listen to me then," she told *Interview*. She frankly addressed her bisexuality in lyrics, and even her use of press-on nails wrapped in electrical tape (the better to pick her guitar with) was seen as "a sort of feminist in-joke." "I think it's really important for people to tell their story, so I want to be as frank about it as possible," she told the *Austin Chronicle*. "It's especially important for women, because the dominant history is male."

But DiFranco wanted her audiences to grasp the universal aspect of her music beyond the "feminist folk artist" label. "It's not like I have an agenda in my music," she told *Billboard*. "It's just that to me, the world is political. Politics is music—is life! That's the lens I look through." On 1993's *Puddle Dive*, she attacked complacency in "Willing to Fight," while "Blood in the Boardroom," on the same album, was a wry commentary on her experiences with the "suits" who wanted to sign her; she declines their offer and leaves behind a "statement" of her power—a menstrual blood stain on a chair. Musically, she played her acoustic guitar with the intensity of an electric one, a style aptly described in a press release calling DiFranco "a punk folksinger who writes songs that can appeal to old folkies and simultaneously climb the college radio charts."

By the mid-'90s, DiFranco showed she was ready to climb the pop charts as well. After releasing *Out of Range* (1994) and *Not a Pretty Girl* (1995) to increasing critical acclaim, *Dilate* (1996) became her first album to crack *Billboard*'s Top 100, peaking at number 87. The live album *Living in Clip* (1997) eventually went gold, and both *Little Plastic Castle* (1998) and *Up Up Up Up Up Up* (1999) hit the Top 30. A front page story in *Billboard* ("Righteous Babe: An Indie Success Story") pointed out that while DiFranco's sales might pale in comparison to what a major could achieve, financially she almost certainly came out ahead, for while a typical major label act might make $1.25–$2 per album, DiFranco, it was estimated, could make $4.

But as her popularity grew, DiFranco did face some criticism for "selling out," particularly when she began a relationship with a man whom she later married. She had previously noted her discomfort with the more rigid elements of the lesbian-feminist community, telling *The Advocate* about a woman at the Michigan Womyn's Music Festival who had heard DiFranco say "I'll see you guys at the tent" and chastised her for using "malecentric" language. "A lot of my fans do want it simple, they want it easy," she told Jonathan Van Meter. "And when I insist on my own stupid personality quirks it can be offensive to them." She addressed the matter on "In or Out" (from 1992's *Imperfectly*), matter-of-factly spelling out her interest in both "spots" and "stripes" and asserting that, depending on her mood, she just might choose to go home alone. After winning an Outmusic Award at 1999's Gay/Lesbian American Music Awards, she said, "I think being queer is much bigger than who you're sleeping with at any given moment. . . . I still consider myself queer."

Today, Righteous Babe releases albums by other artists as well, such as Sara Lee, a member of British band Gang of Four who has played with the Indigo Girls, Joan

Osborne, and DiFranco, and folk artist Bruce "U. Utah" Phillips. DiFranco's own subsequent albums on the label include *To the Teeth* (1999), *Swing Set* (2000), and *Revelling/Reckoning* (2001). And she continues to affirm her desire to work in her own niche. "People have told me for years, 'You are holding yourself back,'" she told *Billboard*. "But that's not the point. The point for me is about not supporting and instead actively challenging a system of big business that I think co-opts and commercializes and is contradictory toward revolutionary art of any kind."

Despite the mainstream acceptance of lesbian performers like k. d. lang and Melissa Etheridge, sexuality could still become the focal point in stories about musicians in the same way that the women-in-rock label indiscriminately lumped together performers of different genres. Some were able to ultimately transcend such categorization. Nearly all the initial articles about Me'shell Ndegéocello, the first female artist signed to Madonna's Maverick label, drew attention to her bisexuality, but such observations were eventually dropped, and the subject became less of an issue in stories on DiFranco as well.

But Britain's Skunk Anansie felt that the repeated media focus on their lead singer, Skin, came at the expense of attention to the band's music. "They'd felt pigeonholed because of Skin's identity, not just as a lesbian but as a black lesbian," explains Meryl Wheeler, then a publicist at the band's U.S. label, Virgin. "They wanted to be in music magazines and grassroots metal fanzine publications, and really focus on the music. Skin was sick of talking about gender politics or identity politics; she's like, 'I've been in *The Advocate*, and if they want to review my record that's great, but I don't want to do another feature for them talking about me—we're a band.'"

It was a problem that Wheeler felt played a major role in the band's lack of stateside airplay. "They made a record [*Post Orgasmic Chill*] that the music press was very receptive to; they'd always been critical favorites," she says. "I think the greatest problem for them lay probably in small-minded people at radio; radio people will come right out and say something as mind-bendingly stupid as, 'We don't want to play any music by that bald lesbian chick.' And Skin told me when they were at Epic they had been told—at Epic—that there was no way they could get on the radio, and they weren't even going to bother working them for radio because of Skin. And she was like, 'Gee, if that's the kind of support you're getting at your own label, why be there?'"

But there were performers—exclusively on indie labels—who deliberately carved out a gay niche in the alternative rock scene. And zines like Donna Dresch's *Homocore* provided another rallying point for those inspired by what was dubbed the "queercore" music scene, such as Kaia Wilson, who read *Homocore* in her teens, became a musician, and eventually founded the queer record label Mr. Lady.

Wilson, born in 1974, was raised in the small town of Jasper, Oregon. With two parents who played instruments (her mother played piano and guitar, her father accordion), Wilson grew up surrounded by music, played piano, and began writing songs at age nine. By high school, Wilson realized she was a lesbian and had discovered the burgeoning queercore scene. "I wrote to Donna [Dresch] and I started to be turned on to different kinds of music," she recalls. "Then, my last year in high school, I befriended Molly and Allison, who at the time were in Bratmobile, but we also were talking about being in a band together, and we had a couple practices out in my parents' garage, which was pretty funny. Through them I met a whole bunch of other people, and I started going to more parties and stuff, and I gradually found myself in this indie punk scene. I started getting into Bikini Kill, L7, and Tribe 8."

It wasn't long before Wilson, who was now playing guitar, decided to get her own band together. "Other people were doing it, so it seemed as though I could do it, because of the examples that were in front of me," she explains. "I felt like it was something I could do and maybe it would be fun. And maybe I'd get some girls—I'm just kidding!" In 1992, Wilson eventually hooked up with Sara Shelton on bass and Nalini "d. d." Cheriel on drums to form Adickdid, a raw, punky trio that stayed together about a year and a half.

When Adickdid split, Wilson decided she wanted her next band to be an all-gay one. "You just have this level of understanding with each other that's unspoken," she explains. "Part of it was also, politically, it seemed like it would be really effective to reach out to folks who needed to have what Team Dresch could provide, which was, I think, good music with good strong political views centering on queerness." Wilson finally met Dresch in Olympia ("It was like, 'Oh my God, I'm meeting *the* Donna! The Donna that I've heard about for so many years!'" she says) and suggested they form a group with Jody Bleyle, who played drums in the Portland band Hazel.

Formed in the fall of 1993, the band featured Wilson on guitar and vocals; Bleyle on guitar, bass, and vocals; Dresch on guitar and bass; and, after trying out others, Marci Martinez on drums. The name Team Dresch was chosen as both a tongue-in-cheek homage to Donna and "team" being a subtle allusion to the lesbian interest in team sports. Team Dresch's first release was a single on the Kill Rock Stars label (with Scott Plouf of the Spinanes and Guided By Voices on drums), with cover art that spoofed the "lesbian pulp" novels of the '50s. Their first album, *Personal Best*, came out in 1995, a joint release by Dresch's Chainsaw and Bleyle's Candyass record labels.

The album's title referred to the lesbian-themed film of the same name, and song titles like "Fagetarian and Dyke," "She's Crushing My Mind," and "Hate the Christian Right" showed that Team Dresch wore their lesbianism like a badge of honor. "We were determinedly and outspokenly a dyke band," says Wilson. "We came around right in that 'lesbian chic' moment, '93, '94," when magazines like *New York* celebrated "The Bold, Brave New World of Gay Women"; "We were at the right place in the right time, definitely."

Team Dresch released their second album, *Captain, My Captain*, in 1996 (with Melissa York on drums), another album of rousing punk that featured a tribute to "Uncle Phranc" (who, after being dropped by Island, would go on to record for Kill Rock Stars; Team Dresch backed her on her 1995 EP *Goofyfoot*) and a pointed observation about "lesbian chic" in the liner notes: "Don't let the media make you think that homosexuality was invented last night just to sell magazines." But the band would break up not long after, something Wilson attributes to "interpersonal relations." "It's tough to be in a band," she says. "It's kind of like a relationship. The first year is like, 'Everything's going great,' but then after that—you know how a lot of relationships fall apart."

Wilson put out a solo acoustic album of her own, *Kaia* (billed on the back cover as "a dyke album for the whole family!"), the same year as *Captain, My Captain* and, after leaving Team Dresch, planned to release another. Wilson was then living in Durham, North Carolina, with her girlfriend, filmmaker Tammy Rae Carland, who was looking for an outlet to sell her videos. The two decided to form a company to release their various projects, and Mr. Lady Records & Videos was born.

Wilson's first release for the label was the 1998 solo album *Ladyman*, another acoustic record, which also featured Team Dresch's Melissa York on drums. The two played together on a tour supporting the album and afterward decided to put together a new band. "When we came back from touring, we were like, 'God, we really want a bass player, we really want a band!'" Wilson recalls. "And I asked one of my friends if she knew any dyke bass players, because, again, we just wanted to play with a lesbian. We just like lesbians! We're biased."

A friend told Wilson and York about Alison Martlew, then playing in a band called Poor Valentino. "In '98 on Valentine's Day we went to scope out her band," says Wilson. "It was pretty funny, we felt like such scouts, like we were gonna go get her for our basketball team or something. She was also playing with, we used to call them 'the teenagers,' and they hated us for it, but they *were* teenagers, they were like fifteen and sixteen, all these little cute, queer punkers that were doing music stuff. So we went and saw that show, and it was really awesome. We just instantly fell in love with Al, and asked if she'd play with us."

Martlew agreed, and the trio settled on the name the Butchies, releasing their first album, *Are We Not Femme?*, in the fall of 1998, with the group pictured in matching red skirts and sleeveless blue blouses on the front; subsequent albums include *Population*

The Butchies, 1999, (left to right): Alison Martlew, Melissa York, Kaia Wilson
Photo by Tammy Rae Carland

1975, released in 1999, and *3,* released in, 2001. The band's spirited rock and lesbian-feminist agenda updated "womyn's music" for a new generation. But the band, and the Mr. Lady label, always honored their predecessors. *Are We Not Femme?* included a cover of Cris Williamson's "Shooting Star," and the cover art of Mr. Lady's 1999 compilation *New Women's Music Sampler* echoes the cover of the 1970 feminist anthology *Sisterhood Is Powerful* and was compiled, in the words of the album's liner notes, as a tribute to "all the women-run labels who came before us paving the road and making what we do more meaningful."

Mr. Lady has gone on to release albums by Le Tigre (an electronic pop trio co-founded by Kathleen Hanna), the hard rock band the Haggard, and singer-songwriter Sarah Dougher, among others. The Butchies themselves broadened their audience after hooking up with Amy Ray, who had been referred to the group by Kill Rock Stars' Slim Moon. Ray had expressed an interest in releasing the Butchies' debut on her own label, Daemon, but Wilson decided she would rather use it to help establish Mr. Lady. But the Butchies did end up playing on Amy Ray's solo album, 2001's *Stag* (she returned the favor, singing on Wilson's third solo album, 2002's *Oregon*), and the Butchies later opened for the Indigo Girls on tour.

"That was such a different experience and so scary," says Wilson. "But so good. I think some people didn't like us, but they have such a polite audience, and I think we won over some fans too. It helped us to cross over to folks that wouldn't know about the kind of music we release, 'cause it can be so underground. And it was also, for me, full circle: 'Oh my God, I used to love them when I was in high school and now I'm actually playing music with them!' And boy, did we talk about being lesbians! We make jokes about it; there's tons of funny stories we can tell. We're definitely not scared about it. Then we would get e-mails from people like, 'It was so great to see you guys with the Indigo Girls—you said "lesbian" onstage!' People who went to their shows, some of them, were more closeted than we're used to playing for. So we had a good effect with that too."

Despite the difficulties of running a small business, Wilson and Carland plan to keep Mr. Lady an ongoing concern. "It can get really tough," she says. "But we're going to do it while it still seems fun for us. If the bad starts to really outnumber the good of the label, we'll dump it. I feel that way about the band too; I don't want to ever be involved in something where you feel like you have to be in it forever. But right now we're still connecting musically, we still feel like we're growing musically, and we're enjoying what we're doing.

"We're not making a living off of what we do, but it's making us enough money to feel good about it," Wilson continues. "But it's hard after a while; it's not all about money, but when you put a lot of time into something you kind of feel like, 'Okay, now can I please make a living off of this?' It can be hard politically too. We've definitely gotten our fair share of criticism, for being this outspokenly feminist and queer. People think we're pigeonholing ourselves. And we *are* pigeonholing ourselves, but we make these decisions for really important reasons. We made the decision to be outspoken about our queerness and our feminist ideologies because it's something that we're not seeing in the world. People don't criticize any other kind of niche label, people don't criticize other people for focusing in on their heterosexuality. You focus on what's important to you. Why do you have to call that exclusionary or pigeonholing or whatever? Also, people don't understand that when you're part of an oppressed group, you need positive reinforcement, you need to see positive examples of people like yourself existing in the world."

Carla DeSantis, editor and publisher of *ROCKRGRL*, has also faced charges of being "exclusionary" with her magazine, which focuses on women in the music business, both on stage and off. "I have gotten that a *lot* over the years," she says. "To be honest, my feeling is that I wish that women *weren't* excluded. But the fact is that they are. My goal has never been to separate women out, but to call for their inclusion in magazines like *Spin* and *Rolling Stone* as artists to be taken seriously."

DeSantis had been working in the music industry for years prior to starting *ROCK-RGRL*, but as a performer, not a writer. Born in 1958 in Massachusetts, DeSantis grew up in New Jersey and California, where she began to play guitar, following years of piano lessons. By high school, she was writing songs. "I just wrote and wrote all the time," she says. "In college I used to write songs in the stairwell. I auditioned for different bands but I never got in because I was terrible. So I started playing my guitar in pizza parlors and just wherever I could. And then when I moved up to Eugene I actually got into my first band. And once I got bitten by that bug that was all I wanted to do. I wanted to be a professional songwriter and if I had a career being a performer, well, that would be fantastic too."

DeSantis eventually returned to California, and in the early '80s joined Lady, a San Jose covers band that played at county fairs and other festivals. It was her first experience with an all-female band. "Audiences always expected us to sound like the Go-Go's!" she says. "They'd say, 'Here are the Go-Go's,' or 'Are you the girlfriends of the guys in the band?' 'Are you lip synching?' At first it really surprised me, and then it just pissed me off. I mean, at *every* gig somebody would say something stupid like that. I thought, 'Why is it that people think girls can't play?' I just found that so strange, especially because it was at a time when there were a lot of women who were really popular."

Later in the decade, DeSantis took a break from music, getting married (she later divorced) and having a son. In 1989, she and the keyboardist from Lady formed another oldies band, the Charms. But she found that attitudes toward women musicians had not changed. "I remember walking into a music store one day, and I went to get a bass down, and the clerk ran over and told me not to touch it," she says. "I was with a guy friend and he couldn't believe it. He goes, 'Whoa! I've never seen that happen before.' And I'd been playing professionally for about eight years at that point. These little things would happen and I thought, 'Am I the only person stuff like this happens to? There are probably other women out there who've experienced the same thing, I just don't know where they are.'"

DeSantis began to find those other women in the mid-'90s, when she signed on to the Internet and discovered Hole's music. "I bought *Live Through This*, which I really related to enormously because I was getting divorced at the time," she says. "It was great to hear an album with so much yelling, and so many references to being a mom, and being a woman, that I hadn't heard since Chrissie Hynde." She was also struck by Courtney Love's experiences as a woman-in-rock. "After Kurt died, the media was very, very cruel to Courtney," she contends. "I didn't understand why. I thought it was terrible that they were making fun of her at a time when she was really vulnerable. I do think that a lot of the criticisms of her were very misogynist. And that was a hot button for me because guys had been weird and mean to me in my own music career. So I felt an obligation to defend her."

DeSantis ended up first "meeting" Love in cyberspace, and she eventually connected with other women online who were equally interested in the new music female artists were making, giving her the idea of launching a label specializing in women artists, with a magazine on the side. But when her call for submissions online drew more articles than music, she decided to focus on the magazine. *ROCKRGRL*'s debut issue (the name being taken from DeSantis's online name) was published in January 1995.

The first issue (initial run: sixty copies) was fourteen pages long and featured former Mary's Danish singer Gretchen Seager on the cover. Seven years later, circulation reached fifteen thousand, and a typical issue was fifty pages and on glossy paper, with a full-color cover and instrument ads featuring performers like Meredith Brooks and Shannon Curfman. But the underlying philosophy remained the same: along with profiles of musicians, *ROCKRGRL* featured editorials and articles on music equipment and business/legal issues.

"My goal has always been to empower women who are already playing music, and to reach out to women who were isolated, because I spent so many years feeling isolated from other musicians," DeSantis says. "I would have given anything to be able to talk to other women about what their experiences were. I think that sixteen-year-old girls who want to play guitar are discouraged; they're discouraged when they walk into a music store and nobody waits on them, they're discouraged when the women they

Amy Ray and Carla DeSantis
November 2000 at the ROCKRGRL Music Conference, Seattle, Photo by Gillian G. Gaar

admire are put down in some way by the press. That may be part of the reason why it was hard for me to see myself as a musician. Because I think I realized at some level, maybe not consciously at the time, that if I wanted to be a musician, I was setting myself up for ridicule. And I didn't particularly like being ridiculed."

ROCKRGRL also features stories that focus on a performer's musicianship. "How come nobody asks women about music?" says DeSantis. "They're always women first and musicians second, third, or fourth or fifth. I can't believe this is still going on, so many years after—well, since rock began. Why is this always an issue and why are women never considered real musicians?" DeSantis would like to reach a larger audience but finds remaining true to her vision of greater importance. "You can find money if you're willing to compromise, but I'm not willing to compromise," she says. "I think if I sexed up *ROCKRGRL* a little bit I could get bigger money and that's kind of gross. I don't think that people understand my motivation. My motivation is really to give people a resource that is going to make them feel good about playing music. Is this something a musician is going to get something out of? Is this going to make a difference in people wanting to play? Is somebody going to care about this?"

In 2002, facing rising printing costs and fewer outlets, DeSantis decided to scale back *ROCKRGRL* from a bimonthly to a quarterly. It was a sobering reflection of the times. By the end of the '90s, the five major record labels controlled over eighty percent of the market and were in turn owned by other companies whose diverse interests squeezed smaller businesses out of the running and made music almost a secondary concern to a label's operation. As publicist Meryl Wheeler, who has worked with both major labels and independent publicity firms, observes, "Labels are now part of major corporations that had so much debt, they became like any other corporation. Which means that for the main part, they're very concerned with short-term gain. Because they have quarterly profit statements, and shareholders, and they're all public companies, they started acting a lot more like tire manufacturers or widget manufacturers; there was less freedom to do other things. I mean, people [in the music industry] had said to me in the '80s, 'Oh this is nothing like it was in the '70s, when the coke flew freely,' and supposedly the '80s were doom and gloom compared to what the '70s had been like. But the '80s were amazing compared to what the late '90s turned out to be."

Wheeler, born in 1959, got her first job in the music industry while in college in the early '80s. "I was always one of those people who pored over record labels, and liner notes," she explains. "I was really fascinated by the music industry. It seemed very foreign to me and very mysterious—how did people meet rock stars and how did records get made?" A major Beatles fan, she was thrilled with her internship in L.A. at Capitol

Records, the Beatles' U.S. label. "Going to the Capitol Records tower at Hollywood and Vine was like going to a shrine!" she says.

Wheeler interned in publicity, and after graduation was hired by Warner Bros. to work in their publicity department. "I thought, 'Wow, talking to writers on the phone about music—that sounds like something I could do,'" she says. "Because I was a history major, I had no marketable skills, except that I knew how to work in an office and I had a strong work ethic. In some ways, I was as much a writers' groupie as I was a rock stars' groupie—I don't mean that in a sexual way, but just being somebody who really admires what they do. I had thought about writing for the UCLA paper about music, but I don't have the discipline necessary to become a writer. I found out later that no writer actually likes to write; if I had known that, I might have tried to do it! But it seemed a lot easier to just talk to writers than to actually become one."

With record sales more dependent on radio and television play, Wheeler did not feel a lot of pressure in her job. "It was kind of understood that publicity didn't necessarily help sell records, except for booking someone on the *Tonight Show*," she explains. "But it was really a lot of fun. You sent your advance records out and waited for people to write about your band. I didn't really have to worry about pitching anything, because most of the artists that I had anything to do with were the superstars that people wanted to write about."

Some of those artists included country supergroup the Trio (Linda Ronstadt, Emmylou Harris, and Dolly Parton) and George Harrison ("I managed to be professional and hold it together when I met him, but after his first day of interviews, I went out to the parking lot, got in my car, sat in it, and screamed!"). Wheeler moved to New York in 1989 and worked at Enigma Records, at the publicity firm Shore Fire Media, and at Virgin Records, where she eventually became National Head of Publicity, working on albums and tours by such artists as Julian Lennon, the Rolling Stones, Iggy Pop, and David Bowie.

Wheeler largely attributes any resistance she felt to pitching female artists as being more because of space than gender. "I never had to deal with the question of an artist's legitimacy because they were a woman; it was more like, 'Do we have space to cover this completely unknown artist?'" Nonetheless, she adds there is a tendency to see female artists, particularly those who are not musicians, as not "equally legitimate." The perception, she explains, is that "It's okay to sing, but anyone can sing. But not anyone can play an instrument. And if you consider yourself a serious fan of the music, you don't want to be part of some magazine that covers a bunch of chick dilettantes—you want serious musicians and that by definition is going to be men."

Even more of a problem, Wheeler feels, is the media's unadventurous approach. "There were fewer music outlets [in the '80s], but they were willing to take more of a chance on things," she says. "The outlets hadn't gotten all corporate and professional, in all the most horrible and negative ways those words apply, as they became later. There was maybe just as limited space in *Rolling Stone* as there is now, but *Rolling Stone* still, at that time, saw itself as a champion of music. In the late '80s and early '90s, it may not have seemed so compared to how *Rolling Stone* was in the early, committed '70s, but it's all relative; it's better than it was in the late '90s and today.

"The other thing that started happening was consolidation in other aspects of the music business," she continues. "Like radio being swallowed up by Clear Channel, and then concert promotion also by Clear Channel, so you had these huge entities controlling all aspects of the music business. So it was harder to break a new artist. The major artists were expected to have the hits, and when they weren't as big as expected, considering the amount of money poured into them, you felt like something bad was going to happen—you can't be spending all this money and not see any return for it to continue on. And of course it hasn't continued on; Virgin had a major corporate shakeup last year [2001] and it's still continuing into this year [2002]."

Wheeler also says that more women are moving into other departments at major labels, though the publicity department remains a female stronghold. "I don't know whether it's a less respected department because women are in it, or, because women are in it, therefore it's less respected," she says. "It might have something to do with the nature of the job. You have to play host—you get coffee, you set up parties, you cater to the artist, you cater to the heads of the label. So there's a lot of subservience you don't have in the sales or promotions department. Though there are powerful and amazing women publicists that I imagine don't have to do a lot of begging—but I imagine they got started that way and are probably good at it." On the other hand, she notes, "You could just as easily say that because you have to deal with writers, people who are actually literate, it takes smarter people to be in the publicity department."

As major labels were swallowed up by international corporations, a fiercely independent music scene continued to exist. And more people working in that scene were learning how to interact with the mainstream with minimal compromise. Julie Butterfield's work as a publicist with such avowed indie companies as K Records and Mr. Lady exemplified how the often contentious relationship between the two realms could be bridged.

Butterfield, born and raised in Nebraska, was introduced to music through her older sister's record collection, which encompassed punk and new wave acts like the Clash and the Cars as well as classic rock. "She would give me records and say, 'Take these home and listen to them,'" Butterfield recalls. "I remember distinctly one day she gave me the Rolling Stones and said, 'Don't play this one around mom!'"

After graduating from the University of Nebraska, Butterfield moved to Minneapolis in the mid-'80s, working in record stores and partaking of the city's vibrant music scene, seeing acts like Babes in Toyland and the Northwest groups Fitz of Depression and Bikini Kill. She also briefly ran her own record label, Skinny Girl. "I don't know if I ever recouped any of the money that I put into it, but it was really important that these bands be documented in the Minneapolis history!" she says of her work putting out singles by such local bands as Lily Liver, Lefty Lucy, and Hot Date.

By 1994, Butterfield felt she was at a crossroads and, looking for a way out of Minneapolis, sent out a résumé designed as a fanzine to various record labels. In July 1994, Calvin Johnson invited Butterfield to Olympia to work at the town's latest indie music festival, Yoyo a Go Go, organized by Yoyo Records' founder Pat Maley. Butterfield worked at the festival's record booth. "It wasn't the most glamorous job, but I knew how to do it," she says. "The labels made money, everybody was happy, and I got to see bands and meet people. And I was really enchanted by Olympia. The second to last day, Calvin pulled me aside and said, 'We're thinking about hiring you to be our in-house publicist; do you think you could do that job?' And I was like, 'Oh yeah, I can do that,' not knowing what to do but knowing that I could do it."

At the time, K Records had offices above a Chinese restaurant. "We all had space heaters—those were the good old days!" Butterfield jokes. Her biggest challenge was not giving structure to the office environment but coaxing musicians wary of outsiders into accepting that publicity did not have to be a destructive force.

"For the first year, people were a little bit suspicious of what I was doing," she admits. "People in Olympia had been really burned by the riot grrrl thing, and the backlash was extreme, like, 'We hate media!' And here I'm telling them, 'I'm gonna get you in a magazine, all right!' I just thought, growing up as a kid in Nebraska, the only way I found out about bands was from *Rolling Stone*; if Elvis Costello was like, 'Fuck *Rolling Stone!*' I don't know if I would have heard about him. I didn't think it was like the Bible, but an information source; there wasn't a lot of info when I was stuck in junior high, you know? Yes, fanzines are amazing, the communities and the network you have built up are amazing, but there are kids who don't have these things going on in their communities. So if you're in this magazine it's not a bad thing."

Education worked the other way as well. "Radio people would call and asked to get 'serviced,'" Butterfield remembers. "And I would say, 'If you want records from me, I suggest you do not asked to be "serviced,"' because that is really gross to me. Just ask, "Hey, send me your new Lois record," or whatever. Most of them were college freshman or something, and they were very eager, so I don't think they were offended. It was like I was trying to school them: 'Don't be a cookie cutter radio guy, have some personality.'"

Sleater-Kinney, (left to right): Janet Weiss, Corin Tucker, Carrie Brownstein
February 1998 in Portland, Oregon, Photo by Diana Adams

When Butterfield's work resulted in higher attendance at shows and greater record sales, artists not on K began to approach her and ask if she could do publicity for them. Butterfield eventually left K and started her own publicity company, 24 Promotions (now Miss Butterfield PR). Her contacts within the music industry meant she was rarely hurting for clients; Molly Neuman at Berkeley's Lookout!, Jody Bleyle at Portland's Candyass Records, and Donna Dresch at Olympia's Chainsaw label were among those who referred their artists to Butterfield.

One of the bands on Chainsaw was Sleater-Kinney, who had formed in Olympia in 1994, founded by guitarists Corin Tucker and Carrie Brownstein. Tucker, born in 1972 in Pennsylvania, moved to Eugene, Oregon, at age 11. She knew about Olympia's music scene from having seen Beat Happening in Eugene and meeting Allison Wolfe and Molly Neuman from Bratmobile, and enrolled at Evergreen after she graduated from high school.

Tucker began working with a classmate on a video about Northwest grunge bands, but the focus changed when she saw the early performances of Bikini Kill and Bratmobile. "They were challenging the sexism in the grunge scene, and I started getting more interested in that, and we ended up making two totally different videos," she explains. "Mine was all about girl bands and how they were going to change everything; this was before riot grrrl had even started, but I could just see it, I knew something really interesting was about to happen. The things Bratmobile and Bikini Kill were saying instantly validated all these things that I felt—suddenly I was like, 'Whaaaaa!' It really inspired me."

When Tucker returned to Eugene in the summer of 1991, she started the band Heavens to Betsy with her friend, Tracy Sawyer; Tucker played guitar, and Sawyer, drums. The group made their debut at the IPU convention on the opening night all-female show. "It was totally crazy," she remembers. "Tracy almost passed out, she was so nervous; she was literally white and could hardly walk onto the stage. And I was like, 'We can do this. I believe in us.' And we did it and it was awesome. Everyone started screaming after we played."

Molly Neuman offered to produce Heavens to Betsy's first demo, and one of the tracks, "My Secret," became the band's first release, appearing on a split single with Bratmobile. In the fall of 1992, Heavens to Betsy played a show in Bellingham, Washington, which was seen by Western Washington University student Carrie Brownstein. Born in 1974 in Seattle and raised in Redmond, a suburb of Seattle, Brownstein had been trying to get a band together since learning to play the guitar in high school. "I'd always loved music, but had never really felt like there was an instrument or a genre of music that spoke to me," she says. "So when I discovered punk rock it seemed to fill in a lot of blanks. And listening to the Ramones, where the songs and

Carrie Brownstein of Sleater-Kinney
at the 1997 Bumbershoot festival, Seattle, Photo by Gillian G. Gaar

chord progressions seemed very accessible, I just realized, 'Oh, this'll be a really good way to do something creative and express some of the things that I'm feeling.'"

Brownstein had formed an all-female band in high school called Born Naked ("Horrible name!"), but says of the group, "We didn't take ourselves very seriously because we felt like no one else was really taking us very seriously." But as she learned about the Olympia music scene, she realized there were places where female musicians were supported, and after a year at WWU she transferred to Evergreen.

Brownstein soon formed Excuse 17 with Becca Albee on vocals and guitar and C. J. Phillips on drums; they later toured with Heavens to Betsy and found that not every place was as supportive of female musicians as Olympia. "Sometimes the people putting on shows just assumed you didn't know how to play," Brownstein recalls. "Facing a lot of sexism and a lot of condescension was really difficult. We were a righteous group of people, thinking that everybody was as evolved as we were, and if they weren't, we were just so indignant. We got in a lot of fights with sound guys and with promoters at shows. It made me appreciate the place that I lived, but I also wanted to figure out how could other places have that. There was always a girl coming up to us and being like, 'I hate living here' and 'No women are playing music.' They had seen what was going on in other places, like Olympia, but they hadn't found a way of politicizing their own scene yet."

Brownstein and Tucker eventually formed Sleater-Kinney (named after the road where their practice space was) as a side project. "We slept and ate and breathed music all the time, so it was just really normal to have a band and have like three other bands," Brownstein explains. With Brownstein and Tucker on guitar and vocals and Misty Farrell on drums, the band recorded a single and compilation tracks for the Villa Villakula label, started in Boston by Tinuviel, who had helped Slim Moon run the Kill Rock Stars label.

In the fall of 1994, Brownstein and Tucker went to Australia, where they worked with a new drummer, Lora MacFarlane, whom they knew solely from exchanging letters. During their two-and-a-half-month stay, they ended up recording their self-titled debut album, released the following year on Villa Villakula (vinyl) and Chainsaw (CD). The album, just under twenty-three minutes, had the raw excitement of a band discovering its own voice, with bristling guitar work, Tucker's arresting vibrato, and potent attacks on sexual politics in "A Real Man," "How to Play Dead," and the casting-couch nightmare "Sold Out." Tucker and Brownstein also discovered their "side project" band had an undeniable chemistry. "I remember playing 'Be Yr Mama' at a show in Australia, and people just going *insane*," Tucker says. "That had never happened with my other band. It just had this kind of hugeness to it that was really exciting. The combination of my rhythm guitar style and Carrie's hot licks, it was just like, 'Oh wow, our strengths as writers really complement each other.' It was just apparent instantly—'Whoa, this could be something really amazing.'"

As a result, Tucker and Brownstein decided to make Sleater-Kinney their main band. When MacFarlane came to the U.S. in the summer of 1995, the band toured and recorded their second album, *Call the Doctor*, which displayed an impressive leap in Brownstein and Tucker's songwriting. The band's new strengths were immediately evident on the album's title (and opening) track; brooding guitar riffs give way to Tucker's sharp vocal parrying with Brownstein's lower one, and after the first verse a rush of guitars swell into the chorus, which has the two trading scream for scream. Feminist themes continued to play a key role in their work; the protagonist of "Anonymous" is shut down by societal expectations, and the taut "Little Mouth" is a clear successor to "Sold Out." But the track that generated the most acclaim was "I Wanna Be Your Joey Ramone," the band's irreverent take on rock stardom.

Even Brownstein and Tucker were impressed with their work. "Corin and I were just like, 'Oh my God, whoa! We just made a really amazing record!'" says Brownstein. "Neither of us had ever done anything like that before, and we were really really excited. I would just be jumping around the apartment to 'I Wanna Be Your Joey Ramone.'" Julie Butterfield, now working as the group's publicist (she would eventually become their manager), was equally thrilled. "Corin made a tape for me, and I said, 'Everybody has to hear this!'" she remembers. "People were probably just like, 'We should listen to it because she's so excited about it.'"

As interest in Sleater-Kinney grew, it became increasingly impractical to have a third member in another country. Toni Gogin became the band's drummer for the *Call the Doctor* tour, but in the fall of 1996 she was replaced by Janet Weiss, a Portland resident (where Tucker had moved after graduating from Evergreen, with Brownstein eventually moving to the city as well) and the veteran of several bands. Her high-powered drumming added a visceral excitement to Sleater-Kinney's music, both aurally and visually.

Weiss, born in 1965 in Hollywood, had been interested in music while growing up but did not pick up an instrument until attending college in San Francisco, when she taught herself to play guitar. She joined her first band, the Furies, when a friend of the group mentioned they were about to go on tour but had lost their drummer. "I borrowed a drum kit, and sat down with their record and tried to see if I could feasibly pull it off," she says. "And I got advice from Chuck Prophet—he was in Green on Red at the time. He talked me into it by saying how easy the drums were and you really only need to know one beat anyway. And I always remembered that; if not for him I might be a secretary."

The Furies only lasted six months, but Weiss soon moved on to other bands, though learning to play drums was not quite as easy as she had been told. "I remember being

Janet Weiss of Sleater-Kinney
August 1998 at Pier 62/63, Seattle, Photo by Gillian G. Gaar

humiliated at sound checks and during shows," Weiss admits. "I knew I was pretty bad. But the first year of playing the learning curve is large; you learn a lot, to the point where you feel like you're making progress every day. So within a year I was feeling like I was a pretty good drummer. If someone had said I was 'good for a girl' on my first tour, I would've agreed. But as time went on and I progressed as a musician, people would still say that. And I can still hear those kinds of things being said, although it's much less frequent. I don't think that sort of mentality is gone from music at all. It just makes me kind of sad at this point. I wish there were so many bands with women that it was not even an issue."

In 1989, Weiss moved to Portland. "I was young, I knew I wanted to be in a band and get a job, and that was about it," she says. "I always had that mindset of, 'You have a job, you're in a band, you play on the weekends, you take time off, you go on tour, you do it because you love it, not because you're gonna be a star, or you're gonna be able to support yourself." She formed the band Motorgoat with Sam Coomes (who was also her husband from 1990–94); they subsequently formed the two-piece band Quasi, of whom *Rolling Stone* once observed, "Quasi put the 'rock' in rocky relationships."

Weiss also drummed for the band Junior High and first heard Sleater-Kinney when the two bands played a show together. She joined the band in time to record their third album, *Dig Me Out*, released in 1997. The record's exuberance was infectious; with Weiss on drums, the band's aural punch had more power than ever, and songs like "Words and Guitar" reveled in the pure joy of rock & roll's energy. Critical response to the album was overwhelmingly positive, and coverage of the group crossed over from music publications to mainstream magazines. Major record companies also expressed interest in signing the band, who had moved from Chainsaw to Kill Rock Stars for *Dig Me Out*. But while creative control was promised, the band members felt that signing with a major would mean they would have to forgo overseeing other aspects of their career. It was a compromise they were not willing to make.

"The people that we talked to wanted us to be in charge of the music, but they wanted to be in charge of everything else," Tucker explains. "Like, 'Okay, I think it'd be a good idea if you guys toured here, and did these interviews, and we'll make a video for MTV . . .' And they would work with us, but they would have the master plan. And that is the major problem—we want to be in charge of everything! It's important to us that we are in control. Especially since the music industry has really changed in the past few years; it's like they sped up the process of trying to make a fast buck off you and then kick you off the label when things aren't selling so well. We really believe in our music, and we want to keep making records together, so we've taken this route so that we can keep going and make a reasonable living for ourselves at the same time."

Still, though the group chose to remain on an indie label, they continued to receive the kind of attention more common for a major label act. In their July 9, 2001, issue *Time* even lauded them as "The Best Band in America" ("It was horribly ridiculous, but it was really funny," says Brownstein of the accolade). The band members occasionally found it challenging to hold on to their indie ethic while still allowing Sleater-Kinney to grow in ways their original fans might not always support.

"For some people, *Dig Me Out* was the first time we sold out," Brownstein says. "We came from a community where people were hardly selling any records, were not even trying to get press, didn't tour with sound people, didn't have their own booking agents. I felt like we were betraying our Olympians—'Oh my God, we're getting a booking agent, what are people gonna think?' Other bands would be like, 'Why don't you guys have a booking agent yet?' but it was really weird coming from such a fiercely independent, anti-corporate community. Which thank God we did, because those values are permanently instilled in us."

Nor was the band interested, in Brownstein's words, in "making *Call the Doctor* five times in a row." *The Hot Rock*, released in 1999, is more subdued than the energetic *Dig*

Me Out but still pulses with a nervy intensity. "Those songs were really hard to play, and it really pushed us as musicians, I think, in a good way," says Tucker. 2000's *All Hands on the Bad One* had a more pronounced political edge. Songs like "You're No Rock n' Roll Fun" and "Ballad of a Ladyman" addressed sexism in the music industry; "Was It a Lie?" dealt with media harassment; and "#1 Must-Have" was both a sobering look back at the commercialization of the indie scene and a wish for a future where women can "write more than the next marketing bid." The band's sixth album, *One Beat*, was released in 2002.

By the time Sleater-Kinney recorded *One Beat*, they had fashioned a career that paid off in artistic—and job—satisfaction in a manner they could not have achieved on a major label. In addition to performing with Sleater-Kinney, each member has per-formed in other bands: Weiss with Quasi, Tucker with Cadallaca, and Brownstein with the Spells (and a memorable appearance in a Priceline commercial with William Shatner). While aware of the indie scene's limitations and a major's financial power, they are happy with their choices, despite the occasional obstacle.

"We had just played a show in Portland, and it was in the midst of a hailstorm," Brownstein recalls. "We were unloading our equipment into Janet's house, across the muddy lawn into her basement, in pouring rain, and Janet was like, 'This is the worst part about being in a band.' And I was like, 'Yeah, I'm sure this wouldn't happen if we were the best band in America!' It's just so funny, the disparity between this weird freaky *Time* magazine thing and what our lives are actually like. And for how much exposure we've had, sometimes you feel like, 'Oh, we might as well have been on a major label.' But, you know what, I'm so glad we're not. We've put in a lot more work than, maybe, some of our counterparts who are on majors, but I feel like the rewards have been really great. We've definitely forged our own path and really expanded the notion of what you can do on an independent label."

Artists like Sleater-Kinney and Ani DiFranco had helped change the perception of what it meant to be on an independent label. No longer was it necessarily seen as settling for "second best," a sign of one's inability to move to a larger arena. Given the opportunity to work with a major label, both had declined, forgoing the possibility of mainstream success, but they were nonetheless able to earn a comfortable living. DiFranco even set up her own label, while other artists on both ends of the indie-major spectrum created their own projects to fill perceived gaps—from Kaia Wilson's Mr. Lady label to Sarah McLachlan's Lilith Fair to Carla DeSantis's *ROCKRGRL* magazine. Perhaps as a result of seeing artists on the "outside" take matters into their own hands, major labels more frequently encouraged artists to move in directions that best suited them; Sheryl Crow was able to scrap two albums she wasn't happy with, and Tori Amos was sent to England to find her muse. For an increasing number of artists, the distribution power and financial potential that a major label offered wasn't enough enticement to sign on the dotted line. And artists on major labels had an increasing sense of their own power. It was a power that women working in both indie—and major—label realms felt freer to draw upon in charting their own destinies.

Girl Power?

"There is a real hunger, especially in young women, for the questions of sexism and gender to be raised, to be part of their culture. . . . In the early '90s it was chic to be a feminist. In the late '90s it is tired. We are consumers, always hungering for something new."
—Tristin Laughter, "Punk for Sale," *Punk Planet,* July 1999

"THE NEW POP DIVAS. They have chefs, masseuses and private shoppers. Here's how today's singing superstars play, work—and spend!"
—*People* cover story, January 18, 1999

On March 3, 2000, the Spice Girls were honored at the BRIT Awards for their "Outstanding Contribution to Pop Music." It was a remarkable honor for a group that had been together barely six years, had only released three albums, and was on the verge of breaking up. But the statistics during that time had been equally remarkable: nine of their ten singles had topped the U.K. charts, the tenth peaking at number 2, their first two albums topped the U.K. charts, the third peaking at number 2, and worldwide album sales totaled over thirty-eight million. At the height of "Spice-mania" in Britain it was said a front-page story on the group could increase a paper's sales by ten percent, and certainly the frenzy surrounding the group's rise solidified their position as Britain's biggest pop phenomenon since the Beatles.

Though the group's success was not as stratospheric in the U.S., the chief idea they espoused—"Girl Power," no longer a call to arms on the cover of a Bikini Kill zine but a kinder, gentler feminism for the end of the millennium—was consumed by the mainstream and sold back to its audience in the form of "Girl Power" t-shirts, among other Spice Girls ephemera. It was no small irony that this girl power was initially manufactured by men, with no intention of generating anything beyond a sizeable profit.

The Spice Girls' birth was due to the efforts of three men: Bob Herbert (who had managed the group Bros), his son Chris, and financier Chic Murphy. Despite initial stories to the contrary, none of the future Spice Girls had worked together before they answered an ad in the London show business paper the *Stage* in March 1994: "R U 18-23 with the ability to sing/dance? R U streetwise, ambitious, outgoing, and determined?" The women who made the cut had varying degrees of entertainment experience: Victoria Adams (born 1975) had studied dance, attended Laine Theatre Arts School in Surrey, and was briefly a member of the pop group Persuasion; Melanie Chisholm (born 1974) had also studied dance and sought work as a session singer; Melanie Brown (born 1975) had attended several dance/performing arts schools, worked as a dancer in men's clubs, and had appeared in commercials; and Geri Halliwell (born 1972) had worked as a model, been a dancer in Majorca, and had presented prizes on a Turkish TV game show (and had met Adams at auditions for the film *Tank Girl*).

The Herberts arranged for the women to live together as they worked with vocal and dancing coaches. Soon the group's original fifth member, Michelle Stephenson, left (as with many events in the Spice Girls' story, varying explanations are given; some accounts say she was fired). She was replaced by Emma Bunton (born 1976), who had been a

Spice Girls, (left to right): Melanie Brown, Melanie Chisholm, Emma Bunton, Victoria Beckham June 1998 at the Palace, Auburn Hills, Michigan, Photo by Jennifer Jeffery

child model and had appeared in commercials. Initially called Touch, the group was later renamed Spice either at Halliwell's suggestion or from an early Spice Girls song, "Sugar and Spice." (After the group became famous, a couple living in a neighboring house claimed the name actually came from their Lakeland terrier, also named Spice.)

After a 1995 showcase performance drummed up interest in the group, Spice decided not to formally sign with their original managers and instead took on Simon Fuller of 19 Management. (*Rolling Stone's* cover story on the Spices claimed that they switched managers because the Herberts were planning to replace one of the members.) When Fuller, the man who looked after the careers of British talents like Annie Lennox, asked what Spice wanted to achieve, Halliwell made the group's priorities clear. "World domination might just be enough for us," she told him, as recalled in her autobiography, *If Only*. "We wanted movies, merchandising, TV specials and to conquer America." From the beginning, music was seen as a means to an end—less a career than a career move, toward the larger goal of becoming famous. The possibility of long-term success in pop music was apparently not considered. "The biggest music buyers are teenagers and their tastes change quicker than street fashions," Halliwell wrote. "Why would the Spice Girls be any different? . . . Two years seemed to be the general consensus. We'd give it everything in that time. In, out and shake it all about—that was the philosophy."

The group (now renamed the Spice Girls) signed with Virgin that July. Two weeks later, before recording a note, the group was in the U.S., fielding film and television offers. But they soon set to work on their first album, *Spice*, and were credited as co-writers on every track. In a *New York Times* article, producer Richard Stannard (a member of one of the album's two production teams) compared the songwriting collaboration to assembling a jigsaw puzzle; "They had all the ideas for the songs, and we'd sort of piece them together," he explained. The end result was a collection of ten songs that broke no new ground musically but were undeniably catchy.

This was especially true of the album's lead track and the group's first single, "Wannabe." This lighthearted romp kicks off with the Spices ostensibly in full control; they'll tell you what it is they "really really" want. But their chief request of a potential lover goes little deeper than asking him to be a friend as much as a romantic partner, and it transpires that all the group really wants is to "zigazig ha," a phrase coined by Brown. Though "Wannabe" was clearly *Spice's* strongest track, Fuller and Virgin had wanted the mid-tempo "Love Thing" to be the first single. But the Spices insisted on "Wannabe" and were rewarded with watching the single top the charts in over twenty countries (including the U.K. and U.S.) on its release in the summer of 1996.

Spice was released in Britain in November 1996, entering the charts at number 1. Slogans on the inner sleeve like "She who dares wins" and "Future is female" could easily have come from a riot grrrl zine, but the difference was the attitude. Whereas riot grrrls questioned the societal roles into which women had been cast, the Spice Girls appeared to celebrate them. Anna Louise Golden was only one of many writers who castigated the riot grrrls for being "so dour and dire" in contrast to the sunny, cheeky Spices. Girl power in the Spice book was again a means to an end, using, as Halliwell wrote, one's "brains and femininity and most importantly inner strength and determination" to "help you achieve your goals." Not a challenge to the system, but a friendly suggestion on how to use it to your advantage—a philosophy called "sexy feminism lite" by *Vogue*.

Their next three singles, "Say You'll Be There," "2 Become 1," and double A-side "Who Do You Think You Are"/"Mama," all entered the U.K. charts at number 1. They quickly parlayed this musical success into other arenas. Though Chisholm might have complained about people who "treat us as a product," the Spices weren't shy about promoting a wide array of products themselves, including cameras, phone cards, choco-lates, perfume, potato chips, soft drinks, and Aprilia scooters (though the latter endorsement deal would result in a lawsuit), not to mention their own line of Spice Girls items (including dolls). The media was invited to not only observe but also par-ticipate in the group's commodification. It wasn't the group's management, but Peter Lorraine, editor of *Top of the Pops* magazine, who gave the members their distinctive nick-names in an article entitled "Spice Rack"—Ginger Spice (Halliwell), Posh Spice (Adams), Sporty Spice (Chisholm), Scary Spice (Brown), and Baby Spice (Bunton)—nicknames that caused the group to further exaggerate the inherent cartoon character quality of their personas.

An article in the *Spectator* pushed the debate to a new level by asking the group about their political views; Halliwell called former prime minister Margaret Thatcher the original Spice Girl and "pioneer" of Girl Power. The article prompted discussion about a newly discovered youthful demographic dubbed "the Spice vote," and the rush was on to deconstruct the group's social significance. The Spices made the U.K. papers every day for months, in stories ranging from one in the *Sunday Telegraph* that called ads appearing to depict violence against men "a case of advertisers leaping on to the 'girl power' bandwagon started by the Spice Girls" to "exclusives" like the news that Halli-well got a false fingernail stuck in her ear following a video shoot.

While enjoying the attention and coming across as larger-than-life friendly in their interviews, the Spices expressed some irritation about the condescending tone of the coverage. "Spice Girls make brilliant pop music, only it's not considered 'serious' by people who like Oasis and The Verve," Chisholm told *Q*. All the Spices expressed irri-tation along the lines of Brown's complaint to the *New York Times*: "Sometimes we get treated as bimbos and we're not bimbos." Once the media learned that a managerial team had put the group together, a further assumption was hinted at: the Spices couldn't sing, or, if it was conceded that they did sing on their own records, that they couldn't sing well.

In truth, the Spice Girls gave very few live performances until they launched their world tour in October 1997; their spots on television or awards shows rarely required them to sing more than three songs. And the group's reception in the U.S. was less frenzied than overseas. Though "Wannabe" and *Spice* both topped the charts (the latter case marking the first time a British female act, and the third time an all-female group, had topped the album charts in the U.S.), subsequent releases did not fare as well. Neither their music nor their "social significance" was taken seriously. Rather, the Spices were treated as Britain's latest disposable pop culture trend, and stateside girl power would prove as transitory as the popularity of another trendy British import, the children's TV show *Teletubbies*.

The Spices' world tour coincided with the release of their second album, *Spiceworld* (U.K. number 1, U.S. number 3), and repeated the catchy pop/smooth ballad mix of the first album. *Spiceworld* was also the name of the group's sole feature film, a fictional day-in-the-life-of-a-Spice-Girl with a mediocre script that fell short of the Spices' obvious comedic skills. The film quickly earned back its twenty-five-million-dollar budget on its European release in December 1997 (the U.S. release followed in January 1998). In the U.K., "Spice Up Your Life" and "Too Much" topped the charts, making the Spices the first act whose first six singles all reached number 1.

But cracks in the Spice veneer were beginning to show. In November 1997, the group fired their manager, a move the media called "the ultimate act of Girl Power." Then, in May 1998, having struggled with stress and bulimia for a number of years, Halliwell left two weeks prior to the group's U.S. tour. Halliwell, who had been called "Podge Spice" in the press, was not the only Spice Girl to have her weight scrutinized. Chisholm, whose rigorous dieting had triggered a depression, was tagged "Sumo Spice." And Adams, defending her slender figure following the birth of her son, had to insist to the press, "I'm not anorexic, I'm not bulimic, and I'm not a skeleton."

The Spices continued as a foursome, though they would not release another album until *Forever* in 2000 (U.K. number 2, U.S. number 39). By then, though not formally announced, the group was, for all practical purposes, split up. Some members had already released solo projects, and each Spice Girl would eventually become a solo artist. Yet the media frenzy remained, at least in Britain. When Adams married soccer star David Beckham, the two became tabloid fodder as "Posh 'n' Becks," dubbed "the Jesus, Mary and Joseph of twenty-first century Britain" in the *Evening Standard*. Adams's wedding dress would later be displayed in London's historic Victoria and Albert Museum.

Britney Spears prompted the kind of debate in the U.S. that the Spice Girls did in the U.K., chiefly about whether her perceived influence was a good or bad thing. But, unlike the Spices, Spears had a substantial entertainment background before she pursued a music career. And key to the Spears controversy was her youth; when her first single and album topped the charts, she was just seventeen years old.

Spears was born in Kentwood, Louisiana, in 1981 and began performing in school (making her debut singing "What Child Is This" at her kindergarten graduation), in local talent shows, and in the church choir. When she was eight, she auditioned for a role on the '80s version of the TV show *The Mickey Mouse Club* but was rejected for being too young. So Spears moved to New York City with her mother and sister, studying at the Professional Performing Arts School. She also found work in commercials and had a role in the off-Broadway show *Ruthless!* At eleven, she finally joined *The Mickey Mouse Club* cast, sharing the bill with fellow Mouseketeers Christina Aguilera, who would also become a singing star, and future *NSYNC members J. C. Chasez and Justin Timberlake (who would later become Spears's boyfriend).

After the show was canceled, Spears's lawyer suggested she consider a singing career, and in June 1997 she auditioned for Jive Records with a powerful performance of Whitney Houston's "I Have Nothing." Jive signed Spears and set her up with a number of producers, including Max Martin, who wrote " . . . Baby One More Time" and had worked with the Backstreet Boys (who were also on Jive), and Eric Foster White, who had worked with Whitney Houston, one of Spears's favorite performers. In the summer of 1998, Spears began a tour of shopping malls around the U.S., performing to backing tracks and building a core audience months before the October 1998 release of " . . . Baby One More Time." The album of the same name was released in January 1999, and both the single and the album debuted at number 1, the first time a solo artist had topped both charts at once. The title came from the song's chorus, which actually went "Hit me baby, one more time." Though Spears insisted that "hit me" meant "just give me a sign" and not physical violence, the words were nonetheless dropped from the title lest they cause offense.

But eyebrows were raised over the schoolgirl-in-heat persona Spears projected in her first video, along with an increasingly revealing series of stage outfits. The photos illustrating an April 15, 1999, *Rolling Stone* cover story, with the suggestive title "Inside the Heart and Mind (and Bedroom) of America's New Teen Queen," provoked considerable outrage. The American Family Association charged that the pictures, which showed Spears in push-up bras and a minuscule pair of shorts with "Baby" in rhinestones on the bottom, presented "a disturbing mix of childhood innocence and adult sexuality" and asked that all "God-loving Americans" boycott stores carrying her albums.

Spears, an avowed Baptist who called the satiric cartoon series *South Park* "sacrilegious," evinced surprise at such reactions. She explained the risqué clothing as "playing a part," though admitting that the attention such outfits attracted from older men "kind of freaks me out." She also contended it was her own idea to tie her shirt up, exposing her midriff, in the "Baby" video, "so it wouldn't be boring and cheesy."

Along with the leers, Spears drew a fair measure of condescension, ranging from the expected claims that she either could not sing or was lip synching (Spears did admit she occasionally relied on "assistance" from her backing vocalists when she was out of breath onstage) to rumors of breast implants, coupled with a constant reminder that teenybop music was the ultimate in disposable pop and that, despite her initial success, Spears's career would undoubtedly be short-lived.

Britney Spears
September 1999 at the State Theatre, Detroit, Photo by Jennifer Jeffery

Baby would go on to sell over twenty-one million copies and produce three more Top 40 hits, "Sometimes," "(You Drive Me) Crazy," and "From the Bottom of My Broken Heart." Her subsequent albums did not match that success but still performed respectably. 2000's *Oops! . . . I Did It Again*, which had more of an edge than its predecessor, reached number 1 and sold over seventeen million copies, and the accompanying singles ("Lucky," "Stronger," and the title song) all hit the Top 40. 2001's *Britney*, which hit number 1 and sold over four million copies) had an altogether tougher sound, displaying a clear hip-hop influence, and offering blunt responses to her critics; songs like "Overprotected" and "I'm a Slave 4 U" reminded her audience that she did have feelings (though her assertion that the latter song referred to being a "slave to the rhythm" was not entirely convincing).

Tongues wagged that none of the album's singles reached the Top 10, but the success of her first feature film, *Crossroads*, released in 2002, quelled fears that her career was fading. The film was a teenage road flick, with Spears as the high school valedictorian and, more important, a virgin, who finds both love and the ability to write a hit song ("I'm Not a Girl, Not Yet a Woman") by the last reel. Spears's likeable performance won over critics despite the decidedly corny plot, and the film earned a tidy thirty-seven million dollars (more than earning back its twelve-million-dollar budget). Spears also expressed a desire to have further control over her career, having co-written some songs on her second album.

Spears was the first in a string of solo female teenage successes of the era. Christina Aguilera's self-titled debut album and the single "Genie in a Bottle" both topped their respective charts on release in 1999. The following year she beat out Spears for the Best New Artist Grammy. Her appearance on a cover of Labelle's "Lady Marmalade," which also featured Lil' Kim, Mya, and Pink, featured in the film *Moulin Rouge* (with a single remix produced by Missy Elliott) was another chart-topper and won a Grammy for Best Pop Collaboration. Mandy Moore and Jessica Simpson, were two other teens who landed records in the Top 40, and Moore had a hit movie of her own with 2002's *A Walk to Remember*, prompting *Time* to remark "Girl power is back in the 'plexes and this time it sings."

Born in 1969, No Doubt's lead singer Gwen Stefani could well have been Spears's or Aguilera's older sister, a sassy, Americanized version of a Spice Girl, whose girl power philosophy was espoused in the track "Just a Girl," in which she sarcastically noted that being "pretty and petite" meant she should not have any rights. It was a bolder statement than the teen singers dared to make, but the soothing musical backing meant the message could also pass unnoticed.

No Doubt was formed in Anaheim, California, in 1986. Stefani's brother, Eric, the group's main creative force (and keyboard player), persuaded his reluctant sister to join as backing vocalist; another friend, John Spence, served as the original lead singer (one of his catchphrases, "No doubt," also supplied the group's name). No Doubt had been inspired by the early '80s British ska movement, and it was easy for a ska band to find work on the local party circuit. In 1987, Tony Kanal joined on bass, and he and Stefani became romantically involved. The group suffered their first major setback when Spence committed suicide on December 21, 1987. The remaining members decided to continue, with Gwen becoming lead vocalist, Tom Dumont joining on guitar, and Adrian Young on drums.

The band's first release was a self-titled recording sold at shows. In 1991, they signed

Gwen Stefani
June 2000 at the opening of the Experience Music Project museum, Seattle, Photo by Gillian G. Gaar

to Interscope, but their self-titled debut, released the following year, was not a success. The label had no interest in their new songs, which the group eventually released themselves in 1995 as *The Beacon Street Collection*. By then, Eric had left the band, and Stefani and Kanal had split up, but the group had reconciled with their label, and a new album, *Tragic Kingdom*, was released that same year.

Gwen Stefani wrote or co-wrote all but one song on *Tragic Kingdom*. Many dealt with her breakup with Kanal, and, for all the music's liveliness, it had a noticeable undercurrent of melancholy. Sales were slow at first, but constant touring built an audience sufficient to send the album to number 1 the following year, eventually selling over ten million copies. But with the success came an unwelcome side effect: an intense media focus on Stefani, due to her position as lead singer and songwriter and her eye-catching appearance (alternately sporting bleached-blonde or shocking-pink hair) and her new celebrity boyfriend (Gavin Rossdale, lead singer in Bush). Most of the album's photographs did put Stefani in the foreground, but they at least included the rest of the band. Other profiles of the group routinely cut the band members out of photo spreads, and interviewers would direct all their questions to Stefani.

The group addressed the situation in the video for "Don't Speak," which had the band members all vying for attention, but inner tensions remained. The turmoil and touring left Stefani with a mild depression ("I was like, 'I don't want to get up, and I'm going to eat all the ice cream in the house and I'm going to lay in bed,'" she told *Rolling Stone*), which perhaps contributed to the darker sound of *Return of Saturn*, released in the spring of 2000. A number of the songs tapped into the anxiety of a young woman whose life does not yet encompass marriage and raising a family. In "Six Feet Under," the singer flirts with the idea of motherhood even as she contemplates death—on her birthday—and "Marry Me" ponders giving in to "my conventional side." The video for "Simple Kind of Life" visualized these anxieties and had Stefani, dressed as a bride, running away from men in tuxes; in other sequences, she sang in front of a birth control pill dispenser.

The album received good reviews and reached number 2 in the charts but had a fraction of the sales of *Tragic Kingdom*. So the group set out to record a lighter, more danceable album on the next outing: *Rock Steady*, released in 2001. A number of songs featured a reggae influence, such as "Hey Baby," a wry commentary about the jousting for position that occurs backstage between a band and their fans after a show. The album hit the Top 10 and was followed by a successful tour that had Stefani back on stage as a high-kicking, athletic, potential best friend to audiences composed primarily of adoring teenage girls.

Other artists of the period aspired to all-around entertainer status, aiming for success in different areas of the entertainment industry. Jennifer Lopez was already the highest paid Latina actor in the country before launching her singing career in 1999, having spent the decade working extensively in television and film. Lopez was born in 1970 in the Bronx and began taking dance and singing lessons at age five. After high school she moved to Manhattan and found dance work in videos and at clubs; in 1990, she was hired as a "Fly Girl" dancer on the comedy TV show *In Living Color*.

After *In Living Color*, Lopez landed roles on the TV shows *South Central*, *Second Chances*, and *Hotel Malibu* and on the made-for-TV film *Nurses on the Line: The Crash of Flight 7*. She also appeared as a dancer in Janet Jackson's "That's the Way Love Goes" video. She had her first major role in the 1995 film *My Family (Mi Familia)*, and in subsequent films she worked with Jack Nicholson (*Blood and Wine*), director Oliver Stone (*U-Turn*), and a giant snake (*Anaconda*).

The 1997 film *Selena*, about the Tejano singer murdered by her fan club president at age twenty-three, would prove to be Lopez's breakthrough. She won the title role out of a reported twenty-two thousand who auditioned. Making the film also led Lopez to an epiphany; while filming the opening concert scenes in the Houston Astrodome, she realized she also wanted to become a singer. "I don't just want to do one thing, I want to do it all," she told *Vista*. Tommy Mottola, chairman and CEO of Sony Records, had the same idea. After seeing *Selena*, he set up a meeting with Lopez and various producers, which went so well Lopez began working on her album the next day, before the record deal had even been signed.

Mottola was not the only person impressed with Lopez's performance. Her *Selena* role would win her a Best Actress honor at the Latino Media Arts Awards, a Best Breakthrough Performance honor at the MTV Movie Awards, and a Golden Globe nomination for Best Actress. Lopez kept up her work in films (including the critically acclaimed thriller *Out of Sight* with George Clooney, the graphic horror film *The Cell*, and the battered wife drama *Enough*), and launched her recording career with *On the 6*, released in 1999. Lopez co-wrote four of the songs on the album (Gloria Estefan co-wrote the peppy "Let's Get Loud"), which was a mix of love songs and danceable pop. The album reached number 8 and sold over seven million copies; the accompanying singles reached the Top 10 ("If You Had My Love" topping the charts for five weeks).

Yet Lopez's headlines were more often unrelated to music. In December 1999, Lopez and then-boyfriend Sean "Puffy" Combs were arrested when they fled a New York club after a shooting; after police pulled them over for running eleven red lights, they found an unregistered gun in Combs's SUV. (Charges against Lopez were dropped, and Combs was later acquitted of weapons possession and bribery charges). And at the 2000 Grammy Awards, Lopez showed up wearing little more than a silk "gown" barely held together by a pin a few inches below her navel, which also provoked comment.

But Lopez rarely rose to the bait of explaining her personal life in detail ("There are some things you have to keep sacred and private"). She was franker in discussing her career, especially the subtle prejudices faced by ethnic performers. In Lopez's case, these comments focused on her hips, which some saw as "too big" (one rumor even claimed her hips had their own insurance policy). "It's because we see all those actresses who are so thin and white," she told the online site *Mr. Showbiz*. "Latinas have a certain body type. Even the thin ones, we are curvy. I've always had trouble with wardrobe people!"

But the attention did help keep her in the spotlight, and both *J.Lo*, released in 2001, and *J to tha L-O!: The Remixes*, released in 2002, debuted at number 1. Lopez co-wrote more songs on *J.Lo* than on its predecessor, and the album was even more firmly planted in the dance groove (a groove that was emphasized on the *Remixes* album); it sold over two million copies. Lopez also became the first female artist to have a number 1 movie and album in the same week; the romantic comedy *The Wedding Planner* was the top grossing film during *J.Lo*'s release.

Conversely, Mariah Carey, who started out as a singer and then moved into film, did not make the transition as easily. She received a critical drubbing for her role in *Glitter* (2001), and the poor sales of the soundtrack album led to her being dropped by her label, Virgin. Yet this failure paled in comparison to Carey's accomplishments; by the time of the ill-fated *Glitter*, Carey was established as the biggest female singing star of the '90s, having sold more than 140 million albums worldwide. The nine albums she released during the '90s all reached the Top 4, with four of them topping the charts, and fifteen of the singles she released during the decade also reached number I. Only Elvis Presley and the Beatles have had more number Is.

Carey was born in 1970 in Long Island, New York, to a white mother and a black Venezuelan father who divorced when Carey was three. Her mother, a former opera singer and vocal coach, encouraged Carey's interest in music, so Carey listened to classic vocalists like Billie Holiday, Sarah Vaughan, and Aretha Franklin in addition to contemporary rap and R&B. A day after graduating from high school in 1987, Carey moved to Manhattan to pursue a singing career, working as a waitress and eventually landing a job doing backing vocals for Brenda K. Starr.

In 1988, Starr brought her to a Columbia Records party, where Carey handed a demo tape (featuring early versions of "All in Your Mind," "Prisoner," and "Someday," which would appear on Carey's first album) to Tommy Mottola, then a Columbia executive. Mottola played the tape on the way home and was impressed enough to return to the party and look for Carey. She was quickly signed to the label, and released her self-titled debut in June 1990.

Carey had written songs since her backing singer days and co-wrote all the songs on her debut, along with arranging, producing the track "Vanishing," and providing her own backing vocals. In early 1991, the album topped the charts, where it stayed for 11 weeks, spawning four consecutive number 1 singles. That February, Carey received two Grammys, for Best New Artist and Best Female Pop Vocal Performance (for "Vision of Love"). Carey released an album a year for the rest of the decade (except 1996, though release of the single "Always Be My Baby" gave her another number 1). The ballads and love songs that were Carey's forte provided a perfect showcase for her immaculate soul-pop, enhanced by an impressive seven-octave vocal range.

In 1993, she married Mottola, who was twenty years her senior (and had been married when he and Carey met), and the two moved to a mansion in Bedford Hills, New York. Soon after, rumors began circulating about Mottola's control over Carey, which reportedly extended to having her followed and monitoring her daily activities. Two *Rolling Stone* stories revealed that Carey was forced to talk to her friends in code on the phone, and her home was nicknamed "Sing Sing." Carey finally regained control over her life and career when she separated from Mottola in 1997 (they later divorced) and changed her management team. She played down her domestic difficulties in interviews, but the video for her next single, "Honey" (another number I), did feature a sequence with Carey being held prisoner in a house by an intimidating man. But she insisted the video's similarities to her own life were "unintentional."

Carey's next albums, 1997's *Butterfly* and 1999's *Rainbow*, displayed more hip-hop influences than her previous work. On *Butterfly* she worked with Sean "Puffy" Combs and co-wrote "Babydoll" with Missy Elliott, and on *Rainbow*, Elliott and Da Brat appeared on "Heartbreaker" and Snoop Dogg on "Crybaby." When "Heartbreaker" reached number I, Carey became the only artist to have had a number I hit in every year of the decade; she also broke the Beatles' record for the most weeks spent at number I on the singles chart. In December 1999, she was honored as Artist of the Decade at the *Billboard* Music Awards.

Rainbow would be Carey's last album with Columbia. In April 2001, she signed a reported eighty-million-dollar contract with Virgin, with her first album for the label set to be the soundtrack to her film *Glitter* (originally titled *All That Glitters*), planned for release that summer. (Carey had made her film debut in the 1999 film *The Bachelor*.) But the strain of Carey's demanding career was beginning to show. In a *Newsweek* story, producer Jimmy Jam marveled at Carey's ability to work all night recording (in three different studios), get four hours of sleep, spend the day shooting a video, and return to the studio in the evening after dinner. That Carey was so devoted to her career was commendable, but maintaining such an intense schedule (especially for an insomniac, as Carey admitted she was) was bound to become punishing, both physically and mentally.

In the summer of 2000, Carey openly complained on her website about her problems with "corporate people," saying of her career, "I do it for you, and I don't want to have to stop because I'm afraid." But a year later stress had pushed Carey to the point where she admitted, "I really don't feel that I should be doing music right now" in a statement on her website that was quickly removed. A later statement insisted "nothing's wrong," but at the end of July Carey checked into a hospital suffering from "extreme exhaustion." *Glitter*, set to open in August, was pushed back to September.

Carey's recovery from what was now being called an "emotional and physical breakdown" meant she was unavailable to promote her new film. Her presence may not have helped *Glitter*'s fate, for the film was widely panned. The story was a semi-fictionalized version of Carey's own rise to fame, but the film suffered from not only retreading familiar ground (yet another rags-to-riches story) but also from Carey's wooden, uninspired performance; her character only seemed to come to life when singing. Within days of its release, the film was the subject of numerous jokes. One, on *Saturday Night Live*'s "Weekend Update" segment, alluded to the recent September 11 attacks on

America, the newsreader stating that the military was searching for Osama bin Laden, the Muslim leader behind the attacks, in places likely to be deserted, "Like theaters showing Mariah Carey's film."

The *Glitter* soundtrack failed to reach the Top 10 and sold poorly. Almost immediately rumors began to circulate that Carey's contract with Virgin would be terminated. The rumors were initially denied; in August, Nancy Berry, then vice chair of the Virgin Music Group, had issued a statement saying "Virgin Music Worldwide continues to give its absolute commitment and support to Mariah on every level." But on January 23, 2002, it was announced that Carey and Virgin would indeed part ways. Carey retained the twenty-one million dollars she received on signing in April 2001 and another twenty-eight-million-dollar settlement. But things looked up for Carey as the year progressed. When the film *Wisegirls* screened at the Sundance Film Festival in February 2002, Carey's performance received good reviews, and she signed a new recording contract with Island Def Jam Music Group in May.

The end of the '90s also saw the emergence of a number of African-American artists whose music resisted categorization, drawing on rap, funk, R&B, reggae, and soul. Macy Gray (born Natalie Renee McIntyre in 1970) did not start singing until she was a film student at University of Southern California. Work in local clubs led to her recording an album with what she called "a funky rock band" for Atlantic in 1994, but it was never released. She eventually signed a deal with Epic, who released *On How Life Is* in 1999. The inventive album included such tracks as "I've Committed Murder," in which Gray coolly detailed killing her boyfriend's boss with the theme from *Love Story* as the musical backing. It sold over seven million copies and reached number 4. The single "I Try" (which reached the Top 5) won a Grammy for Best Female Pop Vocal Performance. The provocative album *The Id*, released in 2001, also received high praise, for Gray's distinctive voice ("like Daffy Duck with soul," according to *Rolling Stone*, the writer hastening to add that such a sound was "endearing") and confrontational sentiments, readily seen in song titles like "Relating to a Psychopath" and "Gimme All Your Lovin' or I Will Kill You."

Alicia Keys's *songs in A minor* created a sensation on its release in 2001, when it debuted at number 1 on the pop charts, topped the R&B charts, spawned a number 1 single, "Fallin'," and quickly sold over six million copies. Keys, born in 1981 in New York to an Italian mother and an African-American father (her parents split when she was two), began playing piano at age five. By the time she enrolled in New York's Professional Performing Arts School she had begun writing songs. She also formed a group, called Ambition, with two friends. The group's vocal coach, Conrad Robinson, introduced Keys to his brother, Jeff, who became her manager.

Keys graduated from high school at sixteen and won a scholarship to Columbia University, but she soon dropped out to focus on her music career. She signed with Columbia Records but ran into conflicts with the producers with whom the label wanted her to work. "The producers would be like, 'Just get in the booth and sing,' and that got her frustrated," Robinson told *Rolling Stone*. Keys finally insisted she could produce herself, and she completed an album in 1998, which Columbia rejected. Arista bought Keys out of her Columbia contract, and Keys went with Arista head Clive Davis when he left to form a new label, J Records.

Keys's work reflected her training as a classical pianist, especially on tracks like "Fallin'," with its underlying Chopin melody. But such a style initially made it hard for Keys to find a place on the radio. Discussing "Fallin'," Davis explained to *Q* that "Urban radio wanted a faster tempo song, pop felt it was too urban" (the album's original title, *soul stories in A minor*, had been changed out of a concern it might limit radio exposure to black stations). In an effort to "get around radio," Davis booked Keys on *Oprah Winfrey* and *The Tonight Show*, which resulted in advance orders for the album doubling overnight.

The sensual pull of "Fallin'" made it an irresistible introduction to the rest of the album, which, aside from two songs, Keys produced, arranged, and wrote. She expertly blended classical piano and gospel harmonies with funky beats and flourishes like a string and flute arrangement by '70s soul star Isaac Hayes. Keys received six Grammy nominations and won five, including Best New Artist, Best R&B Album and Song of the Year, Best R&B Song, and Best Female R&B Vocal Performance (for "Fallin'").

Keys credited artists like Lauryn Hill, who had found success with "alternative rap" group the Fugees before launching a career as a solo artist, for paving the way for her neo-soul style. Hill was born in 1975 in South Orange, New Jersey. She began singing as a child, improvising lyrics over instrumental songs. She also spent hours investigating her parents' collection of '60s and '70s soul 45s, citing Aretha Franklin, Sam Cooke, and Stevie Wonder as particularly influential. At thirteen, she made her singing debut, singing Smokey Robinson's "Who's Lovin' You" at the Apollo. She also pursued acting, eventually winning roles on the TV soap opera *As the World Turns* and in the film *Sister Act 2: Back in the Habit*. She also formed the rap outfit Tranzlator Crew with a friend, Prakazrel "Pras" Michel; they were soon joined by Nelust Wyclef Jean and renamed themselves the Fugees.

The trio's first album, *Blunted on Reality* (released in 1994 on Ruffhouse), fared poorly. But their second, 1996's *The Score*, was a smash, topping both the pop and R&B charts and selling over eighteen million copies, making it the best-selling rap record of the time. The group's cover of Roberta Flack's "Killing Me Softly with His Song" was also a Top

Lauryn Hill
August 1999 at Pine Knob, Clarkston, Michigan,
Photo by Jennifer Jeffery

5 hit and won a Grammy for Best R&B Performance by a Duo or Group with Vocal (*The Score* also won a Grammy for Best Rap Album). But after the release of *Bootleg Versions* that same year, which failed to reach the Top 40, the group split (though the door was left open for a possible reunion), and the members pursued their own projects.

Hill initially began writing songs she planned to give to other artists but eventually decided to record them herself. In 1998, *The Miseducation of Lauryn Hill* (which she wrote, arranged, and produced) was as big a success as *The Score*, topping the pop and R&B charts and selling over seven million copies. She later told *Rolling Stone* that she wanted to "write songs that lyrically move me and have the integrity of reggae and the knock of hip-hop and the instrumentation of classic soul," a concise description of *Miseducation*. Mixed in with love songs (including a smooth cover of the standard "Can't Take My Eyes Off You") and a tribute to her son ("To Zion") were statements of independence like "Lost Ones" and "Doo Wop (That Thing)," a number 1 single that explored conflict between the sexes. The album topped numerous "Best Of" lists, and Hill was nominated for ten Grammys and won five: for Best New Artist, Album of the Year, Best R&B Album, and Best Female R&B Vocal Performance and Best R&B Song for "Doo Wop."

But Hill would take four years to release another record, *MTV Unplugged No. 2.0*, which documented her live appearance on the show. In the extended monologues that introduced each song, she appeared to disparage her stardom, referring to herself as a "prisoner": "I had created this public persona, this public illusion, and it held me hostage." Many critics admitted to finding this stance baffling, but Hill, by then married with two children, was clearly dedicated to setting her own priorities.

Like Keys and Hill, Missy "Misdemeanor" Elliott was heavily involved in every aspect of her career, which extended to substantial writing and producing for other artists. Melissa Elliott was born in Portsmouth, Virginia, in 1971. A highly intelligent child who could have skipped two grades in school if she had not wanted to remain with friends her own age, Elliott began singing as a child and writing what she called "story songs" in high school. She also formed her first group in high school with three female friends, initially called Fay Z and then Sista. The group attracted the attention of Devante Swing, a producer and member of the R&B quartet Jodeci, who brought them to New York and then sent them to Rochester to record an album for his Swing Mob label. The deal fell apart, and Elliott went home to Portsmouth. But she soon returned to New York, writing songs with Timbaland (Tim Mosley), who had worked with Elliott on material for Sista.

The duo's big break came when R&B singer Aaliyah had a hit with their song "If Your Girl Only Knew" on her album *One in a Million*. Elliott and Timbaland were initially going to contribute one song to the album; they ended up providing eight. As the duo continued writing songs, Elliott began appearing on records as a guest vocalist/rapper, but she could not land a deal of her own, which she attributed partially to her size; "I wasn't 5'6", size three, with a tiny waist," she told *Pulse*. She eventually signed with Elektra in 1996, initially as a songwriter, and was given her own label, Gold Mind (a coup for a largely unknown artist). Elektra head Sylvia Rhone encouraged Elliott to launch a solo career, and in 1997 *Supa Dupa Fly* was released on the Elektra subsidiary EastWest.

Timbaland produced the album (and Elliott's next two albums), while Elliott received a co-executive production credit. Elliott alternated rap with singing and offered guest vocal spots to Aaliyah, Lil' Kim, and Busta Rhymes, among others. The record topped the R&B charts and hit number 3 pop; the single "Sock It 2 Me"/"The Rain (Supa Dupa Fly)" (the latter song sampling Ann Peeble's "I Can't Stand the Rain" to good effect) was also a substantial hit. The video for "The Rain" further revealed Elliott's playful side; she wore an inflatable vinyl suit pumped up by attendants at a gas station near the set (the suit was later given to the Rock & Roll Hall of Fame museum). "I just got tired of seeing all these rappers in videos driving around in Mercedes and drinking champagne," she explained to *VIBE*.

The album's success won her a spot on the 1998 Lilith Fair bill (making her the first hip-hop artist to appear on the tour), and she continued guesting on other artists' records. She also began producing such artists as Destiny's Child, Whitney Houston,

Me'shell Ndegéocello, and Spice Girl Melanie Brown (with her solo single "Hot"). Elliott's next album, *Da Real World*, released in 1999 on Gold Mind, was another Top 10 on both the pop and R&B charts, and the teasing "Hot Boyz" was the album's biggest hit (number 5 pop, number 1 R&B). Aaliyah and Lil' Kim again appeared as guest vocalists, as did Da Brat, Eminem, and Beyoncé from Destiny's Child. *Miss E . . . So Addictive*, released in 2001, reaffirmed Elliott's position as a hit maker with "Get Ur Freak On," touted by *Rolling Stone* as "the weirdest, loudest, funkiest and just plain best single of the summer so far."

Still, conventionally tailored groups like Destiny's Child proved that, with the right combination of performer and song, commercial success could be "created." Two aspiring managers in Houston formed the all-female group in 1989, by holding a series of auditions. Billed variously as GirlsTyme, Somethin' Fresh, and Cliché, the group performed at school functions and other local events, culminating in a 1992 appearance on the TV talent show *Star Search*. At this point, the group, consisting of Beyoncé Knowles, LeToya Luckett, LaTavia Roberson, and Kelendria (Kelly) Rowland, all born in 1981, began working under a new name, Da Dolls, and with a new manager, Knowles's father, Mathew.

Da Dolls signed with Elektra but were dropped before completing their first album. The group soon landed a new deal with Columbia under the name Destiny's Child. Their first song, the lush ballad "Killing Time," appeared on the 1997 *Men in Black* soundtrack, and they released their self-titled debut album in 1998. The album hit the R&B Top 20, and the single "No, No, No" reached the Top 5 in both the R&B and pop charts. But it was 1999's *The Writing's on the Wall* that proved to be the group's breakthrough, selling over seven million copies. The album reached the Top 10 in both the R&B and pop charts and produced four Top 40 singles, including "Bills, Bills, Bills" and "Say My Name," both of which topped the pop and R&B charts. The latter song would also win a Grammy for Best R&B Performance by a Duo or Group with Vocal.

The group's poppy R&B featured plenty of harmonizing and playful lyrics (and on their second album, the members began to receive co-writing credits). In "Bills, Bills, Bills," the group complained about a boyfriend who does not pull his financial weight (and repeatedly uses his girlfriend's cell phone—not to call other women, but to call his mother), while "Say My Name" lays down the law to a boyfriend suspected of cheating. The group received some flak for frequently seeming to be castigating men, but Luckett explained that "Bills, Bills, Bills" was based on her own experiences with a boyfriend, adding, "We ain't asking guys to just straight out pay our bills or anything like that. . . . just don't start taking advantage of each other." And Beyoncé told *Rolling Stone*, "A lot of people have thought we're man haters. But we're singing about what

Destiny's Child, (left to right): Farrah Franklin, Kelly Rowland, Beyoncé Knowles, Michelle Williams
May 2000 at Pine Knob, Clarkston, Michigan, Photo by Jennifer Jeffery

women go through. And a lot of the time it isn't all lovey-dovey."

But at this point the group's story became enveloped in backstage drama. On turning eighteen, Roberson and Luckett tried to fire Mathew Knowles as their manager. The two ended up being fired themselves, though they claimed they only learned this when they saw the video for "Say My Name" and discovered, to their surprise, that they had been replaced by Farrah Franklin (born 1981) and Michelle Williams (born 1980). The two filed a lawsuit against the group and Mathew in response (the suit against the group was later dropped, and the suit against Mathew was settled out of court) and formed a new group, Angel.

The new Destiny's Child lineup recorded the song "Independent Women, Part 1" for the *Charlie's Angels* film (co-written and co-produced by Beyoncé, and another pop and R&B chart-topper). But five months after joining, Franklin was fired, reportedly for missing performances; Franklin claimed she had been ill and added that she found Mathew domineering. She later announced plans for a solo album. But though the shakeups were frustrating, the group's members were not necessarily dismayed by them. Beyoncé even recognized their commercial value. "Our story was very squeaky clean, so

I thank God for the controversy," she told *Newsweek* (Articles on the group not only touted their religious beliefs but also stressed the fact that the members didn't drink, smoke, or swear). "I'm happy because it helps me sell records."

The group decided to remain a trio, and their next album, 2001's aptly named *Survivor*, debuted at number 1. The album's more aggressive stance was visible in the title track (another number 1 hit), which could be directed toward a former boyfriend but could also be read as a message to previous members of Destiny's Child (and Luckett and Roberson sued over the song, claiming it violated an arrangement precluding either side from making "disparaging comments"; the suit was settled out of court). "Bootylicious" has the group celebrating the sex appeal of their curvaceous hips, though another number, "Nasty Girl," chides a woman for her risqué clothes—ironic given the group's own penchant for revealing outfits. *Survivor*, largely co-produced by Beyoncé, would sell over three million copies, but after the release of the holiday album *8 Days of Christmas* in 2001, the group announced they were taking a break to work on solo projects. Williams was the first to release a solo album, *Heart to Yours*, in 2002. Rowland appeared on the TV sitcom *The Hughleys*, while Beyoncé, who had starred in a "hip-hopera" update of *Carmen*, landed a co-starring role as "Foxxy Cleopatra" in the spy movie satire *Goldmember*.

But, as usual, artists who fell outside the well-defined parameters of radio and video station playlists found it difficult to get wide exposure and thus build an audience beyond a cult level. Lucinda Williams released her first album in 1979, but it took almost twenty years before her first major critical success. Williams was born in 1953 in Lake Charles, Louisiana. Her father, the poet Miller Williams, was an English professor, so the family moved a number of times; when her parents divorced, she and her siblings remained with him. At age six, Williams began writing poetry, and by twelve she was playing the guitar, listening to artists ranging from Bob Dylan and Joan Baez ("One of my idols") to Loretta Lynn, Hank Williams, Robert Johnson, and Muddy Waters. "Anything I could get my hands on in terms of folk, blues, or country, I just ate it up," she says. "Once I learned how to play the guitar, I spent every waking hour just sitting in my room with my guitar and all my songbooks." Williams's mother, a pianist, also contributed to her musical development. "Just having the piano there as an outlet had a major impact on me," she told *No Depression*. "I got the music from my mother and the words from my dad. I got the best of both worlds."

By her mid-teens, Williams had started playing local coffeehouses. She briefly attended the University of Arkansas, then dropped out and moved to New Orleans, where she began singing in clubs. In the early '70s, she spent time in Austin and Houston, performing a mix of originals and covers in local clubs, while waitressing, housecleaning, and "selling sausages in grocery stores, doing those little demonstration things, just anything and everything," she says. "I didn't really know anything about the music business. The people I surrounded myself with and the world I was in wasn't music-business-oriented. We played for ourselves and for each other. That's what the folk music scene is all about really, just people sitting around playing and trading songs and listening to each other's work and that sort of thing."

In 1978, she recorded her first album, in Jackson, Mississippi. *Ramblin' on My Mind* was released the following year on Folkways, consisting entirely of cover songs, including Memphis Minnie's "Me and My Chauffeur Blues," Hank Williams's "Jambalaya," and the title track (by Robert Johnson). Her second album, *Happy Woman Blues*, was released the following year on the same label but featured all-original material. The albums received little promotion and were sold primarily at shows. In 1984, Williams decided to move to Los Angeles. "I felt like I'd pretty much gone as far as I could go in Austin," she explains. "Even though I liked it a lot there. But I saw other opportunities when I came out to L.A. I was exposed to some different things I hadn't been exposed to before, and I realized, 'Here's an opportunity, take advantage of it.'"

It took some time for the opportunities to appear. A proposed development deal with CBS did not pan out. The atmosphere in L.A. also differed from the more laid-back Texan environment, where "there was just a lot of support," Williams remembers. "I was in my own little support group of other songwriters and stuff. When I came out to L.A. was really the first exposure I had to an actual 'music industry.' And it was pretty frustrating and disillusioning, to tell you the truth. 'Cause something you've done all your life that's real natural, that's second nature to you, all of a sudden you start analyzing it and trying to figure it out, and verbalizing it. And other people are trying to do the same thing, and trying to put rigid controls on things as opposed to just letting things go and happen on their own time. That's the way I'd always lived my life."

She also initially had trouble breaking into the L.A. musicians' "boys club." "I went to this party at some musician's house," she says. "Nobody knew who I was yet. It was all these kind of well-known men musicians and most of the women were either girl-friends or just standing around while the guys passed the guitar around, trading off songs. I was like, 'Well, give me the guitar so I can sing a song,' and somebody handed me the guitar, but it was like this attitude, 'Okay, that's all fine and good, now give it back to us.' There was definitely this kind of vibe, the boys' club kind of thing. I had the feeling like I was the only woman trying to relate on their level.

"It's not like blatant stuff where I don't get paid as much as somebody else," she says of her other encounters with sexism at the time. "It's more subtle. Like when I was growing up playing guitar, guys would say, 'Hey, you're pretty good for a chick.'" On

Lucinda Williams
1990 at the Palomino, North Hollywood, Photo by Sherry Rayn Barnett

another occasion, she thought she had a gig lined up at an Austin club only to be told, "'We've already got one chick singer for the month and they all sound alike anyway.' There's a lot of condescension. But it's the same kind of thing that exists in general anywhere. You do have to work harder to get people to take you seriously."

Another reason Williams had to work harder to attract attention from a record label was that her music could not be readily classified. Her mix of country, blues, and rock was not easy to plug into prevailing radio formats. "Nobody really knew what to do with it," she admits. But in the wake of Suzanne Vega's success with "Luka," Williams was offered a deal with Rough Trade, and her self-titled album came out in 1988, just in time for her to be lumped in with other singer-songwriters of the period like Tracy Chapman. But, as she points out, she shared little with them stylistically. *Lucinda Williams* had much more of a roots music feel than Vega's *Solitude Standing* or *Tracy Chapman*.

"I don't like being categorized, and I don't like the whole female singer-songwriter thing," she says. "In fact, I really hate it. It really surprised me that I got thrown in with Tracy Chapman and Suzanne Vega, because I didn't identify musically with them. But because we're female singer-songwriters and we're singing more serious-oriented songs, we get thrown in together. The music business is ridiculous. It's like a bunch of people sitting around—mostly men—trying to figure out how they can market something and get an angle. 'Hey, we see a little connection between this and this and this, so there must be something going on here. It's a scene. Hey, we have a movement now.' It's all stuff that's created by the music industry to make money. It doesn't mean anything. I'm still going to be doing this when they decide it's not popular anymore. And that's the tragedy of it. Because they decide it's not popular anymore, other women singer-songwriters get left out in the cold because suddenly they don't fit in."

Rough Trade released Williams's *Passionate Kisses* EP in 1989 (the title track would earn Williams a Best Country Song Grammy when Mary Chapin Carpenter covered it), but then her association with the label ended, and she would not release another record until 1992's *Sweet Old World*, on Chameleon. When that label folded, it would take six years for Williams to release another album, but *Car Wheels on a Gravel Road* proved to be her artistic breakthrough.

Its birth had not been easy. She first recorded the album in Austin, co-producing with her then-guitarist, Gurf Morlix, but was unhappy with the results ("Something was missing," she told *Rolling Stone*). After recording a duet with Steve Earle in Nashville ("You're Still Standin' There," which appeared on Earle's 1996 album *I Feel Alright*), she took him on as producer and re-recorded the album. But she still was not pleased, and Morlix quit in frustration. The album was finally finished in L.A., with Roy Bittan, keyboardist with the E Street Band, producing, and was released on Mercury.

Gravel Road is the kind of album music critics love: intelligent, well-crafted, bucking mainstream music industry conventions. The songs were steeped in melancholy and regret; even "Joy," with its more aggressive musical drive, depicted the singer in limbo between love affairs. Though the album did not come close to the Top 40 and only surpassed half a million in sales, it was hailed as a masterpiece and won a Grammy as Best Contemporary Folk album (along with a nomination for Best Female Rock Vocal Performance).

Gravel Road's follow-up, *Essence*, came together much quicker and was released in 2001. The ache of loss was beautifully conveyed on the opening track, the world-weary "Lonely Girls," while "Out of Touch" provided a poignant depiction of how the passing of time erodes relationships. The album was Williams's first to crack the Top 40, reaching number 28. But by then, Williams's dedication to making music that satisfied her own expectations showed that chart placements were not the motivating factor in her career.

Kirsty MacColl was another artist whose music could not always be defined easily. But by the end of her life she was nonetheless acclaimed as one of Britain's finest songwriters, though she bristled at the "female singer-songwriter" tag. "There's a lot of sexist old crap in this business," she told *Record Collector*. "I'm always described as a 'female singer-songwriter.' You don't see all these other singer-songwriters described as male singer-songwriters. I mean, what's your genitalia got to do with it?" She presumably would have found less fault with U2's Bono describing her as "the Noel Coward of her generation."

MacColl was born in 1959 in England, the daughter of folksinger Ewan MacColl. Her parents divorced when she was young, and she was raised by her mother, Jean, a choreographer. She became a fan of pop music while growing up, particularly the records of the Beach Boys. "The first record I ever had was 'Good Vibrations,' which my brother bought," she said. "I was so into it, I was allowed to play it, and I used to play it to death. Surf culture was something that was very fascinating to me for a long time, because I didn't live anywhere near the sea. It was like another world. It sounded incredible." Other favorites were the Beatles, Frank Zappa and the Mothers of Invention, a Charlie Parker album her father had given her, and a '50s-era album of a Mariachi band. "That's my favorite album of all time, I think," she said. "It's the happiest music. Music was the only thing that gave me a great deal of pleasure. It was escapism. I'd sit at home—I was alone a lot—and I'd play a lot of records."

MacColl played violin and oboe at school and also studied classical guitar. She formed her first group, the Drug Addix, while at art college in the late '70s. "A very subtle name, but you had to have a name like that to get gigs in the punk era," she said. "Everybody was in a band. If you didn't have a band already, you just started one. I didn't have any equipment, so I had to be a singer. It was exciting. It was really an attitude, like, 'You can do anything you want and don't take any crap.' But basically we were an R&B band—which was a bit disappointing to people who came expecting us to spit at them!"

The band released an EP, *The Drug Addix Make a Record*, in 1978, with MacColl credited as "Mandy Doubt." The band then recorded some demos for Stiff Records, which turned them down. But the label liked MacColl's voice, and when they learned she had been kicked out of the Drug Addix, they asked to hear her own material. She signed with the label, which released her first single, "They Don't Know," in 1979. Though a MacColl original, its sound was straight from the girl group era—a bittersweet pop song about loving the wrong boy, backed with a lush music arrangement and rich harmonies.

The single received a lot of airplay but did not make the charts (Tracey Ullman later covered the song, with MacColl on backing vocals, and had a Top 10 hit in the U.K. and U.S.). A follow-up single was recorded but not released, and MacColl was dropped. She then signed with Polydor, her first single for the label a cover of Goffin and King's

"Keep Your Hands Off My Baby." But it was a rollicking country & western number that gave MacColl her first chart success, with the unlikely title of "There's a Guy Works Down the Chip Shop Swears He's Elvis," released in 1981. The single reached the U.K. Top 20, but two subsequent singles (including a cover of the Beach Boys' "You Still Believe in Me") and the 1981 album *Desperate Character* failed to chart. She nevertheless recorded a second album for Polydor ("It was totally different from *Desperate Character*; it was quite electronic and quite depressing"), but the label decided not to release it and MacColl was again dropped (some tracks later surfaced on the 1985 U.K. album *Kirsty MacColl*).

MacColl returned to Stiff in 1983 and the following year had a Top 10 hit with a cover of Billy Bragg's "A New England." On the day the record peaked, she gave birth to her first son. The father was Steve Lillywhite, who had co-produced the single with MacColl; the couple married in 1984. She had a second son in 1987, by which time Stiff had folded, and record companies were unwilling to invest in a woman with two young children.

"They weren't particularly interested because they thought, 'She's got kids, she's not really a committed artist,' and all this crap," she explained. "It never seems to bother them that Sting has children. It seems to be perfectly acceptable for a man to have nothing to do with his family whatsoever as long as he's churning out records, but for a woman, they won't trust you to do that."

But MacColl was able to work as a backing vocalist with artists as varied as the Rolling Stones, Robert Plant, John Wesley Harding, Talking Heads, and Happy Mondays. Her guest appearance on the Pogues' 1987 single "Fairytale of New York" led to her touring with the band, which inspired her to write songs again. In 1989, she had a new deal with Virgin, who released her album *Kite* the same year.

Though MacColl said of her work, "I think of myself primarily as a songwriter and secondly as a vocal arranger. And singing comes somewhere down the line," the material on *Kite* demonstrated how much her skill in all three areas had grown. Her cover of the Kinks' "Days" charted the highest in the U.K. (peaking at number 12), but MacColl wrote or co-wrote most of the album's songs, casting a wry eye on romance in both the country & western–flavored "Don't Come the Cowboy With Me, Sonny Jim" and "Innocence" (a deceptively upbeat song about ending a relationship); attacking the entertainment world for its shallowness in "Fifteen Minutes"; and offering a bitter critique of the social climate in modern Britain in "Free World." The lyrical wit and catchy melodies were bolstered by MacColl's glorious harmonies, layering her vocals to achieve what she calls "an ethereal sound," which made even words like "hopeless" sound uplifting.

Kite reached number 34 in the U.K., but though receiving good notices in the U.S. on its release in 1990 (on Charisma), it failed to chart in the States. 1991's, *Electric Landlady* and 1994's *Titanic Days* broadened MacColl's musical palette. On the former, "Walking Down Madison" set its look at the division between rich and poor to a dance-rock beat, and "My Affair," a jaunty look at infidelity, had an equally lively Latin beat. The latter featured black-humored portraits of characters like the "dreadful daughter and hopeless wife" of "Bad" and the creepy serial killer in "Can't Stop Killing You."

Though a much-admired songwriter in Britain, MacColl's records failed to find strong commercial success. Her personal life was changing as well. In 1994, she and Lillywhite separated (they later divorced), and MacColl considered quitting the music business in favor of pursuing a degree in Latin American Studies. Instead, she opted for less formal study by traveling extensively in Cuba and Brazil, which provided suitably sunny inspiration for *Tropical Brainstorm*.

"I made a decision after *Titanic Days* not to do another album until it was a happy one," she said at the time of the album's U.K. release in 2000 (2001 in the U.S.). "I didn't want to make a miserable, cold English weather record; I want to make something that people can dance to." *Tropical Brainstorm* certainly offered plenty of danceable melodies, and songs that celebrated love and desire with all their attendant ups and downs, though MacColl stressed, "It's not a purist Latin album, because it mixes up the influences so much; it's more a case of introducing these styles into my pop songs."

Sadly, the album would be MacColl's last. On December 18, 2000, she was killed by a speedboat while swimming off the coast of Cozumel, Mexico. MacColl was forty-one. Tributes extolled her songwriting, but it was MacColl's love of making music that remained the most important to her. "I like making records more than anything else," she said. "Starting out with a blank piece of tape and then building it up. It's like starting with a piece of white paper, and you're going to draw the Sistine Chapel, and it's like, 'Where do you put the first line?' Because if the first line isn't right, the rest of it's going to fall down. That's what's exciting to me."

Laura Love's music style similarly spanned genres. But after signing with a major label, she found she was happier working on the indie circuit, where she was able to make a comfortable living without making artistic compromises, something an increasing number of artists had come to realize. Love was born in Omaha, Nebraska, in 1960; while still a child, she moved with her mother and sister to Lincoln, Nebraska. Love's mother had sung with a number of swing and jazz bands, so music was regularly heard around the home. "It just seemed like it was all around me," says Love. "My mom would walk around the house occasionally singing a song, and I'd think, 'Whoa, that's the coolest stuff.'" Love's own musical interests at the time included mainstream acts like the Beatles and the Monkees and the cool vocal stylings of Petula Clark. "I liked the way she rhymed 'Bossa Nova' and 'o-vah' in 'Downtown,'" Love says. When their favorite songs would air on the radio, Love and her sister would frequently sing along.

Love also began experimenting with guitar on a toy plastic model she received when she was eight. "I learned three chords," she says. "And I did this solo when I was in the seventh grade, 'Anticipation,' by Carly Simon. 'Anticipation' was about three chords!" But music was more often the backdrop to a troubled upbringing; Love's mother was frequently hospitalized for mental illness, and Love and her sister spent much of their childhood in foster homes.

At sixteen, Love's interest in music and performing took a step in a more serious direction when she learned that her father, whom her mother had said had died in a car accident, was still alive. "I was looking through a newspaper, and it said, 'World-renowned saxophonist Preston Love returns to Midwest,'" Love remembers. Intrigued, Love went to the bar and approached her father when his band went on break. "I went up and said, 'Umm, did you ever know a Winnie Winston?' And he said, 'Uh-huh.' And I said, 'Well, I think I'm your daughter.' And he just about spat his drink all over me!"

When Love's father learned she was an aspiring singer, he brought her onstage at subsequent shows, where she sang songs like the Ohio Players' "Fire" and "Too Much, Too Little, Too Late" by Johnny Mathis and Deniece Williams. These guest spots led to Love's first "professional" gig at the Nebraska State Penitentiary with Leroy Critcher and the Oklahoma Drifters, after the band's members saw Love performing with her father's band. "We did a whole album of Chaka Kahn covers," she says of the prison show. "I can almost remember every song I did on that gig 'cause it was a huge deal to me."

In 1980 Love moved with the guitarist from the band to Portland, Oregon, where she sang with various groups like the Inner City Funk Band, Desire, and other short-lived outfits. But despite her earlier interest in playing an instrument, Love had put her guitar aside, partly because of her lack of skill ("I was terrible," she admits) and partly because there were few role models. "I couldn't see any women playing anything other than an acoustic guitar," she explains. "And I noticed that men all played electric instruments. I didn't see any women playing electric instruments. So I came to the conclusion that that's not what girls did—that was men's work! Girls stood up in the front and sang. So that's what I did."

Love's next stop was Seattle, where a stint in a pop band inspired her to learn electric bass. "And then once I learned how to play the bass and sing at the same time, I realized I wanted to do something else," she says. An encounter with a musician who admired Love's motorcycle at a local convenience store led to the formation of Love's next band, Boom Boom G.I., a name taken from the call Vietnam prostitutes would use to hail U.S. soldiers. Love, still learning the bass, had not planned on singing, but when the band's original singer dropped out, Love took over on lead vocals (the mixed-gender band also featured a female drummer).

The band released two albums of gnarly blues-rock, *Slide a Little Closer*, in1988, and *Don't Know What I'll Wear*, in 1989. But the most memorable aspect of Love's time with the band was being castigated in a local review for singing "annoyingly pointless" lyrics such as "hot sex poodle in a sleazy little suit." "That was a wake-up call for me," she recalls. "I thought, 'Wow, I didn't even know anybody out there heard the lyrics.' *I* hadn't heard the lyrics! I'd always divorced myself from the meaning of words. And I went, 'You know, there's got to be more to life than singing bad lyrics and playing bad music.' I started to want to say stuff that was more reflective of my own experience."

As a result, Love entered the University of Washington, majoring in psychology and taking a number of women's studies classes. For one class, "Women, Words, Music," she recorded a twenty-minute set of songs that became her first solo tape in 1989, *Menstrual Hut*, an acoustic album featuring traditional numbers like "I Never Will Marry" and Love's own "I'm Your Daughter's Lover."

The development of Love's musical career coincided with her realization of her lesbianism, and in turn, her discovery of the lesbian-feminist community. "When I first put out *Menstrual Hut* and *Z Therapy* [her first solo album], women responded first," she says. "They started telling their friends about me, and then radio stations started playing the music, and then Mary McFaul [Love's manager] started booking us, and the audience got bigger. But women were the first to say, 'Hey! Check this out!' And I'll be eternally grateful to the women's community for listening to me first."

Love recorded *Z Therapy* with local musicians in Austin, where she was visiting a friend who had AIDS, an experience that inspired the song "Things I've Heard People Think." The acoustic sound on her first release now gave way to a livelier, funkier music that reflected Love's diverse musical influences. She released the album in 1990 on her own label, Octoroon Biography, "octoroon" being a person of one eighth African descent, referring to her own mixed-race heritage. "I liked the way the words sounded together," Love explains. "But people come up to me at concerts, like in Kentucky, and say, 'Octoroons, I love them! Them little cookies.' So I just go, 'Yeah, they are good, aren't they?'"

Back in Seattle, Love formed the Laura Love Band, releasing the albums *Pangaea*, in 1992, and *Helvetica Bold*, in 1994. She also played with the all-female satirical band Venus Envy, best known for their holiday release, *I'll Be a Homo for Christmas*. Love gave her musical sound a name—Afro-Celtic—and she was as likely to do a spiritual like "Swing Low, Sweet Chariot" as she was to break into a yodel in her own "Anyway" ("I put the 'yo' back in 'yodel,'" she joked). Her songwriting addressed broader concerns as well, in the anti-war "Bang Bang" and "Nelson," a tribute to South African leader Nelson Mandela. "With *Menstrual Hut*, I just said, 'I'm going to talk about some of the stuff I've learned that has raised my consciousness,'" she explains. "And then on *Z Therapy* I was in love for the first time with a woman, and I went 'Wow! This is cool!' and I wanted to talk about that a little bit. And then I started thinking, 'Well, love's a beautiful thing, but there's other things to write about too.'"

More important, Love found she could actually make a living playing music. "Mary said, 'That's how I make my living. I send people like you out and get them gigs, they come back and bring the money, and we divvy it up and that's how we live.' But I just didn't think that was possible." A date at a local women's music festival changed her mind when she saw how many CDs she could sell after a show. "I just couldn't believe it—people were buying them!" she says. "I had my rent after that one gig. And that's when I thought, 'Maybe there is something to this!'"

Love also found she had become the kind of role model she had missed as a budding musician. "People would come up to me, and they'd bring their daughters and say, 'I wanted my daughter to see that there were strong women playing musical instruments,'" she says. "And that's when I started thinking that I had really been shaped by the predominant culture. Without even knowing it, I had developed some sexist and racist and gender role ideas. And it woke me up to all the biases and stereotypes that I carried. These women would say,

Laura Love
Summer 2000, Seattle, Photo by Gillian G. Gaar

'My daughter's told me she's going to be a bass player,' or 'She's going to be a musician,' or 'She wants to write songs.' And I started realizing, you can't even dream it, unless you see it."

Love's blend of musical styles and the band's female element led to regular work at women's festivals and folk/ethnic events. She did not consider large-scale success. "I wanted to be a famous singer," she says. "But I knew early on the chances of that were pretty slim. For me, it was fun to do regardless if there was two people or two million people in the audience. I just wanted to sing. And great if I got to be famous, but I didn't think that would happen."

Nonetheless, Love did get an unexpected opportunity to step up to a major label. After her song "I'm A-Givin' Way" appeared on the Putumayo Records compilation *Shelter: The Best of Contemporary Singer-Songwriters*, she was invited to perform at the record release party at Carnegie Hall in October 1994. But the label could only afford to fly Love to New York, not her band. "I was told, 'It's solo or not at all,'" she recalls. "And I thought, 'Well, it's a free trip to New York City. It's four minutes out of my life. And if I fail miserably, nobody from Seattle's going to be there.'"

To her surprise, Love was the hit of the evening; the *New York Times* wrote that she "stole the show." Love eventually signed with Mercury, impressed by the attitude of the label's president, Danny Goldberg (formerly one of Nirvana's managers). "He said, 'I don't see you being a big hit. I just like your music,'" she says. "I thought that was really refreshing, because I don't see me as a big hit maker either. So I didn't feel a lot of pressure to be, like, Mariah Carey—thank God! He was basically saying, 'I understand what you do. And to me, it's not just about signing people that are going to make huge hits, it's about signing people that I like.' And they just left me to do whatever I wanted. I thought, 'Wow, what a gift.'" .

Love released two albums while on Mercury: 1997's *Octoroon* and 1998's *Shum Ticky*. But while Love liked the greater exposure that being on a major label offered, she was not as happy with the more workaday aspects. Used to charting her own career, she did not entirely adapt to doing things the label's way. "I didn't like all the schmoozing," she admits. "I'd play industry shows, like a *Billboard* convention; they trot you around, and we would have to talk to everyone and ask them to play our record. It's just such a fucked up, fake-o experience. You feel that you're pretty much paid to smile. Your face would get tired and you'd just get sick of talking to people. And those kind of shows just sapped me of the will to live!"

A greater problem was that Goldberg, Love's strongest supporter at Mercury, left the label before *Shum Ticky* was released. *Octoroon* had sold only about seventy thousand copies, "Which is nothing by their standards," she says. "Ours, it was great! I couldn't believe I sold that many records." With no promotional support, *Shum Ticky* did not even sell that many copies, and Love was dropped, which did not entirely disappoint her. "I really wanted to see what the experience of being on a major label would be like," she says. "Who the hell knows, maybe I could've sold fifty gazillion records. But I had a sneaking suspicion that my time there would be limited. So it was good to see it and it was real good to be done with it."

Love has gone back to working at her own pace, touring and, in 2000, releasing the album *Fourteen Days* on Zoë, an imprint of Rounder Records. For Love, success as a musician has come by redefining "success" to fit her own needs. "When I first started out, in the mid-'80s, it was all, 'You have to be on a major label to be legit,'" she says. "But I think there are a lot of people getting hipper to the fact that you don't have to have a hit to make a good living at music."

But while musicians were able to find their own level of success, it was different for those working within the music industry. By the end of the '90s, mergers among the major labels had led to an increased corporate outlook, not to mention the loss of jobs. "Part of what I see is that as the corporations get larger, the jobs are actually becoming fewer," says Cheryl Pawelski, who until spring 2002 was Senior Director of A&R and Catalog Marketing for the EMI Music Catalog Marketing Group. "And the jobs that are truly getting scarce are the most creative jobs. There may be opportunities in the financial end of the business, but the A&R-type jobs are down to a handful. And historically, when jobs get scarce, gender equity goes out the window—and I don't see things getting better for the music business anytime soon! So I guess if a woman is interested in getting into the music business, she will still be most likely hired in publicity, advertising, or back office/legal affairs rather than the flashy creative jobs. But that's not to say that women aren't the presidents of labels and that there is no creative presence at all."

Pawelski, born in Milwaukee in 1966, began her career in the music industry as a musician, though she was always a keen record fan. "As soon as I could get out of the door and buy records, I just started buying copious amounts and sneaking them into the house," she recalls. "I was a waitress, and I'd make one hundred fifty dollars on a Friday night and it'd all be gone the next day. My mom would come in and be like, 'You bought more records didn't you? What do you need all this stuff for?' I like to remind her of that now."

Pawelski began playing with bands in high school and college, playing "guitar and dulcimer and banjo and things with strings." In 1990, she moved to California and started another band, the Bumpin' Uglies, who recorded and toured until the mid-'90s but never quite made enough for the band members to live on. "I wanted to so badly, but either you have the right people or you don't," she says. "And Greg [the band's co-founder] and I just turned out to be like mom and dad in the band with a bunch of really crazy bad kids. And we just couldn't do it anymore. In the middle of our last tour the crazy drummer quit in Phoenix, and the singer was crying, and our bass player kept forgetting his shoes, and it was too much. I completely appreciate what bands go through because it was ugly; I don't want to do that again."

One of the band's singers also worked in the Human Resources Department at Capitol Records and helped Pawelski get a job there in 1990. She eventually wound up in the Sync Licensing department, licensing songs from the company for use in commercials, television, and films. "Which was great, because in a job like that you basically learn everything you never wanted to know about the business," she jokes. "You're soliciting clearances from artists and looking up contracts to see what the restrictions and parameters are. That was really good, because it was two and a half years of answering somebody's phone and getting to know the Capitol catalogue. And one day I was sitting around shooting my mouth off with some music supervisor, talking about Sidney Bechet. And Pete Walding, who was the A&R guy in Special Markets, came out of his office—and this is the big Hollywood moment—and he said, 'How do you know who Sidney Bechet is? You're too young.' And I said, 'Well, Mr. Walding, anybody can buy records.' And he goes, 'You're hired.' So that's how I got into A&R, because Pete heard me talking about Sidney Bechet."

Pawelski's work in Special Markets involved putting together compilations, often for non-traditional retail outlets. "They do things that are premiums—get a free country cassette with a tank of gas, and the sorts of things you see at Starbucks and Pottery Barn," she explains. "So it was my job to know the entire catalogue well enough to be able to pitch my clients with stuff, come up with a repertoire, produce the package, and oversee the mastering. And it's not just compilations like *Women in Rock* or *Bad Metal in the '70s*, it's also, like, *Songs about Blue Jeans*. I've done records for dogs, for blue jeans, shoes, eyes, all kinds of stuff. The weirdest has to be the dog songs. There's less than you'd think. And let's look at the blue jean thing. Sure, you can get Mel McDaniel's 'Baby's Got Her Blue Jeans On,' but Neil Diamond is not going to give you 'Forever in Blue Jeans'—he's just not going to do it. Or 'Blue Jean' by David Bowie—he's not going to want to be on a compilation about blue jeans. So you've got to get pretty creative. But it was a good job for learning all kinds of stuff."

Pawelski also began producing frontline catalogue reissues, starting with a series of Smithereens reissues in the mid-'90s. "Basically they said, 'If you can handle it, you can do it,'" she says. "So I made a point of handling it." Pawelski has produced over twenty-five hundred recordings since then, working on reissues by artists like the Band and the long-awaited *Pet Sounds* box set by the Beach Boys. But, as her career progressed, she saw few changes as far as the number of women working at the top of the industry.

"I don't think the ratio of women to men in this business is ever going to have any parity, especially in the top positions," she says. "Unless women start entering the business in dramatic proportions, I just don't see us getting the corner office chairs. There are many great people working in this business, there just aren't a lot of women. I wish there were more. I think if the whole dot-com music business would have taken off— and maybe it will in the future—there would have been more opportunity for women because there were so many little companies springing up and so many opportunities. But since the digital download world seems to have crashed and the record companies are reducing personnel, it seems likely that men are going to be hanging on to their positions much more firmly."

Changes in attitude also came about as the major record companies were purchased by corporations that had never dealt with the music industry before. "I feel like I have had to work my ass off to prove myself," Pawelski says, "and the ironic thing about that is now there are a lot of people in positions I would be trying to prove myself to who haven't a clue about the catalogue. You have people in this business now that don't know anything about music. It's sales and it's marketing. There's people that have come from Hershey's and Nabisco, and all these other corporations that are very savvy with branding, and it doesn't seem to matter to them that they don't know the artist, the music, or the audience. They seem to think they have a formula to plug these things into, which is why I think a lot of stuff doesn't work. I think it all has to fall down before it becomes the music business again, because it's gotten to such a debilitated state that even if you have people that are walking encyclopedias of musical knowledge, they're devalued by the people that haven't the foggiest notion of who Nancy Wilson is."

Pawelski now has her own company, Filthy Mouth Music: Consultancy/A&R/Production/Licensing. "I thought it would be fun to independently represent artists I like—that own their own masters and publishing—to the film, television, and advertising world, as they wouldn't necessarily have exposure the way they would if a publisher or record company were out plugging away for them," she says. Pawelski also continues to record, releasing children's records under such names as the Mistletones (Christmas music) and the Sleepytones (lullabies). "And I still think I have a solo record in me someday," she says. "It's called *Cheryl Pawelski Throws Like a Girl*. Someday I'll get to that."

In November 2000, Pawelski moderated a panel called "Special Markets & Alternative Ways to Get Heard" at the first *ROCKRGRL* Music Conference (RMC) held in Seattle. The conference was Carla DeSantis's response to the male-dominated panels at

Leslie Ann Jones and Cheryl Pawelski (left to right)
November 2000 at the *ROCKRGRL* Music Conference, Seattle, Photo by Gillian G. Gaar

other music conventions and a result of her desire to see such conferences discuss a wider range of subjects. "There were things I thought were really important issues," DeSantis explains, "like, what do you do when you're a mom and you want to go on tour? And how do you stay true to your own image, why aren't there more women on the radio, what's going on with the Eminem generation? These were things I wanted to explore. And what better way to do that than to bring a bunch of women together who are all in the same boat to talk about it?"

The conference, which ran three days, attracted over twenty-five hundred attendees and did indeed feature panels on being a "rock mom" and staying true to one's image, in addition to panels on marketing, the rise of the Internet, stalkers, self-defense, "Woodstock '99 to Eminem: When Did Women Become the Enemy?," and "The Secret Life of Groupies." Two hundred and fifty artists, including Wanda Jackson, June Millington, and Exene Cervenka, performed at RMC shows over the weekend, and keynote speakers included Ronnie Spector, Amy Ray, and, as a surprise guest, Courtney Love. Ann and Nancy Wilson received *ROCKRGRL's* first Women of Valor Award at a banquet in their honor. "We've never gotten a Grammy," said Ann. "This is the first thing we've ever gotten, so it really means a lot, because it comes from you and not from the industry."

"I figured if we had something cool to come to people would come," DeSantis says, "though I didn't think there would be as many people coming from Europe as there were. People found it worthwhile because you're in a room with other people who are trying to do what you're doing in a totally noncompetitive environment. That's unusual in itself, to be around other musicians in a noncompetitive environment, so I think that's what made it kind of magical. Then of course Courtney called at the last minute and wanted to come. It actually turned out really cool because the success of the conference wasn't based on her being there—that was like an added bonus. It was all a total dream come true. Some of the most influential people, musically, in my life were all in one room. There was Ann Wilson, there was Courtney, there was Bonnie Hayes, who I worshipped in the Bay Area as a songwriter, Pamela Des Barres, Exene performed, the Gossip performed—it was so incredible."

Another, more indie-oriented music conference was held three months before RMC—Ladyfest, held in Olympia, August 1–6, 2000. Inspiration had come from a few sources. In the summer of 1999, Tristin Laughter, a publicist at Berkeley-based Lookout Records, wrote an essay dealing with misogyny in the rock community. "I wanted to address, in particular, the subculture of punk rock and the appropriation of it by totally sexist forces," she explains. "Because to me, it was inherent that punk rock would be part of a critique of culture, not just a marketing ploy which embodied the most virulent strains of mainstream culture, like sexism. Even though it's a hard thing to try to say: 'This is punk' or 'This isn't punk.' But in the light of the Warped Tour with Blink-182 asking female fans [in the audience] 'Show us your tits!' and right after that Woodstock [the Woodstock 1999 festival, which ended in a riot and reports of numerous sexual assaults], I wanted to write something about it. So I did."

Prior to the publication of Laughter's essay in the magazine *Punk Planet*, she sent Allison Wolfe an early draft. "It almost made me cry, it was so amazing," Wolfe says. "I was so proud of her for writing that, because I felt so many of us who had been riot grrrls and had been outspoken hadn't spoken out publicly about anything like this in a long time. I said, 'She's right, this is a total monster that we have been turning a blind eye to. Is there some way we could combat that?' So I thought we could put on the kind of event that we would like to attend and have it be okay to be openly political again. Things just felt so sexist; I was sick of these young testosterone-driven youths saying, 'We're radical, man, because we listen to Slipknot or Limp Bizkit.' I just thought, 'We have to be responsible for creating our own entertainment. We have to start getting vocal and political and start connecting with each other again.'"

Further inspiration came in December 1999 when Wolfe, along with many of the original riot grrrls, returned to Olympia to be filmed for a feature on riot grrrls put together for the Experience Music Project, Microsoft co-founder Paul Allen's Seattle rock museum. Discussions among the participants helped the festival take shape, and Ladyfest was born. "I definitely wanted 'Lady' something," says Wolfe of the name. "It was just a word to reclaim in the same vein as reclaiming the word 'girl.'"

Ladyfest offered an eclectic range of panels, workshops, discussion groups, fashion shows, and daily performances, featuring artists like Lois, the Butchies, and Gina Birch of the Raincoats. The festival hit the national press when *Time* magazine ran a three-page story on the event (illustrated with a large photo of Sleater-Kinney), dubbing Olympia "the hippest town in the West" in the process. More meaningfully, the event also inspired women around the U.S. and overseas to stage their own Ladyfests. "Now it's sprouting up all over the place!" says Wolfe. "Bratmobile went to the one in Glasgow [in 2001]. It was cool, 'cause all the organizers' moms were involved; it was a much more intimate affair. We also played at the one in Chicago [in 2001], which was bigger than the one in Olympia. It might go the way of riot grrrl but that's cool—then someone can start something new."

Bratmobile had performed at the original Ladyfest as well, after re-forming in 1999. After the band's breakup in 1994, Wolfe and Erin Smith had played together in Cold Cold Hearts; Wolfe later performed in the band Deep Lust. Smith eventually went to work at Lookout alongside Molly Neuman, by then the label's general manager. The idea for Bratmobile's reunion came about when the three attended a show by the Donnas, one of Lookout's bands. "People kept going, 'Oh, that's Bratmobile!'" remembers Wolfe. "We hadn't thought of ourselves as a unit like that for a long time. And we talked about it and said, 'Look at the state of music in the late '90s—there are even fewer girl bands now than there were in the early '90s. Maybe instead of complaining about it we should get back together and do something about it.'" Since re-forming, Bratmobile has released two spirited, politically charged albums, 2000's *Ladies, Women and Girls* and 2002's *Girls Get Busy*, both on Lookout.

Meanwhile, Bratmobile's former labelmates, the Donnas, signed with Atlantic in early 2002. Brett Anderson (vocals), Allison Robertson (guitar), Maya Ford (bass), and Torry Castellano (drums) had met at school in Palo Alto, California, and formed their first band, Raggedy Anne, in the eighth grade. The group was later renamed the Electrocutes, and then the Donnas, after the band met their first manager, Darrin Raffaelli, who wrote and produced their first records for his own Super*Teem Records label (their self-titled debut was released in 1996, and reissued on Lookout in 1998). The group also dispensed with their real names in favor of the joint name "Donna": Donna A., Donna R., Donna F., and Donna C.

Neuman first met the Donnas when her band the PeeChees played shows with them. "They were like a local phenomenon, because they were these teenagers playing Ramones-style punk, and they looked cool," she says. "But we didn't know if they were into it, and they were still in high school. So when they graduated from high school that's when we started talking to them." Lookout eventually signed the band and released their second album, *American Teenage Rock 'n' Roll Machine*, in January 1998. Subsequent releases include *Get Skintight*, in 1999, and *The Donnas Turn 21*, in 2001.

On their second album, the Donnas began writing their own songs as well as co-producing. The band's energetic garage rock quickly won them a following, with coverage soon moving beyond zines and alternative magazines to mainstream outlets like *People*. "They had so many opportunities presented to them that were so beyond what our normal bands had," says Neuman. "Appearing in movies [including the film *Jawbreaker*], being on soundtracks, tour opportunities—the level of interest was just beyond anything else we'd ever had to deal with." And Neuman, due to her experience with Bratmobile, was determined to see that the band never felt exploited.

"That was where I think I had a special sensitivity because of my background," she says. "They came into it being into riot grrrl bands and L7 and Shonen Knife, and they were like, 'We were so afraid of you, we saw you at shows and we thought you were so cool!' Now they don't think I'm that cool. They're like, 'Why are you making us do this, it sucks, we're not gonna play tonight,' and I'm like, 'Yeah, you are!' But I also knew that girls in their early twenties were going to have a lot of problems that maybe guys in their early twenties weren't. I had a special place in my heart for not wanting what happened to us to happen to them. It's just really hard, friendships are so fragile, and it's so intense, and it's so easy to feel when you're making decisions that you have to win all the time. I think that's a lot of what we had to deal with, and it was just a crazy way to be. And they have blossomed so amazingly; they're tighter than ever towards one another, and they really have been able to get through the little bumps. I'm not taking credit for that at all, but I think being able to be there for them and help them has been a good thing."

The Donnas signed to Atlantic in the interest of reaching a larger audience with Lookout's blessing. "I think it's a good time," says Neuman. "Because we really gave it our all with the last album; we invested a lot and we had a strong distribution company behind us. But it costs a lot of money to have a hit on a major scale, and we don't have it, and we don't want to go broke trying." The Donnas' major label debut was set for release in late 2002.

Over thirty years before, when Fanny became the first all-female band signed to a major label, they had toured incessantly, in part to prove to their audiences that women could, in fact, play rock & roll. But by the start of the new millennium that fact was largely taken for granted (aside from the occasional disparaging remark that a musician was merely "good for a girl"). Indeed, the inroads women had made in the music community gave them greater power in determining their own fate. While the punk movement of the '70s had been predicated on challenging the mainstream, the indie scene of the '80s and '90s had encouraged the formation of an alternative to the mainstream (as the womyn's music movement of the '70s had also done). Women who found opportunities, both on- and offstage, in that indie scene, could then choose to go on to mainstream positions or to remain where they were. The Donnas chose to sign with Atlantic; Sleater-Kinney chose to stay with Kill Rock Stars. Neither choice was "better"—each group simply had an equally valid way of defining success on their own terms.

Even hugely successful mainstream artists were able to have more of a hand in their careers. It was not unusual to find artists ranging from Destiny's Child and Lauryn Hill to Mariah Carey, Gwen Stefani, and even the "pre-packaged" Spice Girls co-writing, and often co-producing, their own material. The numbers of women working in non-performing areas in the music industry also increased; no longer limited to the publicity ghetto, women can be found working at every level, from being roadies to the heads of record labels.

Still, it could easily be argued such progress has been slow and incomplete. Though there are more women working in the music industry, they are too frequently defined as women-in-rock, a phrase that, however intended, conveys a sense of "otherness," a group apart from the norm. That Sarah McLachlan was told, in the '90s, that radio stations could not add her record because Tori Amos was that week's designated female artist, and that a show with more than one female act on the bill would not make money, provides a clear illustration of the obstacles women still face. Neither argument would have been made to a male artist.

But one of the lures of rock & roll is that it is a game with no rules. This generalization is not entirely true, of course. But it is true that rock & roll is a profession where if you don't like the rules, you can fight them, break them, and write your own. This is how women have survived in the music industry since rock & roll's birth—by rising to the challenge of setting their own rules. As long as they continue to do so, rock & roll has a rich future indeed.

Bibliography

[All U.S. chart positions referred to in the book are from *Billboard* magazine and appeared in various editions of Joel Whitburn's *The Billboard Book of Top 40 Hits*, *The Billboard Book of Top 40 Albums*, *Top Pop Singles*, and *Top Pop Albums* (Record Research, Inc.). U.K. chart positions were taken from *The Complete Book of the British Charts* by Tony Brown, Jon Kutner, and Neil Warwick (Omnibus Books).]

BOOKS:

Adler, B. *Rap: Portraits and Lyrics of a Generation of Black Rockers*. New York: St. Martin's Press, 1991.

Andersen, Mark and Mark Jenkins. *Dance of Days: Two Decades of Punk in the Nation's Capital*. New York: Soft Skull Press, 2001.

Anderson, Christopher. *Madonna Unauthorized*. New York: Simon & Schuster, 1991.

Archer, Robyn and Diana Simmonds. *A Star Is Torn*. New York: E. P. Dutton, 1987.

Azerrad, Michael. *Our Band Could Be Your Life: Scenes from the American Indie Underground 1981-1991*. New York: Little, Brown & Co., 2001.

Baez, Joan. *And a Voice to Sing With*. New York: Plume Books, 1988.

Baker, Glenn A. and Stuart Coupe. *The New Rock 'n' Roll: The A-Z of Rock in the '80s* . New York: St. Martin's Press, 1989.

Becker, Scott, ed. *We Rock So You Don't Have To*. San Diego: Incommunicado Press, 1998.

Bego, Mark. *Aretha Franklin: The Queen of Soul*. New York: St. Martin's Press, 1989.

Betrock, Alan. *Girl Groups: The Story of a Sound*. New York: Delilah Books, 1982.

Bolton, Cecil, ed. *Kate Bush Complete*. London: EMI Music Publishing Ltd., 1987.

Brite, Poppy Z. *Courtney Love: The Real Story*. New York: Simon & Schuster, 1997.

Brown, Ashley, ed. *The Marshall Cavendish Illustrated History of Popular Music* (reference ed.). Freeport, Long Island, New York: Marshall Cavendish Corp., 1989.

Buckley, Jonathan, Orla Duane, Mark Ellingham, and Al Spicer, eds. *Rock: The Rough Guide* (2nd ed.). New York: Penguin Books, 1999.

Burchill, Julie and Tony Parsons. *The Boy Looked at Johnny: The Obituary of Rock and Roll*. London: Pluto Press, 1988.

Buskin, Richard. *Sheryl Crow: No Fool to This Game*. New York: Billboard Books, 2002.

Cann, Kevin and Sean Mayes. *Kate Bush: A Visual Documentary*. London: Omnibus Press, 1988.

Chapple, Steve and Reebee Garofalo. *Rock 'n' Roll Is Here to Pay: The History and Politics of the Music Industry*. Chicago: Nelson-Hall Inc., 1977.

Childerhose, Buffy. *From Lilith to Lilith Fair*. Vancouver, B.C.: Madrigal Press, Ltd., 1998.

Clemente, John. *Girl Groups: Fabulous Females That Rocked the World*. Iola, Wisconsin: Krause Publications, 2000.

Clifford, Mike, ed. *The Harmony Illustrated Encyclopedia of Rock*. New York: Harmony Books, 1986.

Coleman, Ray. *Lennon*. New York: McGraw-Hill, 1986.

Coleman, Ray. *The Man Who Made the Beatles: An Intimate Biography of Brian Epstein*. New York: McGraw-Hill, 1989.

Cott, Jonathan and Christine Doudna, eds. *The Ballad of John and Yoko*. Garden City, New York: Doubleday & Co./Rolling Stone Press, 1982.

Crampton, Luke and Dafydd Rees. *Q Rock Stars Encyclopedia*. London: Dorling-Kindersley, 1999.

Cranna, Ian. *The Rock Yearbook 1986*. New York: St. Martin's Press, 1984[AD1].

Dannen, Fredric. *Hit Men: Power Brokers and Fast Money Inside the Music Business*. New York: Vintage Books, 1990.

Davis, Clive with James Willwerth. *Clive: Inside the Music Business*. New York: Ballantine Books, 1976.

Davis, Sharon. *Motown: The History*. Enfield, Middlesex, England: Guinness Publishing Ltd., 1990.

Denselow, Robin. *When the Music's Over: The Story of Political Pop*. London: Faber and Faber Ltd., 1988.

Des Barres, Pamela. *I'm with the Band: Confessions of a Groupie*. New York: Jove Books, 1976.

Duncan, Patricia J. *Jennifer Lopez*. New York, St. Martin's Paperbacks, 1999.

Echols, Alice. *Daring to Be Bad: Radical Feminism in America 1967-1975*. Minneapolis: University of Minnesota Press, 1989.

Ehrenstein, David and Bill Reed. *Rock on Film*. New York: Delilah Books, 1982.

Evans, Liz. *Women, Sex and Rock 'n' Roll*. San Francisco: Pandora, 1994.

Faludi, Susan. *Backlash: The Undeclared War Against American Women*. New York: Crown, 1991.

Friedman, Myra. *Buried Alive: The Biography of Janis Joplin*. New York: Bantam Books, 1974.

Garland, Phyl. *The Sound of Soul*. Chicago: Henry Regnery Co., 1969.

Garratt, Sheryl and Sue Steward. *Signed Sealed and Delivered: True Life Stories of Women in Pop*. London: Pluto Press, 1984.

George, Nelson. *Where Did Our Love Go?: The Rise and Fall of Motown Records*. New York: St. Martin's Press, 1985.

George-Warren, Holly and Patricia Romanowski, eds. *The Rolling Stone Encyclopedia of Rock & Roll*. New York: Fireside, 2001.

Gilbert, Bob and Gary Theroux. *The Top Ten: 1956-Present*. New York: Fireside Books, 1982.

Gillett, Charlie. *The Sound of the City: The Rise of Rock and Roll*. New York: Outerbridge & Dienstfrey, 1970.

Golden, Anna Louise. *The Spice Girls*. New York: Ballantine Books, 1997.

Gonzales, Michael A. and Havelock Nelson. *Bring the Noise: A Guide to Rap Music and Hip-Hop Culture*. New York: Harmony Books, 1991.

Greig, Charlotte. *Will You Still Love Me Tomorrow?: Girl Groups from the '50s On*. London: Virago Press Ltd., 1989.

Handler, Herb. *Year by Year in the Rock Era*. Westport, Conn.: Greenwood Press, 1983.

Hanhardt, John G. and Barbara Haskell. *Yoko Ono: Arias and Objects*. Salt Lake City, Utah: Peregrine Smith Books, 1991.

Hadeigh, Boze. *The Vinyl Closet: Gays in the Music World*. San Diego: Los Hombres Press, 1991.

Halliwell, Geri. *If Only*. New York: Delacorte Press, 1999

Hayes, Dermott. *Sinead O'Connor: So Different*. New York: Omnibus Press, 1991.

Herbst, Peter, ed. *The Rolling Stone Interviews: Talking with the Legends of Rock & Roll 1967-1980*. New York: St. Martin's Press/Rolling Stone Press, 1981.

Hirshey, Gerri. *Nowhere to Run: The Story of Soul Music*. New York: Viking Penguin Inc., 1985.

Hoberman, J. and Jonathan Rosenbaum. *Midnight Movies*. New York: Harper & Row, 1983.

Hoffman, Elliot L., Eric M. Todd, and Frank Weimann. *Backstage Pass: A Non-Performer's Guide to Rock 'n' Roll Touring Careers*. Belle Mead, New Jersey: Backstage Pass Inc., 1989.

Holt, Sid, ed. *The Rolling Stone Interviews: The 1980s*. New York: St. Martin's Press/ Rolling Stone Press, 1989.

Hopkins, Jerry. *Yoko Ono*. New York: Macmillan Publishing Co., 1986.

Humphrey, Clark. *Loser: The Real Seattle Music Story*. Seattle: MISCmedia, 1999.

Joe, Radcliffe A. *This Business of Disco*. New York: Billboard Books, 1980.

Johnston, Ian. *The Wild Wild World of the Cramps*. New York: Omnibus Press, 1990.

Jones, Allan, ed. *The Rock Yearbook 1985*. New York: St. Martin's Press, 1984.

Juno, Andrea, ed. *Angry Women in Rock, Volume One*. New York: Juno Books, 1996.

Juno, Andrea and V. Vale, eds. *Angry Women*. San Francisco: RE/Search Publications, 1991.

Karlen, Neal. *Babes in Toyland: The Making and Selling of a Rock and Roll Band*. New York: Times Books, 1994.

Kilcher, Jewel. *Chasing Down the Dawn*. New York: HarperEntertainment, 2000.

Kimball, Gayle, ed. *Women's Culture: The Women's Renaissance of the Seventies*. Metuchen, New Jersey: The Scarecrow Press, Inc., 1981.

Kort, Michele. *Soul Picnic: The Music and Passion of Laura Nyro*. New York: Thomas Dunne Books, 2002.

Logan, Nick and Bob Woffinden. *The Illustrated Encyclopedia of Rock*. New York: Harmony Books, 1977.

Martin, Linda and Kerry Segrave. *Anti-Rock: The Opposition to Rock 'n' Roll*. Hamden, Conn.: Archon Books, 1988.

Marsh, Dave. *50 Ways to Fight Censorship & Important Facts to Know About the Censors*. New York: Thunder's Mouth Press, 1991.

Marsh, Dave. *The First Rock & Roll Confidential Report*. New York: Pantheon Books, 1985.

McDonnell, Evelyn. *Army of She: Icelandic, Iconoclastic, Irrepressible Bjork*. New York: AtRandom.com Books, 2001.

McFarland, P. J. *Angel Standing By*. New York: St. Martin's Griffin, 1999.

Miller, Jim, ed. *The Rolling Stone Illustrated History of Rock & Roll* (revised and updated). New York: Random House/Rolling Stone Press, 1980.

Morgan, Robin, ed. *Sisterhood Is Powerful*. New York: Vintage Books, 1970.

Morton, Andrew. *Posh & Becks*. London: Michael O'Mara Books Ltd., 2001.

Near, Holly with Derk Richardson. *Fire in the Rain . . . Singer in the Storm*. New York: William Morrow & Co., 1990.

O'Dair, Barbara, ed. *Trouble Girls: The Rolling Stone Book of Women in Rock*. New York: Rolling Stone Press, 1997.

Pavletich, Aida. *Rock-a-Bye, Baby*. Garden City, New York: Doubleday & Co. Inc., 1980.

Picardie, Justine and Dorothy Wade. *Music Man: Ahmet Ertegun, Atlantic Records and the Triumph of Rock 'n' Roll*. New York: W. W. Norton & Co., 1990.

Raphael, Amy. *Grrrls: Viva Rock Divas*. New York: St. Martin's Griffin, 1996.

Rapport, Steve and Johnny Waller. *Sweet Dreams: The Definitive Biography of Eurythmics*. London: Virgin Books Ltd., 1985.

Ribowsky, Mark. *He's a Rebel*. New York: Dutton, 1989.

Robbins, Ira A., ed. *The New Trouser Press Record Guide* (3rd ed.). New York: Collier Books, 1989.

Robbins, Ira A., ed. *The Trouser Press Record Guide*. New York: Collier Books, 1991 (4th ed.); New York: Fire Books, 1997 (5th ed.).

Rogers, Kalen. *Tori Amos: All These Years*. New York: Omnibus Press, 1994.

Rooney, Jim and Eric Von Schmidt. *Baby, Let Me Follow You Down: The Illustrated Story of the Cambridge Folk Years*. Garden City, New York: Anchor Books, 1979.

Rossi, Melissa. *Courtney Love: Queen of Noise*. New York: Pocket Books, 1996.

Savage, Jon. *England's Dreaming: Anarchy, Sex Pistols, Punk Rock, and Beyond*. New York: St. Martin's Press, 1991.

Sinker, Daniel, ed. *We Owe You Nothing: Punk Planet: The Collected Interviews*. New York: Akashic Books, 2001.

Smith, Joe and Mitchell Fink, ed. *Off the Record: An Oral History of Popular Music*. New York: Warner Books Inc., 1988.

Spector, Ronnie with Vince Waldron. *Be My Baby*. New York: Harmony Books, 1990.

Stambler, Irwin. *The Encyclopedia of Pop, Rock and Soul* (revised ed.). New York: St. Martin's Press, 1989.

Stevenson, Ray, ed. *Sex Pistols File*. London: Omnibus Press, 1987.

Stokes, Geoffrey, Ken Tucker, and Ed Ward. *Rock of Ages: The Rolling Stone History of Rock & Roll*. New York: Summit Books/Rolling Stone Press, 1986.

Szatmary, David P. *Rockin' in Time: A Social History of Rock-and-Roll* (2nd ed.). Englewood Cliffs, New Jersey: Prentice Hall, 1991.

Singleton, Raynoma Gordy, with Bryan Brown and Mim Eichler. *Berry, Me, and Motown*. Chicago: Contemporary Books, 1990.

Taylor, Derek. *It Was Twenty Years Ago Today*. New York: Fireside Books, 1987.

Tomashoff, Craig. *You Live, You Learn: The Alanis Morissette Story*. New York: Berkley Boulevard Books, 1998.

Thomson, Liz, ed. *New Women in Rock*. New York: Omnibus Press, 1982.

Turner, Tina with Kurt Loder. *I, Tina*. New York: Avon Books, 1987.

VIBE magazine, eds. *Hip Hop Divas*. New York: Three Rivers Press, 2001.

Wenner, Jann. *Lennon Remembers*. Harmondsworth, Middlesex, England: Penguin Books Ltd., 1980.

Wiener, Jon. *Come Together: John Lennon in His Time*. New York: Random House, 1984.

Wilson, Mary, with Ahrgus Julliard and Patricia Romanowski. *Dreamgirl: My Life as a Supreme*. New York: St. Martin's Press, 1986.

Wilson, Mary, with Patricia Romanowski. *Supreme Faith: Someday We'll Be Together*. New York: HarperCollins: 1990.

Wolf, Naomi. *The Beauty Myth: How Images of Beauty Are Used Against Women*. New York: William Morrow & Co., 1991.

MAGAZINES:

U.S.: *The Advocate*, allmusic.com (online), *Austin Chronicle*, *BAM*, *Billboard*, *Bitch*, *Boston Globe*, *Boston Sunday Globe*, CDnow.com (online), *Ebony*, *Elle*, *Entertainment Weekly*, *Goldmine*, *Guitar Player*, *Harper's Bazaar*, *Hot Wire*, imdb.com (online), *Interview*, *Jump Cut*, *Ladyslipper Catalog and Resource Guide*, *Los Angeles Daily News*, *Los Angeles Times*, *Mother Jones*, *Ms. *, *Musician*, *New Music*, *New Times*, *New York Times*, *Newsweek*, *No Depression*, *Option*, *Outlook*, *Pulse*, *Request*, *The Rocket*, *Rockpool*, *ROCKRGRL*, *Rolling Stone*, *San Francisco Examiner*, *Sassy*, *Seattle Gay News*, *SF Weekly*, *Sojourner: The Women's Forum*, *Soul Underground*, *Spin*, *Stereo Review*, *Time*, *Traffic*, *Trouser Press*, *URB*, *Us*, *Village Voice*, *Vogue*, *Wall Street Journal*, *The Wire*.

U.K.: *The Face*, *Melody Maker*, *Mojo*, *Mojo Collections*, *New Musical Express*, *Q*, *Record Collector*, *Sounds*.

VIDEOS:

The Changer: A Record of the Times (1991), directed by Judy Dlugacz and Frances Reid (Olivia Records).

The Decline . . . of Western Civilization (1980), directed by Penelope Spheeris (Media Home Entertainment).

The Decline of Western Civilization Part 2: The Metal Years (1988), directed by Penelope Spheeris (RCA Columbia Pictures Home Video).

D.O.A.: A Right of Passage (1980), directed by Lech Kowalski (Harmony-vision).

Girl Groups: The Story of a Sound (1983), directed by Steve Alpert (MGM/UA Home Video).

Janis: A Film (1974), directed by Howard Alk and Seaton Findlay (MCA Home Video).

Monterey Pop (1968), directed by D. A. Pennebaker, James Desmond, Barry Feinstein, Albert Maysles, Roger Murphy, Richard Leacock, Nick Proferes (Sony).

Motown 25: Yesterday, Today, Forever (1983), directed by Don Mischer (MGM/UA Home Video).

Screaming Fields of Sonic Love (1995), various directors (Geffen Home Video).

Selena (1997), directed by Gregory Nava (Warner Home Video).

Spice Girls-Girl Power (1997), various directors (Warner Home Video).

Spice World (1997), directed by Bob Spiers (Columbia Tri Star Home Video).

The Weavers: Wasn't That a Time (1981), directed by Jim Brown (MGM/UA Home Video).

Women in Rock (1987), directed by Stephanie Bennett (MCA Home Video).

General Index

Song Title Index

Album Title Index ·

About the Author

Photo by Diana Adams

GILLIAN G. GAAR is an award-winning freelance writer and photographer based in Seattle. Gaar's work has appeared in *Rolling Stone, CDnow, Q, No Depression,* the Experience Music Project museum, *Goldmine,* and *The Rocket* music magazine in Seattle, where she was a senior editor. She has appeared in the anthologies *Trouble Girls: The Rolling Stone Book Of Women In Rock; The Nirvana Companion; Goldmine: The Beatles Digest; The Scribner Encyclopedia Of American Lives;* and *Encyclopaedia Britannica,* among others.

Selected Live Girls Titles from Seal Press

Film Fatales: Independent Women Directors by Judith M. Redding and Victoria A. Brownworth. $16.95, 1-878067-97-4. A comprehensive reference book and biography with profiles of Lizzie Borden, Allison Anders, Jane Campion, Mira Nair, Susan Seidelman and many others.

Listen Up: Voices from the Next Feminist Generation edited by Barbara Findlen. $16.95, 1-58005-054-9. A revised and expanded edition of the Seal Press classic, featuring the voices of a new generation of women expressing the vibrancy and vitality of today's feminist movement.

The Chelsea Whistle by Michelle Tea. $14.95, 1-58005-073-5. In this gritty, confessional memoir, Michelle Tea takes the reader back to the city of her childhood: Chelsea, Massachusetts—Boston's ugly, scrappy little sister and a place where time and hope are spent on things not getting any worse.

Sex and Single Girls: Straight and Queer Women on Sexuality edited by Lee Damsky. $16.95, 1-58005-038-7. In this potent and entertaining collection of personal essays, women lay bare pleasure, fear, desire, risk—all that comes with exploring their sexuality, with empowering and often humorous results.

Body Outlaws: Young Women Write About Body Image and Identity edited by Ophira Edut, foreword by Rebecca Walker. $14.95, 1-58005-043-3. Filled with honesty and humor, this groundbreaking anthology offers stories by women who have chosen to ignore, subvert or redefine the dominant beauty standard in order to feel at home in their bodies.

Cunt: A Declaration of Independence by Inga Muscio. $14.95, 1-58005-015-8. An ancient title of respect for women, "cunt" long ago veered off the path of honor and now careens toward the heart of every woman as an expletive. Muscio traces this winding road, giving women both the motivation and the tools to claim "cunt" as a positive and powerful force in the lives of all women.

Shameless: Women's Intimate Erotica edited by Hanne Blank. $14.95, 1-58005-060-3. Diverse and delicious memoir-style erotica by today's hottest fiction writers.

Young Wives' Tales: New Adventures in Love and Partnership edited by Jill Corral and Lisa Miya-Jervis, foreword by bell hooks. $16.95, 1-58005-050-6. Wife. The term inspires ambivalence in many young women, for a multitude of good reasons. So what's a young, independent girl in love to do? In a bold and provocative anthology, 20 and 30somethings attempt to answer that question, addressing who the wedding is really for, how to maintain one's individuality and the diversity of queer unions.

Seal Press publishes many books of fiction and nonfiction by women writers. Please visit our Web site at www.sealpress.com.

19.95
4/03